COGNITIVE DEVELOPMENT
FOR ACADEMIC ACHIEVEMENT

Also from James P. Byrnes

*Language and Literacy Development,
Second Edition: What Educators Need to Know*

James P. Byrnes and Barbara A. Wasik

*Minds, Brains, and Learning:
Understanding the Psychological and Educational
Relevance of Neuroscientific Research*

James P. Byrnes

Cognitive Development for Academic Achievement

Building Skills and Motivation

JAMES P. BYRNES

THE GUILFORD PRESS
New York   London

Library of Congress Cataloging-in-Publication Data

Names: Byrnes, James P., author.
Title: Cognitive development for academic achievement : building skills and
    motivation / James P. Byrnes.
Description: New York : The Guilford Press, 2021. | Includes
    bibliographical references and index. |
Identifiers: LCCN 2021016452 | ISBN 9781462547135 (paperback) |
    ISBN 9781462547142 (hardcover)
Subjects: LCSH: Academic achievement—Psychological aspects. | Motivation
    in education. | Cognition in children. | Cognitive neuroscience. |
BISAC: EDUCATION / Educational Psychology | EDUCATION / Secondary
Classification: LCC LB1062.6 .B87 2021 | DDC 370.15—dc23
LC record available at *https://lccn.loc.gov/2021016452*

*In memory of Representative John Lewis
and Supreme Court Justice Ruth Bader Ginsburg,
who inspired us all to fight for social justice,
stand up for the oppressed, and seek equality for all.
Everyone should have the educational
and career opportunities that I have enjoyed.*

About the Author

James P. Byrnes, PhD, is Professor of Educational Psychology and Applied Developmental Science in the College of Education at Temple University. He was a Fellow of Division 15 (Educational Psychology) of the American Psychological Association between 2002 and 2018, has served as Vice President of the Jean Piaget Society, and was Associate Editor of the *Journal of Cognition and Development*. Dr. Byrnes has published over 100 books, chapters, and articles on areas of cognitive development, including language development, logical reasoning, and mathematical learning. His most recent work has focused primarily on developing and testing a comprehensive theoretical model of academic achievement (the opportunity–propensity model) in order to provide insight into ways to eliminate or substantially reduce gender, ethnic, and racial gaps in achievement. Dr. Byrnes has received awards for his teaching and mentoring of undergraduate and graduate students.

Preface

The primary goal of this book is to provide useful information to educators, parents, psychologists, and policymakers about the cognitive and motivational processes that occur in children's minds when they try to learn skills in educational settings (e.g., classrooms). A related goal is to identify the factors that provide answers to the question "Why do some children acquire more information across an academic year than other children?" Both goals are intended to make the "black box" of children's minds less mysterious to educators. By identifying the factors that produce different levels of achievement in students, educators gain insight into how to *help all children learn*.

As a simple example to illustrate this point, imagine that you are a piano teacher with six students. After giving piano lessons to them for a year, you discover that three students learned piano skills faster than the other three. You investigate a little further and find that the three who learned more skills practiced 20 minutes a day while the other three practiced for only 10 minutes every other day. With this knowledge, you now know that all your students could be performing better if they all practiced 20 minutes every day. As this example illustrates, it is possible to help educators *make better instructional, curricular, and policy decisions* by providing them with information about skill-promoting factors such as practice.

Why would providing such kinds of information matter? Consider another analogy from the medical field. Responsible adults would not tolerate physicians prescribing medicines without really understanding the effect of these medicines on the body (and whether the medicines are safe and effective). In a similar way, responsible adults should not tolerate teachers teaching in particular ways without having an understanding of why one teaching method would work better than another. Teaching is a form of procedural knowledge (how to do something). Highly skilled experts in any domain not only have procedural knowledge, they also have conceptual knowledge that explains why procedures work. This book is designed to complement so-called "methods" courses in teacher education programs that explain procedural knowledge of teaching (how to teach) by providing a conceptual framework for understanding why certain teaching methods should work better than others.

Another theme that will be apparent by the end of this book is the fact that students in the United States do not acquire the kinds of cognitive and academic skills they need to be successful in the modern world. Instead of attaining the kinds of skills we would want (usually called a "proficient" level), the majority of students acquire only a basic or rudimentary skill level in all of the subject areas examined in this book (literacy skills, math skills, science skills, and history skills). This troubling level of achievement has serious consequences for the economic well-being of individual students and the United States as a whole. Another goal of this book is to consider the implications of the psychological theories and research for insight into how to elevate the performance of students to the proficient level. I believe that we have learned enough to make modifications in curriculums, instructional approaches, and public policy that will actually work better. There is unfortunately a large gap between what researchers know and what teachers and school systems do.

A fourth goal relates to the idea of social justice. Another troubling fact about the American education system is that low-income children begin their formal education far behind their more affluent peers. Income-related differences in both domain-general and domain-specific skills are large at the start of formal schooling and remain that way through the high school years. The information in this book is intended to provide insight into how to eliminate income-based differences in research-supported ways. The final chapter presents a summary thesis regarding what has to happen to make this goal a reality.

The content of the book is subdivided into four major sections. In the first section (Foundations), the material is designed to (1) provide an overview of the book and the benefits of a developmental approach and (2) explain the nature of brain development to help readers understand some of the neuroscientific claims that one hears in the scholarly literature on learning and in the popular media. The second section (Domain-General Theories of Cognitive Skills and Motivation) examines cognitive skills and dispositions that are applicable to the learning of any subject area. The third section (Domain-Specific Academic Skills) focuses on theories and research that are specific to particular subject areas (reading, writing, math, science, and history). The goal of the third section is to describe age trends in the acquisition of skills in each of these subject areas and discuss the implications of this research for how to teach better and elevate the achievement levels of students. The final chapter attempts to integrate all the information from prior chapters into a single coherent framework (the opportunity–propensity model of achievement).

The intended audiences for this book include (1) advanced undergraduates interested in careers in education; (2) master's-level students in teacher education, educational psychology, or applied developmental science; as well as (3) others interested in finding out more about children's school-related learning in order to make informed decisions about educational policies.

I have numerous people to thank for helping me identify key theoretical constructs, research findings, and implications for instruction. I have grown as a scholar and an applied developmental psychologist from conversations and discussions with graduate students and colleagues. These individuals include Barbara Wasik, Kristie Newton, Doug Lombardi, Carol Brandt, Janelle Bailey, Avi Kaplan, Shanta Hattikudur, Christine Woyshner, Jennifer Cromley, Pat Alexander, Steve Graham, Karen Harris, Allen Wigfield, Kathy Wentzel, John Guthrie, Nathan Fox, Bruce Van Sledright, Scott Paris, Susan Gelman, Marilyn Shatz, John Coley, David Uttal, Mitch Rabinowitz, David Miller, Ty Boyer, Dana Miller-Cotto, Matt Bernacki, Tony Perez, Brad Litchfield, Ben Brock, Ben Torsney, Abbey Auxter, and Jen Eaton. I also thank Craig Thomas and his team at The Guilford Press for excellent advice and support before and after I wrote this book.

Contents

PART III. Domain-Specific Academic Skills

PART IV. Conclusions

PART I
Foundations

CHAPTER 1

Introductory Issues

On the first day of school in any given academic year, children bring with them a set of psychological characteristics that affect how much they will learn that year. To be sure, the content presented by teachers and how this information is presented matters as well, but there is ample evidence that student characteristics such as their existing knowledge, ability to attend, memory ability, natural aptitudes, and motivation all play a strong role in how much they will learn in the classroom (Byrnes, Miller-Cotto, & Wang, 2019). Researchers sometimes refer to these learning-related characteristics as *propensities* because they make students prone to or apt to benefit from the instruction they receive (Byrnes, 2020; Byrnes, Wang, & Miller-Cotto, 2019; Corno et al., 2002).

A second key finding of the literature besides the fact that propensities are highly determinative of learning is that all of the propensities improve with age (see Chapters 3 through 14), so it would be expected that older children and adolescents would be likely to get more than younger children do out of the same learning opportunities. A related prediction would be that older students could handle learning more information because their more advanced propensities make them more efficient processors of information and enable them to engage more with the material, even when it is difficult and abstract. Given these two sets of findings, it is important that preservice and inservice teachers learn about these propensities and discover ways to promote their development. That is the primary overall goal of this book.

The specific goal of the present chapter is to provide an overview of the rest of the book as well as describe the benefits of taking a developmental approach to studying these propensities. In the next two sections, this overview and a description of a developmental approach are provided.

OVERVIEW OF THE BOOK

The chapters in this book are organized into four logically sequenced parts. Part I includes two chapters on introductory or foundational matters: the present overview chapter and Chapter 2 that focuses on developmental neuroscience (mind–brain connections and brain development). Part II includes six chapters that focus on domain-general theories of learning (Chapter 3), the nature and development of memory (Chapter 4), the nature and development of motivation (Chapter 5), executive function and self-regulation (Chapter 6), intelligence, aptitude, and expertise (Chapter 7), and spoken language competence (Chapter 8). The information in Chapters 3–8 is relevant to the learning of any subject area, so regardless of whether children are about to learn key concepts in math, science, or history, these chapters help teachers answer questions such as "Why do children fail to understand this topic?" and "Why do students forget information between one year and the next?"

Because this book is specifically geared toward teachers, the chapters in Part III might be considered the core chapters. Unlike the theories in Part II that are applicable to any subject area (i.e., they are "domain-general"), the theories and findings in Part III are more domain-specific and focus on the subject areas and skills taught in most elementary, middle, and high schools. In particular, the subject areas include reading (Chapters 9 and 10), writing (Chapter 11), math (Chapter 12), scientific reasoning (Chapter 13), and history (Chapter 14).

Another way to think of the information presented in Chapters 3–14 is to consider the fact that if (1) we were trying to predict which students will show the highest level of achievement in some subject area (e.g., math) at the end of the school year, (2) had measures of the constructs in the domain-general chapters in Part II (e.g., working memory), and (3) had measures of student's initial skill level in the subjects presented in Chapters 9–14, we would be able to predict each student's end-of-year achievement level in each subject area with a great deal of accuracy. However, it is also the case that other factors besides the factors presented in Chapters 3–14 are determinative of achievement.

The final part of the book is the last chapter in Part IV (Chapter 15). To have a more refined understanding of who learns in school and why, we also need to consider socioeconomic differences in achievement and cross-cultural differences in achievement and motivation. Chapter 15 includes a discussion of sociocultural factors that provides a more complete understanding of school-related learning trajectories than if this discussion were omitted and it also introduces the opportunity–propensity model of achievement. Although it is not essential that the chapters be read in sequence, there is a logic to reading about domain-general issues first, specific subject areas second, and sociocultural issues third.

THE BENEFITS OF TAKING
A DEVELOPMENTAL PERSPECTIVE

A central premise of scholars in fields such as developmental psychology and human development is that important insights into people can be gained by viewing them in a developmental perspective. In contrast to cataloging the skills, dispositions, and social relationships that adults have at a particular time and linking these characteristics to current levels of functioning, developmental scientists try to situate the current state of propensities within a developmental trajectory that also specifies where a person "has been" and where they "seem to be going" next. Teachers of a particular grade level can appreciate this perspective because they are the ones who inherit a cohort of students from a prior grade and think about what they need to do to get these students ready for the next grade. When a current cohort, as a group, seems to have a particular problem understanding a key concept that should have been initially covered and mastered in a previous grade, it is natural to wonder how they were taught in that grade (or if the prerequisites for that concept had been covered at all). Similarly, if cohort after cohort seems to be particularly anxious about learning skills in a particular domain (e.g., science), it is natural to wonder if they had unpleasant experiences when they learned that subject in prior grades. So, knowing where students "have been" can provide useful insights into their current state.

But knowing where they are going next in the curriculum is also important. Most curricula are sequenced for a reason. Some topics are foundational for later topics. Some topics are easier for children to understand than others because they are more familiar or less abstract. If we arrange a set of skills into a developmental sequence (fewer skills to more skills, lower-level skills to higher-level skills, less proficiency to more proficiency), and chart this sequence as a graph, we can view the progression as a *developmental trajectory*. When children are getting better and better at some ability (e.g., writing, playing the piano), this is typically what we mean by *development*. However, research shows that individual children experience a range of trajectories, some more positive than others. Teachers need to know what the more positive trajectories look like, so they can help get children on these trajectories as opposed to getting them off-track or slowing down their progress.

Developmental scientists are particularly prone to thinking of any skill or disposition as being on a trajectory. Skills and disposition often change over time, often for the better but sometimes for the worse. Developmental scientists also like to zoom in on parts of the trajectory and take "snap-shots" or *developmental states* of the skill or disposition at particular points in time. For example, they might assess the level of some skill at ages 5, 7, and 9. These snapshots or developmental states (expressed as scores on some test) can then be plotted on a graph that represents the average trajectory of the skill between ages 5 and 9.

Developmental scientists are not only concerned with describing the development of skills and dispositions in terms of a sequence of developmental states, but also interested in explaining how and why one state (e.g., skill level at age 5) gets transformed into the next state in the sequence (e.g., skill level at age 7). In other words, they develop theories that explain changes or the sequence of states over time. These theories posit so-called *developmental mechanisms* that explain how and why skills or dispositions change over time in the manner that they do (Klahr & MacWhinney, 1998). Particularly useful theories explain why skills change more rapidly in some children than others, or why some trajectories have a positive slope (things get better) while others have a negative slope (things get worse). One example of a developmental mechanism that could explain increases in skill is practice. As will be discussed in Chapter 7, people who attain the highest levels of expertise in some domain (e.g., chess playing, sports, music) practice an average of 3.5 hours per day. People who practice less attain lower levels of proficiency. So, if one were to take a snapshot of the average skill level at Time 1 for a group of learners, then take another snapshot at Time 2, and finally measure the amount of practice each student engaged in, we could explain why some showed a steeper learning curve (i.e., learned faster) than others using the developmental mechanism of practice.

It is in this way that a developmental perspective not only provides the snapshots of skill development so that teachers can see where students have been and where they are going, but also provides insight into developmental mechanisms that explain how to create the more optimal trajectories. Instruction should be designed to take advantage of, or harness, developmental mechanisms that have been identified in developmental theories, if doing so is possible. Teachers can create opportunities for practice and thereby harness that developmental mechanism, but other developmental mechanisms happen somewhat independently of a teacher's actions. For example, some developmental scientists argue that brain maturation is a developmental mechanism that explains why certain abilities improve over time (e.g., Steinberg, 2008). Teachers obviously cannot control or harness brain maturation. That said, as we will learn in Chapter 2, experience can affect brain development.

Another important way that a developmental perspective should frame considerations of student learning and classroom instruction is that, for about the last 20 years, there has been a tendency among faculty in colleges of education and psychology departments to counteract earlier arguments that younger children are often not "ready" to understand a topic. At one time, many teacher educators assumed that waiting to teach something until children were ready was a major implication of Piaget's theory (see Chapter 3). At the same time, there was also a long-standing "reading readiness" view about waiting to teach anything about reading until children were about 6.5 years old (see Chapter 9, on beginning reading skills). Critics of Piaget's theory argued that he underestimated children's skills, and teachers unnecessarily taught children basic skills first (e.g., sounding out letters) before they taught them higher order skills (e.g., comprehension). The argument became that we should instead examine how skilled performers in some discipline (e.g., adult readers, practicing mathematicians, practicing scientists, practicing historians) carry out their work or perform tasks, and teach children to emulate them. The problem with the latter view is that novices do not really understand what experts are doing. Education faculty and psychologists soon discovered that perhaps you do want to have children, for example, understand whole numbers before you get them to understand rational numbers, negative integers, or algebra (see Chapter 12, on mathematics learning). Now there is a clear emphasis on creating *developmental progressions* that lay out precursor concepts and skills and all the subsequent skills that build on these precursor or foundational skills (Lehrer & Schauble, 2015). Doing so is consistent with a developmental perspective.

In Chapters 3–14, the goal is to not only chart the development domain-specific and domain-general propensities (listing the sequence of developmental states) but also describe theories that posit developmental mechanisms that explain how and why skills and dispositions change over time in both positive and negative ways. These mechanisms will be directly linked to teaching strategies when they are in fact under the control of teachers.

It is important to note how different it is to think of teachers as "facilitators of development" as opposed to "information providers." When teachers think of their job as merely covering the content in the required curriculum and think of students as receptacles into which this information can be "poured," they are not apt to promote development as described in this chapter. There would be no effort to understand what students know at the beginning of the year so that they can adjust up or down what they are about to present. Rather, they would just cover the same content regardless of what students know. Similarly, they might be puzzled as to why some students struggle. In addition, they might likewise cover content (because it should be covered) rather than understand where students are in the developmental sequence for some skill and where they should be going next to keep progressing in the appropriate manner.

It is further worth noting that the mandated curriculum of a school district may take into account the idea of an optimal developmental progression for some skill, but it may not. It is often the case that scholars in academia challenge the prevailing wisdom of what should be taught in school and how. Over the past 20 years, scholars in multiple fields have argued that the endpoint of instruction should be the acquisition of the skills and dispositions of highly skilled individuals or professionals in a given field such as reading, mathematics, science, or history. What kinds of skills and attitudes do these individuals have? We will see regularly in this book that the ideal set of skills in each of the fields of reading, math, and so on are rarely mastered by students by the time they reach the end of high school. A final goal of this book is to foster a different understanding of the endpoint of development than what seems to be fostered in standard curricula.

CHAPTER 2

Brain Development
and Cognitive Neuroscience

Why study brain development and cognitive neuroscience in a book about the development of school-related cognitive skills and motivation? There are at least two reasons. The first is that the fields of developmental, cognitive, and educational neuroscience are all burgeoning (Byrnes & Vu, 2015) and many researchers in these fields have conducted studies on topics that are included in this book (e.g., memory, language, reading skills, math skills). We would be remiss not to address relevant findings discovered by these researchers. As will be discussed later, however, the key term here is *relevant,* because not all neuroscientific findings are relevant to psychological and educational theories and some of these findings are, in fact, often uninformative and distracting.

The second reason for focusing on neuroscientific findings is that the brain "makes" cognition and emotion in a way analogous (but not identical) to the way electric currents running through wires makes electromagnetic waves (Byrnes & Vu, 2015). Psychologists not giving some attention to neuroscientific findings would be a little like physicists not trying understand the source of electromagnetic waves in wires. Scientists often find it useful to examine the articulation between two levels of analysis. For example, sociologists who study group-level phenomena (e.g., conflict among ethnic groups) would be wise to give at least a little attention to the psychologies or minds of individual people in groups. Just as group-level phenomena are one level above psychological phenomena, psychological phenomena are one level above brain-level phenomena in traditional levels-of-analysis discussions (Putnam, 1975). Some have argued that it is reductionistic for scholars at one level (e.g., sociologists) to focus on phenomena at one level below (e.g., the psychological level). However, taking into account certain findings from one level below is not the same as collapsing levels and no longer focusing on phenomena at the higher level (Byrnes & Eaton, 2020). So, when we want to explain why a young girl does not participate in class, for example, we should remain at the psychological level and appeal to psychological constructs to explain her behavior (e.g., "She does not *believe* she can do the task" or "She finds the material *boring*"). Beliefs and interests are psychological constructs. It would not be helpful to say, "She is not participating because her ventrolateral frontal lobe is not very active," which is a biological explanation. It is common for people in the media or educators to skip over the psychological level ("My brain makes me do it").

So how should educators approach neuroscientific findings? In what follows, we will examine three ways in which brain research has the potential to be informative to educators, and we will also briefly discuss some of the informative findings. The first way in which brain research has the potential to be informative is to think about *brain maturation* as a developmental mechanism (as discussed in Chapter 1). The second way is to consider how the *areal structure* of the brain can be sometimes exploited to help determine which of two competing psychological theories is correct. The third way is to introduce the idea of *learning disorders* and their possible origin in brain development. Each of these three potentially informative routes is discussed next.

BRAIN MATURATION

Teachers and parents have long recognized what appear to be qualitative shifts in abilities and understandings. For example, at one point a child has no spoken words in her vocabulary and then around 1 year of age she says her first word (see Chapter 8). At one point a child cannot hear the individual phonemes in a word and then can hear these phonemes (see Chapter 9). Moreover, it sometimes is the case that these emergent abilities appear at around the same age in many children (e.g., 1 year of age in the case of the first word), and one also discovers that attempts to have younger children demonstrate the ability (e.g., 9-month-olds say their first words or 4-year-old children hear phonemes in words) end up being futile. Further, there are age periods when diverse sets of abilities emerge at the same time. For example, between the ages of 3 and 5, children show significant improvements in their theory of mind, executive function, and use of complex syntax (see Chapters 6 and 8). Similarly, there are concomitant increases in other sets of abilities between ages 5 and 7. These age trends have been given labels such as the "3-to-5 shift" and the "5-to-7 shift" (e.g., Sameroff

& Haith, 1996). Collectively, all of the aforementioned phenomena have led some to infer that brain development is the likely cause of the emergence of an ability or sets of abilities. Some psychologists and philosophers have characterized the emergence of such skills as indicating that the ability has come "online" (e.g., Fodor, 1975), the way a website or computer program comes online and can be utilized. But what does it mean for the brain to mature and support the emergence of skills? The next section provides an answer to that question.

Eight Processes of Brain Development

One way to think about brain development is to consider what it means to say that "everything went well" when the processes responsible for producing a brain have all completed their tasks. A reasonable response to this thought experiment is to say, perhaps a little too simplistically, that the goal of brain development is to produce a brain that has the *right number* of the *right types* of brain cells located in the *right brain areas* and connected to each other in the *right ways*. We currently do not have a complete picture of what this properly configured brain looks like (so that we could say that Person 1's brain is more similar to the optimal brain than Person 2's), but we do know that certain disorders have been associated with having too many or too few brain cells in certain areas of the brain, and also with having atypical structural connections within and among brain regions (Byrnes & Eaton, 2020). So, this characterization of the goal of brain development is a good place to start. There are eight processes that collectively produce a brain that has the right number of the right types of brain cells located in the right areas and connected to each other in the right way.

The first process, *proliferation*, begins early in the prenatal period when a neural tube appears on the outer surface of an embryo, about 30 days after conception (Byrnes, 2001). The neural tube will eventually turn into the brain and spinal cord. Within one end of the neural tube, there are proliferative zones out of which brain cells are produced. If you divide the total number of brain cells produced by the amount of time that transpires between when the first and last cells are produced prenatally, the average rate of production is 250,000 cells per minute! Genetic instructions are probably behind the timing and amount of cells produced if we consider how species differ in terms of the total number brain cells, which, in turn, is determined by the number of days in which proliferation occurs in each species (Geshwind & Rakic, 2013). Proliferation lasts approximately 100 days in humans, 60 days in macaque monkeys, and 6 days in mice. With the exception of cells produced across the lifespan in the area of brain called the hippocampus, proliferation is largely over by the fourth prenatal month (Byrnes, 2001). But as we will see later, environmental factors could also interfere with proliferation. In any case, proliferation is responsible for

having the right number of cells. Although it can be quite difficult to estimate of the total number of brain cells with accuracy, recent advances using
modern radiological, computational, and other techniques suggest that the
adult human brain contains 86 billion neurons (16 billion of which are in
the cerebral cortex), 50 billion glial cells, and 20 billion epithelial cells (von
Bartheld, 2018).

But a brain will not be properly produced if cells remain near the proliferative zone in the neural tube. To make sure they move away from the
proliferative zone and end up in their correct locations, we need the second
process called *migration* (Byrnes, 2001; Geshwind & Rakic, 2013; Johnson
& de Haan, 2015). There are two kinds of migration: passive and active.
The passive kind occurs as newly proliferative cells emerge from the proliferative zone and push the already-produced cells away (think of popcorn
here; already popped corn gets pushed up to the top of the popper by newly
popped corn). The second kind, active migration, is fascinating because
clusters of cells crawl along spindles of glia cells that radiate away from the
proliferative zones. Genetic instructions are also once again largely responsible for migration occurring as it should, but note how both the passive and
active kind have enough physical qualities to them that one could imagine
two scenarios that illustrate the probabilistic, "bump and grind" aspect of
migration. One real scenario is that identical twins do not have identical
brains. Sometimes they are mirror images of each other, and brain scans
show they do not have exactly the same shapes and curves (Byrnes, 2001).
The second scenario is more hypothetical: if it were somehow possible to
(1) rewind the process of your own brain development back to when only
one brain cell had been produced and no migration had yet occurred, and
(2) we let proliferation and migration happen again, it is entirely possible
that your second brain would be at least subtly different than your current
brain. Later-produced cells migrate past earlier-produced cells, and line up
into columns (Geshwind & Rakic, 2013). Ultimately, the laminar, 6-layer
structure of the brain is produced that will contain the right mixture of
specific kinds of cells in each layer.

That brings us to the third process. Once the right number cells are
in the right locations, we next have to ensure that the right types of brain
cells are produced. The process responsible for this part of the goal of
brain development is called *differentiation* (Byrnes, 2001). A properly configured brain has different kinds of cells that are classified by their shape,
function, and orientation. Some cells are conical and therefore called *pyramidal* cells, while others look like starbursts so are called *stellate* cells.
Some are involved in processing information (e.g., pyramidal), but some
mainly serve the role of providing structure, myelin, and nutrition to the
processing cells (e.g., *glial cells* such as oligodendrocytes). Readers should
Google "pyramidal cells," "stellate cells," and "glial cells" to see what
these cells look like (e.g., *https://en.wikipedia.org/wiki/Pyramidal_cell*).

Some neurons excrete the neurotransmitter dopamine while others secrete serotonin. Some are excitatory (i.e., when they excrete their neurotransmitter the next neuron in a chain of neurons "fires"), while some are inhibitory (i.e., when they excrete their neurotransmitter the next neuron does not fire). At the point of proliferation, brain cells are called *progenitor* cells because they have not turned into one of these various kinds of cells. The progenitor cells are like stem cells in that they have not fully turned into the right kind of cell until they get to their proper location. But if migration goes awry and a cell ends up in the wrong place, it could still change into the right kind of cell for that location. Chemical signals from surrounding neurons and glial cells combined with genetic instructions instigate the process of differentiation. The chemical signals help correct any problem with migration if differentiation has not started yet (e.g., the cell goes to the wrong place).

In addition to being the right type, brain cells have to grow to their adult length, width, and weight in order to function correctly and make connections with other neurons. Thus, *growth* is the fourth process of brain development. Neurons start out much smaller and lighter than what they become by adulthood. Even so, a 1-year-old's brain weighs about 66% of the weight of a 22-year-old's brain, and a 2-year-old's brain weighs 75% (Borzage, Blüm, & Seri, 2014). By age 10, this figure is 98%. Hence, there is a threefold to fourfold increase in the size of the brain from birth to age 6 (Heiss & Olofsson, 2019). In addition to overall volume and weight increases, however, the human cortex increases in surface area as well, and this increase in surface area is the primary reason for the folds, or *sulci*, in the cortex. However, we not only have a larger surface area than other mammals, we also have considerably more neurons within the cortex, and these additional neurons give us our unique cognitive abilities (Herculano-Houzel, 2017). Surface area increases from early childhood to age 12, when it levels off (Amlien et al., 2016).

But neurons also have to grow in length in order to connect with other neurons, and this lengthening occurs throughout childhood and adolescence. Thus, growth is a prerequisite for the fifth process, *synaptogenesis* (Byrnes, 2001). Part of the intrinsic process of brain development is the fact that young brain cells spontaneously fire and release their neurotransmitters near adjacent cells in the small gap between axon terminals and dendrites called the *synapse* (see Figure 2.1). In addition, long-distance fibers from the extremities (eyes, limbs, ears, and so on) bring afferent stimulation to the brain and cause all the neurons with which they have formed synapses to fire. It takes some time for a fully functioning and efficient synapse to form between two neurons, and correlated firing over time causes the synapse to change. According to an old saying among neuroscientists, "neurons that fire together wire together." Yet another fascinating aspect of brain development that was found in experimental studies with animals

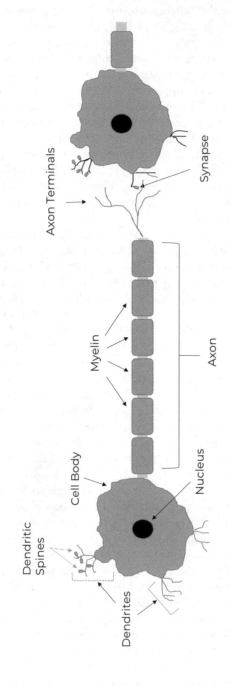

FIGURE 2.1. Schematic drawing of a neuron.

is that even transplanted neurons will grow toward, seek out, and find their proper targets to which they are supposed to be connected. Genetics probably specify these targets; but also, it would appear that a gradient of chemical signals along the way guide neurons toward their target (Byrnes, 2001; Geshwind & Rakic, 2013; Johnson & de Haan, 2015).

One key aspect of synaptogenesis is the formation of synapses on the spines of dendrites (Phillips & Pozzo-Miller, 2015; Stein & Zito, 2019). In a typically developing brain, spines take on several different forms, including a mushroom shape. The formation and elimination of synapses along dendritic spines is what neuroscientists mean by the terms *plasticity* and *learning* (Phillips & Pozzo-Miller, 2015). That is, when we learn something, it means we either created, eliminated, or reorganized a set of synaptic connections along the dendritic spines of excitatory (glutamatergic) neurons in the brain that are connected to the axon terminals of presynaptic neurons. With development, experience, and learning, increasing numbers of dendrites and spines along dendrites form. This increase in dendritic matter is called *dendritic arborization* (because postmortem slices of brain tissue show a "sprouting" of dendrites). So, to say that neurons are connected to each other in the right way means they have formed stable synapses with fully developed dendritic spines.

Another aspect of neurons being connected to each other in the right way is that when a neural network in the brain has been created to perform some task (e.g., interpret words or recognize faces), the neural tracts within these networks have to fire efficiently and quickly. To increase speed and efficiency, neurons must develop a fatty-acid coating called *myelin* (see Figure 2.1). When neurons become myelinated, the electrical conduction along a chain of neurons improves (Bercury & Macklin, 2019) and they can fire up to 100 times faster (Byrnes, 2001). Glial cells called *oligodendrocytes* have the job of wrapping myelin around axons, and this usually occurs in response to neural activity. Thus, the sixth process of brain maturation is *myelination*. To see the importance of myelin in an adult brain, consider an unfortunate consequence of having the neurodegenerative disease multiple sclerosis (MS): the immune systems of people diagnosed with MS attack their own neurons, causing a degradation of myelin. Patients with MS lose the ability walk, develop blurred vision, and so on. Conversely, it is possible to observe that people who have more myelin can perform tasks more rapidly than those with less myelin certain areas. For example, experts in particular fields (e.g., musicians) have more myelin in brain areas supporting particular skills (e.g., recognizing musical notes) than non-experts (Zatorre, Douglas Fields, & Johansen-Berg, 2012), and many studies have shown that one key characteristic of expertise is speed (see Chapter 7). Similarly, adolescents and adults have more myelinated fibers than children, and studies show that adolescents and adults perform a variety of tasks faster than children (Kail, Lervåg, & Hulme, 2016).

How do we know that experts have more myelin than non-experts or that adolescents have more myelin than children? The myelin coating along axons shows up as "white matter" when brains are scanned using magnetic resonance imaging (MRI). Neuron cell bodies show up as "grey matter." Because brain activity is a catalyst for myelination, myelination is assumed to occur throughout adulthood (Bercury & Macklin, 2015).

Whereas processes such as proliferation, growth, synaptogenesis, dendritic arborization, and myelination can be considered *progressive processes* because they build up a brain, the final two processes are called *regressive processes* because they try to "undo" or reverse two kinds of excesses: too many cells and too many synaptic connections (Franke, Luders, May, Wilke, & Gaser, 2012). Research shows that it is normal for developing human brains to have perhaps twice as many neurons and synaptic connections among cells than is needed (Byrnes, 2001; Johnson & de Haan, 2015; Riccomagno & Kolodkin, 2015). Such forms of overproduction probably occurred over thousands of years of evolution as a protective mechanism (Buss, Sun, & Oppenheim, 2006). As we will discuss in the next section, environmental events can interfere with processes such as proliferation, migration, and growth. So, instead of genes specifying the exact optimal number of cells and synapses ahead of time and hoping for the best, during prenatal development our brains create more cells and more connections than needed in case anything goes wrong. To the extent that cells fire and successfully compete for specific chemicals in the brain (trophic factors), they will end up surviving. Those that fire in an uncorrelated way (or not at all) end up dying off. This process of cell death is called *apoptosis*. Apoptosis also occurs in the basal ganglia of Parkinson's patients, but note how this produces serious debilitation in adults. In contrast, apoptosis in the brains of children and adolescents is a good thing; it whittles the brain down to the correct number of cells. Perhaps 40% of the cells that are proliferated will die off by adulthood.

The same can be said for having too many synapses. A brain will not function properly and efficiently with too many synapses, so it is important for excess synapses to be "pruned" (Geden, Romero, & Deshmukh, 2019). As noted above, the extended arms of neurons (axons) form synapses with dendrites (see Figure 2.1). Excess synapses are pruned by microglia that remove excess synapses via phagocytosis (de Silva, 2018). Also, neurons retract some of their axons away from other neurons. So, *apoptosis* and *axon retraction* are the two primary regressive processes that complete brain development.

Until recently, it has not been possible to precisely determine when regressive processes are most likely to occur during the lifespan because early studies relied on sporadically performed autopsies, uneven numbers of available autopsies conducted at particular ages, and the difficulty of counting neurons and synapses from slices of brain tissue (Azevedo et al.,

2009; von Bartheld, 2018). Newer techniques such as MRI can be used to assess changes in total grey matter and white matter with development. However, different labs have used different scanning techniques, which made comparisons across studies difficult. Using improved normalizing and standardization techniques, Franke et al. (2012) showed that grey matter volume shrinks 9% between ages 5 and 19, thereby demonstrating a fairly monotonic cortical thinning. Ball, Beare, and Seal (2019) found that thinning was fastest in the dorsolateral frontal and parietal cortex, precuneus, and primary visual cortex, and slowest in primary and supplementary motor, primary sensory, and superior temporal cortex. It is not clear from MRI results whether the thinning is due to apoptosis or synaptic pruning, but Ball et al. (2019) consider pruning to be more likely. However, others argue that pruning is usually followed by apoptosis (Riccomagno & Kolodkin, 2015). Amlien et al. (2016) found that thinning followed a monotonic loss from age 5 all the way to age 30 at a rate of about 1.5% a year (about 3.1 millimeters down to about 2.5 millimeters).

In contrast to grey matter thinning, white matter volume increases 14% between childhood and adolescence, but the increase plateaus by age 14 (Franke et al., 2012). Tamnes et al. (2017) reported that cortical volume increases during the first 2 years of life but decreases later in childhood and adolescence. Amlien et al. (2016) found that volume was relatively stable between ages 5 and 12, but then decreased between 12 and 20, and again between 20 and 30 at a slightly slower rate. Jetha and Segalowitz (2012) proposed that there are three phases in synaptic pruning: Phase I is birth to 2 years, Phase II occurs during adolescence, and, finally, Phase III occurs when people are in their early 20s.

Factors That Can Affect Brain Development

In the previous section that discussed the eight processes that (if all goes well) collectively produce a properly configured brain, references were made to some of the factors that seem to play a role in how these processes are carried out (e.g., genes). In this section, these factors and others are discussed in more detail. We will begin with genetics, and then examine chemical signaling, environmental experience, nutrition, steroids, and teratogens in turn.

Genetics

As described above, the three maturational processes that most clearly seem to implicate a role for genetics are proliferation, migration, and differentiation. Our genes specify the start and end dates for how many cells are produced, where progenitor cells should migrate to, and the kinds of cells that progenitor cells should turn into when they reach their intended destination. Genes are also implicated when we consider specific developmental disorders that are produced, in part, by problems in proliferation such as Down syndrome (DS) or trisomy 21 (Nakano-Kobayshi et al., 2017). When gametes (i.e., sperm and eggs) are produced, each parent's chromosomes are halved during meiosis in order that their offspring end up having the right amount of genetic material and chromosomes when sperm and eggs are joined during conception (Mom's half and Dad's half make a whole). In trisomy 21, however, one of the chromosomes in the 21st pair fails to completely separate (88% of the time in the egg), such that the offspring end up having 47 chromosomes rather than 46. The extra chromosome expresses a particular kinase that slows proliferation, and children diagnosed with DS end up having too few brain cells. One recent study using a chemical to inhibit the expression of this kinase prenatally in the mouse model of trisomy 21 showed that proliferation can return to its normal rate and the brains of these mice have the right number of cells produced (Nakano-Kobayshi et al., 2017). If this finding could be replicated in human offspring, this would be a remarkable achievement. Imagine if pregnant women who discover that their unborn child has trisomy 21 could take the kinase inhibitor and prevent abnormal brain development and learning disorders in their children.

However, genetics also seems to be implicated in the malformation of dendritic spines in children diagnosed with several learning disorders, such as DS, autism spectrum disorder (ASD), fragile X syndrome, and Rett syndrome (Phillips & Pozzo-Miller, 2015). Children with these disorders not only develop fewer spines on their dendrites, but the spines of their dendrites have different shapes than in typically developing children. Given that *the physical manifestation of learning is the development and reorganization of synapses along dendritic spine*s, it should be clear that having fewer and misshaped spines could be the leading cause of learning problems in these children. But problems in synapse formation and maintenance could also lead to other problems, such as faulty synaptic pruning or apoptosis (de Silva, 2018).

Chemical Signaling

It was noted earlier in this chapter that there are several points in which there appear to be backup systems in place in case genetic instructions fail to be carried out properly. In particular, sometimes neurons fail to migrate properly and end up in the wrong location. When this occurs, chemical signals from surrounding neurons instigate an altering of cell differentiation such that the out-of-place neuron turns into a different kind of cell, one that is appropriate for that location. For example, genetic instructions may have specified that the progenitor cell migrate to Level IV in the brain and become a pyramidal cell, but the cell migrates to Level III instead.

The chemical signals from neighboring neurons might cause the misplaced progenitor cell to differentiate into a stellate cell. Chemical signaling is also important for (1) directing migrating progenitor cells to their correct location (the concentration of the chemical gets stronger as the neuron gets closer to its destination), (2) providing guideposts for growing axons to find their targets, and (3) directing glial cells to envelope the axons of neurons with myelin.

Environmental Experience

The human brain is unique among animals, including other primates, in the length of time it takes to fully mature (Geshwind & Rakic, 2013). The "wiring" is by no means complete at birth, and it takes environmental experience to finish the "wiring." Synapses will only form among neurons if there is correlated activity among them. Some of this activity seems to be genetically encouraged by spontaneous, random firing during early prenatal development, but much of the correlated firing comes later, through experience in the world, and continues throughout one's life.

As we will see in Chapter 8, for example, auditory input is essential in promoting the development of receptive language skills to recognize the unique phonemes and phoneme combinations of one's native tongue. Children appear to be equipped to learn any language early in the postnatal period, but the auditory system is winnowed down to be attuned to just one's own language, perhaps through the regressive processes of synaptic reorganization, synaptic pruning, and apoptosis. Other instances of apoptosis and pruning are likewise heavily dependent on environmental input. It was also noted above that environmental input, learning, and practice instigate the process of myelination.

In the specific subject areas of math and reading, the classroom experience of learning these skills seems to "sculpt" the brain down from activating large areas in both hemispheres to activating smaller, highly specific areas in a single hemisphere (Byrnes & Eaton, 2020). Researchers who study executive function skills (see Chapter 6) likewise explain socioeconomic differences in these skills in terms of environmental differences in children's homelives (Lawson, Hook, & Farah, 2018).

All such findings demonstrate how it would be an inferential fallacy to conclude that whenever structural MRIs or autopsies reveal anatomical differences between the brains of individuals or groups (e.g., men versus women; poor versus rich; Einstein versus the rest of us) that these structural differences have to be due to genetic differences. People who have different experiences or practice different skills over time would naturally have brains that are structurally different (e.g., more myelin within and between brain regions; more glial cells in one area than in another). This is not to say, of course, that some optimal combination of genetic instructions, progressive brain development processes, environmental input, and regressive processes could not produce networks of neurons that process information better or underlie high levels of cognitive skills. But it is clearly the case that "neither genes nor input is prescriptive or determinative of outcome" (Stiles & Jernigan, 2010, p. 328).

Nutrition

In order for any cell in the human body to be produced, RNA "reads off" DNA instructions in chromosomes to construct proteins that eventually form the building blocks of the cell through complex and dynamic chemical and physical processes. Our body parts (including our brains) could not be produced if cells lacked access to the nutrients that subserve this building block process. Some of the required nutrients include proteins, carbohydrates, and fatty acids, but also micronutrients such as iron, iodine, zinc, and folic acid (a B vitamin) (Prado & Dewey, 2014). Developing babies would initially get these substances via the blood supply of the pregnant mother after she consumed foods rich in these substances (meats, complex carbs, spinach, broccoli, etc.). Postnatally, infants would initially get these nutrients and micronutrients via breast milk (if they are able to breast feed) and later via formula and solid food (Prado & Dewey, 2014).

Nutrition is important not only for building and proliferating brain cells, but also for later processes such as myelination (Deoni, Dean, Joelson, O'Regan, & Schneider, 2018). In addition, the availability of certain nutrients has been found to have different effects on brain development depending on when the nutrients have been ingested (or not). In experiments with mice, for example, malnutrition during the prenatal period has been found to slow the proliferation process such that fewer brain cells are actually produced (Byrnes, 2001). In addition, a recent study showed that protein restriction prior to the point in which a mouse embryo even implants in the placenta was found to permanently alter brain cell proportion and affect later short-term memory (Gould et al., 2018). Other studies have shown that lack of access to other nutrients or micronutrients had differential effects depending on when the restrictions occur pre- and postnatally (Prado & Dewey, 2014). In other words, there appear to be critical periods in the operation of certain brain development processes (e.g., proliferation, myelination) when essential nutrients need to be present.

It is also the case that some 25% of our daily caloric intake is utilized to maintain our brain functions (the other 75% is used for movement and maintenance of other bodily functions) (Herculano-Houzel, 2017). Positron emission tomography (PET) and functional MRI (fMRI) scans that rely on blood flow to active brain areas also show that younger children seem to have even higher caloric needs because much larger, bilateral areas are active in their brains than in those of older children and adults who are performing the same task (or even resting in the scanner). Thus, mothers need to have adequate diets throughout pregnancy and breastfeeding, and children require adequate nutrition to promote healthy brain development and learning in school. In addition, however, a recent study showed that a modest amount of neurogenesis is still present even in adult brains (in the hippocampus) and adequate nutrition is required to maintain the process of creating new brain cells out of stem cells as older cells die off (Ferreira, Sousa, Bessa, Sousa, & Marques, 2018). Lack of adequate nutrition combined with lack of use of particular skills ("lose it or use it") are jointly responsible for monotonic losses of brain cells in late adulthood and old age, and poor nutrition also contributes to cognitive impairments as older adults attempt to reason, use language, or try to remember something.

The importance of diet is further apparent when one considers the consequences of the genetic disorder phenylketonuria (PKU). Children diagnosed with PKU lack the enzyme needed to convert the amino acid phenylalanine into the important nutrient tyrosine (Al Hafid & Christodoulou, 2015). As a result, phenylalanine builds up in their brains, causing brain defects that, in turn, cause intellectual impairments. In most developed countries, genetic screening tests are conducted to see if children have the recessive gene for PKU. If they do, they are immediately placed on a special diet to limit the substances that metabolize into phenylalanine (certain proteins). Newer approaches have also relied on the ingestion of enzymes and even gene therapy.

Throughout this chapter, what becomes immediately apparent is the extent to which all of the processes of brain development and factors affecting these processes work together in complex and interacting ways. When all factors are working together in the intended direction, there are cascading benefits. However, when one or more factors are adversely affected (dendritic arborization), other factors are affected as well (synaptic pruning and cell death). In the case of nutrition, we see that nutrition, too, should be understood as interdependent with other processes. In particular, nutrition should be viewed as part of the newly emphasized *microbiota–gut–brain axis* (Heiss & Olofsson, 2019; Wang et al., 2018).

There are billions of colonies of gut microbes, including bacteria and viruses (Heiss & Olofsson, 2019). Which microbes are abundant in a child's intestinal system depends on what they eat, because different microbes thrive on different nutrients. We rely on microbes to digest hard-to-digest material such as whole-grain fibers. Moreover, the metabolites that are the product of microbial digestion are not only used for energy, they also serve as signals to the brain. These signals in turn are involved in direct communication along afferent neural pathways that begin in the intestinal tract and connect with the vagus nerve, which in turn connects with brain areas (Heiss & Olofsson, 2019).

But the microbial metabolites are also involved in modulating neurogenesis (in utero) and synaptogenesis and regressive processes (postnatally) (Heiss & Olofsson, 2019). When antibiotics are used experimentally in mice, they have been found to have more neurons that survive longer than animals not exposed to antibiotics. Interestingly, gastrointestinal symptoms and altered gut microbial composition are found in children diagnosed with several developmental disorders, such as ASD (Heiss & Olofsson, 2019). Perhaps these intestinal problems that contribute to abnormalities in brain development occur via the microbiota–gut–brain axis. Understanding this potential link could have important consequences, in which a correction of the microbial composition early in life could help interfere with faulty synaptogenesis, dendritic arborization, or regressive processes.

All of the above findings have implications for breast feeding, since breast milk in healthy mothers contains not only the right kinds of needed nutrients for brain development, but also initial immune system antibodies, important metabolites of gut bacteria, and the microbes themselves in the proper composition and proportion (Heiss & Olofsson, 2019). Formula-fed infants eventually do acquire the adult-like composition of gut microbials by age 2, but early on their microbiotas are distinct from those of breast-fed infants. A large, international, multisite study funded by the Bill and Melinda Gates foundation (i.e., "MAL-ED") found that iron deficiency, home sanitation, and maternal education were all predictive of cognitive development by age 5, but early enteric pathogens and diarrhea were predictive at age 2 but not age 5. There is obviously much more to learn about the important interrelationships between nutrition, gut microbes, brain development, and cognitive development.

Steroids

The two major classes of steroids produced in the body are corticosteroids (e.g., glucocorticoids) and sex steroids (e.g., androgens, progestogens, and estrogens). The former steroids are informally called *stress hormones* and are produced by the adrenal glands that sit on top of the kidneys. When we feel stressed or afraid, the adrenal glands secrete the glucocorticoids, which in turn make our hearts race, pupils dilate, and so on. The sex hormones are produced in the brain (e.g., by the pituitary gland) or by gonads (i.e., ovaries and testes) and are responsible for the development of secondary sex characteristics (e.g., pubic hair), sexual drive, and menstrual cycles.

Both kinds of steroid hormones have been of interest to researchers who study brain development because there are receptors for these hormones in multiple areas of the brain. Given the presence of receptors, researchers have hypothesized that perhaps steroids may play a role in brain development. More precisely, researchers have wondered whether stress hormones could have a deleterious effect on brain development (Lupien, McEwen, Gunnar, & Heim, 2009) and whether sex hormones might cause anatomical sex differences in the brains of males and females (Etchell et al., 2018).

To truly discern the effect of either type of hormone on the brain, it would be necessary to conduct experimental studies in which people are randomly assigned to either a treatment group or a control group, and the groups only differ in terms of whether or not participants were exposed to steroids (or different amounts of the steroids). Doing so would be unethical (and immoral), so the two usual alternatives are (1) to conduct experiments with animals (usually mice) or (2) to compare groups of people who naturally experience different levels of hormones (e.g., institutionalized children versus typically developing children; males versus females). The problem with using animals as subjects is that their brains differ from human brains in nontrivial ways (Herculano-Houzel, 2017; Lupien et al., 2009). For example, the neuronal and synaptic density of mice brains is much lower than in humans, and processes such as neurogenesis and apoptosis play a more prominent role in mice brains than in human brains. These differences suggest that mice brains could be more or less vulnerable to, or reactive to, hormones than human brains.

The problem with comparing preexisting groups is that they often differ in other ways than simply the level and kind of hormones in their blood. Institutionalized children in Romania, for example, are not only separated from parents, but their diets are also often substandard, and the institutions are quite removed from what would be considered an enriched environment. Similarly, mothers who experience considerable stress during pregnancy and pass on these stress hormones via the placenta might be less educated, of lower income, and so on. And if they are prone to anxiety because of a genetic predisposition, their children would likewise share this genetic predisposition.

And as noted above, when the role of experience is considered, different experiences could sculpt the brain in different ways. If men and women engage in different kinds of activities (or differing dosages of experience), it would be expected that their brains would be structurally different (e.g., more extensive myelination in areas related to different skills). These differences could have nothing to do with sex hormones. In addition, however, men tend to be 9% taller and 9% heavier than women, on average. Any difference discovered in the thickness of cortical areas would have to be corrected by this factor. Orangutans have larger brains than humans, but not when you correct for body size.

With all these provisos in mind, there is some evidence that the volume of the hippocampus tends to be smaller in children and adults who are exposed to high levels of stress hormones both prenatally and postnatally (even through old age) (Lupien et al., 2009). Recall that the hippocampus seems to be the one brain area in which neurogenesis still occurs, and stress hormones do cross the blood–brain barrier. These findings suggest that stress hormones may interfere with neurogenesis, or could affect the extent to which other, later, processes occur (e.g., myelination, synaptogenesis). A recent study also seemed to show that the cortical thinning that occurs during adolescence was correlated with the levels of both stress and sex hormones (Wong et al., 2018).

With respect to sex hormones, one occasionally sees an article in which males and females are reported to differ with respect to the size of some brain area (or thickness of the cortex in that area), but it is important to rely on meta-analyses of multiple studies, because gender differences arising from a single sample could happen as a result of chance factors in sampling. As noted above, it is also important to correct for body size. Wong et al. (2018) reported sex differences in cortical thinning during adolescence but did not correct for body size. One recent meta-analysis of the brain areas associated with language development showed no overall sex differences (Etchell et al., 2018).

Teratogens

The category of teratogens includes any substance that is implicated in producing physical abnormalities in developing fetuses, including alcohol, cocaine, lead, nicotine, viruses, and so on. Attempts to establish a causal role for any of these substances run into the same interpretative difficulties described above for hormones. In particular, experiments can only be ethically carried out in murine studies (mice as subjects); in correlational studies of humans, it is nearly always the case that mothers and children who are exposed to many teratogens differ in important ways from mothers who can avoid these substances (e.g., income level, education level, diet). Thus, when differences are revealed in children's brains or behaviors, we need to ask if these differences are due to the teratogens or to the confounding factors (e.g., mother's diet or education level).

We know from retrospective studies of notorious factors such as the morning sickness drug thalidomide or the rubella (German measles) virus, it clearly matters when a developing fetus is exposed to either of these teratogens. Body parts such as limbs or brain regions seem to have critical periods. If exposure to thalidomide occurs during a critical period for limb development, for example, children might be born with a deformed or missing limb. Other kinds of teratogens are also expected to affect developing bodies and brains in similar ways, depending on such factors as timing and dosage. One of the latest identified is the Zika virus, which is strongly associated with microencephaly (*www.cdc.gov/zika/healtheffects/birth_defects.html*).

Due to ethical concerns, it is obviously not possible to create experimental groups of pregnant women that differ only in terms of how much alcohol they consume (e.g., one drink versus two drinks per day) and when they consume it (e.g., during the first trimester versus during the third trimester). Such designs would be the only way to definitely answer the question of whether a substance is a teratogen for human infants. We know that fetal alcohol syndrome (FAS) can be an outcome of heavy drinking, but not all babies exposed to heavy amounts of alcohol develop FAS and related disorders (Howe et al., 2019). The findings have been inconsistent as to whether low to moderate levels of exposure are linked to some of the facial and cognitive deficits of FAS (Howe et al., 2019). One study showed that low levels of exposure may be related to modestly lower IQ scores only if mothers and children were carriers of one of four genes related to the metabolism of alcohol (Lewis et al., 2012). The IQ scores for nondrinking women who had the genes were 103.1 (2 or less alleles), 103.5 (3 alleles), and 103.2 (4 alleles) (no significant differences). For the women who drank one to six drinks per week, the IQ scores were 107.5 (2 or less alleles), 105.4 (3 alleles), and 104.0 (4 alleles). Whereas these differences are statistically significant because of the large sample size in the study, the largest gap relates to a small effect size ($d = 0.23$) and is not practically meaningful. In addition, these same groups also differed in their socioeconomic level, and the researchers did not control for socioeconomic status, education, and age.

That said, the combination of (1) significant dosage- and timing-related effects for the aforementioned substances and viruses in murine studies and (2) the possibility that the findings are at best uncertain because of the existence of confounds in correlational studies of humans has led to the recommendation that to be entirely safe, pregnant women should abstain from alcohol, cigarettes, and other substances, and do their best to not be exposed to the rubella and Zika viruses.

Exploiting the Areal Structure of the Cortex

As a final topic to explore, it is important to recognize that a mature brain comprises a large number of areas that perform highly specific tasks. For example, some areas process visual stimuli (area V1) while other areas process auditory stimuli (area A1) (Oleary, Stocker, & Zembrzychi, 2013). In addition to these general areas, however, beginning in the 1800s, neurologists began to document case studies that demonstrated so-called "double dissociations" (McCarthy & Warrington, 1990). In particular, patients who suffered a brain injury in one part of the frontal lobe (Broca's area) lost the ability to speak (aphasia) but retained the ability to sing; others who suffered an injury in a spot of the frontal lobe just above Broca's area lost the ability to sing but retained the ability to speak. Other examples of double dissociations include the fact that injury to one brain area affects memory for multiplication facts but not the ability to add; damage to another area affects the ability to add but not memory for multiplication facts. In an effort to compile all such findings and identify these distinct areas, the neurologist Korbinian Brodmann created a "map" that included numbers for the different areas (e.g., Brodmann area 44 vs. Brodmann area 45; see Figure 2.2).

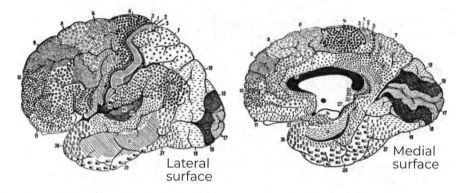

Lateral surface

Medial surface

FIGURE 2.2. Brodmann areas.

With the advent of modern neuroscientific techniques such as electroencephalography (EEG) and fMRI, researchers have largely confirmed the functions of the areas identified by Brodmann and researchers who conducted numerous studies of double dissociations. Educators might be particularly interested in the studies that have identified the areas of the cortex that seem to be involved in the execution of school-related skills such as reading or mathematics, or even more domain-general competencies such as memory, language, or attention. We will describe some of these areas in later chapters on both the domain-specific and domain-general competencies.

The work that has identified these areas is perhaps less informative than research that helps decide among competing psychological theories (Byrnes & Eaton, 2020). If we wanted a psychological explanation for why a baseball pitcher threw a curve ball to a batter who had two strikes, we would not be satisfied by a biological or physical explanation of how his arm moves (Pylyshyn, 1984). Similarly, if we wanted to know whether the mind of a child registers all of the individual letters in a word when reading, we should not care whether a researcher showed that the *visual word form area* in the left hemisphere was active during reading. Such a finding by itself is fairly meaningless, psychologically or educationally speaking. It becomes more meaningful when it can be shown that the visual word form area has the specific job of identifying individual letters and only has that job. And if one theorist argues that readers do not process individual letters but, rather, unanalyzed wholes (or visual "gestalts") while another says they do process the individual letters, the fMRI evidence suggests the latter theory is more accurate than the former theory. So, the most informative neuroscientific findings help us decide among psychological theories, in much the way that findings of psychological studies do. Knowing locations of active areas cannot help a teacher understand the development of reading or math skills. Nor is it helpful to show a difference in activation patterns between typically developing children and those diagnosed with learning disorders.

In this book, we will often consider whether neuroscientific findings help us decide among competing psychological claims. We will not spend much time showing where in the brain a task is performed. But it is important to note at the outset that this logic of exploiting the areal structure of the brain only works when an area only performs one job. If it is active when many different tasks are performed, the evidence is not particularly reliable or useful. It turns out that most areas of the brain have multiple functions rather than a single function. Thus, readers should always remember to interpret neuroscientific evidence with a certain degree of caution.

PART II

Domain-General Theories of Cognitive Skills and Motivation

CHAPTER 3

Domain-General Theories of Learning

A domain-general theory is one that has applicability to the learning of any subject matter (e.g., math, science, social studies). It is useful to begin our discussion of how to apply psychological theories to school learning by first considering domain-general theories of learning, memory, and motivation before we examine more domain-specific theories later in the book (e.g., of how people learn math). It is not possible to fully describe each of the five theories to be discussed in this chapter in a single chapter (or even a single book!) but doing so is not necessary for our purposes. Rather, the goal is to present just the fundamental ideas of the theories that have relevance for school-related learning. To help structure the discussion and provide a framework for readily comparing theories, each theory will be described in turn by providing answers to the following five questions:

1. How does or did the theorist define knowledge?
2. How does knowledge get into the mind according to the theorist?
3. How does or did the theorist explain knowledge growth?
4. What instructional practices are consistent with this theory?
5. How might we evaluate this theory?

We will discuss additional domain-general theories such as information-processing (IP) theory, expertise theory, and theory theory (not a typo) in Chapters 4 (memory development), 6 (executive function and self-regulation), 7 (intelligence, aptitude, and expertise), and 13 (scientific reasoning skills), so they will not be discussed here. The five to be discussed in this chapter include Thorndike's theory, Skinner's theory, Piaget's theory, schema theory, and Vygotsky's theory. Although most of these theories were proposed many years ago, they achieved a considerable amount of empirical support in their day and can still be considered influential as opposed to moribund. Comparing these theories also allows us to see how different paradigms can look at the same child in different ways.

FIVE INFLUENTIAL DOMAIN-GENERAL THEORIES OF LEARNING

Thorndike's Theory

Edward Thorndike (1874–1949) was a highly influential professor who held a position at Teachers College, Columbia University. He is considered the father of educational psychology, which is defined as the field in which psychological principles are applied to educational practice (*www. apadiv15.org*). As we will see by the end of this chapter, learning theorists differ in terms of the extent to which they focus on rote versus meaningful learning. Thorndike was a prominent advocate for rote learning and was often a target for criticism from scholars and practitioners who advocated more meaningful forms of learning. However, it is also the case that rote learning can and does (and should?) occur in educational settings, so a fair-minded approach would be to consider both the rote learning and meaningful learning perspectives in this chapter. In addition, many modern theories of learning in the field of cognitive psychology seem to emphasize rote learning (e.g., John Anderson's ACT-R model; Anderson, Betts, Bothell, Hope, & Lebiere, 2019), and Thorndike's approach can be considered one of the first in this regard. In what follows, we will learn more about his theory by way of the five questions listed above.

How Did Thorndike Define Knowledge?

To answer this question, we shall see that Thorndike and many other psychologists were heavily influenced by philosophers, especially those in the branch of philosophy called *epistemology*. This philosophical influence makes sense because psychology was once a subfield of philosophy before scholars in the 1800s saw the need to collect data and be more scientific (rather than philosophical) to decide among debates regarding the nature of the mind (Byrnes, 1992). In Thorndike's case, he was very much influenced by associationist and empiricist philosophers such as John Locke and David Hume. *Associationists* believe that individual bits of knowledge in the mind exist in a network of associations. For example, in his view, the image of your friend's face and sound pattern of her name are connected via an associative bond in your mind. The same can be said for the answer "9" for the problem "What is 3 × 3?" So, knowledge for Thorndike is simply this network of associated bits of information. This network contains fewer bits and fewer associations in young children but contains many bits and many associations in an adult.

How Does Knowledge Get into the Mind?

This second question invites a consideration of the term *empiricist* that was referenced in the previous section. Empiricists believe that all knowledge in the mind must enter through the senses. So, the one bit of information regarding the image of your friend's face came through your eyes and the visual processing areas of your brain, while the sound pattern of her name came through your ears and auditory processing centers of your brain. Your mind copies sensory experiences such as the face and name, or answer "9" and question, "What is 3 × 3?" that might be printed on a worksheet or flash card.

How Does Knowledge Grow?

According to Thorndike (and modern associationists), all bits of knowledge in your mind are associated to other items of knowledge, but these *associative bonds* can vary according to their strength. When two items are strongly associated with each other, the occurrence of one readily makes you think of the other. So, if you think of your friend's face, her name will immediately come to mind if she is a friend that you see a lot and have known for some time. Philosopher David Hume used the example of a shawl that his grandmother always wore. Even after his grandmother passed away, seeing the shawl made him think of her. However, consider next the examples of trying to remember the name of someone that you just met at a party or recalling an obscure fact that you learned in fifth grade (What is the leading export of Bosnia and Herzegovina?). These bonds may be far weaker, so the new face does not readily evoke the name, and the question about the obscure fact does not readily evoke the answer (car seats, according to Wikipedia).

Thorndike introduced two "laws" to explain why some bonds differ in strength and why bonds can grow in strength over time (Thorndike, 1913). The *law of exercise* actually consisted of two sublaws: the law of use and the law of disuse. To paraphrase the *law of use* in modern terms, it simply suggests that the more often two items of information co-occur or are repeated together, the stronger the associative bond becomes. So, if you form a new friendship, the bond between the face and name would tend to be weak or nonexistent the first time you spend time together with the person, but it should be far stronger after the 50th encounter. The same can be said for any fact learned in school. If you repeatedly study pairings such as "9" and "What is 3 × 3," or "Harrisburg" for "What is the capital of Pennsylvania?" the associative bonds for these pairings grow in strength. Conversely, when the pairings no longer co-occur, that is when the *law of disuse* comes into play. If you learned school facts via rote repetition, then never encounter them or think of them for 20 years, the occurrence of one (a face) does not immediately evoke the other (the name).

However, if you also follow the pairing with something "satisfying" as well, Thorndike argued that this positive event "stamps in" the bond in the brain and makes it stronger than repetition alone. The phenomenon demonstrates his second law, the *law of effect*. So, if a child raises his hand, answers "9" to the question "What is 3 × 3?," and gets praised by his teacher, the law of effect kicks in. But just as the law of exercise has a law of disuse, the law of effect has the subtheme that it is possible to significantly weaken a bond by following it with an event that is "annoying" (Thorndike, 1913). So, keeping with the same example, the bond would be weakened if a child incorrectly says "6" to the question and is scolded by his teacher. We will see later in this chapter that the law of effect laid the foundation for Skinner's theory of reinforcement and punishment.

In summary, according to Thorndike, knowledge grows by continually presenting new information via the senses, repeatedly pairing bits of information, and introducing satisfying states of affairs after correct answers.

What Instructional Practices Are Consistent with Thorndike's Theory?

Well, given the discussion so far, it should be clear that practices such as the use of flash cards, worksheets that require repeated presentation and recall of information, and choral responding (e.g., teacher calls out a question and students respond as a group) would be consistent. In other words, skill-and-drill would be central.

How Might Thorndike's Theory Be Evaluated?

With the advent of constructivism (see below), arguments favoring so-called meaningful learning, and various reform movements in math education, science education, and social studies education, any approach that smacked of rote learning has been roundly criticized. In many ways, Thorndikean teaching is considered to be the antithesis of modern approaches to teaching. That said, his principles are quite in line with many theories in cognitive psychology (as noted earlier). It certainly is true that we do form associations in our minds through repeated encounters and co-occurrences, and that praise and punishments can play a role in how quickly we learn things. Moreover, studies have shown that the switch to meaningful approaches and downplay of rote learning has led to generations of children who do not know basic math facts (their "times tables"), science facts (definitions of different kinds of tree species), or historical facts (when the Civil War occurred). However, we can also learn to associate things repeatedly as we encounter them in meaningful situations, and endless rote learning can be rather boring. Moreover, there is a kind of knowledge called *conceptual understanding*, and Thorndike's theory does not address this kind of knowledge. We will also see that there is nothing in Thorndike's theory that would preclude children learning any topic at any age (which is clearly not possible). That is, Thorndike could not explain why 8-year-olds cannot easily learn algebra, but Piaget or Vygotsky could explain this age difference (see below). Thus, there is a certain truth value to Thorndike's approach, but it only represents one kind of learning that should be supplemented (rather than replaced) by more meaningful approaches.

Skinner's Theory of Operant Conditioning

B. F. Skinner (1904–1990) began to develop his own theory on the heels of waning influence of Thorndike's account. In many ways, he saw his own effort as an improvement over Thorndike's account (Skinner, 1974). Moreover, just as Thorndike was influenced by the philosophical perspectives of associationism and empiricism, Skinner was influenced by the growing movements of behaviorism and arguments of philosophers of science in the 1920s. Philosophers of science argued that an enterprise can only be judged to be truly scientific if (1) claims and evidence are open to refutation and (2) the evidence can be objectively confirmed by other scientists. Skinner looked at the main psychological theories that were developed between the mid-1800s and Thorndike's time and saw that they seemed to rely on introspection, or self-reports of things in the mind (e.g., the image of your friend). Since other people cannot objectively verify what is in your mind, Skinner argued that psychologists who referred to these unverifiable mental entities (i.e., Thorndike) were not being scientific. He agreed with one of the original behaviorists who came before him, John B. Watson (1878–1958), that the goal of psychology was not to explain mental events or how mental events lead to behavior, but rather to predict and control behavior by appealing to environmental events (Watson, 1913).

How Did Skinner Define Knowledge?

As implied above, Skinner disagreed with the theoretical utility of mental constructs such as knowledge. If you want to predict and control behavior, he argued, you can do far better by appealing to things in the environment than by appealing to mental constructs. Regarding mental entities such as concepts, Skinner (1974) wrote, "The referents of concepts are in the real world, they are not ideas in the mind. . . . We do not need to suppose an abstract entity or concept held in mind; a subtle and complex history of reinforcement has generated a specific kind of stimulus control" (p. 106). Some of his predecessors and contemporaries called themselves behaviorists but allowed for some sort of role for mental constructs. Because Skinner argued for entirely ridding psychology of these notions, he was said to advocate a *radical behaviorism*.

We can suppose that the behaviorist analogue to the notion of "knowledge" would be Skinner's construct of a *repertoire* of behavior. All of us, including students, engage in actions all day long. The collection of actions that are under the control of the same stimuli is called a repertoire. So, everything a child does, for example, when filling out a math worksheet would be the repertoire of behaviors related to that worksheet. To Skinner, people do not "have" knowledge or know anything. Rather they simply "do" or "behave." Teachers should care about whether a child successfully completes the worksheet; the goal of instruction is that end. We should not care about or envision something like math skills in the head, he argued.

How Does Knowledge Get into the Mind?

Again, this would not be an appropriate question to ask Skinner. A better one would be, "What should be done to ensure that a student acquires a particular repertoire of behavior such as sit still in class, raise a hand to answer a question, or correctly fill out a language arts homework page?" To answer such questions, we need a few more behaviorist constructs. The first two are the concepts of stimuli and responses. A *stimulus* is some aspect of the environment that has the potential to control behavior (Skinner, 1974). This might be an auditory tone, a spoken word, someone's face, a piece of candy, and so forth. A *response* is simply a behavior emitted in a particular situation. The three key kinds of stimuli include discriminative stimuli, reinforcers, and punishers. *Discriminative stimuli* occur before responses are emitted and serve to signal that reinforcers or punishers are soon to follow. So, in a classic Skinner box experiment with rats, a green light may come on inside the box (discriminative stimuli) before the rat presses a bar (response) and receives a food pellet (reinforcer). But in the classroom, it may be a teacher question (discriminative stimuli) followed by a correct answer (response) followed by teacher praise (reinforcer). When discriminative stimuli signal that a punisher is about to occur, the learner should avoid doing a particular response.

How do you know that a stimulus is a reinforcer or punisher according to Skinner? Not if it is "satisfying" or "annoying," as Thorndike would argue. These are internal, mental responses that are not helpful, in Skinner's view. You never really know what would be judged this way. The key test is whether the response increases or decreases in frequency over time. If teacher praise following a correct answer increases the frequency of correct answers in a particular student, it is a reinforcer. If correct answers do not increase, it is not a reinforcer even if the child seems to like praise (which is irrelevant to Skinner). If whatever the teacher does seems to lead to a decrease in behavior, it is a punisher (even if we might think it should be pleasing or satisfying). So, if praise after a correct response leads to fewer correct responses, it is a punisher. To know which is which, Skinnerians like to chart the frequency of responses pre and post the introduction of a stimulus such as praise.

To add some more complexity to this theory, we will briefly discuss Skinner's notion of *schedules of reinforcement* (Catania, 2013). You can (1) vary the amount of time that elapses before reinforcers (or punishers) are introduced (e.g., every 5 minutes or once an hour), or (2) vary how many times a response has to be performed before a reinforcer is introduced (e.g., every time or after three times), or (3) vary how consistently the amount of time or number of responses are required (e.g., every 5 minutes or varying the time between 4, 5, and 6 minutes). A *fixed-interval (FI) schedule* introduces reinforcers at constant intervals, no matter what the animal (or student) does. For example, an FI(5) schedule might introduce a food pellet every 5 minutes. Or an FI(7) schedule may send a paycheck to an employee every seven days no matter what the employee does. A *variable-interval (VI) schedule* introduces reinforcers at variable times. A *fixed-ratio (FR) schedule* introduces a reinforcer after the person does the required behavior a specific number of times (e.g., FR(3) = always after three correct answers). A *variable-ratio (VR) schedule* introduces a reinforcer after the person does the required behavior a variable number of times (e.g., VR(3) might give reinforcement after two, three, or four responses, with an average of three). Studies with animals suggest that a VR schedule leads to the highest level of responding (Catania, 2013).

How Does Knowledge Grow?

In keeping with the storyline of behaviorism, a more apt question would be, how do students acquire or build up new repertoires? The preceding discussion of discriminative stimuli, reinforcers, punishers, and responses applies when a single behavior is required (e.g., the one-word answer to a fact question) or after a more complex sequence of behaviors is required (solving a multistep math or science problem). How do we create a more complex sequence in order that we can then reinforce it and make it happen more often? That brings us to another important construct of radical behaviorism: shaping. *Shaping* refers to the reinforcement of successive approximations of a behavior.

To illustrate, a new rat that is introduced to a Skinner box does not "know" that a bar in the box will lead to a food pellet if it is pressed. To reach that point, you have to break the process down into successive approximations and reinforce each successive approximation. For example, you might begin by waiting until the animal faces the bar and you drop in a food pellet. Animals have the instinct to repeat behaviors that seem to have produced a reinforcer (Skinner called this "superstitious behaviors"), so they run and get the pellet, go back to the spot in the box where they turned and faced the bar, and do that again. The next step is to reinforce that facing behavior a few more times until it is established. Then you might no longer reinforce simply facing the bar but require the animal to move closer to it and then reinforce that. You then continue reinforcing closer approximations until the animal eventually presses the bar by accident and you reinforce that. Skinner believed that any multistep behavior (e.g., uttering a seven-word sentence, playing a song on an instrument, solving a two-digit subtraction problem) could be shaped in the same way.

What Instructional Practices Are Consistent with the Theory?

Many people who believe that we do have concepts, mental images, facts, and so on stored in our knowledge find the behaviorist account a little off-putting and, well, too behavioristic. And, for the sake of brevity, we need not get into the long arguments that led to the downfall of behaviorism as the dominant paradigm and the "cognitive revolution" of the late 1950s (Byrnes, 1992). Suffice it to say that in developmental, educational, and cognitive psychology (obviously the latter), the dominant paradigms are cognitivist in nature and have amply shown how mental entities can be used to predict and explain behaviors.

That said, there are many students in special education who are unable to benefit from traditional instruction because of cognitive limitations, and they engage in inappropriate or destructive behaviors that need to be modified. The most effective approach for helping these students is called *applied behavior analysis* (ABA) and it relies on the principles of radical behaviorism. It is the method of choice for children diagnosed with DS or ASD (*www.bacb.com/about-behavior-analysis*). In addition, for very unruly regular education students, classroom teachers could structure their classroom-management routine around the ideas of operant conditioning and get an unruly classroom under control. The idea of a *token economy* for classroom management is one strategy. One might create a board with rows of circles next to each student's name. Students receive a new circle every time they are well behaved. Once they reach a certain number, they may get extra recess time.

How Might Skinner's Theory Be Evaluated?

I have already alluded to the fact that most people outside of the field of ABA have little use for radical behaviorism because of its anticognitive slant. Similar to what was said above for Thorndike, most psychologists and teachers believe there is such a thing as meaningful learning and conceptual understanding. In addition, however, behaviorism has been criticized for undermining intrinsic motivation (Ryan & Deci, 2006) and the autonomy of individuals. Skinner wrote a book in 1971 called *Beyond Freedom and Dignity* in which he claimed that it is good for governments to use his behaviorist principles to control people and that there is no such thing as free will.

That said, it would be wrong to conclude that nothing of value could be gained from thinking about the implications of operant conditioning for classroom practice. If the behaviorist approach could be modified to incorporate mental entities such as concepts, interpretations, goals, and emotions, it would not be too far afield from theories (e.g., reward sensitivity theory) that emphasize the behavioral approach system (BAS) and behavioral inhibition system (BIS) in the brain. The BAS and BIS play a central role in modern theories of emotion and mental health (Shahzadi & Walker, 2019). We do seek to engage in behaviors that lead to our experiencing positive emotions such as happiness, pride, and contentment, and seem to avoid engaging in behaviors that lead to us experiencing negative emotions such as fear, anger, and resentment. But reward sensitivity theory suggests that there is a neurobiological basis to the extent to which people are sensitive or respond to rewards. In any event, surely even advocates of meaningful learning recognize that rewards and punishments (and positive and negative emotions) are implicated in learning environments in some manner. It is just that Skinner's claim that his set of constructs explain everything is overly narrow and too focused on external events.

Piaget's Theory

Jean Piaget (1896–1980) was a Swiss developmentalist with training in both biology and philosophy who did his most important work between the years of 1925 and 1975. Similar to Thorndike and Skinner, he was so prolific and wrote on so many topics that it would be impossible to fully explain all aspects of his theory in a short section of a chapter, so once again we will limit the discussion to his most central points of relevance to educators. Also similar to Thorndike and Skinner was his close association with philosophy. As we shall see, Piaget initially was enamored with the rationalist philosophy of Immanuel Kant. Rationalism is the polar opposite of empiricism.

How Did Piaget Define Knowledge?

Piaget was aware of different kinds of knowledge, but he was particularly interested in the development of concepts or conceptual knowledge. Many of his books on the development of thought had the title *The Child's Conception of . . .* (e.g., time, or number, or space). Why concepts? As noted above, in his philosophical training, Piaget became aware of the debate between empiricists such as David Hume and rationalists such as Immanuel Kant. Empiricists argue that all knowledge must come through the senses, but even Hume was puzzled by the fact that the human mind has a conception of causality. Causality cannot be sensed in the same way the shape, color, or size of an object can be sensed. Kant took this fact as a point of departure (*https://plato.stanford.edu/entries/kant-hume-causality*). Kant believed that the world does not make inherent sense; events cannot impose themselves on us in such a way that we understand how things are related to each other. Instead, we are born with so-called a priori principles that we impose on the world to organize things and give them meaning. Thus, ideas such as causality, number, time, and categories are concepts we impose on the world, and they cannot be sensed. Since these things (1) cannot be directly sensed or taught to us by others and (2) appear quite early in development, Kant and other rationalists believe these concepts are innate.

Piaget held this belief, too, until, seeking work after getting his philosophy degree, he became a tester for Alfred Binet, the inventor of one of the original intelligence tests. Children's answers to certain questions surprised him (see the conservation of number task in Figure 3.1 that was an item on Binet's test). His misgivings became even more pronounced as he continued doing small experiments and interviews with children, and after he carefully observed his own infant children develop over the course of their first 2 years. One key idea that was alleged by Kant to be innate is the idea of the distinction between objects and the space between objects. Kant believed that we are born with the idea of objects and derive the idea of space from the gaps between objects and their physical arrangement with each other (e.g., above, below, behind). Piaget discovered in his own infants that children seem to progressively build up a concept of objects over the first year of life, little by little. One key achievement in this regard is the concept of *object permanence,* or the idea that objects continue to exist when they are no longer in view (Piaget, 1952).

If Kant was right that concepts of space, time, number, causality, and so on were innate, these concepts would be present early, be correctly specified, and not slowly develop little-by-little between infancy and adolescence. Piaget found in his studies that this claim was not true. So, if Kant was right that these concepts cannot be learned through the senses (contra empiricists) but Kant was wrong that they were innate (contra rationalists), what other option was there? Piaget came up with a third alternative:

| Child's row of candies: | O | O | O | O | O |
| Experimenter's row of candies: | O | O | O | O | O |

Experimenter: "This is your row of candies and this is mine (points to each row). Do you have more candy, do I have more candy, or do we both have the same?"

Child: "We both have the same."

Experimenter changes the arrangement

> Child's row: OOOOO
>
> Experimenter's row: O O O O O

Experimenter: "How about now? Do you have more, do I have more, or do we both have the same?"

Child: "You have more."

FIGURE 3.1. The conservation of number task.

constructivism. Children do impose their understandings on the world to make it make sense to them, but their early ideas are imprecise, founded on the wrong principles, and need to be progressively revised.

So, Piaget's goal became one of charting the incremental development of the core Kantian concepts until they reached the correct form that was specified by philosophers and experts in disciplines such as science and mathematics. He was particularly interested in the fact that children gained these insights often prior to formal instruction. In other words, they seem to have invented these ideas on their own (hence constructivism). But what he discovered was that these accurate concepts were not fully formed until adolescence and were preceded by three different kinds of knowledge that were qualitatively distinct from each other. *Each kind of knowledge represented the way that children at that level understood or approached the world.* He argued that each form of knowledge predominated for a period of time in childhood and was replaced by a qualitatively distinct form that was better, but not the final form until children reached adolescence. This finding led him to propose the idea of *stages.* Again, children in each stage think about the world in qualitatively distinct ways.

The first stage, or level of thought, was apparent in children between birth and roughly 18 months of age (give or take a few months). Piaget called this kind of thinking *sensorimotor thought* because children came to know the world through what actions they could perform on things. Children engaged in single actions but also engaged in stereotyped action sequences to get a sense of what can be done to objects. These stereotyped actions that were performed in the same way were called *schemes* (Piaget, 1952). Infants were thought to apply schemes to the world the way older children and adults apply their mental concepts to the world. Schemes, then, were the action-based analogues of mental concepts. Piaget thought children grouped or categorized objects according to what could be done to them. Any object that could be inserted into the mouth and sucked became "suckables" when the sucking scheme was applied to them. Anything that could be shaken to make noises were categorized as "shakables" if the shaking scheme could be applied to them. Schemes could also be strung together to solve problems (e.g., the sliding scheme to remove a blanket that covered a toy, followed by a grasping scheme to pick it up). Piaget argued that this kind of thought was comparable to what other primates were capable of but different from higher levels of thought that involved *mental representation*. The lack of the ability to evoke mental representations of absent objects was the source of their inability to solve object permanence tasks. Piaget said the word *representation* meant the child could "re-present" the object to the mind in its absence.

However, Piaget argued that the repeated execution of schemes onto objects promoted the internalization of schemes over time. By around 12 months children could imagine absent objects (e.g., their mothers at work; a hidden toy). By 18 months, they became able to mentally imagine themselves doing actions before they did them. The latter achievements marked the beginning of the *preoperations stage* or level of thought.

Between the ages of approximately 18 months and 5 years, children could do a variety of things mentally that infants could not do. But their thinking fell short in several respects. First, children tended to mentally categorize things based on what they looked like, rather than use the taxonomic criteria of scientists. For example, a dog and a horse might be in the same category, or a whale and a trout might be in the same category. Later, they would have to see that whales and humans are in the same category of mammals, even though they do not look alike and are grouped according to features such as "self-regulating body temperatures." Another limitation of their thought was their failure to provide correct answers to a variety of conservation tasks such as the one in Figure 3.1. The example child in the figure who gives the wrong answer is in the *preoperations stage*. Other similar tasks involve starting with two equal sized balls of clay and rolling one into a cigar shape, or taking two short fat glasses of juice and pouring one into a tall skinny glass. Piaget argued that preoperational children could not solve these tasks because they cannot mentally "undo" the transformations in the second step of the task (their thinking lacks "reversibility").

Between ages 5 and 10, children start passing classification tasks (e.g., "if all of the animals in the world were to die, would there be any dogs left"?") and the various kinds of conservation tasks. When they do, they are said to be in the *concrete operations* stage of thinking. The label "preoperations" that is given to younger children derives from the claim that they lack the mental operations available to children in the concrete operations stage. One such operation involves hierarchical mental structures, in which mental categories (e.g., dog and cat) have subcategories (e.g., collie and Persian) but are also themselves embedded into superordinate categories (e.g., mammals). He even used formulas to represent these operations (e.g., $B = A + A'$ for mammals = dogs + non-dog mammals).

Concrete operational skills come in quite handy in school settings given the centrality of categorization in all school subjects (e.g., rational versus irrational numbers; deciduous versus evergreen trees; democracy versus monarchy) and how the key operations in math and science require reversibility (e.g., subtraction and addition are inverses; $3 + 2 = 5$, $5 - 2 = 3$). A clue to the key limitation of this form of thought is the label "concrete." Children in this level of thought are limited to understanding reality, objects that exist, real things and ideas.

Beginning around age 11, they become able to apply their mental operations to hypothetical things that do not exist or events that did not occur. That is, they realize that reality (the way things are) is just one instance of a set of hypothetical possibilities (Inhelder & Piaget, 1958). Earth happens to be the only habitable planet in our solar system, but maybe there are other habitable planets in other solar systems. And we happen to rely on a carbohydrate metabolism and water to live, but it is possible that other beings could exist that rely on other forms of metabolism and fluids to live. Hypothetical thinking is what led mathematician Descartes to invent negative numbers as part of his Cartesian coordinate system, and also irrational numbers. Hypothetical thinking led the Founding Fathers to invent our current system of democracy that did not exist anywhere on earth.

Once children demonstrate this reasoning ability, they are said to enter the fourth and final stage, called *formal operations*. Other important features of this level of thought are the ability to understand probability and chance, the notion of torque (how distance and force relate to each other as on a seesaw or balance), and also the hypothetico-deductive approach of scientists (Inhelder & Piaget, 1958). To truly know what factor caused an outcome, you need to create two experimental conditions in which everything is held constant while you vary just one thing. For example, to know what factor is most responsible for how fast a pendulum swings, you need to use two identical lengths of string and vary the weights hanging from them. If you compare a short string that has a heavy weight on it to a long string that has a light weight, you will never figure it out what factor truly determines how fast the pendulum swings. That is why in psychological experimental research we create treatment groups and control groups, and randomly assign people to groups. The experimental group gets something the control group does not (e.g., a new way to teach math) but randomization ensures the groups are similar in all other respects.

One further way to characterize the differences in thinking that occur with age is to say that thinking becomes increasingly abstract with development. By *abstract*, Piaget meant "removed from immediate perception and action." Thinking that is closely tied to perception or action is lower-order thinking (e.g., sensorimotor or preoperational thought). Thinking that is less tied to perception and action is higher-order thinking (e.g., concrete and formal operational thought). Moreover, as a child moves between one level of thought and the next, his or her thinking becomes more abstract because each stage transition produces thinking that is one step further removed from immediate perception and action. Thus, preoperational thought is more abstract than sensorimotor thought because the former is one step removed from immediate perception. Similarly, concrete operational thinking is more abstract than preoperational thinking because it is two steps removed from immediate perception (how things look), and formal operational thought is more abstract than concrete operational thought because it is three steps removed.

How Did Piaget Explain Knowledge Growth?

So, we now know that Piaget believed that children progress through four levels of thought between infancy and adolescence, and that thinking becomes more logical and abstract with development. Now we need to consider his explanation for why this occurs. If Piaget were a maturationist, he would argue that this developmental sequence simply reflects the maturation of the brain. As the brain matures, new skills emerge. However, he was not a maturationist because maturationism is simply a particular form of nativism, in which knowledge and skills are thought to be inborn but slowly appear over time, regardless of a child's experiences. Piaget believed that progression through his stages would only occur if children interacted with the world, developed preliminary ideas to make sense of their experiences, received feedback that their current understanding is not correct, and slowly revised their mental structures bit by bit. In other words, he was a constructivist.

He felt that the conservative or slow, progressive nature of change in children's thought was due to two competing tendencies in the mind (i.e., assimilation and accommodation; see below). He believed that we incorporate new ideas into our minds in much the same way that we incorporate food into our bodily systems. Remember that he was trained as a biologist. When we eat something, we break the food down into nutrients and the nutrients are incorporated into our cells. In other words, we find a place for these nutrients in our cells. Biologists call this process *assimilation*. Piaget argued that when children have a learning experience (e.g., a math teacher explains what a fraction is), their minds try to assimilate this information into their current mental structures in an analogous way. In other words, they have to find a "home" for this information in their current knowledge base. Their teacher may present an idea that they already understand (e.g., slices of pizza) to help them understand the new idea (e.g., a fraction). When their existing knowledge is "up to the task" and does not have to be revised, they can find a home for the new information and assimilate it. Note that sociologists also use the notion of assimilation to explain how immigrants change themselves in order to "fit in" to a new culture (how they dress, how they eat, what they wear).

One potential synonym for *assimilation* is understanding. That is, when we assimilate new information, we understand it. However, it is often the case that we think we understand something when we really do not. We have a found a home for new information in our mind, but it is the wrong home. That is why children will think that a horse and dog are the same kind of thing (things that share some similarities in appearance are often in the same category), why the shorter row of candies in Figure 3.1 seems to have fewer candies in it (usually smaller things do have less), and why children add numerators and denominators when adding fractions, just like they do with "regular" numbers (e.g., they wrongly think ⅔ is the answer to ½ + ¼). They assimilate the information, but they are not correct. Assimilation also tends to be partial when children or adults know little about the domain. They will cling to a single aspect of the situation and that is all they take in.

The opposite of assimilation is accommodation. Whereas assimilation is the tendency to keep knowledge structures the same and incorporate information into these structures "as is," *accommodation* is the tendency for our knowledge structures to change to make them more accurate. So, metaphorically, assimilation says, "My mental structures are fine, no need to change them; let's put the new information here (in the wrong spot)." Accommodation says, "My mental structures are wrong and need to change." Assimilation and accommodation are in a battle, in much the same way that our nervous system has the sympathetic system (e.g., speeds up your heart rate) and parasympathetic system (e.g., slows down your heart rate). They work in opposition to each other until homeostasis is achieved.

This battle between assimilation and accommodation is the reason why it can take so long for children to understand some things in school. The strong tendency to keep mental structures the same is the reason why knowledge changes in a slow incremental way. But it is also possible for our minds to overdo assimilation or accommodation. One example of overdoing assimilation is when children (or people with schizophrenia of any age) engage in fantasy. They see things that are not there or believe in things that do not exist. An example of overdoing accommodation is when children directly imitate people, action for action. Note that if we kept readily changing our knowledge structures all the time, we would have no continuity. In fact, people with disorganized schizophrenia demonstrate this continual breakdown. Just as we cannot keep our heart rates racing forever (our hearts would wear out very soon), we cannot keep assimilating or accommodating. Piaget argued that we have a natural tendency to restore the balance between assimilation and accommodation that is analogous to homeostasis. He gave the label of *equilibration* to the process of storing the balance between assimilation and accommodation. In other words, equilibration served as his developmental mechanism for explaining why knowledge becomes more abstract with age and why children progress through the four stages. The catalyst for creating the imbalances is experience in the world, and trying ideas out. Equilibration and knowledge change would not occur without children interacting with the world and others.

What Instructional Practices Are Consistent with Piaget's Theory?

One particularly apt metaphor for the foregoing discussion of Piaget's view of cognitive development is the *child as scientist*. Piaget viewed children as mini scientists who were always trying out their hypotheses about what is true, how to categorize things, what causes what, and so on. Like practicing scientists, children often find out that their hypotheses and theories are wrong. Thus, their knowledge must accommodate. So, one could say that any instructional approach that involves children learning by doing (*active learning*), trying to figure things out on their own (*discovery learning*), by experimenting or gathering evidence, would be consistent with Piaget's theory. Many of the reform and inquiry approaches to teaching math, science, and history would fit this bill.

Given that Piaget discovered sequences of precursory ideas that can be arranged in order by age (e.g., counting in preschool is a precursory activity for understanding arithmetic in elementary school; arithmetic is a precursory set of skills for learning algebra in eighth or ninth grade, and so on), curricula could be arranged so that precursory skills are taught in sequence. In science, there is a related idea of *learning progressions*. In the same way, Piaget's theory supports expectations for what children could understand at given ages. For example, few experienced teachers would attempt to teach abstract ideas to kindergarteners (e.g., the difference between a democracy and a monarchy). However, it is often possible through activities to get certain ideas across. For example, children can learn the basics of democracy through taking votes (which of three books the teacher will read) or the basics of economics by creating a school-wide banking and commerce system with pretend currency that can be used to buy items made by children.

Finally, Piaget's theory underlies the expectation that it will be common for children and teens to develop *misconceptions* as they grapple with ideas that are complex or a little beyond where they are cognitively. Children who master addition, subtraction, multiplication, and division may struggle when they try to apply these operations to fractions and negative integers (see Chapter 12). Teachers can wrongly assume that children are not bright when they have these misconceptions, but Piaget's theory is not about intelligence per se. All of us must progress through complicated topics little by little, and slowly build up the correct interpretation. Note, however, that this expectation does not apply to learning easy-to-understand facts.

How Might Piaget's Theory Be Evaluated?

During the height of the cognitive revolution in psychology in the 1960s, after Skinnerian theory had been overthrown as the dominant paradigm, numerous psychologists and educators flocked to Piaget's theory. Soon, however, scholars who advocated other paradigms (e.g., IP theory) or who advocated other epistemological orientations besides constructivism (e.g., nativists and empiricists) tried very hard to show that Piaget was wrong about a variety of things. Those with a nativist orientation wanted to show apparent comprehension of topics in children much younger than Piaget had found. For example, if Piaget found that children mastered the conservation of number task in Figure 3.1 by age 5, critics wanted to show it in 3- or 4-year-olds. If Piaget found object permanence in 12-month-olds, they wanted to show it in 6-month-olds. The earlier the better.

Those with the empiricist orientation, in contrast, conducted training studies to see if Piaget was right that some topics took a long time to learn, little by little. They tried to show that younger children could be readily taught some concept with a short amount of training. Finally, scholars advocating IP theory wanted to explain the same age trends using the constructs of IP theory (e.g., short-term memory limitations) rather than Piaget's constructs.

So, three kinds of findings eventually led to the downfall of Piaget's theory. The first was the apparent ability of researchers to show various skills in younger children (e.g., concrete operational skills in preschoolers; formal operational skills in 8-year-olds). The second was that there was only weak evidence for across-the-board performance on stage-related tasks. For example, children might pass one conservation task at age 5 but not pass another one until age 10. If children are in the same stage of thought, this uneven performance should not occur, critics argued. Finally, many early studies showed that only about 40% of adolescents pass formal operations tasks. So, we had the odd pairing of findings in which we saw on the one hand very young children were much more skilled than we thought and on the other hand much older adolescents were much less skilled than we thought. Either way, these apparent empirical difficulties led to the downfall of the theory in psychology.

In the field of education, however, there was and remains much more support for the general ideas of constructivism and the educational applications described above. Teachers have found that they cannot seem to teach certain topics to younger children and children do develop a number of misconceptions.

Schema Theory

Schema theory initially acquired some adherents during the 1970s and 1980s because of its applicability for explaining categorization, memory errors, and inference-making during reading. It is constructivist in orientation because of (1) the emphasis on people having knowledge structures that organize and frame their experiences and (2) findings that suggest that people remembered hearing or seeing things consistent with schemata (*schemata* = plural of *schema*), when they actually did not hear or see those things. These findings were an interesting contrast to the realistic, empiricist approach to learning that was first to emerge in cognitive psychology after the cognitive revolution of the 1960s.

How Do Schema Theorists Define Knowledge?

As the name of the theory implies, the central components of knowledge are called *schemata*. There are two kinds of schemata: schemata for categories and schemata for events. Either kind represents what all members of a category have in common (e.g., what all automobiles or cats or diamonds have in common), or what all events of the same type have in common (e.g., what all birthday parties have in common). For example, a schema for automobiles might contain "nodes" for "has an engine," "has a steering wheel," "has tires," "used for transportation," and so on. Schemata for events typically include the order of activities or substeps in an event, such as going to a restaurant, birthday parties, thanksgiving, and so on. The components of the birthday schema might include steps such as "decorate house," "guests arrive," "open presents," "sing 'Happy Birthday to You' after lighting candles on a cake," and "open presents." Schemata for categories are usually arranged in some form of a hierarchy ("terrier" is a kind of "dog," which is a kind of "mammal," which is a kind of "living thing"). The hierarchical structure of schemata for events is the order of events. Both kinds of schemata are very useful for forming expectations (e.g., you expect all cars to have a steering wheel; you expect at some point to sing "Happy Birthday to You" at a birthday party; Elman & McRae, 2019). Schemata are also alleged to "fill in gaps" in descriptions by way of inferences (Elman & McRae, 2019). When we read, for example, that a construction worker fell 20 stories, we infer that he died even when a paragraph describing this event does not explicitly state this fact.

So, to compare it with other theories, schema theory does not provide a description for rote-learning facts as Thorndike does, and the schemata for categories are similar to the categories formed by children who are capable of concrete operational thinking in Piaget's theory. Schema theory is unique among theories for having so-called event representations (i.e., schemata for events). Although schema theory and Piaget's theory are both constructivist, schema theory differs from Piaget's theory in that (1) there is no discussion of more than one level of abstraction, (2) there is only a single level of thought (not four levels), and (3) there is no apparent restriction on what can be learned at different ages. Presumably young children could be just as a capable of forming a schema for an abstract idea (irrational number) as teenagers.

How Do Schemata Form or Get into the Mind?

The key process for forming schemata is *abstraction* across experiences. Our minds are alleged to be able to notice common features across all instances of a category or event. We retain what is common and delete what is not common. For example, our restaurant schema might begin with meeting a hostess who stands behind a tall desk or lectern and asks, "Do you have reservation?" or "How many in your party?" But the first hostess you meet in your first trip to a restaurant might be a tall blonde-haired woman in her early 20s. The next one you meet at your next visit to a restaurant may be a short brunette in her early 30s. The differences in appearance of the two hostess are not retained, but the fact that you are greeted in both instances by a hostess who says similar things is retained.

Similar abstraction processes occur for schemata for categories. For example, there are different kinds of apples that you may try over your lifetime. What is retained is what all varieties have in common (e.g., thickness of skin, starchy and crunchy texture, sweetness; shape and stem); what is not retained are unimportant differences such as color or slight differences in size.

What schema theory has in common with Thorndike is the empiricist idea of the need to experience objects and events. Common elements are perceptible and come through the senses. The abstraction part is where the theories diverge. Thorndike does not allow for the abstraction of commonalities nor for the role of these schemata in further categorization and inference-making.

How Does Knowledge Grow?

All that is required to form schemata is for people to have new experiences in which they encounter new kinds of things that have to be categorized or new kinds of events that have to be categorized. To illustrate, the first time that I visited Starbucks, I asked for a small coffee. I was corrected to ask for a "tall." The next time, I asked for a large coffee and was directed to call it a "vente." Eventually, my schema for Starbucks included all the right terms and where to stand to wait for the fancier drinks (which I did not have to do when just ordering a regular coffee).

What Instructional Practices Are Consistent with Schema Theory?

Schema theorists have not had much to say about instructional practices per se, but we can imagine some activities that would be consistent with the theory. For example, it might be possible for children in science class, or history class, or language arts class to be presented with multiple examples of things such as kinds of leaves (oak, maple, birch), or descriptions of the governments of democracies (e.g., United States, United Kingdom, France), or haiku poems. If people were studying for the Scholastic Achievement Test, perhaps multiple examples of similar kinds of problems could be created so that they could form a schema for that type.

    We shall see in the chapters on mathematics learning and reading that schemata play a key role in problem solving and reading comprehension. When we have a schema for a kind of problem, we can quickly solve it. This process would be similar to what occurs with an experienced plumber or car mechanic who has seen the same problem so many times, they immediately know what to do. In the case of reading comprehension, words in the paragraph elicit schemata from memory. For example, when a story has a line such as "When Samantha got home from work and sat on her couch, Fluffy jumped into her lap and started to purr," the reader makes an inference that Fluffy is her pet cat (see Chapter 9).

How Might We Evaluate Schema Theory?

As was the case for Piaget and Thorndike, schema theory is not without its critics and sometimes the evidence for some of its central claims has been inconsistent or weak (Alba & Hasher, 1983; Elman & McRae, 2019). For example, people do not always make obvious inferences (e.g., not inferring the death of the construction worker who fell in the above example) and they also recall information from stories that are not consistent with an elicited schema (Alba & Hasher, 1983). In other words, memory can be both exact for explicitly stated information but also constructive or distortive for unstated, schema-consistent information. In addition, philosopher Jerry Fodor long ago made a compelling case against something he called the *abstraction fallacy;* that is, you cannot abstract commonalities across a series of objects or events unless you already know what you are looking for (Fodor, 1975). If this is the case, then you are not really learning anything or abstracting commonalities from your experiences. Since that claim was made, however, psychologists have shown how artificial intelligence systems can form abstractions without knowing in advance what they are looking for (Elman & McRae, 2019).

Schema theory can also be criticized for not being particularly developmental in the sense that it fails to account for age-related restrictions on what children can understand at particular ages, and lacks a strong developmental mechanism such as practice (Thorndike) or equilibration (Piaget). Nevertheless, it can provide a cogent account of predictions, problem solving, and inference-making. As a result, it still can be useful for explaining such phenomena (Elman & McRae, 2019). It will continue to gain support if its developmental weaknesses can be strengthened and if psychologists continue to refine the theory to explain how schemata are formed and function in the mind.

Vygotsky's Theory

Lev Vygotsky (1897–1934) was a Russian psychologist who began his career soon after the Russian revolution took place in 1917. Not surprisingly, then, there is a strong Marxist element in his account, especially with reference to the idea of how people internalize cultural norms as they participate in culturally relevant activities such as those in the workplace. He initially rose to prominence for criticizing the predominant behaviorist model of his day, that of Ivan Pavlov of Pavlovian conditioning fame. He also was very much influenced by Piaget's early writings that were published about 10 years before Vygotsky died at the young age of 37. Although he was influential in Russia from the early 1920s onward, he was not influential in U.S. psychology or education until scholars presented his ideas as alternatives to both behaviorism and Piaget's theory in the 1960s and 1970s.

How Did Vygotsky Define Knowledge?

When Vygotsky referred to mental entities related to knowledge and skills, he used two major terms: *functions* and *concepts.* With respect to functions, Vygotsky believed that it was useful to think of a small set of goal-directed, cognitive processes that play certain roles in the mind. The functions of language, for example, included communication and self-regulation. The function of the memory system was to . . . well . . . remember. This tendency to think of the mind in terms of its functions persisted among Vygotsky's students and followers well into the 1970s when one of his students, Alexander Luria, coined the notion of "executive function" (Luria, 1973) that is extremely prominent today (see Chapters 4 and 6).

Vygotsky identified five functions: language, thinking, perception, attention, and memory (Vygotsky, 1978). He argued that interesting new abilities or tendencies emerged when the developmental pathways of these functions intersected in development. For example, thoughts provide the grounding for words, and early in development, children (at approximately 18 months) realize that everything has a name (Vygotsky, 1978). They then pester parents to find out what things in their environment are called. Prior to that point, they may have only a few words in their vocabulary and may not even have a concept of "word." Thus, the intersection of language with thought produces various interesting phenomena. In contrast, when language intersects with behavior, children learn to self-regulate. By way of "inner speech," children can talk to themselves to direct their attention, remember what they were about to do, and think about what they are perceiving. Children are novices about many things, so they use inner speech in a variety of contexts. But inner speech reemerges even in adolescents and adults when they perform new things like drive a car with a manual transmission ("Let see, how do I put it in reverse?").

With respect to concepts, Vygotsky borrowed the distinction between so-called spontaneous concepts and scientific concepts from Piaget. *Spontaneous concepts* are the concepts that children create on their own, based on their experiences, prior to formal education. So, their informal understanding of the concept of "force" might develop from their experiences of trying to open a door that is stuck, or their brother shoving them, or kicking a soccer ball. Spontaneous concepts tend to be idiosyncratic and personalized. For example, not all students would necessarily have experienced struggling to open a door that is stuck or being shoved. A *scientific concept,* in contrast, refers to expert opinion or definitions of a concept in disciplines such as science, math, history, and economics. Scientific concepts tend to be much more abstract, accurate, and generalizable than the informal, spontaneous concepts that children develop. So, when they confront the scientific concept of "force" in physics class, it is often not very similar to their spontaneous concept of force. Similarly, "fractions" and "negative integers" tend not to be much like their informal concepts of numbers that are acquired by counting real things.

In an analogous manner to Piaget's discussion of assimilation and accommodation, Vygotsky argued that children have to work out the differences between their spontaneous concepts and scientific concepts in their classroom experiences. He said that their spontaneous concepts "grow up" (forming an assimilative base for what they are being taught) while their scientific concepts "grow down" (restructuring their understandings to make them more accurate and generalizable). The expectation would be that working out these differences would take some time as children slowly *appropriate* the scientific meanings (appropriate = internalize and make the idea one's own).

How Does Knowledge Get into the Mind?

In contrast to Piaget, who placed a great deal of emphasis on children discovering things on their own as little scientists, Vygotsky argued that all forms of the most valuable kinds of ideas and skills are *socially transmitted* (Vygotsky, 1978). The human species is unique in its ability to pass on solutions to problems, knowledge, and technology to each successive generation so that people do not have to continually reinvent the wheel (literally and figuratively). In fact, Vygotsky proposed the *law of cultural development* that states that all functions appear twice in development: first on the social plane (interpsychologically or between people) and second on the psychological plane (intrapsychologically or within a person). So children learn how to do math, or read books, or buy things at the store in conjunction with their parents. After doing so collaboratively with explanations and support from parents, they eventually internalize these activities and can do them on their own, mentally.

A related notion that was superimposed on Vygotsky's account by later scholars is the idea of *scaffolding*. More skilled people (e.g., parents, teachers, older siblings) can provide supports, guiding questions, and step-by-step instructions to help children learn new skills. Just as brick masons can stand on a scaffold to lay the next layer of bricks on a building's façade and then climb to a higher level to lay yet another higher course of bricks, parents can act as intellectual scaffolds to allow children to perform tasks they cannot do on their own. For example, a parent or tutor could show a child how to solve a math problem. Then, the child could try to do it herself, but with gentle hints ("Okay, do you remember the first step? We have to get the 7 to the other side of the equal sign. How do we do that?"). As the child tries additional steps, the parent or tutor would say less and less. This technique is called *fading*. Scaffolding combined with fading helps a child appropriate and internalize a skill.

How Does Knowledge Grow?

It should be clear that the primary developmental mechanism for knowledge growth for Vygotsky is social interaction between parents, teachers, and more skilled peers. But children have to do their part as well, by receiving instruction, trying things out on their own, and continuing to tinker until they fully understand or perform a skill correctly. Parents also place children in culturally defined settings in which they are asked to learn culturally important skills such as math, reading, music, or dance.

But Vygotsky made one further distinction between two levels of performance: the level of performance that is demonstrated with the help of an adult or more capable peer, and the level of performance when the child is receiving no such help or intellectual support. The gap in performance between these two levels is called the *zone of proximal development* (Vygotsky, 1978). If you really want to promote intellectual development, Vygotsky argued, you need to present information or new skills in a way that falls between the two levels. In other words, you need to challenge students, but not go too far where you would lose them. If you do not challenge them and only ask them about things that they already know or understand, their knowledge will never grow.

Vygotsky argued that the zone of proximal development was the primary reason why he argued against the practice that was common in France at that time of ability grouping on the basis of IQ scores, and then teaching children at the level specified by their IQ levels. In other words, if a group of children have the mental age of 5 (regardless of their actual age), the French method involved teaching in a way that a 5-year-old could understand. Vygotsky (1978) asked us to imagine two children who had the same mental age (e.g., mental age 9), based on their independent level of mastery on an IQ test. He then asked us to imagine their mental age after the tester provided a scaffold of some sort (e.g., gave a hint, started a problem and asked them to finish it, and so on). It is entirely possible that one child might show a mental age of 12 with help while the other showed a mental age of 10 with help. Thus, the two children had two different zones of proximal development. If you presented material that an 11-year-old could understand, you would challenge the first child and promote growth, but you would extend beyond the capabilities of the second child and promote no growth.

What Instructional Practices Are Consistent with Vygotsky's Theory?

From the aforementioned account, it should be clear that scaffolding, fading, modeling of skills, and explanations are all consistent with Vygotsky's account. His view is also similar to Piaget's (and different from Thorndike's) in the sense that teachers should expect children to slowly appropriate higher-order skills rather than master them immediately. Because of his view about spontaneous and scientific concepts, Vygotsky also argued that children should be taught foreign languages to help them think about or understand their own native tongue in a more precise and metacognitive manner. For example, English-speaking children who struggle to understand verbs and verb tenses in Spanish would be expected to have a clearer understanding of verbs and verb tenses in English after they learn Spanish.

Similarly, Vygotsky argued that children's understanding of arithmetic is improved and restructured after they learn algebra, which is a generalized, more abstract arithmetic.

One clear example of how to translate Vygotskian theory into the classroom is *reciprocal teaching* (Palincsar & Brown, 1984; Tarchi & Pinto, 2016). This form of teaching was originally invented through a collaboration between a developmental psychologist with expertise in Vygotskian theory (Ann Brown) and a former classroom teacher and now college professor (Ann Marie Palincsar). The technique involves teachers and students taking turns "playing teacher" within four-person groups as they each describe how to implement four reading strategies (questioning, clarifying, summarizing, and predicting). After everyone in the group reads a passage from a text, the teacher goes first and models one of the strategies (e.g., summarizing). As she demonstrates the strategy, she explains what she is doing and why ("I am going to write one sentence to summarize each of these four paragraphs; a summary is shorter, only contains the main ideas, and omits details"). Then, one of the students goes next and tries to mimic the teacher by modeling the same strategy. Typically, the first attempt at imitating the teacher falls well short. The teacher provides a fair amount of gentle, corrective feedback to these early attempts. Then a second student tries to model and explain the same strategy. Once again, the teacher provides feedback. Next, they move on to the second strategy. The group cycles through the four strategies as often as it takes until they are all mastered. As they proceed, the teacher uses less and less feedback as the students slowly appropriate the strategy. Reviews of the literature have found reciprocal teaching to be highly effective for instilling reading strategies in students and consequently improving their reading comprehension as well (Tarchi & Pinto, 2016).

How Might Vygotsky's Theory Be Evaluated?

Although Vygotsky's theory was far less comprehensive than other accounts, it nevertheless generated the very powerful constructs described above (e.g., scaffolding, fading, zone of proximal development). That said, the profundity of the ideas were not matched by a similar level of detail or specificity. Questions left unanswered include: (1) What kinds of scaffolds are most effective? (2) Why is it that some children show a higher level of performance with help than others (e.g., mental age [MA] of 12 vs. MA of 9)? (3) Why are some concepts easier to learn or more appropriate than others at particular ages? (4) Why are adults better at providing scaffolds than more competent peers are? (5) What other aspects of culture besides language can serve as a medium for the internalization of culturally significant skills? Vygotsky can, of course, be excused for not having a more comprehensive or detailed account that was capable of answering such questions because he died at such a young age. The theories that were available to him at that time (Piaget's early views) were not particularly detailed either.

SUMMARY AND CONCLUSIONS

It was noted earlier that each of the five theories gained a number of adherents because each theory was capable of predicting or explaining a circumscribed set of phenomena. For example, Thorndike could explain rote learning of facts, while Piaget, schema theory, and Vygotsky could explain meaningful learning and conceptual understanding. Skinner could explain the effectiveness of certain forms of classroom management or interventions for children with autism that Piaget, schema theory, and Vygotsky could not. Thus, all of these theories have their own utility but they are insufficiently comprehensive to be able to explain the entire gamut of classroom-related learning. It is for this reason that teachers could incorporate many of the ideas contained in all of these theories to promote learning. It was also shown that all of the theories have other limitations and their share of critics. It remains for modern scholars to overcome their personal preferences and prejudices to attempt to combine two or more of these accounts into a more comprehensive, integrative theory. Note, though, that some of the philosophical assumptions of these theories make them inherently incompatible. Byrnes (1992) provides guidance as to which theories could be coherently combined and which could not be.

CHAPTER 4

Memory Development

The human memory system is operative during every moment of every day, even when we are asleep (Sobczak & Gaskell, 2019). The centrality of memory in our lives becomes tragically obvious when we consider some of the memory-related consequences of brain injuries and neurocognitive disorders such as Alzheimer's disease. Some brain-injured patients develop *retrograde amnesia* in which they cannot remember anything prior to their brain injury. Others who have had part of their temporal lobes removed to stop seizures develop *anterograde amnesia* in which they cannot form any new memories (e.g., they cannot recognize their doctors 5 minutes after spending an hour with them). Still others, diagnosed with Alzheimer's disease, not only have considerable memory problems but also seem to lose their personalities as their disease progresses. What is clear from these examples but also from the experiences of nondisabled persons is that we have to be able to retain our goals, plans, and useful knowledge in order to be successful in the world. Moreover, it is also obvious to teachers and employers how important it is for students to retain the information that they are taught in school.

In this chapter, we will learn about the human memory system and how it develops from infancy to adulthood. Since the 1800s, psychologists have learned quite a lot about how our memories work and have "carved up" the memory system into different components and aspects (e.g., implicit vs. explicit memory; short-term vs. long-term memory; episodic vs. semantic memory). There are also important memory-related terms and constructs that have to be mastered (e.g., cues, encoding, consolidation, metamemory) as well as a variety of experimental effects that researchers have revealed

57

(e.g., the testing effect). We will examine all these aspects of memory as they function in adults first, and then examine developmental trends in memory with this theoretical framing as a backdrop.

THE NATURE OF THE HUMAN MEMORY SYSTEM

We will begin by examining the endpoint of memory development: the human memory system as it operates in an adult. Plato famously once said that any theory or philosophical framework "carves nature at its joints"; that is, theories make ontological distinctions (what kinds of entities or processes exist) (Campbell, O'Rourke, & Slater, 2011). Each of the subsections that follows presents various distinctions or "carvings."

Distinction 1: Encoding versus Consolidation versus Retrieval

When we say that we remember an experience (e.g., being at a friend's wedding), that means we have somehow formed a *mental representation* of the experience and are able to relive it in our minds weeks, months, or even years after it occurred. In Chapter 3, we saw that Piaget intended the term *representation* to mean the ability to "re-present" an object to our consciousness in its absence. Modern psychologists use the term *encoding* to refer to the process of forming a memory trace of an experience. We know from a variety of experiments that encodings are both selective and partial (Eysenck & Brysbaert, 2018). That is, our minds do not operate like video cameras that record and retain all aspects of an experience.

Whereas encoding is the process by which information gets into our memory system, *retrieval* refers to the process of getting it out. If you see a new acquaintance on the street, you may recognize the face but then forget what his or her name is. The inability to remember the name is an example of a retrieval problem. A variety of additional experiments have shown that there is also an intermediary process in between encoding and retrieval that also plays a role in forming permanent memories: *consolidation* (Crowley, Bendor, & Javadia, 2019; Eysenck & Brysbaert, 2018). Memories are not formed, typically, in an all-or-none fashion in one attempt. Rather, they are slowly formed over time. Neuroscientists believe that an inner portion of the temporal lobes called the *hippocampus* plays an important role in binding pieces of information from an experience together and forming more permanent representations of this information until regions of the association cortex take over the job.

The distinctions among encoding, consolidation, and retrieval have played an important role in theorizing how and why we remember something or forget it. You can manipulate what people attend to in a situation and therefore implicate memory problems due to encoding. Or, you can make sure everyone in an experiment attains a high level of immediate memory (e.g., 100% recall) and therefore know that later memory failures could not be due to encoding. Rather, in such cases we would say forgetting is a problem of retrieval. In addition, however, researchers have presented intermediary activities during the consolidation process to either enhance remembering or increase the likelihood of forgetting (Crowley et al., 2019). For example, various experiments have shown that consolidation often happens during sleep. To show this, participants first try to learn information within a set of trials during the day while they are awake. Later that night when they are asleep, half of the participants are exposed to the same stimuli while they are asleep and half are not. Results showed that those presented the material during sleep recalled more information the next day when they were awake again. It is also possible to promote forgetting if new information that is highly similar to the just-learned material is presented during the consolidation phase.

Distinction 2: Recall versus Recognition

The second distinction pertains to the two different ways we can remember something. To understand the difference, we first need to introduce the notion of a *cue*. A cue is a stimulus that occurs in the environment or in one's mind that has the potential to evoke a memory. For example, the question "What is your phone number?" can be a cue for you remembering your phone number. Or, the face of a friend can be a cue for remembering his or her name. When we remember some object or piece of information by way of *recognition*, that means the cue matches our mental representation of that object or piece of information. So, when we recognize a face or a word that we have seen before, that means the actual face of a person or word in a book matches a visual presentation that we have stored in specific areas of our brains (e.g., the ventral temporal cortex for faces, the visual word form area for words; Byrnes & Eaton, 2020). When we can recall something without the benefit of a cue that can match a stored representation, doing so is an example of *recall*. There are cues involved in recall, but they match something that is associated with the stored information, not the stored information itself. For example, a face can serve as a cue for the person's name, but the face matches a representation of the face, not the name (one is a visual representation; the other is an auditory representation). Similarly, we may recognize a tune but forget the lyrics or the name of the tune.

Why are cues not always effective in helping us recall something? For example, why do we sometimes forget names when we see a face or forget the answer to a question that we see on a short-answer test? Here we can introduce several other important memory constructs: strength and activation level. Psychologists argue that our memories are stored in various degrees of *strength*. Some memories are readily recalled, and some are not when confronted with a cue. High-strength memories are readily recalled, and low-strength memories are not readily recalled. What factors affect the strength of a representation? One early claim of both classical theories (e.g., Thorndike, see Chapter 3) and modern cognitive psychologists is that repetition seems to increase the strength of representations. If we dial a particular phone number several times a week for 20 years (e.g., that of our mothers), that amount of repetition increases the strength and retrievability of the number. However, we often forget our own phone number when asked because we never dial it! We will see other factors later in this chapter that also increase the strength and retrievability of memories besides repetition.

The second construct, *activation level,* refers to the hypothesis that memory records have a resting level of activation that can be increased by the presence of a cue. When the activation level of a representation is increased enough, it can be made available to your consciousness. When information comes into consciousness, we have the experience of remembering it. When we struggle to remember and the information just will not come into consciousness, we have the experience of forgetting (or a problem of retrieval). If we assume that the amount of increase in activation level is fixed and finite, then we can combine this idea with strength to explain why we remember some things and fail to remember other things. If the resting activation level for high-strength items is "near" the level of consciousness and a cue raises this activation level by a certain amount, it may bring the information into conscious awareness. However, if a cue raises the activation level of a low-strength item by the same amount, the low-strength item may not come into consciousness.

Distinction 3: Sensory versus Short-Term versus Long-Term Memory

The next set of distinctions derive from the once dominant theory of memory proposed by Atkinson and Shiffrin way back in the 1960s (Atkinson & Shiffrin, 1968). Although this model has been challenged and refined multiple times, it is worth discussing because some of the basic distinctions that it includes are still maintained today.

As can be seen in Figure 4.1, Atkinson and Shiffrin argued that the overall memory system can be subdivided into three kinds of memories or "stores": sensory memory, short-term memory, and long-term memory. Each store can be characterized in terms of (1) whether its capacity is limited or unlimited, (2) how long a memory trace persists, and (3) how information gets into that store.

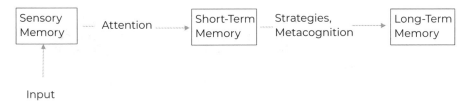

FIGURE 4.1. Atkinson and Shiffrin's (1968) model of memory.

FIGURE 4.1. Atkinson and Shiffrin's (1968) model of memory.

As the name implies, information gets into the five *sensory stores* through the five senses. Each store has a large capacity because it is assumed that the memory trace can stimulate lots of sensory receptors (e.g., many receptors in the retina of your eyes); however, the trace of this experience fades very quickly (usually within a second). To get a sense of this phenomenon, readers should stare intently at something and then close their eyes to see the visual trace fade away.

In order for information to pass from the sensory stores into *short-term memory (STM),* the learner has to attend to some aspect of the stimulation. So, *attention* is the primary process that determines what gets into STM in the Atkinson–Shiffrin model. Researchers originally believed that STM had a limited capacity of 7 ± 2 "chunks" of information. As we shall see below, however, this numerical assumption turns out to be incorrect. What researchers have maintained is the idea of a "chunk."

What is a "chunk" and why is the construct needed or useful? Consider the classic STM test used in many intelligence tests in which a tester calls out a string of letters or numbers, one by one. If the tester called out the 12 letters A-G-M-B-X-K-R-D-E in order, most people would be able to recall only 5–9 of them because of the alleged 7 ± 2 limitation. The limited number of "slots" mean that once 5–9 of the items get into STM, no more items can fit, so the ones that fail to get in are forgotten. In addition, though, it is also possible that the last few items said by the tester could force out or displace earlier ones. However, if the tester called out the string I-B-M-U-S-A-N-F-L-A-B-C, people might recall all 12 letters because they could chunk or group sets of three letters together (i.e., IBM, USA, NFL, ABC). One person in a study even recalled over 80 numbers because he was able to group sets of 9 or so numbers into possible times for runners in a marathon! (Eysenck & Brysbaert, 2018). We will see other examples of chunking in Chapter 7 when we examine how experts in a domain can chunk large amounts of information into a single chunk (e.g., 15 chess pieces into a single image of a memorized game).

Beyond the capacity limitation of STM, it was also argued early on that information fades from STM if nothing further is done with it. To get a sense of this, consider how most people forget the names of people that they are introduced to at parties within a few minutes. They hear the name and pay attention to what the person is saying rather than continuing to attend to the name. Relatedly, sometimes when calling helplines, a recorded message gives a phone number or URL and the person making the call cannot find a pen to write it down. By the time they find a pen, the number or URL is often forgotten.

If our memory systems stopped at only having sensory memories and STM, we would be no different from people who have injuries to their temporal lobes that cause anterograde amnesia, so we need our additional components to create memories that are more permanent. That is where *long-term memory (LTM)* comes in. In the original Atkinson–Shiffrin model, LTM was assumed to have an unlimited capacity because no evidence had accumulated that showed that LTM ran out of space the way STM does.

In addition, the original model assumed that once information gets into LTM, it is never lost. How do we know? One form of evidence is that we can relearn information much faster the second time around than the first. For example, it may take us 3 years to master a foreign language the first time we try (e.g., in high school). Some 30 years later, after no longer using the language, we seem to remember very little but then find we can relearn the language in perhaps 6 months. A second form of evidence of the permanence of LTM memory traces would be that we may not be able to recall a fact at first (e.g., the state capital of Wyoming) but could recognize it if a list of possible cities were presented (e.g., Cheyenne, Casper, Laramie, Gillette, Rock Springs).

How does information pass from STM into LTM? According to the original model, the principal method was rehearsal or repetition. From Chapter 3 on general theories, we saw that repetition was the primary learning mechanism in Thorndike's theory. Anyone who has tried to learn information using flash cards has experience with this memory strategy. But rehearsal is also in evidence in the case of a salesperson who remembers your name at a party and does so by including your name in every one of his or her conversational sentences ("What do you do for a living, Ethan? Ethan, how long have you worked there? Do you have any children Ethan?").

Although the Atkinson–Shiffrin model was useful in that it summarized a number of disparate findings into a comprehensive model and helped to generate hundreds of studies after 1968, it has difficulty accounting for the following (apparently) disconfirming findings (Eysenck & Brysbaert, 2018):

- Subsequent research showed that the STM construct had limited utility because it mainly emphasized passive storage; it was soon replaced by the construct of *working memory (WM)* that combined the storage function of STM with the ability to process or manipulate the information that was temporarily held (Baddeley & Hitch, 1974). An example WM task is the reversed digit-span task, where the instructions are to repeat back a string of digits in the reverse order (e.g., 1-3-7 is repeated back 7-3-1). STM was also unary (had a single component), but research has shown the utility of positing that WM has four subcomponents (central executive, phonological loop, visuospatial sketchpad, and episodic buffer). WM is discussed more comprehensively in Chapter 6 so will not be discussed further in this chapter.

- Various studies showed that the 7 ± 2 limitation was an artifact of the materials and tasks used. It is now believed that the capacity of WM is about four chunks. It is not the number of chunks per se that causes the limitation as much as how long it takes to attend to and rehearse the chunks or individual items before they fade. People can recall seven single numbers but only four 4-syllable words (*reconstitution, emancipation,* etc.). This finding is called the *word-length effect.*

- The Atkinson–Shiffrin model implied that information is processed in STM before it makes contact with LTM information. However, when we chunk, we use information in LTM to form the chunks so the STM-before-LTM claim cannot be true. There are many other findings in the literature showing the importance of prior knowledge to memory (Eysenck & Brysbaert, 2018; Howe, 2015).

- It is also the case that rehearsal is not the only way to get information into LTM and it is not a particularly efficient method to boot. We will discuss such findings for other memory strategies later in this chapter.

Distinction 4: Implicit versus Explicit Memory

If we think of the term *learning* as referring to *improvements or increases in knowledge or skill,* researchers have discovered that we can learn with and without conscious knowledge of these improvements. When we are aware of improvements, we can usually describe what we now know. *Explicit learning* and *explicit memory* refer to information acquisition and retrieval that we are aware of and can articulate (Eysenck & Brysbaert, 2018; Howe, 2015). So, if you are studying material for an exam and can recall most of the information, that experience is an example of explicit memory. However, it is also possible to get better at something or retrieve information outside of conscious awareness. Examples include tracing lines inside a maze, reading text upside down, learning an artificial language, and learning a statistical pattern. In each case, people get better and better over time and are often not aware that they are getting better.

In the case of learning a statistical pattern, it would be easy to learn a pattern in which a computer screen flashed a red light twice on the left and then a blue light once on the right (left–left–right; left–left–right; etc.). Imagine if the participant was asked to type *R* or *L* after seeing two lights flash on the left after learning this sequence. However, people can also learn much more complicated patterns in which they increasingly select the right key after many trials, even when they cannot state the rule or the pattern (e.g., "3 left–1 right" followed by "2 left–3 right" followed by "6 left–2 right" followed by "4 left–6 right," dropping back to "3 left–1 right"). In all such cases of *implicit learning,* we can chart the performance of participants over time and show increases in correct responses that participants are unable to consciously track in their minds.

Another frequently examined form of implicit remembering is called *priming.* As noted above, all knowledge in our memories can be characterized in terms of how readily it comes to mind. If you are asked your name, your name is easy to retrieve. However, if you are asked the capital of Wyoming, it may not come readily to mind. Earlier we noted that cues can temporarily activate information in memory. Priming is the term used for this temporary activation. One example of priming is to have people look at a long list of words and, perhaps, identify how many start with the letter *R.* After doing so, you then ask them to complete a word-fragment task in which they have to supply missing letters to identify a word: "_ _ TC_ _ R." People are much more likely to complete the fragment with the word *catcher* when it was one of the words on the list in the first phase of the experiment than when *catcher* is not on the list (Eysenck & Brysbaert, 2018). When this occurs, we say that seeing the word *catcher* on the list primed the representation of this word in our minds such that when we see the word fragment, the letters in the fragment finish the job and *catcher* is retrieved. Other participants could have seen the word *pitcher* on their list so they would be more likely to complete the fragment using *pitcher* than *catcher.* Priming is a form of implicit learning because it happens outside of consciousness. Researchers have shown that participants are unaware of priming occurring and do not remember seeing the primes on the list.

Researchers originally became interested in the distinction between implicit and explicit memory because of numerous case studies of brain-injured people who showed severed deficits in the ability form new explicit memories (e.g., the names of new doctors) but intact implicit memory (e.g., continual improvements in the ability to trace lines within a maze). Given the development of the brain in which certain cortical areas develop more slowly than subcortical areas (see Chapter 2), developmental psychologists have also become interested in the distinction between implicit and explicit memory because forming explicit memories seems to rely on later developing brain areas (e.g., the hippocampus and frontal lobes). Even young infants show priming affects and the ability to learn statistical regularities (Howe, 2015).

Distinction 5: Declarative versus Nondeclarative Memory

The distinction between explicit and implicit learning is similar to that between declarative and nondeclarative memory. As the name implies, a *declarative memory* is the kind of remembering that you are conscious of and can state (declare). *Nondeclarative memory* is the kind of remembering that you are unaware is happening. The different terminology used in the previous section and present section simply reflects different research traditions within psychology and neuroscience, but they are essentially talking about the same thing. However, scholars who make the declarative/nondeclarative distinction also make further distinctions within each of these two categories.

Within declarative memory, there are distinctions among episodic, autobiographical, and semantic memory (Howe, 2015). *Episodic memory* refers to the ability to remember the details of some event or experience (the time, the place, what happened). So, you use your episodic memory to recall what you ate for lunch today or what happened at your last birthday party. However, you also might use it to remember which specific words occurred at the beginning of a list that you just observed in a psychology experiment. *Autobiographical memory* is the kind of episodic memory that has relevance to the self. So, autobiographical memory would be involved when you remember what happened to you at your birthday party, but not when you are trying to remember the words at the beginning of a list. *Semantic memory* is the knowledge that you acquired in a particular context, but such details have been lost in favor of generalizable, conceptual or factual knowledge. For example, you may have first learned that tigers have stripes during a trip to the zoo when you were 4, but that detail is irrelevant to knowing that tigers have stripes. Semantic memory underlies the meaning that we give to words and helps us engage in reasoning and inference making. Episodic, autobiographical, and semantic memory are all forms of declarative knowledge, because the results of retrieving information from these memories could be stated ("I remember seeing my colleague yesterday"; "There are nine planets in the solar system").

Within nondeclarative memory, one can distinguish between procedural and other kinds of nondeclarative memory. The primary examples of *procedural memory* are skills that we can perform but we may at first be unable to verbally explain to others. For example, riding a bike, tying your shoes, tying a tie, factoring an equation, and making a paper airplane often start out as things we can do and get better at with practice but we may not be able to explain to others. Whereas procedural memory is often called "knowing how," declarative memory is often called "knowing that."

Other examples of procedural memory were alluded to above when implicit learning was discussed. When learning language, for example, young children are adept at picking up patterns and regularities in utterances (see Chapter 8, on language development). Children learning French, Italian, or German, for example, naturally pick up which words are feminine and which are masculine. They do not consciously reflect on this fact. They just follow the lead of others and store this information as part of what they know how to do. Finally, priming is not only a form of implicit learning; it is also an example of nondeclarative memory.

Whereas the distinctions among episodic, autobiographical, and semantic memory were originally made by psychologists who conducted traditional psychological experiments (e.g., learning lists of words), the declarative/nondeclarative distinction initially arose in experiments conducted by neuroscientists (Eysenck & Brysbaert, 2018; Graf & Schacter, 1985). Again, patients with amnesia have severe impairments in declarative memory but often no impairment in various forms of nondeclarative memory.

THE NATURE OF KNOWLEDGE IN LTM

The distinction between declarative and nondeclarative knowledge in memory invites some further consideration of the nature of knowledge in LTM. In Chapter 3, we saw that different theorists have different conceptions of the nature of knowledge. For example, Piaget (1964) proposed that in people who are capable of concrete and formal operations, their knowledge exists in the form of concepts such as time, causality, space, and categories. Categories, in turn, were described in terms of hierarchies in which subcategories (e.g., *dog*, *cat*) were nested within categories (e.g., *mammals*), which were themselves nested within superordinate categories (e.g., *animals*). Each category, in turn, was defined in terms of necessary and sufficient features (e.g., mammals have hair, self-regulating temperature, and bear live young). To be a member of a category, the individual had to have all the defining features (they are necessary) and when you have all of them, that is sufficient to be a member. Thorndike, in contrast, believed that knowledge consists of bits of information that are associated with each other (e.g., "9" is the answer to the question "What is 3 × 3?"). He made no room for concepts. In the case of schema theorists, they argued for schemata for objects (e.g., "dog," "furniture") and schemata for events (e.g., the birthday party script, the department of motor vehicles script). Schemata for objects are similar to Piaget's notion of categories.

Without further modification, none of the theories in Chapter 3 can account for the memory findings discussed so far or for the findings to be discussed later in this chapter. Many studies have shown, for example, that Piaget was right that knowledge exists in the form of hierarchies, but his assertion that all categories are defined by necessary and sufficient criteria does not seem to be correct. Rather, many categories seem to be defined by *characteristic features* rather than necessary and sufficient features. This phenomenon was first identified by the philosopher Ludwig Wittgenstein (1953), who showed that it is not possible to come up with the necessary and sufficient features of common concepts such as *game*. While most (or many) games involve more than one player, some games can be played alone. While most or many games involve rules, some games do not. Thus, the features we come up with for various categories tend to be characteristic features (true of many) not necessary and sufficient features.

Wittgenstein's proposal was further developed by psychologist Eleanor Rosch (1975) into *prototype theory*. A *prototype* resides at the core of any category and tends to contain the majority of highly characteristic features (e.g., flies, is about 3–4 inches in height, tweets, and eats worms, in the case of the prototype for birds). When people are asked to think of instances of a category, they usually think first of the prototype. In addition, when asked to say "yes" or "no" as fast as they can as to whether something is an instance of a category (e.g., "Is a(n) _____ a bird?") they tend to respond faster to prototypical instances (robins) than to instances that share fewer features in common with the prototype (ostriches). Such findings could not be explained by those who advocate necessary and sufficient features. All members of a category would be equally good representatives of the category rather than robins being better representatives than ostriches.

The idea of characteristic features also supports the notion of *family resemblances*. The more an instance looks like the prototype because of having many features in common, the more we can readily identify something as being a likely member. For example, after learning that a *terrier, schnauzer,* and *poodle* are all dogs, a child may surmise that a newly encountered *collie* is a dog as well because of family resemblance. However, the child may wonder at first about whether a *chihuahua* or a *pug* is a dog.

In terms of the hierarchical structure of knowledge, prototype theory specifies that there is a *basic level* that contains the prototype (*dog*), a *subordinate level* that contains different subspecies (*terrier, schnauzer*), and a *superordinate level* (*animal*). We will see in Chapter 8 that when parents talk to their young children and they label things, they often use the basic level terms ("Look at that doggy" rather than "Look at that terrier" or "Look at that animal").

If we combine the notion of the hierarchical structure of knowledge with the ideas of activation level and strength that were discussed earlier, we can add the notion of *spreading activation* to the account of knowledge described so far. When people encounter cues in the environment that increase the activation level of an item in memory, this activation spreads to other items to which it is connected or associated. So, for example, if people are primed with the word *terrier* when they examine a list of words that contains *terrier,* they are faster to respond that the word *dog* is a real word when it is flashed on a screen. Because the subcategory terrier is connected to, and right below the category dog, its activation is thought to spread to dog after the priming. However, the activation only spreads so far. The closer two items are to each other in the hierarchy, the more likely that priming will lead to a facilitation of performance to adjacent items.

SOME OTHER IMPORTANT EXPERIMENTAL FINDINGS OR EFFECTS

Cognitive psychologists have revealed many interesting and important findings over the years, and also sometimes proposed theories to explain these effects. As we shall see, an examination of 10 of these effects can also further illuminate the nature of memory.

1. The Primacy Effect and the Recency Effect

When people listen to a long list of words that are recited to them and are asked to report them back to an experimenter, there is a clear tendency for people to remember the last three to four words in the list the best, the first few words second best, and forget the words in the middle (Eysenck & Brysbaert, 2018). Remembering the last few words is called the *recency effect* and is explained by arguing that those words are still in STM. Remembering the first few words is called the *primacy effect* and explained by arguing that these words were transferred to LTM after being displaced by words in the middle of the list. Students who engage in more meaningful studying can typically overcome the primacy and recency effect and recall all the information.

2. The Phonological Similarity Effect

The phonological similarity effect (PSE) refers to the finding that people perform worse on lists of items that have no overlap in sounds than on lists in which the words share sounds. So, a list with words that rhyme might be recalled worse than a list in which none of the words rhyme with each other (Eysenck & Brysbaert, 2018).

3. Massed versus Distributive Practice

One of the earliest findings of memory researchers that was discovered in the 1800s is that people who "cram" when they study show good immediate memory for the material, but not good retention over time (Eysenck & Brysbaert, 2018). Generally speaking, retention is far better when practice is distributed over time. For example, imagine the case where, for a midterm exam, there were 99 items of information to learn and you had three weekends in which to study. If you studied the first 33 items of information the first weekend, then restudied the initial 33 and studied an additional 33 items the second weekend, then studied the final 33 items of information along with restudying the first two sets as well, you would not only do well on the midterm, you would retain far more of the material over time than "crammers."

Teachers and textbooks can take advantage of this phenomenon by making that sure they regularly ask people to practice material from units that were covered earlier in the year (e.g., in an algebra course, reintroducing homework questions from Chapter 1 while students are also working on homework questions from Chapter 7). Doing so is called *interleaved practice*. Our minds want to forget experiences that do not recur, so occasional reminders tell our minds to retain this material. However, the effectiveness of interleaved practice varies by subject matter and tasks. It has been found to be strongest for pictures ($g = 0.67$), moderate for mathematical problems ($g = 0.34$), and nonsignificant for learning material from expository texts (Brunmair & Richter, 2019). For words, blocking words into similar categories leads to better memory than interleaved practice. Effects of interleaving are stronger when the categories are more difficult to discriminate (list 1 = different kinds of horses, list 2 = different kinds of flowers as opposed to two lists of flowers).

4. The Generation Effect

The generation effect pertains to the finding that people show better recall of information when they actively participate in the creation of a portion of, or embellishment of, that information as opposed to being merely presented with the information (Bertsch, Pesta, Wiscott, & McDaniel, 2007). So, for example, people show better memory for the second term in a word pair such as *dog–leash* when asked to complete the word fragment "dog l__sh" than if they just read the word pair. One meta-analysis of over 80 studies showed that the size of the generation effect was substantial ($d = 0.40$) compared to simply reading the information. This effect is even stronger when people are not constrained by stimuli such as word fragments but can supply whatever meaning they want (McCurdy, Leach, & Leshikar, 2017).

A related finding derives from the technique of *elaborative interrogation* in which people are asked "why?" questions about information (e.g., "Apples are the leading export of Saskatchewan. Why do you think that is?"). The latter technique is normally found to improve learning, but only when people have the knowledge they need to answer the "why" question correctly (Clinton, Alibali, & Nathan, 2016). Both the generation effect and elaborative interrogation effect are explained by appealing to the notion of "*desirable difficulties*" (Bjork, 1994): the more we expend mental effort to understand or process material, the better our memory of it (Fyfe & Rittle-Johnson, 2017).

5. The Testing Effect

This effect refers to the fact that LTM is better when people are immediately tested for the material that they have just read. When participants in one study were asked how they would study material from a textbook for a test, 57% say they would go back and reread a chapter or sections of it multiple times, 21% said they would study the material some other way (e.g., take notes and study the notes), and the final 18% said they would try to recall the material after one reading right on the spot with no further studying. When asked to use one of these strategies, the third one produced the best long-term retention, but it is the least often used (Eysenck & Brysbaert, 2018). A meta-analysis of 61 studies showed the average weighted effect size for people who used the testing method versus those who used some other method was $g = 0.50$ (Rowland, 2014). As was the case for the generation effect, most theorists explain this finding by appealing to the notion of desirable difficulties. Any college professor who has taught material from a textbook knows how his or her own memory for the material is greatly enhanced after teaching it.

6. The Distinctiveness Effect

When presented with a list of words or a story to remember, people tend to remember material that stands out in some way better than information that does not stand out (Eysenck & Brysbaert, 2018). For example, given the list *truck, car, bus, train, bicycle,* and *banana,* people would tend to remember *banana* more than the other items. Similarly, when presented with Bartlett's (1932) classic story about Native Americans called "War of the Ghosts" (see Figure 4.2), people are more likely to recall a strange occurrence at the end the story in which something black and mysterious comes out of the mouth of a character than they are to recall other less distinctive facts.

7. The Levels-of-Processing Effect

Not long after the original Atkinson–Shiffrin model was proposed, it was challenged by researchers who disagreed with the ideas that (1) material passes through STM first before making contact with LTM and (2) rehearsal is an effective or primary mechanism for promoting the transfer of information to LTM. Craik and Lockhart (1972) argued instead that material is more likely to be remembered if it is processed more "deeply" than if it is processed more "shallowly." Information is processed "deeply"

One night two young men from Egulac went down to the river to hunt seals, and while they were there it became foggy and calm. Then they heard war-cries, and they thought: "Maybe this is a war-party." They escaped to the shore, and hid behind a log. Now canoes came up, and they heard the noise of paddles, and saw one canoe coming up to them. There were five men in the canoe, and they said:

"What do you think? We wish to take you along. We are going up the river to make war on the people."

One of the young men said: "I have no arrows."

"Arrows are in the canoe," they said.

"I will not go along. I might be killed. My relatives do not know where I have gone. But you," he said, turning to the other, "may go with them."

So one of the young men went, but the other returned home. And the warriors went on up the river to a town on the other side of Kalama. The people came down to the water, and they began to fight, and many were killed. But presently the young man heard one of the warriors say: "Quick, let us go home: that Indian has been hit." Now he thought: "Oh, they are ghosts." He did not feel sick, but they said he had been shot. So the canoes went back to Egulac, and the young man went ashore to his house, and made a fire.

And he told everybody and said: "Behold I accompanied the ghosts, and we went to fight. Many of our fellows were killed, and many of those who attacked us were killed. They said I was hit, and I did not feel sick."

He told it all, and then he became quiet. When the sun rose he fell down. Something black came out of his mouth. His face became contorted. The people jumped up and cried.

He was dead.

FIGURE 4.2. Bartlett's "War of the Ghosts" story.

to the extent that people supply meaning to it. Meaning, in turn, derives from knowledge in LTM.

To illustrate their experimental approach that was designed to demonstrate levels-of-processing effects, imagine an experiment in which people are asked to listen to a list of words that emanate from a tape recorder. Prior to listening to the recording, people were randomly assigned to one of four conditions. One group is told to say whether the voice saying each word on the recording is a man or a woman. The second group is told to come up with a word that rhymes with each word after each one is said. The third group is told to imagine a picture in their heads after each word is said. And the final group is asked to give a definition of each word. None of the groups were told that they would have to remember the words after performing these activities. Craik and Lockhart would argue that the first group processed the words most shallowly and the fourth group processed it the most deeply. The prediction would be that the fourth group would recall the most words and the first group would recall the least. Results from this and other experiments supported the idea of levels of processing. It is interesting to note, though, that the levels-of-processing effect is only found for explicit learning, not implicit learning (Eysenck & Brysbaert, 2018).

8. The Self-Reference Effect

This effect refers to the fact that LTM for material is enhanced when it is related to the self at the time of testing (Eysenck & Brysbaert, 2018). A meta-analysis showed that compared to a semantic study conditions, people who think about the relevance of stimulus words to themselves recall far more items, $d = 0.65$ (Symons & Johnson, 1997). The survival value of items to the self has particularly strong effects. In a recent study, Nairne, Coverdale, and Pandeirada (2019) asked people to generate survival situations for each word that was presented. For example, for the word *door,* one participant came up with the situation in which his house was on fire but he could escape through the door. Even though people were not told that they would have to remember the words, performance in this condition was far superior (72–75% of words recalled) to that in three other conditions in which people had to (1) rate the pleasantness of the stimulus (45% of words recalled), (2) engage in an autobiographical retrieval task in which they had to recall the last time they saw or interacted with the objects (62–65% of words recalled), or (3) come up with an unusual use for the referent (62% of words recalled). All four of these conditions would represent "deep" processing but considering the survival value of words generated 10–30% more words recalled. Such results are explained by arguing that memory skills would naturally have been selected via evolution because they enhanced our fitness and survival.

9. Context Effects

A *context* is simply a situation in which events or activities occur. In any given day, adults may find themselves in contexts such as driving to work, sitting in an office, chatting with a friend in the hallway, and having dinner with their families. Contexts are culturally defined but occur in specific locations, usually involve people, have norms for what is acceptable behavior, and usually have characteristic objects involved (e.g., a car in the case of traffic; a desk in the case of an office). *Context effects* refer to the fact that people tend to have better recall when the recall phase of the experiment occurs in the same context in which they encoded and perhaps studied information (Eysenck & Brysbaert, 2018). In one particularly dramatic example of context effects, trained scuba divers studied a list of words either under water or above water (Godden & Baddeley, 1975). They then either tried to recall the list in the same or opposite context (in the water or out). Results showed that recall was considerably better when the retrieval context matched the study context. Context effects are an example of the *encoding specificity principle* that states that retrieval is optimized when there is considerable overlap in the information available at retrieval and in a person's memory trace (Eysenck & Brysbaert, 2018). I, for example, have an easier time remembering a student's name in the classroom than when I see a student walking around campus. Such findings also suggest that it might be wise for students to devote some time studying in the same classroom in which they will take a test (if possible). There is less overlap between a context such as their dorm room or bedroom and the classroom.

10. The Typicality Effect

This final effect derives from research examining the predictions of prototype theory. It refers to the fact that the time it takes to judge whether an instance of a category is a member of that category is less for typical members (e.g., "Is a robin a bird?") than for less-typical members (e.g., "Is a chicken a bird?").

When cognitive psychologists conduct experiments to prove the superiority of one theory over another (or explain an interesting finding such as the self-reference effect), care has to be taken that none of the above effects is the real reason for a finding. That is, it may be possible to explain one finding (e.g., the superiority of spaced practice over massed practice) by appealing to other effects (e.g., desirable difficulty) (Maddox, Pyc, Kauffman, Gatewood, & Schonhoff, 2018).

METAMEMORY AND MEMORY STRATEGIES

So far, we theoretically "carved" the human memory system into quite a number of components (e.g., cues, WM, LTM), different kinds of memory (e.g., explicit, implicit, episodic, semantic) and different kinds of processes (e.g., encoding, consolidation, retrieval, priming). To close out the description of the human memory system, we need to consider two final components that are indispensable to remembering things: metamemory and memory strategies.

People's *metamemory* is one aspect of their overall *metacognition*, which refers to their understanding of how their mind works (how they learn, how they remember, and so on) (Bjork, Dunlosky, & Kornell, 2013). There are several aspects of metamemory that could play a role in whether someone remembers an item of information. For example, people differ in terms of how fallible they think their memory is. If you think you are unlikely to forget something or that you always remember, you are unlikely to do anything special to make sure that you will remember (such as write a note or put a reminder in your calendar). College students (especially new students) often think they will remember information in courses without taking notes. Maybe they could avoid taking notes in high school, but they soon find out in college that they cannot remember the content behind lecture bullet points once they begin to study weeks later.

Or, if students think that they have studied for a test well enough ("I know this stuff") but really they have not, they may stop prematurely and then do poorly on a test. Finally, if they have faulty ideas about the best way to study, they will also do less well. As noted above, making flash cards and rehearsing them over and over is neither effective nor efficient, but many students use this method rather than more effective methods. Studying, then, is a function of *whether* you think you need to study and *how* you think you should study. Such choices are strongly influenced by people's metacognition (Metcalfe & Finn, 2008; Schneider & Ornstein, 2019; Tullis, Fiechter, & Benjamin, 2018).

As for the final component of the human memory system, *memory strategies,* there are a variety of strategies that could be used in particular situations to increase the chances that some information is later recalled. As noted above, one strategy was identified in the original Atkinson–Shiffrin model: rehearsal. While it is true that repeating information over and over to oneself will lead to later recall of the information (e.g., using flash cards), it is not a particularly efficient or powerful method (Eysenck & Brysbaert, 2018). Methods that require people to form interacting images or that tap into our prior knowledge work much better and more efficiently (less studying is required). Images have to be interacting because simply forming images of words has been found to be no more effective than rehearsal (Roediger, 1980).

One such strategy that seems to take advantage of familiar information and interconnected imagery was identified thousands of years ago by Socrates' students: the *method of loci* (Caplan, Legge, Cheng, & Madan, 2019). As Socrates walked around the city with his students and taught them, students later were able to remember information that was said to them at particular locations. Today, we would call this episodic or autobiographical memory, but note that when we try this method ourselves for our own familiar route (e.g., our commute home), we can recall images of locations along the way. The technique involves plastering to-be-learned facts at each location along the route (e.g., the train station, the first stop sign, that factory on the left). It was once thought that the visual, navigational aspect of this approach was the key factor that explained why it worked. A recent study showed, however, that it is best to think of the method of loci as just another instance of the *peg method* of studying (Caplan et al., 2019). With the peg method, any well-learned sequence will do, even a purely verbal one. For example, people can memorize the sequence, "One is gun, two is shoe, three is tree . . ." and then "hang" to-be-remembered words from a list by creating an interactive image at each step. For example, if the first word to be studied on the list is *bread,* you can create an image of the gun in "one is gun" shooting a hole through the bread. If the next word on the list is *dog,* imagine a dog wearing or sitting inside the shoe in "two is shoe," and so on.

A second effective strategy that relies on interactive mental imagery and meaning is called *elaboration* (Pressley & Hilden, 2006). Elaboration is often used when people try to study word pairs that have no inherent meaningful connection. For the word pair *cat–truck,* for example, you could create an image of a cat driving a truck. Note that when people create their own image as opposed to being given one by an experimenter, they are also taking advantage of the generation effect that was described earlier in this chapter. Note also that the elaborative interrogation method mentioned above makes use of elaboration, as its name suggests.

A third approach that has been successfully used to remember vocabulary words from a foreign language is called the *keyword method* (Fritz, Morris, Acton, Voelkel, & Etkind, 2007). Here, you create images and relate new vocabulary to something you already know. For example, to remember the Spanish word *carta* (which means letter) you might create an image of a large, addressed and stamped letter inside a shopping cart. Here, the keyword is *cart,* which is embedded in the new vocabulary word, *carta.* However, the keyword method can be used to remember other kinds of words, even unfamiliar English words. For example, for the word *caterwaul* (which means a noisy fight), you might create the image of two cats screeching at each other on top of a wall. The keyword method is argued to work well because of the use of interactive imagery and the generation effect.

The fourth method was also discussed earlier: *self-testing.* The process involves encountering the material in some way (e.g., read a text, read your notes) and trying to recall the information right away. Doing so not only increases your likelihood of remembering the material later, it also provides feedback to your metamemory as to what you remember and what you need to restudy. That said, the feedback we get from immediately testing ourselves can be deceptive. It turns out that waiting 24 hours and trying to remember the information is not only more diagnostic, it also improves memory (Tauber, Dunlosky, & Rawson, 2015).

The final strategy to be discussed is particularly useful when information can be grouped or categorized in some way. For example, imagine being presented with the following list of words and asked to study the words for 3 minutes: *truck, cake, trousers, shirt, candy, ice cream, car, shoes, bus, bicycle, jacket, pudding.* If you simply reread the list in the order presented in the previous sentence (in other words, used rehearsal), you might remember the usual 5–7 words out of 12. However, if you used the *organization strategy* of grouping them first into the categories of vehicles (*truck, car, bus, bicycle*), clothing (*trousers, shirt, shoes, jacket*), and sweet things (*cake, candy, ice cream, pudding*), and then added rehearsal on top of that, you would probably remember all 12. Here, you benefit from accessing your prior knowledge of these categories (a levels-of-processing effect), using category labels as effective cues (e.g., "Let's see; there were four vehicles"), and the generation effect for forming the categories yourself. Any time you can take information and organize it in some way, your memory will improve. Note that this effect would work best for unorganized material that has to be organized. If an instructor provided the organization for you, you would lose the benefit of the generation effect.

Of course, for things you need to do in daily life, you do not always need to use the above strategies and retrieve information from LTM if you do other things, such as write a shopping list to yourself when going to the supermarket, put a doctor's appointment into your calendar in your phone and set a reminder to go off 1 day or 1 hour before, always pay your bills on the same day of the week, and so on. But note that all these examples are also memory strategies as well.

RECOMMENDATIONS OF THE INSTITUTE OF EDUCATION SCIENCES EXPERT PANEL

In 2015, the primary funding arm of the U.S. Department of Education, the Institute of Education Sciences (IES), commissioned a panel of six experts in the field of cognitive psychology (Hal Pashler, Brian Bottge, Art Graesser, Ken Koedinger, Mark McDaniel, and Janet Metcalfe) and a classroom teacher (Patrice Bain) to write a set of recommendations for classroom practice based on well-established findings on memory and learning. These scholars made seven recommendations: (1) space learning over time, (2) interleave worked example solutions and problem-solving exercises, (3) combine graphics with verbal descriptions, (4) connect and integrate concrete and abstract representations of concepts, (5) use quizzing to promote learning, (6) help students allocate study time effectively, and (7) help students build explanations by asking and answering deep questions (Pashler et al., 2007). Recommendations 1, 2, 3, 5, and 6 are well explained in this chapter. We will examine recommendations 2 and 7 in other chapters (e.g., the chapters on math and science learning).

THE FLIP SIDE OF REMEMBERING: FORGETTING

So far, everything discussed in this chapter was about what we can do to remember better. That is, the aforementioned material provides an answer to the question "Why do we remember anything?" In this section, we briefly consider answers to the opposite question: "Why do we forget?" Although it may seem like these two questions are asking the same thing, consider how answers to questions such as "Why did she win the race?" (e.g., She ran faster than the other runners) may not always be the same as answers to questions such as "Why did she lose the race?" (e.g., She pulled her hamstring muscle in an earlier race). In this section, we will see that we need a few more theoretical constructs to explain why we forget. There are four main theories of forgetting: decay theory, interference theory, loss of retrieval cues theory, and retrieval-induced forgetting theory.

Decay Theory

All of us forget and have personal experience with the phenomenon that the passage of time plays a strong role in forgetting. Dating back to some of the earliest studies of forgetting conducted by Herman Ebbinghaus in the 1880s, many studies seemed to show that forgetting follows a negatively accelerating (exponential) function in which we initially forget very little over a period of a few minutes or days, but then rapidly seem to lose much of what we learned (Fisher & Radvansky, 2019). However, several recent experiments combined with a reanalysis of a number of prior experiments suggest that the rate of forgetting is fairly linear or constant over time (Fisher & Radvansky, 2019). Whereas the negatively accelerating or exponential function is still found of meaningless or simple stimuli, the linear drop off has been consistently found for more complex and well-learned material.

Regardless of whether the rate of forgetting is accelerating or constant, both findings confirm that something occurs in our brains that makes well-learned information increasingly difficult to access over time. It is not clear what exactly decays, but one proposal is that the strength of memory traces fades over time if information does not recur. If we consider strength to be measurable by the probability of recall (or metaphorically "closeness" to conscious access) and akin to the idea of resting activation (as noted above), then the strength or resting activation level could decrease over time.

Interference Theory

In order for memory cues such as someone's face or name to work effectively, each cue should be strongly associated with one and only one memory trace. In practice, however, cues often are associated with many memory traces. For example, the cue represented by the question "What is your phone number?" could be associated with your current phone number or the immediately preceding number. In contrast, the cue represented by the question "What is your date of birth?" is only associated with one constant answer. As noted earlier, cues and memory traces work together to help us access information from LTM. We can quantify the connection between cues and memory traces to explain why we can readily retrieve and answer from memory and why we sometimes struggle. When cues are strongly associated with a single memory trace (e.g., a 90% probability), there is no problem. Similarly, when the association between a cue is much stronger for one memory trace (your current phone number) than another memory trace (your previous phone number), there will often not be a problem if you are trying to remember the trace with the stronger association to the cue.

Memory problems arise when other possibilities are the case. When a cue used to be strongly associated with a memory trace that you are trying to forget (e.g., your old phone number) and is more weakly associated with a memory trace you are trying to retrieve (e.g., your new number), the phenomenon of *proactive interference* ensues. A customer service representative on the phone asks, "What is your phone number?" and you stare blankly into the phone and say "Ummmm." In contrast, if the association between a cue and a new memory trace grows over time, you may have trouble remembering older information because of the phenomenon of *retroactive interference*. Here the new information interferes with your ability to retrieve old information (Eysenck & Brysbaert, 2018). For example, after getting a new phone number and using it for a year, you may call up a customer representative who asks, "What is the phone number associated with the account?" which may be the old number. Once again, you stare blankly into the phone.

Interference is a problem when multiple memory traces are competing to enter consciousness. You may have experienced this problem on a test in which you cannot remember, for example, which name goes with which theory (e.g., "Was it Piaget or Vygotsky who advocated the zone of proximal development?"). Interference can emerge on any test in which factual knowledge or a procedure is required and must be retrieved from memory. Sometimes you will forget whether "54" is the answer to "6 × 9" or "7 × 9." Or, you are asked, "What is 6 × 9? "and both the answers "54" and "63" pop into your head. In my immediate family, I have to remember the names of 23 nieces and nephews, their spouses and boyfriends or girlfriends, and three new babies (at this writing!). Interference abounds from multiple name possibilities, so I resort to "Hi, Sweetie" or "Hey, dude."

Loss of Retrieval Cues

The third possibility is that cues may lose their evocative ability over time (Anderson, 2014). For example, for high-strength items in memory, a cue may initially have enough evocative power to bring the item to consciousness. However, it may be possible that the cue loses its evocative power such that it becomes unable to bring the high-strength item to consciousness.

This theory is essentially a decay theory for cues. The decay theory discussed earlier is for the strength of an item in LTM.

Retrieval-Induced Forgetting

Earlier it was noted that asking people to retrieve information right after exposing them to a list or a text is an effective way to promote their memory of the material (the so-called testing effect). One hazard of this effect is that the material that is not recalled during retrieval is more likely to be forgotten later on than is the material that is retrieved (Murayama, Miyatsu, Buchli, & Storm, 2014). Two processes have been proposed as explaining this finding: inhibition and interference. As we will see in Chapter 6 (executive function and self-regulation), inhibition is an important ability that involves the active suppression of information or a response. We will also see in Chapter 9, on reading, that when our eyes fixate on a printed word such as *rose,* our minds initially retrieve all of the meanings associated with the word (e.g., stand up, red flower, great aunt's name) but then retain only the meaning compatible with the context (e.g., "stand up" for the sentence, "When the Queen entered the room, everyone rose."). The factor responsible for eliminating inappropriate meanings is inhibition. A similar effect seems to be at play in retrieval-induced forgetting.

However, it has also been proposed that the material that is retrieved at the testing interferes with the material that is not retrieved. This phenomenon can be controlled in a study by introducing cues that do not activate the material that was retrieved at testing or even using cues that are associated with the material that was not retrieved (Murayama et al., 2014). When interference is not controlled, the average effect size between retrieved and not-retrieved items is $g = 0.50$. When interference is controlled, however, the effect size shrinks to $g = 0.22$. Thus, both inhibition and interference seem to be at work here.

CONSTRUCTIVE MEMORY

So far in this chapter, most of the discussion has been about whether people remember or forget experiences that actually happened to them (e.g., which words were presented to them on a list). Studies have also revealed the natural human tendency to "remember" things that we actually did not experience. Because we mainly do this by relying on our stored knowledge to insert additional meaning into, or reconstruct, our experiences, this phenomenon of remembering things that we did not experience has been dubbed *constructive memory,* in line with constructivist theories such as those of Piaget or schema theory.

One of the earliest examples of constructive memory came from the studies of Sir Frederick Bartlett described above. When people listened to his "War of the Ghost" story and tried to retell it right after hearing it, there was a strong tendency to reconstruct it to make it make more sense. People deleted things that were difficult to process and added and rearranged ideas to make the story more understandable. This process of reorganizing, elaborating, and streamlining became more and more pronounced as people were asked to retell the story multiple times after a few days (Bartlett, 1932).

When Bartlett's work was rediscovered in the 1970s, a variety of experiments showed other interesting effects. For example, one line of research showed that questions about the contents of a short film can cause people to "remember" seeing things in the film that were not there (Loftus & Palmer, 1974). For example, when researchers asked people to watch a short film depicting a car crash, half of the participants were asked one of two very similar questions: (1) "How fast was the car going before it smashed into the other one," or (2) "How fast was the car going before it hit the other one." A week later, all the participants were asked if they remembered seeing any broken glass in the film. Results showed that people asked the question with the word *smashed* were more likely to say that they saw glass than people asked the question with the word *hit*. However, there was no broken glass in the film.

Other examples show that people make inferences and elaborate on things that they hear or read. For example, after hearing the sentence, "The woman spoke to the man behind the counter about the prices," they might be very likely to think they heard the sentence "The housewife spoke to the manager about the high meat prices" (Paris, 1978). Or, if presented with a list of words such as *potato chips, pretzels, peanuts,* and *corn chips,* they may think they heard the word *snack* or *salty* and be as confident that they heard that word as they were for words actually on the list (Schacter, 2012). People also misattribute where they got information, such as when they believe someone told them information, but they actually read it in a newspaper. Older people are particularly prone to such source errors (Schacter, 1999). In one bizarre and tragic example, a woman was raped right after she watched an interview on TV and misremembered the rapist as the person who was interviewed on TV (Thomson, 1988). Other studies have shown how people do not notice when a person who asks them for directions is switched when they look away to point in the direction (Schacter, 1999). Finally, both children and adults are susceptible to the phenomenon of being asked about an event that never happened to them (e.g., getting lost in a shopping mall at age 5; breaking their arm at age 3) that they deny happened to them in their first interview, but then remember with vivid detail the next time they are interviewed, a week or so later (Schacter, 1999). This problem is particularly pronounced in preschool-aged children.

In many respects, these examples of constructive memory derive from the fact that, for reasons of efficiency and cognitive effort, the human mind wants to forget many of the details of an experience and retain just the gist of what we experience (Reyna, Corbin, Weldon, & Brainerd, 2016). For example, people are able to retain the actual words used by someone for only a few minutes but can retain the essential ideas that they expressed for weeks or even longer. People can overcome many of the constructive errors listed above if they can be made to pay closer attention and process the information more deeply (Schacter, 2012). Students are able to memorize the precise definition of terms for tests if they need to do so to get full points. But the default mode, when they have no reason to think they will need to remember something exactly is to discard the full, superficial features of an experience and retain just the gist.

One interesting study of the forgetting curve mentioned above showed how forgetting curves differ depending on whether the stimulus is a list of words or a narrative, and within narratives, whether the surface features or underlying gist was at issue (Fisher & Radvansky, 2018). As will be discussed in Chapter 9, on reading, Van Dijk and Kintsch (1983) proposed that our memory of narratives can be decomposed into three levels of representation: the surface form, text-base, and event model levels. The *surface form* representation contains the exact words and syntax used. In other words, it is the verbatim level. Most studies show this level only lasts in memory for a few minutes. The *text-base* level corresponds to the underlying meaning or gist of what is said in the passage. It can be mapped onto different surface forms (e.g., the actual wording and a paraphrase). The *event model* is a mental representation of what the text describes (e.g., an image of a scene in a book). Fisher and Radvansky (2018) showed that memory for the word list dropped rapidly from the first day to the seventh day, 65% down to 12%, and then dropped more slowly between the seventh day and the 85th day after testing. This is the classic Ebbinghaus power function. For narratives, in contrast, the surface form was lost almost immediately, the text-base gist dropped from 65% recall to 55% recall in the first week, then from 55% to 50% by around the third week and remained there until the 12th week. The event model, however, dropped from 75% to 68% over the first week, and then remained there (around 65%) across the 12 weeks of the study. When we form the text-base gist and the event model, we make inferences, and add things to what we have read. Doing so can cause memory distortions, as a variety of experiments show (e.g., seeing broken glass in the crash film), but it is also an adaptive thing to forget details and retain mental models of what we read or experience (Schacter, 2019).

A further way memory is now conceived as adaptive relates to the fact that there appear to be close links among the brain systems that support memory, thinking into the future, and creativity (Schacter, 2019). We will see that this emphasis on the adaptive nature of memory is also a key theme in the literature on the development of memory in infants, children, and adolescents.

THE DEVELOPMENT OF MEMORY

Having described how the human memory system functions in adults, we can now turn our attention to how memory develops between infancy and adulthood. An efficient way of describing age trends is to utilize the afore-mentioned descriptions of structural and functional aspects of memory as an organizational framework. The goal is to see if each distinction within the memory system (e.g., encoding versus consolidation) or each experi-mental finding (e.g., primacy versus recency effects) or each component of the memory system (e.g., metacognition and strategies) can be thought of as a locus of developmental differences and, therefore, an explanation of the following general trend: between infancy and adulthood, children become increasingly capable of recalling more and more of the information presented to them. Regardless of whether they are asked to memorize a list of words or read a portion of a text, there is nearly always an increase in the amount of information that children can retrieve between each age level (e.g., age 5 to age 7; age 10 to age 15). What are the reasons for such increases in recall with age?

Age Trends in Encoding versus Consolidation versus Retrieval

When children of several age groups are presented with information and older children recall more than younger children, this improved recall could be due to a difference in (1) the manner in which the information was temporarily encoded (how it got into the system and was represented in the mind), (2) the process by which it became consolidated (slowly shifted from a temporary binding in the hippocampus to a more permanent representa-tion in the cortex), or (3) the manner in which it was retrieved. In other words, it is possible that less information got into younger children's minds in the first place, consolidation worked more optimally in older children, or the information got in and was consolidated but younger children had difficulty getting information out (Howe, 2015).

Many studies of children's memory have shown that there are clear dif-ferences in both the amount and quality of information that is encoded by younger and older children (Howe, 2015). So, without special accommo-dations to equate encoding across age groups, age differences in memory could be due to age differences in encoding. Since what we encode is a func-tion of both what we selectively attend to and also how much knowledge we already have, age differences in encoding are to be expected; younger children have less attentional capacity and less knowledge than older children. That said, even when encoding is experimentally manipulated to ensure that older and younger children are equal with respect to encoding, age differences in recall still arise (Howe, 2015). Such findings suggest that age differences could also be due to age differences in consolidation or the ability to recall information.

The hippocampus is part of a complex of structures in the medial temporal lobe that support memory function (Gomez & Edgin, 2016) and was described above as playing an important role in consolidation. Although some aspects of hippocampus development are complete by 24 months, other aspects, such as cortical thinning, neurogenesis, and myelination, continue well into adolescence (see Chapter 2, on brain development; Gomez & Edgin, 2016). These neurological changes are often alleged to be one of the reasons for age differences in consolidation (Gomez & Edgin, 2016; Howe, 2015). In addition, studies have shown that consolidation is enhanced by sleep that occurs within a day of exposure to material. The hippocampus is thought to replay memories during sleep, thereby promoting their consolidation and retention (Gomez & Edgin, 2016; Wang et al., 2018).

As for retrieval, studies suggest that encoding and consolidation differences appear to be more important factors in explaining age differences in memory than in retrieval (Howe, 2015). This finding can be demonstrated by making sure children have encoded material properly and had similar amounts of time and sleep to promote consolidation. When these controls are in place, age differences in memory largely disappear.

Age Trends in Recall versus Recognition

Because recognition involves a matching of a cue in the environment to a stored representation, recognition tests are usually less difficult than recall tests. As such, the usual finding of monotonic increases in memory performance between early childhood and adulthood is less pronounced for recognition tests than for recall tests (Brainerd, Reyna, Howe, & Kingma, 1990).

Age Trends in STM, WM, and LTM

For both STM and WM, studies have shown that there are monotonic increases in the number of items recalled between the preschool period and adolescence (e.g., Gathercole, Pickering, Ambridge, & Wearing, 2004; Swanson, 1999). For example, whereas a 4-year-old could repeat back about two to three digits on the digit-span task, an adult could repeat back about seven digits. Children in between the ages 4 and 7 would recall an amount that steadily increases from two digits to seven digits (Cowan, 2014).

To answer questions about whether there are age differences in LTM, one would have to unpack this question a little further. For example, is the concern about the amount of time that has elapsed since learning (e.g., "Do 10-year-olds retain information for a longer time than 5-year-olds?") or the contents of LTM (e.g., "How much knowledge do 10-year-olds have compared to 5-year-olds?" and "How is this knowledge structured?"; and so on). Even young infants have the capacity to remember things for quite some time with occasional reminders (e.g., a particular mobile for a crib that they shook using a rope tied to their leg) (Howe, 2015). When somewhat older children are tested, their failure to recall has to be decomposed into possible reasons for the lack of recall. Is the information in LTM and they are just having problems retrieving the information or have they truly forgotten it?

With respect to the contents of LTM, we know that knowledge continually grows between infancy and adulthood. As we will see in Chapter 8, on language development, for example, a 1-year-old tends to know just one word while a 5-year-old may know 6,000–10,000 words (quite an increase!). And many words refer to concepts, so this age difference shows clear knowledge growth. In other chapters, we will see that high school students have far more knowledge in domains such as math, history, and science than first graders. In addition, this knowledge tends to be more hierarchically arranged and interconnected (Brainerd & Reyna, 2014; Whitney & Kunen, 1983). Moreover, older children are capable of understanding both concrete and abstract information. It is also the case that definitions in traditional subject areas tend to refer to necessary and sufficient criteria (e.g., all squares have to have four equal sides and four 90-degree angles), so older children will have more of these classically defined concepts in addition to their knowledge of prototypes. Younger children will only have knowledge of prototypes and often will not have the superordinate categories formed yet. All these differences will impact how and whether knowledge in LTM will have effects in memory experiments (as will be further discussed below).

Age Trends in Implicit and Explicit Memory

As noted earlier, the largest age increases in memory occur for explicit memory (Howe, 2015). Researchers can use operant conditioning (see Skinner's theory in Chapter 3) and priming tasks with degraded pictures to show implicit memory in very young children (even infants). Studies show there is very little evidence of age improvements in implicit memory. However, it is necessary to use picture fragments rather than word fragments to show priming in children who are not quite literate.

As for explicit memory, recall that there are three kinds: episodic, autobiographical, and semantic. The necessary ingredients for forming accurate and stable episodic memories include sufficiently developed structures in the medial temporal lobe but also the ability to bind together the elements of an episode (who was there, what they were doing, details of the situation), distinguish real from imagined events, bind items to locations, and avoid confusing elements across similar episodes (Fandakova & Ghetti, 2017; Olson & Newcombe, 2014). For autobiographical memories, in particular, there also has to be a sufficiently developed sense of self (Howe, 2014). These factors collectively explain why the capacity to form autobiographical memories emerges rather abruptly around 2 years of age and gradually strengthens for at least 4 years before eventually becoming more adultlike (Olson & Newcombe, 2014). Prior to age 2 there is the phenomenon of *infantile amnesia* in which people have a hard time remembering anything in their lives that happened before age 2 or 3. One other factor that promotes the development of autobiographical memory is the tendency of parents to reminisce about recent events with their children during conversations during the day or even just prior to bedtime (Hudson & Grysman, 2014). Note that doing so at bedtime could promote the consolidation of autobiographical memory through sleep (Wang, Weber, Zinke, Inostroza, & Born, 2018).

As for semantic memory, we once again have to unpack the question a little further. For example, many studies of semantic memory make a contrast between the verbatim trace of an experience and the gist of the experience (Brainerd & Reyna, 2014), as noted above in the discussion about forgetting. For example, when presented with the words, *apple, banana,* and *grape,* the verbatim trace would contain the information that these three words (and not some other words) were presented. The gist representation, however, might contain the fact that all three words referred to fruits. As time passes, we often forget the verbatim or surface form of the information presented but retain the gist memory that the three words were kinds of fruits (Brainerd & Reyna, 2014). A number of studies have shown that "From the preschool years onward, memory for the surface form of events improves markedly, with the greatest improvement occurring for the standard materials of memory experiments between early and late childhood" (Brainerd & Reyna, 2014, p. 491).

As for gist representations that rely on semantic memory, many studies show there is a slow protracted development. One reason for the slow protracted development was alluded to earlier. To form many gist representations, you have to have the necessary knowledge in place, such as hierarchically arranged categories or schemata (see schema theory in Chapter 3). The second reason is that young children are less likely to link their encodings across stimuli. For example, when encoding they may note that apple is a fruit and banana is also a fruit. However, they may not connect these two encodings to recognize that both words refer to fruit (Brainerd & Reyna, 2014). In other words, they tend to be "piecemeal processors."

Age Trends in Primacy and Recency Effects

As noted earlier, the tendencies to recall the last few items (recency effects) and first few items (primacy effects) but not the middle items of a list are well-established findings. People recall the last few items because they are still in STM. People recall the first few items because they rehearsed them and transferred them to LTM. This analysis suggests that age differences in recency effects would be much smaller than age differences in primacy effects since younger children are less likely to use rehearsal as a strategy than older children (as we shall see below). Many studies have confirmed this prediction when children below the age of 7 are compared to children above the age of 7 (Lehmann, 2015). When children engage in rehearsal in the manner of adults (late childhood and adolescence), they produce comparable primacy and recency effects.

Age Trends in the PSE

Originally, researchers expected that there would be age increases in the PSE, because it was assumed that both speech rate and use of rehearsal promoted the PSE and older children have faster speech rates and use rehearsal more than younger children. However, when care is taken to control for potential alternative explanations, the PSE was found to be age invariant between 5 and 13 years of age (Hasselhorn & Grube, 2003; Jarrold, Cocksey, & Dockerill, 2008). Also, the PSE was found to be smaller when rehearsal was suppressed. These findings show that the PSE is not due to, or strongly affected by, speech rate or rehearsal.

Age Trends in Massed versus Distributive Practice

In both laboratory studies and classroom studies in which children are asked to learn classroom-related content (e.g., math skills or history facts), those who experience distributive practice tend to perform much better on delayed tests than children who do not experience distributive practice do (Pashler et al., 2007).

Age Trends in the Generation Effect

When asked to extend semantic memory across several related instances (e.g., *A wombat is a marsupial,* and *Marsupials keep their babies in a pouch*), about 60% of school-age children in second and fifth grades spontaneously integrate across such sentence pairs (e.g., Wombats keep their babies in a pouch), and 80% do so with scaffolding in the form of forced-choice answers (Bauer, Blue, Xu, & Esposito, 2016). In a related way, explicit instruction in the elaborative interrogation technique (asking "why?" questions) promotes better retention in 10-year-olds and 15-year-olds (Wood et al., 1999). However, elaborative interrogation only works when children have the requisite knowledge in semantic memory to answer "why?" questions correctly. It has also been found that children benefit more when experimenters give them images to remember word pairs (*elephant–pin*) than when the children generate these images themselves (Schneider & Pressley, 1997). For children who lack semantic knowledge, experimenter suggestions for elaboration works better than elaborative interrogation (Wood et al., 1999). College students typically do not need help or scaffolding and benefit more when they actively engage with the material themselves.

Age Trends in the Testing Effect

Several studies examined the testing effect in children and one even demonstrated it in 4-year-olds (Lipowski, Pyc, Dunlowsky, & Rawson, 2014). However, few examined whether the testing effect increases with age. Lipowski et al. (2014) did conduct a developmental study with 7- and 9-year-olds and found that recall performance did improve with age, but the comparison between the restudy alone condition versus restudy plus testing condition was comparably large between these two age levels. Children at both age levels recalled more when they engaged in testing during encoding/studying the material. The lack of age effects could be due to use of two age groups that were both above age 7 and only 2 years apart. However, it could also be due to the use of familiar items in four categories (fruits, body parts, pets, toys). It remains to be seen if age differences will emerge when additional age groups are tested and when different kinds of categorical knowledge are assessed.

Age Trends in the Self-Reference Effect

In their meta-analysis of the self-reference effect that included studies conducted prior to 1997, Symons and Johnson (1997) found only three studies that included children as participants. The effect size for children was significantly larger than zero ($d = 0.37$) but also significantly smaller than for adults ($d = 0.50$). Ross, Anderson, and Campbell (2011) found that, on recognition tests, 4-year-olds were above chance in their ability to remember actions that they actually performed as opposed to observed. Doing so would be an early form of self-reference effect. Using pictures of their faces paired with objects, Cunningham, Brebner, Quinn, and Turk (2014) found that in 4- to 6-year-olds, children performed significantly better, recognizing presented face–object pairs for themselves as opposed to pairs using other children's faces. Additional studies should chart when the self-reference effect approaches adult-like levels.

Age Trends in Context Effects

Edgin, Spano, Kawa, and Nadel (2014) found a nonlinear age trend in context effects. Specifically, they found that recognition memory was 10% better when objects were paired with background scenes than when objects were presented alone for adolescents older than 13 and adults, but not for children in the 4.5, 6, and 10–13 age groups. Edgin et al. explained these findings by saying that older participants had developed expertise in scene perception. Additional studies are needed to confirm this finding.

Age Trends in Typicality Effects

A representative study in this line of work is Bjorklund and Thompson (1983). These researchers presented lists of 11 typical and atypical members of categories to children in kindergarten, third grade, and sixth grade. They also varied the lists according to whether the category members were judged to be typical by children or adults, since there is only about a 40% overlap in the judgments of children and adults (Bjorklund & Thompson, 1983). Results showed age increases in recall, but also that children performed better on child-typical lists than adult-typical lists. The results for child-typical lists is shown in Figure 4.3. In addition to showing how recall improved with age for both typical and atypical exemplars, the gap between the lines illustrates the significant effect for typicality (typical exemplars recalled better than atypical at all ages). In a later study,

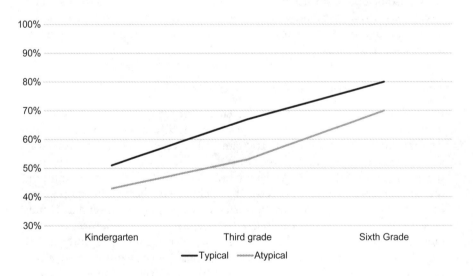

FIGURE 4.3. Age trends in typicality effects for recall using child-typical lists. Based on means presented in Bjorklund and Thompson (1983).

Schwenck, Bjorklund, and Schneider (2009) once again found typicality effects in which 4-, 5-, and 8-year-olds recalled significantly more typical exemplars than atypical exemplars. This finding was not observed in 6-year-olds, however.

Age Trends in Speed of Processing, Metamemory, and Memory Strategies

Many of the aforementioned findings strongly implicate the role of children's knowledge base in memory performance (Bjorklund, 2004; Howe, 2015). As children's knowledge grows and becomes restructured, their memory performance begins to approximate that of adults. However, several other age changes are equally responsible for age increases in memory as knowledge. The first is *speed of processing*. Across a range of tasks, studies show that there are monotonic increases in the speed with which children can perform many behavioral and cognitive tasks (Kail & Ferrer, 2007). This finding has clear implications for memory tasks because memory traces fade as time elapses and if no cognitive operations are performed on these traces. When age differences are found for WM, for example, one reason for these differences could be age differences in speed of processing. The speed of processing effect has not been much of a factor in memory studies of adults but is pervasive in developmental studies. That is why it was not discussed in this chapter until this point.

Besides knowledge and speed of processing, the other two important factors that explain increases in memory are metamemory and memory strategies. In the case of metamemory, there are clear increases in children's understanding of their own memory, as well as their tendency to understand and use memory strategies (Roebers, 2014; Schneider & Ornstein, 2019). At first, children below the age of 7 do not use strategies when presented with material to study because they mistakenly overestimate their memory skills. Overestimation of memory skills is a problem of metamemory. Between ages 5 and 7, it is often possible to teach children strategies and their memory performance improves (a *production deficiency*), but they often fail to use the same strategies at later testing sessions (Schwenck et al., 2009). In addition, even after using a taught strategy spontaneously, there is often a period in which it does not lead to an increase in recall (*utilization strategy*) (Clerc, Miller, & Cosnefoy, 2014; Scwenck et al., 2009). Moreover, when given a choice, children do not seem to know which of several strategies (e.g., rehearsal or organization) would be more effective in a particular situation. All these problems reflect deficits in metamemory that have to be overcome in order for students to use effective strategies and learn more when they study. Students need to acquire other insights as well, such as how long to study, when a particular fact has been mastered so it does not need to be studied anymore, how long it will take to study a large amount of material, and so forth (Roebers, 2014). All these aspects of metamemory improve with age, especially in more successful students.

Once children begin to use the basic form of strategies, usually between the ages of 7 and 10, they continue to grow in their metacognitive understanding of strategies and how to use them most effectively. For example, young children tend not to use the elaboration strategy of creating interactive images spontaneously. When they try to create images after prompting, their images are static rather than interactive. Older children, adolescents, and college students are more likely to use interactive images. In the case of rehearsal, children initially only rehearse the most recent item stated. So, for the string of numbers "3-1-7-4" a child might rehearse "3, 3, 3, 3 . . ." after hearing the experimenter say "3" but then when the experimenter says "1," the child now rehearses "1, 1, 1, 1 . . ." Older children and adults, in contrast, are more likely to use *cumulative rehearsal*. After hearing "3" they would rehearse "3, 3, 3, 3 . . ." but then after hearing the second number, they would rehearse "3-1 . . . 3-1 . . . 3-1 . . ." One further development is that older children are more likely to use multiple strategies to study the same material, whereas younger children are more likely to use a single strategy (Schwenck et al., 2009). For example, in addition to sorting pictures into categories, older students would then use rehearsal or imagery-based strategies to study items one group at a time.

Age Trends in Constructive Memory and False Memory

Recall that constructive memory pertains to the tendency to impose, or add, additional meaning to some experience, and "go beyond the information given" (Bruner, 1973). The constructivist approach is the antithesis of the empiricist approach of the Atkinson–Shiffrin model and Thorndike's associationism (see Chapter 3) that emphasize how all information comes through the senses. In order to impose additional meaning on stimuli, however, two necessary conditions have to be met. First, you have to have the knowledge stored in LTM that supplies the additional meaning that is imposed on a situation. Second, you have to then impose the additional meaning on the situation.

Studies have shown that children younger than 8 often lack the semantic knowledge needed to add additional meaning, but even when they have the necessary knowledge, they are less likely to impose it on a situation than older children, adolescents, and adults (Brainerd & Reyna, 2014; Brod & Shing, 2019; Howe, 2015; Metzger et al., 2008). For example, using the classic Deese–Roediger–McDermott (DRM) paradigm, participants are shown stimuli such as *banana, apple, cherry,* and *orange* (and words from other categories as well). On test trials they are presented with words that they actually saw and words they did not. Participants are then asked to indicate whether each word was actually seen (old) or not seen (new). To elicit the false memory effect, researchers introduce words that were not shown but are strong semantic associates, such as *fruit* for the aforementioned words. As participants grow older, they are significantly more likely to falsely recognize *fruit* as old or as actually been presented when it had not been. In fact, their false recognition rate rivals their accurate recall level, and they are just as confident that they actually saw that word. Thus, there are corresponding increases in both accurate memory and false memory with age (Brainerd, Reyna, & Holliday, 2018; Howe, 2014). The increases in both accurate memory and false memory derive from changes in children's knowledge base. One indirect way of showing the role of knowledge is to use word lists in which children supply the word associations or in which children have more knowledge about the topic than adults (e.g., *Sesame Street* characters). When child-friendly lists are used, false memory rates for young children increase and are sometimes higher than those of adults (Brainerd et al., 2018; Howe, 2014). But a second reason for age increases in both false memory and accurate memory is age increases in speed of processing, as mentioned above (Howe, 2014). Associative strength increases with age and promotes rapid retrieval.

When reading or listening to stories, younger children are less likely to make inferences or fill gaps in the story. As a result, they are more likely to only create surface level (verbatim) traces that rapidly decay, and less likely to create text-base and event model (gist) representations via inference-making (Brainerd & Reyna, 2014; Cain & Barnes, 2017). As such, they are not likely to falsely recognize sentences that contain elaborations supplied by inference-making. For example, if the original sentence that was presented was *Sara's eyes filled up when she learned that she had not been invited to the party,* younger children would be less likely to falsely recognize the sentence *Sara was sad because she was not invited to the party.* Thus, young children may not spontaneously make the inference even when they have the knowledge to do so. However, if you ask children to act out sentences, they can be led to make inferences and then falsely recognize (Paris, 1975).

The preceding descriptions of findings for the DRM paradigm and inference-making suggest young children are always less likely to construct false memories than older children and adults. In fact, research on suggestibility shows that young children are more susceptible to having false narratives implanted in them (Howe, 2015). By simply asking young children a question about an event that never happened to them (e.g., "Do you remember getting lost at the mall?" or "Do you remember breaking your arm and wearing a cast?"), young children show the tendency to later acknowledge the event the second time they are asked, provide elaborate details about it, and express strong confidence that the event happened (Brainerd & Reyna,

2014; Howe, 2015). But once again, the effect is stronger when children have knowledge of the experiences (e.g., they went to the mall many times or had a sibling who broke his or her arm).

The effects of false memory manipulations can also be affected by the emotion content of stimuli. Using the DRM paradigm, Howe, Candel, Otgaar, Malone, and Wimmer (2010) found that when given lists with either neutral terms or terms associated with negative emotions, false memories for neutral terms remained constant over time but false memories for negative information actually increased over time. Another study found that depression, emotional dysregulation, and stress all contributed to deficits in episodic memory and hippocampal volume in adolescents (Barch, Harms, Tillman, Hawkey, & Luby, 2019).

Summary of Age Trends

In summary, then, the four factors that are most responsible for age increases in memory between early childhood and adulthood are (1) increases in knowledge, (2) increases in speed of processing, (3) improvements in metamemory, and (4) an increased tendency to implement multiple effective memory strategies (Howe, 2015; Roebers, 2014). There may also be some role for brain development given the continued development of the hippocampus and frontal lobes through adolescence. The effects of these factors can also be modulated by the emotional content and emotional intensity of stimuli.

IMPLICATIONS FOR EDUCATION

A standard approach used in many school systems to prepare for end-of-year standardized tests is to construct 2-week units on material that are taught across the academic year (e.g., fractions in mathematics, the Melting Pot in social studies, renewable and nonrenewable resources in science) and then reteach material for several weeks prior to administering standardized testing in May. Children may take chapter examinations on a particular unit but may not encounter that material again until the refresher sessions at the end of the year. The theories and research presented in this chapter suggest that this standard approach is not likely to promote long-term retention. Instead, some of the following approaches are more likely to promote retention in an effective and efficient way:

1. *The importance of testing during learning and occasional opportunities to relearn.* As described above, the testing effect is a well-established and moderately strong finding for both children and adults. Quizzes that are presented right after learning can act as a form of both formative

assessment and also a stimulus for the testing effect. However, it is also important not to just test, but also to give ample time for students to learn the material to completely correct recall (Rawson & Dunlosky, 2011). One study compared various combinations of number of testings and relearnings and found that the most efficient and effective combination was to allow students three opportunities to learn material to correct recall followed by three opportunities to relearn the material several days or weeks later (Rawson & Dunlosky, 2011). Doing so led to 80% retention. This technique takes advantage of both the testing effect and distributive practice.

2. *The importance of evoking and scaffolding students' prior knowledge and imagery.* As noted above, many of the powerful findings discovered by cognitive psychologists relate to participants using some mental effort to think about, or add meaning to, material they are learning. This can be done by appealing to impersonal semantic knowledge but also to personally relevant information. One of the least effective approaches to studying is to learn material by rote (e.g., on index cards). It is also important to help students create interactive images to learn material.

3. *The importance of metacognition and strategies.* To be successful and learn material to mastery, students have to have an accurate understanding of their memory limitations and techniques for studying. Even college students overestimate what they will remember for a test and what they have to do to master material. Again, this is where techniques such as self-testing, formative assessments in the form of quizzes, and summative tests come in. Over time, students will slowly understand that they will forget unless they engage in effective study techniques. Parents and teachers can use information in this chapter to help guide their students in studying.

4. *The importance of sleep.* A variety of recent studies of both children and adults show that after encoding material, there is the process of consolidation of memory traces that seems to operate effectively after a good night's sleep. It is well known that many children do not get the amount of sleep they need, especially during high school. Memory research shows that learning and retention would improve if children were to get 8 to 10 hours of sleep in between what they learn during adjacent days of the week.

CHAPTER 5

The Nature and Development of Motivation

Although teachers of all grade levels can occasionally be challenged by students who are resistant to engage in an activity or who are bored, teachers of middle and high school students usually find motivational issues to be particularly difficult to overcome (Eccles & Wang, 2012). Motivation explains a significant portion of the variance in achievement even when other powerful predictors such as prior achievement and socioeconomic status are controlled (Byrnes, Miller-Cotto, & Wang, 2018). Moreover, motivation can be a primary source of both underachievement (i.e., students who achieve less than they could, given their aptitude) and overachievement (i.e., students who achieve more than they should, given their aptitude). Thus, to be more effective, teachers need to understand what motivation is and how to promote it. The goal of this chapter is to provide insight into these "what?" and "how?" questions.

THE NATURE OF MOTIVATION

In a similar way that we theoretically "carved" the human memory system into its components in Chapter 4, we will theoretically carve motivation into its components in this chapter. At the outset, however, it is important to note that researchers have proposed a number of motivational constructs over the past 170 years. The novice can become overwhelmed by the sheer number of constructs and how they differ or relate to each other.

For expository reasons, I shall use a temporal framework to organize constructs. In particular, I will group constructs in terms of whether they are primarily operative before, during, or after a classroom activity is completed. To see the utility of the expository framework, consider the fact that most prominent theories of motivation assume that students are agents who make choices (Wigfield et al., 2015). For example, students choose whether (1) to be compliant and cooperative when a teacher asks them to begin an activity, (2) to do their homework rather than play video games, (3) to keep expending effort and persist in an activity that is difficult or confusing, (4) to take additional math or science classes in high school beyond those that are required, (5) to select particular academic majors in college, (6) to attempt to engage in an activity one more time even though things did not go well the last time, and so on. These examples show motivation theory provides answers to questions such as "Why did she begin that activity in the first place?"; "Why did she choose that activity over other activities?"; "Why is she expending so much effort during the activity?"; and "Why is she feeling ashamed about how she just performed?" These questions show that motivation applies before, during, and after an activity is completed.

Motivation Constructs Operative before Activities Are Initiated

The constructs that explain choices before engaging in an activity include goals and mind-sets, ability beliefs, intrinsic and extrinsic motivation (including needs), outcome expectancies, interest and values, cost, and emotions. Let's examine each of these constructs.

Goals and Mind-Sets

Human behavior is inherently goal-directed (Locke & Latham, 2013). That is, people engage in particular behaviors (e.g., drive to work via a certain route) because they believe that these behaviors will produce particular outcomes (e.g., get to work on time). Motivational theorists focus on goals when they ask, "What is that student trying to accomplish by engaging in that activity?" Sometimes students want to impress or please others (*performance goals*) and sometimes they really enjoy the activity and want to get better at it (*mastery goals*) (Anderman & Patrick, 2012). When students regularly and characteristically pursue certain kinds of goals, they can be said to have a particular *goal orientation* (e.g., a performance-goal orientation or a mastery-goal orientation). Within the performance goal orientation, researchers have found that it is necessary to make a further distinction between *performance-approach goals* and *performance-avoid goals* (Anderman & Patrick, 2012). When students have a performance-approach orientation, they habitually want to engage in an activity to perform better than classmates or demonstrate their competence. When students have a performance-avoid orientation, in contrast, they avoid engaging in an activity in order to not appear incompetent or "dumb."

Logically, one would expect that students who have a mastery-goal orientation or performance-approach orientation would demonstrate higher achievement at the end of an academic year than students who have a performance-avoid orientation because it is not really possible to improve your skill level if you are avoiding engaging in activities that promote skill development. Another ancillary but important consequence of goal orientations besides skill development is the extent to which students seek help from their teachers or peers when they encounter difficulty (Anderman & Patrick, 2012). Students who have a mastery-goal orientation (also called a *learning-goal orientation*) tend to have what has been called a *growth mind-set* (Dweck & Yeager, 2019). People who have a growth mind-set believe that human capacities (e.g., your intelligence or math ability) are not fixed but can develop or improve over time. In contrast, people with a *fixed mind-set* believe that talents are fixed and do not improve or increase over time. These two mind-sets affect how readily you are willing to demonstrate your competence to others or seek help. Those with a growth mind-set recognize that errors and mistakes are common when you are first learning a skill. Moreover, they also recognize that you often need help or advice to overcome a difficulty and doing so is not a sign of incompetence but is a smart thing to do. Those with a fixed mind-set, however, are embarrassed by errors and mistakes because they believe errors are diagnostic of lower aptitude or competence. It is for the same reason that they avoid seeking help from teachers because they wrongly believe that only weaker students seek or need help. Students with the two different mind-sets also are likely to spend different amounts of time voluntarily working on a skill. Research supports these predictions (Anderman & Patrick, 2012).

Beyond the mastery–performance distinction, three further distinctions have also been proposed and shown to be predictive of learning outcomes. The first is the distinction between *specific* (e.g., "get all A's and B's this semester") versus *vague* goals ("do your best"); the second additional distinction is between *difficult* versus *easy* goals (Locke & Latham, 2013). Hundreds of studies have shown that people achieve approximately 250% more when they set goals that are both specific and difficult (e.g., lose 15 pounds in 3 months). The third distinction is between *social* and *academic* goals (Wentzel, Muenks, McNeish, & Russell, 2018). Studies have shown that students perform better academically when they not only set goals to do well in school, but also set goals to get along with, and be responsible to, other people.

What all of these studies show is that people have *multiple goals* that they have to coordinate (Locke & Latham, 2013). Initially, researchers seemed to expect that a single kind of goal would relate to achievement (e.g., mastery goals or academic goals). They now realize that there are often many competing goals at play in any given situation and that various goals are associated with achievement. In addition, correlations between certain goals and achievement do exist, but they are often modest (Anderman & Patrick, 2012; Schneider & Preckel, 2017). As we shall see next, the lower correlations with achievement derive from the fact that goals do not operate in a vacuum. Students may not attempt to pursue goals if other constructs are operative (e.g., they do not believe they have the ability to achieve the goal or if they think teachers are capricious graders).

Ability Beliefs

As alluded to in the previous section, students may not pursue certain courses of action or try very hard if they do not feel that they have the ability to carry out the required actions effectively (Muenks, Wigfield, & Eccles, 2018). In older students and adults, these ability beliefs would vary by the domain in question. For example, a student may feel as though he could effectively carry out a math task but not do well if asked to perform a difficult reading comprehension task. Or, a student may feel that she could effectively execute a corner kick in a soccer match but not be able to remember her lines in a school play. It is interesting that such beliefs are stronger determinants of whether students carry out tasks than objective measures of their ability (Muenks et al., 2018). For example, a student may receive straight A's in math for 12 years but still not rate her ability in math very high. The latter (incorrect) perception may keep her from choosing a STEM career in college.

Ability beliefs not only differ by domain, they also differ in their level of specificity. For example, students can have both global ratings of their competence in a domain (e.g., "I am good in science") as well as more specific ratings of their ability to carry out a particular task in that domain (e.g., "I can solve this physics problem about forces acting on a weight hanging from a spring"). The more specific ability beliefs are called *self-efficacy beliefs* (Bandura, 2013). Global ratings tend to correlate with achievement about $r = .30$, but self-efficacy ratings tend to correlate much higher than that (Schneider & Preckel, 2018). Self-efficacy also predicts career choices rather strongly (Turner et al., 2019).

Intrinsic versus Extrinsic Motivation

According to self-determination theory (SDT; Ryan & Deci, 2017), everyone is born with three basic *needs:* the need to feel competent, the need to feel related to others, and the need for autonomy. Classrooms can be structured, and activities assigned, that either meet these needs or not. When the needs are met, students are predicted to be *intrinsically motivated* to participate; that is, they will participate to engage in the activity because they like engaging in the activity, not to avoid punishment or get rewards.

In contrast, when classrooms fail to meet any of the three needs, teachers have to resort to threats or rewards to gain compliance. When this occurs, motivation is *extrinsic*.

Consider how classrooms can be structured either to meet the three needs or not. With respect to the need to feel competent, for example, tasks can be assigned that are too hard for most students. Assigning such tasks would make the majority of students feel incompetent as they struggle to complete them. To help every student feel competent, tasks can be individualized and differentiated such that they are moderately challenging for all students. The reader should note this point of connection between SDT and the previous section on ability beliefs and self-efficacy.

With respect to the need to feel related, teachers can create an atmosphere of hostility, animosity, and competition among students. Or, they can express warmth and concern for their welfare and using cooperative groups in which students support each other. Finally, teachers can limit autonomy and choice by demanding compliance and acceptance of their rules and choices or afford some autonomy by providing choices where appropriate (e.g., choosing books on which to right reports; choosing math activities that promote the same skills).

Outcome Expectancies

A number of classic and more contemporary theories of learning and motivation have stressed the idea that both humans and nonhuman animals make choices on the basis of the likelihood that an outcome will occur if they engage in a particular behavior (Wigfield, Rosenzweig, & Eccles, 2017). If given a choice between two behaviors in which one behavior is judged to be more likely to produce a desired outcome than another (e.g., studying for an exam using Technique A is more likely to lead to a good grade than studying using Technique B), people tend to choose the more likely option.

But there are two kinds of factors that contribute to outcome expectancies. Some factors are characteristics of the self (e.g., self-efficacy beliefs regarding the likelihood that you have the ability to bring about the desired outcome; the likelihood you will expend the effort), and some are characteristics of others and the environment (e.g., harsh or capricious grading practices on an instructor; inherent difficulty of the material). Studies conducted within the *expectancy–value model* of Eccles and colleagues have shown that outcome expectancies are among the strongest predictors of choices and performance (Wigfield et al., 2017).

Interest and Values

Although interest and values are theoretically distinct, they often appear to be highly correlated with each other and load on the same factor in factor analysis (Eccles & Wigfield, 1995; Kosovich, Hulleman, Barron, & Getty, 2015; Perez, 2012). For this reason, we will consider them in the same section. *Individual interest* is defined as a stable attraction or predisposition toward a topic that you find enjoyable and engrossing. It can be contrasted with *situational interest* that can be fleeting and evoked by situational attributes such as uncertainty, suspense, and curiosity (Bernacki & Walkington, 2018). Studies have shown that individual interest correlates with achievement and work performance about $r = .30$ and continues to predict even when prior achievement is controlled (Nye, Butt, Bradburn, & Prasad, 2018).

Values, on the other hand, pertain to the importance ascribed to a skill or domain. If you want to know what matters to someone, consider how values are often at the heart of conflicts. For example, if it is important for you to be good with your money or be on time, it can be upsetting when someone that you care about is bad with their money or often late. If you do not consider something important, you would be likely to say to yourself, "Who cares?" if the outcome does not obtain. For example, if you do not care about your grades or being on time, you will not get upset if you get a poor grade or are late.

Motivational theorists have defined values in several different ways but, in the aforementioned expectancy–value model, values are decomposed into three components: intrinsic value, utility value, and attainment value (Wigfield et al., 2017). *Intrinsic value* is essentially the same as interest, as described above. *Utility value* has to do with the usefulness of an activity to future outcomes (e.g., taking a math course in high school for a future STEM major in college). *Attainment value* is simply the importance of doing well on the task (e.g., "It is important to me to get an A on this test").

Studies have shown that values do not predict choices and achievement once outcome expectancies have been controlled, but the multiplicative expectancy × value term does predict outcomes even when expectancies are controlled (Wigfield et al., 2017). Even so, the amount of variance explained by the interaction term is negligible. As was noted above for goals, this lack of predictive value makes sense in context. It is possible for a student to care a great deal about getting good grades but not try particularly hard or expend much effort if they do not have the ability. The lack of effort would then lead to lower grades.

Cost

In the earliest iteration of the expectancy–value model, the construct of cost was part of the values component of the model (Wigfield et al., 2017). However, whereas questionnaire items tapping into intrinsic value, utility value, and attainment value all loaded on the same factor and were positively correlated with each other, items tapping into cost loaded on another factor and were negatively correlated with the other value components (Kosovich et al., 2012; Wigfield et al., 2017). The construct of cost refers to beliefs about what you would lose or give up if you engaged in an activity. This might include assessments of the time or effort that could be spent doing other important things, or psychological costs of performing poorly. Recent studies have shown that cost should be included in predictive models because student perceptions of what could be lost predict achievement and choices over and above goals, expectations, and values (Kosovich et al., 2012; Wigfield et al., 2017).

Emotions

Emotions can be felt before, during, and after students complete a task and can affect their motivation. Contemporary psychological and neuroscientific models of decision making and choice emphasize how anticipated emotions (those felt prior to engaging in the activity) play a role in decisions as to which course of action to take (Byrnes, 2013; Poppa & Bechara, 2018). In particular, according to the *hedonic principle* that underlies many long-held accounts of emotion, humans (and other animals) are naturally predisposed to pursue courses of action that lead to pleasurable emotional states and avoid courses of action that lead to unpleasant emotional states (Taquet, Quoidbach, de Montjoye, Desseilles, & Gross, 2016). However, recent studies have shown the actual connection between emotions and choices is not so straightforward. According to the *hedonic-flexibility principle,* it is assumed that

> one of the functions of affective states is to help individuals prioritize among short-term goals (e.g., feeling happy) and long-term goals (e.g., working hard to lose weight). . . . [W]hen they feel bad, people tend to engage in mood-enhancing behaviors. But when they feel good, people seem willing to sacrifice some of their current happiness, engaging in less immediately rewarding behaviors that might promise long-term payoff. (Taquet et al., 2016, p. 1112)

The positive mood and affective states referred to in these accounts include happiness, pride, relief, hope, and enjoyment/interest. The negative mood and affective states include sadness, shame, guilt, fear/anxiety, frustration, anger, jealousy, and boredom. If we link this analysis back to the earlier discussion of goals, we would tend to set goals to feel the positive mood and affective states and avoid courses of action that might evoke the negative affective states if given the option to do so. When students consider how they might feel if they were to solve a math problem at the blackboard or read a passage from a book out loud, different emotions might be evoked given the prior experiences and aptitudes of students. In addition to guiding students toward certain courses of action and away from other courses of action, emotions such as fear and anxiety can cause students to narrow the options they might consider.

Motivation Constructs Operative during Activities

After the constructs described in the previous section promote the adoption of a particular course of action by energizing the student and guiding action selection (Ainley, 2012), some of the same constructs are operative again as the course of action is implemented. However, several additional important constructs emerge as well. For expository purposes, we can begin with the new constructs and reintroduce the already described constructs where appropriate.

Engagement

What does it mean for a student to be engaged in a classroom activity? It depends on which motivation scholar is asked. A perusal of the chapters in a 2012 handbook on student engagement (i.e., Christenson, Reschly, & Wylie, 2012) reveals that prominent motivation scholars define engagement in a variety of ways. That said, one useful way to distinguish between the constructs of motivation and engagement is to say that "Motivation is about energy and direction, the reasons for behavior, why we do what we do. Engagement describes energy in action, the connection between person and activity (Ainley, 2012)." Engagement is about the level of involvement in an activity (Halliday, Calkins, & Leerkes, 2018). Students who are disengaged are not paying attention, not actively and willingly participating, and not giving their best effort. Their minds wander to other thoughts and distractions. Engagement can be enhanced if students have individual interest in the topic, or if a teacher utilizes an instructional technique that at least temporarily promotes situational interest (e.g., have students play roles in a short play in history class).

　　When engagement is characterized as having levels or as falling along a continuum, it is said to range from complete disengagement to a state known as *flow*, in which a student is so engaged that he or she loses all temporal perspective, focuses all attention on the task at hand, and everything else fades into the background (Csikszentmihalyi, Montijo, & Mouton, 2018). Moreover, highly engaged students are likely to experience some of the positive affective states described earlier, such as enjoyment and interest. In contrast, many of the negative affective states, such as sadness, shame, anxiety, frustration, boredom, and anger, are apt to promote disengagement. Sadness can result from personal issues that students are experiencing at home (e.g., parental divorce) or school (e.g., social rejection). Shame can result from a public display of their poor performance on an activity, especially if they do not have a growth mind-set or adopt mastery goals. Frustration results from difficulties and obstacles keeping them from attaining their goals. Boredom can be the result of low levels of individual interest in the subject matter or instructional techniques that do not promote situational interest (e.g., a tedious worksheet). Anger can result from response to perceptions of teacher authoritarianism, unfair grading practices, unfair classroom management practices, or ridicule.

Monitoring of Progress

Earlier it was noted that behaviors are preceded by the goals set by students and that goals are mental representations of some future, desired state of affairs. When classroom tasks require multiple steps or take a certain amount of time to complete, it is important for students to assess how far they have progressed in attaining their goals (Halliday et al., 2018). Although motivation scholars have not devoted much attention to the idea of monitoring of progress, we shall see in Chapter 6 (executive function and self-regulation) that self-regulation researchers have. The basic idea is that successful people set specific and challenging goals (as noted earlier), but they also regularly check on their progress to see if their chosen course of action is working and they are making adequate progress toward these goals (Barrick, Thurgood, Smith, & Courtright, 2015; Martens & Witt, 2004). Motivational constructs are thought to play an important role when students discover that they are not making adequate progress and are struggling to complete a task, as we shall see in the next section.

Effort, Persistence, and Grit

The ideal situation for any teacher is when all students are fully engaged in an activity, trying as hard as they can, and persisting until they succeed. The skills required to be successful in school become increasingly difficult with age, so it is important for students not to avoid tasks or give up too soon in order that they keep progressing in their skill development.

In the same way that engagement can be thought of as consequence of the preactivity constructs that were described above, *effort* and *persistence* have been argued to also derive from constructs such as goals, mind-sets, beliefs, outcome expectancies, and values (Wigfield et al., 2017). Students try hard and persist if the activity is considered important and if they believe there is a good chance that they can be successful. They also recognize that effort and mistakes are all part of the process of becoming proficient and are not indicative of lower aptitude. We will see in Chapter 7 (on intelligence, aptitude, and expertise) that people who become true experts in their fields intentionally practice in ways that are beyond their current capacity and likely to trip them up. Michael Jordan, former professional basketball player and winner of three championships, used to shoot hundreds of jump shots in practice for hours, even after his team won the championships. Even so, his career shooting percentage was just shy of 50%, which means he missed shots about half of the time. There are unfortunately many students who give up or feel embarrassed if they only get a few worksheet or homework problems wrong. If (1) students are encouraged to develop growth mind-sets, (2) tasks are calibrated to student competencies through individualized instruction, (3) the importance of tasks for future learning are emphasized by parents and teachers, (4) goals are collaboratively set and visual representations of progress monitoring are used, and (5) students experience sufficient levels of success that they develop a sense of self-efficacy, they are more likely to expend effort and persist in the face of difficulty (Martens & Witt, 2004; Schunk & Mullen, 2012; Wigfield et al., 2017).

In recent years, there has been an explosion of interest in the related notion of *grit* (Credé, Tynan, & Yang, 2017; Muenks, Wigfield, Yang, & O'Neill, 2017). One of the key figures in this field, Angela Duckworth, left a high-paying job in the business world to become a middle school teacher of math. She was struck by how students differed in their tendency to persist until they successfully learned somewhat challenging concepts such as ratio, fractions, and operations with decimals. She noticed how it was not only IQ or math aptitude that mattered, but something else that she called grit. She left the classroom and decided to pursue graduate training in psychology to see if she could determine who ends up being successful in a variety of settings, such as staying in military training, persisting in spelling bee competitions, and remaining in the teaching profession when one works in challenging schools (*www.ted.com/talks/angela_lee_duck-worth_grit_the_power_of_passion_and_perseverance*). Duckworth has defined *grit* as "perseverance and passion for long-term goals" (Duckworth, Peterson, Matthews, & Kelly, 2007, p. 1087) and the term refers to more than resilience (Credé et al., 2017). The underlying components are said to be persistence of effort and consistency of interest. Whereas most psychologists and educational researchers have their work cited fewer than 1,000 times, at this writing professor Duckworth's publications have been cited over 27,000 times. In recognition of her work, in 2013 she was awarded a MacArthur Fellowship (colloquially known as a "genius grant"). So clearly, there is considerable interest in the construct.

However, this interest has occurred despite the fact that the literature that has attempted to establish the construct validity of grit and its differentiation from other related constructs is relatively sparse and inconsistent (Muenks et al., 2017). Moreover, a recent study of high school and college students showed that a measure of grit yielded no predictive power over other related constructs such as self-regulation and conscientiousness to predict grades (Muenks et al., 2017). In addition, a meta-analysis of over

88 independent samples showed that average weighted correlation between measures of grit and academic performance was only $r = .17$ and between grit and retention was also a similarly modest $r = .18$. In contrast, the average weighted correlation between measures of grit and conscientiousness was $r = .66$, so these measures are tapping into essentially the same concept. Conscientiousness is one of the five general personality traits identified in the Big Five theory of personality. It relates to having self-discipline, being responsible, and striving for achievement (McCrae, 2009). Questionnaire items that tap into this trait include those that ask about being always prepared, paying attention to details, getting chores done right away, liking order, following a schedule, being exacting in work, remembering belongings, being helpful, and giving attention to duties. Thus, there is some connection between achievement and constructs such as grit, conscientiousness, and self-regulation, but far stronger relationships have been found for other factors, such as prior knowledge and self-efficacy.

Emotions

As noted above, anticipated emotions play a role in the courses of action that people take if they have a choice (e.g., academic majors and courses in college), but they also can play a role in the middle of an activity if students must engage in the activity (e.g., have to take a math course to graduate; have to complete a worksheet in elementary school). Which emotions are evoked depends on how students assess their own performance. Were they successful or not? Did they struggle or perform the task with ease? Depending on students' goals, beliefs, mind-sets, and aptitudes, they may either feel pride and efficacy, or feel embarrassed, incompetent, and anxious instead.

Motivation Constructs Operative after an Activity Is Completed

After students have completed an activity, there are two primary outcomes: students successfully completed the task (e.g., attained the correct answer) or they did not (e.g., came up with the wrong answer). For simplicity, we can call these outcomes "success" and "failure," respectively, though these psychological terms do have somewhat problematic connotations in everyday language. *Attribution theory* was developed to explain individual differences in how students respond to success and failure (Weiner, 2010, 2012, 2014). In particular, attribution theorists discovered that not everyone who succeeds or fails on the task feels the same emotions or has the same expectations for succeeding or failing on the same task in the future. The key variable that determined their emotional responses and future expectations was their *causal beliefs* about how and why the outcome was obtained. Causal beliefs, in turn, were said to have three dimensions: *locus* (internal versus external), *controllability* (controllable by the learner versus not controllable), and *stability* (stable versus unstable). The four primary causes of success and failure (i.e., ability, effort, task difficulty, and luck) differ along each of these three dimensions.

Consider the case in which a student attributes doing poorly on a math exam because of his belief that he lacks aptitude for math. Ability is something internal to the student as opposed to something in the external environment (e.g., a teacher who grades harshly). If the student has a fixed mind-set (as opposed to a growth mind-set, see above), he may also believe that his lack of ability is something he cannot control or do anything about. As such he also will assume it to be a stable cause of failure. Based on these attributions, he is likely to experience negative emotions such as shame or sadness, and he will expect to do just as poorly on the next math exam (Weiner, 2014). In contrast, students who attribute the poor grade to other factors would not feel the same emotions or necessarily change their expectations. For example, if a different student perceives herself to have sufficient mathematics aptitude but realizes that she did not spend enough time studying, she will feel not shame or sadness but may be a little angry with herself for not trying as hard as she could. In addition, she is not likely to lower her expectations for the next grade if she expects to study harder next time. Effort is an internal factor but also is controllable. Many other scenarios are possible if one varies the locus, controllability, and stability of causes. For example, attributing the low grade to a harsh grader would shift the anger from oneself to the teacher. Or, if the teacher apologizes for making a hard test and promises to make the next test more accessible, students may not lower their expectations.

THE DEVELOPMENT OF MOTIVATION

As will become evident in this and other chapters, *development* is all about change, and the term typically connotes change for the better (e.g., improvements on some ability or skill). In the present section, the focus now shifts from what motivation is, to changes or improvements in motivation over time. The first section of this chapter appealed to a set of constructs to explain why students begin an activity, choose one over the other, expend effort, or persist until success is attained. To address the issue of whether motivation increases or decreases over time between early childhood and early adulthood, we can next examine research that has focused on age changes in all of the aforementioned constructs. If age changes do occur in the component constructs, we should expect changes in motivation as well.

Age Changes in Goals and Mind-Sets

The key overall developmental pattern discovered in many studies of motivation is that the average levels of motivation for performing well in school drops between first grade and twelfth grade (Wigfield et al., 2017). In other words, most students tend to become less motivated over time. Are goals and mind-sets at least partly responsible for this overall drop? It is difficult to find studies that report how many students endorse mastery goals or growth mind-sets at each age because researchers seem to typically adopt an individual-difference rather than a developmental-difference orientation. That is, they administer a short questionnaire with items that focus on fixed or growth mind-sets (or mastery or performance goals), sort students into groups using a cutoff on the scale (e.g., >3.5 on a scale of 1 to 5), and show how students with one or the other mind-sets show differences in the rate of knowledge growth (e.g., Cain & Dweck, 1995; McCutchen, Jones, Carbonneau, & Mueller, 2016). When this approach is used, it is common to find that about half of students at each grade are assigned into the fixed mind-set group or growth mind-set group (which, of course, should occur if the median score is used as the cutoff). Studies have shown that a growth mind-set sometimes predicts growth in mathematics skills over time (Blackwell, Trzesniewski, & Dweck, 2007; Bostwick, Martin, Collie, & Durksen, 2019), and sometimes predicts a slower rate of decline (McCutchen et al., 2016). Because of its positive role in development, interventions have been conducted to change students' fixed mind-sets into growth mind-sets and have had positive effects on grades (Dweck & Yeager, 2019).

Age Changes in Ability Beliefs

An unfortunate common developmental trend is that students start out in first grade with very positive views of their ability in all subject areas but slowly decline in their self-ratings over time (Muenks et al., 2018). This drop is a function of tasks getting harder and harder as children progress through school (e.g., from sounding out words to comprehending sentences to comprehending textbook chapters), teachers grading performance harder as children age, and social comparison processes (Wolff, Wigfield, Möller, Dicke, & Eccles, 2020). According to the 2 I/E model, students develop their ability beliefs by not only comparing how they perform themselves in the different subject areas (the I is for *internal* in the model name) but also how they perform relative to their peers (the E is for *external* in the model name) and how they used to perform in the past (the 2 in the model name is for two assessment points). The shift from high overall to lower and differentiated is true for most students, but some students do not fit the pattern (Muenks et al., 2018). For example, some first graders start out with less optimism than their peers, and some highly skilled students maintain their high ratings in all subjects over time.

There are relatively few developmental studies of self-efficacy beliefs, and the findings are mixed (Muenks et al., 2018). If material is getting harder to understand and teachers are getting stricter in their grading, all students may become less optimistic (or more realistic) over time. Self-efficacy beliefs derive in part from how successful you have been in the past, but there is also an interpretation that has to occur. There are students who perform well but still rate their ability to be successful to be lower (Muenks et al., 2018). Understandably, self-efficacy beliefs are lower in students who have been diagnosed with learning disabilities, but interventions have been successful in increasing self-efficacy in such students (Bergey, Parrila, Laroche, & Deacon, 2019).

Age Changes in Intrinsic and Extrinsic Motivation

According to SDT, teachers can promote intrinsic motivation in their students if their classrooms are structured to satisfy children's needs to feel competent, autonomous, and related (as noted above). In contrast, if they (1) rely on the provision of rewards and punishments, (2) ask children to perform tasks that are either too easy or too hard, (3) restrict children's choices and autonomy, and (4) create an unaccepting, competitive atmosphere, they will promote extrinsic motivation in their students instead. If SDT is correct, then one would only expect there to be a decline in intrinsic motivation over time if teachers in the later grades are more likely to adopt the second approach that favors extrinsic over intrinsic motivation.

Early studies using Harter's (1981) original or modified intrinsic–extrinsic motivation scale showed that intrinsic motivation declines between the early grades and later grades (Lepper, Corpus, & Iyengar, 2005), though these studies did not include instructional variables to see whether teachers of the later grades are more likely to implement instructional strategies that promote extrinsic over intrinsic motivation. In fact, Lepper et al. (2005) appeal to other constructs and findings to explain this drop (e.g., developmental decreases in interest, developmental increases in performance goals). A more recent study found that intrinsic motivation does decrease between first grade and college, and this decrease was found to be mediated by students' perceptions of how much autonomy they were afforded and whether their teachers differentiated activities according to skill level (Martinek, Hofmann, & Kipman, 2016).

Age Changes in Outcome Expectancies

Studies conducted with the expectancy–value framework have shown monotonic decreases in the mean level of children's expectations for performing well in various subject areas (Wigfield et al., 2017). Highly skilled students, of course, would not be expected to experience as steep of a drop in expectations because they experience more success than their less-skilled peers. However, there is evidence of more harsh grading with age and this practice could lower expectations somewhat.

Age Changes in Interest, Values, and Cost

Studies conducted in the expectancy–value framework have likewise shown monotonic decreases in levels of interest in, and the perceived importance of, most school subjects between first and twelfth grades (Wigfield et al., 2017). Relatively few studies have examined whether perceived cost increases with age; therefore, that finding awaits empirical confirmation in additional studies.

Age Changes in Emotions

Recall that the hedonic principle predicts that, when given the choice, students would tend to pursue courses of action that lead to them feeling positive emotions such as happiness, relief, or pride, and tend to avoid courses of action that lead to them feeling negative emotions such as sadness, disappointment, jealousy, and shame. However, there is a mandated curriculum in all schools that students must follow and relatively few teachers differentiate their instruction or allow choices to pursue activities that are of more interest. In addition, because students differ in their natural aptitudes and tendency to practice skills, it would be predicted that only the most accomplished students in a grade would expect to feel positive emotions on a regular basis.

Age Differences in Engagement

All of the aforementioned age changes in the constructs that are operative before students participate in an activity support the prediction and common finding that students tend to display less engagement in classroom activities with age (Ainley, 2012; Anderman & Patrick, 2012; Eccles & Wang, 2012; Pekrun & Linnenbrink-Garcia, 2012; Wylie & Hodgen, 2012).

Age Differences in Monitoring of Progress

Relatively few studies have been conducted to determine whether older students are more likely to monitor their progress than younger students and then experience either an increase or decrease in motivation. Being able to monitor your progress and revise your plans is an important aspect of self-regulation, as noted earlier. However, being able to do so is both a blessing and a curse. It is a blessing if you make progress or revise your strategies to be more successful. However, it is a curse if you are not making progress and do not feel efficacious about how to improve your performance and progress further. It is likely that students who monitor their progress and realize that they are not succeeding would show a decrease in motivation.

Age Differences in Effort, Persistence, and Grit

Earlier in this chapter, various preactivity constructs such as self-efficacy, mastery (learning) goals, and intrinsic motivation were said to predict the amount of effort expended and the tendency to persist in an activity until success was achieved. It is difficult to find studies in which age declines in effort and persistence are shown to be the result of age declines in ability beliefs, self-efficacy, mastery goals, or intrinsic motivation. Instead, motivational researchers seem to have taken more of an individual-difference (within-grade) stance than a developmental-difference stance (Skinner & Saxton, 2019). Although academic content does become more difficult with age, in the later grades, students are placed in academic tracks and electives are provided presumably to help less-skilled students be more successful in less difficult contexts. However, because (1) intrinsic motivation, interest, and values also decline with age (Wigfield et al., 2017), (2) social comparisons promote drops in competence beliefs (Wolff et al., 2019), and (3) older students may believe that effort is indicative of lower ability, it would be predicted that only the most skilled students would maintain a higher level of effort and persist in the face of difficulties. There do not appear to be published reports of age-related declines or increases in grit, because, again, grit was proposed by Duckworth to explain why students in the same class differ in their tendency to persist in the face of challenges. There are, however, studies that have examined the tendency of students to cope with challenges in either adaptive or maladaptive ways. In their review of the literature, Skinner and Saxton (2019) report that adaptive coping strategies such as problem solving or help seeking tend to be common in the elementary grades and the level is constant through fifth grade. In middle school, however, the adaptive strategies decline and are replaced with more maladaptive ones, such as withdrawal and resistance. By the end of high school, there is some recovery of the adaptive strategies.

One maladaptive strategy that was not reviewed by Skinner and Saxton is *self-handicapping*. Students who self-handicap engage in activities that make it impossible for them to perform well on an exam or other assessment (e.g., party the night before an exam and not study; not even try). The author witnessed a friend who would play basketball rather than study and another fellow student who made designs out of the dots on standardized test answer sheets rather than even try to do well. These alternative behaviors give them an "out" or an excuse for not doing well. A meta-analysis showed that the average weighted correlation between self-reported self-handicapping and achievement was $r = -.23$, meaning more self-handicapping was associated with lower achievement (Schwinger, Wirthwein, Lemmer, & Steinmayr, 2014). However, the correlations divided by grade level were $r = -.29, -.34, -.23,$ and $-.18$ for elementary school, middle school, high school, and university students, respectively.

The correlations for elementary and middle school were significantly higher than those for high school and university, meaning the link between self-handicapping and lower achievement was stronger for younger students. It is not clear why there is a significant drop in the correlation with age, but it could be due to the fact that older students are reluctant to admit that they use this strategy.

Age Differences in Attributions and Postactivity Emotions

Recall that the four main classes of causes of failure in attribution theory are ability, effort, task difficulty, and luck. In the early elementary grades, children tend not to make a distinction between effort and ability (Folmer et al., 2008; Muenks et al., 2018). So, they often think that smarter students expend more effort. Over time, especially if students develop a fixed mind-set and performance goals, they may switch to believing that expending effort demonstrates your lack of ability. In addition, tasks become more difficult in later grades, and doing well or poorly on such tasks is a further indication of your aptitude. Thus, there is good reason to assume that with increasing age, many students who attribute their lower performance to their ability are likely to have low expectations for success and also feel negative emotions such as sadness, disappointment, frustration, and anxiety (Muenks & Miele, 2017). If they cannot avoid participating in contexts that require them to learn new and more difficult skills, they are likely to engage in a variety of maladaptive coping strategies and may even elect to drop out of school after 10th grade.

IMPLICATIONS FOR EDUCATION

The aforementioned review of the literature has shown that motivational factors are important determinants of children's success and failure in school and are also implicated in their emotional well-being. If we recognize that only some students have the aptitudes to get good grades in all subject areas and perform well in the highest academic tracks, it is likely that many middle and high school students experience school-related failures more than they like, experience negative emotions, and will likely disengage from academics. As we will see in Chapter 15, low-income students attain lower levels of achievement than high-income students and are therefore likely to have motivational and emotional problems in later grades. Can anything be done about this state of affairs?

Most school systems assume that there is a required curriculum that all students have to learn. The Common Core movement has further cemented this idea and was originally based on the notion that school curricula in the United States has been "dumbed down" and needs to be made more rigorous and standardized across school systems in order that all students will have the skills they need to be successful in the modern world (Ravitch, 2010). But requiring the same, higher-level content for all students means that only the top students will regularly experience success, feel competent, and feel positive emotions.

So, there is a tension between the goal of making sure all students acquire the skills they need to be successful in today's world, and the fact that many students will struggle acquiring these skills in middle school, high school, and college. SDT, as described earlier, suggests that teachers can play an important role in terms of providing a certain degree of choice in assignments (targeting the need for autonomy), using *differentiated instruction* to align activities to each student's current skill level, and promoting positive social relationships by projecting warmth and support and using mechanisms such as well-managed *cooperative learning* groups. Differentiated instruction and mastery learning along with teacher comments highlighting student responsibility for their own successes has been found to promote self-efficacy in students (Schunk & Mullen, 2012). Even with the use of differentiated instruction and mastery learning, however, students with different aptitudes will progress through content at different rates. It seems impossible to avoid the comparison processes central to the 2 I/E model, but creating a culture in which students recognize that everyone has aptitudes that should be valued may mitigate feelings of inferiority. Parents and teachers can also promote a growth mind-set in students, and various interventions have been successful in teaching parents and teachers how to instill growth mind-sets in students (Dweck & Yeager, 2019). Parents and teachers also play a role in the socialization of values in children, and parent perceptions of the importance of subject areas such as math has been shown to be predictive of students internalizing theses values (Wigfield et al., 2017).

CHAPTER 6

Executive Function and Self-Regulation

The two topics to be discussed in this chapter have several things in common. The first is that they are extremely popular. For example, Müller and Kerns (2015) reported that in the 10-year period spanning 1991 to 2000, approximately 1,200 publications focused on the topic of executive function (EF). In the subsequent 10-year period (2001–2010), the number jumped to over 8,000 and continued to explode through 2015. In the case of self-regulation (SR), I found in the 10-year period spanning 2010 to 2018, according to the search engine PsycINFO, 11,000 publications focused on that topic. The reason for the popularity of both EF and SR derives from the fact that many researchers in a variety of fields (e.g., developmental, educational, social, and clinical psychology; neuroscience; business) have all seen the relevance of these constructs to their own domains.

The second thing that EF and SR have in common is that they both have been theorized to play an important role in academic achievement and many studies have investigated this prediction empirically (Müller & Kerns, 2015; Robson, Allen, & Howard, 2020). The third thing that these constructs have in common is that they both have been related to the ability to successfully attain one's goals in school and many other contexts (Langner, Leiberg, Hoffstaedter, & Eickhoff, 2018; Müller & Kerns, 2015; Robson et al., 2020). As we shall see below, however, the fourth thing that these constructs have in common is that they have been defined in a variety of overlapping and nonoverlapping ways (Müller & Kerns, 2015; Nigg, 2017). These various definitions have led to conceptual confusions that have the potential to limit scientific progress. In the remainder of this chapter, we will delve more deeply into these introductory comments in order to better understand the nature and development of EF and SR.

THE NATURE AND DEVELOPMENT OF EF

The Nature of EF

Overview

As a prelude to discussing the current and most widely accepted definition of EF, it is helpful to briefly discuss the origin of the concept of "executive functions" as elucidated by a former student of Lev Vygotsky, Alexander Luria, in his influential books in the 1970s (e.g., Luria, 1973). Luria was an early neuropsychologist who attempted to summarize the psychological deficits experienced by patients who suffered injuries to specific areas of the brain. What he noted was that patients who suffered injuries to the frontal lobe all seemed to have problems in the ability to control or coordinate more basic tasks. As such, he labeled these abilities "executive," alluding to their top-down management role. As noted in Chapter 3, Luria's mentor Vygotsky was interested in a finite set of cognitive "functions," such as language, memory, and attention. So, Luria adopted this term as well but noted that these executive functions were not unary and could be disrupted through injuries to other brain areas besides the frontal lobes.

With the enthusiastic infusion of neuroscience in the field of psychology in the 1980s and 1990s (see Chapter 2), Luria's work was widely cited and prominent experts on frontal lobe function (e.g., Joaquin Fuster, Patricia Goldman-Rakic) followed in his footsteps (Fuster, 1993; Goldman-Rakic, 1987). Even so, it became widely recognized that there was no set or clear definition of EF and this lack of clarity was problematic for scientific progress (Miyake et al., 2000; Müller & Kerns, 2015). In fact, it has been reported that over 30 different definitions of EF have been proposed (Müller & Kerns, 2015).

In an influential paper that has been cited over 6,000 times at this writing, Miyake et al. (2000) attempted to solidify current conceptions by conducting a confirmatory factor analysis of the nine most frequently used measures of EF to see if they cohered together as a single factor. What they found was that the best-fitting model suggested that a single factor did not fit well; instead, EF can be distilled into three factors that they labeled *shifting* (a.k.a. *cognitive flexibility*), *updating* (a.k.a. WM), and *inhibition*. That is, some tasks require the ability to efficiently shift the focus of attention away from stimuli or change behaviors, others require the ability to update and monitor representations in WM, and still others require the ability to inhibit prepotent responses.

An example of a shifting task is the plus–minus task (Miyaki et al., 2000). Here, subjects are given three different lists of 30 two-digit numbers presented in each of three phases. In the first phase, they are asked to add 3 to each number on the list as fast as they can. In the second phase, they are asked to subtract 3 from each number as fast as they can. In the third phase, they are asked to alternate between adding 3 and subtracting 3 for each successive number as fast as they can. The dependent measure was the difference in response times between the third alternating phase and the two earlier addition and subtraction phases. Faster times on the alternating task (relative to either of the single operations) implied that some people were better at shifting or found it easier to shift.

An example of an updating WM task is the keep-track task. Here, subjects are shown a set of category labels at the bottom of a computer screen (e.g., animals, colors, and metals). Then, words are flashed on the screen that either are, or are not, an instance of these categories (e.g., *green* for color). Their task is to remember the last word that occurred for each of the three categories. This is an example of a classic WM task as discussed in Chapter 4. With the emergence of the Miyake et al. three-component model of EF, working memory (WM) moved from being primarily considered a key aspect of memory, to being considered a key aspect of EF in the field. As noted above regarding conceptual confusions, this is the first instance in which theoretical muddling occurred. Is WM a component of the human memory system or EF? How does EF relate to memory if they are distinct?

An example of an inhibition task is the Stroop task. Here, participants are shown words on a screen that refer to particular colors (e.g., *RED*). However, the color of the font of these letters sometimes does not match the color referred to (e.g., the font is green when the word is *RED*). The task is to either say the name of the word or say the color of the font as fast as they can. For skilled readers, the prepotent response that is difficult to inhibit is the name of the word. For example, for the word *RED,* there is a strong response bias to say "red." This response has to be inhibited in order to describe the color of the letters, "green."

With this three-component fractionation in mind, Friedman and Miyake (2017, p. 186) nevertheless argue that "executive functions (EFs) are high-level cognitive processes that, through their influence on lower-level processes, enable individuals to regulate their thoughts and actions during goal-directed behavior." However, it is not clear how the three component abilities help people regulate their thoughts and actions, though it is often said that to attain your goals you have to remember them or keep them in mind (WM) and avoid being distracted or seduced away from actions that lead to your goals (inhibition). The connection of shifting to goal-directed actions is less apparent. In keeping with the definition of Friedman and Miyake (2017), Lensing and Elsner (2018, p. 188) define EF as "a set of cognitive skills necessary for goal-directed behavior and self-control," that are "correlates and predictors of a large range of social and cognitive developmental outcomes over the lifespan."

Criticisms and Revisions

It was already noted that the original Miyake et al. (2000) study failed to reveal a single-factor solution in confirmatory factor analyses. It was also the case that the correlations among the three tasks that were used to tap into each of the three component abilities were all low (e.g., r's = .15-.32, average r = .24). Subsequent models that were tested in a number of replication studies showed a high degree of inconsistency. For example, some showed a single factor, some showed a two-factor model that omitted the shifting factor, and some showed the original three-factor model (Karr et al., 2018). In fact, across 46 studies, only 72% included a WM factor, 52% included an inhibition factor, and 43% included a shifting factor.

It could also be argued that EF may not be empirically distinct from intelligence. In Chapter 7, we will see that one of the findings that led to the notion of general intelligence (g) is the finding of a *positive manifold*, which refers to the fact that many cognitive tasks correlate about r = .30 with each other. It was noted above that the mean correlation of the alleged EF tasks in Miyake et al. (2000) was r =.24. In addition, a large twin study ($N >$ 800) found that a general latent factor derived from the variance common to the three EF components explained a large percentage of the variance in intelligence that seemed to operate through a genetic pathway (Engelhardt et al., 2016).

Hot and Cold EFs

In addition to subdividing EF into three components, an additional elaboration has been proposed between so-called hot and cold executive functions (Müller & Kerns, 2015). The three-component model described so far is what is meant by cold EF. There is no reference to any affective or motivational aspects of goal-pursuit in that model, which makes cold EF seemingly divorced from the rest of the mind and real-world situations (Barkley, 2012; Müller & Kerns, 2015; Zelazo, 2015). Inspired in part by Damasio's *somatic marker hypothesis* (Bechara, Damasio, Damasio, & Anderson, 1994), researchers argue that goals are inherently linked to anticipated emotional reactions. If emotions are somehow removed from the process (as is the case with patients with frontal lobe injuries), people make poor decisions. Therefore, if EF is a key facilitator of goal pursuit, it must somehow be linked to affect and motivation.

Two common tasks that are used to measure hot EF are the delay-of-gratification task (Carlson et al., 2018) and the Iowa gambling task (IGT; Bechara et al., 1994). The IGT also has a simpler version that can be used with children, called the children's gambling task (Andrews & Moussaumai, 2015). In the delay-of-gratification task, children are given a choice between a smaller food reward that could be taken immediately (e.g., one marshmallow) or a larger food reward that could be obtained if children could wait until an experimenter returned to the room. Children who could delay for the larger reward were found to be more successful in high school and their careers even 30 years later (Benjamin et al., 2020).

The IGT and children's gambling task present two to four decks of cards that differ in terms of both risk and reward. One kind of deck (advantageous decks) yields smaller rewards (e.g., $1.50) but also smaller losses (e.g., –$1.50), and, on average, yielded a net positive gain. The other kind of deck (disadvantageous decks) yields larger rewards (e.g., $25) but also bigger losses (e.g., –$25) and, on average, yielded net negative losses. Whereas many people start off choosing the bigger rewards (disadvantageous) decks during early trials, they soon shift to the safer option (advantageous decks) after experiencing a big loss. People with frontal lobe injuries and young adolescents take a longer time (many more turns choosing decks) to make this shift if they make it at all (Cauffman et al., 2010).

Links to Academic Achievement

Given the relative difficulty in establishing a single-factor solution across measures of the three components of cold EF, there does not appear to be a published meta-analysis that describes the average size of the correlation between composite measures of EF and performance in mathematics or reading. There are, however, meta-analyses that document the average correlation between each of the three components of cold EF and performance in school. Yeniad, Malda, Mesman, van IJzendoorn, and Pieper (2013) report that the average correlation between measures of shifting and mathematics is $r = .26$ and between shifting and reading was $r = .21$. They note further, however, that the average correlation between IQ and these two subject areas were $r = .45$, and $r = .44$, respectively. Note that all four of these are raw bivariate correlations that do not include controls for other strong predictors (e.g., phonological processing in the case of reading). These correlations would likely be smaller with controls. In the case of WM, the average correlations have been found to be $r = .35$, and $r = .29$ for math and reading, respectively (Peng, Namkung, Barnes, & Sun, 2016; Peng et al., 2018). Finally, in the case of inhibition, the correlation has been found to be $r = .27$ (Allan, Hume, Allan, Farrington, & Lonigan, 2014). Thus, these components are clearly correlated with achievement, but by themselves seem to only account for anywhere from 4% to 12% of the variance in achievement prior to controls. In addition, in a large longitudinal study, Willoughby, Wylie, and Little (2019) found that the correlation between a composite measure of EF using shifting and WM was predictive of later math and reading abilities, but mainly because children who were higher on EF were also higher on achievement at both time points. When one controls for these between-children effects, the within-child correlations between EF and later achievement were smaller and often nonsignificant.

As for hot EF, a highly cited study ($N > 500$ citations) by Shoda, Mischel, and Peake (1990) reported that performance on the marshmallow delay-of-gratification test in preschool predicted academic achievement in high school some 10 years later. However, a recent attempted replication study of this finding found that the correlation was half the size of the correlation found in Shoda et al., but also shrank by two-thirds when controls for family background and early abilities were included.

At this writing few studies have examined the correlation between performance on the IGT and school performance, but one study showed that more education was associated with the adaptive decision to more quickly shift to advantageous choices (Davis et al., 2008). Another showed that math performance and IGT performance were uncorrelated in a sample of college students (Buelow & Barnhart, 2017). A third showed that measures of cold and hot EF were uncorrelated with each other in a sample of adolescents in Hong Kong, and also that only a measure of cold EF (cognitive flexibility) predicted school performance. Measures of hot EF (e.g., the Cambridge gambling task) did not (Poon, 2018).

The Development of EF

In keeping with the distinctions among and between components of cold and hot EF, we can examine developmental trends in the three components of cold EF and also the two kinds of measures of hot EF.

Development of Cognitive Flexibility

There have been two primary ways that cognitive flexibility (shifting) has been investigated (Müller & Kerns, 2015). One pertains to children's ability recategorize objects using a different dimension than what was used for the first sorting attempt (e.g., sort them first by color and then by shape). A second way is the Dimensional Change Card Sort (DCCS) test (Zelazo, 2015). In the latter, children are presented with objects that vary along two dimensions (shape and color). In the first set of trials, they are asked by experimenters to sort pictures into one of two piles using shape (e.g., one pile is for ships, one is for rabbits). Then they are asked to sort the same pictures using color. Most studies show that on both kinds of cognitive flexibility tasks, 3-year-olds have considerable difficulty and improvement occurs most rapidly during in the preschool period (Müller & Kerns, 2015; Zelazo, 2015). A variety of explanations have been proposed for these age changes, including insufficient WM capacity to keep the sorting rules in mind, lack of ability to inhibit the prepotent rules that were used during the first set of trials, and insufficiently abstract or robust representations of category dimensions. One recent study tried to improve performance in 3-year-olds by having them attend to and manipulate three-dimensional objects before sorting them along more than one dimension (Beaucage, Skolney, Hewes, & Vongpaisal, 2020).

Longitudinal studies with large national datasets have also shown that when one measures both WM and cognitive flexibility in young children, only WM continues to predict later performance in school when other variables are controlled (Ahmed, Tang, Waters, & Davis-Kean, 2019; Byrnes, Wang, & Miller-Cotto, 2019). Also, a separate cognitive flexibility component fails to emerge in factor analytic studies of young children (Espy, 2016; Müller & Kerns, 2015). However, it may also be the case that the correlations for multiple measures of the same component are often very low (Willoughby, 2016). In any event, the pattern for WM differs from that for cognitive flexibility in which the rate of change for cognitive flexibility is slower and less pronounced after childhood.

Development of WM

Most studies of WM show monotonic increases in this ability from early childhood to late adolescence (e.g., Gathercole et al., 2004; Poon, 2018; Swanson, 1999). So, for example, whereas preschoolers might be able to recall only the last two digits on the reversed digit-span task, adolescents might be able to recall the last five to six. Children between these two ages would recall values in between two items and six items in a slowly increasing fashion with age. The actual number would, of course, depend on the nature of the task. Participants have to recall items before they fade from WM and monosyllabic items ("five") can be articulated faster than multisyllabic items ("five hundred seventy-two").

Development of Inhibition

Inhibition has been assessed in children using a variety of measures, including (1) whispering so others cannot hear, (2) variants of Simon Says and related go/no-go tasks, and (3) stop-signal tasks in which they are told to give certain responses in the presence of stimuli (e.g., a bear) but stop if they see a stop signal, and so on (Müller & Kerns, 2015). As is the case for other measures of EF components, preschoolers show particular difficulty on such tasks, rapidly improve between ages 3 and 6, and continue to show progressive improvements through adolescence (Müller & Kerns, 2015). One longitudinal study, however, suggested that impulse control actually dropped between the ages of 10 and 15, but then increased monotonically between age 16 and young adulthood. The primary developmental mechanisms to explain these age trends have been alleged to be brain maturation (particularly in the frontal lobes) and experiences that promote more efficient and rapid inhibitory responses (Müller & Kerns, 2015; Steinberg, 2008).

Development of Hot EF

With respect to delay of gratification, studies using variants of the classic marshmallow delay-of-gratification task reveal a pattern somewhat similar to that reported above for the cold EF tasks: significant improvement in the ability to delay gratification across the preschool period but few developmental differences after that (Müller & Kerns, 2015). However, this age trend could be due to the simplicity of the marshmallow task that creates a "ceiling effect" in performance after age 6. When one uses more sophisticated measures of delay-of-gratification tasks that are suitable for older participants, one finds that children are more likely than early adolescents (ages 10–15) to prefer immediate over delayed rewards, and early adolescents are more likely to prefer immediate over delayed rewards than older adolescents and young adults (ages 16–25) (Green, Fry, & Myerson, 1994; Steinberg et al., 2009; Water, Cillessen, & Scheres, 2014).

As for performance on the IGT and its more child-friendly variants, most studies show that younger children prefer the larger rewards occasionally afforded by the disadvantageous decks, but this tendency decreases throughout childhood and late adolescence (Cauffman et al., 2010; Lensing & Elsner, 2018). As children progress through adolescence and early adulthood, they show the adaptive tendency to switch from the riskier disadvantageous decks to the advantageous decks.

Summary

As might be expected from the earlier historical, theoretical, and empirical analysis of EF, the developmental findings for each component of EF have similarities and differences. If EF were a unary construct and ability, the developmental trends would be similar if not identical. That said, the general theme appears to be sharpest improvement during the preschool period followed by progressive improvement thereafter. The messiness of the findings probably derives in part from the fact that theorizing has been "bottom up" (from studies using different methodologies) rather than "top down," in which the measures follow from the theory (not the other way around). The fact that all the abilities described so far have some neural underpinning in the frontal lobes should not have been enough to assume that the skills would hang together and have similar effects. Luria did not espouse such a view. As has been known since the time of neuroanatomist Korbinian Brodmann in the late 1800s, all four lobes of the brain have highly specific subregions that are implicated in similar but nevertheless different tasks (Byrnes & Eaton, 2020). For example, area 44 supports the ability to articulate speech, but area 45, just above area 44, supports singing but not spoken language. Would it make sense to lump the two skills into a skill called "executive vocalization"?

THE NATURE AND DEVELOPMENT OF SR

The Nature of SR

Earlier it was noted that scholars from all the major subdisciplines of psychology (i.e., developmental, educational, school, social, and clinical) have demonstrated a considerable interest in the construct of self-regulation. In addition, there are theories that have utilized the construct as part of their overall theory (e.g., Piaget, Vygotsky, information processing; see Chapter 3), but there are also stand-alone theories of self-regulation itself (e.g., Zimmerman, Baumeister, Carver, & Scheier; see below). In what follows, we shall first consider how domain-general theories relied on this construct and then present a consensus view of the nature of self-regulation.

SR within Domain-General Theories

In Chapter 3, we examined three domain-general theories that, as we shall see, referred to the construct of self-regulation as part of their overall explanatory framework. However, their emphasis on SR was not discussed in Chapter 3 so that it could be discussed in this chapter. The first domain-general theory to consider is Piaget's. Recall from Chapter 3 that Piaget (1952) argued that children continually attempt to impose their own understanding on situations. He called these attempts at understanding assimilation. For concepts such as categorical hierarchies, causality, space, time, and number, children's early attempts at understanding are pretty far off. Feedback from the environment causes their conceptual structures to slowly change and become more aligned with the understandings of adults and experts. Piaget called changes to mental structures accommodation. Recall further that assimilation and accommodation are in constant tension with each other and sometimes one process wins out over the other. That is, sometimes we put too much of our ideas into a situation. We think that we understand but we really do not. Other times, we change our structures too much and get things wrong for that reason. In both these instances, assimilation and accommodation are out of balance. When this occurs, equilibration causes things to come back to a balance. This process is akin to our sympathetic and parasympathetic nervous systems working in opposition to each other and reaching homeostasis. Piaget (1952) argued that the combination of assimilation, accommodation, and equilibration keep the changes in our cognitive structures moving in the correct direction, toward the correct adult understanding. This self-correcting or realignment mechanism is what Piaget meant by self-regulation. Our minds are self-regulating systems that are goal-directed toward increasingly more accurate conceptual understandings.

Vygotsky, in contrast, argued that children at first need a lot of adult supervision and scaffolding in order to be successful on most tasks (Vygotsky, 1978). In other words, children start out being "other-regulated" by parents and teachers as new skills are learned (e.g., riding a bike, throwing a ball, reading words aloud). But according to his law of cultural development, any cognitive skill that is regularly performed with assistance and verbal scaffolding of adults eventually becomes internalized in children's minds such that they can do it by themselves without adult help. However, this internalization only occurs if adults "fade" their assistance as children gain mastery. Once children can do the skill on their own, monitor their performance, and correct any mistakes, they are self-regulated in their performance. So, over time, there is a shift from "other-regulation" to "self-regulation" if adults use scaffolding and fading in their helping attempts.

In addition, one other form of self-regulatory behavior that Vygotsky (1978) discussed is the use of *inner speech*. Here, we often talk to ourselves to get ourselves back on track during an activity. This especially occurs when we forget or are just learning a new skill. A new driver may say, "Okay, let's see. How do I put the car in reverse?" Or, adults may walk into to another room to get something and forget what they wanted. They may say to themselves, "Wait, what am I looking for?" Or, when learning a new statistical program after first learning a different one, a learner may say things such as, "Ok, how do I compute a correlation on this program? Where are the tabs for doing that?"

The third domain-general theory that makes references to self-regulation is information-processing (IP) theory. Recall from Chapter 3 that IP theory correctly assumes that human beings are "limited information processors." We forget things and sometimes get "information overload" on a difficult task. The first aspect of self-regulation that IP theorists identify is metacognition. Here, our metacognitive ability helps us recognize when we do not know or understand something, and when we are likely to forget. With such metacognitive insight, learners then try to develop strategies to help them overcome such limitations. So, they may acquire memory strategies such as writing a list or forming mental images of to-be-learned information (see Chapter 4). Or they may ask a teacher to slow down and explain things more simply. In sum, then, self-regulated learners have accurate metacognitive insight and use strategies to be more successful.

Stand-Alone Theories of SR

As noted above, there are also stand-alone theories of SR. That is, self-regulation is not part of a larger theory; the theory is entirely about SR. One problem that arises when one examines the literature on these stand-alone theories is that researchers define SR in different ways (see Vohs & Baumeister, 2016, for multiple examples). Unfortunately, there is also considerable "theoretical drift" in the sense that researchers seem to equate SR with other related constructs (e.g., EF, emotion regulation, self-control) and use SR and related terms interchangeably in the same publications (Nigg, 2017). For example, authors may use the term EF early in a paper and then replace that term with SR later in the paper (e.g., McClelland, Geldhof, Cameron, & Wanless, 2015).

Despite superficial dissimilarities and partial overlap with each other, all of the various definitions of SR in the literature seem to have in common the idea that SR *pertains to the ability to manage, control, or change one's thoughts, feelings, and actions in order to achieve one's goals* (Vohs & Baumeister, 2016). The centrality of the term *self* in SR should also highlight the fact that SR differs from "other-regulation" in which other people (e.g., parents, teachers, spouses, bosses, therapists) intervene to change your thoughts, feelings, or actions to make sure that you achieve your goals.

To further illustrate the differences between SR and other-regulation, consider goals such as getting good grades in school, maintaining your health, and being financially solvent later in life. When children are young, their parents and teachers play an important management role in planning for them, scheduling things on their behalf, and showing them how to engage in behaviors that meet goals such as getting good grades (e.g., how to study for a test). For example, teachers often send home notes about upcoming projects (e.g., science fair projects) early enough so that parents can start working with their children by selecting ideas, finding resource materials, buying needed supplies, and so on. Second-grade teachers would never ask their students to figure these things out on their own and get such a project done well and on time. Moreover, on a daily basis, parents are also the ones who wake children up in enough time for them to get dressed and eat their breakfast to arrive at a bus stop or school on time. With respect to health issues, parents are the ones who decide on the nutritional content of their children's diets, schedule medical and dental checkups, and ensure that their children exercise. Finally, parents save money for their children's education so that they will be able to pay for college when their children are older.

Between kindergarten and young adulthood, however, children are expected to become increasingly self-regulated. That is, young adults should be waking themselves up to be at class or work on time, scheduling their own medical or dental appointments, planning appropriately for class-related or work-related tasks, and saving for their futures. Parents and teachers can provide subtle and occasional reminders by checking in, but the expectation is that part of being an older adolescent and adult is *doing all these things on one's own.*

Beyond this general perspective on SR, we can subdivide the construct into its components further by considering how outside influences can interfere with being self-regulated. In other words, what might get in the way of people accomplishing their goals in classroom-related or work-related settings? The first obstacle relates to the idea of "out of sight, out of mind." When we do not have our goals right in front of us, we often forget them. Consider the example of when a college professor tells her students that there is a paper due at the end of the semester and never mentions this fact again until a week before. It can be easy to forget this fact unless students do something else to help themselves remember and work on this project ahead of time in steps. Relatedly, we often set New Year's resolutions but forget what they are or that we wanted to pursue them. But it is also the case that we can have our goals in mind as we try to make progress toward them (e.g., write a paper, lose 5 pounds, save $100 a month) and we either lack the motivation to get started, or lack the self-control to avoid distractions and "giving in" to behaviors that undermine these goals (read tweets from our favorite Twitter accounts, watch a show, eat a slice of cake that we see in the refrigerator, buy ourselves new clothes that we see in the store that we do not really need).

What all of these examples illustrate are the importance of *goal setting, planning, monitoring of progress,* WM, *metacognition, use of strategies, motivation, inhibitory control,* and *learning from mistakes* to the ability to self-regulate (Dent & Koenka, 2016). Let's examine each of these aspects a little further.

One way to be strategic about goal-setting and planning is to make use of written "things to do" lists with deadlines, and technology such as calendars associated with e-mail and phone accounts. It is also prudent to subdivide larger tasks (e.g., writing a paper) into subtasks (e.g., choose a topic, find resources, write an outline, write a first draft) and then assign deadlines to each of these subtasks. Furthermore, most students in later grades and most employed adults have many competing demands on their time and multiple goals that they have to coordinate. In such cases, it is important to *prioritize tasks* by both importance and deadlines (Carver, Johnson, Joorman, & Scheier, 2015). A related idea is to figure out how to *allocate your time properly* and avoid *procrastinating* (Kim, Fernandez & Terrier, 207; Morris & Fritz, 2015). People who do not engage in such kinds of strategic behaviors are more likely to forget tasks and miss deadlines. In addition, however, there is a need to regularly *monitor your progress,* which again could be accomplished using strategies. For example, you could set a particular day every week to check on progress on your "things to do" list or set automatic alerts of subtasks to appear on your phone. It can also be hard to avoid distractions, but students often find ways to do so, such as leaving a dorm room and finding a secluded place in the library. In the case of dieting, it is good idea to keep tempting foods out of the house. Going to the library and not having the food in the house are both distraction strategies.

Other strategies relate to the ability to *manage your emotions* in order to accomplish your goals. Anger, fear, and anxiety can often be detrimental to attaining your goals to be successful in school, work, and relationships (McRae & Gross, 2020). Another way to be self-regulated, then, is to make use of *emotion-regulation strategies* to change how you feel or express emotions. Imagine the case of being derogated by a teacher or boss just before he or she gives a final grade (in the case of a teacher) or is deciding on your raise (in the case of a boss). Expressing your anger could adversely affect these outcomes. In such cases, you can use an anger-suppression strategy (which was earlier called inhibitory control in the EF section of this chapter). In a different way, succumbing to fear and anxiety could lead someone to not engage in behaviors that could lead to positive outcomes such as working on a paper, seeing a doctor when not feeling well, or making overtures to someone to which you are romantically attracted. People who are depressed will also avoid engaging in goal-related behaviors and often engage in maladaptive behaviors instead. such as staying in bed or self-medicating with alcohol or drugs. There are emotion-regulation strategies to move you out of depression, but when you are unfamiliar with such strategies or they do not work, another strategy is seeking help from a therapist. Suppression or avoidance of your emotional reactions are not as adaptive or effective as other strategies, such as *cognitive reappraisal* (McRae & Gross, 2020). Here, you change the way you think about something by, for example, convincing yourself that something is really not that important (e.g., "Who cares if my team lost? It is only a game"; "Who cares if she got the promotion over me? I will get it next time") and finding a way to reduce the blame if angry at someone ("He was abused as a kid; he can't help the way he acts inappropriately toward me").

One additional SR strategy that helps you accomplish your goals is to *seek advice* or seek help (Byrnes, 2013; Won, Hensley, & Wolters, 2019). If you have never tried to attain a particular goal before and have no idea how to proceed, it is a good idea to ask more knowledgeable people for help. For students at all grade levels, these more knowledgeable people may include parents, teachers, or more accomplished or older peers. In the workplace, these people may include more experienced or accomplished colleagues. For health-related goals, these people may include medical experts and specialists. For financial decisions, these people may include experienced, knowledgeable, and successful financial planners.

But an important prerequisite for using strategies of any kind is to recognize that a problem exists and there is a need for strategies to help overcome this problem. This capacity is a component of what was called *metacognition* when IP theory was discussed (metacognition is also discussed in Chapters 3 and 4). The gaps between your own perception of how you have performed in the past, how well you've prepared, and how well you will do on upcoming assignments is called *calibration* (Byrnes, 2013; Trakhman, Alexander, & Berkowitz, 2019). As was noted in Chapter 4, one key reason why children or struggling students do not use effective study strategies is that they wrongly think they will not forget. This is a defect in their metacognition. But your metacognition also relates to your understanding of a task, what steps are involved, and what are the best strategies to use (Zimmerman, 2008). A related idea is that when students have recurrent issues with depression, anxiety, or anger management that interfere with their learning and social relationships, they need to recognize these problems and seek help for effective strategies that may be suggested by parents, teachers, counselors, or therapists.

Finally, in addition to setting goals, planning, monitoring of progress, avoiding distractions, being calibrated, and using effective strategies, self-regulated people also *learn from their mistakes* and experiences of not attaining their goals (Byrnes, 2013; Zimmerman, 2008). Zimmerman (2008) argues that SR is cyclical and entails three phases: a *forethought phase* in which goals and plans for accomplishing these goals are formulated and set; a *performance phase* in which learners enact plans, monitor performance, and use strategies to stay on task and make progress toward goals; and a *reflection phase* in which the learner reflects upon how things went, whether goals were met, and what to do next time if goals were not met. Given the broader view of SR presented in this chapter, strategies beyond task-related strategies could be used in all three phases (e.g., advice seeking during the forethought and reflection phase; emotion regulation during all three phases).

Byrnes (2013) further argued that just because things did not work out a particular time, that does not mean the original goals, plans, and strategies were bad ideas. For example, you may do everything right when it comes to writing a paper, or seeing a doctor, or working with a financial planner. And yet, you may still get a low grade, be misdiagnosed by a doctor, or lose money in an investment scheme. However, as the adage goes, "the definition of insanity is that you keep doing the same things and expecting a different result." It may be unwise to completely switch an approach after a single failure experience (e.g., no longer seek advice), but it is also unwise to keep using an ineffective strategy multiple times when it leads to failure. Both immediate abandonment and perseveration are maladaptive; self-regulated people strike a balance between them.

With this multifaceted definition of SR in mind, we can see how it is theoretically problematic to equate SR with the more constrained constructs of EF, self-control, inhibition, or emotion regulation. The EF abilities of WM, inhibition, and cognitive flexibility *can help you be self-regulated* as described in this half of the chapter (e.g., keep goals in mind and avoid distractions) but that is only part of the story. So, EF cannot be equated with SR. Similarly, sometimes being self-regulated entails inhibiting a response (e.g., not yelling at a boss) but sometimes it means expressing an emotion (e.g., faking pleasure at getting a gift you do not like; telling someone that you love that you love them). This aspect of emotion regulation is comparable to regulating the temperature of a shower by turning knobs to make the water warmer or cooler, or comparable to pressing and releasing the gas pedal of a car to regulate your speed (Dent & Koenka, 2016). The *self* part of self-regulation once again means that you are turning the knobs or pressing the pedal of your thoughts, behaviors, or emotions, not someone else's. In other words, students are active participants in their own learning (Zimmerman, 2008).

Ego Depletion and Effort

What may not be immediately apparent from the previous discussion of the multiple aspects of SR is that being self-regulated takes a great deal of effort. It can be time-consuming to set goals, make plans, create schedules in phones, work on subtasks, and avoid temptations and distractions. To illustrate, think of the effort involved in getting in shape, losing 10 pounds, or writing a lengthy research paper for a course. Two interesting and often replicated findings are: (1) SR can be thought of as a resource that can temporarily depleted, and (2) it is possible to increase your SR through practice (Baumeister, Tice, & Vohs, 2018). In a variety of clever experiments, Roy Baumeister and colleagues have placed experimental participants in a situation that taxes their self-regulatory abilities (e.g., in a state of mild hunger looking at a really delicious donut for 25 minutes) and then placed them in another situation right afterward that also required self-regulation (e.g., refraining from retaliating against someone who was just mean to you). People who were not taxed in the first phase have been repeatedly shown to use more restraint in the second phase than those who were taxed. In addition, however, people who are placed in interventions that require them to be self-regulated actually seem to increase their ability to be self-regulated over time. In other words, it is possible to strengthen your SR "muscle." Parenthetically, this seems to be the logic behind the season of Lent in Christian denominations or Ramadan in Muslim communities. If you can control or deny yourself during these seasons, this capacity could generalize to other times of the year.

The emphasis on effort also shows once again that it takes a great deal of motivation to be self-regulated. Students' ability beliefs, values, interest, and self-regulation are all key aspects of who exhibits SR and who does not. This connection is reflected in the title of noted self-regulation theorist Barry Zimmerman's 2009 chapter: "Self-Regulation: Where Metacognition and Motivation Intersect" (Zimmerman & Moylan, 2009).

Linkages to Achievement

Before presenting evidence as to whether performance on measures of SR predict achievement in children, adolescents, and young adults, it is useful first to acknowledge several issues that may mitigate expectations. First, as implied above, SR is most relevant in goal-directed activities that (1) involve multiple steps, (2) require metacognitive insight and strategies to figure out what to do and overcome forgetting, distractions, and unhelpful emotional states, (3) require effort, and (4) may not be intrinsically interesting. So, there may be no differences between self-regulated students and their less self-regulated peers when they are completing easy, one-step problems in math or circling answers on a multiple-choice vocabulary task. In contrast, differences in achievement may emerge when they are asked to read entire books on their own or complete lengthy book reports, carry out science fair projects, and solve multistep math or science problems (Dent & Koenka, 2016). Thus, it is important to take into account *person–context interactions* (McClelland et al., 2015).

Second, differences between self-regulated and less self-regulated students should also be most evident in classrooms in which teachers take a step back and require students to be self-regulated. Sometimes, however, teachers worry (often correctly) that their students lack the self-regulatory skills needed to be successful, so they become intrusive and guide students step by step through the tasks (in other words, teachers "other-regulate" them). In such cases, students who are more self-regulated would not necessarily perform better than their peers who are less self-regulated. The latter do not need to be self-regulated because teachers regulate their behaviors. The same could be said for the role of parents. SR is required when students are left to their own devices and are not closely supervised or monitored by their parents or teachers. In sum, we first have to document what students are asked to do across an academic year (how many tasks require SR and how many do not) and how often they are other-regulated while asked to perform tasks that require SR.

This analysis suggests that SR may be more predictive of achievement with age because children tend to be increasingly left to their own devices with age (unless again they have "helicopter" parents or teachers). And if only some of the activities that children complete require high levels of SR, then the correlation between level of SR and achievement should be more muted (Dent & Koenka, 2016).

One further consideration relates to the issue of how SR is operationalized or measured in any given study. If SR is equated with one or more of the EF components (e.g., WM) or emotion regulation, these are only aspects or facilitators of SR rather than the entire ensemble of SR components listed above. Measuring only one or two aspects of SR will also produce lower correlations with achievement (McClelland et al., 2015). In addition, SR in high school students and college students often relies on the use of self-report questionnaires (Dent & Koenka, 2016). If metacognition is a key aspect of SR, poorly self-regulated students will be not be particularly accurate in their reports of their own behaviors related to time management, study techniques, procrastination, and so on. There is also the strong possibility of social desirability when, for example, students are asked to respond to a question such as "I am not very responsible when it comes to deadlines." Questionnaires may not, then, discriminate between truly self-regulated students and their less self-regulated peers.

With all of this in mind, we can consider the findings of meta-analyses that have provided the average correlation between measures of SR and measures of achievement. Robson et al. (2020) located 150 studies that met their criteria for examining the linkage between SR in early childhood and both academic and socioemotional outcomes in early childhood and later on. Studies were included if their measures assessed "the ability to inhibit dominant impulses to modify thought, feeling, and behavior" (p. 4). Thus, Robson et al. limited the definition to the inhibitory control aspect of EF and SR. In cross-sectional studies, the weighted average correlation for mathematics was $r = .42$ (number of studies = 22) and for reading was $r = .34$ (number of studies = 20). In longitudinal studies, the predictive correlations for SR (inhibition) in preschool and later mathematics and reading in early childhood were $r = .31$ and .24, respectively (20 studies each). The predictive correlations between SR measured in early childhood and later reading and math were $r = .20$ and .20, respectively (9 studies for mathematics, 8 for reading). A meta-regression analysis also showed that teacher reports of inhibitory control were more strongly related to achievement measures than task-based assessments or parent reports of their children's ability to self-regulate. Given all the provisos listed above, these lower correlations are to be expected. Children may be more other-regulated when they are young and only the inhibitory aspect of SR was measured in these studies. However, the authors also found that the correlation for math was higher than that for reading. This is opposite of what might be expected given earlier arguments (Dent & Koenka, 2016).

When one distills self-regulated learning into specific components such as planning and strategy use in older children and adults, the following average correlations emerge. Again, contrary to expectation, the mean correlations do not significantly increase with age: elementary school ($r = .24$), middle school ($r = .21$), high school ($r = .18$) (Dent & Koenka, 2016). These means do not differ significantly. The correlations do vary somewhat by content area, but not significantly so: social studies ($r = .34$), science ($r = .26$), language arts ($r = .23$), and math ($r = .21$). As expected from the problems of using self-report questionnaires noted above, the correlations are much higher for recorded self-talk ($r = .48$) and behavioral measures ($r = .37$) than for self-report questionnaires ($r = .17$).

The Development of SR

Studies typically show that self-regulatory capacities (e.g., inhibitory control, planning, emotion regulation) generally improve between preschool and early adulthood. For example, in a large international study conducted of 10- to 30-year-olds conducted in 11 countries, Steinberg et al. (2018) found that a composite measure of planning and the ability to use restraint over impulsivity showed monotonic increases between the ages of 10 and 24 and plateaued thereafter. In a study comparing the performance of 10-year-olds and adults on a measure of inhibition (Stroop task) and planning (Tower of Hanoi), Tsalas, Sodian, and Paulus (2017) found significant improvement with age in these two components of SR. In contrast, another study showed that 10-year-olds reported more frequent use of self-regulatory strategies than 14- to 17-year-olds when it came to resisting temptation for eating unhealthy foods (Tăut et al., 2015). In other words, the teenagers sought out and gave into temptation to eat the unhealthy foods more often. That said, one study of adolescent girls reported using reappraisal of tempting foods to make them less tempting. Activity in the regulatory centers of the frontal lobes correlated with the use of these reappraisal strategies (Giuliani & Pfeifer, 2015). Such seemingly contradictory findings may be explained by the different rates of brain maturation in reward centers of the brain and control centers of the brain (Sinopoli, Schachar, & Dennis, 2011). Another way of characterizing age trends in adolescents, then, is to say that adolescents may have a greater ability to regulate themselves if they want to but may lack the motivation or incentives to do so.

LINKAGES OF EF AND SR
TO DEVELOPMENTAL DISORDERS

One potentially informative way to get a sense of the importance of EF and SR to development is to consider whether children diagnosed with developmental disabilities are more likely to demonstrate deficits in EF and SR than their nondisabled peers. This comparison is a way of metaphorically "taking away" higher levels of EF and SR from children to see what happens developmentally. This inferential leap only makes sense, however, if it can be shown or argued that deficits in EF or SR are partly responsible for the symptomatology of a disorder or if there are good theoretical reasons for linking EF or SR to a disability. Consider, for example, various disorders that fall under the general umbrella of children who demonstrate *externalizing symptoms* such as conduct disorder (CD), oppositional defiant disorder (ODD), and attention-deficit/hyperactivity disorder (ADHD) (Leno et al., 2018). Externalizing symptoms include acting out, misbehaving, being aggressive, violating social norms, resisting the authority of parents and teachers, and other ways of not controlling oneself. Two existing meta-analyses of studies examining EF deficits in ADHD and autism spectrum disorder (ASD) reveal consistent impairments in components of EF such as WM and inhibition (Leno et al., 2018; Velikonja, Fett, & Velthorst, 2019). Studies of other disorders that exhibit externalizing symptoms have been less consistent.

With respect to ADHD in particular, a key expert in the field, Russell Barkley, has argued that ADHD should be viewed primarily as a disorder of self-regulation rather than simply an attentional or hyperactivity disorder (Barkley, 2015). In particular, the characteristic features of ADHD include problems in many of the features of SR listed above, such as poor planning, failing to monitor progress, lack of emotion regulation, failure to inhibit inappropriate responses, failure to learn from mistakes, and poor metacognition. He has also argued that traditional measures of EF, such as the reversed digit-span task, the flanker task, and so on do a much poorer job of predicting problems in real-world contexts than a questionnaire that he developed that taps into the behavioral features of SR such as poor planning and lack of emotion regulation.

One recent study confirmed this finding in college students. When given traditional measures of EF and Barkley's Deficits in Executive Functioning Scale (BDEFS), the latter more strongly predicted ADHD symptoms in college students than the former (Dehili, Prevatt, & Coffman, 2017). The BDEFS has items that focus on the five subdomains of self-management to time, self-organization/problem solving, self-restraint/inhibition, self-motivation, and self-regulation of emotions. That said, one recent meta-analysis of studies that have used the widely used EF measure called the Tower of Hanoi task showed a moderately large effect size ($g = 0.59$) when children diagnosed with ADHD were compared to their typically developing peers (Patros et al., 2019). On the Tower of Hanoi task, participants are shown an apparatus with three pegs and three rings that increase in size on one of the pegs (see Figure 6.1). They have to figure out how to move three rings one by one to another peg and replicate the pyramid arrangement without ever placing a larger ring on top of a smaller ring. Success requires multiple aspects of EF, but it is particularly thought to access the ability to plan.

In addition to externalizing disorders, it is also the case that problems in the WM component of EF is also a key symptom of children diagnosed with mathematics disability and reading disability (Peng & Fuchs, 2016). So, collectively, the results of the aforementioned studies seem to show that problems in components of EF and SR are associated with various

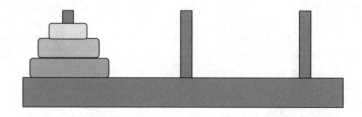

FIGURE 6.1. The Tower of Hanoi apparatus.

childhood disorders and academic achievement. However, the results do not conclusively demonstrate that deficiencies in EF and SR cause the various disorders, since it is possible that a third variable causes both the disorder and problems in EF and SR. For example, if anatomical anomalies in regions of the frontal lobes are associated with the symptoms of a disorder and also EF or SR problems, the correlations between EF problems, SR problems, and a diagnosis could be spurious. One way to more clearly prove causality is to conduct training studies to improve EF and SR. These interventions are discussed next.

EFFECTIVENESS OF INTERVENTIONS TO IMPROVE EF AND SR

Three meta-analyses have been conducted since 2015 of studies that were designed to improve EF or SR and hopefully improve subsequent achievement as well. Jacob and Parkinson (2015) found 43 studies that examined the concurrent and predictive relationship between components of EF and achievement. Similar to what was reported earlier in this chapter, they found moderate relations between EF components and achievement in reading or math (r's = .30). However, they also describe five experimental studies in which a curriculum was created to increase EF components. Whereas some of these curriculums led to improvements in EF, none reported convincing evidence that improvements in EF led to improvements in achievement.

In the second meta-analysis, Takacs and Kassie (2019) reviewed the literature and hypothesized that (1) it is possible to train children's EF skills, (2) they expected smaller but still significant delayed effects, (3) larger effects would be found for atypically developing (AD) children than typically developing (TD) children, and (4) the interventions would not all be equally effective. With regard to their fourth hypothesis, they expected direct computerized training of EF components and training children how to use specific self-regulation strategies (e.g., mindfulness) would be more effective than aerobic exercise and using art to enhance EF. Across 90 identified studies, they found that computerized training was effective for both AD ($d = 0.25$) and TD ($d = 0.60$) children, but contrary to expectations it was more effective for TD children. They also found that mindfulness ($d = 0.46$) and biofeedback relaxation training ($d = 0.93$) were effective. These researchers did not consider whether any of the effective training led to improved academic achievement. The third meta-analysis also considered mindfulness training and found it to be moderately effective in promoting regulation of negative emotions ($d = -0.28$) (Leyland, Rowse, & Emerson, 2019). Again, though, the authors did not consider whether improvements in emotion regulation then contributed to improvements in other aspects of functioning such as social relationships or academic achievement.

IMPLICATIONS FOR EDUCATION

Earlier it was noted that EF and SR have been the subject of thousands of studies over the past 30 years. Given the centrality of goal-directed behavior in human achievement and well-being, this attention is well-founded if indeed it can be shown that EF and SR help people attain their goals. That said, this chapter showed that the correlations among EF, SR, and achievement tend to be fairly modest and no evidence to date has shown that it is possible to increase achievement through training in EF and SR skills. This is not to say that EF and SR skills do not matter. The prior literature review merely points out the considerable lack of clarity and consistency in theorizing about these two constructs. In addition, an earlier discussion in this chapter suggested that higher correlations might emerge in studies if observational studies were to document the frequency with which activities that require EF or SR occur in the classroom. If only some activities require EF and SR, this finding could partly explain the modest correlations. And if self-report measures are problematic from the standpoint of accuracy and social desirability, such measurement imprecision could also contribute to the lower correlations. Finally, the fact that interventions have not been effective to date does not mean they could never be effective. The first steps in increasing the chances of success include (1) the development of accurate consensus theories of EF and SR and (2) increased insight into how and why these two skills improve over time. Note that effective medical treatments (e.g., statin drugs for lowering cholesterol) were not developed until researchers understood how and why medical problems arose (why some people have higher levels of "bad" cholesterol and heart disease than others). The lack of clarity into the nature of EF and SR and how they develop means that interventions to improve them may have been implemented prematurely.

Despite the lack of clarity from researchers and theorists who study EF and SR as stand-alone constructs, we can draw implications from Vygotsky's theory with respect to parents and teachers helping children acquire EF and SR skills. For example, parents can promote the internalization of SR skills by modeling these skills themselves, structuring the environment or choosing contexts in which children's self-regulatory abilities are not exceeded, providing advice on strategies that help, and so on. Over time, parents should also take a step back, little by little, and give children increased autonomy to do things on their own. The same can be said for teachers. There should be a gradual shift between kindergarten and 12th grade in the amount of other-regulation that teachers provide for children when they are engaged in nonroutine activities such as writing a research paper or designing a science fair project. Both teachers and parents can also help children with emotion-regulation strategies by helping children understand how to view situations in ways that minimize maladaptive emotional responses.

CHAPTER 7

The Development of Intelligence, Aptitude, and Expertise

The reader will recall from Chapter 1 that any decision regarding what topics to include or not include in this book was based on whether the topic helps us understand why some students attain higher levels of achievement than other students. In the case of student attributes such as executive function and motivation, we can ask, "Is this characteristic predictive of who learns more across an academic year?" Topics were included if the answer to this question is "yes." Chapters 2–6 of this book showed that students will learn more if, on the first day of school, they walk through the door with higher levels of domain-specific knowledge (e.g., math knowledge), working memory, motivation, executive function, and self-regulation. In the present chapter, we expand on the previous chapters by focusing on three additional characteristics of students that also predict who learns more: their intelligence, their aptitude, and their level of expertise. We shall see that these characteristics are somewhat similar to each other in terms of the role they are expected to play in learning and problem solving, but they are also theoretically distinct. In what follows, we will examine the nature and development of intelligence, aptitude, and expertise in turn. In the closing section, we will consider the implications of the findings for instructional practice and achievement.

THE NATURE AND DEVELOPMENT OF INTELLIGENCE

The Nature of Intelligence

The modern interest in intelligence dates back to the 1800s and received a major catalyst when school systems in Europe and the U.S. military commissioned psychologists to develop tests of mental ability (Sternberg, 2013a). What is interesting about the construct of intelligence is that it has been alleged to be a cultural invention rather than an inherent, universal human attribute (Castles, 2012; Sternberg, 2013b). As Sternberg (2013b) argues, "What is viewed as 'intelligent' differs from one culture to the next, and behavior that is intelligent in one culture may be unintelligent, or irrelevant to intelligence, in another."

The construct of intelligence emerged in the 1800s when there was considerable interest in evolutionary theory and the heritability of traits. Without the cultural context of "nature versus nurture" arguments at that time, combined with differences in the professional success rates of people coming from lower and higher socioeconomic classes, the idea of people being born with more ability than others may have never arisen (or so the cultural argument goes). Once the idea did emerge, practices developed such as grouping students by ability (to make things easier for teachers in France) and aptitude testing in the military and workplace so that military leaders and employers could predict who might do well in specific positions (e.g., drill sergeant versus tank driver). But in line with Sternberg's arguments, the cultural argument says that classrooms and workplaces are also cultural contexts. There would be no reason to think that people doing well in one of these contexts would necessarily do well in another context, if the cultural specificity argument of intelligence is true. Note that these arguments are also in line with the definition of multiple intelligences offered by Howard Gardner. Domain-specific skills (e.g., academic skills, musical skills, athletic skills, and so forth) have to be valued in a culture in order for them to be viewed as a form of intelligence in Gardner's (1993) view.

In contrast to the U.S. emphasis on ability groups and inborn talents, researchers have argued that the Japanese culture is very different (Bempechat, Jimenez, & Boulay, 2002). Japanese parents strongly value the abilities to endure hardships and to be positively engaged in disciplined effort. This emphasis can be contrasted with the U.S. ideal to pursue individual happiness and how grading systems and classroom environments highlight the most successful students. In addition, the cultural definition of intelligence in Japan is not simply mastery of content knowledge; it is also linked to notions of character and behavior. Moreover, Japanese teachers are reluctant to elevate or celebrate students of high ability due to their concerns about equality and unequal distribution of resources. They also strongly emphasize effort and determination over ability. All of these cultural differences suggest that what is judged to be intelligent behavior in the United States and Japan would differ, as also would the way we might measure intelligence in the two countries (Bempechat et al., 2002).

Since the beginning of the intelligence test movement of the early 1900s in the United States, quite a number of theories of intelligence appeared, though only a few survive today that currently drive new research. Even with the winnowed number of theories, however, there continue to be different emphases on how many components of intelligence there are, which components matter the most, and whether it is important to espouse a domain-general aspect of intelligence (*g*) or more specific, lower-level aspects (*s*) such as the speed with which someone performs a task. One of the leading figures in the field, Robert Sternberg (2005), surveyed across the vast literature and proposed a synthetic definition that he believes captures commonalities in the various approaches. He argued that intelligence "is the capacity to learn from experience, using metacognitive processes to enhance learning, and the ability to adapt to the surrounding environment, which may require different adaptations within different social and cultural contexts" (p. 751).

Let's unpack this definition a little. According to the first part, intelligent people have a stronger capacity to *learn from experience*. So, if we relate this idea to students, it would be expected that if one student has more intelligence than another, the former would learn more than the latter across an academic year, according to this part of the definition. A valid measure of intelligence, then, should assess this ability to learn (not just show that some people know more than others or can execute certain already-learned skills better).

As for the second part of the definition, we learned in Chapter 3 (domain-general theories), Chapter 4 (memory development), and Chapter 6 (executive function and self-regulation) that *metacognition* is the ability to know what you do not know and understand the utility of specific strategies. So, when given the opportunity to learn something new, a more intelligent student would be expected to have a better understanding of what they do not know and use more effective strategies to learn the material. Finally, the last part of the definition about *adaptation* pertains to the ability to make adjustments in the environment or change oneself rather than keep trying approaches that are not working. Sternberg shares the emphasis on adaptation in intelligent behavior with Jean Piaget (1952). Intelligent behavior *is* adaptive behavior and vice versa.

To get some additional insight into the nature of intelligence, consider two additional definitions proposed by Linda Gottfredson (1997) and John Mayer (2018), respectively:

> Intelligence is a very general capacity that, among other things, involves the ability to reason, plan, solve problems, think abstractly, comprehend complex ideas, learn quickly from experience . . . it reflects a capability for comprehending our surroundings—"catching on," "making sense" of things, or "figuring out" what to do." (Gottfredson, 1997, p. 13)

> A person's mental capacity to solve problems that concern the inner self and surrounding world. The capabilities include the ability to represent

information relevant to specific topics and contexts accurate in memory and to manipulate that information systematically. The ability further involves identifying the similarities and differences among concepts and contexts, "getting the point," and drawing upon appropriate generalizations so as to relate existing information to new problems; it involves "figuring things out," with the purpose of finding effective solutions. (Mayer, 2018, p. 270)

With these introductory comments in mind, we can now more closely examine three research traditions of intelligence that are still driving new research that appears in the core journals of developmental, educational, and school psychology: the Cattell–Horn–Carroll (CHC) theory of intelligence (Schneider & McGrew, 2012), Sternberg's theory of successful intelligence (Sternberg, 2018), and Mayer's theory of emotional intelligence (Mayer, 2018). We can consider how well the tasks used in these traditions map onto the aforementioned definitions of intelligence supplied by Sternberg (2005), Gottfredson (1997), and Mayer (2018).

According to the Web of Science, the CHC theory has been cited over 1,000 times since 2005 even if one limits the search to just the publications of one of the main proponents of CHC theory, Kevin McGrew. Sternberg's theory of intelligence has been cited over 530 times since 2005. Mayer's model has been cited well over 800 times if you just consider the original paper that presented the theory in 1990 (Salovey & Mayer, 1989). There are many more theories that could be discussed, but they all fall within one of two main traditions represented by the models of Sternberg and CHC (see Sternberg, 2018, for a review). The differences among these three theories also highlights different approaches to theory construction that we can label the "psychometric (bottom-up) approach" and the "a priori (theoretical) approach." Educators may have also heard about Howard Gardner's (1993) theory of multiple intelligences. Gardner's theory has been cited over 1,200 times since 2005, but a close examination of publications that appeared in 2016 or later revealed that none of the citing articles appeared in the primary outlets for developmental, educational, or school psychologists. So, for brevity, we shall just discuss one representative of the psychometric approach and two representatives of the a priori approach in turn.

The Psychometric (Bottom-Up) Approach

Recall that psychologists were initially motivated to study intelligence in the early 20th century because school systems and the military wanted them to construct tests to evaluate the talents and potential of students and recruits. French psychologist Alfred Binet developed one of the first tests and he was followed by many others, including Lewis Terman, Charles Spearman, Louis Thurstone, J. P. Guilford, David Wechsler, Richard Woodcock, and Alan Kaufman (Wasserman, 2018). The term *psychometric* denotes the idea of measuring ("-metric") mental traits ("psycho-"). The process of developing tests of abilities in the early 1900s came on the heels of the "human faculties" perspective of Sir Francis Galton in the 1800s. The basic idea was to divide the mind into basic, distinct "faculties" such as the abilities to remember, to reason, to think spatially, and to perform mathematical computations. One would then develop tests that measured each of these faculties. But after you gave these tests to people, how might one summarize their performance so as to be helpful to teachers and military leaders? Also, is it wise to give a single short test of a mental faculty to measure someone's ability in that area? Such considerations led to the development of a methodological approach and statistical analysis called *factor analysis* that was invented by Charles Spearman (Wasserman, 2018).

When researchers conduct a factor analytic study, they give multiple measures of a particular skill (e.g., verbal ability or math ability) to a sample of participants, compute the correlations among the measures, and submit these correlations to a factor analysis. The output of this analysis shows which tasks had the highest correlations with each other and metaphorically "hang together." To illustrate with a simple example, imagine that there was a theory of intelligence that claimed that intelligence was comprised of just two faculties: verbal ability and math ability. Imagine next that we gave 100 people three measures each of verbal ability (e.g., a vocabulary test, a sentence grammaticality test, and a reading comprehension test) and math ability (e.g., adding two-digit numbers, comparing the relative size of two numbers, and math word problems) and computed the correlations. Table 7.1 shows a fictional set of correlations among these measures to illustrate a possible outcome. The value of correlations shows whether people perform comparably on any two measures (e.g., above average on one, above average on the other). The formula for computing a correlation gives a number that ranges from 0 to 1.0 (for positive correlations). The closer the correlation gets to 1.0, the more correlated the two measures are (demonstrating that people performed similarly on the two measures).

TABLE 7.1. Fictional Correlations within and between Verbal and Math Domains

	VT	SGT	PCT	ANT	RST	MWT
Vocabulary test (VT)	—	.73	.58	.20	.07	.16
Sentence grammaticality test (SGT)		—	.67	.09	.15	.13
Paragraph comprehension test (PCT)			—	.17	.21	.25
Adding two-digit numbers (ANT)				—	.59	.65
Relative size of numbers (RST)					—	.72
Math word problems (MWT)						—

As shown in Table 7.1, people in this fictional study performed similarly on the three measures of verbal ability and the three measures of math ability but did not perform comparably on any measure of verbal ability and any measure of math ability. The within-domain correlations (i.e., verbal test with verbal test, or math test with math test) are bolded in Table 7.1. In this example, the bolded ones are much closer to 1.0 and the cross-domain correlations are closer to zero.

When one then submits these correlations to factor analysis, the output shows columns that depict the alleged "factors" or *latent abilities* that "cause" the comparable performance on the three verbal tests and three math tests. Table 7.2 shows a fictional output of a factor analysis. Each of the numbers in the columns is called a factor loading, and its size indicates how strongly it is allegedly "caused" by the latent factor. In addition, all tests that have loadings above .40 or .50 in the same column are said to be caused by the same latent factor (by convention). The researcher then has to label each factor according to which tests all loaded on the same factor. In this fictional example, two clear factors emerged: one that we can label "verbal ability" (factor 1) and one that can label "math ability" (factor 2).

In real life, researchers almost never get such clear findings, and a good deal of interpretation has to occur to label the factors. But the findings are presented to illustrate the approach. To be more specific, the example above actually demonstrates an approach called *exploratory factor analysis*. In this approach, you submit scores on a number of tests and let the computer tell you which tests "hang together" (i.e., show high loadings on the column for one of the factors). In modern times, researchers are more likely to use a technique called *confirmatory factor analysis* in which you specify ahead of time which tests should hang together (i.e., which ones are caused by the same underlying latent factor) and the output tells you whether these tests do, in fact, seem to have the same underlying factor. It is also common to supplement the numerical results of this test with a graphic or figure such as that in Figure 7.1. The latent factors are usually depicted with ovals and

TABLE 7.2. Fictional Example of Factor Analysis Output

	Factor 1	Factor 2
Vocabulary test	.87	.23
Sentence grammaticality test	.83	.19
Paragraph comprehension test	.89	.06
Adding two-digit numbers	.20	.88
Relative size of numbers	.17	.82
Math word problems	.09	.79

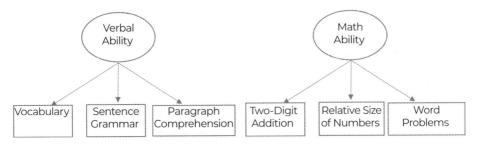

FIGURE 7.1. Graphic showing two latent factors (ovals) and six manifest variables (rectangles).

the scores on specific tests are considered manifest variables, or observable "symptoms" of the factor (depicted as rectangles).

Since the 1920s, various latent factors and subdivisions of intelligence have been proposed. Researchers also disagreed vigorously about whether intelligence is only comprised of a finite set of abilities (such as verbal ability and math ability) or whether it also consists of a general latent factor that is common to and causes the specific latent factors. The inventor of factor analysis, Spearman, denoted the specific factors with an *s* and the general factor as *g* (Wasserman, 2018). The general factor would be depicted in Figure 7.1 as an oval above the two specific factors of verbal ability and math ability. In the exploratory factor analysis output in Table 7.2, there would be three columns: one factor on which all tests load (*g*), one factor in which only the verbal tasks load (s_v), and one in which only the math tasks load (s_m). Spearman was also possibly the first scholar to notice the fact that almost all cognitive tasks correlate with each other in the range of *r* = .10 to *r* = .50 (average of *r* = .30) (Mayer, 2018). Spearman dubbed this phenomenon the *positive manifold*. The positive manifold combined with factor analysis is what led some to infer the presence of *g*, or general intelligence that applies to all tasks.

The reader may already be familiar with a real two-factor solution that was proposed by David Wechsler (1939) in which intelligence was subdivided into verbal and performance components. The tasks that loaded on the *verbal factor* included tests called information, similarities, vocabulary, arithmetic, and digit span. The tasks that loaded on the *performance factor* included tests called block design, matrix reasoning, picture completion, digit-symbol coding, and symbol search. Based on their performance on the verbal scale tasks, people were assigned a Verbal intelligence quotient (IQ). Based on their performance on the performance scale tasks, they were assigned a Performance IQ. Based on their performance across all tasks, they were assigned a Full Scale IQ. So, when you hear that someone has an IQ of 120, that number usually refers to their Full Scale IQ. Until about 20 years ago, the Wechsler scales for both children (Wechsler Intelligence for Children [WISC]) and adults (Wechsler Adult Intelligence Scale [WAIS]) were the most widely used measures of intelligence (Wasserman, 2018).

A different solution was originally proposed by neuroscientist Donald Hebb in the 1940s, and later reaffirmed by Raymond Cattell in the 1970s and John Horn in the 1990s (Horn & Noll, 1997; McGill & Dombrowski, 2019). The tasks used by these researchers and factor analytic solutions revealed one component of intelligence that captured the body of knowledge people had accumulated in their lifetime (*crystallized intelligence* or *Gc*) and another that reflected their ability to solve novel problems and reason (*fluid intelligence* or *Gf*). As will be discussed later in this chapter, making this distinction between Gc and Gf allowed developmental psychologists to reveal some interesting and important age trends in intelligence between childhood and old age.

In addition to Gf and Gc, which were considered second-order abilities, Horn and colleagues also assumed that intelligence consists of 80 primary abilities and six other second-order abilities: short-term apprehension and retrieval (SAR), fluency of retrieval from long-term storage (TSR), processing speed (Gs), visual processing (Gv), auditory processing (Ga), and quantitative knowledge (Gq). Horn and colleagues never advocated for the reality of *g* and instead considered it a statistical artifact (McGill & Dombrowski, 2019). In the 1980s, the Woodcock–Johnson Psycho-Educational Battery—Revised was constructed using Gc–Gf theory as a blueprint.

When one reads all of the numerous other approaches besides those of Wechsler and Horn and Cattell that "carve" intelligence into different components, it can be a little overwhelming to get an overall, coherent sense of what intelligence is. For many years, there did not appear to be a method for determining whose "carving" got it right and whose was wrong. In 1993, however, psychologist John B. Carroll attempted to develop a model that synthesized across all of the competing approaches by combining hundreds of datasets together and conducting one mega factor analysis (Carroll, 1993). After examining the results of this factor analysis, Carroll proposed that intelligence consisted of three hierarchically arranged levels or strata: *narrow abilities,* such as the speed with which someone could perform a task (Stratum III); *broad abilities* that were latent factors that affected performance across sets of narrow ability tasks (Stratum II); and then *general intelligence* sitting at the top of the hierarchy (Stratum I).

THE CHC MODEL

Soon after the Woodcock–Johnson battery was developed and revised several times (Woodcock–Johnson III [WJ-III]), psychologist Kevin McGrew attempted to synthesize the three-level model of Carroll and the two-level model of Horn and Cattell. The result was called the Cattell–Horn–Carroll

(CHC) model (McGill & Dombrowski, 2019; Schneider & McGrew, 2012). The WJ-III soon far surpassed all other intelligence tests in terms of popularity, as did the CHC model itself. As a result, most of the competing measures of intelligence were revised as well to better assess the components of the CHC model (McGill & Dombrowski, 2019; Schneider & McGrew, 2012). See Table 7.3 for a list of the component abilities in different strata.

The CHC model and the WJ-III were specifically designed in the era of *response to intervention* (RTI) to provide more useful insight into the needs of specific students (McGrew & Wendling, 2010). In RTI, the strengths and weaknesses of students are assessed, and students are provided with specific forms of remediation to address the weaknesses. Not everyone who has been diagnosed with a specific learning disability will have the same weaknesses identified. For example, one student may have difficulty with rapid retrieval of information, while another may have difficulty with phonological processing (see Chapters 8 and 9 for discussions of phonological processing). With the WJ-III, these different weaknesses would be identified using different tests that map onto the broad abilities of comprehension-knowledge (Gc) and auditory processing (Ga), respectively. Interventions would then be created to remediate the distinct problems of the two students. Moreover, focusing on a Full Scale IQ score (an index of *g*) would not be helpful in RTI, because the two students could have the

---

TABLE 7.3. Components of the CHC Model of Intelligence

Stratum I
    General Intelligence (G)

Stratum II (Broad Abilities, Latent Factors)
    Comprehension-Knowledge (Gc) (crystallized intelligence)
    Fluid Reasoning (Gf)
    Quantitative Knowledge (Gq)
    Reading and Writing Ability (Grw)
    Short-Term Memory (Gsm)
    Long-Term Storage and Retrieval (Glr)
    Visual Processing (Gv)
    Auditory Processing (Ga)
    Processing Speed (Gs)

Stratum III (Narrow Abilities)
    8 measures of Comprehension-Knowledge
    6 measures of Fluid Reasoning
    2 measures of Quantitative Knowledge
    8 measures of Reading and Writing Ability
    2 measures of Short-Term Memory
    12 measures of Long-Term Storage and Retrieval
    11 measures of Visual Processing
    9 measures of Auditory Processing
    5 Measures of Processing Speed

same IQ but nevertheless have different problems in need of remediation (McGrew & Wendling, 2010; Schneider & McGrew, 2012). This decomposition of intelligence into components that are predictive of school success is probably the reason for the popularity of the WJ-III. School psychologists attempted to use the Verbal IQ, Performance IQ, and Full Scale IQ of the WISC in a similar manner but did not achieve the same level of success in an RTI framework that they are attaining now with the CHC model and WJ-III (Schneider & McGrew, 2012).

So, what exactly is *g*? As noted above, some scholars dismiss the finding as a statistical artifact. Others consider it a real aspect of intelligence that can be equated with *fluid intelligence* (Gf). Noting the high correlation between Gf and working memory (WM), researchers have tried to decompose Gf and WM into their components to see why there is an overlap (Shipstead & Engle, 2018). Using various clever methodological techniques, they discovered that people high on WM are able to maintain more information in mind and avoid proactive interference (see Chapter 4, on memory). People high on Gf are able to more readily forget or disengage old information or rules that are no longer useful. Another approach to *g* is to assume it is not a latent factor that causes more specific broad abilities per se, but is an index of the overlap of processes that are common to all of the tasks (e.g., they all require language, executive attention, and WM) (Conway & Kovacs, 2018).

CRITIQUE OF THE PSYCHOMETRIC (BOTTOM-UP) APPROACH

As will be argued in the next section in which the a priori approach is described, the standard practice in modern psychological research is to begin with a theory in which key components of a construct are defined and then to construct measures that tap into the components so defined. In other words, the preferred order is to begin with a *theoretical definition* and end with an *operational definition*. Questions about the validity of a measure pertain the degree to which the operational definition truly maps onto the theoretical definition. Consider, for example, the theoretical definition of intelligence proposed by David Wechsler (1939): "the global capacity of a person to act purposefully, to think rationally, and to deal effectively with his environment" (p. 229). Then consider the components of his Verbal IQ scale, Performance IQ scale, and the overall Full Scale IQ. It is not at all clear how the 10 scales map onto his theoretical definition.

Rather than start with a theory, beginning with Binet, those in the psychometric tradition seem to have begun with an intuitive sense of some list of mental faculties, and advocates of this approach created tasks to tap into these faculties. But one can well ask, why these faculties and not others? If you compare the list of narrow abilities tested on the WISC to those tested on the WJ-III, there is no principled reason why any of the skills included in one of these measures should or should not be included in the other measure. The models that arise from factor analysis will largely reflect the measures included. Use different measures, different factors will emerge. Or, as famously stated by historian of psychology Edwin Boring, "intelligence is what intelligence tests measure" (Conway & Kovacs, 2018).

Similarly, the manner in which Carroll's model and the Horn–Cattell model were combined has also been closely scrutinized and questioned (Canivez & Youngstrom, 2019; McGill & Dombrowski, 2019). Horn, for one, did not believe in the reality of *g*, while Carroll argued for its inclusion (McGill & Dombrowski, 2019). Neither scholar specifically advocated for the CHC model when they were alive, so use of their names seems a little out of place. Further, the manner in which narrow abilities and broad abilities have been added or deleted from the model seems arbitrary (see Schneider & McGrew, 2012, for example, for a discussion of how new components, such as emotional intelligence, have been added). Had Spearman not used a specific set of measures and invented factor analysis, the idea of general intelligence would never have been proposed. Hence, we return to the idea of intelligence being a cultural invention (Castles, 2012). In addition, other researchers who have attempted to replicate the three-stratum model and broad abilities via other methods have not been successful (Canivez & Youngstrom, 2019).

Note that both the WISC and WJ-III do predict who does well in school, and the WJ-III can identify problems that need to be remediated. Thus, the fact that these measures can be successfully used for prediction does not mean that these measures actually tap into something called "intelligence." Said another way, the manner in which these tests have been utilized seems to follow this logic: children who perform better than other children in school are presumably more intelligent; let's see if we can create tests that identify the smarter children; many (but not all) of the children who perform well in school also perform well on these tests; therefore, these tests measure intelligence. The problem with this logic is that the tests could be measuring something else that is common to the tests and school success.

In addition, however, recall that intelligence tests were initially created to identify children who were fast, medium, and slow learners. Intelligence tests should, then, correlate with the speed with which learners acquire and master skills. A large number of studies conducted between 1905 and 1930 revealed only modest correlations between IQ and learning rate, and mostly for the first few trials when the tasks were still somewhat novel (Ackerman, 1987). The methodology and tasks used by these researchers have been criticized, however. Using a task in which people had to learn to associate Lithuanian words with their English counterparts, Zerr et al. (2018) were able to identify groups of learners that differed by how many trials it took to master all of the pairs: (1) those who reached mastery in five trials, (2) those who reached mastery in seven trials, (3) those who reached mastery in nine trials, and (4) those who reached mastery in 13 trials. The four groups also differed in terms of their retention as well. The more efficient learners also showed better retention over time, including over a 3-year period. Of particular relevance to this section, the correlation between the WAIS Full Scale IQ and a measure of learning efficiency (that combined the number of trials to criterion and retention scores) was $r = .45$. So, perhaps researchers in the early 1900s failed to find a stronger correlation between learning rate and IQ because they did not use the right tests (Ackerman, 1987). However, since the WAIS also includes measures of vocabulary and WM, this correlation could reflect the common content of the two tests.

Finally, a number of researchers have pointed out how racial differences in performance have been used in an inappropriate way to argue for the genetic basis of racial differences in intelligence (Neisser, 1998) and also showed how socioeconomic status is highly correlated with performance on standard IQ tests (Peng, Wang, Wang, & Lin, 2019). These criticisms led to the creation of so-called *culture-free tests* such as Raven's Progressive Matrices, but performance on those measures cannot be considered truly culture free since years of education affect performance on those measures (Peng et al., 2019). If so, children must pick up reasoning strategies in comparable tasks in school and apply these approaches to solve Raven's Progressive Matrices (Flynn, 2018).

The A Priori (Theoretical) Approach

In the second but much smaller research tradition, researchers begin with a theory that distills intelligence into its components, and then develop tests that tap into each of the components (Sternberg, 2018). In the case of Sternberg's model, this more a priori approach was inspired by the work of IP theorists in the 1970s who performed *task analysis* to propose the set of cognitive processes needed to carry out a task effectively (see Chapter 3 for more on IP theory). Once the component operations were identified, IP theorists then attempted to see if overall performance could be predicted by scores on measures of the component operations (Sternberg, 2018). To illustrate this tradition in the case of intelligence, we can consider two models: Sternberg's theory of successful intelligence and Mayer's (2018) model of emotional intelligence.

STERNBERG'S THEORY OF SUCCESSFUL INTELLIGENCE

Sternberg (2018) succinctly defined his perspective on intelligence by arguing that successful intelligence is one's ability to choose, reevaluate, and, to the extent possible, attain one's goals in life, within one's sociocultural context. A successfully intelligent person recognizes his or her strengths and weaknesses and then capitalizes on strengths while compensating for or correcting weaknesses. He or she does so through a combination of analytical, creative, practical, and wisdom-based/ethical skills. (p. 308)

What is immediately apparent from this definition is how different it is from the CHC model. In the CHC model, there is no consideration given to goals, sociocultural contexts, different ways to express intelligence, wisdom, and values. CHC theorists do, however, consider the ideas of strengths and weaknesses within an RTI framework, and create interventions in order to help students be more successful in school. But Sternberg did not develop his model after giving a large battery of tests to people and performing factor analysis. The components derived from his theoretical analysis of what is needed in particular contexts to be successful on particular culturally defined tasks.

There are two ways the theory explains how to be intelligent in particular contexts and both were inspired by IP theory. The first way focuses on the time course of solving a problem starting from the points before, during, and after a problem is worked on. The *metacomponents* of intelligence pertain to figuring out what do, setting up a plan, and monitoring performance (Sternberg, 2018). Smart people are better at this than their less intelligent peers. They properly define a problem, set up a good plan, and allocate their time effectively. The *performance components* of intelligence execute the plans of the metacomponents. Smart people carry out the plan more effectively than less smart people using the appropriate skills and techniques. The *knowledge acquisition* components pertain to how people learn how to carry out the task in the first place and how they learn from their mistakes. Smart people selectively encode relevant information about a task and understand what they did wrong when they made a mistake.

The second way that the theory is contextual pertains to the fact that there are different kinds of intelligence needed in particular situations, according to Sternberg (2018). The kind of intelligence needed on conventional psychometric and achievement tests is called *analytical intelligence*. People high on analytical intelligence may do well on IQ tests and achievement tests but may not be particularly creative or street smart. When novel problems are presented or people focus on problems that require a creative solution, *creative intelligence* is required. Some very creative people may have average or barely passible analytical intelligence. Consider how one of the discoverers of the helix structure of DNA, Francis Crick, reportedly had an IQ of 95. Other times, people need to recognize how an organization functions or social relationships work. People who are street smart recognize how to get ahead and "work" the system to their advantage. These people have *practical intelligence,* according to Sternberg. Practical intelligence is all about the fit between a person and a context. When practically intelligent people detect a poor fit (e.g., an employee wants to spend time with her family but the culture of her workplace wants people to be workaholics who work long hours), they have to figure out how to alter the environment so that there is a better fit (e.g., work to change the culture somehow), or alter themselves (e.g., give up the desire to spend more time with the family), or leave (e.g., move to another workplace or profession that requires less time away from home). Finally, *wisdom-based abilities* are required when considerations have to be given to the common good such that there is a balance achieved between one's own interests, those of others, and the good of society as a whole (Sternberg, 2018). Consideration of the common good requires that one also consider ethics and values as to what is really important. Cutting down a rainforest in Brazil may increase the amount of farmland, for example, but it also contributes to climate change. You may know how to deforest an area (analytical skills), do so in a novel way (creative skills), and work a governmental system to get approval (practical skills), but it is still unwise and unethical (and unintelligent) to do so.

Again, in contrast to psychometric models such as CHC, the theory of successful intelligence began with a theory, and assessments were constructed to tap into analytical, creative, practical, and wisdom-based components. In several projects carried out in high schools, such as the Rainbow Project, Sternberg and collaborators demonstrated how to create such assessments and also demonstrated that these assessments explained performance in school over and above traditional kinds of measures (Sternberg, 2018). He and his colleagues also created different kinds of curricula to the foster analytical, creative, practical, and wisdom-based skills. He has also advocated for broadening the assessment of students applying for admission to undergraduate and graduate programs to measure other kinds of abilities besides the kind of analytical abilities measured by the Scholastic Achievement Test (SAT), Graduate Record Examination (GRE), or Graduate Management Admissions Test (GMAT).

Criticism of Sternberg's Model. There are fewer criticisms of Sternberg's model than models in the psychometric tradition. That said, critics of earlier versions of the model argued that there is little "value added" to appealing to both practical intelligence and analytic intelligence since analytic intelligence is a moderate predictor of success in the workplace (Gottfredson, 1997). Some critics also contended that the model did not have sufficient empirical support when it was originally proposed (Gottfredson, 1997), but that argument would not seem to still be the case (see Sternberg, 2018 for a review). Other critics argue that indicators other than analytic intelligence do add additional explained variance to success in college, but not that much (Niessen & Meijer, 2017).

A rather different model that still exemplifies the a priori approach is Mayer's model of emotional intelligence (EI). Mayer and colleagues consider EI an ability in much the same way that those in the psychometric tradition and Sternberg consider their cognitive intelligence an ability (MacCann et al., 2020). In fact, Mayer (2018) believes EI should be viewed as another broad ability to be added to the CHC model. Schneider and McGrew (2012) agree with this addition. Mayer's model is nevertheless discussed in the present section because it is an a priori rather than bottom-up approach.

The model subdivides EI into four components: (1) the ability to *perceive* emotions accurately, (2) the ability to *use* emotions to facilitate decision making, (3) the ability to *understand* emotions, and (4) the ability to *manage* emotions (MacCann et al., 2020). Mayer and colleagues then proceeded to develop a psychometrically sound measure of each of these four facets called the Mayer–Salovey–Caruso Emotional Intelligence Test (MSCEIT). At this writing, over 700 articles cite the MSCEIT, suggesting that the authors of the citing articles used it in their own research. Several recent meta-analyses show that measures of EI do correlate moderately with outcomes such as workplace success ($r = .24$). The correlation with academic achievement is discussed below. Mayer (2018) argues that a good way to think about EI is that it is a kind of intelligence *about people* (including oneself). All of the other kinds of broad abilities in the CHC model are forms of intelligence *about things*. Both kinds of intelligence exist and are important for being successful in school and the workplace.

Criticism of Models of EI. Perhaps the most consistent concern is whether another new kind of intelligence is really needed (Austin & Saklofske, 2005; Hedlund & Sternberg, 2000). Locke (2005) argues further that the concept of EI is incoherent and does not define an ability at all. Others have failed to demonstrate via factor analysis that EI is an ability separate from other broad abilities in the CHC model (Mayer, 2018).

Relation of Intelligence to Achievement

Recall that one of the original motivations for creating intelligence tests was to be able to predict children's performance in school (and create ability groups). It should be no surprise to learn, then, that the most widely used intelligence tests do correlate with school performance at moderate levels when no other predictors are used. For example, in a meta-analysis in which over 3,000 correlations were located, the average weighted correlations between fluid intelligence (Gf) and reading and math skills were $r = .38$ and $r = .41$, respectively (Peng et al., 2019). However, moderator analyses showed Gf correlates more strongly with more complex tasks than with more fundamental skills. Another meta-analysis summarizing the results of over 160 studies revealed that the average weighted correlation between intelligence and school grades was $r = .44$ (Roth et al., 2015). Correlations of about $r = .40$ suggest that intelligence accounts for 16% of the variance in school achievement when no other predictors are included (leaving 84% of the variance unexplained). However, when one controls for factors such as domain-specific knowledge and phonological processing, the explanatory value of psychometric intelligence shrinks considerably (Cutting & Scarborough, 2006; Fuhs, Hornburg, & McNeil, 2016; Sternberg, Grigorenko, & Bundy, 2001). As noted above, moreover, Sternberg's assessments of other kinds of abilities beyond those measured by standard intelligence tests have been found to explain additional variance (Sternberg, 2018). As for emotional intelligence, one recent meta-analysis found that the average weighted correlation between EI and school performance across 158 studies is $r = .14$ (not very large).

The Flynn Effect, Education, and Transactional Relations

Historical analyses of intelligence scores reveal that the average IQ in the United States and other countries has risen some 30 points over the past 100 years (Flynn, 2018). Dubbed "the Flynn effect" (after the researcher who discovered it), the question is how to interpret this 30-point increase. If indeed there is evidence that g has a strong genetic influence that increases with age (i.e., heritability estimates are higher in adults than children), this 30-point increase has happened far too quickly to be due to evolutionary processes. Flynn (2018) has explained it in terms of education. With education, people give more sophisticated responses to vocabulary and other items that tap into knowledge or require reasoning. For example, instead of grouping things by similar function (e.g., birds and airplanes both fly), more educated people group them according to scientific taxonomies that they learned in school (e.g., birds with animals; airplanes with other forms of transportation).

There are two other findings besides the Flynn effect that seem to demonstrate a strong role of education in determining IQ scores. The first comes from "natural experiments" in which decisions of school systems that are not linked or confounded with children's family or intellectual attributions determine how much education they receive. These decisions, in turn, affect their IQ scores (Bergold, Wirthwein, Rost, & Steinmayr, 2017). For example, many school systems have age cutoffs for school attendance (e.g., must be 6 years old by September 1). Children who have birthdays a few days after the cutoff (e.g., September 1 to 3) are compared to children who have birthdays a few days before (e.g., August 29 to 31). Given the close proximity to the cutoff date, there is no reason to think that those who are held back for another year differ in any meaningful way from those who are allowed to attend (e.g., their socioeconomic status). Studies show that, 1 year later, the children who are not held back end up having higher scores on components of IQ tests (e.g., working memory) than do children who are held back (Burrage et al., 2008). A similar kind of study compared children who were presented with a curriculum across 5 years to children who received the same curriculum across 4 years. The former had higher IQ scores than the latter after the curriculum was completed (Bergold et al., 2017). Another study found higher IQ scores in late adolescence when the length of compulsory education was changed from 7 years to 9 years in Norway (Brinch & Galloway, 2012).

Finally, there are studies that reveal a bidirectional or transactional relationship between schooling and intelligence scores (Peng et al., 2019). If a sample is followed longitudinally for several years and they are given both an intelligence test and measures of academic skills at each time point (e.g., math skills, reading skills, vocabulary), prior intelligence does predict later intelligence, but it also predicts later achievement. In addition, however, prior academic skills predict later academic skills but also later IQ. Some explain this phenomenon in terms of the *mutualism theory* of intelligence, that predicts age-related increases in the size of the positive manifold with age (Kievit et al., 2017). These findings contradict *investment theory* that suggests that Gf promotes the acquisition of Gc, but not the other way around (Peng et al., 2019).

One other intriguing argument suggests that the results of twin studies do support the strong genetic component of intelligence in the manner usually suggested. Instead of there being a direct genetic cause of intelligence, there is a strong genetic contribution to interests and motivation (Bouchard, 2018). Motivation then drives people to spend time on activities that interest them, and they build up skills in that area as a consequence. What all of these studies show is that intelligence is less determinative or unidirectional in its effects than strong advocates of its role have argued.

The Development of Intelligence

All intelligence tests, starting with the one constructed by Binet, ask participants to engage in particular tasks. The notion of IQ is a ratio of a person's *mental age* over his or her *chronological age*. So, if you are actually 8 years old (chronological age) but perform well on items that normally are not passed until you are 10 years old (mental age), your IQ is computed as $^{10}/_8 \times 100 = 125$. Most intelligence tests have these age norms built into them (Kyllonen, 2015). Your score reflects how well you perform *relative to* your same-age peers. So, naturally, children will tend to pass or do well on an increasing number of items on IQ tests with age. In other words, they become more intelligent with age. Piaget (1952) also believed that children become more intelligent with age because, as they construct increasingly more sophisticated mental structures, they are able to solve a wider array of problems and understand more things. In other words, someone capable of formal operational reasoning is more intelligent, in his view, than someone who is only capable of concrete operational thinking (see Chapter 3 for more on Piaget).

Two further findings are that, according to mutualism theory as described above, the components of intelligence may start off being somewhat independent of each other in young children. As they are exercised together in the performance of tasks that require multiple components (e.g., working memory, vocabulary, and math skills when solving math word problems), these components begin to correlate with each other. In other words, the positive manifold should increase with age. However, there is also evidence of increasing differentiation of the broad abilities with age as well (Breit, Brunner, & Preckle, 2020). The final age trend is that whereas both Gc and Gf increase with age between early childhood and young adulthood, Gf shows age-related declines between early adulthood and old age while Gc remains stable or even increases after age 20 (Ackerman, 2018).

If intelligence increases with age (and then declines), why have researchers also shown that there is considerable stability in intelligence scores between childhood and adulthood (Schneider, Niklas, & Schmiedeler, 2014; Yu, McCoach, Gottfried, & Gottfried, 2018)? Recall that there is an implicit age norming in intelligence tests. What the stability shows is that the rank order of people stays the same, especially between two adjacent age periods (e.g., the infancy and preschool periods or late childhood and adolescent periods). So, if we arranged a group of preschoolers from low to high in their IQ, Olivia may have the second highest score behind Emma when they are 4 years old. If we come back in 3 years and test them again, Olivia is likely to still be second behind Emma, even though both have become more intelligent and now can solve more tasks. Correlations between adjacent time periods can approach $r = .90$ while those that are more widely spaced (e.g., infancy and adolescent) might be closer to $r = .50$ or .60 (Schneider et al., 2014).

THE NATURE AND DEVELOPMENT OF APTITUDE

The Nature of Aptitude

Recall that one of the earliest catalysts for the development of theories of ability was the push to create tests that could predict who would do well in school, the workplace, or the military between 1900 and the 1930s. The notion of *aptitude* emerged at that time and was continually refined through the 2000s (see Corno et al., 2002). The root of the word *aptitude* is the word *apt*, which means likely or prone to act in a certain way. Some other related meanings include "readiness to learn" or having a "propensity to do well" (Byrnes, 2020; Corno et al., 2002). When the original predictive tests were created in the early 1900s, there clearly was some expectation that aptitudes are *domain-specific;* that is, people would be expected to do well on specific kinds of tasks, not necessarily all tasks. In fact, domain-specific or role-specific predictions were what employers and the military were interested in. They wanted to know who would be a good drill sergeant and who would be a good lieutenant in the battlefield. There was no expectation that the same person would be good in both roles.

This domain-specificity is one way to distinguish aptitude from intelligence. Aptitude is concerned with who is likely to do well in contexts that call for certain kinds of domain-specific abilities. Intelligence, in contrast, is concerned with who is likely to be successful in a range of contexts and domains. Aptitude is, then, more aligned with Howard Gardner's (1993) notion of multiple intelligences than with Spearman's notions of *g* or the positive manifold.

A relatively unexplored meaning of aptitude is the idea of being able to quickly "pick up" or learn a domain-specific skill. If readers of this book consider their own talents, they can think of skills that come easily to them or that they quickly master, and skills that took much longer to master. Some people readily acquire skills in sports, some readily acquire skills in music, and some readily acquire reading or math skills. There are some unusual individuals who seem to acquire skills in many fields simultaneously, and I suppose we would give them the label of "intelligent" or "Renaissance person," but these people would be the exception rather than the norm.

That said, there was a time when researchers used intelligence tests to measure aptitudes (Corno et al., 2002). Perhaps this decision reflected the idea that people with high levels of Gf or Gc would be most apt to perform well in school given that high levels of intelligence might make one more likely to be successful in school (and not necessarily in other contexts such as manufacturing plants or the football field). According to investment theory, people high in Gf could learn any content better than those with less Gf, and Gc is an index of content knowledge. Note that the Scholastic Achievement Test (SAT) was originally called the Scholastic Aptitude Test because it was designed to help universities make admissions decisions (i.e., who is likely to do well in college in all subject areas).

In any event, the assumption that aptitude was context-specific led to predictions about *aptitude × treatment interactions* (ATIs) (Corno et al., 2002). One ATI prediction was that people with higher levels of aptitude would need less structure and scaffolding to pick up a skill because they could pick it up on their own (i.e., they have high Gf). This prediction was tested by seeing if students with higher levels of aptitude performed better in a subject when their teachers used a form of instruction called *discovery learning,* while students with lower levels of aptitude would learn better with a form of instruction called *direct instruction,* in which teachers explained everything to them and walked them through problems step by step. The idea of *interaction* also meant that high-aptitude students would do worse in direct instruction classrooms, and low-aptitude students would do worse in discovery learning classrooms.

Although some studies demonstrated this predicted interaction, the findings have been generally mixed (Corno et al., 2002). The inconsistencies or noneffects could be due to manner in which aptitudes were assessed. As noted above, aptitudes may best be thought of as domain specific. Many studies used intelligence tests as their measure of aptitude, and earlier it was noted that intelligence tests do not necessarily correlate very highly with learning rates after the first few trials. Given the study of Zerr et al. (2018) described above, their use of a vocabulary-learning task may actually tap into a language-learning aptitude rather than a domain-general learning efficiency rate. Regardless, in that study and earlier studies all students attain the same level of success (on typical, routine tasks that have a common structure).

Other studies used prior achievement in a domain instead of intelligence. If students are given ample time and multiple attempts to learn material, they may end up having the same achievement test scores at the end of the academic year. Perhaps a better measure of aptitude might be the broad ability Gl (learning efficiency) scale of the WJ-III. But that measure does not account for how quickly someone measures skills in multiple domains and may be comparable to the learning efficiency measure of Zerr et al. (2018).

A construct closer to this idea of how quickly students master a skill is *time needed for learning* (Gettinger, 1984). A recent study showed that there were individual differences in how quickly people learned a morphological grammatical rule in a foreign language and how this ability interacted with sleep-mediated memory consolidation (Ben Zion, Nevat, Prior, & Bitan, 2019). Once again, though, such a measure could reflect a domain-specific aptitude for language learning. Clearly, there is a need for additional theorizing, and researchers need to clarify the domain-specific and speed-of-learning nature of aptitude.

One further theoretical elaboration on the construct of aptitude is to recognize that those in the ATI paradigm argue that existing knowledge, Gf, and Gc are not enough to determine who will be successful in school or other contexts. Rather, aptitude has *conative* and *affective* aspects as well (Corno et al., 2002). In other words, it is important to also measure people's motivation, temperament, and emotional intelligence to better predict end-of-year achievement. My colleagues and I likewise consider *propensity* to include prior achievement, working memory, motivation, and self-regulation (Byrnes, 2020). When one measures these multiple aspects of propensity beyond cognitive ability, up to 70% of the variance in achievement is explained.

The Development of Aptitude

Developmental psychologists generally have been less interested in the construct of aptitude described here than educational psychologists have been. As a result, few studies have considered whether aptitude improves over time. Most work has been done to predict performance in school, work, and the military, as noted earlier. This perspective is called an *individual difference* perspective rather than a developmental perspective. That said, it is likely that aptitudes do develop in a transactional manner, with interests, time spent, and educational experiences conspiring together over time in a dynamic manner (Ackerman, 2018; Bouchard, 2018; Peng et al., 2019). For example, if you have a natural aptitude for a skill (e.g., playing soccer or playing the piano) you might be drawn to it and practice the skills frequently. As you get better at it, the attractive value of the skill grows, and you may spend even more time on it and seek out teachers of some kind to get even better at it. Moreover, as we shall see in the final section of this chapter, on expertise, skills "snowball" over time such that once you are really good at something, you can pick up new knowledge and skills in that area even faster. More developmental work to examine this prediction is needed.

Relation of Aptitude to Achievement

It has already been noted that the most recent theorizing and empirical work on aptitude pertained to predicting performance in school and responsiveness to particular kinds of instruction. Moreover, many of these studies used measures of Gf and Gc or prior achievement (Corno et al., 2002). As noted above, measures of intelligence correlate about $r = .40$ with achievement, and measures of prior domain-specific achievement correlate between $r = .50$ and $r = .70$ (Byrnes, 2020). However, it is not clear that intelligence tests or achievement tests measure aptitude per se. Gettinger (1984) reported that a handful of studies have shown that measures of time to learning (how many attempts are needed) predicted achievement over and above measures of intelligence. More work in the area is needed.

Note that aptitude will only be a strong factor in achievement if (1) teachers give a fixed amount of time to learn content (e.g., a 2-week instructional unit) and that amount of time is not enough for low-aptitude students, and (2) students only have one attempt to demonstrate mastery. If students are given ample time, and a *mastery learning* grading system is used (where students keep plugging away until the skill is mastered), there should be no predictive value of aptitude, since all students who persist will learn the material.

THE NATURE AND DEVELOPMENT OF EXPERTISE

The Nature of Expertise

The construct of expertise grew out of a series of studies in the 1970s conducted by researchers in the IP tradition (see Chapter 3). These researchers originally intended to compare the performance of artificial intelligence computer programs for different skills (e.g., playing chess) to that of human experts, as a means of testing their theory of what the skills entailed (Feltovich, Prietula, & Ericsson, 2018). If they wrote the code for the software properly, the computer would make the same moves as the expert. But after these initial studies, follow-up studies were conducted to better understand the nature of expertise itself. In fact, many studies were soon conducted to identify the unique talents of experts compared to novices in very diverse areas (chess, radiology, taxi drivers, waiters, physicists, tennis, etc.; Feltovich et al., 2018; Glaser & Chi, 1988). A Web of Science search conducted for this chapter revealed that, since 2005, over 13,000 publications cite the works of the leading figure in the study of expertise, K. Anders Ericsson. Hence, there clearly is interest in this construct.

An expert in some domain is someone who is capable of "reproducibly superior performance on representative tasks that capture the essence of expertise in real world domains" (Ericsson, 2014). As with other definitions in this chapter, we can unpack this definition a little further. "Reproducibly superior performance" means that the performer did not get lucky and perform extremely well just once. To validate that someone is a true expert, researchers in this area tried to locate domains in which there were credible organizations that certified increasingly higher levels of performance (e.g., novice chess player to Grand Master; tennis rankings). Studies that compare novices to experts should ask novices and experts to perform tasks that capture the essence of expertise in a specific real-world domain (e.g., playing an actual chess game; solving physics problems).

When studies are conducted in this manner, the first distinguishing feature of experts that becomes apparent is *the extent and nature of their knowledge* (Feltovich et al., 2018). Not only do experts know a lot more about a subject area than novices, but also this knowledge is more hierarchically organized, more abstract, and organized around principles of their domain. For example, when presented with physics problems, experts organize them by theoretical principle (e.g., the first law of thermodynamics) but novices group them by superficial features (e.g., both had an inclined plane in them but different principles were involved). In other words, there is not only breadth but also depth of knowledge in an expert. Their knowledge is also more accessible and organized in such a way that it helps them solve problems and reason. Novices, in contrast, not only have less knowledge; their knowledge is also more concrete and less hierarchically organized. Because they are novices, each time they encounter a problem, it is often the first time they have encountered this problem. Experts, in contrast, develop schemata for problems that they have encountered hundreds of times (see Chapter 3 for a discussion of schema theory). Their knowledge is more usable because it is situational or contextual; when confronted with a problem, they recognize being in a similar situation before and how they solved a problem of this type previously. They develop "situation models" of a problem (see Chapter 9 for a discussion of situation models in reading).

A number of advantages accrue to experts because of their extensive knowledge, its organization, and its accessibility. The first is that *experts are able to integrate multiple features of a situation into a single "chunk"* (see Chapter 4, on memory). A chessboard with 15 pieces arranged in a meaningful pattern (a few moves away from checkmate) is processed by an expert as a single chunk that they can reproduce when they are asked to place the pieces back where they were when presented with an empty chessboard. Novices are overwhelmed by having to process the locations of 15 pieces because that information exceeds their WM capacity. However, if experts are asked to remember the locations of 15 randomly arranged chess pieces, their performance matches that of novices (Feltovich et al., 2018).

The second benefit is that *experts can solve problems in their domain much faster than novices can.* They have solved the same problem so many times before that the solution comes to mind automatically and quickly. The third benefit is that *experts' working memories are taxed far less because of the chunking process, the automaticity of their retrieval, and their ability to off-load items in working memory to long-term memory* (Feltovitch et al., 2018). The fourth benefit is that *the reduction in working memory demands allows experts to more readily monitor and evaluate their performance so that adjustments can be made.*

One final point to be made is that expertise is limited to a single domain of knowledge (Feltovich et al., 2018). Experts are not considered to be talented individuals who would perform at a high level on other domains. In other words, they would not be expected to have more *g* than non-experts. Consider the case of one of the greatest basketball players in history: Michael Jordan. Jordan led his team to three NBA championships and accumulated a record of accomplishments that was only surpassed by two or three other players. Yet, when he left basketball to try his hand at baseball, he never performed well enough to ever get out of the minor leagues. When the IQs of chess experts or professional betters were examined, early studies showed no relationship between intelligence and expert performance (Feltovich et al., 2018). So, expertise is highly domain-specific, according to expertise theorists. That said, the behavior of experts in their own domain could clearly be characterized as being highly intelligent, if we appeal to the definitions of Sternberg, Gottfredson, and Mayer discussed earlier in this chapter. In this sense, expertise can compensate for having an average or lower IQ (Schneider & Bjorklund, 1992).

The Development of Expertise

How does one become an expert in a particular domain? Retrospective studies of individuals who reached the level of "reproducibly superior performance" suggested that two factors were particularly important: (1) 3–4 hours per day of *deliberate practice* over a long time span (e.g., 10 years) and (2) access to, and feedback from, a mentor, teacher, or coach who recognized flaws in the current level of performance and suggested new ways of approaching the task (Feltovich et al., 2018). With deliberate practice, a person engages in activities that are very difficult to perform and are designed to extend the current level of execution. Accomplished pianists might try to play an extremely difficult piece by Beethoven that requires extraordinary dexterity. In interviews, both Mia Hamm and Michael Jordan reported practicing skills (e.g., soccer dribbling or basketball shots, respectively) hundreds of times over a 4-hour, daily practice period. But mentors are needed when performance plateaus at a particular level and no further improvement seems to be occurring.

Advocates of expertise theory have argued that these two factors are sufficient to explain who becomes an expert. But the theory has the corollary that anyone can become an expert in any domain (Detterman, 2014). That claim has led to the most criticism of the theory, as we shall see in the next section.

Critique of Expertise Theory

The criticisms of expertise theory are well laid out in a special issue of the journal *Intelligence* that was edited by prominent intelligence researcher Douglas Detterman (Detterman, 2014). Essentially, the authors of the articles contained in that special issue pointed out a number of findings that show how there clearly is an ability or aptitude dimension to expertise. As just one example, multiple studies have found a correlation between IQ and chess playing, contradicting the original finding. In other words, it is not true that anyone can attain the highest level of performance in chess. Only those people who have the requisite skill set can do so. In addition, consider who could or would engage in 4 hours of arduous deliberate practice per day for 10 years. Such an individual must have an extremely high level of motivation, a growth mindset (see Chapter 5, on motivation), and self-efficacy. They also need the support of parents and the financial means to retain a mentor. Consider how Mia Hamm's mother allowed her to travel all around the country with her coach acting as her legal guardian when she was a teenager. In any event, Anders Ericsson was allowed to respond to the criticisms in the special issue and later in Feltovich et al. (2018) but was unmoved by them. He found as many flaws in the studies and argumentation of his critics as they found in the earlier arguments and studies of expertise. So the debate continues.

IMPLICATIONS FOR EDUCATION

If teachers have students who come to their classrooms at the start of a semester with different levels of intelligence, aptitude, or expertise, what are teachers supposed to do? National studies of teachers' self-reported teaching behaviors show that teachers tend to stick closely to a mandated curriculum rather than individualize instruction to the needs of students (Byrnes, 2020). So, if a curriculum adopted in a school district requires that students have certain prerequisite skills in order for the curriculum to be effective (e.g., phonological processing skills in the case of beginning reading instruction; see Chapter 9), teachers report presenting that mandated curriculum even to students who lack the prerequisite skills. In addition, following the lead of Binet in 1905, many schools use ability grouping, especially during language arts instruction, to sort students into groups so that teachers can ostensibly present instruction in a manner appropriate to their ability (what is taught, how it is taught, and the pace of instruction) (Loveless, 2013). Three alternatives to ability grouping are to (1) target the level of instruction toward the mass of students in the middle, thereby teaching beyond the ability of the lowest performers, but below the level needed to help the students at the highest level to progress, (2) create an intervention to equate incoming intelligence, aptitude, or expertise and teaching the same way to all students, and (3) use individualized differentiated instruction.

Ability grouping was commonplace from the 1960s to the early 1990s, until various national groups argued that it should stopped because it was alleged that ability grouping unnecessarily harmed minority students (Loveless, 2013). However, the practice appears to be making a comeback. After examining teacher reports collected during the National Assessment of Educational Progress (NAEP) that is conducted every few years, Loveless (2013) reported that the percentage of teachers using ability groups rose from 28% in 1998 to 71% in 2009. For this chapter I examined the publicly available Early Childhood Longitudinal Study (ECLS) of 2011 database (*https://nces.ed.gov/ecls/dataproducts.asp*). The ECLS-K (ECLS—Kindergarten) 2011 database includes over 18,000 children and their teachers from all across the United States. The percentages of kindergarten teachers reporting that they used reading and math groups 5 days a week were 46% for reading and 17% for math. In first grade, these percentages were 51% and 15%. However, the percentages reporting that they never used ability groups were 12% (reading) and 37% (math) in kindergarten, and 9% (reading) and 30% (math) in first grade. The rest used ability groups 1–4 days a week. When teachers used ability grouping, the average number of reading groups were 4.28 in kindergarten and 4.29 in first grade; for math, the number of groups were 3.40 in kindergarten and 2.79 in first grade. With an average teacher-reported enrollment of 21 students per class (range = 8–33), that means the average numbers of children per group were 4.9 (kindergarten and first-grade reading), 6.2 (kindergarten math), and 7.5 (first-grade math).

Note that the practice of using intelligence test scores to group children largely stopped in the 1980s after lawsuits alleged that minority children were disproportionately assigned to the lowest groups (e.g., the 1979 ruling of Justice Rufus W. Peckham). Moreover, children tend to stay in their ability groups as opposed to move up or move down (Oakes, 1985). These days, achievement test scores or short reading tests are used to assign students to groups.

If you compare the students of teachers in ECLS-K who used ability groups every day in reading to the students of teachers who used it less often, the means are 93.1 for fewer than 5 days and 92.1 for 5 days. This is a statistically significant difference but mostly because of the extremely large sample size. The effect size is $d = 0.05$, which is essentially zero. Thus, it would not appear that the use of ability groups produces a meaningful deficit, but it does not appear to improve reading achievement either, contrary to its intended function. It may also be the case that teachers do not differentiate their instruction by group as noted earlier.

The third alternative mentioned above is differentiated instruction, in which children's strengths and weaknesses are identified and one tailors instruction to their current ability. One promising approach to differentiated instruction, called individualizing student instruction (ISI), was developed by Carol Connor of the University of California, Irvine, and her colleagues at several other institutions (Connor et al., 2013). The ISI intervention consisted of three components: professional development of the teachers, provision of a software package called "Assessment to Instruction" (A2i), and implementation in the classroom. The professional-development component consisted of a half-day workshop at the beginning of the school year, monthly "community of practice" meetings with fellow teachers to discuss instructional issues, and biweekly classroom-based support from certified teachers. The A2i uses three scores from children (word reading, comprehension, and vocabulary) to prescribe the amount of time that they should spend in specific activities (e.g., working with the teacher in small groups versus working on tasks with a peer). For example, it might prescribe 35 minutes of child-managed seatwork on code-focused tasks (e.g., how to pronounce words) for a child tested to be at the kindergarten level for reading skills, but only 5 minutes for a child tested to be at a second-grade level. Teachers were trained in how to use the software to develop activities for each child and how much time to spend on each. There was also an explicit design to focus both on code-related skills (e.g., the alphabetic principle, decoding) and on meaningful reading. Thus, they used a balanced approach to reading instruction (see Chapter 9 for more on a balanced approach). Moreover, Connor et al. used the best experimental method to see if this individualized instruction was causally responsible for improved reading scores over business-as-usual instruction: random assignment to classrooms. Half of the participating teachers were randomly assigned to ISI for reading, and half were randomly assigned to ISI for math. Children and their teachers were then followed from first grade (29 teachers) to third grade (40 teachers).

Results showed that children given individualized instruction outperformed their peers who were given the standard, business-as-usual reading instruction that was not tailored to their needs. In addition, they found that children who were only given the individualized instruction in first grade did not maintain their advantage over time. Rather, it was best for children to have individualized instruction in first, second, and third grades.

CHAPTER 8

The Development of Spoken Language Competence

As discussed previously, Chapters 2–7 all focus on constructs that are highly predictive of success in school. In the present chapter, that focus continues by examining yet another strong predictor: spoken language competence. Spoken language competence not only forms the basis of reading skills (as we shall see in Chapter 9), it should also be seen as a cognitive filter through which all knowledge that is transmitted vocally is acquired (Byrnes & Wasik, 2019). In particular, when students are listening to their teachers teach, they are processing this information via their spoken language skills. As a particularly clear example of how important this ability is, consider the problems faced by immigrants who come to schools in the United States without mastery of English (Byrnes & Wasik, 2019). Or, imagine yourself studying abroad and trying to process what teachers are saying in a foreign language in which you have limited proficiency.

In what follows, spoken language competence will be distilled into its component aspects. As each component is discussed, the nature of that component will be described followed by a consideration of age trends in that component.

THE NATURE AND DEVELOPMENT OF SPOKEN LANGUAGE COMPETENCE

What does it mean to say that a child has spoken language competence? One way to answer this question is to consider what people mean when they say that a friend is fluent in a foreign language, such as Spanish. Informally, people usually mean that the friend (1) knows the meaning of a number of Spanish words, (2) pronounces these words correctly, and (3) puts the right endings on these words and arranges them into proper sequences. Linguists call these three aspects of competence *phonological knowledge, semantic knowledge,* and *grammatical knowledge,* respectively (Byrnes & Wasik, 2019). This triadic definition of spoken language competence is certainly reasonable because it would hardly make sense to say that someone was fluent in Spanish if that person only knew a handful of Spanish words, or pronounced these words awkwardly and incorrectly, or always put the wrong endings on words (e.g., the male ending on adjectives assigned to female nouns, second-person verb endings when speaking in the first person). In addition, however, there are other aspects of spoken language competence that these core aspects are embedded within, such as conversational skills, understanding the different ways to say something and attain your goals, inferring the intent of speakers from what they say, and the understanding and use of figurative language (Byrnes & Wasik, 2019). Linguists use the term *pragmatics* to refer to these additional aspects of spoken language competence. In what follows, we shall examine the development of the phonological, semantic, grammatical, and pragmatic components of spoken language competence in turn.

THE NATURE AND DEVELOPMENT OF THE PHONOLOGICAL COMPONENT

The Nature of Phonological Competence

There are two kinds of phonological processing skills that children have to master to be able to communicate effectively and perform well in school: receptive and productive. Children who have *receptive phonological skills* have the ability to recognize the typical sound patterns of their native language when they serve as listeners in communicative exchanges. In traditional accounts, these recognition abilities are said to occur at four levels: phoneme, syllable, word, and prosody (Nygaard & Pisoni, 1995). When listeners analyze sounds at the *phoneme* level, they can tell the difference between individual phonemes, such as /buh/ and /puh/. Phonemes are the smallest units of sound in a language that, when changed, cause a change in meaning (e.g., *pat* means something different than *bat*). English contains 45 different phonemes that a child eventually has to recognize and discriminate. Children growing up in countries in which English is not the native language usually need to learn phonemes that differ from those in English. Moreover, some languages have fewer than 45 phonemes, while others have more than 45.

At the *syllable* level, a listener can "hear" the number of syllables in a word (e.g., they know that *bod-i-ly* has more syllables than *bo-dy*).

Syllables are composed of phonemes and are, therefore, one level higher up in the sound hierarchy. Spoken *words,* in turn, are composed of syllables (and, by implication, composed of phonemes, as well). At the word level, listeners can recognize words that are already in their vocabularies (e.g., *trouble*) and also know when a word is not familiar. For example, are the words *festiculate, blerpo,* and *evanescent* real English words? If you said "No" or "I'm not sure," that means that you do not recognize the words because sound-based copies are not stored in your memory (or at least not retrieved from memory). To recognize anything (e.g., a face, a song, a word, a scent), you need a copy or representation of it stored in your memory that is matched to what you see, hear, or smell.

At a still higher level of abstraction is the prosody level. *Prosody* includes such aspects as speaking rate, rhythmic patterns, pitch, and intonation changes. For example, you can probably tell when someone is speaking Japanese versus German even if you do not know any Japanese or German words. This characteristic, global "sound" of a language, is what linguists mean by prosody. Having prosodic listening skills is a little like being able to recognize various styles of music (e.g., rock, jazz, folk, rap) even when songs are sung in different languages (e.g., a hip-hop song sung by a German-speaking group sounds a lot like a hip-hop song sung by an English-speaking group).

In addition to the traditional sound categories of phoneme, syllable, word, and prosody, it is also important to acknowledge units of sound called onsets and rimes. The *onset* of a word is the initial sound that can be used to create *alliterations*. For example, in the alliteration "The crocodile cracked crystals," the last three words all have the same onset (i.e., *cr-*). The *rime* of a word, in contrast, is the portion of a word that remains when one removes the onset (and vice versa). As the name implies, one creates words that rhyme by selecting words that all have the same rime or ending (e.g., *cat, hat,* and *fat* all have the *-at* rime). We would say, then, that children who have high levels of receptive phonological skills have the ability to recognize sounds at the phoneme, syllable, onset, rime, word, and prosody levels.

In addition to these receptive abilities, however, phonological processing competence also includes the ability to produce these sound patterns oneself when one serves as a speaker in communicative exchanges. Children would be said to have high levels of *productive phonological competence* if they can (1) produce all of the phonemes of their native language; (2) combine these phonemes into higher units, such as syllables, onsets, rimes, and words; and (3) create multiword expressions that have the characteristic prosodic features of their native language. Note that it is often possible to have some of these abilities without having the others. For example, children may be able to recognize all of the phonemes in their language and be able to produce individual phonemes but still not be able to combine sounds into syllables or words or identify the onset or rime of words. Similarly, comedians such as Billy Crystal or Dana Carvey can sound as if they are speaking French, Japanese, or German without using real French, Japanese, or German words. They can do this because of their deft imitation of the prosodic features of these languages (e.g., speaking rates, intonations, pauses, and sounds common in these languages).

But one key issue in ascribing phonological competence to an individual pertains to the degree of match between (1) that individual's representations and productions and (2) the representations and productions of other speakers with whom the individual comes into contact. Producing sounds that closely match what native speakers expect to hear is what we mean by productive accuracy (Stoel-Gammon, 2011). In order for communication to occur, a person has to have stored representations of sounds, words, and prosody that match the sounds, words, and prosodic features that the person hears in his or her immediate environment. The match does not have to be perfect, but it has to be close enough that intended meanings could be extracted. Depending on the dialect of English (e.g., British, Australian, Scottish, Indian), for instance, U.S. citizens can have more or less trouble understanding what is said. On a tour in Scotland, for example, I could not understand much of what the Scottish tour guide said as he described an infamous battle. Similarly, when college instructors who are from a country other than the United States are still trying to master English and teach in the United States, English-speaking students often complain that they have no idea what the instructor is saying in class (that the person is "hard to follow"). Hence, nonstandard pronunciations coupled with nonstandard prosody can cause a lot of problems for listeners. Children younger than 3 often pronounce words in ways that deviate from standard usage and, as a result, adults other than their parents sometimes do not know what these children are saying (Stoel-Gammon, 2011). These examples of comprehension failures can be contrasted with cases in which the pronunciation is off base but still is interpretable. For example, listeners who grew up in Chicago usually have little trouble understanding the utterances of a Bostonian (e.g., "Oh no! It's raining, and I just washed my *cah*!") or the utterances of the cartoon characters Elmer Fudd (e.g., "Where is that wascally wabbit?") and Sylvester the Cat (e.g., "Thufferin' thuccotash!").

But in addition to issues of communication, a second key issue in ascribing phonological competence is the nature and quality of a child's phonological representations. In particular, a child may be able to match whole words to stored representations in a global manner but may not be able to match portions of words to each other (e.g., phonemes, onsets, or rimes). As explained more fully in Chapter 9, children have to be able to decompose words into smaller portions if they want to be able to read. In addition, however, it is not enough that their brains can register matches of portions of words at an unconscious level. They have to be able to consciously reflect upon sound segments and matches, as well.

The Development of Phonological Competence

Given the answers that were provided to the "nature of" question earlier in this chapter, the "developmental trends" question can be rephrased into the following, more specific variants: What kinds of receptive phonological skills do children have at birth, age 1, age 2, and so on? What kinds of productive skills do they have at the same ages? When do they provide evidence that they can recognize sounds at the phoneme, syllable, onset, rime, word, or prosody levels? When can they combine sounds into syllables and words? When does their speech take on the characteristic prosodic features of their surrounding environment? In what follows, answers to such questions are provided. In keeping with the organizational scheme used for the "nature of" question, age trends pertaining to children's receptive and productive skills are discussed in turn. Before examining these skills, however, it is important to briefly examine the methods used by researchers to reveal receptive and productive skills.

Methods for Assessing Phonological Competence

The need for an introductory discussion on methods becomes apparent when one considers the challenges posed by trying to assess the phonological skills of young infants. Whereas researchers can simply ask adults whether they heard a /puh/ or /buh/ sound emanating from an apparatus, this approach cannot be used with preverbal infants. Instead, researchers have to resort to other methods that try to exploit some of the skills and tendencies that are evident in even in newborns. The most widely utilized skills and tendencies of infants include the facts that (1) very young infants can turn their heads or vary the rate at which they suck on pacifiers in response to particular stimuli, (2) infants have preferences for certain kinds of stimuli, (3) infants get bored when the same stimulus is repeated over and over, and (4) infants show increased interest and attention when a new stimulus is presented after another one had been presented for many trials in a row.

In one experimental approach that makes use of some of these known attributes of infants, researchers repeatedly play one sound for 20–30 trials (e.g., /puh/) and then introduce a different sound (e.g., /buh/) for the next 20–30 trials. If an infant had been sucking on a pacifier at a certain rate when the first sound was presented during the first block of trials, the infant might show less and less sucking over time (indicating boredom).

Similarly, if an infant had been turning his or her head to hear a particular sound coming from a speaker on the right, the infant may turn less and less often each time the sound is repeated during the first block of trials. This phenomenon of diminished response to the same stimulus over time is called *habituation*. However, if a new stimulus is introduced after the old stimulus had been presented for 20–30 trials, the infant may rapidly speed up his or her sucking or turn his or her head to hear the new sound. This phenomenon is called *dishabituation* (also an *orienting response*). When it occurs, we know that the infant can tell the two sounds apart. When the infant shows continued habituation, however, that suggests the infant does not hear a difference in the two sounds. The technique that examines changes in the rate of sucking is called *high-amplitude sucking* (Jusczyk, 1997).

Alternatively, a researcher may use a procedure in which the infant discovers that two different outcomes are linked to two different behaviors. For example, if an infant sucks on a pacifier at a rate of 60 sucks per minute, an experimental apparatus may play a recording of the voice of the infant's mother. In contrast, if the infant sucks at a rate of 30 sucks per minute, the device plays a recording of an unfamiliar female. Alternatively, if the infant turns his or her head to the right, he or she may get to hear someone speaking in English. If the infant turns his or her head to the left, he or she may get to hear someone speaking in Polish. Either way, when infants show differential responding to the two stimuli (e.g., maintaining a sucking rate of 60 sucks per minute to hear the mother), this behavior suggests that the infant can tell the two stimuli apart. The technique that utilizes head turns is called the *conditioned head-turn procedure* (Jusczyk, 1997).

As for productive skills, the typical approach is more observational than experimental. For example, one may merely record the spontaneous babbling of an infant once a month for a year. With older children, one can record a conversation between the child and the experimenter or between two children. Planned discussion topics may be used to elicit certain hard-to-produce words for children of a focal age group (e.g., *spaghetti* or *spring* for 3-year-olds). These recordings can be coded for the phonemes, syllables, and words correctly produced.

Other methods used with older children require them to be more analytical than reactive or spontaneous. The object of such analytical methods is to see whether children can determine the phonemes, onsets, rimes, or syllables in sets of words (Byrnes & Wasik, 2019). For example, researchers may present a word like *pink* and ask children what it would sound like if the final sound (*kuh*) was eliminated (correct answer: *pin*). Or, on some trials, children may be asked to substitute one phoneme for another rather than delete phonemes (e.g., replace the /puh/ in pink with /luh/). To assess children's appreciation of rimes, children may be presented with a triad of words (e.g., *hat, bat, bus*) and asked which one does not sound like the others (correct answer: *bus*). To assess appreciation of individual phonemes, children may be given a word such as *hat* and asked to tap once for each of the sounds (phonemes) it contains (correct answer: three taps for /huh/, /ah/, and /tuh/). Alternatively, they may be given multisyllabic words and asked to clap once for each syllable. Finally, to get a sense of the degree to which the stored representations of words reside in "neighborhoods" and are segmented into syllables, onsets, rimes, or phonemes, a researcher may use a gating task (Magnuson, Mirman, & Myers, 2013; Metsala & Walley, 1998). Here, one presents larger and larger segments of a word until a child can recognize it (analogous to "name that tune"). All the aforementioned analytical tasks have been used to determine the level of phonological awareness in children aged 3–8 (Byrnes & Wasik, 2019). The subset of tasks that specifically require attention to individual phonemes are thought to assess a highly refined form of *phonological awareness* called *phonemic awareness*. Performance on phonological and phonemic awareness tasks has been found to be highly correlated with performance on reading achievement tasks (Byrnes & Wasik, 2019; see Chapter 9, on reading, as well).

Age Trends in Receptive and Productive Competence

Quite a number of studies of the receptive skills of infants have been conducted since the early 1970s using procedures such as high-amplitude sucking and conditioned head turns. For brevity and simplicity, only a broad overview is presented here (see Byrnes & Wasik, 2019, for a more in-depth summary).

The developmental progression for receptive skills is as follows:

1. At birth, infants can recognize the prosodic features of their native languages.
2. By 4 months, they can discriminate several consonantal and vowel contrasts.
3. By 8 months, they can do three new things: discriminate more subtle or hard-to-detect contrasts, use syllables and rhythmic patterns to parse an utterance stream, and hear individual words in passages.
4. By 12 months, they can use phonetic, phonotactic, and syllable stress patterns to parse utterances into individual words.

In addition to these developmental increases, however, children also seem to become less sensitive to some (but not all) non-native vowel contrasts by 6 months and some (but not all) non-native consonant contrasts by 12 months. Between the ages of 1 and 7, children seem to progress from the ability to recognize whole words to the ability to recognize progressively smaller portions of words (e.g., whole words → then syllables, onsets, and rimes, → then, eventually, phonemes).

The developmental progression for productive skills is as follows: (1) *marginal babbling* (e.g., producing strings of sounds they can make) and pronunciation of certain vowels by 7 months, (2) *canonical babbling* between 7 and 9 months, (3) frequent use of 11 consonant and 3 vowel sounds by 12 months (also production of their first word by 12 months), (4) correct pronunciation of nearly all consonants and vowels at least some of the time by age 3, and (5) correct pronunciation of various blends and difficult combinations by age 7. Canonical babbling is distinguished from marginal and other forms of babbling using two criteria: (1) the presence of true syllables and (2) the syllables are produced in reduplicated series of particular consonant–vowel (CV) combinations (e.g., ma-ma-ma-ma- . . .). Canonical babbling is also significant in that it does not emerge in children who are deaf.

These age trends in productive and receptive skills have been explained by appealing to brain maturation, exposure to language in the environment, and children's motivation to communicate. There are four reasons why scientists have appealed to biological explanatory factors to explain some of the developmental trends for receptive and productive phonological skills that were discussed above. The first is that many of these same trends have been found in a number of distinct cultures (Locke, 1993). For example, the *muh* sound is often one of the earliest sounds that infants make in many cultures, and nearly all languages (97%) have this sound in their set of phonemes. Similarly, infants engage in the earliest forms of babbling at similar ages all around the world. Further, the babbling of infants who are deaf is indistinguishable from the babbling of infants who can hear until the point at which infants who can hear start to engage in canonical babbling.

The second reason why scientists appeal to biological explanations is that children's brains are known to go through some of their most significant changes between birth and age 5 (see Chapter 2). As neural networks in various regions of the cortex become reorganized and myelinated (e.g., the auditory processing cortices in the temporal and frontal lobes; the primary motor cortex), infants may show improvements in their ability to (1) process speech quickly and (2) manipulate various component muscles of their vocal tracts. Skills that appear later may involve brain regions and interconnecting neural tracks that mature later (Gierhan, 2013). In addition, changes in the proportional sizes and shapes of an infant's mouth and tongue could contribute to his or her emerging ability to create consonantal sounds that use the tongue (Stark, 1986). Further, neuroscientific studies of healthy adults and adults with brain injuries support the idea of distinct neural networks for many of the skills reported earlier (e.g., initial auditory processing of speech, detection of rhymes and phonemes, motor control of the mouth and tongue).

The third reason why scientists invoke biological explanations is that very young infants show some of the same discrimination abilities that adults have, and also seem to quickly form stored representations of novel sounds (even within the context of an experiment). Thus, it would appear that infants are born with the ability to encode important properties of speech, in much the same way that they are born with the ability to form representations of people's faces or other objects. As such, many scientists think that it is perfectly reasonable to make assertions such as the following: infants' brains must be wired, almost at birth, to hear distinctions in sounds and to create sound categories out of variable input (Jusczyk, 1997). In other words, since infants can perform these tasks, we have to assume that their brains are already configured to carry out these tasks.

However, in acknowledging some or all these points, one need not advocate a strong form of nativism. Radical nativists assume not only that children are born with the ability to do certain things (e.g., hear the contrast between /puh/ and /buh/) but also that children are born with the stored representations for particular sound categories (Jusczyk, 1997). In other words, one would not assume that infants create a neural network that corresponds to a sound like /puh/ after many exposures; one would assume instead that the network for that sound is already created before a child is born and exposed to auditory stimuli (i.e., infants know what /puh/ sounds like before the first time they hear it). By analogy, a radical nativist account of dancing would invite the inference that a person must already know a particular dance step ahead of time (e.g., the tango) if that person is able to learn that form of dancing from an instructor. In other words, if you can learn it, you must have already known the step.

Scientists used to believe such radical nativistic explanations of the abilities of certain animal species (e.g., song birds or ducklings) until they conducted experiments that showed no evidence that these animals are born already knowing the songs of their conspecifics or knowing what their mothers would look like (e.g., by ablating regions of animal brains known to be involved in learning songs or recognizing conspecifics). Other findings that caused problems for radical nativism pertained to the fact that nonverbal, nonhuman species (e.g., chinchillas) can make many of the same vowel and consonant discriminations that human infants can make (Jusczyk, 1997; Vihman, 2017). People used to think that only humans had such skills because we were the only species to have the spoken language competencies described in this chapter.

These days, many scientists advocate a much weaker form of nativism called *innately guided learning* to explain how various species (including humans) learn certain things (Johnson, 1997; Jusczyk, 1997). The basic premise is that many organisms are preprogrammed to learn particular things and learn them quickly. Part of this preprogramming may simply be a bias toward, or strong interest in, particular kinds of stimuli (e.g., speech in the case of humans; songs in the case of songbirds). Another part of the preprogramming may be the ability to create and store representations of recurrent stimuli. By orienting a young organism to attend to certain categories of recurrent stimuli, the organism can then extract the kinds of information it needs to adapt to the demands of its environments (e.g., the frequency and phonotactic properties of one's native language).

Advocates of innately guided learning also believe that this approach explains the general pattern of findings reported earlier:

> The picture that seems to emerge from developmental studies of speech perception is that infants begin with a language-general capacity that provides the means for discriminating potential phonetic contrasts in any of the world's languages and then winnow the set of contrasts down to the ones most relevant to their native language. This notion is consistent with learning-by-selection accounts [in the neuroscience literature] . . . where it is claimed that the nervous system begins with an overexuberance of connections that are pared down in the course of development. (Jusczyk, 1997, p. 73)

The preceding section suggests, then, that biological factors may well contribute to age changes in receptive and productive skills. However, a purely biological account could not explain all the findings reported earlier. For example, children do not progressively master the phonology of all languages (even those they are never exposed to); rather, they progressively master the specific phonology expressed by others in their rearing environments. Hence, it is exposure to, and internalization of, sound patterns in one's ambient environment that explains why (1) children show a preference for recordings of their own mothers' voices, not the voices of strangers (because they were exposed to their mothers' voices in utero); (2) canonical babbling takes on the prosodic characteristics of a child's own native language rather than those of some other language; (3) children who are deaf do not reach the canonical babbling stage; (4) children can use the characteristic syllable-stress patterns, phonetic features, and phonotactic restrictions contained within their native languages to parse an utterance stream into individual words; and (5) children seem to become less sensitive to non-native contrasts over time. The more exposure a child has to the ambient language-related sounds in his or her environment, the more his or her internal representations will eventually correspond to this ambient environment.

But there are other ways to construe the construct of "experience" besides the idea of passive (yet attentive) exposure to the utterances of others. For example, when children babble, utter a single word, or create multiword utterances, they provide themselves with additional auditory input that they can analyze (Vihman, 2017). In other words, children serve as their own audiences. The quality of this input will, of course, be rather restricted when children are 12 months old (due to their partial mastery of pronunciations), but eventually children will promote growth in their stored representations by exposing themselves to their own utterances. In addition, however, children can use these experiences as feedback regarding their productive attempts. For example, if children want to say *rabbit* and know that adults say *rabbit,* their early flawed attempts (e.g., *wabbit*) can provide them with feedback that can be used to modify how they produce this word. Thus, just as children will never become good at shooting basketballs, writing in cursive, or playing an instrument unless they practice and observe their own mistakes, they will also never become proficient in pronunciation unless they repeatedly try to pronounce a wide range of words (Vihman, 2017). And children show a preference for attending to words with sounds that they can make. Thus, production seems to drive attention and reception. Different children can make different sounds and show different preferences.

A third way to view the role of experience is to consider the ways in which adults respond to or interact with children. Researchers have found that infants vocalize more when their mothers are responsive to these vocalizations (Bornstein & Tamis-LeMonda, 1989; Rheingold, Gewirtz, & Ross, 1959). Conversely, infants growing up in impoverished households babble less than infants growing up in households with higher income levels (presumably because the former receive less verbal stimulation than the latter; Oller, Eilers, Basinger, Steffens, & Urbano, 1995). In older children, experiences such as reading a broad array of books with parents, watching television shows that focus on letters and vocabulary, and playing computer games that focus on prereading skills, all predict the level of rime awareness and phonemic awareness in 4- and 5-year-olds (Foy & Mann, 2003; Scarborough & Dobrich, 1994).

A final way to consider the role of experience is to consider the effect of vocabulary development on children's phonological processing skills. According to Metsala and Walley's (1998) lexical restructuring model, children's phonological representations of words are thought to become more segmented over time as a result of children gaining new vocabulary words. Each time a new word is learned, it has the potential to promote the segmentation of existing representations if the onset, rime, or phonemes in the new word also occur in words that are already in a child's vocabulary. For example, a child who already has the word *snake* in his or her vocabulary might segment the holistic auditory representation for this word into /sn-/ + /-ake/ in response to learning the new word, *rake.*

Because the segmentation process is a function of the words already in a child's vocabulary, each new word may or may not promote segmentation. Given the word-by-word nature of this mechanism, the model further suggests that the restructuring process is likely to take many years instead of happening in an all-or-none, abrupt manner. In addition, the model predicts that words that exist in dense neighborhoods (e.g., *hat, mat, cat, rat*) are likely to be more segmented than words that exist in sparse neighborhoods (e.g., *orange*).

Whereas studies have found a consistent correlation between the size of a child's vocabulary and his or her performance on gating tasks (a measure of the degree of segmentation), several studies reviewed earlier in this chapter suggest that older children's representations may not be substantially more segmented than younger children's representations. However, the study by Ainsworth, Welbourne, and Hesketh (2016) resolves this controversy by showing that level of segmentation and access to phonemes is correlated with vocabulary size, and that access to the phoneme plane emerges over time. If so, it would be interesting to see whether several programs that are known to increase a child's vocabulary also lead to higher levels of segmentation.

Finally, besides biological and experience explanations, researchers have also argued for a role for motivation in phonological competence. Earlier it was argued that the human communication system is inherently goal directed. In particular, the claim was that people engage in communicative acts because they want to accomplish particular goals (e.g., get a listener to do something). One of the benefits of viewing communication from the perspective of goals is that additional implications can be derived from the work of scholars who place a heavy emphasis on goals in their theorizing. For example, scholars who study motivation appeal to goals to explain why people differ in their tendencies to initiate certain activities, expend effort in these activities, and persist in the face of failure (see Chapter 5). Others who emphasize goals are those who study problem solving. These scholars argue that people engage in the following four processes when they try to solve a problem: (1) setting a goal, (2) devising and evaluating alternative ways to accomplish this goal, (3) choosing and implementing the best alternative, and (4) observing the effects of this decision (Byrnes, 1998).

These motivational and problem-solving perspectives help provide insight into two sets of findings that have emerged in the literature on the development of phonological processing skills: (1) individual differences in the level of phonological processing skill manifested by children at particular ages, and (2) individual differences in the phonological processing strategies used by children to solve the same phonological problem. To illustrate the former finding, if one 3-year-old manifests a higher level of phonological skill than another 3-year-old, motivational theory leads one to hypothesize that (1) one child used language to accomplish his or her goals more often than the other child, (2) one child was more interested in engaging in communicative exchanges than the other, and (3) one child was more perfectionistic than the other (and cared whether his or her pronunciations matched those of adults). Motivational theory can also be used to explain why some infants are "intonation babies" who engage in extended bouts of canonical babbling (complete with prosody), while others are "word babies" who produce much shorter babbles (Dore, 1975). Motivational differences may also be at the root of the finding that children who can make the same set of sounds sometimes differ with respect to the frequency with which they make particular sounds (Vihman, 1993). Such differences in the relative frequency of sounds in babbles may reflect personal preferences for making these sounds.

To illustrate the findings regarding strategy choices within problem solving, two equally motivated children may use different strategies to solve the same pronunciation problem. For example, one child may decide to simply not use a hard-to-pronounce word (e.g., *spaghetti*) while another may decide to use the word in a reduced or altered form (e.g., *pagetti* or *bisketti*). Such individual differences in problem-solving solutions are to be expected according to phonology scholars who advocate a problem-solving perspective. The problem-solving perspective on phonology arose as an alternative to nativist proposals (Menn & Stoel-Gammon, 2005). Instead of observing all children using the same strategy to solve particular phonology problems (as strong forms of nativism would predict), children are found to utilize a variety of creative solutions to the same problem (as problem-solving theorists would predict). In addition, children have been found to progressively master the phonology system little by little as they tackle one problem after another. Nativist accounts have a hard time explaining progressive mastery (they imply faster and more systemwide mastery). Further, children differ in terms of the problems they wish to solve at any point. Some may choose to stop substituting /wuh/ for /ruh/ sounds while others may focus on correctly pronouncing blends (e.g., *spr-*). Finally, children sometimes show regressions in their pronunciations after they discover a pronunciation rule that they overgeneralize. Such regressions would not be predicted by nativists. Why would children be preprogrammed to first pronounce a word correctly and then pronounce it incorrectly?

THE NATURE AND DEVELOPMENT
OF THE SEMANTIC COMPONENT

The Nature of Semantics

Earlier in this chapter it was noted that competent speakers of a language have stored phonological representations for words (and parts of words) that they match to sounds that they hear. For example, a woman who turns around when someone calls out her name engages in this matching process. She hears her name, recognizes it, and then turns around. But communication of ideas requires other kinds of representations besides phonological representations. To understand what someone is saying to you, you also need to know the meanings associated with particular sound patterns. For example, to respond appropriately to the question "Can you speak French?," you need to know what *can, you, speak,* and *French* mean. Contrast your ability to answer such a question with the situation in which someone says to you, "Parlez-vous Français?" Many people have heard this familiar expression before and may even have stored phonological representations for some of the words. However, they may not know the meaning of *parlez, vous,* or *Français*. Without stored representations of the meanings of these words, a listener could not provide an appropriate response. Conversely, the tip-of-the-tongue phenomenon demonstrates that people can have an idea that they want to express but sometimes fail to access the phonological word form associated with this idea (Saffran, 2003).

Although most philosophers, linguists, and psychologists have agreed for many years that people need to have stored representations of both phonological word forms (PWFs) and word meanings, there have been many disagreements over the precise nature of the latter. Many scholars have assumed that meaning arises when people map PWFs onto their conceptual knowledge (Bloom, 2000; Perszyk & Waxman, 2018). For example, English-speaking people are said to derive the meaning of PWFs, such as *dogs* and *cats,* by mapping these words onto their concepts of dogs and cats, respectively. In countries where English is not the native language, of course, different PWFs would be mapped onto these same concepts (e.g., *hunde* and *katzen* in Germany, *chiens* and *chats* in France, and *perros* and *gatos* in Mexico).

Further reflection on this mapping process prompted many scholars to contend that (1) conceptual knowledge seems to be a precondition for learning new words (e.g., children need to have a certain amount of conceptual knowledge of dogs and cats before they can learn the words *dogs* and *cats*) and (2) the connection between word forms and concepts is both conventional (i.e., a community of speakers all agree that a particular word shall be used to refer to a particular concept) and arbitrary (i.e., any PWF could have been used besides the one that happened to have been selected in a given community).

One of the benefits of this conceptual knowledge account of word meaning is that it helps us see that word meaning is more than simply the overt labeling of objects, actions, and properties. To the average person, it certainly seems like we are referring only to a specific dog when we say to a toddler, "Look at that cute doggy!" But in reality, the word also refers to the category of things called *dogs* (Perszyk & Waxman, 2018). In other words, the speaker is really saying, "Look at that thing that is a member of the category of dogs!" In essence, one could say that the referent of the word is not "out there" in the real world per se; rather, it is inside a person's head (though noted philosophers, such as Hilary Putnam and Willard

Quine, have vigorously disagreed with this claim). If common nouns do, in fact, refer to members of categories and not just specific individuals, we often do not need to have an actual referent of a noun present in order to have a meaningful conversation about the referent (Sloutsky, Yim, Yao, & Dennis, 2017). For example, mothers and children often discuss animals they have seen at the zoo well after the trip to the zoo occurred (Nelson, 1996).

A second benefit of the conceptual knowledge account is that it helps us see that there is nothing in the act of applying a label (e.g., "dog") to a particular object (e.g., your neighbor's dog) that provides the definition of the word (Pan, 2005). Similarly, there is nothing in the act of describing a particular painting as being "cubist" that is informative as to what it means for a painting to be cubist. Categories are mental representations that specify what members of that category (e.g., dogs) have in common (Smith, 1989). These commonalities might be things that we can detect with our senses (e.g., has four legs, barks, and wags tail), but they might not be. For example, U.S. presidents have applied the term *dictator* to Adolph Hitler, Benito Mussolini, Saddam Hussein, and Vladimir Putin. These leaders are not in the same category because they look alike, sound alike, smell alike, or taste alike; rather, they are in the same category because they ruled with supreme and unrestricted authority. Supreme and unrestricted power is not something that we can sense in the way that we can see that two apples are both red. Note also that the term *dictator* gets part of its meaning through the contrast between that category and the category of leaders who (1) are selected in free elections with multiple candidates, (2) can be turned out of office without force, and (3) have many of their policies rebuffed or rejected by others who share power with them (e.g., congressional representatives). As the foregoing examples illustrate, meaning often derives from the *relations within concepts* (e.g., membership relations, similarity relations) and *relations among concepts* (e.g., contrastive relations, such as that between dictators and other leaders). In noting that shared commonalities may not be perceptible or visual, we can see that word meaning is not simply the association between a word and a "picture in the head," as the average person tends to assume (Bloom, 2000; Pan, 2005). However, it does seem to be the case that we imagine prototypical situations in which we usually experience a referent when we hear a word (e.g., the sky in the case of a bird; Ostarek & Vigliocco, 2017).

There are, then, several important benefits that accrue from casting meaning in terms of the mapping between word forms and categorical concepts. However, this account is not without its problems. The first problem is that scholars disagree about the precise nature of categories. According to the *classical view of concepts* that dates back to the ancient Greeks, membership in a category is determined by a set of *necessary and sufficient criteria* (Smith & Medin, 1981). In other words, all members of the category need to have these criteria and the condition of having all of them is sufficient grounds for saying that an object is a member of the category. For example, the necessary and sufficient criteria for being a member of the category of "square" are (1) having four angles, (2) all of these angles are 90 degrees, (3) having four sides, and (4) having sides that are all the same length. If we change the number of angles, the size of the angles, the number of sides, or the equilateral criterion, the shape is no longer a square. Note that with such a scheme, categorization is all-or-none. In other words, something either is or is not a member. Moreover, all objects that have the necessary and sufficient criteria are equally good representatives of the category. It would make little sense, for example, to say that one square is a better example of the category of square than another.

Based on both philosophical arguments and empirical research, however, it is now believed that only certain scientific or mathematical concepts are defined through necessary and sufficient criteria (Bjorklund, 2004). The vast majority of our concepts need to be defined in some other way because it is often impossible to come up with necessary and sufficient criteria for these concepts (Rosch, 1975; Wittgenstein, 1953). To illustrate, consider the classic case of the category of "games." What makes something a game versus something else? Does it need rules? Do you have to keep score? Can one person or more than one person play? You could try to develop a set of necessary and sufficient criteria, but you would eventually learn that there are always exceptions. Next, consider the category of "dogs." Do dogs have to be pets or bark? What about wild dogs and species of dogs that do not bark? Once again, the set of necessary and sufficient features for even this familiar category does not exist.

Instead of being defined through necessary and sufficient criteria, most of our concepts seem to be defined through *characteristic features* (Murphy, 2002; Rosch, 1975). Characteristic features are attributes that many (but not all) members of a category seem to have. For example, most dogs bark and most birds fly. These criteria are pretty good clues to category membership, but an object does not need to have these criteria to be considered members. As such, membership in a category is more graded and probabilistic than all-or-none. In a related way, whereas it does not make sense to say that one member of a classically defined category (e.g., "square") is a better representative of the category than another, it does makes sense to say that a particular kind of dog or bird is a better example or better representative of its category than other kinds of dogs or birds. For example, a terrier seems to be a better example of the category of dogs than a chihuahua. Similarly, a robin seems to be a better example of the category of birds than an ostrich. The best representatives in a category tend to be those individuals that have more of the characteristic features (e.g., typical size, typical shape, typical behaviors). One would even say that the best representatives are stereotypical or prototypical for the category.

The prototypes of a category are said (metaphorically) to reside at the core or center of the category; less typical members are said to reside at the periphery, close to the border with other categories (Murphy, 2002; Rosch, 1975). So, a robin would reside at the core of the category of birds, close to other prototypical instances of birds (e.g., canaries, sparrows). Ostriches, chickens, and so on would reside near the periphery. This "distance from the core" metaphor has been used to explain differences in the speed with which people respond to questions such as "Is a robin a bird?" and "Is an ostrich a bird?" People respond much faster to the former question than to the latter. The features of prototypes are also highly correlated. For example, features such as long snout, barking, and tail wagging tend to co-occur a lot. It is thought that these features bundle together in children's minds the way phonemes cluster together in spoken words.

Regardless of whether categories are defined using necessary and sufficient criteria or characteristic features, categories can often be organized into hierarchies (Murphy, 2002). For example, categories such as "dog," "cat," and "cow" are subcategories of the superordinate category of "mammal," because dogs, cats, and cows have in common the following features: (1) bear live young, (2) have hair, (3) have mammary glands, and (4) have self-regulating temperature (once called "warm-blooded"). "Mammals" and "reptiles," in turn, are subcategories of the superordinate category of "animals" due to their sharing features common to animals (e.g., locomotion, respiration). The category of "animals," in turn, is itself a subcategory of its superordinate category, of "living things." Hence, many categories have subordinate categories beneath them (e.g., "terriers" and "German shepherds," in the case of "dogs") but also superordinate categories above them (e.g., "dog" and "cat" have "mammal" over them). This hierarchical arrangement of categories has been used to explain the different speeds in which people answer questions such as "Do birds fly?" and "Do bird birds breathe?" The attribute of flying is thought to be linked to the category of "birds," but the attribute of breathing is thought to be linked several tiers up the hierarchy to the category of "living things" (Rosch, 1975).

In considering the features that define particular levels of a conceptual hierarchy, it has been argued that the *basic level* might be the most conceptually primitive or easiest to acquire (Mervis & Crisafi, 1982). Why? Instances of basic levels stand out because basic levels maximize within-category similarity (e.g., a dog is more similar to another dog than it is to a cat) as they highlight between-category differences that are not too difficult to detect through visual inspection. In contrast, it can be harder to understand the basis of similarity for superordinate categories such as "living things" (e.g., the similarity between dogs and trees) and harder to see differences between instances of subordinate categories (e.g., the differences between oak trees and maple trees). Recent computer simulations have shown that categories do seem to form in ways that are the best combination of being simple to learn and maximally informative, just as prototypes are (Regier, Kemp, & Kay, 2015).

The preceding discussion of the classical view of concepts and prototype theory suggests that children know the meaning of various nouns when they map these nouns onto categories that are defined by either necessary and sufficient criteria or characteristic features (depending on the category). In addition, it has been suggested that children's understanding of other types of words (e.g., verbs and adjectives) may also be supported by probabilistic representations. For example, actions such as jumping and pushing can be illustrated through both good and bad examples. Similarly, there are very good examples of the color red and colors that lie more on the periphery of the color category of "red" (as a trip to the paint store can easily demonstrate). The graded quality of membership in such cases suggests that some version of prototype theory may apply to actions and attributes, as well. However, this suggestion has been challenged through counterarguments and by findings that provide less-clear support for a prototype theory of verbs than has been found for nouns (Tomasello & Merriman, 1995).

Hence, the mapping-to-categorical-concepts account seems to work best for nouns that clearly refer to categories of things. What about other common kinds of words, such as adverbs? Do we derive the meaning of *quickly* from a mental representation of what all actions done *quickly* have in common? Probably not. Then, there are determiners (e.g., *the*), prepositions (e.g., *to*), and question words (e.g., *what* or *how*) that do not seem to have any kind of meaning associated with them at all. Further, there are other important concepts that are not really categories, such as numerical concepts (e.g., *three*), causal concepts (e.g., X *caused* Y), spatial concepts (e.g., X *is next to* Y), and temporal concepts (e.g., X *happened before* Y). Thus, there must be some sort of mapping between these concepts and word forms, but the concepts are not categories. At present, we know much more about children's understanding of categories and nouns than we know about children's understanding of other kinds of concepts and word forms. A recent proposal is that the human species shares with other animal species so-called core knowledge capacities for representing objects, causality, agency, spatial relations, and numerosity that appear to be present in preverbal infants. Only the human species maps these relations onto language, which allows integration across, and generalization beyond, these modularized abilities (Perszyk & Waxman, 2018).

Finally, a good case has been made that meaning usually derives from units of discourse that are larger than individual words (Bloom, 2000). Consider, for example, the sentence about dogs that was utilized above: "Look at that cute doggy!" The part of this sentence that does the referring is the noun phrase (NP) *that cute doggy*. The listener must access his or her knowledge of the category of "dogs" in this instance (e.g., in order to know what dogs look like), but to understand the sentence or even the NP, the meaning derived from the category of "dogs" must be augmented and fixed using the determiner *that* (which points out a specific dog, not just any dog) and *cute* (which describes the dog's attribute and says something about the speaker's attitudes). Thus, it would appear that the acquisition of vocabulary is really part of a larger story of making meaning out of larger units of discourse, such as phrases and sentences. By narrowing the study of meaning to just individual words, philosophers, linguists, and developmental psycholinguists may have been "seeing the trees but not the forest." Perhaps this tendency is why words such as *what, to,* and *that* have been (wrongly) said to be semantically "empty." They actually contribute to the meaning of larger units such as NPs, prepositional phrases, and sentences. In a similar way, it is sometimes the case that the meaning of a whole phrase or sentence is larger than, or different from, the sum of the individual meanings of words. Consider how the individual meanings of *pretty* and *stupid* combine into the phrase *pretty stupid*. The phrase does not mean an attractive but unintelligent person.

In essence, then, it would appear that traditional accounts of semantics have placed too much emphasis on the categories that supply meaning to common nouns. The story that seems to hold true for common nouns may not provide an adequate account of other kinds of words (e.g., verbs, adverbs, adjectives, question words, determiners) or larger units such as NPs, verb phrases (VPs), or prepositional phrases. The inadequacy of the categorical account does not mean that categories are not involved. Rather, it means that scholars need to develop accounts of other kinds of concepts besides categories that match the categorical account in their level of detail. In addition, scholars need to move beyond the level of individual words to understand how children figure out the meaning of phrases and sentences. In any event, an important aspect of semantic development is children's acquisition of categories and other kinds of concepts that PWFs, phrases, and sentences can be mapped onto.

The Development of Vocabulary and Word Meaning

The literature on the development of word meaning is too large to summarize in a section of a single chapter (see Byrnes & Wasik, 2019, for a comprehensive review). For brevity, some notable age trends in vocabulary development include the following:

1. Children's first words appear around 12 months of age and they may add only about 50 others by the time they are 18 months old.
2. By the time middle-class children are in first grade some 54 months later, however, they have 10,000 words in their vocabularies (an average of 184 words per month!).

3. However, close examination of the changes with age show that the rate of word learning seems to speed up after age 3 and then slow down after age 12.

4. There are large individual differences in the size of children's and adults' vocabularies at different ages.

5. There is a preponderance of *nominals* (names for categories and individual people) in the first words of many U.S. children from middle- to high-income homes but not in the first words of middle-class children from several Asian countries.

6. Some children adopt a referential communicational style (i.e., their first words are nominals), while others adopt a more expressive style (i.e., their first utterances are *Bye-Bye* and *wuv you*)

7. Word meanings become progressively more elaborated, abstract, and integrated with age.

There are quite a number of factors that can be used to explain all of these age trends. For brevity, it can first be noted that *children learn words that they are motivated to learn*. Between 9 months and 18 months of age, children slowly come to realize that they can make utterances to have others respond to their needs. Also, children learn words related to topics in which they are interested (Mani & Ackerman, 2018). Another key factor is that *other components of the spoken language system can help promote vocabulary acquisition* (Byrnes & Wasik, 2019). In particular, *children tend to learn new words that they can pronounce and at least partially match to existing phonological representations in memory*. They also can use *existing grammatical structures to help them learn new words*. For example, in an experiment, one group of children might be shown a stuffed animal and told, "This is blurpie. He likes to eat chocolate worms." Another might be shown the same animal but told, "This is a blurpie. Blurpies like to eat chocolate worms (Naigles & Swenson, 2007). Because of syntax, the first group would think that Blurpie is a proper name. The second, however, would think that Blurpie refers to a category of stuffed animals.

A third factor that promotes vocabulary acquisition is the development of *an aspect of social cognition called theory of mind* (Bloom, 2000). Between ages 3 and 5, children develop the capacity to infer the mental states of other people. This will help them understand communicative intents and recognize that communities of people share the understanding of what words refer to (Tomasello, 2011). Children who lack theory of mind skills, such as those diagnosed with ASD, have a great deal of difficulty learning language (Bloom, 2000). *Last but not least, children need to be exposed to new words*. This exposure can occur through conversations with peers and adults, and through forms of book reading in which the book acts as a catalyst for conversations (Wasik & Hindman, 2020).

THE NATURE AND DEVELOPMENT
OF GRAMMATICAL SKILLS

The Nature of the Grammatical Component

As will be emphasized more clearly in the section below about the pragmatics component of spoken language competence, *people make utterances to accomplish particular communicative goals* (Tomasello, 2011). For example, when speakers have the goal of informing listeners of something that they believe to be true (e.g., the traits of a friend), they often accomplish this goal using a declarative format that contains an explicit subject (e.g., "Rosa" in "Rosa is very nice"). In contrast, when speakers want listeners to do something as soon as possible (e.g., move away from something dangerous), they often express this goal using a subjectless imperative format (e.g., "Get out of the way!"). In order for communication to be successful, both speakers and listeners have to be familiar with the conventional formats that are normally used to express various goals. There are, of course, several ways to accomplish the same goal (e.g., using the declarative format "I wish I knew what time it was," instead of the interrogative format "Can you tell me the time?"), but this fact does not undermine the need to know how to create multiword structures that are likely to be interpreted as intended (Hopper, 2015).

Up to this point in the chapter, we have said that competent speakers know how to produce the PWFs of their language (e.g., /fa/-/ther/) and also know the meanings associated with these PWFs (e.g., male caregiver). Whereas having such phonological and semantic knowledge is necessary for successful communication, it is not sufficient. To see this, consider the hypothetical case of an adult male who only had four words in his vocabulary (but could pronounce them perfectly!): *you, give, money,* and *me.* Imagine next that he wanted his boss to pay him his weekly salary (= his communicative goal). If he said to his boss on payday, "You give me money," the boss would probably interpret this utterance to mean that the employee wanted his weekly salary. However, if the employee used the same words but said, "Me give you money," the boss would probably not hand over the check. In fact, the boss would probably expect that the employee would be handing him money instead. As a second example, consider the case of a woman who was a witness to a criminal assault but only has three words in her vocabulary: *Bill, hit,* and *Joe.* When asked by a prosecutor during a trial to describe what happened, it clearly matters whether she says, "Bill hit Joe" or "Joe hit Bill."

As these two examples illustrate, competent speakers need to know more than individual words. They also need to know how to combine words in ways that are (1) likely to be interpreted correctly by other listeners and (2) judged to be acceptable or well formed by other listeners. One aspect of this combinatorial knowledge for English speakers is made evident in the examples above: *word order.* Different meanings emerge from different word orders. However, grammatical knowledge involves more than arranging words in conventional orders. It also involves knowing how to (1) add endings onto words (called *inflections*) and (2) insert various grammatical function words (GFWs) in appropriate places in an utterance (Tomasello & Brooks, 1999). To illustrate the role of inflections, consider our four-word employee again. Imagine that the next time he saw his boss, he merely wanted to express his delight over getting paid a few days earlier. If he said with a broad smile, "You hand me money!" (to mean "I like you because you gave me money the other day!"), the boss may incorrectly infer that the employee wanted to get paid again (too soon). It would be useful, then, to know how to indicate additional meanings in some way. One way to convey new meanings in this example would be if the employee inserted tense into his utterance. In English, speakers often indicate tense by adding -ed onto the ending of verbs. Note how the utterance "You handed me money!" would be interpreted differently by the boss than "You hand me money!" Other important endings include the -s attached to the end of verbs when utterances are about things other than the speaker or listener (e.g., "You walk home once a week but John walk<u>s</u> home every day"), the -s attached to the end of nouns when utterances are about several countable entities (e.g., "I have one chicken but you have 10 chicken<u>s</u>"), and the -ing that is attached to verbs to indicate that the utterance is about an ongoing activity as opposed to something that happened in the past or will happen in the future (e.g., "You are count<u>ing</u> chickens").

Comparison of these four endings (i.e., -ed, third-person singular -s, plural -s, and -ing) reveals that whereas some endings add meanings to utterances that probably could not be inferred without them, other endings seem to be redundant or unnecessary. For example, one could not take away the -ed or -ing from verbs and know for sure when the event described in an utterance took place. In contrast, listeners often can still understand the main message of an utterance even when speakers leave off the third-person singular or plural -s (e.g., Q: "How much does this gum cost?" A: "It cost 10 cent"). Most languages have similar kinds of inflections or designations that seem to have little to do with the meaning of the utterance (Maratsos, 1983). For example, Spanish-speaking listeners could probably understand the meaning of *La gato es grande* (i.e., "The cat is large") even though the proper wording is *El gato es grande*. Thus, gender is one aspect of grammar that carries little if any meaning. In fact, the connection between gender assignment and meaning has been said to be completely arbitrary. As a result, speakers have to learn gender assignment by rote.

In contrast to gender assignment, most aspects of grammar relate to the overall meaning of a sentence in an important way. In particular, it is sometimes said that grammar pertains to using word order and inflections to describe "who did what to whom" (e.g., Saffran, 2003). In our two examples, this connection between word order and agency in English is apparent. For example, Bill is the hitter in "Bill hit Joe," but Joe is the hitter in "Joe hit Bill." But there are many languages that rely less on word order and more on inflections to carry information about agency and so on (e.g., Turkish, Russian, and Latin). For example, there would be different endings on the Russian word for *hammer* in a sentence depending on whether (1) it is the subject of the sentence (e.g., "That hammer is rusty"), (2) it is an instrument (e.g., "He hit it with a hammer"), or (3) something is located on the hammer (e.g., "Her coat is lying on the hammer"). Notice how hammer is spelled the same way in English regardless of these differences in the grammatical role of hammer. In contrast, the Russian word might have endings such as *-e* or *-im* added to the end of the word. Similarly, in Latin, the word for *father* would be spelled *pater* when father is the subject of a sentence, *patris* when some object in a sentence belongs to the father, and *patrem* when father is the recipient of an action. Use of these endings obviates the need for determiners (*a, the*) and prepositions (*to, of, with*) in Latin and other heavily inflected languages. In addition, one could say the words in any order in heavily inflected languages and still get the proper meaning across (unlike English).

Because English and certain other languages are not heavily inflected, there is a need for determiners, prepositions, and other GFWs (also called *closed-class words*). These words contribute to the overall meaning of an utterance but do not themselves have meaning in the way that so-called *open-class words* such as nouns, verbs, and adjectives have meaning (Hoff, 2013). Examples of GFWs besides determiners and prepositions include complementizers (e.g., *that*), conjunctions (e.g., *because, and, when, if*), auxiliaries (e.g., *can, do, should*), and question words (e.g., *what, when, how*). The labels "open class" and "closed class" pertain to differences in the size of, and limits on, these two categories (Bates, Bretherton, & Snyder, 1988). Whereas children learn nearly all of the limited number of closed-class words that they will ever learn by age 6 or 7, they continue to learn new nouns, verbs, adjectives, and adverbs for the rest of their lives.

To see how closed-class terms add to the meaning of an utterance beyond that supplied by open-class terms, compare the following pairs of sentences:

1a. "Hand me an apple, would you?"
1b. "Hand me the apple, would you?"

2a. "Hand me the painting of Jake, would you?"
2b. "Hand me the painting for Jake, would you?"

3a. "You saw a man yesterday. That same man has just arrived."
3b. "The man that you saw yesterday has just arrived."

4a. "Today is Tuesday. I have to go to class."
4b. "If today is Tuesday, I have to go to class."

Speakers say (1a) above when there are several apples present and apples have not been the topic of conversation earlier (here, the inference is that any apple will do). In contrast, they say (1b) when a particular apple has been discussed before or when there is only one among other fruits. In (2a), Jake's likeness has been captured in a portrait. In (2b), we do not know the subject of the painting, but we do know that the painting seems to be a gift for Jake. Use of the complementizer in (3b) allows a speaker to say two things about a subject at the same time in the same utterance. In such cases, complements function almost as adjectives by modifying the noun (compare "The tall man" with the adjective *tall* and "The man that you saw yesterday"). In (4a), the speaker seems pretty sure about what he or she knows (that it is Tuesday and that he or she has to go to class). In contrast, in (4b), the speaker is not sure about the truth of the first clause (whether it is, in fact, Tuesday). The speaker is, however, sure about the connection between the day and classes held that day.

Thus, grammatical knowledge involves knowledge of open-class words, closed-class words, and inflections. It also involves knowing the proper temporal order of words within phrases and larger units (e.g., adjectives usually before nouns in the case of English, adjectives usually after nouns in the case of French) and knowing where to place inflections in order to get certain ideas across (e.g., -ed is placed on verbs, not on nouns or determiners). Speakers who have this knowledge and use it to formulate declaratives, imperatives, interrogatives, and so on will be more likely to accomplish their communicative goals than speakers who lack some or all aspects of this knowledge. Consider how beneficial it would be for a tourist in France to know how to construct expressions such as *Excusez-moi, où sont les toilletes?* ("Excuse me, where are the restrooms?").

Implicit in the foregoing discussion of grammatical competence, however, is the idea that adult speakers have knowledge of different *kinds* or categories of words such as nouns, verbs, determiners, and question words. Why is this assumption of *grammatical categories* necessary, according to some linguists? Consider the following analogy: When people make themselves sandwiches, they typically implement a procedure that has steps. First, they assemble all the ingredients (e.g., find two slices of bread, some lunch meat, and mayonnaise). Second, they place the lunch meat on one slice and spread mayonnaise on the other. Third, they place the slice with mayonnaise on top of the slice with the lunch meat. In order to carry out these steps, the person has to have mental categories of the kinds of ingredients that are normally used to make sandwiches (e.g., bread slices as opposed to chocolate syrup). Moreover, when certain steps are carried out, reference is made to specific categories (e.g., mayonnaise is spread on the bread, not on the lunch meat). Well, the same applies when people construct sentences and questions. They assemble specific kinds of words and carry out procedures that apply to these particular words. For example, to formulate the question "What did you eat for breakfast?" speakers need to retrieve the proper question word from memory (i.e., *what* rather than *how*) and place it at the beginning of the question. Placing some other kind of word at the beginning (e.g., an adverb) is a little like using two bunches of broccoli to make a sandwich instead of two slices of bread. Second, speakers have to retrieve the proper auxiliary from memory (e.g., *do* rather than *can*), place it right after the question word, and apply tense markings to it (e.g., *did* rather than *do*). Again, placing a word from a different category would either lead to the wrong question being asked (e.g., a preposition would lead to a question such as "What in the world did you eat?") or to an ungrammatical question (e.g., "What happily did you eat?"). Similarly, applying tense to words other than the auxiliary in the question would be ungrammatical, as well (e.g., "What do you ate?"). Next, the proper pronoun has to be retrieved from memory (e.g., *you* rather than *we* or *they*) and placed next in line, and so on.

Language scholars make use of this assumption of categories and procedures when they argue that language production is highly *generative* or creative (Chomsky, 1965; Lidz, 2007; Pinker, 1994). Just as there are many possible ingredients that can be combined in various ways to make sandwiches (e.g., different kinds of breads, different kinds of dressings, different kinds of filling), speakers can combine words together in productive, creative ways, as well. The only alternatives to the assumption of categories and procedures are proposals that require specific word-by-word constructions to be stored in memory. If people stored millions of specific sentences rather than a much smaller number of procedures for making them, doing so would be a little like a chef having hundreds of separate recipe cards that each describe the ingredients for one specific sandwich (e.g., Sandwich 1 = wheat bread + ham + lettuce + mayonnaise; Sandwich 2 = wheat bread + ham + lettuce + mustard; Sandwich 3 = wheat bread + ham + lettuce + Russian dressing) as opposed to a single card that lists the possible categories of ingredients (e.g., breads, lunch meat, toppings, dressing). Moreover, proposals that require highly specific word combinations stored in memory have a hard time explaining people's ability to make *new* statements or formulate new questions that they have never said before.

Note, though, that in saying that speakers (including young children) have knowledge of grammatical categories, such as noun and verb, one need not assume that this knowledge is explicit or that speakers use the same category labels as linguists. Most people become explicitly aware of grammatical categories during school only in the following kinds of situations: (1) when their essays are corrected by teachers (e.g., a marginal comment says, "There is no verb in this sentence"); (2) during foreign language instruction when they learn about determiners (e.g., *la* and *le*), verb endings and other inflections (e.g., *-e, -es, -e, -ons, -ez, -ent*), and so on; and (3) when they are asked to diagram sentences. But note that children can often learn how to perform many things before they know the labels used by experts to refer to specific objects or actions. For example, they might kick a soccer ball for years before their first coach refers to specific kinds of kicks using terms such as *dribble, pass,* and *cross.* If children are observed to always add *-ed* to all regular verbs when taking about past events and never add *-ed* to nouns or adjectives in such situations, it seems reasonable to conclude that they must have at least implicit knowledge of verb-like entities (though this knowledge may be something such as the overly specific notion of "names for actions"). This inference that children have grammatical categories when they add inflections only to the right kinds of words seems particularly warranted when children only hear a specific verb used in the present tense (e.g., a made-up experimental word such as *blick*) but later apply the *-ed* rule to this new term (e.g., *blicked*).

In addition to being a central element in explanations of the generativity of language, however, grammatical categories and procedures are also useful when it comes to understanding the utterances of others. Utterances are easier to understand when groups of words in these utterances are bundled together. For example, when someone says, "The brown dog that you hate is up the street," it is helpful to subdivide the words in this utterance into two major sections or phrases: "The brown dog that you hate" and "is up the street." If nothing else, these sections refer to two holistic, component ideas in the utterance (one about the dog and the other about its location). Consider how *parsing* the sentence in this way provides a more direct or efficient mapping to these two ideas than if word meanings for each word in the utterance were retrieved one-by-one (e.g., *brown + dog + you + hate + is + up + street*). When all the individual meanings are retrieved, it is not clear how they should be combined. *Brown* and *dog* should go together, but what is to stop *dog* and *you* or *hate* and *street* from being combined when they are accessed in an unbundled manner? Moreover, as discussed above, the individual words in this sentence are not specifically the elements that do the referring—rather, the elements that do the referring are the constituent NP ("The brown dog that you hate") and the VP ("is up the street"). Thus, it would seem that people have to have some mental processes that help them bundle groups of words into such constituents (Lidz, 2007).

Many common models of language processing assume that people create bundles using *grammatical rules* such as the following:

1. Sentence = NP + VP.
2. NP = (determiner) + (adjective) + noun.
3. VP = verb + (NP) + (prepositional phrase).

Whereas the entities that are not in parentheses in each rule are required elements, the entities that are in parentheses are optional. For example, an NP could have both a determiner and an adjective in addition to a noun (e.g., *the big dog*) or it could just have a noun (e.g., *Abe*). The basic idea is that people assign incoming words to phrases based on the grammatical category of each word and the categories that have been already assigned to words that were processed up to that point. For example, when listeners hear the sentence above about the brown dog, they are assumed to start creating an NP using Rule 2 above (e.g., *The . . . brown . . . dog . . .*) because they hear the word *the* first (which is a determiner). They keep building this NP word-by-word until the speaker utters the word *is* (Hopper, 2015). At that point, Rule 3 kicks in and they start to build up a VP. After both phrases have been built, they are combined together using Rule 1 above. Hence, listeners are believed to use such rules to create meaningful bundles of words in their mind.

The proposed existence of such rules and the nesting of components of some rules within others (e.g., NP within the sentence rule) show that human language is also *hierarchical* in addition to being generative (Lidz, 2007). Linguists in this tradition illustrate this hierarchical feature using "tree" diagrams such as those in Figure 8.1. One further way to prove the existence of rules is to show how the multiple meanings of ambiguous sentences can be mapped onto different tree diagrams. Figure 8.1 shows tree diagrams for the two interpretations of the ambiguous sentence "The sailor saw the pirate with binoculars."

However, not all language scholars advocate the existence of such rules or grammatical categories such as verb and preposition (Ambridge & Lieven, 2015; Tomasello, 1992). Some scholars, for example, advocate

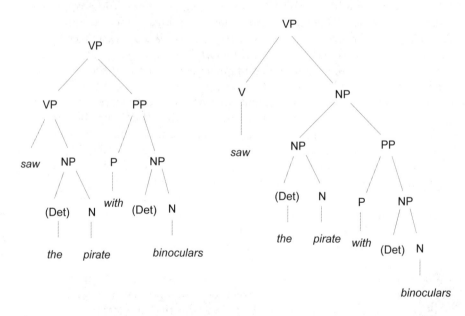

FIGURE 8.1. Partial tree diagrams for the two interpretations of the sentence *The sailor saw the pirate with binoculars.*

mental processes that rely on so-called *argument structures*. In these views, the central element of any expression is a verb. Verbs are the linchpins that describe the relationship between entities that are referred to by other words in an utterance. For example, in the sentence "Darth Vader is Luke's father," it is fine to know that (1) *Darth Vader* and *Luke* refer to particular individuals, (2) *father* means something like "male caregiver," and (3) the -*s* attached to *Luke* is possessive (the parent *of* Luke). But to really understand the meaning of the sentence, the listener has to make the identity connection between the first two words and the last two through the verb *is*. Often, advocates of argument structures convey this meaning using formalisms such as *(Darth Vader, Luke, father of, is)*. The general format is Argument 1, Argument 2, . . . , verb. Depending on the theorist or the age of the speaker, these structures might be only somewhat abstract and general (e.g., *hitter, person hit, hit*) or fairly abstract and general (e.g., *agent, patient, action*).

Hence, scholars differ in the answers they would provide to the question posed at the beginning of this section regarding the nature of grammatical knowledge. Despite these differences, most would agree that people use their grammatical knowledge to create and interpret multiword utterances that (1) portray the relationships among entities in visible, ongoing situations or in mental "scenes" that they envision (Tomasello, 1992); (2) demand responses on the part of themselves or their listeners; or (3) request information that can be used to clarify relationships among entities. As we discuss in the next section on developmental trends, however, the different models adopted by researchers determine the kinds of skills that they look for at different ages. For example, people who believe in grammatical rules often conduct studies to determine when children seem to follow particular rules (Lidz, 2007). In contrast, scholars who advocate argument structures often focus on age changes in verbs—those who advocate for *emergentist* or *constructivist* accounts often focus on the slow, progressive acquisition of grammatical rules and unevenness in development (Ambridge & Lieven, 2015).

The Development of Grammatical Skills

Again, there are simply too many findings regarding grammatical skills development to discuss the concept fully in a single section of a chapter, so we must limit ourselves to describing some notable age trends:

1. Prior to 15 to 24 months, children are in the *holophrase* period in which they only utter one word at a time. Since there is no word order in one-word utterances and they do not use inflections or GFWs, there is no evidence of grammar prior to 15 months.
2. Between the ages of 15 months and 24 months, most children begin

to put two words together; when they do, we can say that grammatical competence has begun to emerge.

3. Early utterances are *telegraphic* (i.e., children include only the most
   important content words in their utterances and omit inflections
   and GFWs).

4. Between 24 and 36 months, children create expressions around
   focal verbs, place inflections on the ends of words, and acquire
   words that serve particular grammatical functions.

5. Children often learn how to say things grammatically before they
   learn a grammatical rule (e.g., *He went home*) but then *overgeneralize* rules to the exceptions after they learn the rule (e.g., *He
   goed home*) followed by eventually using the correct forms again
   (e.g., *He went home*); this age-related pattern, of correct followed
   by incorrect followed by correct, is called *U-shaped development*.

6. Although children have initial difficulty mastering questions, nega-
   tion, and complex constructions, they usually demonstrate full
   mastery by first or second grade.

How might these age trends be explained? It turns out there are several categories of theories of grammatical development that can be grouped
according to similarities in their core philosophical orientations. Some theories, for example, are grounded in the idea that children learn languages
in much the same way that they learn anything else: through observation,
imitation, and corrective feedback. In the language development literature,
these approaches are often called *learning theories*. Other theories, however, are based on the idea that general, empiricist theories of learning cannot explain the acquisition of language. Moreover, theorists in this camp
argue that important aspects of grammatical knowledge are innate. These
theories are, as we discussed above, called *nativist* in their orientation.
Still other theories have their origins in attempts to refute both the nativist
and learning-theory perspectives. Some of these alternatives place a heavy
emphasis on children's agency and conscious problem-solving abilities as
they use language and build up their grammatical structures step by step.
These approaches are said to be *constructivist* or *usage-based* in their orientation. In what follows, these three orientations are briefly described and
critiqued in turn.

Learning Theories of Grammatical Development

In the 1950s, the predominant views of learning placed a heavy emphasis
on the contingencies among environmental stimuli, the behavior of people
or animals, and outcomes. B. F. Skinner was a leading advocate of this
approach (see Skinner's theory in Chapter 3). At the same time, advocates
of these views were extremely reluctant to explain behaviors using mental

constructs, such as imagery, intentions, concepts, and rules. To illustrate this behaviorist approach, consider how theorists in this camp would explain the following behavioral regularity evident in a young female soccer player: Every time the player has the ball in the corner of the field near her opponent's goal and she sees several teammates standing in front of that goal, she makes a crossing pass to them. The sensory perception of her players in front of the goal would be called a *discriminative stimulus* (or S^d). The crossing pass would be called a *response* (or R). Her teammates scoring off of the pass (or her coach yelling, "Nice cross, Amber!") would be called a reinforcer if the frequency with which the pass is executed when the child is in the corner of the field increases over time. To behaviorists, there is no substantive difference between the child's behavior in this situation and the behaviors of other kinds of animals in analogous situations. For example, pet cats often come running (R) when they hear the whirring sound of a can openers (S^d) because running is often followed by an outcome that increases the frequency of running (i.e., dinner). Hence, cat food operates as a reinforcer. Similarly, rats can learn that if they press a bar (R) immediately after a green light (S^d) comes on, a food pellet will be delivered into their cage (reinforcer).

Behaviors such as crossing passes, running, and bar presses cannot be considered behavioral reflexes (i.e., hard-wired responses, such as knee-jerk reactions), so principles of classical (or Pavlovian) conditioning do not apply. In contrast, principles of *operant conditioning* (championed by B. F. Skinner, 1957, and others) do apply. These principles not only explain the regular, predictable sequence of events in such situations (S^d followed by R followed by reinforcer), they also explain how it is that (1) soccer players progress from never making crossing passes in relevant situations to nearly always making crossing passes in such situations, (2) cats progress from never running to the kitchen when the can opener is operating to running nearly every time, and (3) rats progress from never pressing the bar after the green light comes on to always doing so.

To explain such progressions, behaviorists utilize the construct of *shaping*. Shaping involves the reinforcement of successive approximations to the end behavior. For example, to get a rat to press a bar in a cage to dispense food (end behavior), an experimenter would begin by placing a rat in a cage and waiting for the animal to merely face the bar from any point in the cage. When the animal faces the bar (R), an experimenter makes a food pellet come out of a small opening in the side of the cage (a reinforcer). Normally, the animal runs over to get the pellet but then returns to the same position and faces the bar again (this is called *superstitious behavior*—it is built into animal species). The researcher continues to reinforce this facing behavior for a few trials until it is well-established. Then, the experimenter waits for the animal to not only face the bar but now move a bit closer to it, as well (the next successive approximation). When the animal stumbles across this new behavior (face bar + move closer), it is reinforced using a food pellet. This process proceeds for a few trials. Next, the experimenter waits until the animal faces the bar and moves even closer before reinforcing, and so on. Eventually, experimenters can get an animal to reliably press a bar in a cage through such reinforcements of successive approximations. Similarly, one would explain the development of crossing passes and running in the same way (successive approximations are reinforced).

After 20 years or so of successful experimentation with both animals and human subjects on a variety of behaviors, prominent behaviorists eventually turned their attention to language. In the 1957 book called *Verbal Behavior*, B. F. Skinner (1957) explained the development of language in children using principles of operant conditioning. In particular, Skinner argued that the following progression is a paradigmatic example of shaping: making babbling sounds (da-da-da-da-ma-ma-ma-ma) at 6 months, to uttering first words at 12 months (*Mama*), to putting two words together at 18 months (*Mommy kiss*), to putting three words together at 24 months (*Mommy kiss Daddy*), to adding inflections and GFWs somewhat later (*Mommy is kissing Daddy*). In addition, the sight of his or her mother might be an S^d for a child. If the child engages in the behavior of uttering *Mama* after seeing his or her mother (R), and this behavior is somehow reinforced (e.g., the mother looks at or smiles at her child), the label *Mama* would be expected to increase in frequency.

Note that behaviorists would assume that any word or utterance that is used by a speaker is part of that speaker's behavioral repertoire because of a history of reinforcement. According to behaviorists, words and syntactic constructions that are retained in a person's oral repertoire are continually reinforced. Words and constructions that drop out are assumed to be followed by a stimulus that acts as either a punisher or a neutral stimulus (i.e., neither a reinforcer nor a punisher).

Note also that reinforcers and punishers are defined by their effects on behavior, not by whether they seem pleasant or negative, respectively. For example, if a parent angrily says, "Stop that!" every time a child touches an electrical outlet, this utterance is a punisher only if the frequency with which a child touches the outlet decreases over time. If the frequency stays the same, the warning is a neutral stimulus. This point is important because critics of the behaviorist account often refer to a study conducted by Brown and Hanlon (1970) as providing evidence against the behaviorist account of language development. Brown and Hanlon found that parents rarely corrected their children when they spoke ungrammatically (e.g., the child says, "Her curl my hair" instead of "She is curling my hair"). What's worse, they actually responded to such utterances in a seemingly positive way (e.g., "That's right. She is curling your hair"). Nonbehaviorists argued that if the behaviorist account were correct, the frequency of such ungrammatical utterances should either stay the same or increase over time because these utterances are followed by reinforcements. The fact that ungrammatical utterances become less frequent over time was taken by nonbehaviorists to mean that the behaviorist view was wrong. But note that a behaviorist could easily dismiss this criticism by saying that seemingly positive statements could not be properly viewed as reinforcements since the frequency of ungrammatical utterances did not increase.

A second criticism that is often lodged against the behaviorist account is that it seems to leave little room for novelty. In reality, however, animals (including humans) are alleged to always be engaging in randomly emitted behaviors that possibly involve new combinations of old elements. Just as a rat does not "know" that facing the bar will lead to reinforcement (the rat just randomly does it), humans do not always know that their utterances (e.g., "Mama" or "That dress looks nice on you") will be reinforced. Note how this unintentional account is the exact opposite of the perspective of this book (and usage-based theories) in which utterances are constructed to fulfill communicative goals and intentions.

A third criticism is that the behaviorist account could not easily explain the U-shaped age trend for over-regularizations that was described earlier in this chapter. Behaviorists would argue that there must be stimuli in the environment that extinguish the proper term (*went*) at a particular point in time, then others that reinforce the incorrect term (*goed*) at a later point in time, and finally others that punish the incorrect term and reinforce the correct term (*went*) at a still later point in time. To behaviorists, the frequency of behaviors does not increase or fall in an unexplained manner. Rather, increases mean that reinforcers are operative; decreases either mean that either these reinforcers are no longer present or that punishers are present.

But what about the ability of children to add suffixes to novel words such as *blick*? Some early studies showed that when shown a picture of one bird-like creature and told, "This is a blick," then shown two of them and told, "Now we have two of them, There are two____" children say "blicks" (Byrnes & Wasik, 2019). Doesn't that finding cause problems for behaviorism because it seems to demonstrate the use of cognitive rules? Here, behaviorists would apply the construct of *generalization* (Catania, 1998). If a particular S^d is followed by a behavior and then a reinforcer (e.g., a musical E note corresponding to 440 hertz (Hz) is followed by bar pressing and then food), it is often possible to elicit the reinforced behavior (bar pressing) using S^ds that are similar but not identical to the original (e.g., an E-flat or F note of, say, 400 or 500 Hz, respectively). The ability of S^ds to elicit the behavior falls off as the similarity between an S^d and the original training S^d decreases (e.g., a C note of 250 Hz would not elicit it). So, when children correctly say *blicked*, behaviorists would argue that they are merely engaging in the process of generalization (e.g., "He kicked the ball" got reinforced, so "He blicked the ball" would be reinforced, too).

Many readers may not be persuaded by the foregoing behaviorist account of language development. Certain camps of psychologists tend not to be persuaded either. In the 1960s, a different paradigm that was still within the general category of learning theories emerged to deal with two claims of the operant-conditioning account that were judged to be problematic: (1) the idea that behaviors are randomly emitted, then reinforced; and (2) the idea that all complex behaviors need to be built up through reinforcement of successive approximations. To understand objections to these claims, consider the case of a soccer player who never made a crossing pass in her life but does so right after she observes her coach praising a teammate for making such a pass during a game. Such imitative sequences clearly occur in everyday life. The phenomenon is called *vicarious learning* (the child did not get reinforced herself, but someone the child judges to be similar to herself did). In contrast to radical behaviorists who resist attributing mental constructs to people, *social learning theorists* (e.g., Albert Bandura, 1986, in earlier days) argued that imitative behaviors can be explained by appealing to constructs such as goals (e.g., I would like to be praised, too). When imitation occurs sometime after the observed behavior, theorists in this camp argue that mental imagery needs to be invoked, as well (i.e., one models one's memory of what was observed). Social learning theorists use constructs such as goals, imitation, and mental imagery to explain the development of language in children. Note, though, that they still retain the idea of reinforcement.

NATIVIST ACCOUNTS OF GRAMMATICAL DEVELOPMENT

In 1959, linguist Noam Chomsky wrote a scathing review of Skinner's (1957) book *Verbal Behavior*. In addition to arguing that constructs such as reinforcement were vague and circular (and, therefore, the existence of reinforcers is unprovable), Chomsky made a case for the *generativity* of the human language faculty that was widely accepted. As noted earlier, this generativity is said to derive from people's ability to use a finite number of grammatical rules to generate an infinite number of possible sentences. For example, using Rules 1–3 that were presented earlier in this chapter, a person could generate an infinite number of well-formed and novel declarative sentences (e.g., *Sue kissed Eric, Eric kissed Sue, Sue ate the food, Eric hit the ball*). Importantly, these novel sentences need not bear any similarity to sentences that have been uttered and allegedly reinforced in the past (e.g., *The green Martian tackled the fine young sarcastic motorist*). The ability to utter novel sentences that are very dissimilar to sentences said in the past causes problems for behaviorist explanations, such as those involving generalization.

Whereas many scholars readily accepted the validity of Chomsky's critique of behaviorism and the notion of rule-based generativity, some of these scholars found it difficult to accept another claim that he made: Children are innately endowed with grammatical knowledge. Why did Chomsky (1957, 1965) and many others after him (e.g., Fodor, 1983; Gleitman, 1990; Lidz, 2007; Pinker, 1994) adopt a nativistic stance? Some of their reasons include the following:

* *The poverty-of-the-stimulus argument.* Inasmuch as young children demonstrate generativity and systematicity in their utterances, it is reasonable to assume that they have knowledge of grammatical and morphological rules. However, children only hear or experience the surface form of sentences produced by others; the underlying rules that others use to generate these utterances are neither observable nor directly taught to children. Moreover, the utterances of parents are not terribly complex (in grammatical terms) and often contain errors, omissions, and slips of the tongue. If children have to make hypotheses about these rules, what constrains them from making wrong guesses? The poverty-of-the-stimulus argument, then, pertains to the gap between what children come to know and what they experience (Crain & Thornton, 2012). Taken together, these claims about language imply that simplistic notions of imitation could not be correct. Whereas one could get children to parrot complete utterances such as *Je m'appelle Jacques*, this ability to mimic a continuous string of unparsed sounds would not allow children to create similar sentences in a productive manner on their own (e.g., *Il s'appelle Bernard, tu t'appelles Bernice*). If it is the case that (1) children do not learn rules via observation and imitation and (2) they nevertheless use rules to produce sentences, it follows that they must already know these rules or at least know the key elements of these rules. In other words, grammatical knowledge must be innate.

* *The parsing problem.* Before children can create grammatical constructions (i.e., strings of properly order words with inflections), they must have stored representations of individual words. After all, words are the building blocks of sentences. Unfortunately, parents often do not talk to their children using single-word constructions such as *Bottle?* (though they sometimes do; see below). Instead, they use multiword, seamless constructions such as *Doyouwantyourbottle?* To create building blocks for themselves, children have to parse these seamless sentences down into individual words (i.e., *Do/you/want/your/bottle*). How do they do this? Some nativists argue that children can use their innate knowledge of grammatical categories to map portions of input onto these categories (e.g., *dog* onto noun, *bark* onto verb). Hence, grammatical categories and rules (e.g., Rules 1–3 above) help children solve the parsing problem (Fodor, 1975; Pinker, 1989).

* *The inadequacy of domain-general developmental mechanisms.* To develop the structure of language that is evident in well-formed expressions, children need two things: (1) richly structured and systemic input

from adults and (2) a developmental mechanism that is capable of fostering the development of language-specific structure. On the basis of the poverty-of-the-stimulus argument above, nativists argued that the first condition is never met for most children. As for the second condition, Chomsky (1980) argued that domain-general mechanisms—such as Skinner's operant conditioning or Piaget's equilibration (see Chapter 3)—are not specific enough or consistent enough across children to generate language-specific knowledge and structures.

• *The universality and species specificity of language.* Whereas other species such as crickets, birds, whales, apes, and bees engage in bona fide forms of communication, no other species communicates using the complex pragmatic, semantic, and grammatical knowledge utilized by humans. For example, bees can communicate about the location of pollen only by using a very circumscribed dance system. Humans, in contrast, can talk about anything they want in various ways. Moreover, there is a fair amount of consistency in the ages at which children master particular milestones across all cultures (e.g., babbling at 6 months, first words at 12 months, two-word combinations at 18 months). If people are willing to admit that physical milestones, such as walking or puberty, are encoded in the genes to emerge at particular ages, why not language? Further, there appear to be dedicated systems in the brain for language functions (see Chapter 2). Damage to these areas in adults often produces language problems that are difficult to overcome. Together, the findings of species specificity, regular developmental sequences, and brain regions for language are taken by nativists to mean that there is a "language module" in the brain that matures over time.

• *The relative speed and ease with which children acquire language.* Language scholars spend a great deal of time reading works that describe complex grammatical rules and systems (e.g., Chomsky, 1965). Many scholars are struck by the fact that children master this complex system between the ages of 1 and 5 (Crain & Thornton, 2012). They argue that all one has to do is converse with children and they seem to pick up the skills they need. Moreover, whereas very young children learn grammatical rules relatively quickly and tend to make very few errors once they do, older children take much longer to learn most other topics and tend to make many errors, as well. For example, whereas 3-year-olds never apply the "verb + -ed" rule to nouns by mistake, 8-year-olds often misapply addition rules for whole numbers to fractions (e.g., ½ + ¼ = ²⁄₆). The latter error continues well into adolescence despite low grades on tests (see Chapter 12).

• *Three aspects of all languages strongly support the nativist, abstract rules account.* (1) All languages have a hierarchical structure (as described above), (2) rules of grammar make reference to abstract relations that are defined over these hierarchical structures, and (3) some abstract properties of syntactic representations help explain a wide variety of syntactic phenomena (Lidz, 2007). Using knowledge of embedded rules, for example, allowed researchers to devise experiments and show that 18-month-olds had to have something like these rules in mind in order to correctly respond to statements such as "I will play with this red ball and you can play with that one" because *that one* refers to the NP constituent *this red ball* (Lidz, 2007). The property that rules of grammar define abstract relations over structures can be illustrated by examples of how to interpret pronouns. In the two sentences "Hillary decided that she will run for president" and "After she moved to New York, Hillary decided to run for president," the "she" refers to Hillary, but not in the sentence "She decided that Hillary will run for president" (Lidz, 2007). Abstract rules constrain such referring relationships.

- *No one has come up with a better explanation.* In a famous debate with noted developmentalist Jean Piaget, Chomsky (1981) argued that explanations of language development differ in terms of their adequacy. Whereas nativist accounts are not perfect and leave many questions unanswered, Chomsky argued that no one has proposed a better alternative. Until that alternative is proposed, he argued that it is reasonable to maintain the nativist perspective.

In sum, then, nativists have generated a number of arguments against the viability of seemingly simplistic accounts that appeal to constructs such as imitation and reinforcement. Moreover, they have supplied a number of arguments in favor of the idea that children are born with considerable insight into the nature of language. But to be useful to practitioners, nativists have to propose specific kinds of developmental mechanisms that explain the age trends reported earlier in this chapter. For example, they need to supply viable answers to questions such as, "Why do children progress from (1) one-word utterances to (2) two-word utterances without inflections to (3) multiword utterances with inflections, and so on?"

Constructivist and Usage-Based Alternatives to Nativism

A key difference between constructivists and nativists pertains to their level of conservatism (and skepticism) regarding the need to attribute competencies to young children. Whereas nativists tend to be generous in their attributions (even when the competencies of newborns are at issue), constructivists tend to be more minimalistic. In other words, the latter attribute competencies and knowledge to young children only when the evidence strongly supports this attribution. Some constructivists, however, do believe in progressively abstract grammatical schemata but argue one need not believe that children ever acquire categories such as noun and verb (Ambridge & Lieven, 2015).

To illustrate the general approach of constructivists, consider the account of grammatical development proposed by Tomasello and Brooks (1999). These authors argue that there are three basic components of the ability to communicate: (1) mental representations of "scenes," (2) communicative goals regarding aspects of these scenes, and (3) linguistic devices for accomplishing communicative goals. Scenes are schematized representations that involve multiple participants (e.g., people, inanimate objects) that are related to one another in clearly differentiated ways. The participants may be visible in the immediate environment or may be part of a child's memory of an event. In addition to specifying the roles of participants, children's representations of scenes may also take into account various perspectives (their own, that of the listener, or that of one of the participants). The theory assumes that children are motivated to talk about these scenes by commenting on them, requesting or demanding changes in them, or asking for more information about them. These goals are accomplished through the use of word order, inflections, GFWs, and intonation.

For example, given a scene involving a manipulative activity (e.g., a parent knocking over a small tower of blocks), children may partition this scene into participants that play respective roles (e.g., the parent is the agent, the action is knocking over, the patient is the tower of blocks). In addition, children may decide to highlight the outcome rather than the action or the agent (i.e., children may take the perspective of the blocks). If so, they may decide to accomplish this descriptive goal using the passive construction (e.g., *The blocks were knocked over by Daddy*). On another occasion, the child may decide to highlight the agent using the active voice (e.g., *Daddy knocked over the blocks*). On yet another occasion, the scene may represent an unexplained outcome that motivates the goal of finding the person responsible for this outcome. When such a goal arises, a child may try to fulfill it by asking a question about the scene (e.g., *Who knocked over my blocks?*). It is argued that with age, children acquire an increased ability to use language to (1) partition scenes into objects and their roles and (2) highlight individual components of scenes. Which participants and perspectives are highlighted in speech is a matter of a child's communicative goals. As goals change, children discover the need to expand their repertoire of structures and linguistic devices.

After reviewing the evidence regarding age changes in children's grammatical knowledge, Tomasello and Brooks (1999) argued that children progress through four major levels:

1. During the *holophrase level,* children between the ages of 12 and 17 months use single linguistic symbols and intonation to express declarative and imperative goals. These symbols (e.g., *Jenna!*) are distilled from

the larger expressions used by their caregivers (e.g., *Here comes Jenna!*). Which symbols are distilled depends on issues such as the salience of referents in particular scenes, the frequency of terms in discourse, and the phonological stress placed on these symbols in the ambient language. For example, as noted above, first words tend to be nouns in U.S. homes but tend to be verbs in many Asian homes. Inasmuch as children do not use word order or inflections in a productive manner at this level (e.g., they do not always add the plural -*s* to nouns where appropriate), there is no need to attribute grammatical categories to children.

2. During the *word-combination level,* children between the ages of 18 and 23 months accomplish their communicative goals using two-word utterances. These utterances often partition scenes into two components. Observational and experimental studies show that children combine words using the same word orders utilized by adults in their environment. For example, if they hear adults say *That's Daddy's shoe,* they tend to say *Daddy shoe* rather than *Shoe Daddy.* Moreover, the existence of consistent patterns of "pivot-word" combinations (e.g., *More* + _____) suggests that these combinations are productive and that children are starting to form the grammatical categories of noun and NP. Because children do not generally demonstrate similar kinds of productivity with verbs, there is no need to assume that they have created the grammatical category of verb as yet. Similarly, inasmuch as they do not contrastively use alternative word orders or inflections to denote distinct grammatical roles (e.g., "agent," "patient"), there is no need to posit knowledge of these roles either.

3. During the *verb-island construction level,* children between the ages of 24 and 35 months use word order, verbs, and inflections to explicitly indicate several participant roles in scenes but do so in a scene-specific and verb-specific manner. If there were an overall, organized system of verbs, one would expect similar levels of complexity and productivity across all verbs. What is observed, however, is a pattern in which some verbs occur in a single, simple frame (e.g., *Cut* _____) while others occur in a variety of more complex frames (e.g., *Draw* _____; *Draw* _____ *on* _____; *Draw* _____ *for* _____). Similarly, prepositions such as *by* occur only with certain instrument verbs, not all the instrument verbs that appropriately use this preposition. Thus, the words that can fill particular slots in instrument verbs are better captured by concrete categories such as "things to draw with" rather than the more abstract grammatical category of instrument.

4. Finally, during the *adult-like construction level,* children who are 36 months and older accomplish their communicative goals in ways that suggest they have knowledge of abstract grammatical categories and roles. They engage in discourse about scenes using a range of grammatical devices that partition these scenes into two or more participants. Moreover, there

is clear evidence of productivity and systematicity in their spontaneous use of word order, inflections, and GFWs across verbs, as well as evidence of generalization across categories of scenes. The most compelling evidence, however, for the claim that children have moved beyond the verb-island level is in their occasional overgeneralizations and performance in experimental training studies. In the case of overgeneralizations, a child may say *He falled me down* when constructing simple transitive expressions of the form NP–verb–NP (e.g., *Amber kicked the ball*).

Thus, in contrast to nativists who argue that children must be born with abstract grammatical categories, constructivists (and usage-based theorists) argue that children slowly and painstakingly construct these categories over time through finding patterns, creating schemata, and abstracting across these schemata. There is little evidence that children acquire grammar easily and quickly, as nativists argue. Development is protracted, uneven, and contains errors. If a child created a category such as verb from the get-go, why would he or she apply verb-related rules only to some verbs (Ambridge & Lieven, 2015)? In the most recent formulation of usage-based accounts, Tomasello (2011) appends the original proposal that was heavily based on goals, pattern finding, and abstraction to include children's ability to mind read the intentions of others (referred to earlier as theory of mind).

However, as was argued in the prior section on nativist approaches, the constructivist account can be useful to teachers only if it gives a sense of developmental mechanisms. What factors cause children to progress through these four levels of grammatical knowledge? Can these factors be manipulated by teachers in the classroom? At present, comprehensive and detailed models of developmental mechanisms have not been proposed by constructivists who study language development (Tomasello & Brooks, 1999). Tomasello and Brooks, however, speculate that children may eventually acquire abstract grammatical categories and roles in the same way that they form schemata, event representations, and categories in other domains: by "extracting commonalities of both form and function" (p. 179). For example, children might notice that for all their transitive constructions, the participant responsible for an action or state is in the preverbal position and the participant being affected is in the postverbal position. Given the variety of verb islands that children create, the extraction of commonalities and construction of abstract categories would be expected to take some time (which it does).

Other possible factors that could promote the development of abstract grammatical categories and roles include frequent adult modeling of structures in joint-activity or joint-attention situations (e.g., talking about the same scene) and children engaging in frequent discussions about similar scenes. Moreover, the literature on transfer (e.g., Singley & Anderson, 1989) suggests that people are likely to transfer the same solution to a problem across different situations when their goals are the same in the two situations (e.g., Situation 1: locking one's keys in one's own car; Situation 2: locking your parents' keys in their car). If adults talk about scenes in similar ways (e.g., highlighting similar aspects of the scene, such as facial expressions and clothing), they provide models that can be imitated. Similarly, if adults ask children to comment in similar ways across scenes (e.g., ask how the person is feeling), adults may evoke similar communicative goals in children. In general, however, constructivists need to devote considerable energy to the problem of developmental mechanisms before this perspective can be practically and systematically implemented in the classroom.

Although researchers who study the role of parental input in grammatical development are not necessarily all aligned with the constructivist perspective, research on child-directed speech (parentese) is clearly relevant to the contrast between nativists and constructivists. If all that has to happen for innate knowledge to be activated is for parents to talk to their children, then grammar acquisition would emerge comparably and quickly in all children, regardless of how often and in what manner they are spoken to. However, a large number of studies have accumulated that have shown that both the quantity and quality of child-directed speech has an effect on grammatical development (Ambridge, Pine, Rowland, Chang, & Bidgood, 2013; Hoff, 2006; Huttenlocher, Vasilyeva, Cymerman, & Levine, 2002; Huttenlocher, Waterfall, Vasilyeva, Vevea, & Hedges, 2010; Rowe, 2015). Parental speech that is repetitive, contains short expressions, and recasts what children say in the proper format initially helps bootstrap the process. Later, more complex speech (i.e., more clauses and verbs per utterance) and move diverse speech (i.e., different kinds of constructions modeled) leads to more complex syntax. Over the past 10 years, this input focus has gained a certain amount of ascendency in the field.

THE NATURE AND DEVELOPMENT OF PRAGMATICS AND CONVERSATIONAL SKILLS

The Nature of Pragmatics and Conversational Skills

As noted earlier, there is more to being a competent speaker of language than knowing the meaning of words, how to pronounce them, and combining them into grammatical structures that have appropriate word orders and affixes. You also have to be an effective conversationalist, understand different communicative intents, understand the different ways that you can express the same ideas, and also understand nonliteral expressions that involve humor, deception, metaphor, and idioms (Byrnes & Wasik, 2019).

Let's unpack these additional abilities a little further. To begin, think of friends to whom you would assign the label "good conversationalist." What is it about these individuals that causes you to believe that they are skilled in the area of conversations? Do they initiate conversations themselves, or are they provoked reluctantly into making polite banter? Do they dominate conversations and "talk through" partners, or do they engage in a more egalitarian give-and-take? Do they take the needs of the listener into account, or do they drone on about topics that are unfamiliar, too complicated, or of little interest to their conversational partners? Answers to these questions show that communicative competence involves more than phonology, semantics, and grammar. It also involves (1) a desire to communicate with others (i.e., convey ideas to them and receive ideas back), (2) respect for others, (3) a desire to get along with others, (4) reciprocity and turn taking, and (5) lack of egocentrism (Ninio & Snow, 1999). Egocentric individuals have a difficult time putting themselves in someone else's shoes and think everyone knows what they know. In light of these five additional aspects of spoken language competence, one might expect shy and socially isolated individuals to have deficiencies in conversational skills (Ninio & Snow, 1999), or expect that these individuals would not come to mind when one thinks of good conversationalists. One might have similar expectations for overly assertive, rude, and self-centered individuals.

A third way to understand spoken language competence is similar to the second in that it connects language abilities to social competence in general. However, it adds important new insights, as well. As noted earlier, the central idea involves the recognition that *language use is a form of goal-directed or intentional behavior* (Bloom, 1998; Ninio & Snow, 1999; Searle, 1983; Tomasello, 2011). In other words, the claim is that we *use language in order to have certain effects on listeners*. For example, sometimes we communicate because we want to provide information to others (e.g., "Hey, Otto, did you know that World Cup tickets are on sale?"). Here, the primary intended outcome is a change in the listener's knowledge base (though these knowledge changes sometimes provoke changes in the person's behavior, as well). Other times, we communicate to change people's opinions or persuade them to a particular point of view (as in argumentative essays or congressional debates). Still other times, we say things to alter people's behavior or make them do things. For example, Hart and Risley (1995) found that a large percentage of the utterances directed toward children by parents have to do with either getting children to do something (e.g., wash their hands) or getting them to stop doing something (e.g., stop yelling). Conversely, children often say things to parents to have their own needs met (e.g., as when a child says, "Mommy, I'm hungry" as a means of getting something to eat). To get a sense of a speaker's intentions or communicative goals, one merely needs to ask, "Why did he say that?" or "What was she trying to accomplish by saying that?"

But, as many parents of teenagers and spouses fully understand, there are many ways to express the same intention and have an effect on listeners. Although a direct, brutally honest way of expressing an idea gets the point across (e.g., "Dad, you won't be wearing *that* shirt when you chaperone at the school dance tonight, will you? You look like a nerd!"), it is usually the case that a less direct, gentler utterance can have the same effect without hurting a person's feelings (e.g., "Hey, Dad, how about wearing that new blue shirt I got you for your birthday? You look great in it and it would mean a lot to me"). It can be argued that an important part of spoken language competence is "building up a toolkit" of possible ways to express the same communicative intention (Ninio & Snow, 1999). In other words, *competent speakers know a lot of different ways to express themselves, and they choose their utterance options wisely in particular situations.* In general, the idea is to *figure out how to accomplish primary communicative goals* (e.g., get the listener to do something) *while maintaining positive social relationships with others.*

The converse ability is also useful—that is, individuals with high levels of spoken language competence are adept at correctly inferring the communicative intentions of others when they serve as listeners or recipients of utterances directed toward them. For example, a wife might say the following to her husband one week before her birthday: "I just finished a book by Anita Shreve. It was great. I'd like to read more of her stuff." The husband, if he is skilled at picking up indirect requests or hints, might realize that in saying this statement, his wife was hoping that he would buy her another Anita Shreve book for her birthday. Or sometimes people in dating situations say things like "I think we should spend a little time apart" or "Can we be friends instead of lovers?" as ways of expressing the idea that the relationship is close to over. So, if we connect our previous discussion with the present one, it appears that one way to demonstrate a lack of social skills is to be routinely dominating and rude as a speaker (as described earlier in this chapter). A second way is to be a listener who regularly fails to "get the hint."

Linguists and philosophers who study the "meaning behind the meaning" and the use of expressions as instrumental, goal-directed acts are in the field of *pragmatics* (Matthews, 2014; Ninio & Snow, 1999). These scholars sometimes attempt to delineate various "rules" of conversation, such as the four principles of cooperation proposed by Grice (1975):

1. *Quantity principle:* Be informative, but use the right amount of information in doing so (i.e., say no more or no less than what is required).
2. *Quality principle:* Be truthful, and avoid making assertions for which you have insufficient evidence.
3. *Relation principle:* Be relevant (i.e., don't introduce random thoughts that have little to do with the current topic of conversation).
4. *Manner principle:* Avoid ambiguity by being brief and orderly.

In regard to the quantity principle, saying too little can be a problem, as in the case in which a letter of recommendation for a professor has the single line: "Mr. Jones has excellent penmanship." The reader is left to infer that the applicant has no other notable abilities, including those that would be useful for being a successful college professor (e.g., research skills, writing skills, teaching skills). Conversely, saying too much can be a problem, as well. For example, a listener would not want a lengthy dissertation on the history of watches in response to the question "Do you happen to know the time?"

Some have argued that various communicative devices—such as *irony, sarcasm, metaphor, lying,* and *humor*—become effective, in part, through an intentional violation of Grice's cooperative principles (Cameron-Faulkner, 2014). As noted earlier, one need not be direct or brutally honest to accomplish one's communicative goals. Sometimes one can be equally or more effective using sarcasm and humor, which often have the effect of muting or softening the message (Creusere, 1999). The interesting aspect of irony, sarcasm, metaphor, and humor is that the speaker and listener know that the speaker does not really mean what is being said. For example, when a father says to his children in an annoyed tone, "Well, isn't this fun!" after being stuck with them in a traffic jam for one hour, the father does not really mean that being in a traffic jam is fun. Hence, speakers who use devices such as irony or sarcasm intentionally violate Grice's (1975) quality principle to have an effect on their listeners.

Similarly, metaphors and other forms of figurative language (e.g., idioms) are not intended to be taken literally. For example, a speaker who uses the idiom *let off steam* within the sentence "He went outside to let off some steam," does not mean the person actually let off steam (as a teakettle would). Rather, the speaker means that the person was angry and left the situation to calm down. As for jokes, they often bend, distort, or exaggerate the truth for comic effect (e.g., as when Woody Allen said in the movie *Annie Hall* that he was expelled from New York University for looking into the soul of the boy next to him during a philosophy exam). Other times, jokes require holding in mind two meanings of the same expression (e.g., "Why did Snoopy quit his job as a cartoon character?" "Because he was tired of working for *Peanuts*"). Because the speaker and listener know that the speaker is not telling the truth or being literal as a means of getting some other idea across or to make the listener laugh, no harm is usually done.

In contrast, lies are intentionally false utterances that only the speaker knows, at first, are not true. Moreover, the goal of a lie is not to get the listener to focus on the opposite meaning (as in irony or sarcasm), or to enhance understanding through a mapping to a familiar analogous idea (as in metaphor), or to make the listener laugh (as in a joke). Rather, the goal of a lie is to deceive the listener for some other purpose (e.g., the speaker wants to avoid getting in trouble or wants to avoid hurting someone's feelings). In any event, these aspects of spoken language competence illustrate once again that speakers have many options at their disposal to accomplish their communicative goals. These options include being direct, polite, indirect, ironic, sarcastic, metaphorical, idiomatic, humorous, and deceitful.

Whereas some scholars who study pragmatics focus on such communicative options, others delineate the various kinds of *speech acts* that people use (e.g., Cameron-Faulkner, 2014; Searle, 1969). For example, any given utterance can serve to (1) express the speaker's beliefs about some state of affairs (e.g., "It's raining outside"), (2) request information from others (e.g., "Do you know what time it is?"), (3) cause a formal or legal definition to take effect (e.g., "I christen you *Queen Elizabeth II*" or "I now pronounce you man and wife"), or (4) demand that others perform some behavior (e.g., "Stop that at once"). Competent speakers of a language know the usual grammatical form and intonation patterns of such declaratives, interrogatives, imperatives, and so on. For example, interrogatives in English have a rising intonation and either a fronted auxiliary (e.g., *can* or *do*), a fronted verb (e.g., *is* or *are*), or a question word (e.g., *what* or *where*). Thus, the choice of words, intonations, and structures clearly matters when one wants to have a desired effect on a listener. For example, you may not get an answer if you do not execute a question correctly (the listener may not know it was a question). Competent speakers acquire the knowledge they need to accomplish their communicative goals and execute a variety of speech acts.

In stressing the goal-directed aspect of language in this book and discussing this perspective alongside the traditional topics of phonology, semantics, and grammar, the approach becomes aligned with that of a variety of scholars in the *functionalist* perspective on language acquisition (Ninio & Snow, 1999; Tomasello & Brooks, 1999). At one time, functionalists represented a controversial minority in the fields of linguistics and philosophy. The latter fields were once dominated by scholars who take a strong *formalist* orientation (e.g., linguist Noam Chomsky) and are still somewhat dominated by them. Formalists stress the autonomy of language (from the rest of cognition and specific situations) and consider it important to develop rule-governed models that could generate well-formed utterances "on their own." In addition, these scholars tend to believe in the innate origins of language skills, and they also tend to consider goals, context effects, and implicit meanings as epiphenomena or tangential to the core or "real" issues in linguistics (such as phonology, semantics, and grammar). In contrast, functionalists argue that children learn new pronunciations, words, and grammatical structures precisely *because* they are interested in specific topics, want to communicate more effectively, and want to get along more effectively with others (Bloom, 1998; Ninio & Snow, 1999; Tomasello, 2011). In the field of developmental psychology, the functionalist or usage-based theories (Tomasello, 2011) now predominate. As we shall see, formalist and functionalist orientations have very different implications for instruction. As such, it clearly matters who is "right" in this regard. Instruction based on one of these perspectives is more likely to be effective than instruction based on the other perspective.

The Development of Pragmatics and Conversational Skills

Again, it is not possible to fully summarize all the relevant studies focusing on these remaining aspects of spoken language competence, but we can list some important developmental trends. To begin, few children younger than the age of 5 show high levels of insight into ideas such as utterances having multiple or implicit meanings. Moreover, young children tend to be literal, concrete, and largely truthful. After age 5, use of more varied communicative devices (e.g., sarcasm, indirect requests, white lies) increases steadily and seems to level off by late childhood (but sometimes later). The key aspect of children's mastery of these communicative devices is their ability to comprehend and control utterances that are figurative or intentionally false. Depending on the communicative goal of a speaker, false statements may be expressed to (1) convey a negative attitude in a muted way (as in sarcasm), (2) make someone laugh (as in humor), (3) spare someone's feelings (as in white lies), or (4) avoid punishment (as in other kinds of lies). As children grow in their ability to recognize the multiple goals of other speakers (and "get inside their heads" more generally), children also become more apt to respond correctly to nonobvious indirect requests and to possibly express themselves in more polite ways, as well.

The developmental mechanisms responsible for the developmental trends in communicative skills include (1) multiple opportunities to converse with others and fulfill their communicative goals, (2) increases in vocabulary, and (3) increased exposure to examples of sarcasm, indirect requests, and so on with age.

IMPLICATIONS FOR EDUCATION

It was mentioned earlier that spoken language competence is not only important because language is the filter through which information is acquired in a classroom, but also because spoken language is the foundation on which reading skills are built between kindergarten and third grade. As will be discussed in Chapter 15, children differ in terms of the spoken language skills that they bring to the classroom. In particular, higher-income children enter kindergarten with much more advanced phonological, semantic, and grammatical competencies than low-income children (Byrnes &

Wasik, 2019). The same is true for native English speakers compared to non-English speaking children who immigrated a short time before kindergarten.

The main implications of the preceding summary of language development derive from all the previous discussions of the developmental mechanisms that promote improvement in phonological, semantic, grammatical, and pragmatic skills. If children are not engaging in language-promoting activities at home (e.g., frequent conversations and other activities in which new words are presented and more complex syntax is modeled), these activities need to be a core part of their experiences at day care centers and preschools. But it is not mere passive exposure to language that matters. Children have to be active participants in these conversations and practice their increasingly sophisticated language skills repeatedly between the ages of 1 and 5.

A good example of an evidence-based preschool program that promotes language development in low-income children is Story Talk (Wasik & Hindman, 2020). Story Talk includes four key components: (1) *Story Maps* that guide teachers through book readings and extension activities that support children's vocabulary development, (2) *carefully selected books* that present stories that reflect specific themes (e.g., the weather) and new vocabulary words (e.g., *canopy*), (3) *professional development* that provides group trainings to explain the conceptual and procedural components of the program and targeted one-to-one coaching addressing each teacher's strengths and weaknesses in implementing the practices; and (4) *ongoing assessments* of the extent to which teachers implement the program as it was designed to be implemented, as well as children's progress in learning the target vocabulary words presented in the books. Story Maps are detailed guides that include (1) *key vocabulary* words identified from books; (2) *Story Starters,* which contain three to four open-ended questions and comments that promote discussion of the book; (3) *guiding prompts through stories,* which both provide open-ended questions and engaging comments about new words and ideas that teachers can use before, during, and after book reading to engage children in rich language exchanges; and (4) *extension activities* that reinforce and increase the contextualized exposure to vocabulary words. Story Maps capitalize on basic research by organizing instruction around themes and providing repeated exposures to a dense array of thematically related key vocabulary within and across book readings. For each reading, Story Maps guide teachers in three particular vocabulary-building strategies, including (1) specifying open-ended questions or comments that model rich language for children and prompt children to think and talk about new vocabulary, (2) suggesting follow-up remarks to ensure that children use vocabulary in meaningful contexts and get feedback on their language, and (3) guiding teachers to explicitly define or recast words and to invite children to relate them to their own prior knowledge. Since repeated readings (see Morrow, 1985; Vadasy & Sanders, 2008) are critical to learning vocabulary, each Story Map contains three distinct versions to guide three separate readings of the book.

Studies have shown that Story Talk significantly improves children's vocabulary compared to business-as-usual instruction (Wasik & Hindman, 2020). It seems to simulate the activities that happen more often in higher-income homes than in lower-income homes. If implemented during preschool and kindergarten, it has the strong possibility of getting all children ready to read.

PART III
Domain-Specific Academic Skills

CHAPTER 9

The Development
of Beginning Reading Skills

The present chapter marks the transition in this book from descriptions of the set of foundational (and predictive) abilities that play a role in the learning of any subject matter (e.g., memory, executive function, motivation) to summaries of theories and research on the nature and development of specific school-related skills such as reading, mathematics, and science.

Reading skills, the focus of this chapter, are crucial to success in school and life (Byrnes & Wasik, 2019). What makes a high level of literacy all the more important in today's world are the demands placed on readers when they attempt to comprehend materials of a more specialized or technical nature in school or the workplace. The world is very different than it was even 50 years ago, and it is important to consider whether reading skills have kept pace with these changing demands. In the most recent (2019) National Assessment of Educational Progress (NAEP) that was administered in all 50 U.S. states and includes measures of the kind of basic and advanced reading skills required today, results showed that only 35% of fourth graders and 36% of eighth graders scored at the proficient level. What is worse, since the last assessment that was conducted in 2017, only one state (2%) showed a statistically significant increase in performance, 20 states (38%) showed no change, and 60% showed a significant *decline*. (NAEP data are available at *www.nationsreportcard.gov/highlights/reading/2019*.) Clearly, it is useful for educators and parents to better understand what it means to be a proficient reader and how to promote reading proficiency in students.

So much is known about reading that it is traditional to subdivide the research into two foci: the acquisition of beginning reading skills (i.e., learning to read) and reading comprehension (i.e., reading to learn). Children in grades 1 to 3 usually spend most of their time learning to decode words (i.e., map letters onto sounds) and becoming more fluent. After third grade, they are expected to become independent readers who can comprehend narratives and textbook material on their own. Again, because of the large amount of research, this chapter focuses on beginning reading skills, and Chapter 10 focuses on reading comprehension skills.

THE NATURE AND DEVELOPMENT
OF BEGINNING READING SKILLS

The Nature of Beginning Reading Skills

In order to know how to help children become good readers, we first need to know what good reading entails. The task of defining good reading is approached in four ways. First, we shall consider a consensus view of reading that emerged from a panel of experts convened by the National Research Council (NRC; Snow, Burns, & Griffin, 1998). Then, we shall examine a list of the component operations involved in reading a single sentence that have been discovered by cognitive psychologists. Next, we discuss a model of proficient reading that emerged in the 1980s and that influenced many comparable models that are in use today (i.e., Seidenberg & McClelland's [1989] connectionist model). Finally, we examine a model that demonstrates the inherent connection between spoken language and reading (i.e., the simple view of reading).

A Consensus View of Reading

The field of reading research has been continually plagued by deep divisions among camps of researchers who hold diametrically opposed perspectives. Given this history, one would think that it would be impossible to come up with a consensus view of reading on which most scholars could agree. In the late 1990s, however, a group of 17 experts on reading did just that (Snow et al., 1998). Although these experts approach reading from a variety of perspectives, they readily agreed that, at a general level, reading should be defined as "a process of getting meaning from print, using knowledge about the written alphabet and about the sound structure of oral language for purposes of achieving understanding" (p. vi). What should be noticed about this definition is the combined emphasis on (1) meaning and understanding (as opposed to an exclusive focus on sounding out words), (2) knowledge of alphabetic characters (as opposed to suggesting that letter knowledge is less important than whole, undifferentiated words), and (3) knowledge of sounds (as opposed to minimizing the role of these sounds). The expert panel, in conjunction with a number of reviewers and consultants, elaborated on this general definition by suggesting that skilled readers:

- Rapidly and automatically identify written words through visual processes, phonological decoding processes, semantic processes, and contextual interpretive processes.
- Use their general world knowledge and extensive sight vocabulary to comprehend texts literally and draw inferences.
- Demonstrate the ability to accurately assess and monitor their own understanding.
- Use a common set of syntactic and inferential processes to comprehend both spoken language and text, as well as text-specific processes to comprehend texts.

So what this definition means, minimally, is that a literacy curriculum should be designed to promote (1) the rapid and automatic identification of written words, (2) use of world knowledge and sight vocabulary to comprehend texts literally and to draw inferences, (3) metacognitive monitoring of understanding, and (4) the accessing of spoken language competences and text-specific competencies. Teachers should always ask themselves, "Am I promoting all of these skills?" and "What are the best ways to do so?"

Component Skills of Reading Sentences

Cognitive psychologists who study the process of reading sentences have subdivided themselves into camps of researchers who study interesting but separate phenomena, such as mentally grouping sets of words into syntactic structures, accessing the meaning of each word of a sentence, acknowledging the role of phonology in parsing a sentence and controlling eye movements, and so on. However, there is no comprehensive theory that captures and integrates all of these processes into a single theoretical model (Rayner & Reichle, 2010). As such, we cannot present such a model here, but we can list some of the consistent findings of these researchers to give a sense of what skilled readers do when they read sentences:

- *As we read a sentence in a culturally prescribed direction (e.g., left to right in English), we build up a syntactic structure for that sentence in a step-by-step manner; this structure combines individual word meanings into an arrangement that helps people compute the overall meaning of the sentence* (Staub, 2015). There was some debate in the field about whether people create an entire structure very early in the process and plug words into this structure, or whether they build up a provisional structure step by step and phrase by phrase until they have reason to reconsider this provisional structure upon encountering a particular word that does not fit. The latter seems to be the case.

What does it mean to build up a syntactic structure step by step? Recall from Chapter 8 the notions of grammatical categories and rules. We learned that these categories and rules are used to parse a sentence into its constituents and then combine these constituents in a hierarchical structure that specifies "who did what to whom" (Staub, 2015). The fact that linguists can write the rules for forming certain sentences means that there are certain types of sentences and each type can be produced using a specific set of rules. For example, each of the following sentences can be produced by using the same three rules:

1. *The tall boy hit the round ball.*
2. *The girl chewed an apple.*
3. *A man drew a picture.*
4. *A woman dropped the cup.*

These three rules are:

Rule 1. Sentence = Noun Phrase + Verb Phrase (i.e., S → NP + VP).
Rule 2. Verb Phrase = Verb + Noun Phrase (i.e., VP → V + NP).
Rule 3. Noun Phrase = Determiner + (optional adjective) + Noun (i.e., NP → D + (adj) + N).

To depict the hierarchical arrangement of a set of rules, linguists have used tree structures. Figure 9.1 depicts a tree structure for the three rules above. By nesting one component (e.g., a determiner) within another (e.g., a noun

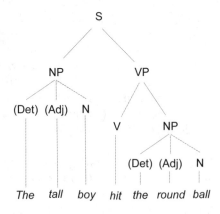

FIGURE 9.1. Tree diagram for the three formulas S → NP + VP, NP → (det) + (adj) + N, and VP → V + (adv) + NP.

phrase), the structure shows how the former is part of the latter. It should be noted, however, that other kinds of syntactic theories besides those that entail rules have been proposed (including connectionist models; Caplan & Waters, 1999). The rule-based theories are presented here for illustrative purposes, but other kinds of models would also provide the basis for grammatical expectations.

To create a tree structure step by step, the process would proceed as follows. Upon reading the word *the,* for example, the rule for producing NPs is elicited. Unconsciously, the mind says, "Okay. A noun phrase must be starting." Given that a determiner has already been encountered, Rule 3 (above) sets up the expectation that either an adjective or a noun will be encountered next. When the word *tall* is next read in Sentence 1, it is assigned the slot for adjective. Having organized the words *the* and *tall* together, Rule 3 now sets up the expectation that the next word will likely be a noun (to complete an NP), and so on. In order for this system to work, written words (e.g., *tall*) have to be mentally associated with grammatical classes (e.g., adjective) in addition to word meanings.

Over the years, various researchers have doubted the existence of a mental parser, grammatical rules, and grammatical classes. Although these doubters have made some good points, there is considerable evidence that syntactic knowledge is an important aspect of sentence comprehension (regardless of whether the parser relies on rules or other kinds of representations). In the first place, there is the syndrome called *Broca's aphasia* that results from injury to the Broca's area of the cerebral cortex (located in the left frontal lobe). Individuals who have this disorder are able to comprehend the meanings of individual words but have trouble with the syntax of sentences (Caplan & Waters, 1999; Just & Carpenter, 1987). For example, they see no difference between the following two sentences:

1. *They fed her the dog biscuits.*
2. *They fed her dog the biscuits.*

Although these two sentences have the same words, they have different tree structures and, therefore, different meanings. In addition, there are many well-known "garden-path" sentences, such as the following:

3. *Since Jim jogs a mile seems like a short distance to him.*
4. *The old train the young.*

Most people read these sentences and then get confused when they reach the word *seems* in Sentence 3 and the second *the* in Sentence 4. That's because the mind initially thinks that *jogs a mile* is a VP and *the old train* is an NP. Both the sentences were parsed incorrectly.

Further, there are studies that show how syntax affects both the meaning and pronunciation of a word that is encountered. For example, read the following sentences:

5. *Cody said, "Does are in the park, aren't they?"*
6. *Tomorrow was the annual one-day fishing contest and fishermen would invade the place. Some of the best bass guitarists in the country would come here.*

In sentence 5, grammatical rules suggest that *Does* is an auxiliary verb. Instead, it turns out to be the plural noun referring to female deer. The noun and the auxiliary have different pronunciations and meanings. In the sentences in 6, grammatical rules and prior context suggest that *bass* is a noun that labels a type of fish. Instead, it turns out to be an adjective in this instance that modifies a type of guitar. The noun and adjective have different meanings and pronunciations.

Finally, grammatical relations are evident when a reader encounters ambiguous sentences, such as:

7. *Visiting relatives can be a nuisance.*
8. *The burglar saw the cop with binoculars.*

Does sentence 7 mean that it can be a bother to go see your relatives, or that relatives who come to see you can be a bother? Theoretically, the only way someone could "see" the multiple readings of these sentences is if he or she constructed multiple syntactic structures for each one.

   • *Eye movements can be very diagnostic about the processes of lexical access and the construction of syntax* (Clifton, 2015; Staub, 2015; Taft, 2015). Using sophisticated eye-tracking equipment and software, we now know that when readers move their eyes across a page, they do not do so in a smooth sweep of words; rather, their eyes jump from one word to the next (like jumping across rocks in a creek) and remain on each word for different amounts of time. These eye movements are called *saccades,* from the French word *saquer* for jerky movements. Each time our eyes land on a word, our minds first have to visually recognize it (i.e., "I have seen the group of letters *DOG* before"), access the meaning of the word (i.e., "a cute, furry pet that barks"), access a phonological representation of the word (i.e., /dawg/), and place the word in a spot of an emerging syntactic structure for the entire sentence (e.g., an NP). When our eyes remain on a word for a short amount of time, that means a skilled reader is doing all four of these processes very quickly. When we stay on a word longer, something is slowing down one or more of these processes.

   Cognitive psychologists have been very clever in their studies to show that all four of these processes occur during saccades. For example, they have contrasted eye-fixation times on (1) real words that very frequently occur in texts (e.g., the word *the*), (2) real words that occur infrequently in texts (e.g., *octogenarian),* (3) homonyms for real words that are inserted into sentences (e.g., *The camper was surprised by an angry grizzly bare),*

(4) pseudohomonyms for real words (e.g., *gerl* for *girl*), (5) pseudowords that are not real words but obey the pronunciation rules of English (e.g., *strime*), and (6) non-words that are random combinations of letters (e.g., *qtlr*). Fixation times are far shorter on words that occur often in texts. Studies have shown that a variety of fixation times vary according to frequency. So, highly frequent words such as *the* might be fixated on for a quarter of a second (250 milliseconds) or even skipped (Clifton, 2015), while an infrequent or unfamiliar word might be fixed on for 1 second or longer. The average fixation time for words is around 300–500 milliseconds.

Although it is easy these days to determine the frequency of words in texts that are likely to be encountered by the average adult because computers and word-processing programs can count the words automatically and quickly, at one time, teams of researchers actually counted words by hand after compiling popular books, magazines, and newspapers that are read by lots of people! This painstaking work took months to complete. Researchers then created lists of words that vary in their frequency (e.g., frequency of 25 per million vs. 5 per million) from which researchers can select when designing an experiment with test sentences.

Researchers can also use reading times to detect when people started one syntactic structure but then realized that this structure was not correct, as was the case with the garden-path sentences listed above (Sentences 3 and 4). Returning to the jogging example, when you read this sentence the first time, your mind starts to construct a sentence in which the words in the phrase *jogs a mile* were grouped together into the same VP (VP = V + NP; *jogs* [V] + *a mile* [NP]). However, when your eyes reached the word *seems,* your mind realized that something was wrong. Note that you would not have constructed the initial syntactic structure had there been a comma after the word *jogs.* The eye-fixation procedure can also tell researchers when people reach a problem in the sentence and go back to read the first portion again, as is the case with this and other garden-path sentences.

Other factors that determine fixation times on words besides frequency include *predictability* (Staub, 2015) and *semantic priming* (Henderson, Snowling, & Clarke, 2013). In studies that include both highly frequent words and words that are predictable from the context (e.g., *Since she was out of cash, Mary Carmen went to the* _____; words such as *bank* or *ATM* are predictable). Because word meanings are interconnected in a semantic network (see Chapter 8), the presentation of a semantically related word (e.g., *bark* or *wag* in the case of *dog*) just prior to presenting test sentences "primes" the meaning of *dog,* and this meaning is activated from memory much faster. Thus, eye-fixation time on *dog* is shorter for people primed with the word *bark* than for people in an unprimed, control condition of the experiment. But priming would not work for people who do not have a rich, interconnected network in which, for example, *bark* and *wag* are ideas connected to *dog*.

Of course, priming with the word itself speeds up reading even faster because both the orthographic (i.e., letter combinations) and phonological representations of the word (i.e., the component sounds) are primed from memory. This phenomenon can be shown using a *display change* technique (Clifton, 2015). When we read, our eyes fixate on each word, as noted above. The area of the sentence just outside (to the right) of the fixation zone for a word is called the *parafoveal area*, which is functionally blind (subjects cannot report what is flashed in that area). If the actual word that is about to be fixated on is briefly flashed in the parafoveal area, doing so primes the word such that fixation times are faster.

• *Readers are sensitive to the frequency with which particular syntactic structures are encountered in texts; commonly observed structures tend to be started first in the mind using the word-by-word process; however, less frequent syntactic structures can be "primed" and override the more common construction.* So, if people very frequently read simple declarative structures (S → NP + VP), such as *The man ate the apple*, they will tend to start the components of these structures when they encounter signals such as determiners (*the* or *a*) in the case of NPs, or verbs (e.g., *ate*) in the case of VPs. However, these expectations can be overridden if participants in a study are exposed to less frequent alternative structures one or two times just before encountering the target sentence in the experiment. So, for example, if normally people tend to be confused and slow down their reading when they read a sentence with a less common reduced relative clause structure, such as *The soldiers warned about the dangers conducted the midnight raid*, this effect can be eliminated if participants are primed first with sentences with unambiguous relative clauses, such as *The soldiers who were warned about the dangers conducted the midnight raid* (Arai, Nakamura, & Mazuka, 2015; Fine & Jaeger, 2016; Traxler, Tooley, & Pickering, 2014). The priming effect is even stronger if there is overlap in the verbs used across test sentences in the study. The centrality of verbs for the composition of syntactic structures during reading is consistent with the finding of the centrality of verbs and frequent verb schemata or frames in the early spoken grammars of preschool children (Tomasello, 2011; see Chapter 8).

• *When the eyes fixate on a word during reading, all of the multiple meanings of particular words are activated; however, only the meaning that is consistent with the meaning of the sentence remains active until the meaning of the sentence is computed; the incompatible meanings are inhibited very quickly; this pattern of parallel activation of multiple possibilities followed by inhibition of incorrect possibilities does not seem to be the case for syntax.* So, when reading the sentence *The people rose when the queen entered the room,* all of the meanings of the word *rose* are activated when the eyes fixate on *rose,* including the flower, the color rose, the past tense of the act of standing, and so on. However, only the meaning of standing up is consistent with the rest of the sentence, so that one meaning is retained while the other meanings are actively inhibited (Gernsbacher & Kaschak, 2013). Note that the aforementioned priming technique was used to show how multiple meanings are accessed upon eye fixation, but unrelated meanings are soon inhibited in good readers (Henderson, Snowling, & Clarke, 2013).

In contrast, when the first few words of a sentence are read, the mind does not construct all possible syntactic structures that are compatible with these first few words, such as the simple declarative sentence or the syntax of complex sentences involving *when* and a subordinate clause, and so on. Instead, the mind of a reader constructs the first proposed structure word by word, and phrase by phrase, and revises the first possibility when the eyes encounter a word that shows them that this first proposed structure is not correct (Staub, 2015).

Note that these findings suggest that people can only do both of these tasks (i.e., activate possible meanings and create particular syntactic structures) if they already have these forms of knowledge in mind and, in the case of semantics, actively inhibit the wrong meanings as quickly as possible. As such, the findings show once again how important it is to have spoken language in order to read. But the findings also suggest that if people do not inhibit incorrect word meanings that are activated shortly after an eye fixation, they will have trouble computing the meaning of the sentence. As we shall see in a later section of this chapter, some poor readers who can decode (sound out) sentences sufficiently well will still have comprehension problems because of the relative levels of activation of particular meanings in their semantic system. When the dominant meaning is too strongly active in memory (e.g., "place to put your money," in the case of *bank*) while the subordinate meaning is not sufficiently strong (e.g., "side of a river," in the case of *bank*), the incorrect dominant meaning will not be suppressed and the correct meaning will not be sufficiently activated (Henderson, Snowling, & Clarke, 2013).

• *Phonology seems to play a role in accessing word meanings, building up syntactic structures, and controlling of eye movements.* There is a long-standing debate in the field of reading research on two hypotheses regarding word meanings: (1) whether skilled readers rely on phonological representations of printed words to access word meanings after fixating on these words, or (2) whether people access word meanings directly from orthography without phonology intervening (Clifton, 2015; Harm & Seidenberg, 2004; Price, Witzel, & Witzel, 2015). The claim that skilled readers do not rely on an orthography → phonology → meaning route led some to argue against teaching children how to sound out words in the 1970s and 1980s. However, many clever studies conducted since that time have shown how phonology does play a central role in accessing word meaning and sentence processing, even in skilled adult readers (Clifton, 2015). For example, when people are asked to categorize words that are flashed on a screen as quickly as they can, they often miscategorize homophones. For example, for the category of edible things, they correctly say " 'yes' " to *apple* and " 'no' " to *truck,* but then incorrectly say " 'yes' " to *meet.* Or, when they are presented with a word such as *couch* before *touch,* the reading time for *touch* is slowed because of the difference in vowel pronunciation. The same is true for sentences that contain a number of rhyming words or words containing the same first consonant (or onset). So, if you control for word length, frequency, syntactic structure, and so on, the sentence *Red-headed Ned said Ted fed in bed* takes more time to read than the matched sentence, *Dark-skinned Ian thought that Harry ate in bed* (Price et al., 2015).

Using the aforementioned display change technique, if a homophone of a word is briefly flashed in the parafoveal area just prior to the time when eyes fixate on the word, fixation times are shorter. So, for example, people fixate less on the word *beach* if primed with *beech* in the parafoveal area but not when primed with *bench* (Clifton, 2015). Similarly, if people who are about to fixate on the word *rack* are primed with a pronounceable non-word such as *raff,* they read it faster than if primed with a pronounceable non-word that has a different vowel sound, such as *rall.* It has also been found that highly frequently five-letter words are often skipped when reading (as noted earlier). However, this is only the case for one-syllable five-letter words. When the words have two syllables, they are not skipped. This unconscious decision to skip or not occurs when incoming information enters the parafoveal area. Thus, this finding is one further demonstration that phonology affects reading processes.

Finally, whereas the central role of phonology in reading is now beyond dispute, it is also the case that there are many common words that do not follow the regular phonological patterns of pronunciation, such as *was, have, the, yacht, busy,* and *sew.* The distinction between regular and irregular words has led many theorists to propose *dual routes* to pronunciation: a phonologically mediated route (orthography → phonology → meaning) and a direct route (orthography → meaning) (Harm & Seidenberg, 2004; Pritchard, Coltheart, Marinus, & Castles, 2018). At one time researchers sided either with models that only had a mediated route or with models that only had direct routes, but now everyone acknowledges that our minds have to learn and store both kinds of routes in order to be a proficient reader. Where researchers differ is how they model these different routes in the mind.

Two Influential Models of Reading

The third way to understand the nature of skilled reading is to examine theoretical models of this ability. Although there are a number of such models in existence (Rayner & Reichle, 2010), it is most efficient to examine just two of these models here for illustrative purposes. Both have had considerable impact on reading research, and both highlight important constructs. The first is Seidenberg and McClelland's (1989) connectionist model. Whereas this model has been strongly endorsed in several influential publications (e.g., Adams, 1990; Pressley, 1997), certain kinds of empirical problems have caused it to be refined over the years (Brown, 1998). Regardless, connectionist models predominate in many areas of the reading literature. Figure 9.2 depicts the key elements of the original model. The second model that will be discussed is the simple view of reading proposed by Gough and his colleagues (e.g., Gough, Hoover, & Peterson, 1996).

A CONNECTIONIST MODEL OF READING

Connectionist models are based on the idea that when people read, they process many different types of information (e.g., letters, word meanings, syntax). More important, the model shown in Figure 9.2 implies two things: (1) that processing is divided among relatively autonomous subsystems that perform their own tasks (indicated by the ovals), and (2) that each

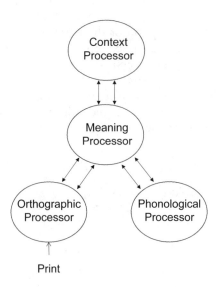

FIGURE 9.2. A connectionist model of the four processors that are operative during reading.

subsystem sends what it "knows" or has "figured out" to at least one other subsystem (indicated by the arrows). The former point means that readers have many different clues they can use when they read words and derive the syntax of a sentence. The latter point means that one processor can send its clues to other processors to help them make sense of and constrain their own clues—that is, the processors work interactively with one another (Perfetti, 1985). With this in mind, let's examine the jobs performed by the orthographic, meaning, phonological, and context processors in turn.

The Orthographic Processor. Orthographic knowledge consists of knowing the individual symbols of a written language. For example, a child in the United States who knows the letters of the English alphabet has orthographic knowledge, as does a child living in China who knows all of the logographic characters of Chinese. The orthographic processor shown in Figures 9.2 and 9.3 can be thought of as a storehouse of orthographic knowledge. The single oval for the orthographic processor in Figure 9.2 is shorthand notation for the more detailed set of connections shown in Figure 9.3. More specifically, the orthographic processor has the job of processing and recognizing strings of letters (i.e., words). It accomplishes this feat by means of small *units* that recognize individual letters and parts of letters (McClelland & Rumelhart, 1981; Seidenberg & McClelland, 1989). As noted above, the system is designed according to connectionist principles.

Word recognition occurs when the units for each letter of a word attain a sufficient degree of activation. The main way that each unit becomes activated is through direct perception of the letter it represents in the mind. Using the model in Figure 9.3, for example, any of the units in the lowest row (representing portions of letters) become activated when readers perceive any of the individual portions in text in front of them. The second way that units can be activated is through *spreading activation*. A unit can spread its activation to another unit if the units are linked in an associative relationship. Associations form between units when certain letters (e.g.,

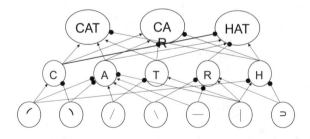

FIGURE 9.3. Details of the orthographic processor.

q) frequently co-occur with other letters (e.g., *u*). Any unit that has been partially activated by spreading activation turns on faster than it would have if the letter were presented alone. As noted earlier, memory researchers and psycholinguists refer to this process as *priming*. For example, when someone sees a *q* while scanning a word left to right and then sees a *u* next, the unit for *u* is turned on, or activated, faster than it would have been if *u* were perceived alone. Thus, associations and spreading activation promote faster reading.

In connectionist models, moreover, units spread their action either to increase the activation of units they are connected to (the lines with arrowheads in Figure 9.3) or to decrease or inhibit the activation of units they are connected to (the circular ends of connecting lines in Figure 9.3). For example, since a slanted vertical line (/) is part of the letter *A*, the unit for the slanted line is connected to the unit for *A* with a connection ending in an arrowhead. Since a completely vertical line is not part of the letter *A*, the link between the two units has a circular (inhibitory) end to it. In effect, when the vertical line unit is activated, it inhibits the unit for *A*. Any familiar word, then, is really a highly associated pattern of letters, and each letter in the word primes the perception of the others. As a result, the entire word is recognized very quickly and automatically as a result of perceiving every one of the letters. After many years of research using sophisticated technology, we now have a better sense of how the orthographic processor works in skilled readers. Here are some of the findings:

1. Contrary to a common belief held among nonscientists, skilled readers process the individual letters of the words they are reading. They are not aware of this because word recognition has become automatic and subconscious for them. However, skilled readers do not recognize the letters of a word independently of one another. Rather, after many years of reading, associations form between the units for one letter in a word and the units for other letters. As a result, a familiar word is perceived as a whole.

2. The strengths of the association between the units for letters reflect the frequencies with which these letters co-occur in written texts. For example, when the letter *t* occurs as the first letter of a three-letter word, it is extremely likely that the next letter will be an *h* (Adams, 1990). People who read a lot develop mental associations between letters. Once associations form, they allow the activation from the units for one letter to "spread" to the units for another. As a result, skilled readers recognize familiar words very quickly and automatically. In contrast, someone who has never read a book and only knows letters would not recognize words as fast as a skilled reader because no associations have formed among the units for letters. Such a person would, however, recognize isolated letters as fast as a skilled reader.

3. Letter associations also help skilled readers process the proper order of letters in a word (e.g., *the* vs. *hte*), as well as perceive association-preserving pseudowords (e.g., *mave* and *teel*). A pseudoword is a made-up word created by researchers. It uses combinations of letters and sounds that appear frequently in real words (e.g., the *-ave* in *mave*).

4. Finally, letter associations also help a reader divide a word into syllables. For example, whereas *dr* is an acceptable combination of letters that maps onto the sounds of spoken English (e.g., the /drrr/ sound in the word *drive*), *dn* is not. As a result, a skilled reader who encounters the word *midnight* would visually divide this word into *mid* and *night* (splitting between the *d* and *n*, which do not make a combined sound like *dr*). In contrast, skilled readers would not visually divide *address* into *add* and *ress*. Moreover, a skilled reader implicitly knows that vowels seem to "pull" their adjacent consonants into a cluster of association patterns. For example, the *a* in *party* perceptually pulls the *p* and *r* toward itself. This fact combined with the fact that *rt* is an unacceptable spoken combination means that *party* would be divided into *par* and *ty* (Adams, 1990).

It is interesting to note that, historically, written language did not use spacing and punctuation to delineate words (Just & Carpenter, 1987). As a result, readers had to exclusively rely on their orthographic knowledge to make sense of a sentence. To see how this might work, consider the following sentence: *Thatmanhatesveggies.*

The Meaning Processor. Of course, comprehending a sentence requires far more than the ability to determine whether letter strings are orthographically acceptable or familiar. For example, the pseudosentence *Trat distle quas* contains combinations of letters that appear in real words (e.g., the *tr-* in *trat* also appears in *truck* and *tree*), but it is meaningless. Similarly, the sentence *The octogenarian insinuated himself into our organization* would be meaningless to a person who knows that he or she has seen the written words *octogenarian* and *insinuated* before, but cannot remember what they mean. Thus, sentence comprehension requires both an orthographic processor to recognize letter strings and a meaning processor to access word meanings.

Several views have been proposed regarding how meanings are assigned to words. The structure of the meaning processor is analogous to that of the orthographic processor, but this time sounds are not decomposed into smaller segments and interconnected—word meanings are. According to connectionist views, word meanings are represented in the meaning processor as associated sets of primitive meaning elements, in the same way that spellings of familiar words are represented in the orthographic processor as associated sets of letters and parts of letters (Adams, 1990). A person's experience determines which meaning elements are associated and stored for a given word (Hintzman, 1986). For example, a child who hears the word *dog* applied to a specific dog in a specific context might associate the whole experience with the word *dog*. The next time he or she hears the word *dog* applied, however, it might be with a different dog in a different context. According to the connectionist view, those aspects of the second context that are similar to aspects of the first context (e.g., both dogs had a flea collar) would become associated and stored with the word *dog*. Over time, a consistent set of *meaning elements* would be distilled from these repeated encounters with dogs. Each element would be highly associated with the others and would, therefore, prime one's memory for the others. Moreover, some aspects of the meaning of dog would be more central to its meaning and reflect consistent correlations of attributes (e.g., "has fur" and "barks"). Such attributes would be accessed the fastest when the single word *dog* is read. Other meaning elements that are somewhat less central (e.g., "has an owner") would also be accessible but would be accessed more slowly, if at all, when the word is read in isolation.

As Figure 9.2 shows, the meaning processor is directly linked to the orthographic processor. This means that the output of each processor can help the other do its job better. In support of this claim, Whittlesea and Cantwell (1987) found that when a pseudoword is given a meaningful definition, subjects perceived this word faster than they did when it lacked a definition. This improved perceptibility lasted for at least 24 hours, even when the supplied meaning had been forgotten. A more recent study with children showed that providing meaning to a non-word that shared an onset with a known word (e.g., *biscal* with *biscuit*) sped up the rate at which the non-word was integrated into children's lexicons (Henderson, Weighall, & Gaskell, 2013). Thus, the meaning processor helped the orthographic processor do its job better. But the reverse can happen, as well. As we show in the section on the development of reading ability (see the Developmental Models and Trends section below), students who frequently read text with new words can dramatically increase the size of their vocabularies. Thus, orthographic knowledge can improve the capacity of the meaning processor.

The Phonological Processor. Analogous to the orthographic and meaning processors, the phonological processor consists of units that form associations with one another. In this case, however, the basic units correspond to phonemes in the reader's spoken language. As depicted in Figure 9.4, phonemes such as /ba/ and /tuh/ can be combined into syllables such as *bat* and also into words such as *battle* (phonologists and linguists prefer the convention of encasing sounds in a pair of backslashes and representing these sounds with a set of symbols such as /θ/, which represents the sound corresponding to *th*; most of us do not know these symbols so they are not used in this book). A word can also be composed of an initial sound (onset)

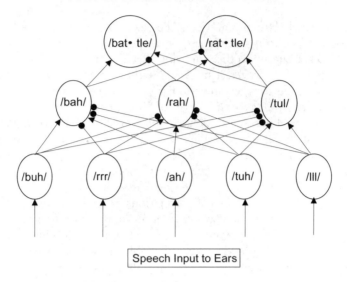

FIGURE 9.4. Details of the phonological processor.

and a final sound (rime) that it may have in common with other words. For example, the rime of *cat* and *hat* is /-at/, while the onset of these words are /k/ and /h/, respectively. The auditory representation of a word, syllable, onset, rime, or phoneme is composed of an activated set of specific units in the phonological processor (Adams, 1990).

Studies suggest that phonemes and larger sound units take on different levels of importance in reading and oral language. In particular, Treiman and colleagues have found that many words seem to be represented in terms of an onset and a rime, perhaps because certain vowel–final consonant combinations occur in texts more often than chance (Kessler & Treiman, 1997). Both children and adults make fewer errors and respond faster when they utilize onset–rime information in words (especially rime information). They appear to be less reliant on the more specific connection between graphemes and individual phonemes (Treiman, Mullennix, Bijeljac-Babic, & Richmond-Welty, 1995; Treiman & Zukowoski, 1996). In a related way, other studies suggest that the level of the syllable often overrides the level of the phoneme in early writing (Treiman & Tincoff, 1997). In light of the centrality of syllables, some modern connectionist computer simulations utilize this level as predominating over the level of phonemes (Taft, 2015).

As noted earlier, when skilled readers see a written word, they do not have to translate it phonologically in order for its meaning to be accessed. Many studies have shown that meaning can be accessed simply by a visual pattern of letters (Adams, 1990; Clifton, 2015; Seidenberg & McClelland,

1989). And yet, skilled readers of a variety of languages often do translate words phonologically when they read. This tendency to create phonological representations even occurs in languages such as Chinese that use logographic symbols that do not map onto sounds the way English graphemes do (Chow, McBride-Chang, & Burgess, 2005). The connectionist assumption that orthography, phonology, and semantics all work together and mutually constrain each other is clearly consistent with the findings of cognitive psychologists reported earlier in the chapter.

The Context Processor. The context processor has the job of constructing an online, coherent interpretation of text (Adams, 1990). The output of this processor is a mental representation of everything that a reader has read so far. For example, upon reading the sentence *When Queen Elizabeth entered the chamber, the MPs all rose,* the context may be a mental image of Queen Elizabeth walking up to the podium in the British House of Commons. Whereas some researchers (e.g., Just & Carpenter, 1987) call this image a *referential representation* of the text, others (e.g., van Dijk & Kintsch, 1983) call it a *situation model.* For simplicity and consistency with other chapters, we shall use the latter term.

According to Seidenberg and McClelland (1989), semantic, pragmatic, and syntactic knowledge all contribute to the construction of a situation model (Seidenberg & McClelland, 1989). For example, when skilled readers encounter the sentence *Juan went to the store to buy a _____,* they use their semantic knowledge to access the meanings of all of the words in the sentence. In addition, they use their pragmatic knowledge to expect that Juan will buy something that people usually buy at stores. If the blank were filled in by *savings bond,* readers would likely be surprised when their eyes reached the word *savings.* Syntactic knowledge also prompts the reader to form certain expectations about what will occur next, as discussed earlier in the section on the findings of cognitive psychologists (Garrett, 1990; Just & Carpenter, 1987).

In sum, then, syntactic, pragmatic, and semantic knowledge all contribute to the construction of a situation model (a mental image of what has been described in a text). Once in place, this model prompts a reader to form expectations about what will occur next in the text. As each new segment of text is encountered, skilled readers interpret what is read in a way that makes it consistent with the current situation model.

The model of proficient reading in Figure 9.2 shows the two-way relationship between the context and the meaning processor. The model implies that the prior context can influence the meaning assigned to a word and that current meanings influence the construction of a situation model. Thus, when skilled readers process the sentence *Chloe removed the thorn from the rose,* they assign a different meaning to *rose* than they would if they read the sentence *The crowd rose to sing the national anthem.*

However, research has shown that the context-meaning effects are weak relative to the orthography-meaning and phonology-meaning effects; that is, readers are much better at predicting possible meanings of a word based on its perceived spelling than they are at predicting which word will follow a preceding context (Adams, 1990; Snow et al., 1998). When context-meaning links conflict with orthography-meaning links, the latter wins. Thus, *skilled reading consists, first and foremost, of learning the correspondences between written words and their pronunciations and meanings.* Context effects occur after words are perceived and various possible meanings are accessed. But overall, context, orthography, meanings, and phonology all work in concert to help a reader construct the best possible interpretation of a text.

In sum, the original Seidenberg and McClelland (1989) model has gained acceptance in part because it correctly specifies the interacting roles of orthography, phonology, semantics, and syntax. It has been revised over the years to account for many phenomena described in the first part of this chapter, including the notion of a phonology-mediated route to meaning and a direct route between orthography and meaning (e.g., Harm & Seidenberg, 2004). It inspired many additional connectionist models that continue to explain other phenomena (Rayner & Reichle, 2010). However, there is still a need for researchers to come up with a model that puts all of the findings of cognitive psychologists together—the original model and various revisions can explain or predict some findings but not all. Moreover, there are still debates about whether (1) there is a need to posit rules, (2) phonological representations are segmented versus undifferentiated wholes, and (3) other matters. Connectionist models do a better job for tasks such as pronouncing individual words and parsing ambiguous sentences than other tasks, but the field continues to develop.

THE SIMPLE VIEW OF READING

The second theoretical perspective, the simple view of reading, begins with the insight that reading comprehension and listening comprehension have much in common (Gough et al., 1996). For example, the same lexicon is used when reading and listening; sentences or words that are ambiguous in one modality (e.g., reading) are often ambiguous in the other modality (e.g., listening); both modalities rely on sequential processing (one word at a time) and on word order to compute syntax (at least in English); and the same background knowledge supports the interpretation of both printed and spoken words. These commonalities suggest that reading can be subdivided into two parts: that which is unique to reading (i.e., *decoding* or translating text into sounds) and that which is shared with listening (i.e., comprehension).

This suggestion can be integrated with the connectionist model by noting that listening comprehension involves the context, meaning, and phonological processors of the connectionist model in Figure 9.2. Reading skills are made possible by "grafting" the orthographic processor onto the other three processors. Decoding is represented by the links between the orthographic and phonological processors; knowledge of the *alphabetic principle* is also represented by the links between these two processors. The alphabetic principle is the understanding that graphemes (single letters or groups of letters) map onto phonemes (sounds) in systematic ways.

We know that decoding and comprehension are separable because a typical 5-year-old or older child with a reading disability can comprehend spoken language but cannot decode. Conversely, there are conditions such as hyperlexia in which an individual can decode but not comprehend (Gough et al., 1996). And if you measure decoding skill and listening comprehension separately, both these factors are found to strongly predict reading ability (Lonigan, 2015). To be able to read, then, a student has to be skilled at both decoding and comprehending.

To capture the fact that decoding and comprehending are both necessary but not individually sufficient for reading, Gough and colleagues proposed a multiplicative hypothesis. If reading skills (r), decoding skills (d), and comprehending skills (c) can be placed on three hypothetical continua that range from 0 to 1 (e.g., someone who has more skill would receive a score closer to 1), reading must be the product of decoding and comprehension and not simply the addition of these components, as the formula $r = d \times c$ suggests. Both decoding and comprehending have to be greater than 0 for reading to take place. In their studies, Gough and colleagues found that the correlations between reading scores (r) and the product of scores for decoding and comprehending ($d \times c$) were higher (r's = .84–.91) than the individual correlations between decoding and reading or between comprehension and reading. Decoding was measured by having students read pseudowords. Listening comprehension was measured by having students listen to stories and answer questions about these stories. Reading was measured using standardized reading tests.

In addition to having very good empirical success as a model, the simple view of reading is strongly supported by neuroscientific evidence that shows that many of the brain areas that are active when we comprehend spoken language are also active when we read (Price, 2012).

Summary

Collectively, the definitions and component skills of reading evident in the conclusions of the NRC, the findings of cognitive psychologists, the connectionist models of reading, and the simple view of reading all emphasize the importance and integration of orthographic skills (including decoding), spoken language comprehension skills (phonological processing, semantics, syntax), and background knowledge. When do these skills emerge in development, and when does their integration seem evident? We address these developmental trends questions in a subsequent section.

The Development of Beginning Reading Skills

Now that you know what skilled reading involves and why it is important, you have a sense of the "endpoint" of reading development (but, of course, reading always improves a little with continued practice and experience). The beginning point of reading development is that point in a child's life when he or she has no idea what reading involves and lacks even emergent literacy and spoken language skills (e.g., infancy). After spoken language begins, children acquire preliteracy skills during a period of emergent literacy (see below) that occurs between age 1 and kindergarten. Emergent literacy is described in the next section. Then, we consider some relevant evidence regarding precocious reading that may also occur before the start of kindergarten. Finally, in the third section of this chapter and the next chapter, we fill in the next two developmental time periods (learning to read between first and third grade, and reading to learn from fourth grade to adulthood, respectively).

Emergent Literacy

Whitehurst and Lonigan (1998) define *emergent literacy* as consisting "of the skills, knowledge, and attitudes that are presumed to be developmental precursors to conventional forms of reading and writing . . . and the environments that support these developments" (p. 849). The construct of emergent literacy was originally proposed in the 1980s as an alternative to the idea of *reading readiness* that has existed in educational circles since the early 1900s (at least). According to the readiness concept, it is not possible to teach reading to children until they are maturationally "ready" to benefit from this instruction. Some researchers went so far as to use IQ tests to determine when the brain was ready (Morphett & Washburn, 1931).

Notwithstanding the merits of this brain-based proposal, a readiness conception implies an all-or-none dichotomy between readers (i.e., first graders who are ready) and nonreaders (i.e., preschoolers who are not ready). Teachers did not attempt to teach anything about reading during the years between birth and age 6 because it was believed that children were not ready. Somewhere during their sixth year, advocates argued, their brains became ready and instruction could begin.

The emergent literacy conception, in contrast, implies a *continuum* of skills that have their origin well before formal reading instruction begins in first grade (Teale & Sulzby, 1986). Some examples of such skills include knowing that (1) the words in a book tell the story, and the pictures are just an accompaniment to the words; (2) English readers read words from left to right and lines of words from the top of a page to the bottom; (3) written words correspond to spoken words; (4) one reads all of the words on a page before reading the words on the next page; (5) pages are read in a specific order from the first to the last page; (6) there is someone (i.e., the author) who had the story in his or her mind and decided to write it down so that children could know the story, too; and (7) writing is like speaking because it is way of communicating ideas (Clay, 1985; Sulzby, 1991; Teale & Sulzby, 1986; Whitehurst & Lonigan, 1998). These insights are collectively called *conventions of print* or *print concepts*.

Whitehurst and Lonigan (1998) elaborated on the original conception of emergent literacy to suggest that it also involves other kinds of skills, such as an oral vocabulary, knowledge of syntax, knowledge of letters of the alphabet, the alphabetic principle, phonological processing, pretend reading, reading motivation, and verbal processing skills (e.g., rapid automatized naming and verbal working memory). As noted above, children who know the alphabetic principle understand that there is a relationship between graphemes (i.e., individual written letters or groups of written letters) and phonemes (i.e., individual sounds or groups of sounds). One assesses alphabet knowledge by presenting individual letters to children and asking for their names and/or the sounds they make. As described in Chapter 8, phonological processing abilities include knowing the number of syllables in a word, knowing which words rhyme, recognizing alliteration, and adding or deleting sounds from words. For example, a phonological processing task might be to ask children the question "What does the word *pink* sound like when you take off the last sound?" *Rapid automatized naming* (RAN) is the ability to rapidly give the names of a series of letters, objects, numbers, or colors.

To this list of emergent literacy skills, we can add several more. Children who can recognize *environmental print* can recognize their favorite DVD or a McDonald's restaurant without actually reading the words on the DVD or the restaurant sign. *Print awareness* is a composite measure that combines alphabet knowledge, concepts of print, and the ability to partially sound out a word using, for example, just the first letter. Finally, there is *invented spelling*. Before children acquire the ability to spell out a word as it is conventionally spelled, they show an intermediate ability in which they use an incomplete set of letters to characterize an entire word. For example, they may spell *kindergarten* as *KDN* or *flowers* as *FLAWRS* or *summer* as *SUMR*.

Researchers have found that all of these aspects of emergent literacy are highly predictive of who learns to read well in grades 1 to 3 (Whitehurst & Lonigan, 1998). Thus, it is important that the preschool years are devoted to improving emergent literacy skills to get children ready to read when formal instruction begins in kindergarten and first grade.

Precocious Readers

It is common for teachers and parents to report that most preschoolers vigorously resist being taught to read. In addition, experimental and informal attempts to teach young children how to read have generally failed when children are younger than 5 (Feitelson, Tehori, & Levinberg-Green, 1982; Fowler, 1971). There are, however, documented cases of precocious readers who ranged in age from 2 to 5 when they began reading (Aram & Besser-Biron, 2017; Fowler, 1971; Goldstein, 1976; Jackson, 1992; Tafa & Manolitsis, 2012), as well as a few experimental programs that have been seemingly successful with 4- and 5-year-olds (Feitelson et al., 1982; Fowler, 1971). It has been estimated that only 1% of the population are precocious readers (Olson, Evans, & Keckler, 2006). If we combine this evidence with the fact that it is often straightforward to teach (nondisabled) 6-year-old children from low- and middle-income households to read (Snow et al., 1998), the data as a whole can be interpreted in two ways. According to the reading readiness view that was discussed above, there is a neurological basis to being ready and willing to read. According to a motivational view, in contrast, the age trends do not reflect neurological maturation but reflect normative trends in reading motivation.

With regard to the reading readiness view, it was noted earlier that well-controlled studies have found that age alone is not a very good predictor of responsiveness to reading instruction when factors related to knowledge and experience are taken into account (Adams, 1990; Bryant, MacLean, Bradley, & Crossland, 1990; Stanovich & Siegel, 1994). Early studies (e.g., Fowler, 1971; Morphett & Washburn, 1931) showed that it was a child's *mental age,* not his or her chronological age, that mattered (e.g., a 2-year-old who could answer questions for 5-year-olds on an IQ test could learn to read better than a 5-year-old who could only answer questions for 4-year-olds). Moreover, mental age and intelligence were soon replaced in later studies with better predictors of reading in typically developing first graders, such as letter knowledge and phonological processing.

Children are clearly not born with knowledge of letters, and they need to acquire a substantial productive vocabulary (through experience) to create the segmented, phonetic representations of spoken words that were described earlier (Metsala, 1999). Segmented representations, in turn, are required for creating links between graphemes and phonemes. Thus, a lack of receptivity to instruction could reflect a lack of exposure to relevant information, not biological maturation. Surprisingly, however, there does not appear to be a strong association between family SES and precocious reading (Olson et al., 2006). What may matter more than being rich or poor may be parents being responsive to their children's interest in books, letters, and spelling, and scaffolding their early attempts at reading-related skills (e.g., Aram & Besser-Biron, 2017; Olson et al., 2006). In addition, however, there is some evidence that precocious readers have higher IQs than their nonprecocious peers (Olson et al., 2006), so perhaps the developmental pathway from emergent literacy skills to formal reading is sped up in these children, given appropriate environmental support. There is an inherent aspect of precociousness in the scoring of IQ tests, given that smarter children know what older children know (so they learned it faster).

Thus, the lesson to be learned from the research on precocious readers is that it is generally rather difficult to teach formal reading to children prior to kindergarten. We still do not know whether the difficulty arises from maturational issues, motivational issues, or the simple fact that time is needed for children to acquire important kinds of emergent literacy and spoken language competencies before they can learn to read. That said, these prereading competencies must be embodied in the form of neural assemblies in the brain (i.e., clusters of neural groups that have formed synaptic connections with one another). In order for neural assemblies to form, there has to be a sufficient number of neurons located in certain regions of the brain that have matured to the point that they can form synaptic connections with neighbors. Studies of brain development suggest that only the neurons in the frontal lobe continue to develop substantially beyond infancy (see Chapter 2), so the primary temporal constraint related to maturation may well be the time it takes for synapses to form after repeated encounters with the same kind of stimulation (e.g., the sight of a given letter). Conversely, it is possible that skills like phonemic awareness and decoding are subtended by areas in the frontal lobes (Shaywitz et al., 1998). If these areas take some time to finish their development, there may be two kinds of factors that explain why it is hard to teach children below the age of 4 to read: (1) experiential factors (e.g., insufficient exposure to letters and spoken words) and (2) maturational factors (e.g., continued development of the frontal brain regions). Again, however, we cannot discount the potentially important role of motivation. Children who read early have an unusually strong desire to read as preschoolers and seek out support from parents and siblings (Olson et al., 2006).

Developmental Models and Trends

As noted in Chapter 1, a developmental analysis of literacy development provides both a description of age trends (i.e., snapshots of ability levels at different ages) and explanations of these age trends. One common way to characterize age trends is to appeal to Chall's (1983) six-phase model of reading development that, for the purposes of the present chapter, we can limit to just the first three phases: emergent literacy, beginning reading, and fluent reading. The emergent literacy phase (birth to kindergarten) was described above. What we can say is that successful readers enter first grade with strong oral language skills, phonemic awareness, syntactic awareness, the ability to rapidly name letters, and knowledge of the alphabetic principle. Early reading development consists of putting all of this entering knowledge together with written words and sentences—that is, it can be characterized as the progressive acquisition of letter–sound correspondences, as word-meaning correspondences, and learning how to parse sentences to derive the overall meaning of sentences.

The beginning reading phase (first to third grade) pertains to the time when children are first taught how to read in a formal manner, and they show all of the signs of a typical novice learner. The goal of instruction is to move them from being a beginning reader to being a fluent reader by the time they reach fourth grade. Children in the beginning reading phase are relatively slow in their ability to decode words, have relatively few sight words in their vocabulary, tend to read in a halting and monotone manner, and devote most of their attention to decoding rather than comprehension (Perfetti, 2007).

A more detailed analysis of the progressive changes in the ability to decode is given by Ehri's (1995) phase model. To begin with, Ehri notes that mature readers have at least four ways to read words. For unfamiliar words, they can use *decoding* (i.e., transforming graphemes into phonemes and blending the phonemes into pronunciations), *reading by analogy* (i.e., using already known sight words to pronounce new words that share letter clusters), and *reading by predicting* (i.e., making educated guesses about words based on context clues or initial letters). For familiar words, however, they tend to use *sight reading* because it is fast and automatic. The goal is to become a reader who shifts from relying mostly on the first three approaches to relying primarily on sight reading. When readers acquire an extensive sight vocabulary, they can allocate most of their cognitive resources to tasks such as accessing word meanings and creating mental models. Sight vocabularies are acquired through extensive reading and repeated exposure to the same words. In effect, connections form between printed words and their meanings, spellings, and pronunciations, and the sight of a word triggers rapid retrieval of the latter four kinds of information (Ehri, 1995).

After conducting numerous longitudinal studies with young children that extend from the preschool period to the point many children are fluent readers in the third grade, Ehri (1995) suggested that the connection-forming process proceeds through four phases: prealphabetic, partial alphabetic, full alphabetic, and consolidated alphabetic. The term *alphabetic* is used to denote the fact that (1) words consist of letters and (2) letters function as symbols for phoneme and phoneme blends in words. During the *prealphabetic phase,* "beginners remember how to read sight words by forming connections between selected visual attributes of words and their pronunciations or meanings and storing these associations in memory" (p. 118). For example, they may see the tail of the letter *g* in *dog* and associate it with real dogs, or see the two humps in *m* and associate *camel* with real camels. This phase is called prealphabetic because children are not really focusing on letters and their association to phonemes. This is also the phase when children engage in reading environmental print, such as stop signs and fast-food symbols. During the *partial-alphabetic phase,* "beginners remember how to read sight words by forming partial alphabetic connections between only some of the letters in written words and sounds detected in their pronunciations" (p. 119). For example, they might recognize the *s* and *n* of *spoon,* associate these two letters with their names (not their sounds), and retrieve the word *spoon* based on prior encounters (e.g., the last few times *s* and *n* co-occurred this way, the word was, in fact, *spoon*). Relatedly, they might pronounce the letter string *KDN* as *garden* because *k* and *g* are articulated using the same region of the mouth. During the *full-alphabetic phase,* "beginners remember how to read sight words by forming the complete connections seen in the written forms of words and phonemes detected in their pronunciations" (p. 120). For example, in reading *spoon,* a child in this phase would recognize that the five letters correspond to four phonemes and that the double *o* corresponds to the sound /oo/. Finally, in the *consolidated-alphabetic phase,* growth in a child's sight word vocabulary produces fully connected spellings for an increasing number of words. After this occurs, letter patterns that recur across different words become consolidated. For example, the connection between the *-at* in *bat, cat,* and *hat* and the common rime of these words prompts a consolidation of that pattern. Consolidation of many such patterns helps a reader become facile with multiletter units that correspond to morphemes, syllables, and subsyllabic units. Studies suggest that second grade may be the time when many children's sight vocabularies are large enough to support the consolidation process (Ehri, 1995).

If all goes well between first and third grades, children will learn how to quickly access the meanings and pronunciations of words as their eyes fixate on them and correctly compute the correct syntactic structure to derive the overall meaning of sentences they read. Because of the constraints of working memory, this generally means performing lexical access of all words and computing syntactic structures in 2 seconds or less (Perfetti, 1985). When they do, they are said to attain the level of *reading fluency.* If decoding, lexical access, and parsing are too slow, children may correctly pronounce all of the words but have no idea what they just read.

At one time, the construct of fluency was limited to the idea of efficient and automatic lexical retrieval (Ashby, 2016; Schwanenflugel & Kuhn, 2015). Recall that lexical retrieval pertains to the process of pulling up the proper meaning and pronunciation of a written word when the eyes fixate on that word during reading. *Efficient* lexical retrieval pertains to the ability to quickly and accurately pull up the right meanings and sounds of words from memory for a particular sentential context. *Automatic* lexical retrieval pertains to the ability to retrieve lexical information without devoting cognitive resources, such as attention. To get a sense of how a skill can shift from being effortful to automatic, consider how beginning drivers have a hard time using a manual stick shift and talking at the same time. After lots of practice, driving actions become automatic and drivers do not need to allocate attention to these actions. As a result, experienced drivers can talk and drive at the same time. To the notions of efficient and automatic lexical retrieval, Perfetti (2007) added the notion of *lexical quality*. Once lexical access is efficient and automatic, there can still be comprehension problems for some readers. Reading requires high-quality lexical representations that are stable and contain rich connections among orthography, phonology, and word meanings. Studies show that good readers have higher-quality lexical representations than poor readers, and this difference produces comprehension difficulties for poor readers.

More recently, the construct of fluency has been further expanded to include the abilities to (1) construct syntactic structures of sentences quickly and accurately and (2) read sentences with expression and prosody rather in a monotonic way (Ashby, 2016; Klauda & Guthrie, 2008; Schwanenflugel & Kuhn, 2015). Consider Schwanenflugel and Kuhn's definitions:

> Fluency combines accuracy, automaticity, and oral reading prosody, which, taken together, facilitate the reader's construction of meaning. It is demonstrated during oral reading through ease of word recognition, appropriate pacing, phrasing, and intonation. It is a factor in both oral and silent reading that can limit or support comprehension.

To understand why prosody should be considered part of fluency and how it promotes comprehension, Ashby (2016) added phases in the development of fluency: decoding, recoding, and precoding. All readers (including beginning readers) decode (sound out) a word they have never encountered before. Once the word has been decoded multiple times, a reader simply recodes it (i.e., translates it from text to sound) on additional encounters. To understand precoding, we return to the eye-movement techniques described earlier in the chapter. Recall that material in the parafoveal area can speed up reading (i.e., shorten fixation time). Earlier we saw that this can be done via priming using either a meaning element (e.g., *bark* for *dog*) or a sound element (e.g., *beech* for *beach*). A similar priming works for prosodic elements, such as how words are subdivided into syllables. A good prime for *demand* would be a stimulus briefly flashed in the parafoveal area such as *deXXXX* rather than *demXXX* because we pronounce *demand* as "de-mand" rather than "dem-and." Studies show that reading times for words are shortened using the proper syllabic prime presented in the parafoveal area.

One final developmental trend worth noting is that in the early elementary grades, decoding ability, word retrieval fluency, and listening comprehension predict reading comprehension. In the later grades when decoding, parsing, word retrieval, and prosody have become automatic and fluent, listening comprehension takes on a much stronger predictive role (Silverman, Speece, Harring, & Ritchey, 2014). The latter finding supports the simple view of reading, but it should also be noted that the original model excluded processes such as fluent word retrieval, quality of lexical representations, and prosody. Moreover, the applicability of the simple view of reading in other cultures with other languages has led to further proposed revisions. For example, whereas decoding and listening comprehension were found to predict reading comprehension in Dutch children, two other language skills added significant variance: vocabulary and knowledge of morphology (Verhoeven, Voeten, & Vermeer, 2019). Similarly, listening comprehension and decoding explained about 50% of the variance in the reading performance of children learning to read in Arabic, but orthographic and morphological knowledge explained an additional 20% (Asadi, Khateb, & Shany, 2017). *Morphological knowledge* consists of knowing root words, prefixes, suffixes, and grammatical inflections in one's own language (e.g., -*s* or -*es* for plurals in English). All of these morphemes which can be added or taken away from a word to alter its meaning (e.g., In English, adding -*er* to *read*, makes it *reader* or someone who does the reading).

IMPLICATIONS FOR EDUCATION

In the previous section that described developmental trends in the acquisition of beginning reading skills, we learned the following: (1) it is important for children to acquire emergent reading skills such as phonemic awareness and concepts of print, (2) there seem to be maturational, experiential, and motivational obstacles to getting children to read prior to age 5; (3) children progress through four phases in their acquisition of decoding skills (i.e., prealphabetic, partial alphabetic, full alphabetic, and consolidated alphabetic); and (4) many (but not all) children progress from being slow decoders to eventually becoming fluent readers by the end of third grade. We can now ask the developmental mechanism question: What factors promote changes in beginning reading skills? For specific age trends we can ask questions such as what factors could explain the shift from the prealphabetic to the partial-alphabetic stage? And, what do children have to do to become fluent readers?

The most obvious answer to such questions is that children progress when they are provided with repeated *opportunities to learn* about books, letters, and printed words at home and school, and multiple *opportunities to practice* decoding and sentence-processing skills (Kuhn & Rasinski, 2015). The meaning and pronunciation of printed words will only be accessed from long-term memory in less than a second if they are repeatedly encountered. Middle-class children come to school with higher levels of emergent literacy skills precisely because of having many opportunities to converse with their parents and read books with them (Byrnes & Wasik, 2019). And lower-income preschool children would benefit from evidence-based instructional techniques in their Head Start centers and preschools such as Story Talk, which was described in Chapter 8.

Similarly, the work on priming of syntax and developing expectations shows that frequency and exposure matter. In the 1960s, researchers thought it was a good idea to create books that only contained highly frequent words within very short sentences that combined these words via a simple syntax (e.g., the "Dick and Jane" books). Researchers and publishers used so-called *readability formulas* to create these books. This idea made a certain amount of sense if the goal was to have children reading books and experiencing success as early and often as possible. Because books for older children, such as the *Harry Potter* series, contain many unfamiliar words and sometimes long and convoluted sentences, most children in grades below fourth grade would struggle with these texts.

But the problem with the made-up, more readable books is that children cannot become generally fluent for any kind of book until they build up a lexicon with both frequent and infrequent words, and build up syntactic competence that includes the ability to correctly parse frequent and infrequent structures, and simple and complex syntax. One way to combine both of these ideas is to utilize trade books that were written by real authors that tell real stories, but are also kind in terms of vocabulary and syntax. Of course, some of these books will present some infrequent words and will occasionally use infrequent syntax. If all of these books present different words and different examples of syntactic structures, children will eventually progress in their speed at decoding, lexical access, and syntactic parsing. But the mantra should be *practice, practice, practice,* combined with lots of different books. If children read actual books for 20 minutes in school, 20 minutes at home, and do so 200 days a year, that amounts to 133 hours of practice per year and 400 total hours between the start of first grade and the end of third grade. If they engaged in practicing any kind of skill—such as shooting a basketball from different spots on the court or playing songs on the piano for a total of 400 hours—they would be pretty good at those skills, too, after 3 years.

In addition to practicing reading of the same text and different texts at least three times a week for 15 minutes, Kuhn and Rasinski (2015) argued that teachers should also (1) model expressive reading for children so children can hear what proper expressive reading sounds like, (2) have children read along with the teacher in an echoic manner, and (3) take care in selecting books for children (educator and author Timothy Rasinski gives many good recommendations for books at *www.timrasinski.com*).

Finally, it is a bit disheartening to hear reports in the news media that the so-called reading wars are beginning to reemerge over discontent with the lack of improvement in reading proficiency as described in the beginning of this chapter (see, e.g., *www.edweek.org/ew/articles/2019/09/11/ what-the-new-reading-wars-get-wrong.html*). As this chapter shows, there is so much evidence for the role of phonological processing not only as a component of emergent literacy but also as an aspect of skilled reading that it would almost be malpractice to abandon any aspect of reading instruction that promotes decoding and phonological process. Teachers were supposed to be advocating a *balanced approach* in which both decoding and meaning were emphasized ever since an influential book by Marilyn Adams appeared in 1990 (Adams, 1990). If teachers have gone a little out of balance to neglect meaningful reading of real books, that by no means should encourage teachers to advocate a return to the whole-language approach once again. Doing so would be misguided and not based on any well-supported theory or evidence that has accumulated to date.

CHAPTER 10

The Development
of Reading Comprehension Skills

In Chapter 9, we examined "beginning reading" and characterized it in terms of the skills needed to process individual words and sentences. In this chapter, we examine how readers comprehend larger segments of text, such as paragraphs, chapters, and full books. Before proceeding further, however, it should be noted that the distinction between "beginning reading" and "reading comprehension" is somewhat artificial and was made for expository purposes only. Although it has been traditional to characterize the former as "learning to read" and the latter as "reading to learn" (e.g., Chall, 1983), this characterization might prompt someone to draw two unwarranted conclusions: (1) that beginning reading never involves the extraction of meaning or information from text, and (2) that beginning reading only involves the proper pronunciation of words. Teachers and publishers who have drawn these conclusions have sometimes assumed that young readers do not have to read meaningful text in order to learn how to read (i.e., any text or string of words will do). In contrast, one of the major premises of contemporary approaches to reading is that any form of reading can, and should, be meaningful. We share this view but note that it is the case that some children leave third grade with adequate decoding skills but nevertheless have comprehension problems in fourth grade and beyond (Spencer & Wagner, 2018). Moreover, certain skills arise in the context of reading full paragraphs and stories that do not arise when single words or sentences are read. We examine these emergent skills and consider what happens after many children gain fluency in the second and third grades through an assessment and evaluation of the literature on multisentence reading comprehension.

THE NATURE AND DEVELOPMENT OF READING COMPREHENSION

The Nature of Reading Comprehension

A useful way to describe reading comprehension is to first give an overall sense of what it entails, and then describe some of its structural and functional aspects. The *structural aspects* of a system pertain to its component parts and their interrelations. In the case of reading, such aspects would emerge in response to questions such as "What do proficient readers know, and how does this knowledge affect their reading?" Functional aspects, in contrast, pertain to the goal-directed or processing aspects of a system. In the case of reading, the latter aspects would emerge in questions such as "What do proficient readers do when they read?"

To get an initial sense of what reading comprehension entails, it is helpful to examine the three-way relation among writers, written language, and readers. Writers usually begin with the goal of creating certain ideas in their readers' minds. To fulfill such a goal, writers ask themselves questions such as "If I want my readers to have such-and-such thoughts, what words can I use?" Writers choose certain words, phrases, and sentences based on their beliefs about conventional ways to say things and presume that their readers know these conventions. Thus, if the conventional way to state a prediction is to use an "if–then" construction and writers want their readers to know their prediction, they will use an if–then construction to make this prediction in print (e.g., *If the economy worsens, the next president will be from the opposite political party*). We can say that readers comprehend some written text when they understand what the writer was trying to say (Graesser, Millis, & Zwaan, 1997). In a sense, then, when a reader comprehends a writer, there is a "meeting of minds." Relatedly, we can say that comprehension involves knowing what is going on in some extended portion of text.

In contemporary theories, readers are assumed to achieve this kind of understanding by mentally representing text at five different levels of analysis (Graesser et al., 1997). The first level is called the *surface-code level*. Here, readers temporarily store a verbatim trace of some segment of text. How do we know? Studies show that readers can tell the difference between actually presented text and paraphrases, as long as test items are presented shortly after test takers read a segment of text. The second level is called the *text-base level*. Here, readers represent the content of text in a stripped-down format that preserves meaning but not the exact wording or syntax. The text base may also include a small number of inferences that are generated to create coherence between a pair of successive sentences (see below). The third level, called the *situation model,* "refers to the people, spatial setting, actions, and events" of a mental microworld that is "constructed inferentially through interactions between the explicit text and background world knowledge" (Graesser et al., 1997, p. 167). So, a situation model for the sentence *The grandmother looked up at her tall grandson* would be a mental representation of an older woman looking up at a tall young man (Cain & Barnes, 2017). The fourth level is called the *communication level.* Here, a reader represents the author's communicative intent (e.g., "The mystery novelist is probably telling me this now to throw me off the trail of the killer"). The fifth and final level is called the *text-genre level* because it reflects a reader's ability to categorize texts into different types (e.g., newspaper article, expository text, fiction). The operation of all five levels is essential for achieving a higher-level or "deep" understanding of text.

One further way to describe comprehension at a general level is to note that textual interpretation is very much a process of creating a coherent representation of the ideas contained in a passage or book (Cain & Barnes, 2017; Carpenter, Miyake, & Just, 1995; Graesser et al., 1997; McNamara & Magliano, 2009; Rapp, van den Broek, McMaster, Kendeou, & Espin, 2007). Psychologists argue that there are two kinds of coherence: local and global. *Local coherence* refers to an integrated representation of the ideas contained in a pair of adjacent sentences. *Global coherence,* in contrast, refers to an integrated representation of ideas that appear across widely dispersed segments of a text (e.g., ideas in the first and last chapters of a book). Two common ways to create coherence among sentences is by way of *reference relations* (e.g., the pronoun *she* in a sentence referring back to "Monica" in a preceding sentence) and *causal relations* (e.g., inferring that a glass broke after reading *Sasha tripped as she walked with her glass of juice. Her mom cleaned up the mess;* Rapp et al., 2007).

Structural Aspects of Comprehension

Structural aspects of comprehension pertain to aspects of the mind related to either processing capacity or the knowledge possessed by readers. Structural aspects provide the parameters within which the functional aspects of reading can operate. As we discuss later in this chapter, the functional aspects refer to the processes that readers perform when they read (e.g., inference making, reading strategies). As noted above, then, structural aspects largely pertain to *what readers know;* functional aspects pertain to *what readers do.* Readers who have limitations in their structural aspects (e.g., they have low WM capacity or low knowledge) will be hampered in their ability to carry out functional aspects, such as implementing a reading strategy. In contrast, readers with enhanced structural aspects have the resources they need to carry out the functional aspects effectively. Two important kinds of structural aspects are discussed next in turn: memory related and knowledge related.

Memory-Related Structural Aspects

As noted in Chapters 4 and 6, working memory (WM) is considered a short-term, transient form of memory that places an important structural limitation on the processing that occurs when people read or engage in other kinds of mental activities. In the same way that a large workshop enables a skilled carpenter to work on a wider array of projects of different sizes than a very small workshop does, the mind can carry out more elaborate cognitive operations when it has access to greater WM capacity than when it has access to less WM capacity. WM acts as a buffer to temporarily retain previously read successive items of information until the integration of these items can occur (Cain, Oakhill, & Bryant, 2004; Perfetti & Stafura, 2014). In addition, however, skilled readers constantly update their WM by (1) adding or retaining items of information that are particularly relevant to understanding the text as a whole, and (2) deleting items that are no longer relevant (Carretti, Cornoldi, De Beni, & Romano, 2005). They also adjust their level of processing, depending on the purpose of reading, by expending more effort and resources when reading to study versus reading for entertainment (Linderholm & van den Broek, 2002; Rapp et al., 2007).

Knowledge-Related Structural Aspects

Reading scholars often characterize knowledge in terms of cognitive structures called *schemata* (singular = *schema*) (see Chapter 3). A schema is a mental representation of what multiple instances of some type of thing have in common. For example, a schema for a house specifies the things that most houses have in common, and a schema for birthday parties specifies the things that happen at most birthday parties. Besides having schemata for types of objects and events, it has been claimed that skilled readers and writers have schemata for specific types of texts, too. Reading-related schemata are thought to support the ability to create global coherence (Carpenter et al., 1995; Graesser et al., 1997). The two main schemata that have been examined closely are those for *narrative* and *expository texts,* although there are also schemata for other genres, such as *argumentative essays*. In what follows, we discuss how schemata for specific topics (e.g., houses), narratives, and expository texts help students comprehend and remember what they are reading, and then examine several other kinds of knowledge that are important for skilled reading.

TOPIC KNOWLEDGE

When people read, they bring their existing knowledge to bear on a particular passage. This preexisting knowledge is often called *prior knowledge, background knowledge,* or *world knowledge* by text processing researchers. These researchers argue that a significant portion of this knowledge is represented in the form of schemata. When readers have schematized knowledge for objects and events, they are better able to assimilate the information presented in some text than when they lack this knowledge. In particular, when readers try to process some text, their minds try to find mental "spots" for each successive idea that is expressed in the text. For example, consider the truncated schema for a concept of "dog" below. If you are reading a passage that says, *Dogs are one of the most common pets,* your mind might metaphorically say, "I knew that because my 'dog' node is attached to a 'common pet' node by way of an 'is–a' link" in my 'dog' schema. However, if you next read the line *Dogs were first domesticated by ancient peoples,* your mind might say, "I didn't know that; let's add that piece of information to my 'dog' schema."

In addition to providing an assimilative base for incoming information, schemata for topics also help readers make inferences when things are not explicitly stated by an author. For example, if you read the line *The suspect handed Ralphie a "milk bone"* . . . , you would probably use your "dog" schema to make the inference that "Ralphie" is a dog. Similarly, if you were to read the line *Nobody came to Naomi's birthday party,* you might use your knowledge of people to infer that "Naomi" became sad as a result.

This schema–theoretical description of topic or background knowledge has been extended in recent years by considering other forms of declarative and conceptual knowledge that could enhance comprehension. Schemata correspond to an important form of conceptual knowledge (i.e., categorical relations among types of things or events), but there are other kinds of conceptual knowledge that could influence comprehension, such as the core principles of some domain (e.g., *adaptation,* in the case of biology), causality, temporal relations, spatial relations, mathematical relations, and so on (Gernsbacher & Kaschak, 2013; Guthrie et al., 2000). Causality, explanations, and core principles tend not to be modeled via schemata these days. Instead, researchers posit structures such as naïve or expert theories in readers' minds, or even connectionist node–link structures (Rapp et al., 2007; see Chapter 9 for examples of connectionist models and Chapter 13 for a discussion of naïve theories and causality).

Regardless of the theoretical model used, most scholars argue that prior knowledge promotes more extensive processing during reading (Cromley & Azevedo, 2007; McNamara & Magliano, 2009; Miller, Stine-Morrow, Kirkorian, & Conroy, 2004; Talwar, Tighe, & Greenberg, 2018). Evidence for this claim comes from the fact that high-knowledge readers allocate more time to conceptual integration during "wrap-up" and to global inference making. *Wrap-up* is the term for the processing that takes place at major syntactic constituent boundaries, such as clauses and sentences. But Talwar et al. (2018) also found it was necessary to augment the simple view of reading (see Chapter 9) by adding background knowledge to the two standard predictors of decoding ability and spoken language skills in order to fully predict the reading skills of struggling adult readers.

SCHEMATA FOR NARRATIVE TEXTS

Authors of narratives attempt to communicate event-based experiences to their readers. In most narratives, there are (1) *characters* who have goals and motives for performing actions; (2) *temporal* and *spatial placements* in which the story takes place; (3) *complications* and *major goals* of the main characters; (4) *plots* and *resolutions* of complications; (5) *affect patterns* (i.e., emotional and other responses to the story line); (6) *points, morals,* and *themes;* and (7) *points of view* and *perspectives* (Graesser, Golding, & Long, 1991).

One tradition within the text processing literature assumes that authors of narratives have schematized knowledge of the above components of a story and rely on this structure to "fill in" the components as they write a particular story. It is further assumed that an author does so with the expectation that his or her readers have this schematized knowledge, as well. As each part of a story unfolds, readers rely on their narrative schemata to form expectations as to what will come next. Skilled writers play off these expectations to occasionally surprise readers or "leave them hanging" (as cliff-hangers do). Schemata may be responsible for the feeling that readers may get after reading any of the individual portraits of characters in James Joyce's (1914) book *Dubliners* (i.e., wishing that each of the short stories did not end where it did, unfinished). Moreover, readers are thought to use their schemata for narratives to help them judge whether a story is a good one and also to create a *situation model* of what they have read.

SCHEMATA FOR EXPOSITORY TEXTS

Whereas the main goal of narratives is to tell a story to entertain readers, the main goal of expository texts is to provide information so that readers can learn something (Weaver & Kintsch, 1991). Thus, *Snow White* or any of the *Harry Potter* books are examples of narrative texts; this book or a biology textbook are examples of expository texts.

Just as skilled writers and readers are thought to have schemata for narrative texts, they are also thought to have schemata for expository texts.

The two most cited theoretical models of expository schemata are those of Meyer (1985) and Kintsch (1982). In Kintsch's model, there are three main relations that make up the schemata for expository texts:

1. *General–particular relations* that have to do with identifying, defining, classifying, or illustrating things (e.g., *A schema is a mental representation* . . .).
2. *Object–object relations* that have to do with comparing or contrasting things (e.g., *WM differs from long-term memory in that* . . .).
3. *Object–part relations* that have to do with causal relations, how the parts of something are put together, and how the parts work individually and collectively (e.g., *There are three types of memory: short term, working, and long term* . . .).

In Meyer's (1985) model, the ideas in a passage are also said to stand in certain relations to one another. Analyses of many common expository texts show that writers arrange their ideas into five common relations:

1. *Collection:* a relation that shows how things are related together into a group (e.g., *There are seven types of vehicles on the road today. First, there are* . . .).
2. *Causation:* a relation that shows how one event is the antecedent cause of another event (e.g., *The tanker spilled all its oil into the sea. As a result, the sea life* . . .).
3. *Response:* a relation that shows how one idea is a problem and another is a solution to the problem (e.g., *A significant number of people who are homeless have a substance abuse problem. It should be clear that homelessness will not diminish until increased money goes toward the treatment of this addiction* . . .).
4. *Comparison:* a relation in which the similarities and differences between things are pointed out (e.g., *Piaget and Vygotsky both emphasized egocentric speech; however, Vygotsky viewed it more as* . . .).
5. *Description:* a relation in which more information about something is given, such as attributes, specifics, manners, or settings (e.g., *Newer oil tankers are safer than they used to be. These days they have power steering and double hulls*).

Because these relations pertain to how the ideas are arranged in some text, they are said to make up the *prose structure* of the text. Writers hope that the arrangement of ideas in their readers' minds is the same as the arrangement of ideas in the text.

According to schema–theoretical models of comprehension, an individual who writes an expository textbook has schematized knowledge of the relations identified by Kintsch (1982) and Meyer (1985) and also knows the conventional ways of communicating these relations. The most common way to prompt readers to recognize a relation is to place sentences close together. When one sentence follows another, skilled readers try to form a connection between them (Carpenter et al., 1995; Graesser et al., 1997). If a writer fears that his or her readers will not make the connection even when sentences are placed in close proximity, he or she can use various *signaling devices* to make the connection explicit. For example, to convey Meyer's (1985) comparison relation, a writer might use the words *in contrast* to signal causal relations, or might use the words *as a result*. Of course, readers do not always need signals to make the connection. Consider the following two passages:

1. *There are two main causes of heart disease. Fatty diets promote the formation of plaque deposits on arteries. Cigarettes enhance the formation of plaque by constricting blood vessels.*
2. *There are two main causes of heart disease. First, fatty diets promote the formation of plaque deposits on arteries. Second, cigarettes enhance the formation of plaque by constricting blood vessels.*

For most people, the words *First* and *Second* in the second passage are not needed in order for a reader to connect the ideas in the three sentences into Meyer's (1985) "collection" relation. However, reading times are enhanced in low-knowledge readers when such devices are used (Graesser et al., 1997).

Over time, it is assumed that readers gain knowledge of the common relations found in expository texts, such as collection, causation, response, comparison, and description. In a sense, their mind unconsciously says, "Okay, how is this sentence related to the one(s) that I just read? Is it a causation relation? A comparison?" If the closest sentence does not provide an immediate fit, people read on until they find a sentence that does.

In addition to helping readers form expectations, knowledge of prose structure is thought to help readers comprehend and retain more of what they read (Meyer, 1985; Weaver & Kintsch, 1991). In particular, the five relations identified by Meyer often serve as an author's main point or thesis. Main ideas are connected by one of these five relations, and lesser ideas are subsumed beneath this overall relation. People who first encode the main point and then attach additional ideas to the main point demonstrate superior comprehension and memory of the ideas in a passage. People who treat paragraphs as a string of individual ideas show inferior comprehension and memory. Meyer, Wijekumar, and Lin (2011) showed that children's reading comprehension can be improved using a web-based tutoring system that promotes knowledge of text structure and signaling.

OTHER KINDS OF KNOWLEDGE

Three other kinds of knowledge that have been shown to be predictive of comprehension include knowledge of vocabulary and morphology, knowledge of acceptable grammatical structures, and metacognitive knowledge of reading (Cain et al., 2004; Perfetti & Stafura, 2014; Proctor, Carlo, August, & Snow, 2005; Spencer, Quinn, & Wagner, 2017; van Gelderen et al., 2004). The predictive links between reading comprehension and the two aspects of linguistic ability (i.e., vocabulary and grammatical knowledge) are certainly consistent with the simple view of reading presented in Chapter 9 (i.e., that reading consists of listening comprehension skills combined with decoding skills). But it is also consistent with Perfetti and Stafura's (2014) reading systems framework in which the lexicon (that contains information about word meaning and morphology) mediates between (1) the system of interconnected orthographic and phonological representations for words; and (2) the system of comprehension processes related to parsing sentences, making inferences, and constructing a situation model. *Metacognitive knowledge* of reading pertains to knowing the correct and incorrect ways of approaching the task of reading (e.g., recognizing the utility of using context to figure out the meaning of unfamiliar words). *Morphology* pertains to knowledge of morphemes, which are the smallest units of meaning in a language. The word *happy,* for example, has one unit of meaning. The word *unhappy* has two. Readers who have *morphological awareness* have explicit knowledge of how affixes and other word components change meaning. Morphological awareness, or the ability to explicitly describe such morphological relations is an independent predictor of reading comprehension (Spencer et al., 2017).

Functional Aspects of Comprehension

In addition to having structural knowledge of topics and the various kinds of texts (e.g., narrative vs. expository), readers also need to engage in a variety of active mental processes in order to enhance their reading comprehension (Graesser et al., 1997; Paris, Wasik, & Turner, 1991; Pressley et al., 1994; Pressley & Hilden, 2006). For descriptive purposes, these processes can be organized into three main clusters: orienting processes, coherence-forming processes, and reading strategies. We examine each of these clusters in turn.

Orienting Processes

The first thing that people have to do before they read is orient their cognitive processing toward some textual passage. For example, they need to *engage their attentional mechanisms* and, hopefully, motivational components, such as interest, as well (see Chapter 5 for more on motivation). Attention is a key component of executive function (see Chapter 6) and a recent meta-analysis showed that executive function correlates $r = .36$ with reading comprehension (Follmer, 2018). Next, they have to *set a goal* for reading (Pressley et al., 1994). Reading is a *purposeful* activity in that we read things for different reasons (Paris et al., 1991; Rapp et al., 2007). For example, whereas we usually read a newspaper to find out what is happening in the world, we read spy novels simply to be entertained or take our minds off work. Similarly, sometimes we only want a rough sense of what an author is trying to say, so we just skim the pages for major points. Other times we really want to process everything that an author says, so we read every line carefully (e.g., as when we read a textbook right before a test). Goal setting is crucial because the goals we set can either enhance or limit what we get from reading. For example, if someone sets the goal of "pronouncing all of the words correctly" but does not set the goal of "learning something," he or she is unlikely to engage in any of the reading strategies that are described later in this chapter and, therefore, will not comprehend very much of what he or she reads.

Coherence-Forming Processes

Recall that a central goal of reading is to create a coherent mental representation of the ideas in a passage (i.e., a situation model). There are several key processes that facilitate the construction of coherent representations, though *inference making* is probably the most widely studied of these processes (Gernsbacher & Kaschak, 2013; Graesser et al., 1997; Paris et al., 1991). Readers make inferences in order to (1) elaborate on the meaning of an individual sentence and (2) integrate the meanings of several sentences in a text (Alba & Hasher, 1983). For example, when readers encounter sentences such as *The man stirred his coffee,* many of them elaborate on the ideas presented by inferring that he used a spoon. In addition, when presented with a pair of sentences such as *Nigel smoked four packs a day. After he died, his wife sold her Phillip Morris stocks,* many readers infer that smoking caused Nigel to die. Thus, the two ideas of smoking and dying are integrated together through a causal relation. Moreover, as mentioned above, the principal source of inter- and intrasentence inferences is a reader's knowledge of topics such as "coffee" and "cigarettes." The second source is the reader's knowledge of text structures and genres.

Why do readers make inferences when they read? It seems that a reader's mind is always trying to make sense of what it is encountering (Rapp et al., 2007). One way of making sense of things is to make the information presented more concrete and specific. So, when people read the sentence above about stirring coffee, their minds naturally ask questions such as "What kind of thing do people usually use to stir their coffee?" Notice that the inference that a spoon was used is merely probabilistic. People sometimes use whatever is handy, such as the handle of a fork. Recent models of language processing also place a strong emphasis on *embodied cognition*, in which we use our perceptual areas of the brain to mentally simulate events (Glenberg, Gutierrez, Levin, Japuntich, & Kaschak, 2004). When we read about someone using a spoon, there is brain activity in the motor area of our cortex. We also tend to envision where we often see or encounter objects when we read nouns (e.g., *Birds are often found in the sky;* Ostarek & Vigliocco, 2017).

As to why we make intersentence inferences, it is helpful to repeat a point made earlier: It seems that the mind is always asking, "How does this new sentence relate to the sentences that I already read?" When two events co-occur close in time, it is natural to think that the prior one caused the later one (Bullock, Gelman, & Baillargeon, 1982; Graesser et al., 1997; Rapp et al., 2007). For example, by stating the first sentence above about smoking and then the second one about dying right after it, it is natural to assume that smoking killed Nigel. Similarly, if one reads the two sentences *The floor was just mopped. I fell,* it is natural to assume that the speaker slipped on the floor. It is possible, however, that smoking did not kill Nigel and that the person fell because of something else (e.g., tripping over a bucket). Thus, once again we see that inferences are not necessary conclusions—they are merely probabilistic guesses.

In addition to causal connections, various other intersentence connections could be inferred on the basis of one's knowledge. These include inferences regarding the (1) goals and plans that motivate a character's actions, (2) traits or properties of characters or objects, (3) emotions of characters, (4) causes of events, (5) likely consequences of actions, (6) spatial relationships, (7) global theme or point, and (8) attitude of the writer (Graesser et al., 1997). Do readers make all these inferences? It depends on whom you ask. Some "minimalist" theorists believe that only causal inferences are made routinely (e.g., McKoon & Ratcliff, 1992). Other more "constructionist" theorists believe that readers usually make inferences related to character goals, inferences as to why certain events occurred, and inferences that establish coherence at the local or global levels (Gernsbacher & Kaschak, 2013; Graesser et al., 1997).

As one further illustration of an inference-based coherence process, note that readers naturally link up a pronoun in a second sentence to a person's name in a first sentence (e.g., *Maya saw the doctor. She said . . .*). Similar to causal inferences, such *anaphoric inferences* about pronouns are also probabilistic (i.e., the doctor in the prior sentence could be a woman, so *she* refers to the doctor, not Maya). Anaphoric expressions are one kind of class of textual entities called *referring expressions* (Gernsbacher, 1996). Other types include *cataphoric expressions* that refer to future text elements and *deitic expressions* that refer to things in the world. Writers and readers recognize that referring expressions conform to a small set of rules. For example, when a new entity is first introduced in a text, the referring expression usually contains an indefinite determiner (*a* or *an*), a richly specified noun, and a descriptive set of adjectives or prepositional phrases (e.g., *A massive man with a bushy mustache*). The next time this entity appears, however, it usually contains a definite determiner and just the noun (e.g., *The man . . .*).

The final way that coherence is established and maintained is by making use of *inhibition* processes that suppress ideas that are incompatible with the current situation model (Gernsbacher, 1996). In Chapter 6, inhibition was said to be one component of executive function. When words are read in succession, the multiple meanings of each word are temporarily activated. For example, when people read *The woman smelled the rose,* they temporarily activate meanings such as "thorny flower with soft petals" and "stood up" when they reach the word *rose.* However, only the former meaning is compatible with the overall meaning of the sentence. To achieve coherence, readers need to suppress or deactivate the inappropriate meanings (Henderson, Snowling, & Clarke, 2013). Poor comprehenders have difficulty accessing less common meanings and suppressing dominant meanings.

Reading Strategies

So far, we have seen that readers set goals for reading and engage in processes such as inference making and inhibition to create a coherent situation model. One further way readers enhance their understanding is to apply a number of *reading strategies* (Edossa, Neuenhaus, Artelt, Lingel, & Schneider, 2018; McNamara, 2017; Schünemann, Spörer, Völlinger, & Brunstein, 2017). Most theorists argue that a strategy is a deliberate, goal-directed operation that is directed at solving a problem (Bjorklund, 2004). In the case of reading, the "problem" to be solved is achieving a deep and accurate understanding of some text. To say that a strategy is deliberate implies that a reader has some control over it. In other words, he or she intentionally tries to apply it and decides when and where to do so. The converse would be reading processes that happen automatically or implicitly, such as inhibition. Some of the reading strategies that have been investigated include *identifying the main idea, summarizing, predicting, monitoring,* and *backtracking,* though there has been some debate as to whether all of these processes are under a reader's control (Magliano, Trabasso, & Graesser, 1999; Rosenshine & Meister, 1994). Inference making has been called a reading strategy, too, and there is evidence that it is partially under a reader's control (Magliano et al., 1999). It was discussed in the prior section because it is so central to the coherence-forming processes. Rather than engage in unproductive taxonomic debates regarding which processes are strategies and which are not, it is best to think of strategies and pro-cesses being arrayed along a continuum of deliberateness and explicitness, with some being more deliberate and explicit than others. We now consider those strategies and processes that are perhaps farther along the continuum than others.

In order to *identify the main idea* of some passage, readers need to assess the relevance of each idea in the passage and then rank ideas in terms of their centrality or importance (Schünemann et al., 2017; van Dijk & Kintsch, 1983). Consider the following paragraph taken from Steven Pinker's (2011) book *The Better Angels of Our Nature: Why Violence Has Declined*:

> Self-control, then, is a stable trait that differentiates one person from another, beginning in early childhood. No one has done the twin and adoption studies that would be needed to show that performance on standard tests of self-control, such as the marshmallow test or the adult equivalent, are heritable. But it's a good bet that they are, because pretty much every psychological trait has turned out to be partly heritable. Self-control is partly correlated with intelligence (with a coefficient of about 0.23 on a scale from −1 to 1), and the two traits depend on the same parts of the brain, though not exactly in the same way. Intelligence itself is highly correlated with crime—duller people commit more violent crimes and are more likely to be the victims of a violent crime—and though we can't rule out the possibility that the effect of self-control is really an effect of intelligence or vice versa, it's likely that both traits contribute independently to nonviolence. Another clue that self-control is heritable is that a syndrome marked by a shortage of self-control, atten-tion deficit hyperactivity disorder (which is also linked with delinquency and crime), is among the most heritable of personality traits. (p. 601)

What is the main idea of this paragraph? Is it contained in the first sentence? The last? The fourth? How do you know? If this were an item from the verbal section of the SAT, one of the questions about this para-graph would ask which sentence was the main idea. Apart from the practi-cal reality that important standardized tests require the ability to identify the main idea, readers also need this skill in order to construct the prose structure for a text (see the previous section on structural aspects). Pinker (2011) rank ordered the ideas in his paragraph in a particular way (in his own mind), and he wanted us to get his point about self-control. To say that we comprehended his paragraph is to say that we rank-ordered ideas in the same way that he did.

In addition to determining the prose structure of a passage, a second way to identify main ideas is to locate various signals in the text. Sometimes signals are graphic (e.g., italics), sometimes they are lexical (e.g., using the word *essential*), and sometimes they are semantic (e.g., explicit topic sen-tences). Readers expect that the main idea will occur early in a paragraph, but location is not always a very good predictor. In fact, studies have shown that as few as 25% of children's textbooks have main ideas located near the beginning of paragraphs (Garner, 1987). Thus, it may be a better idea to rely on prose–structure relations and prior knowledge to find the main idea than to rely on text signals.

Besides being central to comprehension, an additional reason why identifying the main idea is an important strategy is that it is a prerequisite skill for performing the second important reading strategy: *summarizing* (Schünemann et al., 2017). In order to create a summary, you need to be able to delete unimportant ideas and retain just the gist of what is written. The gist, in turn, comprises mostly the main ideas. Note that the text-base level described earlier helps one distill the gist of a passage.

To see why identifying the main idea is a prerequisite skill for summarizing, consider the five rules for forming a good summary proposed by Brown and Day (1983). The first two rules specify that readers should delete trivial, irrelevant, or redundant information. The third rule suggests that readers should find a superordinate term for members of a category (e.g., *automobiles* for Ford, Jeep, and Honda). Rules 4 and 5 specify that readers should find and use the main ideas of a passage in their summary. If main ideas are not explicitly provided by an author, readers should construct their own main ideas. Thus, one could not construct a good summary without being able to identify the main ideas.

Studies suggest that readers adopt different strategies when asked to read a passage and write a summary of it from memory (Hyönä, Lorch, & Kaakinen, 2002). Whereas some readers skim quickly through the passage, others read more slowly or reread portions of the text. The best summarizers have been found to be students who (1) have greater WM capacity and (2) spend a good deal of time processing topic sentences.

The third important reading strategy is *predicting*. Predicting consists of simply forming expectations regarding what will happen next in a narrative story or anticipating what the author of an expository text will say next (McNamara, 2017). Good writers are skilled at helping readers make predictions and also skilled at violating expectations in such a way that it is entertaining. To illustrate, consider the following lines taken from the 2013 book *Dad Is Fat,* written by the comedian Jim Gaffigan: "Having five children has really made me appreciate the more important things in life. Particularly the sublime state of being alone" (p. 17). Gaffigan's humor works well because readers expect him to say one thing and he frequently says another.

The fourth reading strategy is called *comprehension monitoring.* Simply put, comprehension monitoring is the ability to "know when you don't know"—that is, it is the ability to detect a comprehension failure (Edossa et al., 2018; Markman, 1981). As discussed in Chapter 9 and earlier in this chapter, reading does not consist of simply knowing how to sound out words. Rather, reading consists of extracting meaning from texts. If a portion of a text does not make sense, readers should recognize that the main goal of reading (i.e., extracting meaning) has not been met.

When readers recognize that something that they just read does not make sense, they have two options: (1) they could simply read on, or (2) they could decide to do something about their lack of comprehension. The latter option brings us to our fifth and final strategy: *backtracking*. Backtracking consists of rereading a portion of a text when a lack of comprehension occurs. Garner (1987) suggests that readers backtrack in response to four judgments and beliefs:

1. They do not understand or remember what they just read.
2. They believe they can find the information needed to resolve the difficulty in the text.
3. The prior material must be scanned to locate the helpful information.
4. Information from several prior sentences may need to be combined and manipulated to resolve the comprehension problem.

In Chapter 9, backtracking was shown to be a key indicator of comprehension problems, such as when readers are presented with "garden-path" sentences (e.g., *Since Jim jogs a mile seems like a short distance to him*). Eye-tracking tools demonstrate when people encounter a problem (e.g., at the word *seems*) and when they go back and reread the sentence.

Summary

In contemporary reading theories, it is assumed that reading comprehension is greatly aided when readers (1) set goals for understanding; (2) have declarative and conceptual knowledge of the topic; (3) have adequate WM capacity and knowledge of the different types of texts (i.e., narrative and expository); (4) have linguistic knowledge and metacognitive knowledge of reading; and (5) employ a variety of active mental processes, such as inference making, inhibition, identifying the main idea, summarizing, predicting, monitoring, and backtracking.

The Development of Reading Comprehension Skills

As a means of summarizing the development of reading comprehension skills, we first examine the research concerned with developmental differences in structural aspects of reading comprehension, then the developmental research related to functional aspects, and finally, the research related to the role of extensive reading in the development of reading skills.

Development of Structural Aspects of Comprehension

In discussing the development of structural aspects of reading comprehension, one asks questions such as "How do the schemata of younger children differ from those of older children?" and "Do older children have more conceptual knowledge than younger children?" We attempt to answer such questions by first focusing on research pertaining to the development of WM capacity, and then considering research on the development of schemata for specific topics, schemata for stories, and schemata for expository texts.

WM CAPACITY

Studies have shown that there are monotonic increases in the capacity of WM that occur between the ages of 5 and 25 (see Chapter 4). In addition, children show an increased ability to update WM and inhibit the activation of irrelevant information, two key aspects of executive function (see Chapter 6). These increased abilities in memory have been found to be associated with improved reading comprehension skills (Cain et al., 2004; Carretti et al., 2005). However, there are also individual differences in memory retrieval, such that good readers are more likely to access the right word meanings, read fluently, and inhibit improper meanings than poor comprehenders (Perfetti & Stafura, 2014).

TOPIC KNOWLEDGE

Reading theorists assume that a substantial portion of children's knowledge of various topics (e.g., animals, fractions, baseball) is arranged into schemata. Thus, their knowledge of birds might be represented by a node for "bird" connected to a node for "canary" by an "is–a" link, and so on. With age, experience, and increased education, children's schemata for various topics become more and more elaborate. Relatedly, other forms of conceptual and declarative knowledge increase with age as well (Lehrer & Schauble, 2015; McCormack, 2015; Nunes & Bryant, 2015; Sloutsky, 2015). This increased topic knowledge greatly facilitates children's comprehension. But, of course, since older children acquire much of their knowledge via reading in school, there is reason to think that reading increases topic knowledge, and increased topic knowledge improves comprehension further.

STORY SCHEMATA

Although several theoretical models of schemata for stories have been proposed over the years (Graesser et al., 1991), the models that have generated the most developmental research are those based on the classic *story grammars* proposed by Mandler and Johnson (1977) and Stein and Glenn (1979). Stein and Glenn (1979) has been cited over 1,000 times at this writing, according to Web of Science, and Mandler and Johnson (1977) has been cited over 1,200 times. In Stein and Glenn's classic account, a story grammar is a theoretical description of what most stories have in common. It is not intended to reflect an actual knowledge structure in a young reader's mind. Rather, it is a representation of an expert's knowledge of what all stories have in common (Stein, 1982). To get a sense of the formal, abstract character of a story grammar, consider the following example: If an adult were to sign up for a writing workshop to learn how to write a book for children, he or she would probably be presented with some form of a story grammar by the workshop leader. The workshop leader would say things like, "Any successful story has seven parts. The first part is. . . ."

Although children do not start out with a formal, explicit story grammar in their minds, it has often been said that they do develop *story schemata* in response to listening to and reading many stories. A story schema contains personalized, implicit knowledge about what most stories have in common (Stein, 1982). Given the personalized nature of story schemata, any two children could develop different schemata if they listened to very different types of stories during their lives. However, as children read more and more stories and gain increased knowledge about people, their story schemata should become more similar to a formal story grammar.

The original story grammar proposed by Stein and Glenn (1979) specified that stories have seven main components: (1) a *major setting* that includes the introduction of characters (e.g., "Once upon a time, there was a beautiful young woman called Cinderella"); (2) a *minor setting* that includes a description of the story context (e.g., "She lived in a modest house with her stepmother"); (3) *initiating events* that include changes in the environment or things that happen to the main characters (e.g., "One day, the prince invited everyone to a ball"); (4) *internal responses* that include the character's goals, plans, and thoughts that arise in response to the initiating events (e.g., "Cinderella said, 'Oh, I want to go the ball too!'"); (5) *attempts* that include the character's actions to fulfill the goal (e.g., "So she started to fix an old gown to make it more presentable"); (6) *direct consequences* that specify whether the goal was attained (e.g., "But her stepmother made her clean the house instead of fix her gown"); and (7) *reactions* that include the character's feeling or thoughts about the direct consequences (e.g., "When it came time to go to the ball, Cinderella was sad because she could not go"). The first two elements are usually grouped together to form what is called the "setting" part of a story, and the last five elements are grouped together to form what is called the "episode" part of the story. Hence, prototypical stories contain both a setting and at least one episode.

Research has shown that when stories conform to the canonical structure specified above (i.e., they have all seven of the components arranged in the same order as above), few developmental differences emerge. In particular, even 4- and 5-year-olds show good recall of the events in a story when it has all of the components outlined in Stein and Glenn's (1979) story grammar. Older children do, however, recall more information in the story than younger children and also make more inferences than younger children. The majority of these inferences seem to be attempts to fill in category information that was missing in the actual text (Stein, 1982). For example, if the "reaction" portion of a story was missing, older children tend to fill in this component through inference. A longitudinal study of Swedish children showed a steep increase in the inclusion of the main macrostructure of narratives between ages 4 years, 4 months and 5 years, 10 months, but then leveling off thereafter (Lindgren, 2019). In addition, some studies suggest that whereas children are likely to recall the action elements of a story schema (part of the "attempts" node), adults are more likely to recall internal responses, such as a protagonist's goals and the events that initiated these goals (van den Broek, Lorch, & Thurlow, 1996).

When noncanonical stories are used, developmental differences become even more pronounced. For example, when a story is artificially disorganized (e.g., the "initiating event" is placed after the "direct consequence"), older children are more able to recover the canonical structure of the story in their retellings than younger children are (Stein, 1982). Similarly, when children are given the initial portions of a story and asked to complete it, older children are more likely than younger children to add the components that the story grammar would suggest are missing (Eckler & Weininger, 1989). Finally, when presented with stories that are missing some of the components specified in the story grammar (e.g., "direct consequences"), older readers (who have well-developed story schemata) are more likely than younger readers to say that the story was not a good one (Stein & Policastro, 1984).

Thus, developmental differences are most pronounced when children are asked to comprehend a story that does *not* conform to a story grammar. It would seem that a canonical story minimizes the amount of processing that has to be done in order for the story to be comprehended. The argument is that this minimization would occur only if children had something like a story schema in their mind. Since older children tend to have greater processing capacity than younger children, the former can take a noncanonical story and mentally fill in components or rearrange them to make it into a more canonical story.

In sum, then, story schemata have been thought to play two important roles. First, they minimize the processing that has to occur when a story is read. When presented with a canonical story, readers need not devote all of their mental resources to comprehending the basic facts in the story.

Instead, readers can use any additional processing resources to perform other mental tasks, such as inference making (Stein, 1982) and metaphor comprehension (Waggoner, Messe, & Palermo, 1985). Second, story schemata set up expectations as to what will occur next in a story. For example, if the "initiating event" component has just occurred in a story, readers tend to expect that the "internal response" component will be encountered soon. Although older students can make better use of the two roles played by story schemata than younger students, even preschoolers seem to have a rudimentary story schema. In most cases, however, it is necessary to use auxiliary pictures and probing questions to reveal a story schema for children below the age of 6 (Shapiro & Hudson, 1991).

Many school systems have incorporated the story grammar model into their reading curriculum. In fact, teachers frequently ask students to identify the parts of a story that they just read (e.g., "Who can tell me what the setting is?"; "What is the initiating event?"). Thus, students learn the parts and then get a lot of practice finding the parts in actual stories. If the schema theory is correct that the mind "naturally" abstracts common elements on its own, perhaps this explicit instruction would not be necessary. And yet, at the very least, we would expect that this practice would certainly help students acquire a story schema faster than they would on their own. Research supports this expectation, especially for younger students or students with disabilities (Dimino, Taylor, & Gersten, 1995; Lauren & Allen, 1999; Pressley, Johnson, Symons, McGoldrick, & Kurita, 1989).

SCHEMATA FOR EXPOSITORY TEXTS

In its purest form, a developmental study of prose structure would take groups of children at two ages and give them well-organized and poorly organized expository passages to recall (e.g., Danner, 1976). In such a study, one could examine whether older children are more likely than younger children to (1) use the author's prose structure to help their recall (i.e., to find the author's main thesis and use it to organize their recall of subordinate ideas), (2) need explicit text signals to derive the prose structure, and (3) derive the prose structure in poorly organized passages. All these findings would support the idea that, with age and increased reading opportunities, children acquire schemata for expository texts.

Unfortunately, such "pure" developmental studies are hard to find. Instead of using multiple age groups, many researchers have used just one age group. In addition, many researchers seemed to be more interested in reading ability than age because when they compared children of two age groups, they usually added reading ability as a variable (e.g., they compared fifth-grade, struggling comprehenders to third-grade, skilled comprehenders). Further, many researchers provided instruction on how to derive prose structure to see whether children's comprehension could be improved. As a result, few of the existing studies can be used to say whether children "naturally" acquire schemata for expository texts simply by reading many of them (as seems to be the case for story schemata).

Nevertheless, the existing research suggests that the derivation of prose structure is often not an easy task for children at any age. Meyer, Brandt, and Bluth (1980), for example, found that when given four well-organized passages to remember, only 22% of ninth graders consistently used the strategy of using the author's main thesis to organize their recalls. More than 50% of these students did not use the strategy even once. As a result, even the best readers recalled 70% or fewer of the ideas in the passages. Similarly, Zinar (1990) found that fifth graders recalled only about 20–25% of the content of short prose passages, suggesting that they, too, did not use the prose structure to guide their recall.

This is not to say, however, that children's performance is always so deficient. For example, Garner et al. (1986) found excellent knowledge of prose structure in a group of seventh graders. In particular, 75% could provide a meaningful description of a paragraph, 98% could exclude topically unrelated sentences from a paragraph, 87% knew where to place a topic sentence in a paragraph, and 87% could arrange a set of sentences into a cohesive whole. Similarly, Spires, Gallini, and Riggsbee (1992) found that fourth graders in a control group recalled 60% or more of the content of expository passages arranged in the form of problem–solution or compare–contrast formats. Welie, Schoonen, and Kuiken (2018) found that Dutch eighth graders correctly answered 68% of questions on a measure of expository text comprehension and the two strongest predictors of comprehension were their understanding of connectives and metacognitive knowledge of prose structure.

The finding that children can perform both extremely well and extremely poorly suggests that something other than schemata for expository texts might be at work. One possible explanation for such variable performance is children's knowledge of the passage topic (Roller, 1990). For very familiar passages, being aware of common formats such as problem–solution or compare–contrast may add little to one's knowledge of the topic—that is, a reader might show excellent comprehension of a familiar passage even when he or she lacks knowledge of common formats (i.e., lacks a schema for expository passages). For example, a young child who is enthralled by dinosaurs might show very good comprehension of a passage about the extinction of dinosaurs even though this child lacks knowledge of the format in which the ideas are arranged (e.g., "causal" relations). Conversely, a reader may show very poor comprehension of an unfamiliar passage even when he or she has knowledge of common formats. For example, an adult who is unfamiliar with computers but familiar with compare–contrast formats might show poor comprehension of a passage about the similarities and differences between two kinds of computers.

If both prior knowledge and schemata for expository texts affect comprehension, the effects of schemata for expository texts should be most pronounced when readers are only moderately familiar with a topic. In reviewing the literature on prose structure, Roller (1990) found two findings in support of this notion: (1) presenting disorganized paragraphs has its strongest effects when readers are moderately familiar with the topic, and (2) providing instruction of the different types of prose structures (e.g., problem–solution) has its strongest effects when readers are moderately familiar with a topic. When readers are either very familiar or very unfamiliar with a topic, these effects are considerably weaker.

In sum, then, there is evidence that children in the later grades have at least implicit knowledge of various prose structures. Whether they make use of this structure to aid their comprehension and recall seems to depend on their familiarity with a topic. Because most studies in this area have neither controlled for familiarity nor used a "pure" developmental design, it is hard to say what the "natural" developmental course of schemata for expository texts is. Nevertheless, a number of studies have shown that when children are told about the various types of relations in prose passages and asked to identify these relations (e.g., "Look at this paragraph. Where is a collection relation? How about a cause–effect relation?"), they show improved comprehension (Welie et al., 2017). So, just as teaching story grammar elements can help improve children's comprehension of stories, teaching children the common expository elements can help them better comprehend expository passages. However, given the role of familiarity, it would make sense that pointing out expository relations should be done only when the passage contains content that is moderately familiar to students. It would be a waste of time for content that is either highly familiar or highly unfamiliar. One way a teacher could check the familiarity of a topic is to have students generate a group-concept map or web prior to reading (Guthrie et al., 2000). Here, students would say everything they know about a topic, and the teacher would depict this knowledge using a node–link schema on the board.

Development of Functional Aspects of Reading

In what follows, developmental research on the three categories of functional aspects (i.e., orienting processes, coherence-forming processes, and reading strategies) is described in turn.

Orienting Processes

Research shows that young children do not set optimal reading goals for themselves. For example, instead of reading something to increase their knowledge about the topic or be entertained, young readers say that the goal of reading is to "pronounce all of the words properly." Other students act as if their goal is to simply "get the assignment done" (Paris, Byrnes, & Paris, 2001; Paris et al., 1991). With these goals, students who read all the words properly and finish reading an assigned passage will not be bothered if they do not comprehend what they read. Over time, children replace their suboptimal goals with more appropriate ones regarding meaning. Typically, however, this shift takes too many years to complete. It should be clear that teachers need to help students set goals that are more appropriate for themselves early on in the elementary grades. It is also the case that with developmental increases in executive functions, the ability of children to allocate attention effectively during reading would increase as well (Follmer, 2018).

Coherence-Forming Processes

Given the fact that (1) declarative and conceptual knowledge underlies inference making and (2) declarative and conceptual knowledge increases with age, it should not be surprising to learn that many studies have found that children in the later grades (e.g., fourth, fifth, and sixth grades) are more likely to make inferences than children in the earlier grades are (Paris et al., 1991; van den Broek, 1989). For example, when reading the sentence *The man stirred his coffee,* older students are more likely than younger students to infer that the man used a spoon (Paris, 1978). Inference making, in turn, predicts degree of comprehension even after controlling for other factors, such as WM (Cain et al., 2004).

However, the common finding of developmental differences in inference making should not imply that younger children are incapable of making inferences. Some studies have shown that young children demonstrate very good inference-making skills when they are presented with stories about very familiar topics or are given instruction on how to make inferences (Dewitz, Carr, & Patberg, 1987; Paris et al., 1991; Wasik, 1986). Thus, the "natural" course of inference making can be altered by way of instruction or by using highly familiar content.

One good way of eliciting inferences is to stop in the middle of stories whenever an inference is required and ask questions. For example, when students read the popular "Miss Nelson" stories (about a teacher named Miss Nelson), they need to make the inference that a mean substitute teacher in the story, named "Viola Swamp," is really Miss Nelson in disguise. Throughout the book, subtle clues are left to help readers make this connection. Young readers often miss these clues, so it would be helpful to ask questions such as "What is Viola Swamp's dress doing in Miss Nelson's closet?" Given the centrality of explanations in the comprehension process, "why" questions would also be extremely helpful (Magliano et al., 1999; McNamara, 2017). Over time, repeated questions that require inferences would ultimately help children make inferences on their own. However, since older students seem to make inferences without much prompting, focused instruction on inference making might be best for kindergartners through fourth graders. The combination of increased WM capacity, knowledge growth, teacher guidance, and changing goals for reading (see above) should lead to the spontaneous tendency to generate inferences.

Other kinds of coherence-forming processes besides inference making (e.g., anaphora and inhibition) have received very little attention from developmentalists. At present, for example, only one study has shown that it is possible to improve the comprehension of anaphora in third graders through direct instruction (Baumann, 1986). Similarly, there are only a handful of developmental studies of the role of inhibition in reading. One study found that (1) seventh graders demonstrated a greater ability to inhibit distracting information than fifth graders, and (2) the ability to inhibit irrelevant information was strongly related to reading comprehension scores (Kipp, Pope, & Digby, 1998). Another study of 6- to 11-year-olds found that inhibitory skills predicted reading comprehension after controlling for age, intelligence, and level of attentional problems (Savage, Cornish, Manley, & Hollis, 2006). Why age changes in inhibition might occur is still something of a mystery. Some have speculated it has to do with the development of the frontal lobes (Dempster, 1992), but connectionist modeling studies suggest it may have to do with the elaboration of neural nets associated with the reading system (e.g., the addition of inhibitory connections).

Reading Strategies

Children in the elementary grades have difficulty recognizing, recalling, and constructing the main idea in passages (Baumann, 1981; Johnston & Afflerbach, 1985; Paris et al., 1991). Moreover, there is evidence that this skill improves throughout the adolescent and early adult years. Once again, however, the identification of main ideas is more likely when familiar content is used (Sternberg, 1985) and when students are directly taught how to perform this strategy (e.g., Baumann, 1984; Schünemann et al., 2017).

As might be expected given the findings for identifying the main idea, there are clear developmental trends in the ability to provide a good summary. Whereas younger students (e.g., fifth graders) tend to create summaries by simply deleting statements and using the author's words, older students (e.g., high school students) tend to combine and reorganize ideas using their own words (Brown & Day, 1983; Paris et al., 1991; Taylor, 1986).

As was found for both inference making and identifying the main idea, however, preadolescent children can be taught how to provide a good summary (Brown, Day, & Jones, 1983; Palincsar & Brown, 1984; Rinehart,

Stahl, & Erickson, 1986). In the Rinehart et al. study, for example, children were taught four rules for summarizing over the course of five 1-hour lessons: identify the main information, delete trivial information, delete redundant information, and relate main and supporting information. The teacher modeled each strategy and then asked students to practice the modeled strategy. They worked first at the paragraph level, and then moved up to combining paragraph summaries into a single summary for the whole text. When training was over, the researchers found that trained children showed better memory for what they read than untrained children did.

With respect to predicting, studies have shown that although many students do not spontaneously make predictions when they read, they can be taught to do so. In support of the claim that good comprehenders make predictions when they read, these studies also show that the reading comprehension of children and college students improves after being told how to make predictions (Fielding, Anderson, & Pearson, 1990; Hansen & Pearson, 1983; McNamara, 2017; Palincsar & Brown, 1984; Pearson & Fielding, 1991).

One way to improve student predictions is to have them make a prediction on what a book will be about after examining the title and cover illustration (Pressley et al., 1994). Then, in the midst of reading the work, children can be asked to stop and make additional predictions. Finally, after the reading is completed, children can be asked to examine their original predictions to see whether they were right. Pressley and colleagues have shown that whereas first graders need a lot of prompting to make such predictions, older students need much less prompting after 3 years of such instruction.

As noted previously, the essence of reading comprehension is the extraction of meaning—that is, one reads *in order* to gain an understanding of a story or some topic area. If students read a story or an informational passage and do not come away with a good understanding of what they read, that means that they did not attain the central goal of reading (Baker & Brown, 1984; Paris et al., 1991). If it were to be found that many children do not detect their comprehension failures or do not try to fix a comprehension failure when it occurs, that would mean that reading instruction is seriously deficient. To see this, consider an analogy: What would we think about a vocational school that constantly produced automobile mechanics who could not detect or repair problems within a malfunctioning automobile? Just as the essence of car repair involves knowing the difference between a well-functioning and malfunctioning car (and knowing how to fix the latter), the essence of reading involves knowing the difference between adequate and inadequate comprehension (and knowing how to fix the latter).

Unfortunately, many studies have shown that children in the early elementary and middle school years have difficulty detecting their own comprehension problems (Baker & Brown, 1984; Garner, 1987; Paris et al., 1991). For example, in a classic study, Markman (1979) showed how even sixth graders can fail to detect logical inconsistencies in expository passages. In one passage, several lines pointed out that there is no light at the bottom of the ocean and that it is necessary to have light in order to see colors. After these lines were presented, the very next line stated that fish that live at the bottom of the ocean use color to select their food. Even with explicit instructions to find such problems in passages, a sizable number of sixth graders could not find them. Using similar materials, this finding has been replicated many times with other age groups (e.g., Baker, 1984). Even college students, for example, fail to accurately recognize that they have not fully comprehended passages they have read (Thiede, Anderson, & Therriault, 2003). One way to improve self-assessments of comprehension is to delay asking students for their assessments until a few minutes have passed. When asked to provide assessments immediately, information from the passage and the ideas evoked by this information may still be available in WM. Having access to seemingly large amounts of information in WM may lead readers to wrongly conclude that they learned something from it. In addition, however, a recent study showed that fourth and sixth graders were able to integrate and detect inconsistent information across multiple texts when an implicit measure of error detection was used instead of an explicit measure (i.e., slower reading times at the point of the inconsistency rather than explicit questions) and when the inconsistencies were made more obvious (Beker, van den Broek, & Jolles, 2019).

Overall, the developmental research on monitoring has revealed the following trends: (1) in the elementary grades and somewhat beyond, children often operate on "automatic pilot" when they read and seem oblivious to comprehension difficulties (Duffy & Roehler, 1987); (2) whereas younger readers tend to use a single standard for judging the meaningfulness of what they have read (e.g., problems with a single word), older readers use multiple standards for judging meaningfulness and consistency (Baker, 1984; Garner, 1981); and (3) older children and college students are more likely to construct coherent representations of texts and benefit from instruction that helps them form such representations (McNamara, 2017; Paris et al., 1991; Schünemann et al., 2017).

In a review of the literature, Garner (1987) argued that backtracking develops substantially between sixth and 10th grade. There are at least three reasons why younger readers tend not to reread a portion of text: (1) they sometimes think that it is "illegal" to do so; (2) they may not realize that they have a comprehension problem (see the prior paragraph on "monitoring"); and (3) they are often unfamiliar with text structure and cannot, therefore, use text structure to help guide their search for clarifying information. In addition, since many young readers think that the goal of reading is not to construct meaning but to "sound out words properly," they would not be troubled by a comprehension failure (Paris et al., 1991). Thus, if some meaningless portion of a text were sounded out properly, there is no need to reread it.

Collectively, the shortcomings in children's structural and functional aspects of reading suggest that they often do not construct adequate situation models in their mind—that is, their mental representation of what is going on in a text does not match the one that the author hoped to create in their mind. To help promote more complete and accurate situation models in young readers, Glenberg et al. (2004) created an intervention in which they used concrete props that corresponded to items in stories (e.g., a toy barn and toy farm animals). Compared to a condition in which children merely reread passages, first and second graders who either manipulated the props or imagined themselves manipulating the props showed markedly improved comprehension.

The Role of Extensive Reading

Studies have consistently shown that students who read frequently tend to have higher scores on reading achievement tests than students who read less frequently (e.g., Cipielewski & Stanovich, 1992; Greany, 1980; Greany & Hegarty, 1987; Nell, 1988; Walberg & Tsai, 1984). How should this finding be interpreted? One approach is to accept the correlation at face value, assume a causal relationship between frequent reading and reading achievement, and infer that a good way to raise test scores is to have students read more often. Another approach, however, is to examine the evidence more critically before drawing any instructional implications from it. The latter approach is adopted here.

The first way to critically evaluate the link between frequent reading and reading development is to ask the question "Is the correlation credible?" A good way to assess the credibility of a correlation is to see whether it is *spurious*. Could the correlation between frequent reading and elevated reading scores be due to some other variable that tends to be associated with both frequent reading and high test scores? One obvious "other variable" would be reading ability (Cipielewski & Stanovich, 1992). Motivation theorists recognize that people are more likely to engage in some activity if they feel self-efficacious (see Chapter 5). Moreover, they have shown that talented individuals tend to feel more self-efficacious than their less-talented peers. If so, then it would be expected that skilled readers would tend to read more than struggling readers. In addition, skilled readers, by definition, have higher test scores than struggling readers. Hence, it is entirely possible that the correlation between frequent reading and reading achievement is spurious.

As noted earlier, researchers determine whether correlation is spurious by seeing whether it maintains its numerical value when the effects of other variables that might be involved are mathematically eliminated. Studies have shown that the correlation between frequent reading and reading achievement does shrink somewhat when the effects of reading ability and other possible factors (e.g., SES) are subtracted out, but it does not shrink to zero (Anderson, Wilson, & Fielding, 1988; Cipielewski & Stanovich, 1992; Heyns, 1978; Taylor, Frye, & Maruyama, 1990; Walberg & Tsai, 1984). Thus, the correlation between frequent reading and higher test scores does not appear to be spurious.

However, statistics alone cannot determine the meaning of a mathematical relationship or the direction of causality. There has to be a well-regarded theory to lend further support to an assumed connection between two factors. It turns out that there are theoretical grounds for assuming that frequent reading promotes the development of reading skills. However, the links between frequent reading and skill development are more complicated than they would first appear.

Contemporary theories of cognition suggest that one of the best ways to become more proficient in some activity is to practice regularly and extensively (Anderson, 1995; Ericsson, 1996; see Chapter 7). In fact, some studies show that a minimum of 4 hours per day of practice is required for someone to attain the highest level of expertise in domains such as tennis, piano, or chess. However, research on the "power law of learning" suggests that practice is particularly important during the earliest stages of skill acquisition. After a certain point in time, practice provides diminishing returns. To illustrate, consider the case of a first grader who makes pronunciation mistakes about 30% of the time in September, but only 15% of the time after 9 months of regular reading in school (a 50% reduction in errors). During the second and third grades, however, the student may find that his or her error rate is reduced down further from 15% to just 10% and 8%, respectively, after 2 more years of practice. The latter represents reductions of only 33% and 20% in the student's error rate, respectively. Thus, the notion of diminishing returns suggests that increased practice would be most beneficial to individuals who are in the earliest stages of learning to read (e.g., first through third graders) and least beneficial to individuals who are in the latter stages (e.g., ninth through 12th graders). If so, then a uniform policy that mandates an increase in reading for all students (e.g., all students should read 15 minutes more per day) would have a greater effect on younger readers than on older readers.

In a related way, the idea of diminishing returns suggests that there would be a higher correlation between frequent reading and test scores in younger children (e.g., second and third graders) than in older children (e.g., fifth and sixth graders). It is notable that most of the studies that have investigated the role of frequent reading have focused on children in the fifth grade or older (presumably because many younger children are not yet fluent, independent readers). However, if practice has its strongest effects early in the process, then the correlations generated from studies of fifth graders may underestimate the potential value of frequent reading for younger children.

One further theoretical point relates to "Matthew effects" (Stanovich, 1986). Cognitive psychologists have shown that the comprehension of sentence-length constructions requires the ability to process and hold in WM the meaning of all of the words in the sentence (Carpenter & Just, 1987). As your eyes fixate on each word in a sentence, all preceding words in that sentence must be retained and maintained in WM before this information fades. If any obstacle to comprehension is encountered before the information starts to fade (in about 2 seconds), comprehension processes usually falter (Baddeley, 1990). One such obstacle is the presence of an unfamiliar word. Whereas highly familiar words can be processed in .25 second or less, unfamiliar words can take considerably longer to process (as noted in Chapter 9). With only 2 seconds to process all of the words, then, unfamiliar words pose quite a problem. However, if a person reads many different types of works and does so on a regular basis, that person tends to convert words that used to be unfamiliar into familiar words (in the same way that unfamiliar faces can become quickly recognized through repeated encounters). Over time, the troublesome words soon become processed nearly as quickly as other words, and comprehension problems are no longer disrupted (Perfetti, 1985). However, an important caveat in this account is that children differ in their ability to use contextual cues to acquire new vocabulary words from text. Children with greater WM capacity acquire new meanings from context more readily than children with less WM capacity (Cain et al., 2004). Thus, wide reading is more likely to increase the processing speed of the high-WM-capacity children than the low-WM-capacity children.

The most significant consequence of this increase in processing speed is that the reader now has better access to the knowledge contained in the texts that he or she is reading. Acquiring more knowledge, in turn, helps the reader make new inferences that further enhance the comprehension process (Pearson & Fielding, 1991). Other benefits of wide reading include (1) the acquisition of new vocabulary words and grammatical constructions that are normally not acquired in conversation (Stanovich & Cunningham, 1992); (2) enhanced phonemic awareness that can be used in the decoding process (Stanovich, 1986); and, as noted above, (3) increased background knowledge.

Thus, regular reading has the potential to increase one's reading speed, vocabulary, knowledge, and phonemic awareness. Such changes, in turn, make one a better reader still. In effect, reading skills tend to snowball over time. This analysis implies that if two individuals were to start out at roughly the same place in the first grade, but only one were to read extensively, it would be expected that the extensive reader would show faster growth in reading skills than the less extensive reader would. Moreover, if we were to plot their reading scores as a function of time, we would see a widening gap between their respective "learning curves" over time. Stanovich (1986) labeled this phenomenon the "Matthew effect" after the New Testament author who refers to the rich getting richer (i.e., Matthew).

However, it is important to note that Matthew effects would not be expected to occur if children were to read exactly the same (unchalleng-ing) works again and again. Similarly, little growth would be expected if children were to read new books each time but select books that contain many of the same words and ideas. Thus, researchers would tend to find a higher correlation between extensive reading and reading achievement in a study if they asked questions such as "How many different books did you read last year?" than if they asked "How many minutes do you spend read-ing each day?" In addition, the idea of Matthew effects suggests that the causal relationship between frequent reading and reading achievement is more appropriately viewed as reciprocal than unidirectional (i.e., frequent reading causes higher achievement, which in turn promotes more frequent reading). However, in general, there does appear to be a solid theoretical basis for assuming that frequent reading would promote higher levels of reading achievement. Yet, the evidence for Matthew effects in reading is somewhat inconsistent (Pfost, Hattie, Dörfler, & Artelt, 2014). Thus, more investigations into this topic are required.

Summary

In sum, we now have a good sense of the developmental trends in reading comprehension: Children seem to develop both structural and functional competencies with age that help them process what they are reading. In particular, research shows that older children demonstrate better reading comprehension than younger children do because they are more likely than younger children to (1) have more WM capacity; (2) have extensive declara-tive and conceptual knowledge of topics; (3) have structural knowledge of the different kinds of texts (e.g., stories and expository texts); (4) engage in functional processes that enhance comprehension, such as inference mak-ing, inhibition, and comprehension monitoring; and (5) have had more extensive practice.

That said, there are many forms of evidence that suggest that cur-rent teaching methods are not developing the reading comprehension skills needed for contemporary society. As noted in Chapter 9, for example, the results of the 2019 National Assessment of Educational Progress (NAEP) revealed that only 35% of fourth graders and 36% of eighth graders in the United States scored at the proficient level. That means that 65% and 64%, respectively, read at the basic or below basic level. According to the NAEP, fourth-grade students scoring as the proficient level when reading narrative texts

> should be able to identify implicit main ideas and recognize relevant information that supports them. Students should be able to judge elements of author's craft and provide some support for their judgment. They should be able to analyze character roles, actions, feelings, and motives. (*https://nces.ed.gov/nationsreportcard/reading/achieve.aspx#2009_grade4*)

When reading expository texts, fourth-grade students

> should be able to locate relevant information, integrate information across texts, and evaluate the way an author presents information. Student performance at this level should demonstrate an understanding of the purpose for text features and an ability to integrate information from headings, text boxes, graphics and their captions. They should be able to explain a simple cause-and-effect relationship and draw conclusions.

IMPLICATIONS FOR EDUCATION

With respect to developmental mechanisms that could explain these age trends, three themes emerge from the research on schemata and strategies. First, it takes considerable time for children to develop schemata and strategies on their own. In the absence of explicit instruction, many middle school and high school students (who have been learning to read for more than 5 years) do not make use of schemata and strategies to guide their comprehension. Second, certain kinds of instruction can substantially decrease the amount of time it takes children to develop schemata and strategies. In particular, a large number of instructional studies have shown that explicit instruction on schemata or strategies can improve the comprehension of even elementary students. That said, a recent meta-analysis showed that whereas the average effect size for children's use of strategies after direct instruction was $d = 0.79$, the average effect size for reading comprehension on experimenter-made tests of comprehension was $d = 0.43$ but for standardized reading tests it was only $d = 0.19$ (Okkinga et al., 2018). It is not clear why the effect was so muted for standardized tests. But if we convert the effect size of $d = 0.19$ into a success rate within a binomial effect size display, it corresponds to 55% of children in the strategy-training groups showing improved reading comprehension, compared to 45% of the children in the control group. This 10% higher success rate applied to large school districts or even the United States would mean a substantial number of children showing improved reading. Third, children's prior knowledge of a topic can influence the degree to which they use their schemata or strategies to enhance their comprehension. Familiarity can compensate for a lack of knowledge of prose structure and can also enhance the chances that strategies will be deployed. Indeed, a variety of studies of adults who are struggling readers show that people who are very knowledgeable about some topic (e.g., baseball) can show excellent comprehension of a passage on that topic (Recht & Leslie, 1988; Talwar et al., 2018; Walker, 1987). But reading many diverse books instills the broad topic knowledge that can promote comprehension, inference making, and predictions. In essence, then, the primary developmental mechanisms include extensive reading and explicit instruction in strategies.

CHAPTER 11

The Development
of Writing Skills

This present chapter on writing is the third in the series of chapters on literacy skills, along with Chapters 9 (beginning reading) and 10 (reading comprehension). To truly understand the nature of literacy, all three chapters should be considered collectively. There is a high correlation between reading skills and writing skills (Williams & Larkin, 2013), and, as we shall see, both forms of literacy share common intellectual resources. Writing skills are vitally important for performing well at the university level and also in the workplace (Ferretti & Graham, 2019; Preiss, Castillo, Grigorenko, & Manzi, 2013). Unfortunately, many students fail to acquire the writing skills they need to be successful in today's world. The most recent NAEP for writing, conducted in 2011, showed that only 28%, 27%, and 27% of 4th, 8th, and 12th graders, respectively, in the United States performed at or above the proficient level (NAEP, 2011a). The results for the 2017 assessment have not yet been released at this writing.

In what follows, we will examine the nature and development of writing skills as a means of figuring out why so many students do not learn what they need to learn in the area of writing.

THE NATURE OF WRITING ABILITY

The goal of this section is to provide a reasonably complete answer to the following questions: "What are the component processes involved in writing?" and "How do highly skilled writers differ from less skilled writers?"

One way to answer these questions is to examine the definition of writing competence that was proposed by the governing board of the NAEP for the 2011 NAEP for writing (p. 4): "Writing is a complex, multifaceted, and purposeful act of communication that is accomplished in a variety of environments, under various constraints of time, and with a variety of language resources and technological tools" (NAEP, 2011b). The governing board further added that writers write to accomplish various goals, including to convey experience (real or imagined), explain, and persuade. Examples of conveying experience include writing personal narratives, biographies, and fictional stories. Writers explain using expository text and persuade in argumentative essays.

Another way to define writing competence is to examine influential models of writing (e.g., Abbott, Berninger, & Fayol, 2010; Hayes, 1996, 2012; Hayes & Flower, 1986; Scardamalia & Bereiter, 1986) and distill major components from these models. At a global level, these models suggest that there are two kinds of variables that affect the writing process: those that pertain to characteristics of *writing environments* and those that pertain to characteristics of *individual writers* (Hayes, 1996). In what follows, these two types of variables are discussed in turn. Then, we briefly consider some of the neural correlates of writing to see if neuroscientific research provides any additional insights.

Characteristics of the Writing Environment

When people write, they write in particular *contexts* or situations. For example, whereas some do their writing on a computer in a secluded cabin in Vermont, others do their writing in the midst of a classroom full of peers using a pencil and paper. Similarly, whereas some are attempting to write to a large, popular audience (e.g., a novelist), others may be writing to a single person (e.g., a teacher, a peer, or a pen pal). As a writer moves from one context to another, it is typically the case that the audience, medium (i.e., computer vs. paper), and individuals who are present in that context change, as well. Such contextual variations are thought to affect the writing process in important ways (Hayes, 1996, 2012).

With respect to the shift from paper to computer, for example, a meta-analysis of 32 studies showed that word-processing packages help all writers (especially weaker writers) to produce higher-quality pieces (Bangert-Downs, 1993). Other significant contextual variations include the text that has already been produced and the availability of collaborators (Hayes, 2012). Obviously, the task of adding the last line to a five-line paragraph is different than the task of adding the very first line to a blank page. Moreover, studies show that writers continually reread what they have already written in order to set the stage for the next portion of text (Graham, 2006; Hayes, 1996, 2012). As such, a change in the initial portion would lead to a change in the portion added on. In addition, having a collaborator changes the writing process significantly. For example, children write very differently when they collaborate with a teacher than when they collaborate with a peer (Daiute, 2002), and peers and professional colleagues can be helpful resources in the revision process (Atwell, 1987; Graham, 2006; Hayes, 2012).

Characteristics of an Individual Writer

Psychological theories typically explain changes in behavior by appealing to changes in some mental entity. For example, if a person performed behavior X at one time (e.g., studied really hard) but now performs behavior Y (e.g., did not study at all), psychologists usually appeal to changes in mental entities such as concepts, values, and beliefs to explain this behavior change (e.g., he or she no longer believes that studying is effective). Relatedly, psychologists often explain differences in behavior across two individuals (e.g., one studies but the other does not) by appealing to the same sorts of mental entities. To explain variations in the outputs of the writing process (e.g., a well-written essay vs. a poorly written essay), psychologists have appealed to five clusters of *person-related variables:* (1) motivation factors, (2) forms of knowledge held in long-term memory, (3) writing-specific cognitive processes, (4) components of working memory (WM), and (5) transcription processes (Graham, 2006; Hayes, 1996, 2012). Let's examine each of these five kinds of variables in turn.

Motivational Aspects of Writing

People engage in writing for particular reasons. Whereas some write for pleasure, others write because they have been given an assignment by a teacher or an employer. Regardless of whether people write because they want to or have to, it is clear that writing is very *goal-directed* (Hamilton, Nolen, & Abbott, 2013; Hayes, 1996, 2012). This assumption suggests that a change in goals would lead to a change in writing output. Notice how a goal such as "I want to write a summary of current research on learning" would lead to a different paper than a goal such as "I want to critically evaluate current theories of learning."

More generally, however, one of the primary aims of education is to produce students who habitually engage in literate activities such as reading and writing (Anderson et al., 1988). Hence, it has been of interest to determine the factors that cause students to regularly engage in writing on their own (Hayes, 1996). Inasmuch as most prolific writers find the writing process intrinsically satisfying, they engage in it as often as possible. Whereas it is relatively easy to get students to write by giving them an assignment, it is quite another to get them to write frequently on their own (or select an occupation because it requires regular writing). In order for students to make the latter kinds of choices, they need to hold positive attitudes toward the writing process and themselves as writers. Moreover, they need to believe that writing affords more benefits than costs. Whereas the tendency to write a particular assignment relates to specific goals, the tendency to write frequently might be called a predisposition to write (Hayes, 1996). However, it is important to note that writing is a difficult task even for the most accomplished writers (Graham, 2006). Intrinsic interest in the act of writing and interest in the topic of an assignment certainly helps and has been found to predict writing quality (Hidi & Boscolo, 2006), but the difficulty of writing implies that other characteristics of motivation such as self-efficacy and values would matter as much if not more (Graham, 2006; Hidi & Boscolo, 2006). In other words, in order to succeed, writers have to believe that they have the skills and persistence needed to accomplish their goals. They also have to be able to deal with failure and rejection. Consider how J. K. Rowling's first *Harry Potter* book was reportedly rejected by 12 major publishers in England over the span of 20 years! Writers should anticipate this rejection, according to novelist Stephen King, but writers should write to please themselves and write about things they care about (King, 2000). Thus, motivation is crucial.

Knowledge Structures in Long-Term Memory

Of course, a well-written document would not be produced if a person merely had the motivation to write. Such a person also needs certain kinds of writing knowledge and skills. Writing researchers have argued that there are five main types of knowledge that successful writers store in their long-term memories: (1) knowledge of task schemata, (2) knowledge of topics, (3) knowledge of audiences, (4) knowledge of genres, and (5) knowledge of language (Glover, Ronning, & Bruning, 1990; Graham, 2006; Hayes, 1996; Scardamalia & Bereiter, 1986). Contemporary theories suggest that an alteration in one of these kinds of knowledge (e.g., an absence of topic knowledge in one person vs. its presence in another) would lead to outputs that differ in their quality (e.g., the high-knowledge author writes a good essay but the other does not).

Task schemata are mental representations of writing tasks that a person regularly encounters. They include global parameters regarding deadlines and length, as well as stored strategies that were successful in the past (e.g., clarifying things with an instructor first, starting at least 3 weeks early, focusing on familiar topics). As noted in Chapter 9, schemata help people accomplish tasks efficiently. Writers who lack schemata need to "reinvent the wheel" each time they are given a particular task.

As for knowledge of topics, readers of this book may have noticed that it is much easier to write a paper when you know a lot about the topic than when you know very little about it. The same is true for even the most skilled writers. Knowledge helps you generate ideas and organize them effectively. To see this, imagine that you were given the assignment of writing an essay on the nature of writing. It should be clear that you would have an easier time writing such a paper after you read this section than before you read it (unless you were already familiar with the literature on writing!). As another example, imagine that you were writing an essay regarding an unfair grade for a friend. If you did not take the class with the friend and experience things the way he or she did, it would be harder to write the essay than if the unfair grade were given to you. Good writers understand the importance of topic knowledge, so they usually do a great deal of research before they attempt to write about an unfamiliar topic. Author James Michener, for example, usually researched a topic for about 3 years before he wrote one of his tomes. But Stephen King has argued that you should not go overboard with research nor have too much of it show up in the book (King, 2000).

However, whereas topic knowledge is necessary for writing a good piece, it is not sufficient. Writers also have to be able to "get inside their readers' minds" in order to be successful. Stephen King likened the process to mental telepathy (King, 2000). That is, writers need to be able to answer questions such as "What do my readers already know?"; "What do they want to hear?"; "How would they probably react to my statements?"; "Do they see in their minds what I see in my mind?" In the extreme, writers who do not understand what their readers know and believe could produce a variety of unwanted responses in their readers. For example, poor writing could make readers of this work feel (1) confused (if the level is too high), (2) belittled or bored (if the level is too low), or (3) angry (if the author's stance runs contrary to their beliefs). In most cases, readers want to learn something new or form a "connection" with something they read. Readers will not learn anything new if the material is either too familiar or too unfamiliar, and they may not have their beliefs confirmed by someone who challenges their opinions. Moreover, readers will gain very little from a piece if they are unable to draw inferences that connect sentences and paragraphs together into a coherent whole (see Chapter 9). When writers egocentrically assume that their readers know what they know, they do not provide enough clues in the text to support required inferences. Thus, *knowing your audience* is a key to being a skilled writer. Note that the element of the task environment related to audience (see above) pertains to who the audience is. Here, the issue concerns a writer's knowledge of that audience.

To appreciate the utility of the next kind of knowledge, consider the following question: If someone asked you to write an argumentative essay, a textbook, a story, and a poem, would you know how to write something in each of these *genres*? As we saw in Chapter 9, genres have their own distinctive structures that skilled readers come to know. For example, we saw that stories have a narrative structure involving components such as settings, characters, and outcomes. Given the fact that there are "standard" ways of organizing ideas in specific genres, and that readers come to expect this standard format when they read a work in that genre, writers need to stick close to this standard format in order to maximize the chance that their readers will like and comprehend what they have read. Of course, the task of writing something in a particular genre is made easier when a writer has a *schema* for that type of work. Where do these schemata come from? They get internalized by reading a lot of examples of that genre (e.g., many novels or poems) and writing multiple pieces in that genre yourself.

Finally, although having knowledge of topics, audiences, and genres is important to writing well, an absolutely indispensable component of good writing is knowledge of your audience's native language. Writers need to know how to place specific words in specific grammatical constructions in order to convey just the right meaning. That is, writers need to have (1) a good vocabulary, (2) knowledge of grammatical rules, and (3) knowledge of the *pragmatics* of a language (e.g., knowing how to be polite, sarcastic). This knowledge helps them ensure that what the reader envisions in their minds as they read, is what the author intended to plant there (King, 2000).

To see how important *knowledge of language* is, consider the following example. Imagine that a French psychologist who is editing a book on cognitive theories asks a U.S. expert on Piaget's theory to contribute a chapter about Piaget to this volume. The U.S. expert is told that the readers of this book will be non-English-speaking French undergraduates. Even if the expert knew a lot about Piaget's theory (i.e., had topic knowledge), had been asked to write chapters many times before (i.e., had a task schema), knew a lot about how French undergraduates think (i.e., had knowledge of the audience), and also had a schema for expository chapters (i.e., had knowledge of that genre), it should be obvious that he or she would be unable to write a good chapter if he or she were not sufficiently fluent in French.

Writing-Related Cognitive Processes

In his reformulations of the seminal Hayes and Flower (1980) model of writing, Hayes (1996, 2012) suggested that there are three important cognitive processes that help writers translate their knowledge and motivation into action: text interpretation, reflection, and text production. *Text interpretation* refers to a set of processes that are used by a writer to create mental representations of linguistic and graphic inputs. These processes include reading, listening, and scanning graphic images. *Reflection* refers to a set of processes that function to transform one internal representation into another. Examples include problem solving, decision making, and inference making. These three processes were included as replacements for the planning component in the original Hayes and Flower 1980 model.

Text production refers to a set of processes that are used when a writer translates internal representations into written, spoken, or graphic outputs.

This revised model places reading skills at the center of effective writing. However, Hayes (1996, 2012) made a distinction between reading to comprehend and reading to evaluate. As noted in Chapters 9 and 10, readers engage in the following sorts of processes when they read to comprehend: decode words, apply grammatical knowledge, apply semantic and schematized knowledge, draw inferences to elaborate on what is written and the author's intentions, and construct a summary. The output of such processes is a representation of text meaning. When people read to evaluate, however, they read with an eye toward problems inherent in the current draft of a document that they have written or someone else has written. Instead of simply decoding words, for example, they also look for spelling errors. Similarly, instead of simply applying grammatical knowledge to form a mental representation of "who did what to whom," they also look for grammatical faults. Components such as semantic knowledge, inference making, schemata, and consideration of the needs of audiences help writers look for unwarranted inferences, schematic violations, incoherence, and inappropriate tone or complexity.

Thus, to revise a document, writers have to engage in (1) critical reading of what they have written, (2) problem solving and decision making (i.e., identification of a problem, consideration of alternative ways to fix it), and (3) text production (i.e., translating these intentions into revised text). These three processes are best coordinated if a writer has a schema for the task of revision. This schema might include a search for common kinds of problems, strategies for locating problems (e.g., not looking at a draft for a few days or even weeks before returning to it), and so on. In addition, carrying out the three core processes of writing requires the capacity resources afforded by WM and knowledge resources contained in long-term memory.

Using this overall framework, a researcher could explain differences between more experienced and less experienced writers. For example, one study showed that college freshmen tend to focus their revisions at or below the sentence level (e.g., fix spelling or substitute a single word). More experienced writers, in contrast, tended to focus on both local and global problems (Hayes, Flower, Schriver, Stratman, & Carey, 1987). Why might this be the case? One place to look might be a difference in the ability or inclination to detect problems in texts. Conceivably, skilled writers could be better readers than struggling writers. Another place might be WM differences. A third might be a lack of revision schemata in inexperienced writers. A fourth might be lack of knowledge of good solutions to writing problems that are identified (e.g., "I know it reads sort of choppy but I don't know how to fix it"). A fifth might be differences at the level of production. Skilled and struggling writers might be similar in their ability to read critically and detect problems, but different in their ability to translate their plans into effective text. Studies have shown, for example, that skilled writers produce segments of sentences that are 53% longer than those of struggling writers (Hayes, 1996).

Thus, the model is useful for locating numerous possible differences between skilled and struggling writers. Are any of these differences particularly crucial? Hayes (1996) suggested that reading skills are important for reasons other than the fact that they help a writer identify problems in a draft. For example, reading skills help writers gain accurate topic knowledge as they do research. In addition, readers often formulate a representation of the author of some work (including such things as the author's personality traits and political orientation). Collectively, these representations help a skilled writer create and revise documents in ways that are different from the methods used by struggling readers and writers.

Components of WM

Kellogg (1996) proposed a model that is similar to that of Hayes (1996) but emphasized the significance of WM to a greater extent. In Kellogg's model, the text production process consists of three subcomponents: formulation, execution, and monitoring. When in the *formulation phase,* a writer plans what he or she is going to say and then translates this plan into an intention to write down a specific segment of text. When in the *execution phase,* the motoric and related responses needed to carry out this intention are put into play. Note that this process is relatively straightforward for someone who has been writing longhand or typing for years. For the beginning or struggling writer, however, effortful execution could disrupt the flow of ideas from mind to paper. In other words, a slow writer or typist could forget the exact phrasing that emerged during the formulation phase. During the *monitoring phase,* the writer reads and edits the text that has been produced. WM could affect such processes, as well.

Transcription Processes

Other researchers likewise revised the original Hayes and Flower model (1980) in response to what they discovered in studying the development of writing skills in the elementary school years. The ability to spell and write fluently has been repeatedly shown to be an important contributor to the quality of children's writing (Abbott et al., 2010; Graham et al., 2008; Kent & Wanzek, 2016). As just noted, if writers have to pause to retrieve spellings or if they take a long time to write each word of a sentence, they could forget what they were going to say. In addition, however, spelling ability may reflect a rich vocabulary system that reflects strong interconnections between orthography, phonology, syntax, and semantics. These findings on transcription processes led Hayes to revise this original model and include transcription processes (Hayes, 2012).

THE DEVELOPMENT OF SKILLED WRITING

The developmental research on writing skills is organized as follows. First, we will examine the early emergence of writing during the preschool period. Then, we will consider developmental studies that used the original and revised models of Hayes and Flower (1980) as their guide. For simplicity, the latter studies are grouped according to whether they examined the knowledge needed for writing or the writing processes.

Early Writing Skills

Consistent with the literature on emergent literacy (see Chapter 9), a number of studies have shown that children develop conceptions of the writing process well before they are exposed to formal writing instruction in kindergarten and first grade (Brenneman, Massey, Machado, & Gelman, 1996; Gombert & Fayol, 1992; Share & Levin, 1999). To assess what preschoolers know, researchers sometimes dictate words to children and ask them to write these words down. Other times, researchers may present a picture and ask children to write the word for it. Studies have shown that children progress through a series of approximations to writing between the ages of 3 and 5. For example, they may begin with scribbles but then progress to wavy lines and pseudoletters.

After reviewing studies of this sort that were conducted in various countries, Gombert and Fayol (1992) proposed that children progress through three phases in their early writing attempts. In Phase 1 (approximately age 3), children produce nonfigural graphics such as scribbling and wavy lines. These markings usually obey principles of writing such as unidirectionality and also sometimes have features characteristic of mature writing such as linearity, vertically short traces, and discrete units. Notably, children do not confuse writing with drawing even at this beginning level.

During Phase 2 (between ages 3 and 4), children's writing may consist of strings of circles or pseudoletters. The distinct characteristic of this phase is the very clear existence of discrete units. These units, however, are used to correspond to verbal dictations in nonphonemic ways. For example, children tend to write longer sequences for words for large things (e.g., an elephant) than for small things (e.g., a mouse). Relatedly, they may write these units using the same color as the object (e.g., a red marker for *apple*; a yellow marker for *lemon*). Near the end of this phase, however, children may start matching sequence strings to phonemic information (e.g., longer sequences for multisyllable words).

During Phase 3 (between ages 4 and 5), children start to produce writing samples that contain actual letters that they know. In most cases, these letters come from children's own first name, but slowly new letters are added. Unlike earlier phases, children no longer attempt to match sequences to dictations in either semantic or phonological ways. The absence of such matching may reflect their having to allocate considerable attention to the task of writing unfamiliar letters (Gombert & Fayol, 1992). With continued practice, however, these matchings reappear, but only in terms of phonological features. For example, they may write "KGN" for *kindergarten*. Interestingly, however, many of the oldest children begin refusing to participate, arguing that they do not know how to spell particular words. This three-phase account is consistent with the findings of Levin and Bus (2003), who found that the drawings and writings of preschoolers become increasingly differentiated with age (i.e., writing looks more like writing; drawing looks more like drawing).

Soon thereafter, children enter kindergarten and receive instruction on writing all letters of their native alphabet or idiographies. In first grade and beyond, many children also receive instruction in spelling and in the alphabetic principle (see Chapter 9; Graham et al., 2008). Of course, good writing involves more than spelling. As noted earlier, writers set goals, rely on schemata, revise, and so on to draft stories, informative passages, and argumentative essays. In the next two sections, we consider children's abilities in these areas during elementary and secondary school.

Further Developments I: Structural Aspects of Writing

In line with the distinction between structural and functional aspects of reading comprehension that were discussed in Chapter 9, it is helpful to consider the development of structural and functional aspects of writing, as well. The structural aspects pertain to developmental changes in WM capacity and knowledge resources. The functional aspects involve changes in writing processes.

It has already been noted that there are monotonic increases in the capacity of WM from early childhood to young adulthood (Swanson, 1999). Such increases provide a processing space within which effortful tasks such as planning and critical reading can take place (McCutchen, 2006; Niedo, Abbott, & Berninger, 2014). In addition, fluency at the level of text generation and transcription helps writers overcome the limits of WM.

As for knowledge-related structural aspects, large- and small-scale studies have found that children become better writers with age (e.g., Applebee, Langer, Mullis, & Jenkins, 1990; Greenwald, Persky, Campbell, & Mazzeo, 1999; Scardamalia & Bereiter, 1986), though there is still much room for improvement in high school and college (Escorcia, Passerrault, Ros, & Pylouster, 2017; Graham et al., 2018). One reason why older students write better than younger students is that they have more of the knowledge needed for writing. As we have seen, writers can have knowledge of such things as topics, genres, audiences, and language (Olinghouse, Graham, & Gillespie, 2014). Let's now examine the developmental literature to see whether there are age differences in these forms of knowledge.

Topic Knowledge

When asked to write a paper on some topic, younger children tend to generate fewer ideas than older children and adults (Scardamalia & Bereiter, 1986). This age difference in the amount of ideas generated derives, in part, from the fact that younger children usually have less topic knowledge than older children and adults. Sometimes age differences are even found within samples of students who are labeled "experts" on some topic. For example, in her study of the effects of knowledge on writing, McCutchen (1986) found that even in a group of children labeled "high-knowledge," her high-knowledge eighth graders still had more pertinent knowledge than her high-knowledge fourth or sixth graders. Thus, it is usually safe to assume that for any given topic, older children will know more than younger children. As a result, the latter will have a greater resource of ideas to tap into.

However, studies have also shown that children seem to generate fewer ideas than their knowledge would warrant. In particular, researchers have found that simply prompting children to think of additional ideas causes them to generate many more things to say (Graham & Harris, 1996; Scardamalia, Bereiter, & Goelman, 1982). Why do children generate fewer ideas than they are capable of? The first reason seems to be that whereas younger students use a somewhat random method of *associative thinking* to generate ideas, older students use a *heuristic or goal directed search* to guide their generation of ideas (Hayes & Flower, 1986; Scardamalia & Bereiter, 1986).

The second reason why younger students generate fewer ideas than they are capable of is that they tend to retrieve only those ideas at the highest levels of hierarchically arranged knowledge (McCutchen & Perfetti, 1982; Scardamalia & Bereiter, 1986). When writing about "animals," for example, younger writers might generate ideas immediately connected to the top-level node "animal" and fail to retrieve ideas below that level (e.g., information associated with different types of animals such as dogs and cats). Prompting seems to move them farther down a hierarchy to retrieve more detailed information (e.g., asking "What can you tell me about different types of animals such as dogs or cats?"). But notwithstanding such tendencies for young writers to not utilize all the knowledge they have about a topic, there are a variety of studies that show that students who have more knowledge about a topic produce better written products (Olinghouse et al., 2014).

Knowledge of Genres

In Chapter 10, we learned that extensive reading seems to cause children to acquire schemata for various types of texts (e.g., stories and expository texts). If children do acquire such schemata over time, it would be expected that when they are asked to write something in a particular genre, older children would be more likely than younger children to write something that conforms to the "ideal" structure for that genre.

The literature on story writing, however, suggests there is a developmental lag between being able to recognize a good story and being able to write one. In particular, even though 5- and 6-year-olds seem to have good knowledge of the canonical structure of stories (Stein, 1982), studies show that much older students (e.g., fourth, fifth, and eighth graders) sometimes have trouble composing stories that conform to this canonical structure. For example, on the 1998 NAEP for writing that examined the skills of over 17,000 students, only 38% gave a "sufficient" response to story prompts in which they produced a clear but underdeveloped story with few details. Only 20% attained the "skillful" or "excellent" ratings for well-developed, detailed, and coherent stories (Greenwald et al., 1999). It is important to note, however, that students were only given 25 minutes to compose each of their stories. The 2011 NAEP only tested the narrative skills of 8th and 12th graders. Stories composed by 8th graders could receive ratings of "marginal," "developing," "adequate," "competent," and "effective." Most (81%) received ratings of "adequate" or below. To be rated as "adequate" the student "used some detail, but detail did not always convey an experience, while organization was somewhat loose, word choices clear rather than precise, and sentence structure relatively unvaried" (National Center for Educational Statistics, 2011). Thus, little seems to have changed since the 1998 assessment, but we must wait to see the results of the 2017 assessment.

In a study in which children were given several class periods to compose and potentially revise their stories, Freedman (1987) found that there was development between the 5th and 12th grades in the degree of realization of the "ideal form" of a story. In the 5th and 8th grades, only 34% and 45% of children, respectively, wrote stories about true personal experiences that included some setting information and at least one complete episode. When asked to invent a story, however, these percentages rose to 55% and 70%, respectively. Finally, Langer (1986) found that whereas there were few differences between the stories of 8- and 14-year-olds in terms of structure, the stories of the 14-year-olds were more elaborated than those of the 8-year-olds. Comparing the NAEP studies with the Freedman and Langer studies, then, we see that the size of the age difference can be large or small, depending on the nature of the writing task. But even in the best of circumstances, there still seems to be a lag of 3 to 4 years between using schemata to comprehend stories and using them to write stories. Further support for the idea that children need to gain independent, explicit control over their genre knowledge comes from the finding that the quality of writing improves when teachers provide scaffolds for children (Donovan & Smolkin, 2006) such as an outline with question prompts (Graham, Capizzi, Harris, Hebert, & Morphy, 2014).

With respect to expository writing, we would expect an even larger developmental lag because of the findings for reading comprehension that show that children seem to comprehend stories better than they comprehend expository texts (see Chapter 10). Several studies support this expectation of relatively poorer performance for expository writing. For example, Langer (1986) found a more marked difference between 8- and 14-year-olds for expository writing than for story writing. At both ages, however, performance on the expository task was generally unimpressive. Similarly, in a highly structured task in which students were asked to complete a paragraph that already contained key elements (e.g., topic sentences and signals), Englert, Stewart, and Hiebert (1988) found that whereas sixth graders performed significantly better than third graders in the generation of textually consistent details (40% vs. 37%, respectively) and main ideas (35% vs. 22%, respectively), students at both grade levels tended to perform poorly on both of these expository writing tasks.

On the 1998 NAEP (Greenwald et al., 1999), only 38% gave "sufficient" responses to informational writing prompts (e.g., designing a television show). Children in this category used simple sentences that conveyed information in a clear, sequential but sparsely developed manner. Only 11% received ratings of "skillful" or "excellent." On the 2011 NAEP, 12th graders could receive ratings ranging from "marginal" to "effective." Only 26% received ratings of "competent" or "effective"; 74% received ratings of "adequate" or below. To get a rating of "adequate," students "developed explanations using some details that do not enhance the clarity or progression of ideas, while organization was somewhat loose and sentence structure simple overall." So, it would appear that performance has improved somewhat since the 1998 assessment, but not by much. This improvement could be due to the fact that students completed the tasks on the 2011 NAEP using computers and were given guidance and prompts.

Across all grades, studies have showed that children are most successful when they write expository texts in the simple description format (i.e., taking information and summarizing it). They had much more difficulty writing essays in the compare–contrast format or other formats that required them to *analyze* information rather than simply *report* it (Applebee et al., 1990; Englert et al., 1988). Moreover, their passages needed work with respect to organization, development, transitions, and grammatical complexity (Greenwald et al., 1999).

Although most developmental researchers have focused on narrative and expository writing, a few have also examined argumentative writing. Argumentative writing is a form in which an author adopts the goal of convincing his or her readers that a particular point of view is a good one (Applebee et al., 1990; Greenwald et al., 1999). For example, a student engages in argumentative writing when he or she writes an essay about deserving an "A." In judging the quality of an argumentative essay, researchers look for the presence of the key elements of a well-structured argument, such as claims, data, warrants, recognition of an opposing point of view, and rebuttals (e.g., Knudson, 1992; McCann, 1989). Most developmental studies have shown that children write better argumentative essays with age.

For example, McCann (1989) asked 6th, 9th, and 12th graders to write argumentative essays and found that the essays of the 9th and 12th graders not only had more overall quality than those of the 6th graders, they also contained significantly more claims and warrants. No significant grade differences emerged for the use of data to support a claim, however. In a similar study, Knudson (1992) found that 4th and 6th graders used significantly fewer claims, data, and warrants than 10th and 12th graders. Thus, both studies showed that children are more likely with age to include the elements of good arguments.

However, the increased use of such elements does not imply that older students always produce high-quality arguments. In particular, on the 1998 NAEP, the percentages of children who received "skillful" or "excellent" ratings for their argumentative essays were 12% (4th grade), 14% (8th grade), and 22% (12th grade). These figures should not imply, however, that little development occurred. The raters used more stringent criteria for assigning the highest two levels for the 8th and 12th graders and also gave different writing prompts. But overall, most children demonstrated only a basic kind of proficiency in argumentative writing. These findings for persuasive writing are troubling considering that the Common Core state standards have placed a strong emphasis on promoting this ability (Newell, Beach, Smith, & VanDerHeide, 2011). Since the earliest findings revealed suboptimal argumentative writing at all age levels, there have been a variety of attempts to improve persuasive writing through the use of strategies such as providing students with specific goals, providing computer-based scaffolds, and having students engage in structured argumentation with peers; these attempts have been generally more effective than business-as-usual instruction (Ferretti, Lewis, & Andrews-Weckerly, 2009; Newell et al., 2011).

In sum, then, most students, even in the high school levels, have difficulty writing stories, expository reports, and argumentative essays. When development occurs, it is usually in the form of an increased use of key elements of a particular genre, greater cohesion, and additional details. In the case of stories, older students are more likely than younger students to include both a setting and a major episode in their stories. In the case of expository reports, older students are more likely to use superordinate structures (e.g., main ideas and supportive details) than younger students. In the case of argumentative essays, older students are more likely to use claims, data, and warrants than younger students. Although even elementary students have been found to use some structure in their writing, older students use more structure and tend to elaborate that structure more extensively. In addition, the quality of argumentative essays of college students can be significantly enhanced by simply giving them goals to include counterarguments and rebuttals (Nussbaum & Kardash, 2005). Across all age levels, students who have more knowledge of genres produce higher-quality written products (Olinghouse et al., 2014). But students who have both knowledge of genres and knowledge of topics create higher-quality written products than students with only one or neither of these forms of knowledge (Olinghouse et al., 2014; Wijekumar et al., 2018).

Knowledge of Audiences

A major difference between writing and having a conversation is that when you have a conversation, you have an actual person to whom you speak. This individual reacts to your statements with facial expressions and also helps keep the conversation going by saying things back to you. When you write, however, you have no one to play these roles for you. As a result, you need to create your own imaginary audience and hypothesize about how these people would probably respond to your statements. Moreover, you need to be able to think about what you have written objectively to see whether someone else might have trouble understanding what you are trying to say (Hayes & Bajzek, 2008). Writing, then, poses greater cognitive demands than having a conversation. If so, then young children may be less-effective writers than older children because the former have a harder time creating and writing to an imaginary audience than the latter (Bereiter & Scardamalia, 1982; Knudson, 1992).

In one of the few studies that investigated possible developmental differences in children's knowledge of how audiences affect what is written, Langer (1986) found that both 8- and 14-year-olds realized that a text would have to be modified if an audience were to change. However, whereas the younger children said that a shift in audience would mean that there would be different requirements regarding neatness and length, the older children argued that the changes would be reflected in terms of language and form. Obviously, more studies are needed to reveal the existence of other age differences in knowledge of audiences. One study of college students revealed the existence of the "knowledge effect": when writers know something technical, they tend to think that others share that knowledge (Hayes & Bajzek, 2008). Writers who adopt this faulty assumption tend to write less clearly than when they do not have this assumption.

Knowledge of Language

Perfetti and McCutchen (1987, p. 130) define writing competence as "productive control over the grammatical devices of language in the service of some communicative intent." This definition nicely captures the central role played by a writer's knowledge of language. In order to have productive control over one's language and convey exactly what one wants to convey, a writer needs to have a good vocabulary and good command of syntax. Is there evidence that older students have larger vocabularies and greater command of syntax than younger students?

In the case of vocabulary, school children add about 3,000 new words to their vocabularies each year (Adams, 1990). Thus, the notion of "choosing just the right word" is more applicable to older children than younger children since only the former are likely to have the range of words necessary to engage in such a selection process.

In the case of syntax, Loban (1976) and Hunt (1970) found that there is development in syntactic maturity throughout the school years. By "syntactic maturity," we mean that older children are more likely than younger children to group separate clauses together into single, more complex constructions. For example, instead of writing the three separate sentences in sentence 1 below, older students are more likely to write the single construction in sentence 2:

1. *Philadelphia has a great baseball team. Philadelphia has a great football team. Philadelphia does not have a good basketball team.*
2. *Philadelphia has a great baseball team and a great football team, but it does not have a very good basketball team.*

Moreover, even 9-year-olds seem to know that Sentence 2 is more acceptable than sentence 1 when asked which is better. However, these same students could not imitate the constructions such as Sentences 1 or 2 when given parallel content (Scardamalia & Bereiter, 1986). Other researchers have found that high school students could not deliberately replicate the very same grammatical errors that they had made on a prior writing assignment. On the 1998 NAEP study for writing that included grammatical complexity, grammatical variability, and word choice in its rating scale, only 27% of 12th graders attained the highest two ratings overall (Greenwald et al., 1999). Recall that on the NAEP, children needed to write well in a short period of time. Thus, one could summarize such studies by saying that syntactic development during the school years seems to be the progressive attainment of *fluency and conscious control over complex grammatical constructions.*

A final aspect of language knowledge that seems to develop with age is the ability to use cohesive devices, which include such things as (1) using pronouns in one sentence to refer back to individuals named in earlier sentences and (2) using the same or related words in several successive sentences. Sentence 3 below illustrates both of these devices. The words that create ties are in bold:

3. *Mary was known as a popular girl. She was so **popular**, in fact, that **she** was named class president.*

A variety of studies have shown that older children are more likely to use cohesive devices than younger children. McCutchen (1986), for example, found differences in coherence between younger students (i.e., fourth graders) and older students (i.e., sixth and eighth graders) even when their knowledge of the topic was statistically controlled.

Summary

Across a variety of studies, older children were found to demonstrate greater knowledge of topics, genres, audiences, and language than younger children were. The major change that seems to occur is not so much the acquisition of these forms of knowledge as it is children's ability to consciously reflect on and manipulate this knowledge (Perfetti & McCutchen, 1987; Scardamalia & Bereiter, 1986). In particular, with the exception of knowledge of audiences, children were always found to know more than they demonstrate in writing. In particular, children were found to generate less content than they know, comprehend texts of a particular type (e.g., stories) earlier than they can write texts of that type, and vocalize or recognize well-formed syntactic constructions before they can write such constructions themselves.

Further Developments II: Functional Aspects (Writing Processes)

The improvements in the structural aspects of writing (i.e., WM and knowledge) provide the resources that help children carry out the functional aspects of writing more effectively. In the original 1980 model of Hayes and Flower, writers were said to engage in three main processes: planning, translating, and revising. The questions that have captured the interest of developmental researchers include, "Are older children more likely to carry out these processes than younger children are?" and "If so, do older children carry out these processes more effectively?" In what follows, we will examine the developmental literature to see what the answers to these questions are. Note that the revised model of Hayes (1996) that emphasized such things as social relations, motivation, and reading skills has not received much attention from developmentalists and educators to date.

Planning

Most developmental studies of writing show that children give very little evidence of explicit planning (De La Paz & MCutchen, 2011; McCutchen,

2006; Scardamalia & Bereiter, 1986). Although young writers may at times "rehearse" what they will eventually write in the form of partial or full sentences, these notes are probably early drafts of eventual lines rather than plans per se.

Instead of forming goals and writing to these goals, children are more likely to engage in what has been called "knowledge telling" (Scardamalia & Bereiter, 1986). Writers who engage in "knowledge telling" write down everything they know about a topic, in the order that ideas come to mind. Knowledge-tellers stop writing when they feel that they have written everything they know.

Because children do not write from goals and plans, they tend to generate ideas by way of associative thinking rather than heuristic searches, and they often do not organize these ideas in any way. As a result, their stories, essays, and arguments often lack both conceptual coherence and rhetorical coherence.

Translation

In the earlier section of the development of writing knowledge, we learned that younger children have smaller vocabularies, a smaller repertoire of syntactic structures and cohesive devices, less fluency, and less conscious control over these language forms than older children have. As a result, younger children are less equipped for translating their personal meanings into precisely interpretable texts. That is, they tend to produce "writer-based" texts rather than "reader-based" texts (Perfetti & McCutchen, 1987). Writer-based prose is "full of idiosyncratic phrases that are loaded with semantic content for the writer—meaning that is not, however, articulated for the reader" (Perfetti & McCutchen, 1987, p. 126). In reader-based prose, in contrast, ideas are well-articulated and there is little ambiguity and a great deal of intersentence cohesion. In fact, the meaning is so well specified that most people who read a segment of the text would come away with the same interpretation of it.

Although few studies have shown that increases in vocabulary and syntax skills with age directly contribute to the production of reader-based prose, several studies have shown that older children are more likely than younger children to use a variety of intersentence cohesion devices. Moreover, the tendency to create more cohesive texts seems to increase linearly with age between the third grade and adulthood (Garner et al., 1986; McCutchen, 1986; Wright & Rosenberg, 1993). These findings are reflected in some of the age trends reported in the 1998 and 2011 NAEP reports.

In addition to these text-generation processes, recall that the original Hayes and Flower model (1980) was revised to include transcription variables such as handwriting (and typing) fluency and spelling. Children show improvements in both of these aspects of transcription, and these improvements are additional factors that produce higher-quality written products (Abbott et al., 2010; Graham et al., 2008).

Revising

The literature on developmental trends in revising has revealed four main findings. First, children, adolescents, and inexperienced college students do very little of it (De La Paz & McCutchen, 2011; Fitzgerald, 1987; Graham, 2006; Scardamalia & Bereiter, 1986). Second, when students do revise, the vast majority of changes are superficial rather than conceptual or organizational. That is, students are more likely to focus on specific words, spelling, or grammar than on deeper issues such as goals, plans, and overall intended meanings (Fitzgerald, 1987; Graham, 2006; McCutchen, 2006; Scardamalia & Bereiter, 1986). Third, the main reason why children tend not to revise is that they have trouble detecting problems in the first place— especially in their own writing (Bartlett, 1982; McCutchen, 2006). When problems are pointed out to them, children can at times be quite good at making appropriate changes (e.g., Beal, 1990), although some studies have found that the changes do not always improve the quality of the text (Scardamalia & Bereiter, 1986). Fourth, a further constraint on children's revising may be that they lack sufficient memory capacity for dealing with multiple issues of content and quality at the same time. When an adult guides them through revisions in a scaffolded way, the quality of revisions improves (Scardamalia & Bereiter, 1986).

In a recent meta-analysis, Kent and Wanzek (2016) examined the relationship between different writing processes and writing quality. They found that handwriting fluency ($r = .49$ overall, $r = .59$ for younger writers), spelling ability ($r = .49$), reading ability ($r = .48$), and oral language ($r = .30$) were all moderately and significantly correlated with writing quality in grades K–12. These findings strongly support the original and revised Hayes and Flower model.

Reading and Writing Connections

The original and revised Hayes and Flower models included the component of reading in their editing and revising phase. Why? Better readers tend to be better writers, and vice versa. When you have refined reading skills, you can detect your own writing errors more readily. In addition, however, the fairly large correlation between reading and writing has been argued to derive from a common set of cognitive resources that both skills can tap into, such as schemata for genres, language skills, and WM (Gillespie Rouse, Graham, & Compton, 2017; Lee & Schallert, 2016). Moreover, just as researchers make a distinction between learning to read and reading to learn (see Chapters 9 and 10), researchers also make a comparable distinction between learning to write and writing to learn. That is, after children master the basics of writing, they can use this skill to promote their comprehension.

To examine writing to learn, a number of researchers have examined whether asking students to engage in writing activities after reading documents could be used to improve their comprehension of those documents. In the aggregate, however, the results of these studies have been mixed; sometimes writing activities improved comprehension and sometimes they did not (Arnold et al., 2017; Gillespie et al., 2017). Arnold et al. (2017) argued that the primary reason for the conflicting findings is that not all post-reading writing activities are the same. For example, taking notes and filling in blanks on worksheets have been considered to be the same as immediate recall and essay tests. When you only consider the post-reading writing activities that require retrieval, the effects are much stronger on comprehension (Arnold et al., 2017).

But one additional claim is that it should be possible to improve reading skills by engaging in extensive writing, and improve writing skills by engaging in extensive reading (Lee & Schallert, 2016). This transactional, interrelationship has been shown in some longitudinal studies (Abbott et al., 2010). In addition, an intervention designed to improve reading and writing skills in English learners (ELs) by increasing the amount of reading in one treatment group and the amount of writing in a second treatment group, resulted in improved reading comprehension in both treatment groups compared to the control group (Lee & Schallert, 2016). However, the writing skills only improved for students who had higher writing skills to begin with. Thus, the inconsistent findings reported above and Lee and Schallert's findings suggest that there does seem to be a connection between reading and writing, but the details of this relationship are still being worked out.

Summary

In sum, then, children not only gain more WM capacity, topic knowledge, and discourse knowledge (e.g., of genres) with age, they also engage in writing processes such as planning, text production, and revising more effectively. These structural and functional aspects, of course, play equally important and interactive roles in the development of writing skills. For example, as children gain more knowledge of their language, they are more equipped for performing the process of translation effectively. Similarly, as they gain more knowledge of audiences, they become more skilled at detecting and correcting possible ambiguities in what they have written. Thus, it is best to think of the development of writing ability as the coalescing of, and interaction among, knowledge and processes, rather than the acquisition of separate components.

According to Berninger, Mizokawa, and Bragg (1991), there are three types of constraints that affect the rate at which writing knowledge and processes coalesce. First, there are neurodevelopmental constraints that influence young children's writing by affecting the rapid, automatic production of letters and hand movements. These low-level constraints are thought to constrain the "transcription process" (i.e., writing down symbols) but not the central "translation processes" (i.e., converting ideas into potential text). After transcription processes have been mastered and automatized, linguistic constraints on words, sentences, and schemata have their effects. Finally, after transcription and translation processes have been sufficiently mastered, cognitive constraints on planning and revising may become evident. Thus, whereas neurodevelopmental constraints have their strongest influence on young writers, older children are influenced mostly by linguistic and cognitive constraints. In a study that examined the direct and cross-lagged effects of reading and writing skills, Abbott et al. (2010) found that prior reading skills and prior writing skills separately predicted later reading skills and writing skills, respectively, but prior reading skills also predicted later writing skills, and vice versa.

Having completed our discussion of how older students differ from younger students in their writing ability, we can now move on to the question, "How do individuals of the same age differ from one another?" In what follows, we answer this question by first comparing skilled and less skilled writers of the same age and then considering the writing skills of immigrant children learning English.

COMPARISONS OF SKILLED AND LESS SKILLED WRITERS

The major findings of the studies that have compared same-aged skilled and less skilled writers are as follows:

1. Although skilled writers and less skilled writers do not differ in terms of grade-point averages (GPAs), achievement test scores, and short-term memory capacity, the former are better at manipulating verbal information than the latter (Benton, Glover, Kraft, & Plake, 1984). In particular, a study of college students showed that when students were asked to (1) reorder strings of letters into alphabetical order, (2) reorder words into a meaningful sentence, or (3) reorder sentences to make a meaningful paragraph, those students who showed skilled writing ability were faster and more accurate than their peers who wrote less well. Cognitive and educational psychologists have referred to such abilities as being indicative of a large WM span for verbal information (Kellogg, 1996; McCutchen, Covill, Hoyne, & Mildes, 1994; Ransdell & Levy, 1996).

2. In elementary school children, the mechanics of writing (i.e., handwriting and spelling) contribute significantly to both fluency and overall

quality (Graham, Berninger, Abbott, Abbott, & Whitaker, 1997; Graham et al., 2008; Greenwald et al., 1999). Skilled writers are able to write and spell more quickly than less skilled writers.

3. As noted above, skilled writers tend to be better readers than less skilled writers are (Abbott & Berninger, 1993; Englert et al., 1988; Hayes, 1996; Langer, 1986; Perfetti & McCutchen, 1987). Writing and reading are not, of course, the same, but they do seem to rely on the same central knowledge structures (Perfetti & McCutchen, 1987). But again, there is a difference between reading for comprehension and evaluative reading (see above). Skilled writers are better at both kinds of reading than less skilled writer are (Graham, 2006; McCutchen, 2006).

4. Just as older writers are more likely than younger writers to use heuristic (i.e., goal-directed) searches to retrieve ideas from long-term memory, skilled writers of a particular age group are also more likely than less skilled writers of that age group to use heuristic searches (Scardamalia & Bereiter, 1986) and also more likely to engage in incomplete searches (Graham & Harris, 1996). When good writers lack knowledge on a particular topic and cannot retrieve information from memory, they may also use their heuristic search methods to delve into the published literature to find what they need. Few studies, however, have demonstrated this phenomenon. Finally, whereas expert writers usually elaborate on an assignment by building in issues, themes, and constraints, novice writers stick very close to the assignment (Scardamalia & Bereiter, 1986).

5. In terms of language competence, expert writers mainly differ from novice writers in three ways: (1) whereas handwriting, spelling, punctuation, and grammar are largely automatized in the former, these processes are still somewhat effortful in the latter; (2) the former have a larger repertoire of sentence constructions and grammatical devices than the latter; and (3) skilled writers add larger segments to their sentential constructions than less skilled writers do (Greenwald et al., 1999; Hayes, 1996; Norris & Bruning, 1988; Perfetti & McCutchen, 1987; Scardamalia & Bereiter, 1986).

6. Whereas skilled writers spend a great deal of time creating goals and organizing their ideas before they write, less skilled writers show little evidence of explicit planning and goals. As a result, less skilled writers tend to "jump right into" the task of writing, and their work demonstrates less sophisticated organization (Graham, 2006; Scardamalia & Bereiter, 1986). Experts are also more likely to comment on how their goals and plans change in the midst of writing.

7. Because expert writers are more likely than novices to create explicit goals and subgoals, the former are more likely to revise than the latter. Why? Deep-level revisions take place when one realizes that a segment of

text does not meet the goals set for that segment (Scardamalia & Bereiter, 1986). For example, if you were writing to a friend to explain that he or she does something offensive, and you had the goal of being polite, you might say in response to reading a draft, "Oh, that's no good. He or she might be offended by this phrasing." In contrast, people who do not write from goals have nothing to compare the text to and will not, therefore, see the need to revise anything. Skilled writers are also better at revising than less skilled writers are because the former tend to have greater topic knowledge (McCutchen, Francis, & Kerr, 1997), greater executive control over revising (Graham, 1997), and greater sensitivity to their audience (Graham, 1997).

Furthermore, because skilled writers often change their goals and plans as they write, they will have a tendency to review what they have written and delete those portions that do not fit with the new plans and goals. Because less skilled writers tend not to change goals while writing, they will not engage in such wholesale revisions.

8. Finally, many of the aforementioned differences really concern a difference in *metacognition* between skilled and less skilled writers. It is probably incorrect to say that less skilled writers do not have goals when they write or that they have little knowledge of genres or language. Instead, it is more correct to say that whereas skilled writers can consciously reflect on and manipulate their goals and knowledge, less skilled writers do not have the same conscious access to their goals and knowledge (Scardamalia & Bereiter, 1986).

WRITING DIFFICULTIES OF STUDENTS DIAGNOSED WITH DISABILITIES AND ELs

Children Diagnosed with Learning Disabilities and ADHD

All of the aforementioned differences between same-aged skilled and less skilled writers are magnified when we look specifically at children who have learning disabilities (LD) or ADHD. Children diagnosed with LD are significantly less likely to (1) plan, (2) generate adequate content, (3) revise, (4) translate content into text, and (5) recognize the deficiencies of their writing than their nondisabled peers are (Troia, 2006). Children diagnosed with ADHD obtained lower scores than their normally achieving peers for writing quality ($d = -0.78$), output ($d = -0.64$), number of genre elements ($d = -0.69$), vocabulary ($d = -0.76$), spelling ($d = -0.80$), and handwriting ($d = -0.62$) (Graham, Fishman, Reid, & Hebert, 2016). The serious difficulties faced by these children as they write, combined with repeated experiences with failure, inevitably lead to serious motivational problems as well. What is particularly unfortunate is the finding that a sizable portion of regular classroom teachers (42%) reported in national surveys that they often do not adapt their instruction to meet the needs of writers with LD (Graham, Harris, Fink-Chorzempa, & MacArthur, 2003; Graham et al., 2008). Fortunately, many of the effective instructional techniques mentioned above have been tried on students diagnosed with LD and ADHD and have had success improving their writing skills.

Writing Problems of ELs

Earlier in this chapter, it was noted that only about 25% of a national sample of high school students were rated as being proficient writers on the NAEP. For ELs, the findings are even starker: only 1% of them were rated as proficient (Beck, Llosa, & Fredrick, 2013; Matuchniak, Olson, & Scarcella, 2014). These findings make sense if you consider combining the tendencies of all students to engage in very little planning or revising with low English vocabularies and developing control over English syntax; this combination would mean that ELs would have trouble with all three phases of the writing process (planning, text production, and revising). One study found, however, that if teachers engaged in 46 hours of professional development to learn how to apply a cognitive-strategies approach to writing in their classrooms, the writing skills of ELs significantly improved relative to ELs in typical classrooms (Matuchniak et al., 2014).

IMPLICATIONS FOR EDUCATION

So, we know that the core processes and knowledge of writing change with age, but we still do not know much about the developmental mechanisms responsible for these changes. Several likely sources of improvement include (1) increases in WM capacity, (2) writing frequency and practice, (3) extensive reading, and (4) instructional techniques. In particular, practice is likely to engender fluency and the automatization of writing skills. If WM is freed up to attend to goals and meaning, or if WM capacity increases, writing is likely to improve, as well. Extensive reading is likely to help because children would be exposed to new vocabulary terms, styles, genres, and syntactic constructions (Stanovich, West, & Harrison, 1995). To make this information explicit, however, children would need to engage in a form of literary criticism.

As for instructional techniques, it should be noted that children historically have not been asked by their teachers to write extensively, and, regrettably, recent surveys show children still only write for about 15 minutes a day (Cutler & Graham, 2008; Graham et al., 2014; NAEP, 2011). Moreover, they tend to get very little feedback on their writing and are rarely asked to submit multiple revisions of their work. Even when teachers report using evidence-based instructional practices, they use these practices infrequently (Graham et al., 2014). Thus, the children who improve may have a natural gift for, and love of, writing. They may also get feedback from sources other than their teachers (e.g., parents).

Whereas traditional instruction tends not to lead to sufficient improvements in writing ability, a variety of programs have been created to explicitly scaffold writing processes such as planning, text production, and revising (De La Paz & McCutchen, 2008). Thus, there is hope for change, but it will require the adoption of more explicit forms of instruction, better preparation in teacher preparation programs, and employment of teachers who are themselves skilled writers. A particularly helpful guide to effective, evidence-based instructional practices is Graham and Perin's (2007) meta-analysis, *Writing Next: Effective Strategies to Improve Writing of Adolescents in Middle and High Schools—A Report to Carnegie Corporation of New York* . Graham and Perin found that the following practices led to significantly improved performance and moderate to large differences between experimental and business-as-usual instruction: (1) explicit instruction on strategies for planning and revising texts (d = 0.82), (2) explicit instruction on how to summarize text (d = 0.82), (3) students collaborating on planning, drafting, and revising text (d = 0.75), (4) setting specific goals for final products such as to persuade using a thesis, supportive arguments, and counterarguments (d = 0.70), (5) using word processing (d = 0.55), and (6) teaching students how to combine individual sentences into a single, more complex one (d = 0.50). Thus, whereas novelist Stephen King has argued that writers do not really need to take courses on how to write (they just need to read, read, read and write, write, write), these findings show that most of us need explicit instruction. Mr. King must have had a natural aptitude that allowed him to detect and distill techniques on his own.

There are several other findings worth noting. One is that a recent meta-analysis showed that reading achievement scores are higher when teachers balance the amount of language arts lesson time between writing and reading, than when teachers devote a disproportionate amount of time to reading, d = 0.39 (Graham et al., 2018). In addition, studies show that writing instruction should begin during the early childhood years as opposed to waiting until the elementary school years. Currently, very little instruction on writing occurs in early childhood classrooms and when it occurs, it is not of a very high quality (Gerde, Bingham, & Pendergast, 2015). However, when teachers engaged in practices that support writing (e.g., by providing materials, giving opportunities for writing in activities), children showed stronger writing skills (Bingham, Quinn, & Gerde, 2017).

CHAPTER 12

The Development
of Mathematical Competence

Although it is often claimed that reading skills are among the most important skills that students can acquire (e.g., Snow et al., 1998), the mathematical skills that children acquire in early childhood and the elementary grades also strongly predict educational, work-related, and health-related outcomes many years later (Blakely et al., 2020; Duncan et al., 2007; Schneider et al., 2017). Math skills are also argued to be extremely important to the economic development of nations (Butterworth, 2017). Moreover, in the complicated and technologically sophisticated world of today, it is important that all students attain a high level of *numeracy*. Unfortunately, only 41% of fourth graders and 34% of eighth graders in the United States attained the "proficient" level on the 2019 NAEP for math (National Center for Education Statistics [NCES], 2020a). On the Programme for International Student Assessment (PISA), the United States performed below the mean for member nations of the Organisation for Economic Co-operation and Development (OECD). Student proficiency was also grouped into six levels on PISA. Whereas 65% of U.S. 10th graders performed at Level 3 or below, only 16%, 7%, and 2% performed at Levels 4, 5, and 6 (the highest levels). The findings on both NAEP and PISA show that students in the United States are not learning what they need to learn in mathematics to be successful in today's world. To understand how to promote a higher level of performance, the rest of this chapter focuses on the nature of mathematical competence, how it develops, and what factors (including methods of instruction) seem to promote it.

THE NATURE OF MATHEMATICAL COMPETENCE

The question of what students need to know and be able to do in mathematics by the time they graduate high school has generated different answers over the years (Karp & Furinghetti, 2016). There have been debates about which students need to learn higher levels of mathematics (e.g., should all students or just college-prep students?) and what kinds of mathematics they need (e.g., just algebra and geometry or also trigonometry and calculus?). Note that people who work in trades (e.g., home construction) often need to be facile in upper levels of arithmetic (e.g., fractions, ratios, percentages), and that many factories now utilize robotics and artificial intelligence. Working with the latter often requires an understanding of statistics. That said, only 60% of high school graduates in the United States attend college, and of those, only about 40% graduated in 2018 with an academic major that relies on having higher levels of mathematical skill (e.g., business, STEM fields) (NCES, 2018).

With all this diversity in career goals and outcomes, the question of who needs math and what kinds of math can be a little complicated. That said, one could argue that there are many problems that have to be solved at home and at work that involve some facility with mathematics. For example, professional carpenters who own their own small businesses not only need to understand rational numbers (e.g., to cut wood to appropriate sizes), they also need multiplication and division skills to buy enough materials, as well as business math skills to understand the consequences of loan decisions, payroll, and so on, so that they do not go out of business. In their personal lives, they have to understand the consequences of decisions related to the personal debt that accrues from credit cards and mortgages. They have to balance their family budgets, save for their children's college tuition, and put enough money away for retirement. Given all these issues facing someone like a carpenter, we can see why early math skills can be predictive of success later in life. If we then consider the mathematical thinking required for STEM-related professions and several professions in the social sciences (e.g., economists, sociologists, and psychologists), we can see that people in the latter professions need even higher levels of mathematical competence.

By embedding math skills within the decision making and problem solving that occurs in daily life at home and work, we can begin to see what mathematical competence truly entails. It is one thing for students to be able to imitate the steps carried out by their teachers as they demonstrate how to solve a particular math problem (e.g., add two fractions; compute an interest rate and growth function; compute an integral to determine the area under a curve), and quite another to solve real-world problems with mathematics on your own. Knowing how to carry out the steps of some mathematical procedure or calculation is called *procedural knowledge*.

Being able to solve problems with mathematics requires another kind of knowledge related to understanding *how and why a particular procedure is useful in a particular situation*. The latter form of understanding is called *conceptual knowledge* (Rittle-Johnson, 2019). As we will see later in this chapter, there are various numerical concepts that students have to master to attain higher levels of proficiency, ranging from the *cardinal value* of sets in kindergarten to concepts such as *functions, cosine, integrals*, and *derivatives* in high school and college. All these formal mathematical concepts are intimately linked to symbolic representations and expressions. Competence involves facility with operations over these symbolic representations and expressions. In other words, an informal, inexact, or intuitive understanding of quantities is not enough. In addition, many of the procedures implemented in math problems result in particular answers (e.g., $3 \times 9 = 27$). The results of such procedures are stored in memory as math facts. Psychologists use the term *declarative knowledge* to refer to the body of factual knowledge that students have.

But being highly proficient in using math to solve real-world problems in an efficient manner requires several other aspects of competence besides the three kinds of knowledge listed above. The first aspect pertains to being *flexible:* competent performers are able to use a single procedure across different situations and recognize how the skill transfers across these situations (Star et al., 2015). When students only learn how to execute a skill a single way in decontextualized classroom exercises, they will not recognize when the skill applies in real-world contexts (Bransford, Brown, & Cocking, 2000). The second aspect of competence that promotes efficiency and success is the acquisition of *schemata* for particular problems that recur (see Chapter 3 for more on schema theory). Students develop schemata for problem types in their math classes by repeatedly trying to solve examples of each type (Quilici & Mayer, 2002). Similarly, when professional carpenters repeatedly confront the same construction or installation problem that has the same mathematical requirements, they develop schemata for that common problem and immediately know what to do. The same can be said for financial planners, economists, or psychologists when they try to solve recurring problems that involve mathematics.

The astute reader will recognize that the foregoing description of mathematical competence is resonant with the description of expertise presented in Chapter 7. Experts are not limited to solving a few, seemingly unrelated concrete problems. They have extensive schemata for problem types, more abstract representations of these problems and the principles underlying them, and a deep conceptual understanding of why certain procedures are called for and "work." But, as noted in Chapter 7, people only acquire expertise through extensive practice and having the motivation needed to (1) regularly engage in domain-specific tasks and (2) persist when they experience difficulties. Engagement and persistence, as was noted in

Chapter 5, require that students develop a strong *interest* in the domain (in this case mathematics), recognize its *importance,* and develop a strong sense of *self-efficacy* and a *growth mindset.* Unfortunately, as the afore-mentioned NAEP and PISA evidence suggests, few students seem to attain a high level of mathematical competence that includes high levels of proce-dural knowledge, declarative knowledge, conceptual knowledge, schemata, interest, and self-efficacy for math. Those students who lack these aspects of competence tend to avoid certain college majors that have good salaries (e.g., STEM fields; Li, Lee, & Snyder, 2018), and this avoidance is problem-atic because the United States cannot remain competitive in the world if it does not attract a sufficient number of undergraduates into STEM fields. Regardless of major, avoidance of higher-level math courses in high school and college further exacerbates the problems of students having insufficient math skills for today's world.

The foregoing summary of mathematical competence was nicely sum-marized by a panel commissioned by the National Research Council (2001) that described five essential components of competence and proficiency:

> 1) conceptual understanding (comprehension of mathematical concepts, oper-ations, and relations), 2) procedural fluency (skills in carrying out procedures flexibly, fluently, and appropriately), 3) strategic competence (ability to for-mulate, represent, and solve mathematical problems), 4) adaptive reasoning (capacity for logical thought, reflection, explanation, and justification), and 5) productive disposition (habitual inclination to see mathematics as sensible, useful, and worthwhile, coupled with a belief in diligence and one's own effi-cacy). (p. 116)

THE DEVELOPMENT
OF MATHEMATICAL COMPETENCE

The preceding description of mathematical competence is a depiction of the ideal endpoint of development (i.e., how students should turn out after 12–16 years of schooling). The goal of the present section is to explain how and why many students fail to acquire the skills they need. The approach will be to describe the kinds of math skills that students seem to demon-strate (or not demonstrate) during the following three age periods presented in sequence: (1) birth to kindergarten, (2) first grade to eighth grade, and (3) high school and beyond.

Birth to Kindergarten

The human species has two cognitive systems for thinking about, and responding to, different quantities: (1) a nonsymbolic (analog) *approximate number system* (ANS) that is an innate part of our biological endowment and shared with other animal species, and (2) a *formal symbolic number system* that only humans develop through enculturation and education (Barner, 2017; Bonny & Lourenco, 2013; Dehaene, 1992; Pantsar, 2019). The ANS is thought to be preserved across evolution and species because even approximate numerical comparisons can be advantageous (e.g., our group has around four members and a rival group seems to have more members, so it is not smart to pick a fight). Studies have shown that, in both nonhuman animal species and humans, approximate comparisons create response patterns that conform to *Weber's law,* which states that subjective differences in intensity between unequal stimuli are propor-tional to their objective intensities (Bonny & Lourenco, 2013). Practically, in everyday terms, this law means that people will be faster at seeing a difference in the approximate size of sets when the gap between the sizes is larger (e.g., 20 vs. 12 as opposed to 20 vs. 17). Across human history, it is interesting that only some cultures developed a formal symbolic system that was passed on to successive generations, and that these systems have differed in their specific details (Pantsar, 2019). There were environmental pressures that must have promoted the development of the formal sys-tems (e.g., economics, trade, and so forth), but even when these pressures existed, it took some time before these systems reached their final forms after multiple iterations.

The questions that have generated considerable debate since Dehaene (1992) first introduced the ANS to psychologists and educators are (1) How early in development is the ANS operative?, (2) In early childhood and the first few grades of school, does the ANS serve as a foundation on which the later formal system is built?, and (3) Which system is more predictive of later mathematics achievement, the ANS or the formal system? (Bremner et al., 2017; Cantrell & Smith, 2013; Carey & Barner, 2019; Pantsar, 2019; Schneider et al., 2017).

Regarding the first question, several lines of studies suggested that even preverbal young infants seem to be able to make comparisons across sets of differing sizes, perhaps by relying on the ANS. Using the *habituation paradigm* described in Chapter 8, Starkey and Cooper (1980) presented young infants with screens that showed one, two, or three black dots. If you repeatedly show the same picture (e.g., two dots) over many trials, infants look less and less at the display (i.e., they habituate). However, if you intro-duce a different picture after habituation occurs (e.g., three dots or one dot), they will look much longer at the new picture if they see a difference. Starkey and Cooper's 3- to 22-week-old infants did just that, but only for arrays with three or fewer dots. Strauss and Curtis (1981) found that 10- to 12-month-old infants seemed to tell the difference between both two and three objects, and three and four objects. Note that people of all ages (including infants) have the ability to *subitize* arrays of one to four objects, which is defined as the ability to immediately identify the exact amount in an array without counting. With older children and adults, it is possible to show response patterns conforming to Weber's law even for set sizes much larger than four (Schneider et al., 2017).

Note, however, that researchers have questioned the validity and meaning of the results using the habituation paradigm by finding other reasons why infants may look longer after new pictures are produced (Cantrell & Smith, 2013; Mix, Huttenlocher, & Levine, 2002). For example, it is possible to equate the total proportionate surface area of black pixels and white pixels in a computerized display such that the number of dots does change but the proportion of white and black pixels stay the same. When this is done, infants do not dishabituate (Mix et al., 2002), which suggests that they are not really registering numbers per se but are recognizing that something had changed.

Another line of research with infants has found results that seemingly show an infant's ability to add or subtract using displays of one or two objects. In this paradigm invented by Wynn (1992), infants observe a small toy being placed on a small stage in front of them. A screen then obscures the view of the toy. Then, infants can see a hand place an identical second toy behind the screen. Finally, the screen is lowered. On "possible" trials, infants see the expected two dolls. On "impossible trials," however, they see only one because the second one was removed surreptitiously. A difference in looking times between the possible and impossible trials is taken to mean that the infant was surprised and could, therefore, perform addition. On other trials for subtraction, the infant sees two toys from the start, but one is taken away after the screen is raised. Again, possible and impossible trials are created for the subtraction trials. A recent meta-analysis of 12 replication studies of Wynn (1992) in other labs showed that infants do seem to look longer at impossible outcomes than possible outcomes, $d = 0.34$ (Christodoulou, Lac, & Moore, 2017).

Once again, however, alternative explanations for the findings have been proposed and examined (Cantrell & Smith, 2013). One recent study showed that in addition to being able to subitize small set sizes, infants are also able to track the identity and location of objects. When you create carefully constructed trials and use precise eye-tracking software, the results of Wynn (1992) and others can be explained by the fact that infants look at the spot where the last object that they examined should have been, not at all objects in the display (Bremner et al., 2017). Thus, with both the habituation methodology and Wynn (1992) methodology, infants do respond in ways that suggest that the ANS is helping them recognize changes in the sizes of small sets. But there remains a debate about whether there are other nonmathematical ways to explain their performance.

Moving next to somewhat older children, a large number of studies have examined preschool children's acquisition of *number words,* their ability to *count,* and their understanding of *cardinality* and *ordinality*.

Some early studies that were designed to counter Piaget's claim (1965) that preschoolers lack a true understanding of number seemed to show that even 2- and 3-year-olds have a rudimentary sense of the meaning of the number words *one, two,* and *three* and can count as high as up to 10 (Gelman & Gallistel, 1978). These same studies also were alleged to show that children know the rules of counting, such as (1) only count each object once, (2) give only one number word to each object, and so on. However, subsequent studies showed that young children really do not fully understand what number words mean, since they are unable to correctly respond to questions such as "Can you give me three chips?" (Barner, 2017; Carey & Barner, 2019). The fact that they can recite counting strings up to 10 is comparable to their ability to recite "Patty Cake" and "Eenie meenie miney mo" (Carey & Barner, 2019). In literature, these children are called "non-knowers." A little later, they may be able to give one object when asked for one, but do not correctly supply the correct number when asked for two, three, or four. But a few months later, some children are correct for both one and two (and are then called "two-knowers"), and then a little later may give three or four objects, but no higher (Barner, 2017). When children can correctly give one, two, or three objects, they are sometimes called "subset knowers" since they only know some of the number words. But when asked to count, these children show little understanding of cardinality, which is the understanding that the number of items corresponds to the last number word said after all objects are counted. At around 3½ or 4, many children in the United States eventually figure out the rules of counting and cardinality, at least for numbers less than 10 (Barner, 2017). Children who reach this stage are called "CP-knowers" since they appear to understand the cardinality principle (CP). But development is not complete, since it still takes children several more years to understand the principle that every number and number word has a successor (*four* comes after *three, one hundred seven* comes after *one hundred six,* etc.) and that the successor principle supplies the subsequent insight into the concept of infinity (Barner, 2017; Cheung, Rubenson, & Barner, 2017).

An intriguing finding that supports the distinction between conceptual knowledge (in this case cardinality) and procedural knowledge (in this case counting) at the preschool level is that children who are in between the subset-knower level and CP-knower level sometimes generate mismatches between their gestures (e.g., holding up two fingers when holding two objects in the other hand) and their words (e.g., saying "three" when asked how many there are). Children showing these mismatches more readily learned how to count and acquire the cardinality principle (Gibson, Gunderson, Spaepen, Levine, & Goldin-Meadow, 2019). In other words, their implicit conceptual knowledge preceded their explicit conceptual knowledge.

The importance of children attaining a sophisticated and complete level of CP and counting competence by kindergarten is that it strongly predicts not only children's readiness to learn math (Geary, vanMarle, Chu, Hoard, & Nugent, 2019) but also how well children do in math many years later, even after controlling for arithmetic skills learned along the way (Koponen, Aunola, & Nurmi, 2019).

There have been various theories proposed to explain (and challenge) this developmental trend in children's concepts of number. Some theorists are *nativists* who propose that the concept of number is innate and appeal to the ANS as evidence. In this view, children merely map number words onto representations in the ANS (Barner, 2017). However, there is considerable evidence against this claim. Other researchers are more *constructivist* in their orientation and assume that children do map the words *one, two,* and *three* onto their subitizing ability, and then inductively infer other aspects of the number system, such as the successor principle from this knowledge and counting experience. Once again, though, there is evidence against this proposal (e.g., Jara-Ettinger, Piantadosi, Spelke, Levy, & Gibson, 2017) as well as the logical problem of *induction fallacy* (Barner, 2017). According to this fallacy, in order for anyone to induce a new idea out of old information, they have to already know what they are looking for, which some philosophers say is impossible. A recent study showed that children do not immediately learn the successor principle after they become CP-knowers but CP-knowers can be taught this principle through training; in other words, training is less effective for children who have not attained the CP-knowing stage (Spaepen, Gunderson, Gibson, Goldin-Meadow, & Levine, 2018).

A third explanation, called the *exact algorithm hypothesis* (Carey & Barner, 2019), is that children progressively build up their concept of number through a combination of their subitizing ability for sets less than four, emerging counting skills, and information gleaned from the way natural languages indicate number, such as singular and plural markings on nouns, and number agreement in verbs (*He is, they are*) (Barner, 2017; Carey & Barner, 2019). Indirect support for this claim comes from a study in which researchers tried to see what factors predicted which preschoolers became early CP-knowers (Geary et al., 2019). The significant predictors, in order of importance, included their ability to discriminate letters, their ability to count up to 20 objects with the correct verbal labels, their IQ (indexed by the vocabulary, block design, and information subscales), their age, and their ability to discriminate sets of dots (using the ANS). Many of these measures tap into children's language skills. Another study revealed very similar results but used knowledge of the count list, nonverbal approximate numerical ability, working memory, executive conflict processing, and knowledge of letters and words as predictors (Mou, Berteletti, & Hyde,

2018). In any event, the debates among the nativists, constructivists, and language-based theorists wages on. For now, we can say that children do progressively build up their understanding of numbers, counting rules, and cardinality between birth and age 5, but theories differ as to how to explain this progressive development.

As for ordinality, Piaget (1965) argued that a mature understanding of number requires that children fuse the concept of set size (cardinality) with the idea that sets can be arranged in increasing magnitude (ordinality). In his studies, he found little evidence that children demonstrate this fusion prior to age 5. This claim was initially challenged by those in the nativist camp described above, but the field has progressively moved back toward Piaget's position. For example, Colomé and Noël (2012) found that preschool children understood the cardinal meaning of number words (e.g., "Give me five___") before they understood the ordinal aspect ("Give me the second one"). In another study, Geary and vanMarle (2018) divided their low-income sample into four groups depending on when the children attained CP-knower status across the first 2 years of preschool (ages 4 and 5). Whereas the CP-knowers at Time 1 were able to correctly judge the relative size of numerals below 15 at a rate of 60% at Time 1, those who attained CP-knower status by Time 2 were not above chance (80%) until the second year. The same was true for those who attainted CP-knower status by Time 3 in the second year (65%). Whereas the two fastest CP-knower groups attained a 90% level by the end of the second year (age 5), the two groups slower to attain CP-knower status were only about 60–70% correct on numerical size comparisons by age 5. Thus, most children in the study mastered cardinality before they mastered ordinal comparisons. This finding is comparable to the finding above that children become CP-knowers before they appreciate the successor principle (which is also a form of insight into ordinality). From a readiness standpoint, it is important to master both aspects of number; a meta-analysis showed that success on numerical comparison tasks correlates $r = .30$ with later math achievement in first grade (Schneider et al., 2017).

One final aspect of the concept of number that both Piaget (1965) and contemporary scholars emphasize (e.g., Carey & Barner, 2019; Sarnecka & Wright, 2013) is the idea of *one-to-one correspondence* of sets. If you can place two sets in one-to-one correspondence, you should know that the two sets have exactly the same number. But when preschoolers are given Piaget's (1965) classic *conservation of number* task (that was actually invented by IQ theorist Alfred Binet for his intelligence test, see Chapter 7), many children below the age of 4 or 5 fail to recognize that sets of objects placed in one-to-one correspondence keep their equal number when the sets are altered out of the one-to-one visual shape. In the conservation task, the experimenter creates two rows of candies in which each piece of candy in the top row is placed above one piece of candy in the bottom row. Children are then asked, "These are your candies (points to top row) and these are my candies (points to bottom row): do you have more, do I have more, or do we both have the same?" Both 4- and 5-year-olds say, "We have the same." But when one row is either stretched out such that it looks longer than the other row, or one row is made into a pile rather than a row, and children are asked, "How about now? Do you have more candy, do I have more candy, or do we both have the same?", only older children recognize that the number of candies has not been changed by this perceptual transformation. Recent studies have shown that children do not recognize the *equinumerosity* of two sets until they reach the stage of being a CP-knower (Sarnecka & Wright, 2013). In other words, insight into the cardinality principle is attained at around the same time that they recognize that two sets have exactly the same number, in a one-to-one correspondence sense.

Where modern researchers disagree with Piaget is the apparent age of onset of these insights. His writings suggest that children do not understand cardinality until age 5. Modern studies of cardinality and equinumerosity suggest that some 4-year-olds have these understandings. In addition, however, Piaget (1965) explained age trends using a developmental mechanism called equilibration (see Chapter 3). Modern scholars argue in favor of subitizing, language, and counting experience as better explanations. Both groups have a constructivist flavor, however, in that they recognize that concepts such as cardinality, the successor principle, ordinality, and equinumerosity emerge progressively across the preschool years and cannot be directly taught to children who are younger than 4 (Nunes & Bryant, 2015). They also argue against nativists who put a heavy emphasis on the early emerging ANS as being the foundation for later math (Carey & Barner, 2019).

One way to summarize all the concepts and skills mastered by children between the ages of birth and 5 is to say that many children acquire *number sense*. As defined by an expert panel convened to understand why children in the United States do not acquire the math skills they need to be successful in college and the workplace (National Mathematics Advisory Panel, 2008), number sense

> entails an ability to immediately identify the numerical value associated with small quantities (e.g., 3 pennies), a facility with basic counting skills, and a proficiency in approximating the magnitudes of small numbers of objects and simple numerical operations. An intuitive sense of the magnitudes of small whole numbers is evident even among most 5-year-olds who can, for example, accurately judge which of two single digits is larger, estimate the number of dots on a page, and determine the approximate location of single digit numerals on a number line that provides only the numerical endpoints. These competencies comprise the core number sense that children often acquire informally prior to starting school. (p. 27)

First Grade to Eighth Grade

Whereas much of the mathematical knowledge of preschoolers is informal and not linked to mathematical symbols (e.g., 3 or +), the move to elementary school requires more formal and symbolic competencies. In order for researchers to examine the declarative, procedural, and concept knowledge of elementary school students, they have to first be aware of the curriculum presented to students at each grade level. For example, it would make no sense for researchers to examine first graders' comprehension of negative integers if children are not asked to learn negative integers until sixth or seventh grade in many school districts (Common Core State Standards Initiative [CCSSI], 2020). Between first and eighth grade, the sequence of topics covered at each grade level include: (1) addition and subtraction of natural numbers (positive whole integers) below 20, (2) addition and subtraction with regrouping, multiplication, and division, (3) rational numbers (fractions and decimals), and (4) irrational numbers, linear equations, and functions (CCSSI, 2020). Children find addition easier to understand than subtraction, single-digit addition and subtraction easier than addition and subtraction with regrouping, arithmetic operations on natural (whole) numbers easier than arithmetic operations on rational numbers, and arithmetic easier than algebra (Nunes & Bryant, 2015). With each grade level and topic area, the same content can be expressed as decontextualized math sentences (e.g., "3 + 7 = ?") or embedded in word problems. Children tend to find word problems harder to understand than decontextualized sentences, though not always (Nathan, 2012). Let's unpack these each of these general age trends in turn.

Addition and Subtraction

When can children perform addition and subtraction? The answer depends on the nature of the task. At one time, young infants were thought to be able to add or subtract one from a display of one or two objects (e.g., dolls) (Wynn, 1992). But as noted above, this finding has been challenged methodologically. Using a different nonverbal task in which (1) an experimenter first slides one to six plastic chips under a mat, (2) the experimenter then slides an additional one to six chips under the mat or removes one to six while the initial chips are still hidden from view, and (3) children are given their own chips and asked to place the same number of chips on top of their own mat so that their chips match what is under the experimenter's mat after chips are added or removed, the number of correct responses steadily improves between age 4 and age 6 (Levine, Jordan, & Huttenlocher, 1992), from about three correct (out of six) to five correct for addition trials, and from two correct to five correct for subtraction trials. When these same children were given short story problems (e.g., "Kim had 5 crayons. She lost 2. How many crayons did she have left?"), they performed worse on the story problems at each age level until age 6. When given standard number-fact problems (e.g., "How much is 3 and 2?"), performance in children below 6 was even worse for subtraction problems, but performance was comparable for addition number-fact and addition story problems. A more recent study using a simplified version of the nonsymbolic chips task revealed children performed in a manner comparable to children in Levine et al. (1992) in which the average performance 3- to 5-year-olds was 64% correct (Gray & Reeve, 2016).

After children enter elementary school as first graders, they are asked to solve single-digit addition "sentences" of the form "3 + 4 = ?" They are often given a finger-counting strategy by their teachers to solve these problems in which they put up the appropriate number of fingers for the augend (3) on one hand, then put up the appropriate number of fingers corresponding to the addend (4) on the other hand, and finally count up all of the fingers on both hands. In the research literature on math learning, this strategy is called the *count-all* strategy (Siegler & Araya, 2005). The goal of instruction and practice on problems is to move children from a reliance on this slow and inefficient procedure to rapid and automatic *direct retrieval* of the answer from long-term memory. Many school systems use a spiral curriculum in which content from the prior academic year is reintroduced in the beginning of the next academic year (CCSSI, 2020). Even with all this repetition and practice (including in seatwork and homework), it takes until about third grade for direct retrieval to be the norm (though we will see below that there is more to the story).

In between the initial count-all strategy and direct-retrieval route, children invent a variety of other strategies such as (1) *count all from first* (start on the last number said when counting the augend and then count on using the fingers of the other hand, such as "3 . . . 4, 5, 6, 7"), (2) *count on from second* (similar to prior strategy but you start with the addend and then count on from that), (3) count on from larger (also called the *min strategy*), and (4) *derived facts* (i.e., use known facts to construct the answer, such as "3 plus 3 is 6, so one more makes 7") (Siegler, 2016).

Initially, many researchers assumed that children progressed from the count-all to the other strategies in an orderly or stepwise fashion where they only used one of the strategies at particular times. However, that false impression was due to the standard way children's arithmetic skills were assessed: testing them in a single session. When a different approach called *microgenetic analysis* was used, in which you individually test children one-on-one and give them repeated attempts to solve the same problems every day over several weeks, researchers found instead that children continued to use multiple (average of three) strategies across multiple consecutive testing sessions, even when they mainly used direct retrieval for most problems (Siegler, 2016). The reader has probably experienced this phenomenon themselves when asked to perform a multiplication task that they had not performed in years (e.g., "What is 7 times 8?"). When direct retrieval fails, we may resort to the derived facts approach (e.g., "Well, I know 7 times 7 is 49, so 7 more is . . . 56"). To characterize the dual tendency to mainly use one strategy but use several others as well, Siegler developed *overlapping-waves theory* (2016). In Wave 1, the predominant but not exclusive tendency may be to use count all, but by Wave 5 the predominant but not exclusive tendency may be to use direct retrieval.

As children progress through these waves of strategies to solve single-digit addition problems between first and third grades, they are also asked to learn single-digit subtraction in earnest in second grade and multidigit subtraction with regrouping in third grade (Caviola, Mammarella, Pastore, & LeFevre, 2018). The goal of instruction is for children to eventually rely on direct retrieval of answers on single-digit subtraction problems and efficient strategies for multidigit subtraction problems. Studies have shown that children utilize a variety of strategies to solve subtraction problems, too, and the overlapping-waves account applies equally well to subtraction (Caviola et al., 2018). Performance declines when (1) subtraction problems are presented vertically (one subtrahend above the other) versus horizontally, (2) both subtrahends have two digits, and (3) children have to engage in regrouping to solve problems (e.g., 21 – 17). These levels of complexity likewise promote the use of different strategies. For example, a child might count down three for the problem 21 – 3, use direct retrieval for 10 – 5, and use *decomposition* for problems such as 64 – 12 (e.g., 60 – 10, which is 50; 4 – 2, which is 2, so take away another 2 from 50, so 48). They may also use the standard right-to-left columnar approach taught in school for two-digit problems requiring regrouping (e.g., for 31 – 17, subtract 7 from 11, yielding 4; then 10 from 20, yielding 10; 10 + 4 = 14).

Earlier in this chapter we considered the importance of conceptual understanding for procedural efficiency and accuracy. In the case of multidigit subtraction with regrouping, children have to understand the concept of *place value* (Chan, Au, Lau, & Tang, 2017). That is, in a number such 324, the "3" is actually 300, the "2" is actually 20, and "4" is 4. Numbers have a value based on their position or place in the digit sequence. Children also have to understand that when you regroup, you are taking away one 10 or one 100 from numbers in the second or first position and combining that amount with the amount in the adjacent position on the right. So, for the problem 374 – 27, the first step is to take away 10 from 70 and combine it with the 4 (10 + 4 = 14) to allow you to then subtract 7 from 14. That is why the 374 becomes 360 + 14 (and the 7 in 374 is changed into a 6). When children are first learning multidigit subtraction with regrouping, they have a lot of trouble understanding why you have to regroup and decrement numbers if they are simply taught the algorithm. They often forget to decrement or, in the case of 374 – 27, subtract the 4 from the 7! They have even more trouble when the regrouping affects multiple columns such as in the case of 205 – 26. They may change the "0" in 205 into "9" but then not decrement the "2" down to "1."

Teachers have found that children have less trouble understanding subtraction when they use various manipulatives such as *base-10 blocks* (Chan et al., 2017). With base-10 blocks, there are equal-sided squares called "units" than can be snapped together making a rod. A unit is meant to represent the numbers in the units column of a multidigit number. When you snap 10 of the units together, they are the same length as a block called a "long," which is meant to represent the number in the 10s column. Ten of the longs connected along their sides make "flats" which are meant to represent the hundreds column. Once children learn to use the blocks to represent a number (e.g., 1 flat, 2 longs, and 3 units for the number 123), they can see why they need to exchange a long for 10 units during a regrouping problem. For example, if asked to take away 14 from 123, they will see they only have 3 units and could only take away those 3 and one of the longs (= 13 total). Being still short by one, they will need to exchange the other long for 10 units. When one of the additional units is taken away from the 10 exchanged units to make the 14, what remains are the flat (100) and 9 units (or 109).

Multiplication and Division

In the United States, children normally begin to learn multiplication and division in the third and fourth grades (CCSSI, 2020). To make the bridge to multiplication from the arithmetic that they already know (i.e., addition and subtraction), children are normally told to think of multiplication as repeated addition (Siegler, 1988; Schulz, 2018). For example, three groups of three objects could represent 3×3 and children could say, "3, 6, 9" as they count the three groups. As was the case for addition and subtraction, however, the goal is to have the answers to recurring multiplication problems stored as facts that can be directly retrieved from long-term memory when presented with a problem (De Visscher, Nöel, & De Smedt, 2016). Along the way, children are found to use repeated addition but also other strategies, such as *decomposition of operands* (Polspoel, Peters, Vandermosten, & De Smedt, 2017; Schulz, 2018; Zhanga, Ding, Lee, & Chen, 2017). An example of decomposition of operands would be solving the problem $3 \times 13 = ?$ by decomposing the problem into two parts (e.g., 3×10 and 3×3) and then adding the results ($30 + 9 = 39$).

With any such arithmetic facts, the general assumption is that children and adults store them in an associative net in long-term memory (see Chapter 4, on memory). Each answer to a problem is stored at a particular level of *associative strength,* often quantified in the form of probability of recall (Siegler, 1988; Van der Ven, Boom, Kroesbergen, & Leseman, 2012;

see Chapter 4). According to overlapping-waves theory, children attempt to recall the answer to a problem via direct recall and assess their degree of confidence in the answer that is retrieved. If confidence is high enough, they state that answer. If it is not high enough, they may continue to search their memories several more times. If to no avail, they then use repeated addition, decomposition of operands, or other strategies.

How do you increase the associative strength of multiplication facts? Practice, practice, practice. One unfortunate consequence of the reform movement in mathematics education is that promoting conceptual understanding of math was given a much higher emphasis than developing automaticity and direct retrieval through practice (Anderson, Reder, & Simon, 1996).

It is interesting that children and adults have an easier time recalling doubles (6 × 6), multiples of 5 (9 × 5), the "1" rule (*Any number times 1 is itself*), and the "0" rule (*Any number times zero is zero*) than they have with other numerical combinations between 0 and 9 (Siegler, 1988). Two other factors that cause difficulty for children and lead them to use alternative strategies besides direct retrieval and make mistakes are problem size (i.e., problems that have larger answers [e.g., 625] are harder than problems with smaller answers [e.g., 9]) and presenting problems in physical text such as 12 × 13 = ? as opposed to questions such as "What is 12 times 13?" (De Visscher et al., 2016).

What makes physical text a problem is the fact that the numbers in these problems are associated with many different problems in memory. For example, the number "3" appears in 3 + 4 = ? and 3 × 4 = ? and many other problems. If we treat the physical numerals on a sheet of paper as *memory cues* (see Chapter 4), the fact that these numbers are associated with many different problems means that children and adults will often experience the problem of *interference* when a problem is presented (De Visscher et al., 2016; Heidekum, Grabner, De Smedt, De Visscher, & Vogel, 2019; Siegler, 1988). If so, then it would be expected that many children would produce the answer "7" to the problem 3 × 4 = ? because that problem only differs from 3 + 4 = ? by one symbol (i.e., "+" instead of "×"). One overcomes interference for any piece of information (e.g., an old phone number interfering with a new phone number) by repetition and practice. It is interesting that there is an overlap in the brain regions that are active not only when we try to recall math facts and other kinds of semantic facts (e.g., the word *dog* is the correct label for a picture of a dog), but also when we try to inhibit interfering information (Heidekum et al., 2019). A related finding is that children diagnosed with *math disability* have a particularly hard time with math fact retrieval and interference (De Visscher & Noël, 2014).

Besides interference, other problems ensue when children move from learning their "times tables" for combinations of numbers from 0 to 12 to larger multidigit numbers and must use an algorithm that subdivides the task into multiple steps. For example, in the problem depicted below, children are taught to first multiply the multiplicand (i.e., 437) by the number in the ones column of the multiplier (the "3" of 23) and place the result below the line in a way that lines up the numbers by place value.

$$
\begin{array}{r}
\overset{1}{2} \\
437 \\
\times\ 23 \\
\hline
1311
\end{array}
\quad\Longrightarrow\quad
\begin{array}{r}
1 \\
1\cancel{2} \\
437 \\
\times\ 23 \\
\hline
1311 \\
874
\end{array}
$$

But, in this algorithm, one also "carries" the "2" of 21 ("three times seven is 21, put down the 1 and carry the 2") and places it above the "3" in 437. Then the 3 in 437 is multiplied by the "3" in 23 (making 9), but you have to remember to add the 2 above the 3 in 437 to that product of 9. In other words, lots to remember and lots of steps in which a mistake could be made. It is common for children to not line up the products below the line and to forget to add the carried numbers to the products in intermediate steps.

In an important sense, the errors that children make with such problems reflect the fact that they do not understand what many of the steps mean (Schulz, 2018). For example, why put down the "1" and carry the "2" in the problem above and not the other way around? Why do the numbers below the line have to be lined up? Over the past 30 years, there has been an increasing emphasis to promote children's conceptual understanding of procedures such as multiplication (Schulz, 2018). The idea is to have them develop *operational sense,* which consists of understanding what operations do. Once children develop facility with addition and subtraction, they may begin to notice patterns, such as the relation between 1 + 5 and 2 + 4. If you increase one of the numbers and decrease the other by the same amount, the same answer is obtained. But it also helps to understand place value. Children cannot understand the decomposition strategy in multiplication, for example, if they do not understand place value, or develop the *part–part–whole schema* for numbers (Cheng, 2012). If you know that 23 can be decomposed into 20 and 3, or 437 can be decomposed into 400, 30, and 7, you can then understand why you can break up the steps of the problem 437 × 23 into pieces and add the results back up. A recent study showed that children of teachers who tried to promote their conceptual understanding of operations were less reliant on the formal algorithm shown above and were able to generate two additional ways to complete the same multiplication problem (Schulz, 2018). Children who were introduced to the formal ("meaningless") algorithm too early or too exclusively performed worse and were less able to generate additional ways to solve the same problem. That said, the percentages of children who used different strategies were 46% (decomposition), 43% (the formal algorithm illustrated above), and 4% (repeated addition).

Because children are (1) reliant on their multiplicative expertise to appreciate division as its inverse and also to perform long division, (2) asked to develop fluency in single-digit division problems ("What is 24 ÷ 6?") before they are asked to solve multidigit long-division problems in a vertical format, and (3) not always taught in a manner that promotes their conceptual understanding of division, we would expect some of the same kinds of problems when children learn long division that were already identified above for addition, subtraction, and multiplication. Research supports this expectation (Schulz & Leuders, 2018). But children also find division to be more challenging and difficult than the other three arithmetic operations, even children in higher grades (Fagginger et al., 2016; Schulz, 2018).

In the Schulz (2018) study mentioned above in which children could come up with several alternative ways to solve the same multiplication problem, they could only come up with one way to solve division problems. Even in countries such as the Netherlands in which the curriculum has been revised to progressively move children from (1) using informal strategies to solve division problems by using their existing addition, subtraction, or multiplication knowledge to (2) using the formal long-division algorithm, children only correctly solved division word problems in year 1 (age 10) 42% and 68% (age 11) of the time (van Putten, van den Brom-Snijders, & Beishuizen, 2005). Many children begin solving division problems using a lower-level and inefficient strategy of repeatedly subtracting the divisor from the dividend (e.g., for 432 ÷ 15, they write 432 − 15 = 417; 417 − 15 = 402) but progressively shift toward a higher-level, more efficient scheme such as multiplying the divisor by 20 and subtracting that amount (e.g., 15 × 20 = 300; 432 − 300 = 132) and then multiplying the divisor by 8 and subtracting (e.g., 15 × 8 = 120; 132 − 120 = 12). In year 1, 22% of the children used the higher-level scheme but by the next year the percentage rose to 54%. Note that both the teachers and their textbooks promoted the use of these strategies as opposed to promoting the formal algorithm, which only 3% of students used in year 2 after two years of instruction in division. The figure for the higher-level informal scheme would probably be much lower in the United States and the figure for the formal algorithm would probably be much higher because different approaches to instruction in the two countries.

Rational Numbers

The category of *rational numbers* includes any real numbers that can exist in the relationship of *a/b* where *b* is not zero (Obersteiner, Reiss,

Van Dooren, & Van Hoof, 2019). So, the category includes *percentages, ratios, fractions,* and *decimals.* Because of the foundational role of rational numbers in learning algebra (Booth & Newton, 2012; DeWolf, Bassok, & Holyoak, 2015) and the considerable difficulty that children experience when they try to learn rational numbers (Obersteiner et al., 2013; Siegler & Pyke, 2013), there has been a literal explosion of studies on children's conceptual and procedural knowledge of rational numbers over the past 10 years, though most of these studies have focused on fractions. This interest is well founded given that a national survey of high school algebra I teachers found that fractions were one of the two largest weaknesses in students' preparation for their course (Siegler & Pyke, 2013) and a national survey of workers from diverse jobs found that 68% of employees reported using rational numbers at their place of employment (Tian & Siegler, 2017). Unfortunately, something is not right with standard instruction given that studies have shown that (1) even high school students report that there are no numbers between $5/7$ and $6/7$, (2) students could not translate .029 to $29/1000$, and (3) only 29% in a national sample could solve the problem "Estimate the sum of $12/13 + 7/8$" when given the options 1, 2, 19, and 21 (Resnick et al., 2016; Tian & Siegler, 2017). Some 55% of 13-year-olds, 36% of 17-year-olds, and 17% of college students estimated the sum to be either 19 or 21 (Resnick et al., 2016). What is worse, studies of teachers have also shown serious weaknesses in their own understanding of rational numbers (Lee, Brown, & Orrill, 2011). Many teachers can correctly perform computations with rational numbers (e.g., invert and multiply with division of fractions) but are unable to explain why these computations must be performed that way and have difficulty linking operations to graphical figures.

What are the sources of students' (and teachers') difficulty with rational numbers? The first source is primarily conceptual. Students have to embed their current conceptual understanding of natural numbers (whole positive integers) within the larger category of rational numbers. This assimilation (to use the Piagetian term) is not easy because of the differences between the properties of natural numbers and rational numbers and the operations that can be applied to them. Whereas you can count whole objects using natural numbers (e.g., "there are one, two, three apples"), it is more difficult to count rational numbers that often refer to parts of objects (Mix, Levene, & Huttenlocher, 1999). With natural numbers, there are no numbers in between each one and each one has a successor (Siegler & Lortie-Forgues, 2015); there are an infinite number of fractions between two successive numbers. In addition, when you add two fractions, the answer is larger than the two addends, as is the case with natural numbers, but when you multiply fractions the answer is often smaller than the multiplicands, and so on.

What is crucial for students' later success in school is that they are able to correctly organize rational numbers into a mental "number line" (Byrnes

& Wasik, 1991), just as their earlier success in school depended on their ability to arrange natural numbers by increasing magnitude (DeWolf et al., 2015; Tian & Siegler, 2017). Success at ordering fractions and decimals by increasing magnitude completely mediates the relationship between prior achievement in the early grades (using natural numbers) and later achievement in high school math. What keeps children from making the change from natural numbers to rational numbers is that many studies of conceptual change in various subjects (math, science, etc.) show that it is hard to promote this change (Obersteiner et al., 2013), especially when children are confident that their misapplications of whole number ideas to rational numbers are correct (Durkin & Rittle-Johnson, 2015). In addition, children also have to develop a conceptual understanding of addition, subtraction, multiplication, and division of rational numbers as to why these operations have the effects that they do (Siegler & Lortie-Forgues, 2015). One aspect of this understanding is comprehending the *direction of effects* of the operations: do the answers get bigger or smaller when the operations apply? Operations with rational numbers sometimes work in the opposite direction to when the operations are used with natural numbers.

But even when students have reasonably high levels of conceptual understanding, they still make mistakes procedurally (Braithwaite, Tian, & Siegler, 2017; Byrnes & Wasik, 1991), and as noted above, adults (e.g., teachers) can be quite skilled procedurally with fractions but not fully understand them conceptually (Lee et al., 2011). The kinds of procedural errors that children make can be traced to their misapplication of whole number strategies (e.g., adding the numbers and denominators of fractions such as ½ + ¼ = ²⁄₆) but also misapplying the procedure for dividing fractions to adding or multiplying them (Braithwaite, Pyke, & Siegler, 2017; Byrnes & Wasik, 1991). One explanation for the latter error is that textbooks in both the United States and China seem to use common denominators in exercises for addition and subtraction, but not common denominators for multiplication and division (Braithwaite & Siegler, 2018).

Positive and Negative Integers

In the United States, it is common for positive and negative integers to be introduced in the fifth, sixth, and seventh grades (CCSSI, 2020). The category of integer is an important but challenging topic in the transition from arithmetic to algebra (Whitacre et al., 2017). Given the story so far in this chapter, it might be predicted that just as children have considerable difficulty moving from understanding whole (natural) numbers to understanding rational numbers such as fractions, they will likewise have difficulty grasping the meaning of negative integers and the new ways that arithmetic operations apply to them (Byrnes, 1992). This is indeed the case.

Conceptually, it is not difficult for children to understand how positive integers can be concretely represented by a set of objects (e.g., "3" can correspond to three toys). But what does it mean for a negative integer such as −3 to correspond to a quantity? How can any quantity be less than zero? (Varma & Schwartz, 2011; Whitacre et al., 2017; Young & Booth, 2015). Historically, it is not entirely clear when negative integers appeared in various cultures. Some assume the construct was useful in trade ledgers to represent debts owed, while others argue that mathematicians in the 17th, 18th, and 19th centuries invented them as part of the Cartesian coordinate system, number lines, and as solutions to algebraic formulas such as $(x + 2) = 0$ (Ifrah, 1998). Contemporaries of these mathematicians often argued that negative numbers do not exist, and many middle schoolers in today's schools wish they would just disappear!

Some of the stumbling blocks for children include understanding that (1) the expression "9 − 2 =" means the same thing as "9 + −2 =," (2) the expressions "12 × 3 =" and "−12 × −3 =" yield the same answer, as do the expressions 5 + 3 = and 5 − −3 = , and (3) the answer to −12/−4 is 3 but the answer to −12/4 is −3. In one of the earliest studies of children's understanding of integers in developmental psychology, Byrnes (1992) found that seventh graders' conceptual understanding of negative integers that they had prior to learning how to apply the four arithmetic operations to these negative integers strongly predicted who learned the procedures better. The conceptual knowledge task asked them to correctly place positive and negative integers on a number line, correctly place them on an analogous staircase where the middle level or ground floor was zero, say which of two integers was a larger amount (e.g., −7 vs. 3), and say who won a quiz show game based on the points they won or lost in the game. In addition, however, on procedural knowledge items that were administered after teachers completed the unit and required children to correctly add, subtract, multiply, and divide integers, children made many procedural errors, such as ignoring negative signs, miscategorizing integers as whole numbers, and incorrectly employing whole-number operations for integers.

In a more recent study, Brez, Miller, and Ramirez (2016) found that just as there is a linear to logarithmic shift in children's placement of positive whole numbers on number line estimation tasks, there is a comparable shift for negative and positive integers as well. This finding contrasts with the findings presented above for rational numbers and suggests that children may have a somewhat easier time understanding quantities as expressed as integers as opposed to rational numbers. Brez et al. did not link children's conceptual knowledge to their procedural competence, however. The findings of Brez et al. (2016) confirm those of Fischer (2003), who found that instruction seems to promote the development of a mental number line that adds zero and negative integers to the existing number line for natural numbers. Gullick and Wolford (2013) found that the same brain areas that are active when children and adults compare positive integers are active when fifth graders and seventh graders compared positive and negative integers. However, Blair, Rosenberg-Lee, Tsang, Schwartz, and Menon (2012) found that the brain areas active for negative integers were much less defined or differentiated than those for positive integers, and frontal lobe areas associated with greater mental effort were more active for negative than positive integers. Older children in Gullick and Wolford (2013) were also more likely to demonstrate the distance effect for negative integers as well (faster responses when numbers were farther apart). But Varma and Schwartz (2011) showed that younger children tended to solve comparison problems by using their established mental number line for positive integer comparisons but supplemented this mental number line with rules for solving other problems (e.g., any negative number is less than any positive number). Older participants, however, responded in a manner that suggested they had restructured their mental representation of positive and negative integers to reflect new understandings (e.g., every integer has an opposite that cancels it out). These findings are consistent with those of Young and Booth (2015), who found that children's ability to construct number lines with negative integers seemed to follow a similar developmental progression as has been found for positive integers, but the estimation of negatives lags behind positives. The findings of Blair et al. (2012) combined with those of Varma and Schwartz (2011) and Young and Booth (2015) suggest that (1) the symmetrical number line around zero that combines negative integers and positive integers together takes time to develop, and (2) repeated experience working on problems that involve integers promotes the progressive development of this symmetrical number line and more differentiated brain regions to support it.

Inversion and Equivalence

The concept of *inversion* relates to the pervasive idea in mathematics that many operations and functions have inverses, that is, the opposite transformation that "undoes" or reverses the initial operation or function. For example, the inverse of addition is subtraction (e.g., $2 + 3 = 5$; $5 - 3 = 2$), the inverse of multiplication is division (e.g., $5 \times 3 = 15$; $15 \div 3 = 5$), the inverse of squaring a number is taking the square root, and the function $g(x) = x/3 + 2/3$ is the inverse of the function $f(x) = 3x - 2$ (Ding & Auxter, 2017; Nunes & Bryant, 2015). The concept of *equivalence,* in contrast, relates to the idea that the quantities or mathematical objects on either side of the equals sign (" = ") correspond to the same amount and are interchangeable (McNeil, Homburg, Devlin, Carrazza, & McKeever, 2019).

   Why group the constructs of inversion and equivalence together in the same section? It turns out that both these forms of conceptual understanding are examples of the idea of *structural relationships among related ideas* in mathematics (Gilmore & Bryant, 2008; Nunes & Bryant, 2015). Or more briefly, they are both examples of relational understandings. What is more, you cannot say that you truly understand one operation (e.g., addition) without understanding how it is the inverse of another (e.g., subtraction and vice versa) (Gilmore & Bryant, 2008). Similarly, you cannot say you truly understand what is on one side of the equals sign without recognizing how it is equivalent to what is on the other side—for example, $(x - 4)^2 = (x^2 - 8x + 16)$. So far in this summary of the development of arithmetic between kindergarten and middle school, we have only considered how children master topics or operations in isolation and in sequence. Now we can consider whether and how they construct conceptual, relational understandings across related topics.

With respect to inversion for arithmetic operations (i.e., addition, subtraction, multiplication, and division), studies show that children slowly integrate or interconnect operations and their inverses between first grade and eighth grade (Ding & Auxter, 2017; Gilmore & Bryant, 2008; Nunes & Bryant, 2015). For example, younger children are less likely than older children to see that an expression such as $15 + 11 - 11$, simply reduces down to 15, and less likely to see how subtraction can be used to solve what seems to be an addition problem (Nunes & Bryant, 2015). For example, given the word problem "Sarah had some apples and her friend gave her 3 more. Now she has 7. How many did she have before her friend gave her more?," the solution requires children to use subtraction. Children are even less likely to show an integration of multiplication and division with age, presumably because they have particular difficulty with division (Nunes & Bryant, 2015). The lack of such integrations across inversely related operations means that children will be hampered in their problem-solving ability and also will lack the conceptual foundation they will need when they later try to comprehend higher forms of math such as algebra.

As for equivalence, children also show considerable difficulty in acquiring the correct interpretation of the equals sign even when in middle school, and they demonstrate progressive mastery over time (Alibali, Knuth, Hattikudur, McNeil, & Stephens, 2007; McNeil et al., 2019). For example, given a problem such as $3 + 4 + 5 = 3 + \_\_\_\_$, some 80% of children between the ages of 7 and 11 gave the incorrect answer. Children seem to assume (and prompted interviews with them has confirmed) that the equal sign can be translated as "the answer," or what you get when you do the operation on the left of the equal sign. As such, a common error is to add all the numbers up (e.g., $3 + 4 + 5 + 3 = 15$) (Alibali et al., 2007; McNeil et al., 2019). As was noted above for inversion, the problem with children failing to acquire the proper relational understanding of equivalence in elementary and middle school is that they are less likely to show higher achievement in algebra (McNeil et al., 2019).

Word Problems

Finally, all the aforementioned findings for whole numbers, rational numbers, integers, and arithmetic operations on them become a little more complicated when we compare children's performance on problems expressed as computational problems (e.g., $7.32 \div 1.6 = ?$) to when these same operations and numbers are embedded in story problems. It can certainly help performance sometimes when the storyline is familiar to children or is easy for them to envision what is going on in the problems (Nathan, 2012), but it is also the case that being able to envision the problem does not immediately translate into a solution for solving the problem (Nunes & Bryant, 2015). It is the case, however, that children's reading comprehension ability is a strong predictor of their math achievement (Fuchs, Gilbert, Fuchs, Seethaler, & Martin, 2018). And Chinese textbooks spend a considerable amount of time presenting problems in the form of drawings of familiar concrete situations (Ding, 2016). But it is possible for some students to be quite proficient in solving computational problems but lack the ability to solve comparable word problems that contain the same operation. In addition, studies suggest that it is important for children to repeatedly solve problems with similar structures to them in order for them to develop schemata for types of problems (see Chapter 3, on schema theory). When you develop a schema, you do not have to "reinvent the wheel" each time you confront a problem with a similar or analogous problem situation that requires the same solution.

Summary and Common Themes

Each of the previous sections on addition and subtraction of whole numbers, multiplication and division of whole numbers, rational numbers, integers, and inversion and equivalence reveal some common themes.

* The first theme is that children need to develop both (1) conceptual understanding of natural numbers, rational numbers, and integers and (2) procedural knowledge of how to correctly perform arithmetic operations on them. That said, even when children had developed both forms of knowledge, they still made computational errors. These two forms of knowledge seem to be distinct in the mind, as one recent factor analytic study of fractions knowledge showed (Lenz, Dreher, Holzäpfel, & Wittmann, 2020). But conceptual understanding is important in itself for motivational reasons (e.g., not feeling "lost"; having a rationale for new rules for addition, subtraction, multiplication, and division of rational numbers and integers) and for problem solving with new problems.

* The second theme is that children need sufficient practice with solving procedural problems in order for solutions to computational problems

to be directly retrieved from memory; they also need sufficient practice to develop schemata for word problems that require the same computations. This practice helps them overcome the aforementioned computational errors.

- The third theme is that performance tends to fall off with age level when children need to associate numerical symbols with their appropriate referents (1, ½, 7.25, –7, etc.) and arrange new classes of numbers into a number line that incorporates these new numbers in a coherent way. Rational numbers and integers have different properties than whole numbers, and all three categories need to be integrated and interrelated to each other.

- The fourth theme is that children need to construct new relational understandings such that arithmetic operations are integrated with their inverses and the notion of equivalence is accurately understood. The third and fourth theme show that mathematics is properly understood as a system of interrelated numerical systems and operations. It is problematic when all the parts of this system are learned in isolation and remain distinct.

- The fifth theme is constructivist in flavor (see Piaget's and Vygotky's theories in Chapter 3); as children learn new topics, they try to understand and assimilate this new information using their existing knowledge. In the case of learning rational numbers and integers, what children know about whole numbers initially interferes with what they learn about rational numbers and integers. They eventually have to accommodate their knowledge to overcome this natural number overassimilation (i.e., reorganize and make their knowledge more abstract).

- The sixth theme is that there are individual differences in mathematical competence at each grade level. Some children master the material easily and avoid making the common computational mistakes. Others struggle. Understanding the differences between these two groups is an important goal of education to make sure all children learn the math skills they need to be successful in today's world. The age trends so far largely explain the findings reported at the beginning of this chapter for NAEP and PISA in which U.S. students do not perform as well as they need to.

High School and Beyond

Far fewer studies have been conducted on the math skills of high school and college students than on preschoolers and elementary students. When researchers do focus on high school and college students, most of the studies have centered on students' understanding and performance in algebra. This focus is sensible given that algebra represents the first mathematical topic area that requires a symbolic, abstract understanding beyond arithmetic and also serves as an important foundation for higher level mathematics in high school and college (Koedinger, Alibali, & Nathan, 2008; McNeil et al., 2010; National Mathematics Advisory Panel, 2008; Rittle-Johnson & Star, 2007; Star et al., 2015). Unfortunately, it is also a subject area in which many students fail to acquire sufficient proficiency to be successful in higher levels of math, much less successful in academic majors that require mathematical proficiency or in STEM careers. For instance, the High School Longitudinal Study of 2009 assessed students' performance in algebra in the fall semester of 2009 when they were 9th graders and then again in the spring semester of 2012 when they were finishing 11th grade. Performance was categorized into seven levels based on the sophistication of student performance. Although student performance increased between 2009 and 2012, most students were proficient only at Levels 1 and 2; in particular, 85% of 9th graders and 92% of 11th graders mastered Level 1 content, but only 58% of 9th graders and 92% of 11th graders mastered Level 2 content. Only 28% of students were proficient in Level 4 skills that seem to be the bare minimum needed for higher forms of math or STEM majors (Ingels & Dalton, 2013). Similarly, on the 2011 NAEP for mathematics, only 59% of 8th graders could find an equivalent equation for $N + 18 = 23$, and only 31% could find the equation of a line that passed through a particular line and had a negative slope (NAEP, 2011; Star et al., 2015).

In the following section on instructional implications of all these developmental findings, there will be more to say about student difficulties with algebra. For now, it can be said that the transition from arithmetic in which concrete entities can be used to model mathematical relations to one in which the relations are symbolic and abstract and not easily modeled is difficult for students. In other words, their conceptual understanding is often lacking (Barbieri, Miller-Cotto, & Booth, 2019; Chu, Rittle-Johnson, & Fyfe, 2017). In addition, they often overgeneralize what they know about arithmetic operations to algebraic operations (McNeil, Rittle-Johnson, Hattikudur, & Peterson, 2010). Furthermore, both their understanding of rational numbers (especially fractions) and negative integers are predictive of their algebra performance (Siegler et al., 2012; Young & Booth, 2020). So, in the former case, knowledge of arithmetic procedures interferes with their learning; in the latter, the two foundational conceptual understandings are not available to provide a foundation for their learning.

IMPLICATIONS FOR EDUCATION

The foregoing summary of developmental trends shows that many children in the United States fail to acquire the kinds of math skills needed to be successful in today's world by the time they graduate high school (National Mathematics Advisory Panel, 2008). The age trends show that infants and preschoolers have surprising competencies for approximate quantity comparisons and for comprehending the cardinal and ordinal properties of whole numbers below 20. Children also attain fairly high levels of competence in addition and subtraction of whole numbers by fourth grade, but then an increasing number of children fall by the wayside with age after topics such as place value, multidigit long division, inversion, equivalence, rational numbers, integers, and algebra are introduced between second and ninth grades. According to the National Mathematics Advisory Panel, these results demonstrate that whereas children in the United States seem to acquire a basic number sense for whole numbers (as noted at the end of the "Birth to Kindergarten" section of this chapter), they fail to acquire a more advanced number sense which would include the following:

> a principled understanding of place value, of how whole numbers can be composed and decomposed, and of the meaning of the basic arithmetic operations of addition, subtraction, multiplication, and division. It also requires understanding the commutative, associative, and distributive properties and knowing how to apply these principles to solve problems. This more highly developed form of number sense should extend to numbers written in fraction, decimal, percent, and exponential forms. Far too many middle and high school students lack the ability to accurately compare the magnitudes of such numbers. (p. 27)

These trends have been true of the United States for some time (since the 1960s at least) and in many (but not all) countries around the world, as the findings of NAEP and PISA show. Can anything be done to improve the mathematical competencies of children, especially for topics introduced in fourth grade and beyond?

In the 1980s and 1990s, reform efforts spurred on by the National Council of Teachers of Mathematics (NCTM) were geared toward replacing the then-prevalent practice of rote memorization of math facts and computational drills with a much stronger, if not exclusive, emphasis on problem solving, conceptual knowledge, and mapping math concepts and procedures onto real-world situations (NCTM, 1989). Analyses of NAEP results and other national and international assessments conducted since 1989 reveal that this reform movement did little to improve performance, as the review in this chapter indicates. Whereas the NCTM standards were not based on well-designed studies of teaching methods, student learning, or the principles of cognitive and motivational science, the following three sets of recommendations are. The first set is from the National Mathematics Advisory Panel (2008) report. The second set come from researchers who have tried different approaches to improve performance. And the third set derive from prior chapters in this book. Let's consider these three sets of recommendations in turn.

Recommendations from the National Mathematics Advisory Panel

- *The gaps in preparedness between income groups at the start of first grade have long-lasting effects and should be remediated using empirically supported interventions.* There are over 20 mathematics interventions funded by the Institute of Education Sciences that have produced large increases in low-income children's math skills (Byrnes, 2020; Ramani & Siegler, 2008). Interventions implemented after first grade have not been effective in eliminating these gaps.

- *The K–8 prealgebra curriculum should focus on more in-depth treatment of fewer more central or important topics.* Comparison of the typical math content covered by teachers in K–8 classrooms in the United States and those of the top performing nations in the world (i.e., Singapore, Japan, Korea, Hong Kong, Flemish Belgium, and Czech Republic) show that the top-performing countries focus on fewer topics in a more in-depth fashion. In the United States, there is a common tendency to use a "spiral" curriculum where the math topics of the prior year are reintroduced at the beginning of the next year (presumably as a refresher). The National Mathematics Advisory Panel suggested dropping this practice and conducting more of a deep dive on whole number, rational number, and integer concepts; problem solving; and developing fluency in performing the four arithmetic operations on the three categories of numbers. And rather than debating which of conceptual knowledge, procedural fluency, or problem solving should be emphasized, they argued that all should be given considerable attention because they are mutually reinforcing. That is, as students repeatedly try to solve problems using procedures, they build up their conceptual knowledge, procedural knowledge, and problem-solving skills simultaneously.

The more in-depth coverage allows for promoting all three kinds of skills and also more attention to other aspects, such as the ability to compose and decompose numbers, and understand place value, equivalence, inversion, and the commutative, distributive, and associate properties of operations. Consider, for example, how comprehension of multiplication of fractions, the distributive property, and equivalence would be needed to solve the algebra problem below (and if you lacked these understandings you would have difficult solving the problem):

1. $3(x + 4) + 3 = 21$
2. $3x + 12 + 3 = 21$ (distributive property)
3. $3x + 15 = 21$
4. $3x + 15 - 15 = 21 - 15$ (equivalence)
5. $3x = 6$
6. $\frac{1}{3} \times 3x = 6 \times \frac{1}{3}$ (equivalence, multiplication of fractions)
7. $x = 2$

And the reduction in the number of topics and more in-depth coverage of the more important topics allows teachers to spend much more time than they currently do on rational numbers and integers. The expert panel argued that fractions, in particular, are not given the amount of coverage and time as they should be given, given their foundational or gatekeeping role for algebra. They also analyzed the textbooks used in the United States and the top six nations and noticed that those in the top six were considerably smaller with fewer pages and fewer topics covered. Topics and exercises should match these recommendations.

- *Children need to develop fluency and automaticity in their execution of mathematical procedures; computers can be a useful in this regard.* As noted in both Chapter 3 (on general theories) and 4 (on memory), there is no getting around practice to attain fluency in arithmetic procedures applied to whole numbers, rational numbers, and integers. Research shows that computer programs that promote practice can be a useful classroom support. As an aside, I wrote a simple program that presented my children with graphics that looked like flash cards with arithmetic problems on them, recorded their answers, and indicated whether they were right or wrong. In the span of 15 minutes, my children were able to practice over 700 problems. I authored this program because my children's school wholeheartedly adopted the NCTM standards and deemphasized practice. One other recommendation of the National Mathematics Advisory Panel, however, was to restrict the use of calculators when children practice solving problems. Calculators do not promote mastery of procedures and facts.

- *Embedding problem solving in real-world situations promotes conceptual understanding and problem solving; certain kinds of graphics can be beneficial as well.* At least with whole numbers, rational numbers, and integers, it is possible to link numbers to real-world referents. For example, "3" could be linked to three children, "¾" could be linked to three equal pieces of a pizza cut into quarters, and –7 could be linked to how much you owe a friend who lent you money. But base-10 blocks and other kinds of manipulatives can be used to promote further understanding of whole and rational numbers, as can number lines. As noted above, base-10 blocks can help children understand place value (e.g., 326 can be represented by 3 flats, 2 longs, and 6 units). Other kinds of plastic, rectangular manipulatives can correspond to ⅛, ¼, ⅓, and ½ (e.g., where two ¼s placed side to side are the same width as a ½ piece) and both base-10 blocks and fractions strips can be used to show why faulty calculations are wrong. For example, a child who thinks the solution to ½ + ½ = ? is ²⁄₄ will see this is wrong when two ¼ strips are placed above two ½ strips.

One kind of graphic used in countries such as Singapore to promote problem-solving skills is called alternatively "strip diagrams," "tape diagrams," or "bar models" by different researchers (Booth & Koedinger,

2012). Figure 12.1 shows below how one could use a bar model to help foster the correct solution to the word problem above it.

Note that children could also be taught a purely symbolic technique to solve such problems in which the story could be translated to expression $N - (\frac{1}{4})(N) = \$27$ and could be manipulated to solve for N.

Whereas bar models have been found to be an effective technique, there are other kinds of models that either do not help or actually hurt performance if, for example, the problem and the graphic are not located close together, as above, or there are extraneous components of the graphic such as cute animals or a picture of Sasha and a coat (Booth & Koedinger, 2012). Some researchers have also found that the purely symbolic approach is actually more effective for more skilled students and is also more efficient (Koedinger et al., 2008). So not all graphics are equally helpful and eventually students have to make the transition to a more abstract, purely symbolic approach as math becomes increasingly abstract in algebra I, algebra II, trigonometry, and calculus.

- *The expert panel also recognized the need to attend to the socio-emotional and motivational aspects of performance as well.* As noted in Chapter 5 (motivation), children will learn more and persist in spite of difficulties if they develop a sense of self-efficacy for math, consider math interesting and relevant, develop a growth mindset for math, and feel supported by teachers and peers. How do elementary and middle school teachers develop these dispositions? Self-efficacy is promoted by success. Classrooms have to be set up to promote mastery of content, however long that takes. In most U.S. classrooms, math content is divided into 2-week modules. If you do not master the material in about 2 weeks, unfortunately, teachers move on to the next topic. With the reduced number of topics and extra time opened up (the second recommendation above), teachers can utilize more of a mastery approach. Students can pace themselves and accept all the scaffolding and tips they need to succeed on all tasks presented to them.

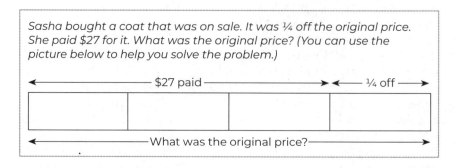

Sasha bought a coat that was on sale. It was ¼ off the original price. She paid $27 for it. What was the original price? (You can use the picture below to help you solve the problem.)

← ——————— $27 paid ——————— → ← —— ¼ off ——→

← ———————What was the original price?——————— →

FIGURE 12.1. A bar model of the algebra problem.

As noted in Chapter 5, increased self-efficacy usually promotes increased interest as well. However, another way to promote interest and a sense that math is relevant and helpful is to embed math in meaningful, problem-solving activities. That was one of the goals of NCTM reforms. There is no need to now revert back to an exclusive emphasis on rote learning and drills, given the failure of NCTM reforms to promote higher achievement. Rather, computers can be utilized to supplement meaningful problem solving. When used as a "treat" or privilege that can be accessed once problem solving is completed, students can engage in more practice on the computer.

As for a growth mindset, entire schools beginning in first grade should promote this understanding of ability. Students should begin to recognize that every time they master a new skill, they get smarter and more able, no matter how long it takes them. Aptitude does not matter as much as expertise when solving problems in the real world (unless there is an occasional need to develop a solution really fast).

As for feeling supported by teachers and peers, teachers can model genuine support, positive affect, and confidence in children as they work on mastery. Praise for good effort and hard work goes a long way. As for support from peers, heterogeneous cooperative learning groups can accomplish that goal as long as groups are working toward common goals and helping each other succeed. One way to promote that effort is to utilize individualized problem-solving sheets (based on what topics have been mastered by each child) in groups as well as average improvement points across groups of four children. Then peers have an incentive to do well themselves but also help their groupmates.

- *The final recommendation was to increase the mathematical competencies of elementary and middle school teachers.* The expert panel aptly noted that it is not possible to teach a topic well that you do not know and understand. Achieving this goal might require recruiting a larger percentage of teachers who have existing math skills (away from STEM majors, for example) or by adding coursework that promotes teachers' own understanding of such things as rational numbers, equivalence, integers, and algebra but also the pedagogical content knowledge for how to present material and create tasks that children can understand and master.

Recommendations from Researchers

- *Procedural competence can be promoted by comparing solution methods.* There are several ways to unpack this general approach into specific recommendations. The first perspective is to say that students generally perform much better when they are shown several *worked examples* before attempting to try to solve similar problems on their own (Barbieri et al., 2019; Booth, Lange, Koedinger, & Newton, 2013). The claim is that worked examples reduce the *cognitive load* of problems. The second perspective is to say that comparing solution methods helps students to identify similarities and differences in solutions and thereby be more apt to generalize or transfer solutions to new problems and develop flexibility in solution methods (Hattikudur & Alibali, 2010; Rittle-Johnson & Star, 2007). For example, Hattikudur and Alibali (2010) showed that children's misconceptions about the equals sign could be reduced by having them compare equality expressions with "=" to inequality expressions with "<" or ">." In addition, comparisons of multiple solutions can also help students to identify the more efficient of a pair of solutions. The third perspective is to say that it can also be helpful when students not only compare two correct solutions, but also compare one correct and one incorrect strategy (Barbieri & Booth, 2016).

- *Conceptual knowledge can be enhanced by having students self-explain solution methods.* The conceptual benefits of the worked-example and incorrect-example effects can sometimes be enhanced by asking students to explain why a solution method is either correct or incorrect (Barbieri et al., 2019; Rittle-Johnson & Loehr, 2017). Note that self-explanations tend to promote conceptual knowledge but not procedural knowledge (Booth et al., 2013). However, there are constraints on when self-explanations are effective. First, self-explanations promote comprehension and transfer in domains that are consistently guided by general principles. This first constraint may mean that self-explanations might work better when students are examining solutions to physics problems (a domain with principles such as the third law of thermodynamics) than when they are studying subtraction solutions. The second constraint is that the solution has to be known to be correct or incorrect as opposed to the learner's own ideas as to what is correct. Self-explaining a student's own incorrect answers may promote continued errors. Third, self-explanations may reduce performance if they promote attention to certain aspects of a problem to the detriment of other important aspects of a problem. And fourth, self-explanations have sometimes been shown to be less effective than some alternatives, such as solving unfamiliar problems and attempting to retrieve their performance.

- *The effectiveness of instructional approaches often depends on the characteristics of the learner.* For example, embedding algebra problems in real-world situations seems to work better for novice learners than for more skilled learners (Koedinger et al., 2008). More skilled learners do better with more formulaic or symbolic solutions. Booth and Koedinger (2012) found that diagrams were more beneficial for older and higher-ability students than for younger and lower-ability students. In years past, these effects were called aptitude × treatment interactions (Corno et al., 2002).

Recommendations Deriving from Prior Chapters

Finally, Chapters 3 (general theories of learning), 4 (memory), and 7 (intelligence, aptitude, and expertise) should be consulted for further insights. For example, Piaget's theory could be used to explain why first graders would have difficulty understanding negative integers and algebraic concepts, but these concepts could be mastered by children in sixth grade or higher (the former require concrete operational thought but the latter require formal operational thought). Piaget would also argue that (1) hands-on active learning is important, and (2) algebraic and integer concepts could be taught using concrete precursors to set the stage. Vygotsky's theory could be useful, using constructs of scaffolding and teaching within each child's zone of proximal development. The chapter on memory would emphasize distributive practice in which practice problems contain a mixture of new and old problems. Such interleaved practice would obviate the need for end-of-year reviews or standardized tests as well as the need for a spiral curriculum that the expert panel recommended dropping.

CHAPTER 13

The Development
of Scientific Reasoning Skills

With very little persuasion, the average person on the street could probably be convinced of the importance of literacy skills and math skills to their own well-being and the economic success of nations. In particular, they would readily appreciate how it would be practically impossible for people in any country to be highly successful in school and the workplace when those people lack basic reading, writing, and mathematics skills.

What about science? Why do people need to learn science, and how might proficiency in scientific thinking help them and their fellow citizens be more successful in their personal, academic, and professional lives? There are several different ways to answer this question. The first is to appeal to evolutionary theory and evidence. As will be discussed later in this chapter, there is compelling evidence that human infants and young children seem to be equipped with basic explanatory frameworks to make predictions and interpret their worlds in terms of biological, physical, and psychological causes (Gopnik & Wellman, 2012). Why would evolutionary processes incrementally promote this early emerging explanatory ability over time if it were not adaptive and useful?

A second way to explain the importance of scientific thinking is to note its close association with *critical thinking*. Critical thinking consists of the ability to evaluate the quality of arguments and evidence that are used to support some claim or position (Byrnes & Dunbar, 2014). A critical thinker might ask questions such as "Should I take an alleged antiviral medication to ward off COVID-19?"; "Is global warming real or a hoax?"; "Is marijuana a 'gateway drug'?"; "Should I take the advice of a friend and move my retirement funds out of the stock market?" All these decisions rely on the accuracy and predictive value of evidence and arguments around this evidence (OECD, 2016). In a related way, it is sometimes argued that there should be no laws to restrict the sale of military-style weapons to people outside of the military because if we allow that to happen, they will next take away all of our guns (a "slippery slope" argument). Does it logically follow that restricting AR-15 rifles will lead to restricting all weapons, including hunting rifles? As we shall see, scientific competence requires the ability to design studies and collect evidence in ways that are credible and accurately reflect what is going on. If so, then people would be more equipped to engage in critical thinking if they developed higher levels of scientific competence. When we can engage in effective critical thinking on our own, we can avoid being given bad advice from doctors, lawyers, financial advisors, and politicians and protect ourselves from being misled (Mercier & Sperber, 2011).

A third way to consider the importance of science pertains to students having access to well-paying jobs in science, technology, engineering, and mathematics (STEM) fields (National Research Council [NRC], 2012). Education is a ticket out of poverty only if it leads to a job that at least pays a living wage. The average starting salary range of college graduates with STEM degrees is $62,000 to $69,000. For graduates earning non-STEM degrees, the average starting salary range is $52,000 to $57,000 (National Association of Colleges and Employers, 2019). STEM majors not only affect their own financial success, they also affect the economic well-being of nations inasmuch as the primary driver of economic prosperity over the last 120 years has been technological advances (NRC, 2012).

In spite of the importance of scientific competence, the story recounted in previous chapters is repeated once again here in the case of science. On the latest NAEP for science (NCES, 2015), 40% of U.S. 12th graders scored at the "below basic" level, 38% performed at the "basic" level, 20% performed at the "proficient" level, and 2% performed at the "advanced" level. If we reasonably assume that the kinds of skills associated with the proficient level are those needed to be successful in the contemporary world (see below), it is a sad state of affairs to say that most students in the United States (78%) fail to acquire the scientific-reasoning skills they need. In addition, student performance in 2015 has not changed from that in 2009, so the United States has made little progress in promoting a higher level of scientific competence. On the 2018 Programme for International Student Assessment (PISA) that assessed the scientific skills of 15-year-olds around the world (OECD, 2020), the United States scored 13 points above the average for 41 nations designated in 2015 as members of the OECD, but 10th overall among these OECD countries (behind Australia, United Kingdom, New Zealand, Finland, Poland, Canada, Korea, Estonia, and Japan). Compared to students from both OECD and non-OECD nations that took the test, the United States performed 25th overall. In addition, after placing students into seven levels based on their performance, 66% of U.S. students performed above the absolute lowest levels of 1a and 1b, but the majority of those scoring above 1b (65%) only scored in the mediocre levels of levels 2 and 3. Only 23% scored higher than level 3.

The rest of this chapter is organized using the format of prior chapters. In particular, we shall first delve further into the nature of scientific competence. Then, we chart the development of scientific-reasoning skills from early childhood to late adolescence. Finally, we consider the implications of theories and research on scientific thinking for instruction.

THE NATURE OF SCIENTIFIC REASONING COMPETENCE

We can draw on three sources for insight into what it means for someone to be scientifically literate. The first is the 2012 report of an expert panel commissioned by the NRC who were asked to define scientific competence, review the literature, and make recommendations for revisions in science curriculum and instruction to improve the performance of students in the United States (NRC, 2012). The second source is the framework for science developed by an expert panel commissioned by the NCES prior to conducting the 2015 NAEP for science (NCES, 2015). The third source is the science framework developed for the 2018 PISA that had a primary focus on science (OECD, 2020).

The NRC (2012) Report

The 18 members of the Committee on a Conceptual Framework for New K–12 Science Education Standards consisted of (1) eight scientists from the fields of biology, physics, chemistry, and engineering; (2) three scholars with expertise in the cognitive science of learning; (3) five education faculty with expertise in science education, math education, or educational policy; (4) a university chancellor; and (5) a school superintendent. Thus, the committee members had insight into the nature of science, how people learn, science curricula, and how to teach science. This group recognized that students graduate high school and college with a limited understanding of the nature of science because they are mostly presented with a myriad of scientific facts and definitions across 12–16 years of schooling. This continual presentation of a string of facts and definitions has led many students to develop misconceptions of what science is and what scientists do.

To alter these misconceptions, the committee recommended reforming the curriculum around three dimensions: scientific and engineering practices, cross-cutting concepts, and disciplinary core ideas. The *scientific and engineering practices* included (1) asking questions (for science) and defining problems (for engineering), (2) developing and using models, (3) planning and carrying out investigations, (4) analyzing and interpreting data, (5) using mathematics and computational thinking, (6) constructing explanations (for science) and designing solutions (for engineering), (7) engaging in argument from evidence, and (8) obtaining, evaluating, and communicating information.

One goal of the educational reforms that the committee proposed was to have students understand how practicing scientists actually carry out these eight behaviors. Another goal was to have students themselves learn how to carry out these behaviors in the design, execution, and communication of their own scientific projects (NRC, 2012). In the middle section of this chapter on the development of skills, we shall consider whether there is evidence that students can conduct the eight scientific practices (i.e., asking questions, using models, and so forth). We will consider the other two dimensions of the NRC framework (i.e., cross-cutting concepts and disciplinary core ideas) in the third section of this chapter, on instructional implications.

The NAEP for Science Framework

Similar to the experts on the NRC panel, the experts who developed the tests and questions for the 2015 NAEP for science likewise had expertise in the natural sciences, psychometrics, and science education. After constructing the NAEP assessment, administering it, and scoring responses, students were placed into the four levels of below basic, basic, proficient, and advanced. According to these experts, the goal of our science curriculum is to have all students attain the proficient level by 12th grade, but as noted earlier, only 38% of U.S. students do. According to the framework,

> Students performing at the Proficient level should be able to demonstrate relationships and compare alternative models, predictions, and explanations. They should be able to explain trends among elements in the periodic table; conservation laws; chemical mechanisms for metabolism, growth, and reproduction; changes in populations due to natural selection; the evolution of the Universe; and evidence for boundaries and movements of tectonic plates. They should be able to design and critique observational and experimental studies, controlling multiple variables, using scientific models to explain results, and choosing among alternative conclusions based on arguments from evidence. They should be able to compare scientific costs or risks and benefits of alternative solutions to problems at local or regional scales. (NCES, 2020b)

The PISA (2018) Science Framework

The expert panel that designed the 2018 PISA assessment that predominantly focused on science defined *science literacy* as the ability to engage with science related issues, and with the ideas of science, as a reflective citizen. A scientifically literate person is willing to engage in reasoned discourse about science and technology. This requires the competencies to explain phenomena scientifically, to evaluate and design scientific enquiry, and to interpret data and evidence scientifically.

Performance in science requires three forms of knowledge: content knowledge, knowledge of the standard methodological procedures used in science, and knowledge of the reasons and ideas used by scientists to justify their claims. Explaining scientific and technological phenomena, for instance, demands knowledge of the content of science. Evaluating scientific enquiry and interpreting evidence scientifically also require an understanding of how scientific knowledge is established and the degree of confidence with which it is held.

The definition of science literacy recognizes that there is an affective element to a student's competency: students' attitudes or dispositions towards science can influence their level of interest, sustain their engagement, and motivate them to take action. (OECD, 2020, p. 50)

A close reading of these three sources that define scientific competence shows that these definitions overlap to a large extent. They all include *scientific content knowledge* (principles, theories, constructs, facts, and models), *scientific procedural knowledge* (the eight scientific processes), *epistemological knowledge* (understanding of the nature and origin of knowledge in science; understand why certain procedures, such as experiments, are central to establishing knowledge in science), *argument and communication skills,* and *positive attitudes* toward science. But the three expert panels and developmental scientists also recognize the important and indispensable interrelations among these five component aspects (Lehrer & Schauble, 2015). For example, it is not possible to conduct well-designed studies or form effective arguments in the absence of appropriate levels of knowledge. In addition, however, philosophers of science, science educators, and educational psychologists also emphasize the importance of epistemological knowledge in the development and evaluation of theories and scientific findings. In the next section, we can consider age trends in these different components of scientific competence, keeping in mind the need for integration among them.

THE DEVELOPMENT OF FIVE ASPECTS OF SCIENTIFIC COMPETENCE

In what follows, we consider what is currently known about five aspects of scientific competence in turn: scientific content knowledge, scientific procedural knowledge, epistemology, argument, and motivation.

Scientific Content Knowledge

It is not easy to answer the question "Does scientific content knowledge increase with age?" in a straightforward matter. Scientific knowledge can exist in the mind in very different formats and at different levels of cohesion and abstraction. As would be expected from the description of expertise in Chapter 7, the scientific content knowledge of practicing scientists would not only be extensive, but their knowledge of *theoretical constructs* (e.g., *adaptation, fitness*) would be embedded in larger *theories* (e.g., *evolution*) and these constructs would be connected to each other in meaningful, cohesive ways. In addition, items of information such as individual facts (e.g., *there are eight species and four genera of great apes*), theoretical constructs, *theoretical explanations* (e.g., *natural selection*), and *theoretical principles* (e.g., *Newton's first law of motion*) would all be mentally represented at different levels of abstraction. This analysis suggests that age comparisons would not only tend to reveal differences in the *amount* of scientific content knowledge that students possess at different ages, but also potentially differences in the *level of cohesion* among ideas, the extent to which both *concrete* and *abstract* ideas are represented, and the level of sophistication of theoretical explanations (diSessa, 2013; Kuhn, 2011). One further complication is whereas educators and policymakers have been interested in what children have seemed to learned from their science classes in school, developmental psychologists have been interested in revealing the kinds of everyday "scientific" ideas that children construct on their own from their personal experiences and conversations that they have prior to formal schooling (diSessa, 2013; Gopnik & Wellman, 2012). The body of knowledge that children and adults abstract from their experiences has been dubbed "folk," "informal," or "intuitive" theories. The body of knowledge evident in practicing scientists that teachers hope to instill in their students has been dubbed "formal" theoretical knowledge. Let's examine these two kinds of knowledge in turn, since doing so follows age trends in knowledge from birth to kindergarten (intuitive scientific content knowledge) and first grade to college (formal scientific content knowledge).

Intuitive Scientific Content Knowledge

At a very basic level, any science consists of a set of *phenomena* it tries to explain and *theories* that are constructed to explain these phenomena (Gopnik & Wellman, 2012). Theories are also used to make predictions to new situations in addition to explaining existing phenomena. Although the claim was once a minority opinion, it is now commonly (but not universally) assumed by many developmental and cognitive psychologists that, by the age of 4, children seem to construct at least three informal or *intuitive theories* out of their personal observations and experiences: an *intuitive biology,* an *intuitive physics,* and an *intuitive psychology* (Coley, Arenson, Xu, & Tanner, 2017; Kamps et al., 2017; Wilkening & Cacchione, 2011). To demonstrate the existence of these intuitive theories, researchers present children with different scenarios (e.g., a child becomes sick with a cold), ask them to explain why outcomes occur, and make predictions to new cases (e.g., if a friend visited, would the friend also get sick?). The key findings that researchers like to demonstrate are that (1) children will use their intuitive theories in one domain (e.g., biology) to only explain phenomena in that domain, and (2) children make sensible predictions to new cases that are consistent with their intuitive theories. So, for example, in studies of intuitive biology, children might be presented with a story in which a child character in the story is sick with a cold and participants are asked whether that child could make another child sick by sneezing on the child (a biological explanation) or having mean thoughts about the child (a psychological explanation).

Researchers who examine the development of these intuitive theories are called "theory theorists" (Gopnik & Wellman, 2012). Theory theorists assume that both formal and intuitive theories have three features: (1) they have a distinctive structure that includes a coherent, abstract, and causal representation of the world; (2) they have distinctive explanatory, interpretive, and predictive functions; and (3) they have a dynamic structure in that there is an interplay between theories and actions in which theories guide hypothesis testing and the gathering of evidence. The evidence, in turn, can promote revisions in the theories in much the same way that evidence can promote revisions of the theories of practicing scientists (Gopnik & Wellman, 2012).

Theory theorists have designed a number of experiments to show that children's intuitive theories have these three features. Examples of the tasks used to measure intuitive theories are presented in Table 13.1. Most studies show that children have rudimentary explanatory frameworks in place for biological phenomena (e.g., germs, inheritance), physical phenomena (e.g., movement of objects, physical supports of objects), and psychological phenomena (e.g., belief revision, emotional reactions) by the age of 4. These frameworks continue to develop beyond age 4 based on children's interactions in the world and their education (Coley et al., 2017; Gopnik & Wellman, 2012; Wilkening & Cacchione, 2011).

However, whereas these studies have demonstrated a surprising level of sophistication in the thinking of preschoolers, it is clearly the case that there is a wide gap between the extent, accuracy, level of abstraction, and sophistication of the content knowledge represented by the intuitive theories of preschoolers and the formal theories of practicing scientists (diSessa, 2013). For example, whereas the intuitive psychology of a preschooler only contains three main constructs to explain behavior (i.e., goals, beliefs, and

TABLE 13.1. Examples of Tasks Used to Measure Intuitive Theories

Theory	Task
Intuitive biology	
Property projection	Told that people have an organ called an *omentum*. Do horses/dogs/worms/etc. have an omentum, too?
Contagion	A child (Susan) was said to have breathed in some germs/poison and had to stay home because of runny nose. Her friend came over. Will her friend also catch a runny nose from Susan?
Intuitive physics	
Weight bias	An apparatus with three holes in the top, three drawers on the bottom, and three tubes connecting top holes to bottom drawers, directly below or not; child asked to search drawers after ball was dropped in a hole.
Day–night cycle	Children read a description of the day–night cycle and were asked to explain what they read in words and draw a picture of the earth, sun, etc.
Intuitive psychology	
False belief task	Small dolls depicting a mother and child in a model kitchen; child leaves a candy on the kitchen counter and leaves. Mother doll comes in and moves the candy to a cabinet. Child doll comes back and subject is asked where the child doll will look for the candy.
Implicit utility task	Two puppets are given choices of trying two fruits; one has tried them before and one has not; one takes a bite and asks to try the other one. Children are asked who tried the fruits for the first time.

Note. Data from Carey (1985); Solomon and Cassimatis (1999); Hast (2018); Vosniadou and Skopeliti (2017); Liu, Wellman, Tardif, and Sabbagh (2008); and Jara-Ettinger, Floyd, Tenebaum, and Schulz (2017).

desires), the formal psychology of a psychology professor contains hundreds of interrelated constructs (as this textbook demonstrates). In addition, the apparent competence of preschoolers has to be reconciled with the large number of studies that have shown the modest level of formal knowledge demonstrated on NAEP and PISA (as noted above), and numerous forms of *misconceptions* in older students, adolescents, and adults even after multiple years of instruction in science (diSessa, 2013; Lombardi, Nussbaum, & Sinatra, 2016; Schneider & Hardy, 2013).

More specifically, Schneider and Hardy (2013) argued that it is important to distinguish three kinds of concepts when tracing the development of scientific concept knowledge: (1) misconceptions, (2) everyday conceptions, and (3) scientific concepts. They define *misconceptions* as ideas constructed by students that are inconsistent with scientific concepts and are easily disproven by experiments. For example, students may think that a small pebble will float on water because it is light, or that a 12-ounce can of diet soda will sink at the same rate as a 12-ounce can of regular soda since they confuse weight with density. An *everyday conception* will match certain experiences and therefore be sometimes correct but will fail more direct tests that entail a proper understanding. For example, they may think that something made of wood will float but something made of metal will not. These students fail to see that hollow metal containers will float while fallen trees will sink. A *scientific concept* that underlies a proper understanding of floating and sinking, such as *density,* is one that is held by the larger scientific community.

Schneider and Hardy traced the development of the concepts of sinking and floating in third graders just before, just after, and one year after learning about floating and sinking in their science classes. They discovered five different groups of students who differed with respect to the number of misconceptions, everyday conceptions, and scientific concepts they possessed. For example, the "misconceptions" group demonstrated an above-average level of misconceptions and a below-average number of everyday conceptions and scientific conceptions. The "fragmented" group, in contrast, were above average on all three conceptions, while the "scientific" group were above average on scientific conceptions but below average on misconceptions and everyday conceptions. At the pretest, 85% of students fell into the misconceptions (51%) or fragmented groups (34%). None were in the scientific conception group. By the posttest after some instruction, however, the percentages were 9% (misconceptions), 20% (fragmented), and 18% (scientific). The remaining children were in other possible combinations of having above-average or below-average levels of the three kinds of knowledge. Note that the concept of density (i.e., mass per unit of volume) is an abstract concept that is difficult to understand and distinguish from weight. Piaget's theory would predict that the 8-year-olds in this study would have difficulty understanding this abstract idea (see Chapter 3).

In a study comparing 13-year-olds and college-level biology majors, Coley et al. (2017) examined the development of intuitive biological thought. They identified three kinds of misconceptions that had been found in younger students and were interested in determining (1) whether these misconceptions were less evident in 13-year-olds and college students and (2) whether several additional years of science education promoted the replacement of three intuitive misconceptions with more formally correct conceptions. The three misconceptions included attributing human characteristics to nonhuman or inanimate objects (anthropocentric thinking), believing that objects existed to serve human goals (teleological thinking such as thinking that earthworms exist to aerate soil for humans), and thinking that members of categories have an underlying essence that makes them more similar to each other than they are (essentialist thinking). Coley et al. constructed a measure that assessed the three kinds of misconceptions as well as correct conceptions and found that whereas correct conceptions did improve, the misconceptions were also evident at comparable levels in 13-year-olds and college students. So, once again, the poor performance of older students has to be reconciled with the alleged high level of performance of preschoolers on tasks constructed by theory theorists.

Further evidence of widespread misconceptions even in adults are the various intuitive physics studies modeled on the work of Michael McClosky (1983). In these experiments, people would be (1) shown a drawing of a ball circling around inside a circular tube and asked to draw its trajectory after it comes out, (2) shown a drawing of a coin tossed in the air and asked to say what forces are acting on the coin, (3) shown a drawing of a cannon ball shot off of a cliff and asked to draw the trajectory of the ball and describe all of the forces acting on the ball, and so on. Even after spending a semester or more taking college-level physics, people reported beliefs that were at odds with the theories and laws of Newtonian physics. For example, they gave responses characteristic of the erroneous "impetus" view of force that was commonplace in the middle ages, prior to Newton's laws being developed. In the impetus view, a thrown ball is thought to be imparted with a certain amount of "force" that dissipates over time, causing the ball to drop.

One question that can be used to critique all of the studies of intuitive theories described above is "How do you know that children and adults have something in their minds that can be called 'theories'?" (diSessa, 2013). The evidence appears to derive from a small set of carefully constructed experimental stimuli in which people are only asked to provide a single response at a single point in time. If they give the formally correct "right" answer on the tasks constructed by theory theorists, or the classic kind of "wrong" misconception response proposed by other researchers, is it accurate to say, in either case, that a coherent, abstract theory guides their responses?

Andrea diSessa, a well-known professor of physics and physics education at University of California, Berkeley, notes that it is relatively easy to show incoherence in responses, if one simply probes answers with different questions across several hours coming at the phenomenon at different angles (diSessa, 2013). Rather than providing evidence of a theory, diSessa has shown instead the existence of hundreds if not thousands of "p-prims" (phenomenological primitives) that are subconceptual schemas evoked by aspects of situations. Examples include the "increased effort begets increased result" (*Ohm's p-prim*) and the idea that "the equalities of quantities should balance each other" (*abstract balance p-prim*) (diSessa, 2014). Ohm's p-prim might be evoked when a person reasons that hitting a nail with a hammer harder will drive the nail in deeper and a variety of related situations (e.g., throwing a ball harder will make it travel faster);

the abstract balance p-prim might be evoked when students examine what happens when weights are removed from one side of a balance. The balance "wants" to return to equilibrium. Rather than showing coherence of thought, diSessa and colleagues have revealed what they called evidence of the *knowledge in pieces* view of science content knowledge.

Perhaps responding to the criticism of theory theory that it may be overly generous to assume that young children have a coherent theory that bears any resemblance to theories of scientists, former advocates of that view now, instead, espouse the existence of implicit causal schemata in both children and adults that determine how they assess causal relationships in a system (Gopnik & Wellman, 2012). These probability-based schemata derive from experience acting on the world and observing what happens. To show how these schemata might be operative in young children, experimenters devised an apparatus in which a box plays music when a yellow square block is placed on top of it but not when a cylindrical red block is placed on top of it. They also see that when both blocks are placed on the box, music plays. Based on these observations, young children readily determine that the causal agent is the yellow block. What this revision to theory theory shows is that both theory theorists and "knowledge in pieces" theorists agree that people can create mental structures that can be useful for making predictions about real events, but will fail to be accurate when put to the test in the kinds of situations studied by practicing physicists, biologists, and psychologists. Even so, rather than calling these implicit mental structures a bad thing leading to misconceptions, researchers are now arguing that these structures can help people understand and assimilate the theories presented in their science classes.

Anyone critiquing this literature on scientific content knowledge will recognize that the debates about the scientific competence of young children and adults are really about what we mean by an aspect of knowledge (in this case what makes something a theory) and how our knowledge of this aspect has been acquired. Both these evaluations rely on our epistemological stances (see section on epistemology below). But the methods used to examine intuitive knowledge also reflect the biases of the researchers (e.g., to show that children are extremely competent versus to show that adults are not particularly competent).

Formal Scientific Content Knowledge

Whereas the previous section focuses on the kinds of scientific notions that children and adults develop on their own based on their experiences, in this section we focus on the kinds of formal scientific content knowledge they should be acquiring in their science lessons at school. When the expert panels mentioned in an earlier section of this chapter referred to scientific content knowledge, they were essentially referring to *theoretical explanations, conceptual knowledge,* and *declarative (factual) knowledge* (OECD, 2016).

A central task of any science is to catalog and explain *different kinds of things* and *different kinds of phenomena.* So, in earth science, students learn that there are different kinds of rocks (e.g., *igneous* vs. *sedimentary*) and different kinds of trees (e.g. *deciduous* vs. *evergreen*); in biology, they learn there are different kinds of organs (e.g., *exocrine* vs. *endocrine*) and different layers of skin cells (e.g., *granular* vs. *basal*); in chemistry, they learn that there are different kinds of elements (*helium* vs. *iron* in the periodic table) and different kinds of chemical bonds (e.g., *covalent* vs. *ionic*); and in physics, they learn that there are different kinds of celestial bodies (e.g., *planets* vs. *asteroids*) and different kinds of energy (e.g., *kinetic* vs. *potential*). But there are also different *phenomena* that occur that also need to be explained, such as earthquakes (earth science), heart disease (biology), rust forming on metals (chemistry), and phases of the moon (physics). Anyone who learns the core ideas of a given science, then, learns about the different categories of things and different phenomena that scientists in each discipline try to explain. Scientists develop *theories* to explain how and why the categories and phenomena come about. And when they posit theories, the theories refer to different constructs or *concepts* such as *gravity, metabolism, evolution, force,* and so on.

More specifically, a key aspect of any scientific explanation is a *model* (Chi, 2008; PISA, 2015; NRC, 2012; Lehrer & Schauble, 2015). For example, Newton's model of the universe contained a substance called ether that filled the space between celestial objects but did not include "black holes." Modern models of the universe do not include ether but do include black holes. One of the earliest models of the atom was J. J. Thompson's plum pudding in which electrons (the plums) existed in a viscous substance (Helge, 2002). Any model describes the components of some system and how the components work together to explain some outcome. Why does an electric spark create water droplets in an inverted tube that is supplied with oxygen on one side and hydrogen on the other? The model of the atom that includes components such as protons, electrons, neutrons, and covalent bonds helps to explain this outcome. Students need to appreciate that the history of science should be characterized by a succession of models proposed to explain specific phenomena that are revised in response to evidence collected. This insight is part of what we mean when we say we want students to have scientific content knowledge (OECD, 2016). But many models, such as those of the atom or even the human mind, can be difficult for young children to grasp because these models are often abstract and metaphorical.

The main way that we can learn whether children actually learn and can apply the science content presented in school is to consider their performance on well-designed national and international tests (and, to a lesser extent, in small-scale studies of researchers). However, federal and state laws that require regular assessments of children mainly require testing of reading and math skills. States differ with respect to whether and when children's science skills are assessed. In addition, the teams that developed NAEP assessments and PISA assessments tried to create test items that required reasoning and the ability to link responses to their implications for experimental designs. Thus, total scores and achievement levels on NAEP and PISA cannot be easily decomposed into rote knowledge of facts versus conceptual understanding. That said, descriptions of performance levels suggest that students performing at the "basic level" for NAEP have a rudimentary level of understanding. Consider the description of the basic level for fourth graders on the NAEP for science (*https://nces.ed.gov/nationsreportcard/science/achieve.aspx#2009_grade4*):

> Students performing at the Basic level should be able to describe, measure, and classify familiar objects in the world around them, as well as explain and make predictions about familiar processes. These processes include changes of states of matter, movements of objects, basic needs and life cycles of plants and animals, changes in shadows during the day, and changes in weather.

This description can be contrasted with that for the next higher level, the proficient level, where there is more of an emphasis on conceptual understanding and coherence among concepts and practices:

> Students performing at the Proficient level should be able to demonstrate relationships among closely related science concepts, as well as analyze alternative explanations or predictions. They should be able to explain how changes in temperature cause changes of state, how forces can change motion, how adaptations help plants and animals meet their basic needs, how environmental changes can affect their growth and survival, how land formations can result from Earth processes, and how recycling can help conserve limited resources.

Unfortunately, 24% of fourth graders on the 2015 NAEP performed at the "below basic" level, 38% at the "basic" level, and 37% performed at the proficient level. Thus, 62% of U.S. fourth graders performed below the proficient level and thereby demonstrated only a rudimentary and largely factual understanding of important science concepts and processes.

To get a sense of whether there is growth in children's scientific content knowledge with age and further instruction, we can consider the descriptions and percentages for eighth-grade performance on NAEP science assessments:

> Students performing at the Basic level should be able to state or recognize correct science principles. They should be able to explain and predict observations of natural phenomena at multiple scales, from microscopic to global.

They should be able to describe properties and common physical and chemical changes in materials; describe changes in potential and kinetic energy of moving objects; describe levels of organization of living systems—cells, multicellular organisms, and ecosystems; identify related organisms based on hereditary traits; describe a model of the solar system; and describe the processes of the water cycle.

The description of the proficient level for eight graders is as follows:

Students performing at the Proficient level should be able to demonstrate relationships among closely related science principles. They should be able to identify evidence of chemical changes; explain and predict motions of objects using position-time graphs; explain metabolism, growth, and reproduction in cells, organisms, and ecosystems; use observations of the Sun, Earth, and Moon to explain visible motions in the sky; and predict surface and ground water movements in different regions of the world. They should be able to explain and predict observations of phenomena at multiple scales, from microscopic to macroscopic and local to global, and to suggest examples of observations that illustrate a science principle. They should be able to use evidence from investigations in arguments that accept, revise, or reject scientific models. They should be able to use scientific criteria to propose and critique alternative individual and local community responses to design problems.

The percentages of eighth graders performing at the below basic, basic, and proficient levels were 32%, 34%, and 32%, respectively. Thus, even though what is required to be assigned to the basic level is more sophisticated at the eighth-grade level than it is for the fourth-grade level, 68% of eighth graders still performed below the proficient level, suggesting only modest improvement between the fourth and eighth grades despite the fact that eighth graders were provided with 4 additional years of science instruction.

Scientific Procedural Knowledge

The second of the five aspects of scientific competence pertains to the ability to design studies in such a way that they provide credible evidence regarding the accuracy of theoretical predictions. Notice from this definition how there is a direct link between the first element, scientific content knowledge (e.g., theory), and the second, scientific procedural knowledge (designing studies). These two forms of competence should not be taught in isolation from each other because of this inherent relationship. We come back to this point later.

To get a sense of what this second ability of scientific procedural ability might entail, imagine that you read an article in which a researcher tries to prove that drinking turmeric tea will reduce inflammation in arthritic knees, so he creates two experimental groups: (1) the treatment group is asked to drink 1 cup of turmeric tea every day for 2 weeks and take a daily dose of ibuprofen, and (2) the control group neither drinks the tea nor takes the pill. Two weeks later, we find that the swelling in the knees of the treatment group is less than in the control group.

It should be easy to see that this is not a properly designed test of the anti-inflammatory properties of turmeric tea since ibuprofen also has anti-inflammatory effects. When one experimental group has two potentially causal agents that could produce an outcome and these are not separated out, we say the two potentially causal agents are *confounded* with each other. As another example, sometimes we hear in the media about a new way to teach science that is supposedly better, but then when we delve further into the study, we find out that the new method was tried out in an upper-income private school with a selective admissions process but the control group was a lower-income public school. In such a study, multiple other variables besides the new instructional technique are confounded with the new technique, which renders the results uninterpretable.

Ever since the time of Sir Francis Bacon (the 1600s), the method typically used to provide more credible results by teasing out the independent effects of an alleged causal factor is called the "isolation of variables" or "*control of variables*" technique. Here, one creates a *fair test* by creating two experimental conditions in which everything is the same between the treatment and control groups except for the one variable of interest (e.g., turmeric tea or the new science technique). One can "unconfound" variables in the turmeric tea example by not giving ibuprofen to just the experimental group, giving it to both groups, or not giving it to either group. In the science teaching example, we can create the proper conditions by *randomly assigning* teachers and children in both schools to the experimental and control instructional conditions.

Jean Piaget (see Chapter 3) was one of the first researchers to examine the ability of children and adolescents to understand and carry out the control of variables technique (Inhelder & Piaget, 1958). However, his constructivist tendencies led him to see if children demonstrated this ability prior to being formally taught it in school (in other words, if they constructed it on their own). Although his findings seemed to suggest that children lacked this ability until after age 12 or so (e.g., children below that age tended to create confounded comparisons), this conclusion was challenged by many researchers in the years to follow (Schwichow, Croker, Zimmerman, Höffler, & Härtig, 2016). A meta-analysis of 72 studies in which researchers tried to teach the control of variables strategy to students in a treatment group and compared their performance to nontaught students in a control group revealed an average effect size of 0.61, which is a pretty strong and consistent effect (Schwichow et al., 2016). The results showed that children as young as 9 could be taught the strategy (3 years earlier than Piaget found) and that two aspects of the intervention were associated with stronger effects: when good examples of well-designed studies were demonstrated for students, and when a cognitive conflict approach was used in which students discovered results that were at odds with their beliefs. In the section below on the instructional implications of the research presented in this chapter, we examine other aspects of interventions that did or did not make a difference in how this strategy is taught. For now it is sufficient to note that it is one thing to teach children the strategy; it is quite another to have it be internalized as a strategy that they regularly use to design new experiments to test the accuracy of theories and models. In addition, many causal systems in the real world are complex and multivariate and do not lend themselves to examination via the control of variables strategy (diSessa, 2014; Kuhn, Ramsey, & Arvidsson, 2015).

Epistemology

The third component of scientific competence pertains to people's beliefs about the nature of science, how knowledge is acquired, and the relationship between evidence and theory revision (Lombardi, Bickel, Bailey, & Burrell, 2017; Stathopoulou & Vosniadou, 2007). To see the importance of this component, consider several real-world examples. Several years ago, I read an article in my local newspaper about a guest speaker who said at a local high school assembly, "Evolution is only a theory," as an argument against evolution. Another example is when I heard a radio talk-show host say, "Global warming is a hoax. Thermometers are just getting better and more accurate since the 1920s so that is why it only *seems* to be getting warmer. And besides there were not any thermometers a couple hundred years ago." The former example about the guest speaker suggests that he believed that there are some facts that are known to be unchanging and true (hence not "just theories"), while anything that is "still a theory" is unproven speculation. The latter statement from the radio host reflects a misunderstanding of how the evidence of climate change is established. Among other things, scientists rely on air bubbles trapped in deep layers of the arctic ice caps and Boyle's law (that links gas pressure to temperature) to determine, with a great deal of precision and accuracy, what the earth's temperature must have been hundreds of years ago. They do not rely on thermometers and they are not simply speculating.

As these examples show, it is not only people's misconceptions about scientific ideas (e.g., concepts such as *force* or *metabolism*) that cause problems, but also misconceptions about the *nature of science* and the links between methodologies, evidence, and theory revision that can also cause problems. Because epistemology requires the ability to *reflect on* knowledge and *evaluate* the information value of particular forms of evidence for theory revision, it is inherently *metatheoretical* (Kuhn, 2020; Lombardi et al., 2017). In other words, it requires thinking about and critiquing a theory rather than just knowing the theory. To have a more accurate understanding of the nature of science, then, it is important for students to develop a deep understanding of not only what scientists know, but also *how scientists know what they know* (Lombardi et al., 2017). The latter is a key aspect of scientific epistemology. Practicing scientists engage in evaluative reasoning every time they think about the manner in which they or other scientists pose questions, make observations, design experiments, collect data, or interpret these data.

Some have argued (e.g., Stathopoulou & Vosniadou, 2007) that a proper understanding of the nature of science requires a *constructivist epistemology,* comparable to that of Piaget (see Chapter 3). Here, scientists do not have minds that are blank slates that simply copy reality. Rather, they slowly increase their understanding of some phenomenon as they test out models of the world. Piaget liked to call children "little scientists" (Gopnik & Wellman, 2012) and called his theory of cognitive development, *genetic* (developmental) *epistemology*. Others have argued that the most apt philosophical stance to take toward scientific theory revision is *pragmatism* (Malachowski, 2004). Here, one comes to know that a particular theory is probably a correct account of some phenomenon by observing how it helps one correctly predict and explain future outcomes. As science advances, we come closer and closer to the truth.

As one example of how epistemology can operate even before people consider evidence, consider the case of *plausibility* (Lombardi et al., 2017). If a layperson or scientist believes that some explanation of a phenomenon such as climate change or evolution is not even plausible, this metatheoretical attitude will affect how they respond to evidence. As another example of such evaluative reasoning, consider how Andrea diSessa (2014, p. 803) discussed the debate between theory theorists who assume coherent, theory-like knowledge structures in children and his own "knowledge in pieces" (p-prims) account that takes the opposite perspective:

> Describing p-prims as "correct" or "incorrect" is a category error. They are plainly not scientific in many ways, but they often make correct predictions in everyday use; that is, their ecological function. P-prims often appear as incorrect predictions and explanations ("misconceptions") in situations of importance in science, but this ignores both their frequent effective use in everyday reasoning and the fact that they may become effective parts of normative scientific understanding.

To say that it does not even make sense to ask the question about p-prims being correct is an example of how scientists evaluate questions before they even begin to design experiments. Reviewers of journal articles submitted for publication in educational and developmental journals often consider whether the research questions asked by researchers are the right ones to ask, will move the field in a new appropriate direction, and so on. They then consider other matters such as the representativeness of the sample, measures used, and so on. I likewise engage in such reasoning when deciding which studies will get presented in this book.

As might be expected from the review of research on intuitive theories provided earlier in this chapter, there is the curious split between (1) researchers who think that even preschoolers can engage in such evaluative, epistemological reasoning (see Tong, Wang, & Danovitch, 2019, for a review); and (2) researchers who document the many ways in which high school students, college students, and lay adults demonstrate flaws in their epistemological reasoning (Lombardi et al., 2017). How could young reasoners be so good while older reasoners be so bad?

The primary reason for the difference was alluded to earlier in this chapter: researchers in the two camps used tasks that had different levels of intellectual demand. For example, one aspect of an epistemological stance is a judgment or evaluation of the reliability of the information that has been presented. Imprecise or unreliable temperature gauges should make one question the reality of climate change, for example, if such instruments are the basis for climate change assertions (which of course they are not). Or, if a scientist is known to be an unreliable source because of a past history of bias or incoherence, information from that individual can be discounted.

To see if young children can demonstrate the ability to judge the reliability of someone as an information source, imagine a task in which two puppets look into a box filled with common objects of which preschoolers already know the names. One puppet correctly labels all the objects, where the other sometimes labels objects incorrectly (e.g., labels an orange a banana). When an unfamiliar object is next introduced, the two puppets give it a name. Studies using this and similar tasks show that children are more likely to adopt the name used by the reliable puppet than the unreliable puppet (Tong et al., 2019). Other studies have found that 4- and 5-year-olds, but not 3-year-olds, are more likely to believe a speaker who uses the word *because* as part of an explanation than another speaker who uses all the same words except for *because* (Bernard, Mercier, & Clement, 2012). Further, 5-year-olds were more likely than 3-year-olds to prefer noncircular explanations (e.g., "Sometimes it rains when clouds in the sky have too much water in them . . .") to circular explanations (e.g., "When it rains water falls from the sky and gets us wet") (Corriveau & Kurkul, 2014).

Although such nascent abilities are impressive, they are a far cry from the kind of epistemological thinking needed to gain a proper understanding of the nature of theories, evidence, and theory revision. In reviewing the literature on the development of epistemological beliefs, researchers have proposed that there appear to be three levels on insight that emerge over time (Stathopoulou & Vosniadou, 2007). In Level 1, scientific knowledge is considered to be a grab bag of beliefs about true facts (e.g., the earth is not flat) and procedures (e.g., the correct way to carry out a lab experiment). Also, people at Level 1 believe that experiments provide unambiguous data in support of true beliefs and do not differentiate between scientific ideas, procedures, and evidence. At Level 2, students begin to demonstrate an understanding of explanation and hypothesis testing, but still expect experiments to confirm basic truths. Moreover, these students still believe in the certainty of knowledge and that absolute truth is attainable. Level 3 is the constructivist view of scientific knowledge and knowledge acquisition (see Chapter 3 on constructivism). Smith, Maclin, Houghton, and Hennessy (2000, p. 350) argued that this level represents an "epistemology in which students are aware of the central role of ideas in the knowledge acquisition process and of how ideas are developed and revised through a process of conjecture, argument, and test." At this level, people realize that all evidence is interpreted through the lens of theories, and no observation can ever be "pure." They also recognize that it is the very nature of theories to be constantly evolving and moving toward ever-increasing accuracy on the basis of credible evidence, as opposed to establishing absolute, unchanging truths. It is this third level that the designers of NAEP and PISA hope to see in students, but few demonstrate this level of understanding into the nature of science and theory revision.

Argument

One important aspect of the professional activity of scientists and scientific progress is a form of interaction that can be called *argumentation* (Berland & Reiser, 2009; Mercier, Boudry, Paglieri, & Trouche, 2017; Nussbaum, 2011). It is a commonplace component of scientific activity that students never see but emerges as competing and collaborating groups of scientists propose models, gather data, and discuss whether theories have to be revised on the basis of evidence. The discussions occur at professional meetings, during the peer-review process, and in professional publications such as books and journal articles. These discussions are crucial not only for finding flaws in other people's work and reasoning, but also in your own. Other scientists help us see our "myside" biases and overcome them. The debate between theory theorists and diSessa described above is an example. The NRC (2012) panel describe the role and importance of argument skills as such:

> Although the practices used to develop scientific theories (as well as the form that those theories take) differ from one domain of science to another, all

sciences share certain common features at the core of their inquiry-based and problem-solving approaches. Chief among these features is a commitment to data and evidence as the foundation for developing claims. The argumentation and analysis that relate evidence and theory are also essential features of science; scientists need to be able to examine, review, and evaluate their own knowledge and ideas and critique those of others. Argumentation and analysis include appraisal of data quality, modeling of theories, development of new testable questions from those models, and modification of theories and models as evidence indicates they are needed.

In classic argument theory, people on two sides of an argument make *claims* and need to back up these claims with *warrants* such as evidence or sound reasoning (Nussbaum, 2011). For example, a critic of Newtonian physics in the late 1800s might claim that "ether does not exist" and provide evidence that it does not by shooting a light beam from earth to another planet to see if the reflected light that comes back is altered by the ether. If the light does not reflect back altered, that finding is evidence in support of the claim that ether does not exist. Newtonians, might then criticize the methodology used by non-Newtonians and conduct their own studies to prove ether does exist (this debate about ether is a true story by the way). Particularly skilled arguers also anticipate criticisms of their claims or warrants, so they often anticipate counterarguments and provide *rebuttals* of these arguments ahead of time.

Evolutionary psychologists have recently contended that the human mind evolved to make us "natural born arguers" as a protective mechanism against being conned (Mercier et al., 2017). We want to know whether, for example, ether does exist because it is a key assumption of Newtonian theory. We should not accept the claims of scientists simply because they are scientists. As noted above, critical thinkers can protect themselves from bad advice from scientists, doctors, lawyers, and financial planners. Our argument skills are a key component of this critical-thinking detection ability.

Although there is reason to believe that argumentation is an evolved ability, it apparently does not come easy to us. A number of studies have shown that even high school and college students have difficulty making sound arguments and counterarguments (Bennett et al., 2010; Kuhn, 2010; Nussbaum, 2011). People have a hard time distinguishing between theories (models) and evidence. They often rely on gut reactions to the *plausibility* of someone's claim rather than on evaluating the evidence in support of the claim (Lombardi et al., 2016, 2017). So, even before they are presented with evidence, a gut reaction of "no way!" can render the evidence inconsequential.

Another hindrance in the development of argument skills is the epistemological stance of learners (and scientists) (Lombardi et al., 2016). If students progress at all, they seem to progress from an *absolutist* stance, to a *multiplist* (relativist) stance, to an *evaluativist* stance after long-term interventions. Absolutists believe that all scientific knowledge is certain and truths are easy to discover and compile. Multiplists believe that it is possible for there to be two or more positions on an issue, and there is no way to resolve the discrepancies ("reasonable people can disagree"). Evaluativists believe that some evidence and arguments are better than others and it is, therefore, possible to decide among the different theoretical perspectives. Students have been found to be more likely to learn the correct understanding of a scientific concept and revise their misconceptions when they are multiplists or evaluativists than if they are absolutists (Lombardi et al., 2016).

Motivation

The final component that contributes to the development of scientific-reasoning competence is motivation. It can take years to master the kinds of knowledge and skills that were identified earlier (in the discussion of NAEP and PISA results) as being indicative of proficiency in scientific competence. Motivation often slips when students struggle to understand, and it is the very nature of science that experiments often produce disappointing results. Thus, it clearly is the case that students will only persist in science-related pursuits during and after high school if they (1) perform well in science, (2) find science interesting, (3) are intrinsically interested in science and fully engage themselves in science coursework, (4) feel efficacious about performing well, (5) consider it worth the effort to try hard, (6) think it is important and useful to them, and (7) have growth mindsets (see Chapter 5; Rosenzweig & Wigfield, 2016). Indeed, the 2015 NAEP for science reported a correlation of $r = .38$ between students' science performance and their endorsing an item that asked how much they like science (NCES, 2015). PISA reported comparable relationships between science scores and other aspects of motivation such as self-efficacy, and utility value (OECD, 2016). That said, only 28% of 12th graders said they liked science a lot on the 2015 NAEP, and the 2011 Trends in International Mathematics and Science Study (TIMSS) found that, around the world, there was a substantial drop between fourth grade and eighth grade in the percentage who "agreed a lot" with the statement "I enjoy learning science" (from 68% to 43%) (OECD, 2016). The monotonic drop in motivation for science between elementary school and high school has also been found in large studies in the United States (Rosenzweig & Wigfield, 2016). PISA reported gender differences in various aspects of motivation for science (OECD, 2016) and even among high-ability students (SATs >650), women were more likely to opt out of STEM careers between high school and age 33 because they had the skills to succeed in other professions (Wang, Eccles, & Kenny, 2013).

IMPLICATIONS FOR EDUCATION

Throughout this chapter, it was noted that most students fail to acquire the kinds of scientific-reasoning skills and dispositions that they need to be successful in today's world. Policymakers and educators in most nations recognize that something must be done, and it is natural to assume that there is something wrong with the way students are taught (Windschitl & Barton, 2016). Observational studies show that science teachers often rely on a "transmission" view of teaching in which they assume that their job is to simply convey the key ideas of some unit of science and ask students to reproduce the idea on a test (Windschitl & Barton, 2016). Moreover, textbooks and lectures tend to convey way too many ideas for students to handle, and often do not distinguish important or central ideas from peripheral ideas. Further, students are typically not asked to engage in authentic scientific practices (asking questions, designing experiments, collecting and analyzing data, etc.) and if they are asked to engage in some of these practices (e.g., carry out the steps of a lab), there are no interconnections among the components (e.g., between the lab and the lectures). But assessments such as NAEP and PISA require students to show how they can engage in authentic, connected practices and, for example, relate theoretical models to evidence and understand the implications of certain kinds of evidence for model revision. The reports of NAEP, PISA, and NRC all specify what we would hope students would know and be able to do in science, but these reports do not provide sufficient and specific advice on how to alter classrooms such that students move toward these ideals (Windschitl & Barton, 2016).

Not that long ago, decisions about how to teach science to children were guided by Piagetian theory (see Chapter 3; Gopnik & Wellman, 2012; Windschitl & Barton, 2016). Educators took to heart the suggestion that young children were not capable of meaningfully engaging in the components of scientific reasoning described above, so there was a tendency to delay asking them to do so until middle school and adolescence. An important shift occurred in the 1990s when policymakers and educators were confronted with disappointing findings from TIMSS, NAEP, and PISA, and the NRC issued their science teaching standards (NRC, 1996). There was a strong push to change the standard model of transmission teaching, overloading of information, and disconnected components, to more of an inquiry-based approach that was thought to have children engage in scientific practices the way scientists do such as asking questions, designing studies, and engaging in arguments about the meaning of evidence for their models (Furtak, Seidel, Iverson, & Briggs, 2012).

A meta-analysis of 37 studies conducted in the 10 years following the publication of the 1996 NRC standards reported that the average effect size between classrooms that used inquiry-based methods and standard science classrooms was 0.50 (Furtak et al., 2012). However, one may question the winnowing process in which the 37 articles were distilled in that article, and the authors did not use the standard formula for computing effect sizes that are also weighted by sample size and variance. Furtak et al. (2012) did, however, report that instruction that tended more toward heavy teacher scaffolding as opposed to child-led discovery learning was more effective, and this finding has been confirmed in a different meta-analysis in which scaffolded, guided discovery was found to be more effective than pure discovery in teaching children the control of variables technique (Martella, Klahr, & Li, 2020).

Other studies have shown that science learning can also be promoted by targeting specific aspects of motivation such as self-efficacy, interest, and values (Lin-Siegler, Ahn, Chen, Fang, & Luna-Lucero, 2016; Rosenzweig & Wigfield, 2016; Shin et al., 2019) or targeting children's metacognition or epistemological beliefs (Lombardi et al., 2016; Zepeda, Richey, Ronevich, & Nokes-Malach, 2015). A somewhat more comprehensive approach has recently been advocated that has its roots in inquiry-based methods but argues for the centrality of scientific models (Lehrer & Schauble, 2015; Windshitl & Barton, 2016). All the other aspects of scientific practices center around models and are motivated by them.

For example, scientists do not simply ask questions; rather, they ask questions motivated by their models and the phenomena that models are attempting to explain. Similarly, they do not simply design studies or collect data and evidence for no reason; rather, the design of experiments, data-collection instruments that are used, and argumentation that ensues about how to interpret evidence are already directly related to their models. Thus, if one starts with models that attempt to explain interesting naturally occurring phenomena, all of the other aspects of scientific practice naturally follow in a coherent, and interconnected way (Lehrer & Schauble, 2015; Windshitl & Barton, 2016). Children can be taught how to use jars of pond water as models of the entire pond, or hand-made distributions of data as a model of some phenomenon (growth of bacteria in the water), or other kinds of models to explain why an opera singer's voice can cause a wine glass to break (Windshitl & Barton, 2016).

Because the translation of global suggestions (e.g., "focus instruction on models" or "focus on big ideas not small peripheral facts") into the classroom is not always straightforward, it can be useful for science researchers to conduct so-called *design experiments* in collaboration with classroom teachers (Lehrer & Schauble, 2015; Windshitl & Barton, 2016). In a design experiment, researchers and teachers work together to develop methods for choosing the big ideas of a unit, appropriate models that are associated with these ideas, concrete models that children can create, and scaffolds for children (such as charts that have columns for the "phenomenon," "research questions," "tentative models," "evidence," and "how models needs to be revised"). Children's epistemology will be enhanced when they see the imperfect relation between models and evidence, use models to explain phenomena, and engage in argumentation with each other about flaws in their data-collection techniques and what their findings mean. But, one will find that the initial attempts of teachers making these ideas work in a real classroom will often be off the mark. Children will not always understand, and teachers and researchers will have to go back to the drawing board to think of better models or scaffolds. It is the collaborative trial-and-error quality of design experiments that will eventually help teachers and researchers create teaching methods that will eventually promote the kinds of scientific-reasoning ability that we aspire to on NAEP, PISA, and the NRC. We have not been ambitious enough and we have often underestimated what children between the ages of 8 and 10 can do.

CHAPTER 14

The Development
of Historical Understanding

In 1905, the philosopher George Santayana wrote the famous aphorism "Those who cannot remember the past are condemned to repeat it" (Santayana, 1905). As an introduction to this chapter, it is useful to unpack this expression to expose several implicit ideas in it. Notice that Santayana does not seem to be saying, "We should study history to see all the wonderful things that human beings have done." Rather, he is suggesting that human beings have a number of tendencies that make them repeatedly prone to make decisions that have led to disastrous consequences. It is notable that Santayana was born the same year that slavery was abolished in the United States (1863) but lived through the Reconstruction and Jim Crow eras, the Great Depression, the rise of fascism in Spain, Italy, and Germany, two world wars, and the destruction of Nagasaki and Hiroshima by atomic bombs. The premise of his aphorism seems to be that comparable kinds of problems are likely to be repeated in the future unless we come to understand why such events happened, recognize signs of their reemergence, and work to prevent them.

But having a deep understanding of the causes of historical events requires that we also understand the economic, political, cultural, and geographical factors that were operative when these events occurred (Thornton, 2017). Consider, for example, that Nazism did not take hold in the 1930s in Germany simply because Hitler was allegedly a persuasive speaker; rather, it was also highly important that (1) there was a worldwide

Great Depression at the time that hit Germany particular hard (economics), (2) the Treaty of Versailles imposed harsh annual reparations payments that Germany could not afford (economics), (3) Germany had only been a democracy for a short time (politics), (4) there had been a recent failed coup led by communist immigrants from Russia (cultural, political), (5) Hitler blamed the Treaty of Versailles and the coup on Jewish Russian immigrants (cultural, political), (6) there was a prevailing anti-Semitism in Germany at the time (cultural beliefs), (7) neighboring France had made military incursions into Germany because Germany failed to make reparations payments (geography, politics), (8) Mussolini's fascism had just taken hold in neighboring Italy in a bloodless coup that Hitler tried to emulate (geography, politics), and so on (Ullrich, 2016).

The suggestion that a proper understanding of history and historical causes requires all of these additional insights from multiple disciplines besides history is one of the reason why there has been a long-standing debate about whether school curriculums should primarily be based in history or in the larger set of disciplines known as *social studies* (Barton & Avery, 2016; Thornton, 2017). There is a debate about what disciplines are included in the social studies, but the National Council for the Social Studies (NCSS, 2020) assumes that the list includes

> anthropology, archaeology, economics, geography, history, law, philosophy, political science, psychology, religion, and sociology, as well as appropriate content from the humanities, mathematics, and natural sciences. The primary purpose of social studies is to help young people make informed and reasoned decisions for the public good as citizens of a culturally diverse, democratic society in an interdependent world.

An underlying assumption of this chapter is that a multidiscipline social studies approach is preferable to a singular focus on history, but regrettably far fewer studies have been conducted on children's understanding of specific kinds of social studies content (e.g., geography, economics) than on reading, math, and science skills, and the majority of studies that have been conducted on social studies have been in the area of history (Barton & Avery, 2016). Thus, we will limit our focus in this chapter to historical understanding because of our decision to only write about a topic when more than a handful of studies have been conducted.

Following the organization of other chapters, we will begin with a description of what historical reasoning competence entails and consider national data regarding how many students in the United States acquire this level of competence. In the second section, we consider age trends in the acquisition of historical reasoning competence. In the final section, we consider instructional implications of this research.

THE NATURE OF HISTORICAL
REASONING COMPETENCE

Historical reasoning is not the same as scientific reasoning (see Chapter 13), but it does share some important similarities. For example, reasoning in both disciplines involves asking questions, looking for evidence to answer these questions, considering the quality of evidence and how to interpret it, making attributions of causality, engaging in critical thinking, engaging in argumentation, and having epistemological insight into the nature of the discipline and how experts know what they know (Reisman, Brimsek, & Hollywood, 2019; van Drie & van Boxtel, 2008; Wiley, Griffin, Steffens, & Britt, 2020). That said, there are some important differences as well. For example, whereas scientists create their own measuring devices that are specifically designed to validly measure a variable and gather new data within controlled experiments, historians must accept the evidence that exists, however flawed, circumscribed, and biased it may be. In addition, aspects that are unique to history include second-tier concepts such as *historical significance,* the *reliability of sources, corroboration,* the difference between *primary* and *secondary sources, contextualization, empathy, historical timelines,* and the difference between the *past* and *history* (Barton & Avery, 2016; Bertram, Wagner, & Trautwein, 2017; van Drie & van Boxtel, 2008). Let's briefly consider these different unique aspects of historical reasoning competence in turn.

Unique Aspects of Historical Reasoning Competence

Historical Significance

Events happen every second of every day in the world. Twenty years from now, historians will not provide detailed accounts of everything that is happening right now but, rather, will make decisions about describing events that mattered and were worth talking about (Seixas, 1994). The Great Depression and World War II were both highly significant events and worth talking about, but how about the Teapot Dome scandal or battles between ranchers and farmers in the West during the westward expansion of the 1800s? All these things have found their way into U.S. history books. Will historians be talking about the impeachment of Donald Trump in 20 years? How about the migration of Syrians out of war-torn Syria or Central Americans out of gang-ridden Guatemala? What makes an historical event worth talking about in an historical account of a time period? Historians make these judgments all the time as part of an *historical narrative* meant to interpret a string of events and make them meaningful (Seixas, 1994). But a little reflection shows that one would fully expect a liberal history professor to make different selections of events and interpretations than a conservative history professor, and male historians to make different decisions than female historians, and American Indian historians to make different decisions than White historians. Histories are replete with accounts that describe events that are alleged to be factual, but whether these accounts become part of the narrative and how they are interpreted depends on the writer. Historians are well aware of this selectivity and the role that values play in judging the importance of an event. Perhaps that recognition explains the long-standing aphorism that "victors get to write histories."

Reliability of Sources

How do we know that a particular event actually happened in the past? How do we know the details of these events? Before the advent of cameras, historians had to rely on different forms of documentary evidence, such as diaries, newspaper articles, letters written by eyewitnesses, minutes of meetings, artwork, and so on. The authors of these forms of evidence and the items themselves are considered *sources,* and we want to know how *reliable* these sources are for reporting things accurately, completely, and without bias (Barton & Avery, 2016). Just as what was said about the selectivity of historians, authors of these forms of evidence also decide what to report about the event and what to exclude, and they use interpretive language to describe the events. Consider, for example, a letter written home by a soldier during the U.S. Civil War. It is easy to see how a northern Union soldier might select different events to report and interpret these events differently than a Confederate soldier who experienced the same battle. Similarly, we know that southern newspapers described the same battles differently than northern newspapers do. Moreover, a recent history of the rise of Hitler contained diary entries from a close associate and fond admirer of Hitler, Herman Hess (Ullrich, 2016). Can these diary entries be given any credibility, given the nature of the relationship between Hitler and Hess? Ullrich's history also includes comments from British foreign service officials who gave accounts that were polar opposites of those of Hess. Historians are aware that their sources tend to be partial and biased. Their role is to try and craft the most accurate account possible across multiple, sometimes conflicting sources, taking into account the weaknesses of the available evidence (Reisman et al., 2019).

Corroboration and Integration of Sources

Because sources are often unreliable or conflicting, an important aspect of being an historian is finding multiple sources of evidence that can corroborate an interpretation, as opposed to relying on a single source (Reisman et al., 2019). For example, if Alexander Hamilton hypothetically wrote a letter to his wife in which he said that a violent fight broke out during a session of the New York legislature, it would be useful to obtain evidence from other sources to see if this account is accurate or an exaggeration.

But once the reliability of sources is determined and one attempts to find corroboration, there is the remaining task of integrating information across sources to produce a coherent and defensible historical narrative account (Nokes, 2017; Rantala & van den Berg, 2015; Wiley et al., 2020). Using the terminology of Chapter 10 on reading comprehension, historical reading comprehension not only requires the construction of a verbatim textbase of what was read and a situation model through inference making, there is also a need to create a coherent representation of an account by means of corroboration (Wiley et al., 2020).

Difference between Primary and Secondary Sources

A *primary source* for an historian would be a document or artifact that existed at the time of an historical event. Examples are listed above, such as a diary entry or letter of an eyewitness. A *secondary source* would be a narrative reconstruction of an event that relies on primary sources. A good example is a history textbook. A key part of historical competence is understanding the advantages and disadvantages of using primary or secondary sources to write a new historical narrative. Primary sources are often preferred since they have not been filtered through the lens of an historian. Yet, they are not often written to preserve history and can be incomplete, partial, or biased. Conversely, it can be useful to examine secondary sources such as historical accounts that were written not long after the events took place, but these narratives cannot replace the unfiltered authenticity of primary documents. Modern historians could well write entirely different narratives using primary sources than those that were written at the time. Secondary sources should be seen as second-hand interpretations of first-hand interpretations.

Contextualization

One of the easiest traps to fall into when reading about the past is *presentism* and the related phenomenon of being *anachronistic* (Levstik & Thornton, 2020; van Straaten et al., 2019). It is natural to impose our current understanding of things back onto historical figures. To understand any historical actor's decisions and behaviors, we need to properly contextualize the individual within the cultural, scientific, and economic milieu of that time period. It can be difficult to not be dispassionate about the mindsets of people when we, in modern times, have a hard time understanding how people could have been so sexist, or racist, or anti-Semitic only just 100 years ago. Historians do not condone immoral stances or ridicule scientific misunderstandings since their only goal is to explain what happened and why those events happened. Note that the above description of 1930s Germany is an example of contextualizing what was going on at that time to explain how Hitler could have risen to power. It is clearly immoral to be anti-Semitic, but one cannot understand the rise of Hitler without understanding the prevalence of that attitude among the citizenry in pre-war Germany, so historians have to refer to this prevailing attitude in their narratives about the rise of Hitler.

Empathy

A notion related to contextualization is the ability to "get into the minds" of past actors, to understand their points of view and beliefs (Levstik & Thornton, 2020). This form of cognitive empathy is different from what psychologists mean when they discuss emotional responses such as compassion and sympathy. Cognitive empathy is the ability to take on another's perspective. When discussing the writing of the U.S. Constitution, for example, it is easy to see how important this ability is for a proper understanding of why the U.S. government was designed as it was. For example, the Second Amendment makes a great deal more sense when one considers how the Founding Fathers had just recently freed themselves from the tyranny of King George and used their meager personal weapons to fight against the well-equipped British army. People at that time may well have reasoned, "Who knows when we might need to have our guns again to fight against a tyrannical ruler." It matters little to an historian whether such a mindset is appropriate now in the current times in order to explain why the Second Amendment was included back in the 1700s. Historians may also try to "get inside the head" of Alexander Hamilton by reading his entries in the *Federalist Papers* or his letters to family members to see whether he included the Second Amendment as a bargaining chip to get votes from the state legislatures of certain states. Modern historians argue that the capacity for this form of empathy helps us overcome the tendency toward presentism (Levstik & Thornton, 2020).

Historical Timelines

An historical timeline is a *representation of a temporal sequence of events* (Barton & Levstik, 1996). It is meant to represent some reality but is distinct from it, the same way that a map is a representation of some landmass but obviously different than the landmass. An historical timeline is analogous to the number line in mathematics, but in a timeline, events are the points on the line instead of numerical quantities. The narrative that an historian constructs about a sequence of events can refer to a timeline because a causal story can be imposed on the sequence to explain why things happened as they did. For example, the timeline for the rise of Hitler might include the defeat of Germany in World War I, the German (communist) Revolution of 1918, the Treaty of Versailles in 1919 that included severe reparations payments, and the Weimar Republic of 1919 to 1933. Within this timeline, the later events could be explained by the earlier events. What to include on a timeline will be based on an historian's assessment of the event's historical significance and his or her historical narrative. Timelines also have a spatial quality to them, in the sense that events that happened 100 years apart should be spaced farther apart on the timeline than events that occurred 10 years apart.

Difference between the "Past" and "History"

Historians consider the *past* to be all the events that have gone on in the world before and *history* to be the practice of interpreting the past on the basis of residues of evidence that we have (Bartram et al., 2017). When a history is written, it is not simply a copy of the past (Stoel et al., 2017). As noted above, historians ask questions about the past, search for and evaluate the available evidence to answer these questions, and write a narrative that provides a causal structure and meaning to the sequence of events wherein they selectively choose to emphasize only those events that they consider to be significant and contribute to the overall meaningful narrative. This description shows that a history is not comparable to an unedited video recording that captures everything but provides no explanatory narrative. Rather, it is more comparable to a documentary film that is created by selecting slices of video that are particularly informative and arranging these slices into an effective sequence that mirrors an interpretive narrative that tells a story.

One succinct way to summarize the foregoing account of the components of historical reasoning competence is to say that it "presents disciplinary reading as an analytic process that involves questioning the reliability and probity of texts, corroborating sources with other pieces of evidence, and weaving an intertextual understanding of the past that takes into account its foreignness and unfamiliarity" (Reisman, 2015, p. 2). When historians, teachers, and students develop this kind of understanding of the nature of historical reasoning competence, they have the kind of epistemological understanding needed to effectively engage in historical inquiry (Stoel et al., 2017).

THE DEVELOPMENT OF HISTORICAL REASONING COMPETENCE

As the previous section demonstrates, historical competence is far more than being able to regurgitate the names and dates of historical events in some already defined period of history (e.g., the Renaissance). Unfortunately, until recently, most achievement tests of history primarily focused on factual knowledge. Even so, a widely publicized statistic in the early 1980s showed that the majority of graduating 12th graders in the United States could not report the dates of the U.S. Civil War. Such findings prompted the Secretary of Education at that time (William Bennett) to pen a now infamous document, titled "A Nation at Risk," in which he referred to the "rising tide of mediocrity" in U.S. schooling. Many have disagreed with the assessment that being unable to recall such facts is as problematic as such critics had alleged. Rather, they argue that it is more worrisome that students cannot engage in more important, higher-level forms of historical reasoning.

For example, we can once again turn to the NAEP reports (a.k.a. the Nation's Report Card) and its familiar performance levels of below basic, basic, proficient, and advanced. The latest NAEP for history was conducted in 2018 and assessed the skills of fourth and eighth graders. Whereas it may be aspirational to hope that eighth graders would all demonstrate the advanced level, it is not too much to ask that they demonstrate the "solid" (NAEP's term) performance indicative of the proficient level (*https://nces. ed.gov/nationsreportcard/ushistory/achieveall.aspx#grade12*):

> Eighth-grade students performing at the Proficient level should be able to explain the significance of people, places, events, ideas, and documents, and to recognize the connection between people and events within historical contexts. They should understand and be able to explain the opportunities, perspectives and challenges associated with a diverse cultural population. They should incorporate geographic, technological, and other considerations in their understanding of events and should have knowledge of significant political ideas and institutions. They should be able to communicate ideas about historical themes while citing evidence from primary and secondary sources to support their conclusions.

Results showed that 34% of U.S. eighth graders performed at the below basic level, 50% performed at the basic level, and only 15% performed at or above the proficient level. So, once again the education system in the United States is not instilling such hoped-for skills.

As for more specific components of historical reasoning competence such as understanding historical significance, the interpretive nature of historical inquiry, the reliability of evidence, corroboration, and so on, history education researchers seem to be arguing against themselves. On the one hand, there is a consensus that prior generations of history researchers were too reliant on Piagetian notions (see Chapter 3) and failed to realize that young children are far more capable of understanding historical concepts than Piaget claimed (Barton & Avery, 2016; Barton & Levstik, 1996). On the other hand, most studies that tried to create instructional techniques to teach students who were 10-years-old or younger ideas such as historical significance, historical timelines, reliability of evidence, the interpretative nature of historical narratives and so on have not met with a great deal of success (de Groot-Reuvekamp, Ros, & van Boxtel, 2018; Seixas, 1994; VanSledright, 2014). Even high school students have difficulty understanding the reliability of sources and how to integrate across sources (Reisman, 2012; Rentala & van den Berg, 2015; Wiley et al., 2020).

Much of what gets in the way of promoting the kinds of competencies described in this chapter is epistemological in nature. That is, children have a difficult time understanding the interpretative nature of historical narratives and assume that if two accounts differ in primary source documents, one account must be wrong and the other is right. A little later, they come to assume that everything is relative, and it is not possible to find out what actually happened (i.e., all historical accounts are biased). Finally, with much scaffolding students in middle and high school can come to understand the true nature of historical reasoning (Reisman, 2012; Reisman et al., 2019; Rentala & van den Berg, 2015; VanSledright & Maggione, 2016). Children also fall prey to presentism and anachronistic thinking.

But epistemological issues are only part of the problem, given that measures of epistemology only correlate an average of $r = .16$ with achievement (Greene, Cartiff, & Duke, 2018). At a more basic level, large numbers of studies show that children do not seem to apprehend time as an abstract dimension until they are at least 7 or 8 years old (McCormack, 2015). For example, although they can correctly distinguish between events that happened recently (e.g., their own birthdays) and events that happened further in the past (Christmas), they are unable to engage in a similar kind of proportional thinking when gauging events that will happen in the future. Such findings suggest that children do not seem to have a mental spatial timeline that integrates the past, present, and future along a single trajectory the way adults do (D'Argembeau et al., 2015; McCormack, 2015). Similarly, the fact that children can sort pictures into appropriate piles or broad categories (e.g., "happened long ago" vs. "more recent") by relying on the clothing of those pictured (Barton & Levstik, 1996) does not mean they can interpret an historical timeline as a *representation* of history nor understand why the events on the timeline are significant or part of an interpretative causal story. Similarly, although 5-year-olds perform well on intuitive psychology tasks, suggesting they have some ability to engage in cognitive empathy (see Chapter 13), that is not the same as getting inside the mind of an historical character to understand how that individual thought about some issue at the time.

IMPLICATIONS FOR EDUCATION

In many respects, history educators face some of the same dilemmas that confront science educators (see Chapter 13). Whereas there are some studies that suggest younger students are capable of more competence than we gave them credit for in the past, other studies suggest that the core skills in each domain are easier to develop after age 9 or 10 than before those ages. It is interesting as well that the percentages of 12th graders attaining the proficient level are comparable for both NAEP for science (i.e., 20%) and NAEP for history (16%). In the United States, moreover, whereas third-grade teachers report that they spend an average of around 10 hours per week teaching language arts and 6 hours per week teaching mathematics, they report spending only 3 hours per week on social studies and 3 hours on science. In the eighth grade, the figures are 6.5 on language arts, 5 hours on mathematics, 4 on social studies, and 4 on science (Hoyer & Sparks, 2017). Perhaps part of the reason why children struggle learning the modern conceptions of science and history is that school curricula focus less on these subjects than reading or math, especially in the earlier grades.

Although various reform movements in both science and history call for a great reduction in the number of facts presented to children and an increased focus on a smaller number of "big ideas" or themes, it is not at all clear that such calls have actually been heeded by textbook publishers, authors of state-mandated curriculums, or teachers in contemporary science or history classrooms. Perhaps that is why the percentages of students attaining the proficient level on the NAEP for history has changed little between 1994 when new teaching standards were proposed and now. The original standards that were proposed in 1994 created a storm and were met with fierce opposition by conservative voices such as Lynne Cheney (wife of former Vice President Dick Cheney) and radio host Rush Limbaugh (Nash, 2004), who strongly disagreed with the idea that heroic narratives about key figures (e.g., Christopher Columbus, George Washington) should be counterbalanced by more problematic truths associated with the lives of these individuals (e.g., large-scale death of the original inhabitants of Hispaniola when Columbus "discovered America"; Washington owned slaves). In response to the firestorm, the 1994 standards were subsequently revised and promulgated in 1996.

The 1996 standards proposed that instruction should be focused around five interconnected dimensions of historical thinking: (1) chronological thinking, (2) historical comprehension, (3) historical analysis and interpretation, (4) historical research capabilities, and (5) historical issues (*https://phi.history.ucla.edu/nchs/historical-thinking-standards*). *Chronological thinking* is the ability to recognize the sequence of historical events and, as noted earlier, is a prerequisite for considering the causal relations between earlier and later events. Children below the middle school grades are encouraged to read engaging historical narratives to get a sense of chronology; students in middle school and high school are encouraged to create their own representational timelines. *Historical comprehension* is also argued to be facilitated by providing engaging historical narratives that require the ability to recognize the motives, intentions, hopes, and fears of key historical figures. While students engage their cognitive empathy skills reading such works, teachers are encouraged to help students avoid presentism. Connor et al. (2017) showed that an innovative, technology-based approach to personalizing reading instruction for children not only increased their social studies and science knowledge, it also improved their overall reading comprehension skills. Thus, carefully designed instruction based in narratives could be a good way to improve the historical skills of younger children.

To overcome the tendency to think that there is a single settled account of some historical event, *historical analysis and interpretation skills* should be developed by having students read, critique, compare, and reconcile multiple primary and secondary sources. If this is done properly, students will come to understand that

> written history is a dialogue among historians, not only about what happened but about why and how events unfolded. The study of history is not only remembering answers. It requires following and evaluating arguments and arriving at usable, even if tentative, conclusions based on the available evidence. (1996 Standards)

Fostering *historical research capabilities* might evoke the most interest in students, since they get to "do history" or "act like a practicing historian." Students can be encouraged to ask questions such as who produced a document and why; what contextual factors of that time period are important to understand when interpreting the document; and what is the evidence of the authenticity and credibility of the document. The final aspect proposed by the authors of the 1996 standards, *historical issues,* pertains to the dilemmas facing historical figures, the decisions they made, and decisions they did not make but could have made. Values and moral issues often arise in such discussions.

As should become clear, teaching in ways consistent with these five standards requires a level of skill, epistemological insight, and disciplinary knowledge that few teachers may have, especially elementary school teachers, who tend to be generalists rather than experts with degrees in history or history education. If mandated curricula also foster the older style of lecturing about historical periods and requiring that students read textbooks that likewise present lots of detail and a particular "accepted" narrative, it may be difficult for teachers to change their ways. Moreover, it may be difficult to disabuse students of the idea that history merely records what happened in a direct and complete way and may make it hard for them to understand ideas such as the unreliability of evidence, need to corroborate evidence, and interpretive role of historians. In addition, history shows that proposed changes in the curriculum have provoked some of the strongest reactions from parents and politicians (Nash, 2004; Thornton, 2017). When students learn about two sides of the same story (e.g., about the Manifest Destiny of White settlers moving out to the western frontier of the United States versus the perspective of Native Americans who were displaced when this occurred), parents and politicians may object that the information is too negative or gloomy (Nash, 2004). Furthermore, "acting like an historian" as described above may require much more time than is allotted each week, even in eighth grade (4 hours).

To help overcome the difficulties of implementing history instruction that is more consistent with the 1996 standards, a number of researchers have developed new curricular materials and professional development for teachers. As one example, consider the Reading Like an Historian (RLH) curriculum of Reisman (2012). The RLH curriculum is designed to be a radical departure from traditional textbook-driven instruction; it uses a new activity structure called the document-based lesson, in which students use their background knowledge to critique, ask questions about, and then reconcile, historical accounts from multiple texts. The instructional materials include multiple primary source documents plus scaffolds for students as they engage in forms of interrogation and reconciling of the multiple texts. In particular, in line with Vygotskian theory (see Chapter 3), teachers are trained to model and explicitly name and explain four history-specific reading strategies for students (sourcing, contextualization, corroboration, and close reading). Then teachers ask students to engage in guided practice in small groups where students try out the strategies as the teacher facilitates and scaffolds. Finally, students are asked to engage in independent practice of the strategies on their own. Each document-based lesson further consists of four components in which students develop background knowledge through reading or teacher lectures, then they are presented with a central research question to guide their investigations (e.g., "Why did the Homestead strike of 1892 turn violent?"), then they examine and critique historical documents using the four strategies (sourcing, contextualization, corroboration, and close reading), and finally engage in discussion and argumentation. Prior to implementing the RLH curriculum during an academic year, teachers attended a 4-day training session and received follow-up coaching several times during the year. Teachers promised to use the RLH curriculum at least 50% of the time in their history lessons.

Teachers in five high schools were randomly assigned to either the RLH curriculum or the business-as-usual (control) classrooms. After 6 months of implementation, the performance of students receiving the RLH curriculum was compared to that of students in control classrooms on four outcome measures: (1) students' historical thinking, (2) their ability to transfer historical thinking strategies to contemporary issues, (3) their mastery of factual knowledge; and (4) their growth in general reading comprehension. Results showed that students in the RLH classrooms significantly outperformed students in the control classrooms on all four measures.

While these results are encouraging and demonstrate how it is important for researchers to create the conditions for change through the provision of materials and professional development for teachers, it is not entirely clear how to alter instruction in the elementary and middle school grades where researchers have not been as successful implementing the changes based on the 1996 standards (VanSledright, 2014). What may be needed is the strategy adopted by curriculum designers of reform mathematics and science instruction (see Chapters 12 and 13). In other words, history educators could ask: what prerequisite skills and activities might lay the foundation for students' understanding of the core second-order concepts of historical significance, the reliability of sources, corroboration, the difference between primary and secondary sources, contextualization, empathy, historical timelines, and the difference between the past and history? If students have trouble understanding what historical significance may mean for an event such as the U.S. Civil War or the Emancipation Proclamation, could they be made to understand it using a more familiar recent event in their lives? Similarly, could they be made to understand the concept of "evidence" using concrete materials about familiar experiences (e.g., who spilled milk in the cafeteria) wherein some forms of evidence are more diagnostic than others?

As for understanding timelines, de Groot-Reuvekamp et al. (2018) created a curriculum called Timewise for children in grades 2 and 5 in the Netherlands. The curriculum contains specific objectives for each lesson, as well as activities to accomplish these goals. For example, children are regularly asked in each lesson to arrange pictures in chronological order into four boxes named "a very long time ago," "a long time ago," "not so long ago," and "our times." With comparable props, stories, pictures, and videos, lessons have the four primary objectives of (1) teaching them the vocabulary of time, (2) placing objects, situations, events, and people on a timeline, (3) identifying the characteristics of historical eras, and (4) comparing and contrasting different historical periods. Results showed that children randomly assigned to the Timewise curriculum performed significantly better than children enrolled in control classrooms on posttests of the ability to construct timelines.

Thus, it is possible to reform instruction in different grades to improve performance in the manner of Reisman (2012), Connor et al. (2017), and de Groot-Reuvekamp et al. (2018). However, it is only when reformed curricula for elementary, middle, and high school students are created, aligned, and articulated that we can have any hope that more than 16% of U.S. students will demonstrate the proficient level of performance on the NAEP. More importantly, it is also only when history can be fully integrated with social studies content from anthropology, archaeology, economics, geography, history, law, philosophy, political science, psychology, religion, and sociology that we will have hope that the vast majority of graduates of high schools in the United States will become active, empathic, and culturally sensitive citizens.

PART IV
Conclusions

CHAPTER 15

Putting It All Together

AN OPPORTUNITY–PROPENSITY MODEL
OF ACHIEVEMENT

Having described the nature and development of six domain-general cognitive skills in Chapters 3–8 (e.g., memory, motivation, self-regulation) and six domain-specific cognitive skills in Chapters 9–14 (e.g., reading, writing, math), we are now in a position to come back full circle to a unifying principle that was mentioned in Chapter 1: all of the topics discussed in Chapters 3–14 were included in this book because they provide a partial answer to the question, "Why are some children more likely to demonstrate higher levels of achievement than others on end-of-year assessments?" In other words, the topics in Chapters 3–14 can be thought of as a list of factors that collectively predict which children in a classroom will learn the most over an academic year.

To see why it would be useful for teachers, parents, and policymakers to have such a list, we can make a medical analogy. In the field of epidemiology, researchers often begin to solve a health problem by first following a sample of people longitudinally and seeing if these people have certain characteristics that make them particularly prone to develop a condition such as heart disease over time (e.g., their diet, amount of exercise, weight, and so on). If the predictors are "malleable" (i.e., people can change this factor), recommendations then ensue to make changes so that high-risk people do not develop the disease. For example, once epidemiologists discovered that limited exercise, diets high in saturated fats, and obesity predicted heart disease, recommendations soon followed that people could

avoid getting heart disease if they exercised more, took cholesterol medicines to counteract the effects of saturated fats (or limited saturated fats in
their diet), and lost weight.

But it is also true that it is not only important to create such a list; it is
also necessary to put all of the factors together into a coherent story that
explains how all of the factors work together to produce different levels
of achievement (Byrnes, 2020). In the remainder of this chapter, a model
that coherently integrates the literature on the predictors of academic
achievement is described: the *opportunity–propensity (O-P) model*. We
will see how the predictors mentioned in Chapters 3–14 promote achievement, but we will also see that it is important to introduce several additional important predictors in the model beyond those discussed so far.
Because the predictors of Chapters 3–14 have been already described in
detail, they will be only briefly reintroduced in this chapter in terms of
their place in the model and how they promote achievement. More space
will be devoted to the factors that have not already been introduced in
previous chapters.

THE O-P MODEL OF ACHIEVEMENT

The O-P framework was originally proposed by me and my colleagues in
the mid to late 2000s (Byrnes & Miller, 2007; Byrnes & Wasik, 2009;
Jones & Byrnes, 2006). These researchers relied on four sources of existing evidence and theories to construct and revise the current iteration. The
first source was the scholarly literature on academic achievement. The goal
was to locate all variables identified by educational psychologists, developmental psychologists, teacher education scholars, and educational policy
scholars as being predictive of achievement.

The second source was multivariate longitudinal studies in which
researchers attempted to predict achievement in particular subject areas in
later grades from a set of variables assessed in earlier grades (e.g., Aunola,
Leskinen, Lerkkanen, & Nurmi, 2004; Duncan et al., 2007; Fuchs et al.,
2008; Geary, 2011). These studies were extremely useful not only for identifying consistent sets of predictors, but also for showing the relative importance of predictors that remained significant after all other predictors were
included in the model.

The third basis of model development were existing comprehensive
models that were constructed by other research groups. Rather than reinvent the wheel, O-P researchers considered whether models such as (1) Carroll's (1963) model of school learning, (2) Walberg's theory of educational
productivity (Parkerson, Lomax, Schiller, & Walberg, 1984; Young, Reynolds, & Walberg, 1996), and (3) Cronbach and Snow's (1977) aptitude
× treatment interactions (ATIs) theory (as updated in Corno et al., 2002)

contained all of the identified factors and arranged them in a chronological and interconnected manner.

The fourth source was, unexpectedly, Gottfredson and Hirschi's (1990) self-control theory of crime that specifies that crime occurs when individuals not only have the opportunity to commit a crime, but also when they are prone to engage in the criminal behavior. Gottfredson and Hirschi argued that many people have the opportunity to commit crimes, but only some people take advantage of that opportunity. Hence, the self-control theory is an O-P model. At the same time that the O-P model of achievement was initially being constructed, I was also conducting a parallel line of research on adolescent risk-taking and recognized how Gottfredson and Hirshi's model could be extended and modified to explain not only risk-taking but also academic achievement as well. It was fortuitous that, at that time, both the self-control theory (Gottfredson & Hirschi, 1990) and the updated ATI account (Corno et al., 2002) identified the construct of *propensity* as a powerful determinant of behavior in classrooms and other contexts.

With these four sources in mind, my colleagues and I considered various possible ways to organize all the identified predictors of achievement into a single model that attempted to describe how these predictors related to each other and to achievement (Byrnes, 2020). The Walberg model had considerable merit for identifying nine categories of predictors but did not specify how the predictors related to each other, nor did the model arrange the factors in a chronological order that fully specified how certain predictors mediated between other predictors to affect levels of achievement. The other existing comprehensive models also targeted key factors but did not include the full set of 20 predictors that have been identified to date, nor did these models arrange the factors in a chronological and proposed causal order. In any event, the task became one of considering ways to build on prior attempts that actually identified variables that correlated with skill development, include more factors that these models excluded, and arrange the factors in a way that could predict developmental changes in skills and propensities.

After initial tentative models were constructed, my colleagues and I (and other groups of researchers who subsequently adopted the O-P model) then conducted a number of multivariate studies to see which predictors remained significant after controls and which dropped out because they were found to be spurious (e.g., Baten & DeSoete, 2018; Byrnes & Miller-Cotto, 2016; Morgan, Farkas, Hillemeier, & Maczuga, 2016; Ribner, Harvey, Gervais, & Fitzpatrick, 2019; Sackes, Trundle, Bell, & O'Connell, 2011; Wang, Shen, & Byrnes, 2013). After identifying these nonspurious predictors, O-P theorists then tested proposed relationships among these predictors using hierarchical regression, structural equation modeling, and hierarchical linear modeling. The original version and current iteration of the model are shown in Figures 15.1 and 15.2.

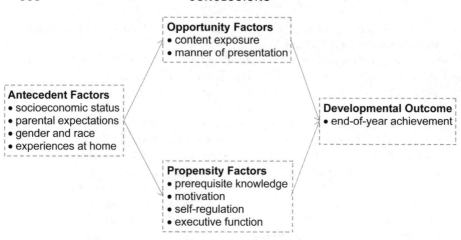

FIGURE 15.1. The original O-P model.

To understand how the distilled factors were eventually organized into a coherent model that effectively captured their interrelationships, it is helpful to note that the O-P model, like any other model, has both metatheoretical and theoretical aspects. At the metatheoretical level, model building began by asking the question "At any given time (e.g., the end of an academic year), why do some children show a higher level of skill in some domain than others?" After due consideration of prior theories and

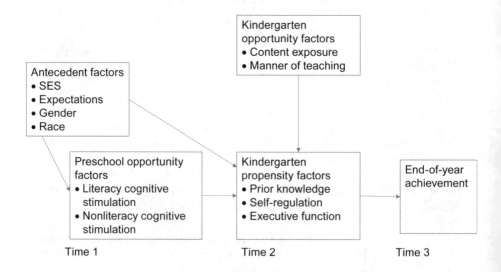

FIGURE 15.2. Current iteration of the O-P model.

multiple literatures, the original answer provided by O-P theorists was, "Those with higher levels of skill were given more high-quality opportunities to learn these skills and were more prone to take advantage of these opportunities." Note that this answer represented one of the first attempts at synthesizing the normally distinct literatures of (1) educational policy scholars who emphasize the construct of *educational opportunity,* and (2) applied developmental psychologists, educational psychologists, and special education faculty who study personal characteristics of children that make them likely to benefit (or not) from educational opportunities (i.e., propensities). But this synthesis also incorporated the basic O-P premise of the self-control theory of crime that was extended, by analogy, to explain the development of academic skills.

In the O-P model, *opportunity factors* were defined as aspects of learning contexts at home and school that promote skill acquisition such as content exposure (*what* content is taught or presented) and evidence-based teaching methods (*how* this content is taught) (Byrnes & Miller, 2007; Byrnes & Wasik, 2009; Byrnes et al., 2018). Defined as such, learning contexts would include classrooms, parents reading books to their children, trips to museums, and so on (any context in which children have the opportunity to learn something). This part of the model demonstrates the alignment of the O-P model with the educational policy literature that emphasizes educational opportunities but also extends these accounts by including contexts beyond schools and classrooms. It also aligns with the teacher education literatures and ATI model that attempt to describe characteristics of instruction that matter. In Chapters 3–14, we saw that there were direct implications for what parents and teachers can do to create better learning opportunities at home and school to promote skills in children. We will briefly revisit these opportunity (instructional) factors again in the next section of this chapter.

Propensity factors, in contrast, are defined as characteristics of children that make them prone to acquire skills in these contexts such as existing domain-specific knowledge (e.g., math or science skills), motivation, executive function, intelligence, and self-regulation. In other words, propensity factors are the key child-level variables described in Chapters 3–14. This part of the model focusing on propensity factors shows the alignment with the educational and developmental psychology literatures. This book so far has primarily placed a strong emphasis on describing propensity factors, but each chapter also described the implications for instruction (or opportunity factors) as well. We will also briefly revisit the propensity factors again in the next section.

The model further assumes that *opportunity factors and propensity factors are both necessary conditions for knowledge growth.* In the case of school-related skills, for example, children will only show high levels of achievement if they are not only exposed to the content required on end-of-year assessments in an effective manner (the opportunity condition), but they are also willing and able to benefit from these learning opportunities (the propensity condition). The inclusion of the propensity condition shows that the O-P model extends beyond the traditional explanations of educational policy scholars who tend to only emphasize educational opportunities (e.g., Guiton & Oakes, 1995; Palardy, Rumberger, & Butler, 2015). It is also consistent with the key premise of ATI scholars, especially in their proposal that propensity can be considered a form of *readiness to benefit from instruction* (Corno et al., 2002). The O-P model builds on this premise by identifying additional aspects of propensity than those identified by ATI scholars and embedding these variables in a larger model that specifies chronological and mediational relationships among the full set of factors.

But to fully account for achievement and include additional variables identified in multiple literatures, it is necessary to ask a follow-up question to the answer provided to the first question above: "Why are some children exposed to more learning opportunities than other children, and, when they are, why are they more willing and able to benefit from these opportunities?" *Antecedent factors* are variables that provide answers to these questions. These factors include socioeconomic status (SES), gender, race/ethnicity, and parental expectations for their children's education. By including variables in all three of the antecedent, opportunity, and propensity categories, the model effectively integrates across the scholarly literatures of educational psychologists, developmental psychologists, teacher education faculty, and educational policy faculty. In the next section, we will consider these factors a little more fully given that they have not been considered so far in this book.

Beyond identifying nonspurious predictors and categorizing them into the three categories of antecedent, opportunity, and propensity factors, however, several further steps are required to explain achievement and gain insight into how and when to intervene. The first additional step would be to arrange the predictors into a hypothesized network that takes causal sequences and temporal precedence into account (e.g., Figures 15.1 and 15.2). Implicit in the two questions that guided the development of the antecedent, opportunity, and propensity categories is the idea that antecedent factors operate earlier in time than opportunity and propensity factors. So, for example, higher-SES families can afford to move to neighborhoods with schools that have effective teachers and a curriculum aligned with the instructional principles advocated in this book. Hence, the antecedent factor SES was originally alleged to precede and lead to exposure to high-quality instruction (an opportunity factor). And scholars who study the effects of gender and race (antecedent factors) on achievement often argue that even children in the same classrooms are not afforded the same learning opportunities by teachers because of culturally determined racial and gender biases (Minor, 2015; Tate, 1997). Teachers might favor, call on, praise, and hold higher expectations of students of certain demographic categories (e.g., White males).

In the same way that the model assumes that antecedent factors operate earlier in time than opportunity factors and propensity factors, it further assumes that opportunity factors and propensity factors operate earlier in time than end-of-year achievement. Thus, antecedent factors such as SES operate at Time Period 1 (e.g., birth to age 5), opportunity factors and propensity factors operate at Time Period 2 (e.g., across the kindergarten year), and the outcome is measured at Time 3 (at the end of the kindergarten year).

Statistically, the model that has been described so far implies that variations in antecedent factors (e.g., lower vs. higher SES) *should lead to variations in both the levels of opportunity factors* (e.g., lower-quality vs. higher-quality instruction) *and levels of propensity factors* (e.g., lower vs. higher levels of prerequisite skills at school entry). *Variations in opportunity and propensity factors, in turn, should lead to variations in the level of skill at the end of the academic year.*

The third step in constructing O-P models, beyond distilling the set of nonspurious predictors, placing them into the three categories, and arranging them in a chronological and hypothesized causal sequence, is to appeal to theoretical accounts as to *why* each of the variables in the categories is predictive of achievement and in what manner. Otherwise the model would lack coherence and be merely an eclectic mixture of factors. We will discuss the explanatory role of each factor in the next section.

THE ROLE OF ANTECEDENT, OPPORTUNITY, AND PROPENSITY FACTORS IN PROMOTING ACHIEVEMENT

Given the temporal sequence assumed in the model (i.e., that antecedent factors beget opportunities and propensities, and opportunities and propensities, in turn, promote achievement), we can begin by first considering how antecedent factors play a role in promoting achievement and then briefly consider the theorized role of opportunity and propensity factors. Antecedent factors were also not given much attention in earlier chapters, so we give them their due consideration next.

Antecedent Factors

As noted above, the O-P model assumes that antecedent factors are variables that are likely to explain two outcomes: (1) why some children are exposed more often to high-quality learning opportunities than other children and (2) why some children are more prone to benefit from high-quality learning opportunities because they enter these opportunities with higher levels of propensities. To illustrate how antecedent variables could produce both outcomes, consider two hypothetical first graders named Emma and Olivia (the top two baby names for girls in 2014). We do a little investigating and find out that Emma attends an elementary school in which her teachers implement many of the reformed ways of teaching mentioned in this book and are also good classroom managers. We also find out that prior to first grade, Emma's parents read many different books to her, spent a lot of time having conversations with her, and took her to places such as museums and the zoo. Emma attended both a preschool and a kindergarten where she learned some academic skills but also got a sense of what it is like to participate in classroom settings.

Olivia, in contrast, attends a school in which her first-grade teachers teach in the traditional ways and sometimes use faulty classroom-management strategies. In addition, prior to first grade, her parents read to her only a few times a week using a smaller number of books. They also conversed with her less often and did not take her to visit museums and other places such as the zoo. Olivia did not go to preschool but did enroll in kindergarten at her local public school.

How might we explain Emma's and Olivia's different levels of exposure to high-quality learning opportunities at home and school? According to the O-P model (and the *family investment model* of Vasilyeva, Dearing, Ivanova, Shen, and Kardinova [2018]), three antecedent variables—*family SES, parental beliefs,* and *parental teaching behaviors*—play an important role (Byrnes, 2020; Wang et al., 2013). Family SES, but in particular parental education level, is associated with parental beliefs about the kinds of skills that their children need to learn prior to school and their parental role as provider of information and enrichment experiences (Vasilyeva et al., 2018). The income component of SES, however, is more related to having the means to afford (1) houses in neighborhoods associated with top-performing schools, (2) enrichment materials such as books and computer games, and (3) the tuition for private preschool programs. When we investigate further, we discover that Emma came from a family in which her parents had a higher income and attained higher education levels than Olivia's parents.

Because of such differences in educational opportunities, we investigate further and find out that Emma entered first grade already knowing how to read and count to 50, seemed really interested in learning, and showed a high level of self-regulation (i.e., could pay attention, avoid distractions, and exercise self-control over her behavior). Olivia, in contrast, could not read when she entered first grade but did know most of the letters of the alphabet and could count to 10. She seemed fairly interested in learning, but sometimes had trouble paying attention or staying in her seat. In other words, Emma entered first grade with a higher level of readiness to learn the content presented in first grade. How might we explain such different levels of readiness to learn in Emma and Olivia?

Once again, we can turn to the three antecedent variables of family SES, parental beliefs, and parental teaching behaviors. Because Emma's parents thought it important to get her cognitively ready for school and to deal with the classroom environment, they read to her, played math games with her, conversed with her, and took her to museums and the zoo. They also put her in both preschool and kindergarten so that she could learn self-regulatory behaviors in classroom settings. In sum, then, the model assumes that antecedent factors explain why children such as Emma and Olivia come to first grade with differing levels of readiness, but could also explain a widening achievement gap between Emma and Olivia (if that occurred) between each successive grade level because, in our example, Emma is exposed to a higher-quality education than Olivia in elementary school.

Opportunity Factors

However, a number of studies conducted by O-P scholars and other research groups suggest that low-income and high-income children do not seem to be exposed to vastly different classroom environments. As noted above, O-P models have been examined using hierarchical regression (e.g., Byrnes, 2003), structural equation modeling (e.g., Byrnes & Wasik, 2009; Wang et al., 2013; Wang & Fitzpatrick, 2019), and hierarchical linear modeling (e.g., Byrnes & Miller-Cotto, 2016; Morgan et al., 2016). The data have derived from individual classrooms (Auxter, 2016; Ding, Byrnes, & Ke, in preparation; Jones & Byrnes, 2006), large-scale national studies such as the NAEP (Byrnes, 2003), the National Educational Longitudinal Study of 1988 (NELS:88; Byrnes & Miller, 2007), the Early Childhood Longitudinal Study—Kindergarten (ECLS-K; Byrnes & Wasik, 2009; Byrnes & Miller-Cotto, 2016), the 2011 ECLS-K (Byrnes et al., 2018; Byrnes et al., 2019), the Early Childhood Longitudinal Study—Birth Cohort (Wang et al., 2013), and several smaller studies (N's of 100–600 students) conducted in Massachusetts (Star et al., 2015), Quebec (i.e., the Quebec Longitudinal Study of Child Development; Ribner et al., 2019), Flanders (Baten & deSoete, 2018), and China (Ding et al., in preparation).

In every case, regardless of the different ages involved (preschoolers, kindergarteners, third graders, fifth graders, and high school students), measures used, analytic strategy used, and content areas (reading, math, science, history, vocabulary), *the strongest predictor of later achievement has been the knowledge and skills that children bring to a grade at the start of a year.* This finding is consistent with the findings of Walberg and colleagues (e.g., Parkerson et al., 1984). The next strongest predictors have been three other propensity factors (working memory, self-regulation, and perceived competence/interest) and one of the antecedent factors (SES). In a typical O-P study in which 50–70% of the variance in end-of-year achievement is explained, opportunity (instructional) factors only account for about 2–5% of the variance when other factors are controlled. Again, these findings are consistent with those of Walberg and colleagues (e.g., Parkerson et al., 1984) but also the findings of ATI studies (Cronbach & Snow, 1977; Gage, 2009) and other researchers (Hanselman, 2018; Yeh, 2017).

This somewhat surprising finding regarding the strong roles of propensity factors and SES, on the one hand, and seemingly inconsequential role of instruction, on the other, runs contrary to the beliefs of most nonscientists (e.g., parents) and policymakers who seem to think that achievement hinges almost exclusively on the quality of instruction (Tyack & Cuban, 1995; Yeh, 2017). That is, when achievement data show that one school has substantially higher achievement scores than another school, nonscientists assume that this difference must be due to the fact that the higher-achieving school has better teachers. *The results of many O-P studies, however, suggest that the higher-performing schools had more affluent, more knowledgeable, and more motivated students to begin with.* This is why the arrow (pathway) pointing from the antecedent box in Figure 15.1 has been dropped from the original model to the revised model shown in Figure 15.2. It does not appear that higher-income children are exposed to higher-quality teaching environments than low-income children (otherwise the path from antecedent to opportunity would be statistically significant).

What does this mean? In order for opportunity factors to emerge as significant predictors of achievement, variation in opportunity factors (e.g., from low-quality to high-quality instruction) has to correspond with variation in achievement. In other words, there has to be significant and systematic covariation between opportunity factors and achievement. However, sufficient covariation will only emerge if there is sufficient variance in both opportunity factors and achievement. By "variance" we mean teachers of high-income children cover different content and do so in different ways than teachers of low-income children.

There are several sources of evidence that suggest there is insufficient variation in standard instructional practice to currently detect an effect for instruction. With the exception of Jones and Byrnes (2006), Auxter (2016), and Ding et al. (in preparation), who measured quality of instruction by observing teachers in their classrooms, in other O-P studies large numbers of teachers reported on what content they presented and their style of instruction by way of questionnaires. There is a strong tendency for teachers to overreport their use of particular behaviors for reasons including misunderstanding questions, recall issues, and social desirability (Camburn, Han, & Sebastian, 2017; Mayer, 1999). Overreporting the frequency of behaviors should lead to a statistical problem called "restriction of range," which in turn would lower covariation and correlations.

In addition, however, there is evidence that *teaching is a deeply engrained cultural activity that becomes slowly internalized as teachers participate themselves in classrooms as students for at least 16 years.* In video studies, researchers have noticed the striking within-nation similarity of teaching styles (Stigler, Gallimore, & Hiebert, 2000). This finding is corroborated in questionnaire studies as well. Byrnes and Miller-Cotto (2016) showed that the amount of variance in self-reported teaching behaviors was considerably smaller than the variance in propensity factors or SES. So, variance seems to be already small due to cultural effects and it is probably reduced further by overreporting on questionnaires.

One further constraining source on teaching variance is very likely the use of common textbooks and mandated curricula in school systems. Teachers who follow textbooks and curricula closely would tend to look very similar at least in terms of content coverage. Byrnes and Miller-Cotto (2016) found that teachers of low-performing students reported that they frequently presented essentially the same content as teachers of high-performing students (i.e., they did not modify their presentations to the level of their students). What is worse, some studies have shown that teachers often present material that many students have already mastered, such as colors, shapes, and print concepts in kindergarten (Byrnes et al., 2018; Engle, Claessens, & Finch, 2013). Yeh (2017) argued that most estimates from value-added models suggest that the contribution of individual teachers to achievement is "not distinguishable from zero."

The lack of variance problem may be more of a statistical issue than a problem of lack of influence per se. Imagine the hypothetical case in which all teachers in a study taught the same content in an effective manner. Teaching would not emerge as a significant predictor because of the lack of variance but such a finding would not mean that teaching had no effect. The fact that teachers exposed children to content and children learned this content means that teaching had an effect. The only alternative to recognizing the necessity of content exposure is a form of nativism in which the theorist believes children were born with the knowledge assessed on achievement tests.

In addition, *the findings from most of the O-P studies pertain to what teachers in the United States say they ordinarily do, as they enact culturally internalized teaching norms and a mandated curriculum.* This standard way of teaching has been dubbed "business-as-usual" instruction. The variance accounted for by teaching variables would probably be higher if comparisons were made between teachers whose instruction was transformed via effective professional development interventions to implement powerful methods that derive from the principles of cognitive science. We have seen such differences emerge in previous chapters. Moreover, in their review of randomized control experiments designed to improve the math skills of low-income children, Wang, Firmender, Power, and Byrnes (2016) found that many programs produce effect sizes near $d = 1.0$ compared to business-as-usual instruction. Some of these programs were comprehensive curricula such as the Building Blocks math curriculum coupled with professional development (Clements, Sarama, Wolfe, & Spitler, 2013) but some only involved children playing a specially designed board game three times a week (Ramani & Siegler, 2008). If researchers were to examine the effects of such instructional approaches within an O-P study, the amount of variance explained by instruction would likely increase. This is an empirical question that is open to refutation. There is some optimism for a stronger role for instruction given the amount of IES funding spent on RCTs to promote the use of techniques based on the principles of modern cognitive and motivational science. At this writing, IES has already funded 139 RCTs just within the Cognition and Student Learning program (*https://ies.ed.gov/ funding/grantsearch/index.asp*).

We have repeatedly seen in this book that most teachers engage in the standard, business-as-usual approaches that they themselves learned rather than use the various new ways to teach reading, math, writing, science, and history that are (1) advocated in this book, (2) based on principles of cognitive science, and (3) endorsed by major teacher education and policy organizations such as the NCTM, the NRC, and the NCSS.

Thus, whereas prior studies conducted by O-P scholars and other research groups have not found a strong effect for opportunity factors, that does not mean a stronger effect will not be found if teachers adopt some of the teaching approaches presented in this book that are grounded in principles of cognitive and motivational science. Indeed, a recent cross-cultural O-P study conducted in China and the United States found that instruction grounded in rich worked-examples and prompts for deep explanations explained 16% of the variance in children's understanding of the inverse relationship between arithmetic operations after controlling for pretest understanding of inverses (Ding et al., in preparation). This is over eight times the amount of variance found in other O-P studies in which most teachers engaged in business-as-usual teaching. If additional studies show comparably strong effects for instruction grounded in cognitive science and only schools serving the highest-income children adopt these new, more powerful approaches, then the arrow that was dropped from the original model in Figure 15.1 may have to be reinstated in Figure 15.2. That would obviously be an undesirable outcome because it would mean income would be not only associated with the skills children bring to school, but also associated with access to a higher-quality instructional environment.

Propensity Factors

Since teachers currently do not differ very much in their instructional approaches and content coverage, it stands to reason that the only source of achievement differences that appear on end-of-year tests are the propensities that children bring with them to the classroom at the start of the academic year. In other words, some children start out ahead and end up still ahead at the end of the year. But the role of propensities in producing individual and group differences in achievement needs to be understood in two ways. *The first way is to recognize that antecedent variables produce differences in propensities that are evident from the start of first grade* (Byrnes, 2020). Because of the similarity of teaching styles and content coverage among teachers, the size of the gap between low-income and high-income children in their propensities does not appear to grow in size between 1st and 12th grades (thankfully). Rather, the gaps are comparable at each grade level. Figure 15.3 illustrates this phenomenon for reaching achievement in grades 1–3. Notice how the gaps between the lines stay about the same size rather than increase over time (an effect size of about d = 0.30 between each quartile for family SES) and that the gap between the top 25% for family income (the richest families) and bottom 25% (the poorest families) remains at a large but constant d = 1.0. *What this means, of course, is that if the United States were to create highly effective universal preschool and kindergarten programs, the gaps would not emerge in the first place and instructional interventions would not be needed in later grades to eliminate the gaps.*

The second way to understand the role of propensity factors is to say that they mediate the role of instruction. What does mediation mean? Let's

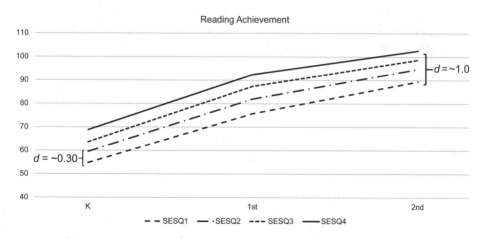

FIGURE 15.3. Evidence of achievement gaps at the beginning of kindergarten that stay fairly constant over time rather than widening. SEQ1 = bottom 25% in terms of family SES (low-income families); SESQ2 = next higher 25% for family SES; SESQ3 = next higher 25% for family SES; SESQ4 = top 25% for family SES (highest income families). Data from a secondary analysis of publically available ECLS-K 2011 database.

again return to our two hypothetical students Emma and Olivia. As we saw when we examined Piaget's theory, expertise theory, and Vygotsky's theory in Chapter 3, the amount and kind of knowledge that students have in their heads determines what they attend to in a lesson, how they process and understand the information, and how much is remembered. Using the famous example of chessboards when expertise theory was discussed, let's say that when Emma and Olivia are 10 years old, Olivia is a novice chess player and Emma is an expert chess player. When Olivia, the novice, is shown a chessboard from an actual game in which 15 chess pieces are arranged on the board in a meaningful way (e.g., three moves away from checkmate), she will only be able to correctly place five to six of the pieces back where they were on the board after she is asked to replicate the arrangement of pieces from memory. Emma, the expert, on the other hand, will be able to "chunk" the arrangement of pieces into a single meaningful whole and rearrange all 15 of the pieces back to their positions. *So, both are presented with the same information, but they process the information in different ways and therefore show different memories.* This example shows how level of expertise (knowledge) can mediate what is learned or remembered from a situation. If we think of classroom lessons taught by a teacher in reading, math, science, and history as comparable to chessboards presented to children, we can begin to understand how the propensities in children's heads mediate what they learn. This explains why the (bolded) arrow from first-grade opportunity factors (instruction) in Figure 15.2 passes to the propensity oval first before passing on to later achievement by way of the propensity oval (also a bolded arrow). The indirect relationship of passing through propensity factors is what is meant by mediation.

So, briefly, how do all the propensity factors in this book mediate the information presented by teachers in their lessons? Let's examine them one by one:

- *Knowledge at the start of the year (Chapters 3, 4, 7, 9–14).* We already saw above how chess knowledge can mediate what is learned or remembered about a situation. But in a similar way, the reading, writing, math, science, and history knowledge that children have at the start of the year is the assimilative base on which new knowledge is built. In other words, students who know more at the start of the year will learn more. Existing knowledge is the strongest predictor of the set of propensity factors and accounts for about 40–50% of the variance in achievement when all other predictors are controlled (Byrnes, 2020).

- *Motivation (Chapter 5).* Motivation is assumed to affect what is attended to in a lesson, how engaged students are in learning, and how long they persist in the face of difficulties (Carroll, 1963; Corno et al., 2002;

Eccles et al., 2003; Wentzel & Wigfield, 2009). If two students start the year with the same level of initial skill but one is more highly motivated, the more motivated student should show higher levels of skill at the end of the year. Motivational variables such as interest and self-efficacy account for about 10–15% of the variance in end-of-year achievement when other predictors (including prior knowledge) are controlled (Byrnes, 2020).

- *Executive function (Chapter 6).* The theoretical case for why executive function (EF) would predict achievement has been made difficult by the fact that EF has been defined in a variety of ways using different measures that vary in their psychometric properties (Müller & Kerns, 2015). The most common models of EF assume that it consists of three component abilities: working memory, cognitive flexibility, and inhibition. There have been inconsistencies across studies with respect to which of these components of EF are the most predictive (Müller & Kerns, 2015). Some have argued that the WM component acts like a bottleneck filter that determines how much information children can attend to and store (Alloway & Alloway, 2010). Others have argued that the ability to shift attention or inhibit incorrect responses should also promote skill development and memory retrieval (Müller & Kerns, 2015). O-P and other longitudinal studies have shown that WM accounts for about 10% of the variance in end-of-year achievement with other variables controlled (Byrnes, 2020; Peng et al., 2016).

- *Self-regulation (Chapter 6).* Measures of self-regulation show that it, too, is predictive of achievement, but the theoretical case for its role is also made difficult by the fact that it, too, has been defined and measured in a variety of ways. Some equate it with EF (Langner et al., 2018), others equate it with emotion regulation (Eisenberg & Zhou, 2016), others equate it with behavioral self-control (Nigg, 2017), and still others equate it with the tendency to plan, be strategic, and monitor performance (Schunk & Zimmerman, 2013). A number of O-P studies have found that a measure of self-regulation called "approaches to learning" is the second strongest predictor after prior knowledge (Byrnes, 2020). The approach to learning variable pertains to teacher ratings of a child's ability to pay attention, inhibit inappropriate behaviors (e.g., sit still, obey classroom rules), and be engaged in learning.

- *Intelligence, aptitude, expertise (Chapter 7).* With all other variables controlled, measures of IQ explain about 8% of the variance (or less) in achievement (Sternberg et al., 2001). It is not clear how predictive aptitude is since so few studies have measured it in ways that are independent of prior achievement or general intelligence. But Gettinger (1984) reported that a few studies have found that measures of "time to learn" predict achievement over and above measures of IQ. As for expertise, its predictive value was described above in terms of the powerful role of prior knowledge.

Having more prior knowledge also means you will not have to rely so much on WM to process classroom material.

• *Spoken language competence (Chapter 8).* We saw in Chapter 8 that spoken language competence is the foundation on which reading skills develop. This close connection between spoken language and reading is confirmed in studies supporting the simple view of reading. One additional obvious form of evidence that shows the importance of spoken language competence to achievement is the finding that children who are English learners (ELs) have a particularly difficult time adjusting to school and acquiring the skills they need to be successful. The reader can imagine themselves sitting in a classroom in which the teacher is presenting material in a language that is unfamiliar to them to get a sense of how language is a filter and similar to prior knowledge in terms of how it can affect how well and how easily the information is processed. As a further illustration, consider the gaps in math achievement shown in Figure 15.4, in which children who were native-English speakers were compared to children who were designated by their schools as "limited English proficient" (LEP) and spent one academic year in a program to support their English learning (LEP-1), and children who spent 2 years in programs for LEP students (LEP-2). As can be seen, the gap between native-English speakers and LEP-2 children at the start of kindergarten in math skills was preexisting and fairly large ($d = 0.71$). By the end of second grade, however, the gap narrowed somewhat to $d = 0.56$, but that is still a worrisome gap in terms of size.

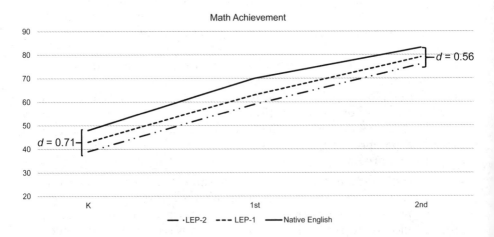

FIGURE 15.4. Math achievement in grades K–3 by English language proficiency. LEP-2 = children designated as LEP and received services for 2 years; LEP-1 = children designated as LEP and received services for 1 year. Data from a secondary analysis of publically available ECLS-K 2011 database.

Interdependence among Factors

A final point about the variables in the antecedent, opportunity, and propensity factors is that they are often interdependent and correlated with each other. For example, we have already seen how SES is associated with reading and math achievement, but it is also associated with all other subject areas and entering levels of executive function, self-regulation, and spoken language competence. To illustrate one case, in preparation for writing this chapter, I conducted a secondary analysis of the publicly available ECLS-K 2011 dataset and found that the effect size between the average WM scores of children in the top and bottom quartiles for SES at the start of kindergarten was $d = 0.66$; for self-regulation (approaches to learning) it was $d = 0.29$. Other studies have shown that low-income children are already behind higher-income children in their spoken language skills by age 4 (Byrnes & Wasik, 2009). There is also a close association between English-language status and SES. My secondary analysis of the ECLS-K 2011 database showed that whereas only 17% of native-English speakers in the sample were in the lowest quartile for SES, the corresponding percentages were 48% for LEP-1 and 65% for LEP-2 (all percentages should have been 25%).

In addition, all the propensity factors mentioned above are correlated with each other $r = .30$ or above. Even math and reading achievement are correlated at the very high level of $r = .70$ and early math skills predict later reading skills (Purpura, Logan, Hassinger-Das, & Napoli, 2017). The latter finding was found to be due to the mediating role of children's mathematical language, which once again implicates the role of spoken language competence. One additional interesting finding is the close association and transactional relationship between WM and academic skills. Math skills in one grade not only predict the level of math skills in the next grade, they also predict WM in the next grade. Similarly, WM in one grade not only predicts WM in the next grade, it also predicts academic skills in the next grade (Miller-Cotto & Byrnes, 2019).

FINAL THOUGHTS AND IMPLICATIONS FOR EDUCATION

We have covered a lot of ground in this book and the implications of the findings are manifold. There are too many to discuss in this final brief chapter. To keep the discussion going and hopefully move things forward, the following most important summary implications are offered:

1. It is entirely possible to eliminate achievement gaps through the provision of high-quality preschool programs for low-income children. These

programs should target not only emerging math and reading skills, but also spoken language, WM, and self-regulation skills. All the skills together form the foundation for readiness to learn in school.

2. It is clear from the summary of achievement performance on the NAEP and international assessments that something has to change in instructional practices to increase the overall academic competencies of U.S. students. Too many students fail to attain the proficient level in every subject area examined in this book. There is every reason to believe, however, that if instructional practices were to be reformed to be more consistent with the principles of cognitive science as described in this book and we were to become more ambitious in what we expect of students, many more students would attain the proficient level.

3. However, it is extremely important that political barriers to implementing needed reforms be addressed and removed. Many teachers agree that the new ways of teaching described in this book are much needed and sensible, but the reforms are often impeded at the federal, state, local, or even school levels by legislators, policymakers, superintendents, school boards, principals, and parents.

References

Abbott, R. D., & Berninger, V. W. (1993). Structural equation modeling of relationships among developmental skills and writing skills in primary- and intermediate-grade writers. *Journal of Educational Psychology, 85,* 478–508.

Abbott, R. D., Berninger, V. W., & Fayol, M. (2010). Longitudinal relationships of levels of language in writing and between writing and reading in Grades 1 to 7. *Journal of Educational Psychology, 102,* 281–298.

Ackerman, P. L. (1987). Individual differences in skill learning: An integration of psychometric and information processing perspectives. *Psychological Bulletin, 102,* 3–27.

Ackerman, P. L. (2018). Intelligence-as-process, personality, interests, and intelligence-as-knowledge: A framework for adult intellectual development. In D. P. Flanagan & E. M. McDonough (Eds.), *Contemporary intellectual assessment: Theories, tests, and issues* (4th ed., pp. 225–241). New York: Guilford Press.

Adams, M. J. (1990). *Beginning to read: Thinking and learning about print.* Cambridge, MA: MIT Press.

Ahmed, S. F., Tang, S., Waters, N. E., & Davis-Kean, P. (2019). Executive function and academic achievement: Longitudinal relations from early childhood to adolescence. *Journal of Educational Psychology, 111*(3), 446–458.

Ainley, M. (2012). Students' interest and engagement in classroom activities. In S. L. Christenson, A. L. Reschly, & C. Wylie (Eds.), *Handbook of research on student engagement* (pp. 283–302). New York: Springer Science + Business Media.

Ainsworth, S., Welbourne, S., & Hesketh, A. (2016). Lexical restructuring in pre-literate children: Evidence from novel measures of phonological representation. *Applied Psycholinguistics, 37,* 997–1023.

Al Hafid, N., & Christodoulou, J. (2015). Phenylketonuria: A review of current and future treatments. *Translational Pediatrics, 4,* 304–317.

Alba, J. W., & Hasher, L. (1983). Is memory schematic? *Psychological Bulletin, 93*, 203–231.

Alibali, M. W., Knuth, E. J., Hattikudur, S., McNeil, N. M., & Stephens, A. C. (2007). A longitudinal examination of middle school students' understanding of the equal sign and equivalent equations. *Mathematical Thinking and Learning, 9*, 221–246.

Allan, N. P., Hume, L. E., Allan, D. M., Farrington, A. L., & Lonigan, C. J. (2014). Relations between inhibitory control and the development of academic skills in preschool and kindergarten: A meta-analysis. *Developmental Psychology, 50*(10), 2368–2379.

Alloway, T. P., & Alloway, R. G. (2010). Investigating the predictive roles of working memory and IQ in academic attainment. *Journal of Experimental Child Psychology, 106*(1), 20–29.

Ambridge, B., & Lieven, E. (2015). A constructivist account of language acquisition. In B. MacWhinney & W. O'Grady (Eds.), *The handbook of language emergence* (pp. 478–510). New York: Wiley.

Ambridge, B., Pine, J. M., Rowland, C. F., Chang, F., & Bidgood, A. (2013). The retreat from overgeneralization in child language acquisition: Word learning, morphology, and verb argument structure. *WIREs Cognitive Science, 4*, 47–62.

Amlien, I. K., Fjell, A. M., Tamnes, C. K., Grydeland, H., Krogsrud, S. K., Chaplin, T. A., . . . Walhovd, K. B. (2016). Organizing principles of human cortical development—thickness and area from 4 to 30 years: Insights from comparative primate neuroanatomy. *Cerebral Cortex, 26*, 257–267.

Anderman, E. M., & Patrick, H. (2012). Achievement goal theory, conceptualization of ability/intelligence, and classroom climate. In S. L. Christenson, A. L. Reschly, & C. Wylie (Eds.), *Handbook of research on student engagement* (pp. 173–191). New York: Springer.

Anderson, J. R. (1995). *Learning and memory: An integrated approach*. New York: Wiley.

Anderson, J. R. (2014). *Cognitive psychology and its implications* (8th ed.). New York: Worth.

Anderson, J. R., Betts, S., Bothell, D., Hope, R., & Lebiere, C. (2019). Learning rapid and precise skills. *Psychological Review, 126*, 727–760.

Anderson, J. R., Reder, L. M., & Simon, H. A. (1996). Situated learning and education. *Educational Researcher, 25*, 5–11.

Anderson, R. C., Wilson, P. T., & Fielding, L. G. (1988). Growth in reading and how children spend their time outside of school. *Reading Research Quarterly, 23*, 285–303.

Andrews, G., & Moussaumai, J. (2015). Improving children's affective decision making in the Children's Gambling Task. *Journal of Experimental Child Psychology, 139*, 18–34.

Applebee, A. N., Langer, J. A., Mullis, I. V. S., & Jenkins, L. B. (1990). *The writing report card, 1984–1988: Findings from the national assessment of educational progress*. Princeton, NJ: Educational Testing Service.

Arai, M., Nakamura, C., & Mazuka, R. (2015). Predicting the unbeaten path through syntactic priming. *Journal of Experimental Psychology: Learning, Memory, and Cognition, 41*, 482–500.

Aram, D., & Besser-Biron, S. (2017). Parents' support during different writing tasks: A comparison between parents of precocious readers, preschoolers, and school-age children. *Reading and Writing, 30,* 363–386.

Arnold, K. M., Umanath, S., Thio, K., Reilly, W. B., McDaniel, M. A., & Marsh, E. J. (2017). Understanding the cognitive processes involved in writing to learn. *Journal of Experimental Psychology: Applied, 23,* 115–127.

Asadi, I. A., Khateb, A., & Shany, M. (2017). How simple is reading in Arabic?: A cross-sectional investigation of reading comprehension from first to sixth grade. *Journal of Research in Reading, 40,* 1–22.

Ashby, J. (2016). Why does prosody accompany fluency?: Re-conceptualizing the role of phonology in reading. In A. Khateb & I. Bar-Kochva (Eds.), *Reading fluency: Current insights from neurocognitive research and intervention studies* (pp. 65–89). New York: Springer International.

Atkinson, R. C., & Shiffrin, R. M. (1968). Human memory: A proposed system and its control processes. In K. W. Spence & J. T. Spence (Eds.), *The psychology of learning and motivation* (Vol. 2, pp. 89–195). London: Academic Press.

Atwell, N. (1987). *In the middle: Writing, reading, and learning with adolescents.* Portsmouth, NH: Heinemann.

Aunola, K., Leskinen, E., Lerkkanen, M.-L., & Nurmi, J.-E. (2004). Developmental dynamics of math performance from pre-school to Grade 2. *Journal of Educational Psychology, 96,* 699–713.

Austin, E. J., & Saklofske, D. H. (2005). Far too many intelligences?: On the communalities and differences between social, practical, and emotional Intelligences. In R. Schulze & R. D. Roberts (Eds.), *Emotional intelligence: An international handbook* (pp. 107–128). Boston: Hogrefe & Huber.

Auxter, A. E. (2016). *The problem with word problems: An exploratory study of factors related to word problem success.* Dissertation submitted to Temple University, Philadelphia, PA.

Azevedo, F. A. C., Carvalho, L. R. B., Grinberg, L. T., Farfel, J. M., Ferretti, R. E. L., Leite, R. E. P., . . . Herculano-Houzel, S. (2009). Equal numbers of neuronal and nonneuronal cells make the human brain an isometrically scaled-up primate brain. *Journal of Comparative Neurology, 513,* 532–541.

Baddeley, A. D. (1990). *Human memory: Theory and practice.* Boston: Allyn & Bacon.

Baddeley, A., & Hitch, G. (1974). Working memory. *Psychology of Learning and Motivation, 8,* 47–89.

Baker, L. (1984). Spontaneous versus instructed use of multiple standards for evaluating comprehension: Effects of age, reading proficiency, and type of standard. *Journal of Experimental Child Psychology, 38,* 289–311.

Baker, L., & Brown, A. L. (1984). Metacognitive skills and reading. In P. D. Pearson, M. Kamil, R. Barr, & P. Mosenthal (Eds.), *Handbook of reading research* (Vol. 1, pp. 353–394). White Plains, NY: Longman.

Ball, G., Beare, R., & Seal, M. L. (2019). Charting shared developmental trajectories of cortical thickness and structural connectivity in childhood and adolescence. *Human Brain Mapping, 40,* 1–15.

Bandura, A. (1986). *Social foundations of thought and action: A social cognitive theory.* Englewood Cliffs, NJ: Prentice-Hall.

Bandura, A. (2013). The role of self-efficacy in goal-based motivation. In E. A. Locke & G. P. Latham (Eds.), *New developments in goal setting and task performance* (pp. 147–157). London: Routledge.

Bangert-Downs, R. L. (1993). The word processor as an instructional tool: A meta-analysis of word processing in writing instruction. *Review of Educational Research, 63,* 69–93.

Barbieri, C., & Booth, J. L. (2016). Support for struggling students in algebra: Contributions of incorrect worked examples. *Learning and Individual Differences, 48,* 36–44.

Barbieri, C. A., Miller-Cotto, D., & Booth, J. L. (2019). Lessening the load of misconceptions: Design-based principles for algebra learning. *Journal of the Learning Sciences, 28,* 381–417.

Barch, D. M., Harms, M. P., Tillman, R., Hawkey, E., & Luby, J. L. (2019). Early childhood depression, emotion regulation, episodic memory, and hippocampal development. *Journal of Abnormal Psychology, 128,* 81–95.

Barkley, R. A. (2012). *Executive functions: What they are, how they work, and why they evolved.* New York: Guilford Press.

Barkley, R. A. (2015). *Attention-deficit hyperactivity disorder: A handbook for diagnosis and treatment* (4th ed.). New York: Guilford Press.

Barner, D. (2017). Language, procedures, and the non-perceptual origin of number word meanings. *Journal of Child Language, 44*(3), 553–590.

Barrick, M. R., Thurgood, G. R., Smith, T. A., & Courtright, S. H. (2015). Collective organizational engagement: Linking motivational antecedents, strategic implementation, and firm performance. *Academy of Management Journal, 58,* 111–135.

Bartlett, E. (1982). *Children's difficulties in establishing consistent voice and space/time dimensions in narrative text.* Paper presented at the meeting of the American Educational Research Association.

Bartlett, F. C. (1932). *Remembering: A study in experimental and social psychology.* Cambridge, UK: Cambridge University Press.

Barton, K. C., & Avery, P. G. (2016). Research on social studies education: Diverse students, settings, and methods. In C. A. Bell & D. Gitomer (Eds.), *Handbook of research on teaching* (5th ed., pp. 985–1038). Washington, DC: American Educational Research Association.

Barton, K. C., & Levstik, L. S. (1996). "Back when God was around and everything": Elementary children's understanding of historical time. *American Educational Research Journal, 33,* 419–454.

Baten, E., & deSoete, A. (2018). Mathematical (dis)abilities within the opportunity-propensity model: The choice of math test matters. *Frontiers in Psychology, 9,* 1–16.

Bates, E., Bretherton, I., & Snyder, L. (1988). *From first words to grammar: Individual differences and dissociable mechanisms.* New York: Cambridge University Press.

Bauer, P. J., Blue, S. N., Xu, A., & Esposito, A. G. (2016). Productive extension of semantic memory in school-aged children: Relations with reading comprehension and deployment of cognitive resources. *Developmental Psychology, 52,* 1024–1037.

Baumann, J. F. (1981). Effect of ideational prominence on children's reading comprehension of expository prose. *Journal of Reading Behavior, 13,* 49–56.

Baumann, J. F. (1984). The effectiveness of a direct instruction paradigm for teaching main idea comprehension. *Reading Research Quarterly, 20,* 93–115.

Baumann, J. F. (1986). Teaching third-grade students to comprehend anaphoric relationships: The application of a direct instruction model. *Reading Research Quarterly, 21,* 70–90.

Baumeister, R. F., Tice, D. M., & Vohs, K. D. (2018). The strength model of self-regulation: Conclusions from the second decade of willpower research. *Perspectives on Psychological Science, 13,* 141–145.

Beal, C. R. (1990). The development of text evaluation and revision skills. *Child Development, 61,* 247–258.

Beaucage, N., Skolney, J., Hewes, J., & Vongpaisal, T. (2020). Multisensory stimuli enhance 3-year-old children's executive function: A three-dimensional object version of the standard Dimensional Change Card Sort. *Journal of Experimental Child Psychology, 189.*

Bechara, A., Damasio, A. R., Damasio, H., & Anderson S. W. (1994). Insensitivity to future consequences following damage to human prefrontal cortex. *Cognition, 50,* 7–15.

Beck, S. W., Llosa, L., & Fredrick, T. (2013). The challenges of writing exposition: Lessons from a study of ELL and non-ELL high school students. *Reading and Writing Quarterly: Overcoming Learning Difficulties, 29,* 358–380.

Beker, K., van den Broek, P., & Jolles, D. (2019). Children's integration of information across texts: Reading processes and knowledge representations. *Reading and Writing, 32,* 663–687.

Bempechat, J., Jimenez, N. V., & Boulay, B. A. (2002). Cultural-cognitive issues in academic achievement: New directions for cross-national research. In A. C. Porter & A. Gamoran (Eds.), *Methodological advances in cross-national surveys of educational achievement* (pp. 117–149). Washington, DC: National Academies Press.

Ben Zion, D., Nevat, M., Prior, A., & Bitan, T. (2019). Prior knowledge predicts early consolidation in second language learning. *Frontiers in Psychology, 10,* Article 2312.

Benjamin, D. J., Laibson, D., Mischel, W., Peake, P. K., Shoda, Y., Wellsjo, A. S., & Wilson, N. L. (2020). Predicting mid-life capital formation with pre-school delay of gratification and life-course measures of self-regulation. *Journal of Economic Behavior and Organization, 179,* 743–756.

Bennett, J., Hogarth, S., Lubben, F., Campbell, B., & Robinson, A. (2010). Talking science: The research evidence on the use of small group discussions in science teaching. *International Journal of Science Education, 32,* 69–95.

Benton, S. L., Glover, J. A., Kraft, R. G., & Plake, B. S. (1984). Cognitive capacity differences among writers. *Journal of Educational Psychology, 76,* 820–834.

Bercury, K. K., & Macklin, W. B. (2015). Dynamics and mechanisms of CNS myelination. *Developmental Cell, 32,* 447–458.

Bereiter, C., & Scardamalia, M. (1982). From conversation to composition: The role of instruction in a developmental process. In R. Glaser (Ed.), *Advances in instructional psychology* (Vol. 2, 1–64). Hillsdale, NJ: Erlbaum.

Bergey, B. W., Parrila, R. K., Laroche, A., & Deacon, S. H. (2019). Effects of peer-led training on academic self-efficacy, study strategies, and academic performance for first-year university students with and without reading difficulties. *Contemporary Educational Psychology, 56*, 25–39.

Bergold, S., Wirthwein, L., Rost, D. H., & Steinmayr, R. (2017). What happens if the same curriculum is taught in five instead of six years?: A quasi-experimental investigation of the effect of schooling on intelligence. *Cognitive Development, 44*, 98–109.

Berland, L. K., & Reiser, B. J. (2009). Making sense of argumentation and explanation. *Science Education, 93*, 26–55.

Bernacki, M. L., & Walkington, C. (2018). The role of situational interest in personalized learning. *Journal of Educational Psychology, 110*(6), 864–881.

Bernard, S., Mercier, H., & Clément, F. (2012). The power of well-connected arguments: Early sensitivity to the connective because. *Journal of Experimental Child Psychology, 111*(1), 128–135.

Berninger, V. W., Mizokowa, D., & Bragg, R. (1991). Theory-based diagnosis and remediation of writing disabilities. *Journal of School Psychology, 29*, 57–79.

Bertram, C., Wagner, W., & Trautwein, U. (2017). Learning historical thinking with oral history interviews: A cluster randomized controlled intervention study of oral history interviews in history lessons. *American Educational Research Journal, 54*(3), 444–484.

Bertsch, S., Pesta, B. J., Wiscott, R., & McDaniel, M. A. (2007). The generation effect: A meta-analytic review. *Memory and Cognition, 35*, 201–210.

Bingham, G. E., Quinn, M. F., & Gerde, H. K. (2017). Examining early childhood teachers' writing practices: Associations between pedagogical supports and children's writing skills. *Early Childhood Research Quarterly, 39*, 35–46.

Bjork, R. A. (1994). Memory and metamemory considerations in the training of human beings. In J. Metcalfe & A. Shimamura (Eds.), *Metacognition: Knowing about knowing* (pp. 185–205). Cambridge, MA: MIT Press.

Bjork, R. A., Dunlosky, J., & Kornell, N. (2013). Self-regulated learning: Beliefs, techniques, and illusions. *Annual Review of Psychology, 64*, 417–444.

Bjorklund, D. F. (2004). *Children's thinking: Developmental function and individual differences* (4th ed.). Pacific Grove, CA: Brooks/Cole.

Bjorklund, D. F., & Thompson, B. E. (1983). Category typicality effects in children's memory performance: Qualitative and quantitative differences in the processing of category information. *Journal of Experimental Child Psychology, 35*, 329–344.

Blackwell, L. S., Trzesniewski, K. H., & Dweck, C. S. (2007). Implicit theories of intelligence predict achievement across an adolescent transition: A longitudinal study and an intervention. *Child Development, 78*, 246–263.

Blair, K. P., Rosenberg-Lee, M., Tsang, J. M., Schwartz, D. L., & Menon, V. (2012). Beyond natural numbers: Negative number representation in parietal cortex. *Frontiers in Human Neuroscience, 6*, Article 7.

Blakey, E., Matthews, D., Cragg, L., Buck, J., Cameron, D., Higgins, B., . . . Carroll, D. J. (2020). The role of executive functions in socioeconomic attainment gaps: Results from a randomized controlled trial. *Child Development, 91*, 1594–1614.

Bloom, L. (1998). Language acquisition in its developmental context. In W. Damon

(Series Ed.), *Handbook of child psychology: Vol. 2. Cognition, perception, and language* (pp. 309–370). Hoboken, NJ: Wiley.

Bloom, P. (2000). *How children learn the meanings of words.* Cambridge, MA: MIT Press.

Bonny, J. W., & Lourenco, S. F. (2013). The approximate number system and its relation to early math achievement: Evidence from the preschool years. *Journal of Experimental Child Psychology, 114*, 375–388.

Booth, J. L., & Koedinger, K. R. (2012). Are diagrams always helpful tools?: Developmental and individual differences in the effect of presentation format on student problem solving. *British Journal of Educational Psychology, 82*, 492–511.

Booth, J. L., Lange, K. E., Koedinger, K. R., & Newton, K. J. (2013). Using example problems to improve student learning in algebra: Differentiating between correct and incorrect examples. *Learning and Instruction, 25*, 24–34.

Booth, J. L., & Newton, K. J. (2012). Fractions: Could they really be the gatekeeper's doorman? *Contemporary Educational Psychology, 37*, 247–253.

Bornstein, M., & Tamis-LeMonda, C. S. (1989). Maternal responsiveness and cognitive development in children. *New Directions for Child Development, 43*, 49–61.

Borzage, M., Blüm, S., & Seri, I. (2014). Equations to describe brain size across the continuum of human lifespan. *Brain Structure and Function, 219*, 141–150.

Bostwick, K. C. P., Martin, A. J., Collie, R. J., & Durksen, T. L. (2019). Growth orientation predicts gains in middle and high school students' mathematics outcomes over time. *Contemporary Educational Psychology, 58*, 213–227.

Bouchard, T. J. (2018). Hereditary ability: g is driven by experience-producing drives. In R. J. Sternberg (Ed.), *The nature of human intelligence* (pp. 15–29). New York: Cambridge University Press.

Brainerd, C. J., & Reyna, V. F. (2014). Dual processes in memory development: Fuzzy-trace theory. In P. J. Bauer & R. Fivush (Eds.), *The Wiley handbook on the development of children's memory* (pp. 480–512). New York: Wiley Blackwell.

Brainerd, C. J., Reyna, V. F., & Holliday, R. E. (2018). Developmental reversals in false memory: Development is complementary, not compensatory. *Developmental Psychology, 54*, 1773–1784.

Brainerd, C. J., Reyna, V. F., Howe, M. L., & Kingma, J. (1990). The development of forgetting and reminiscence. *Monographs of the Society for Research in Child Development, 55*(3–4), v–93.

Braithwaite, D. W., Pyke, A. A., & Siegler, R. S. (2017). A computational model of fraction arithmetic. *Psychological Review, 124*, 603–625.

Braithwaite, D. W., & Siegler, R. S. (2018). Children learn spurious associations in their math textbooks: Examples from fraction arithmetic. *Journal of Experimental Psychology: Learning, Memory, and Cognition, 44*, 1765–1777.

Braithwaite, D. W., Tian, J., & Siegler, R. S. (2017). Do children understand fraction addition? *Developmental Science, 21*, 1–9.

Bransford, J. D., Brown, A., & Cocking, R. (2000). *How people learn: Brain, mind, experience, and school: Expanded edition.* Washington, DC: National Academies Press.

Breit, M., Brunner, M., & Preckel, F. (2020). General intelligence and specific cognitive abilities in adolescence: Tests of age differentiation, ability differentiation, and their interaction in two large samples. *Developmental Psychology, 56,* 364–384.

Bremner, J. G., Slater, A. M., Hayes, R. A., Mason, U. C., Murphy, C., Spring, J., . . . Johnson, S. P. (2017). Young infants' visual fixation patterns in addition and subtraction tasks support an object tracking account. *Journal of Experimental Child Psychology, 162,* 199–208.

Brenneman, K., Massey, C., Machado, S. F., & Gelman, R. (1996). Young children's plans differ for writing and drawing. *Cognitive Development, 11,* 397–420.

Brez, C. C., Miller, A. D., & Ramirez, E. M. (2016). Numerical estimation in children for both positive and negative numbers. *Journal of Cognition and Development, 17,* 341–358.

Brinch, C. N., & Galloway, T. A. (2012). Schooling in adolescence raises IQ scores. *Proceedings of the National Academies of Science of the USA, 109,* 425–430.

Brod, G., & Shing, Y. L. (2019). A boon and a bane: Comparing the effects of prior knowledge on memory across the lifespan. *Developmental Psychology, 55,* 1326–1337.

Brown, A. L., & Day, J. D. (1983). Macrorules for summarizing texts: The development of expertise. *Journal of Verbal Learning and Verbal Behavior, 22,* 1–14.

Brown, A. L., Day, J. D., & Jones, R. (1983). The development of plans for summarizing texts. *Child Development, 54,* 968–979.

Brown, G. D. A. (1998). The endpoint of skilled word recognition: The ROAR model. In J. L. Metsala & L. C. Ehri (Eds.), *Word recognition in beginning literacy* (pp. 121–138). Mahwah, NJ: Erlbaum.

Brown, R., & Hanlon, C. (1970). Derivational complexity and order of acquisition in child speech. In J. R. Hayes (Ed.), *Cognition and the development of language* (pp. 11–54). New York: Wiley.

Bruner, J. S. (1973). *Beyond the information given: Studies in the psychology of knowing.* New York: Norton.

Brunmair, M., & Richter, T. (2019). Similarity matters: A meta-analysis of interleaved learning and its moderators. *Psychological Bulletin, 145,* 1029–1052.

Bryant, P. E., MacLean, M., Bradley, L., & Crossland, J. (1990). Rhyme and alliteration, phoneme detection, and learning to read. *Developmental Psychology, 26,* 429–438.

Buelow, M. T., & Barnhart, W. R. (2017). The influence of math anxiety, math performance, worry, and test anxiety on the Iowa Gambling Task and Balloon Analogue Risk Task. *Assessment, 24,* 127–137.

Bullock, M., Gelman, R., & Baillargeon, R. (1982). The development of causal reasoning. In W. J. Friedman (Ed.), *The developmental psychology of time* (pp. 209–253). New York: Academic Press.

Burrage, M. S., Ponitz, C. C., McCready, E. A., Shah, P., Sims, B. C., Jewkes, A. M., & Morrison, F. J. (2008). Age- and schooling-related effects on executive functions in young children: A natural experiment. *Child Neuropsychology, 14,* 510–524.

Buss, R. R., Sun, W., & Oppenheim, R. W. (2006). Adaptive roles of programmed cell death during nervous system development. *Annual Review of Neuroscience, 29,* 1–35.

Butterworth, B. (2017). The implications for education of an innate numerosity-processing mechanism. *Philosophical Transactions of the Royal Society of Britain, 373,* 1–16.

Byrnes, J. P. (1992). The conceptual basis of procedural learning. *Cognitive Development, 7,* 235–257.

Byrnes, J. P. (1998). *The nature and development of decision-making: A self-regulation model.* Hillsdale, NJ: Erlbaum.

Byrnes, J. P. (2001). *Minds, brains, and education: Understanding the psychological and educational relevance of neuroscientific research.* New York: Guilford Press.

Byrnes, J. P. (2003). Factors predictive of ethnic differences in mathematics proficiency in White, Black, and Hispanic 12th graders. *Journal of Educational Psychology, 95,* 316–326.

Byrnes, J. P. (2013). *The nature and development of decision-making: A self-regulation model.* Hillsdale, NJ: Erlbaum.

Byrnes, J. P. (2020). The potential utility of an opportunity-propensity framework for understanding individual and group differences in developmental outcomes: A retrospective progress report. *Developmental Review, 56.*

Byrnes, J. P., & Dunbar, K. N. (2014). The nature and development of critical analytical thinking. *Educational Psychology Review, 26,* 477–493.

Byrnes, J. P., & Eaton, J. T. (2020). Educational neuroscience. In R. Sperling, A. Martin, & K. J. Newton (Eds.), *Handbook of educational psychology and students with special needs* (pp. 655–683). New York: Routledge.

Byrnes, J. P., & Miller, D. C. (2007). The relative importance of predictors of math and science achievement: An opportunity–propensity analysis. *Contemporary Educational Psychology, 32,* 599–629.

Byrnes, J. P., & Miller-Cotto, D. (2016). The growth of mathematics and reading skills in segregated and diverse schools: An opportunity–propensity analysis of a national database. *Contemporary Educational Psychology, 46,* 34–51.

Byrnes, J. P., Miller-Cotto, D., & Wang, A. H. (2018). Children as mediators of their own cognitive development: The case of learning science in kindergarten and first grade. *Journal of Cognition and Development, 19*(3), 248–277.

Byrnes, J. P., & Vu, L. (2015). Educational neuroscience: Definitional, methodological, and interpretive issues. *Cognitive Science WIRES, 6,* 221–234.

Byrnes, J. P., Wang, A., & Miller-Cotto, D. (2019). Children as mediators of their own cognitive development in kindergarten. *Cognitive Development, 50,* 80–97.

Byrnes, J. P., & Wasik, B. A. (1991). Role of conceptual knowledge in procedural learning. *Developmental Psychology, 27,* 777–786.

Byrnes, J. P., & Wasik, B. A. (2009). Factors predictive of knowledge growth in mathematics in kindergartners, first graders, and third graders: An opportunity–propensity analysis. *Contemporary Educational Psychology, 34,* 167–183.

Byrnes, J. P., & Wasik, B. A. (2019). *Language and literacy development: What educators need to know* (2nd ed.). New York: Guilford Press.

Cain, K., & Barnes, M. A. (2017). Reading comprehension: What develops and when? In K. Cain, D. L. Compton, & R. K. Parrila (Eds.), *Theories of reading development* (pp. 257–281). Amsterdam, the Netherlands:John Benjamins.

Cain, K. M., & Dweck, C. S. (1995). The relation between motivational patterns and achievement cognitions through the elementary school years. *Merrill–Palmer Quarterly, 41,* 25–52.

Cain, K., Oakhill, J., & Bryant, P. (2004). Children's comprehension ability: Concurrent prediction by working memory, verbal ability, and component skills. *Journal of Educational Psychology, 96,* 31–42.

Camburn, E. M., Han, S. W., & Sebastian, J. (2017). Assessing the validity of an annual survey for measuring the enacted literacy curriculum. *Educational Policy, 31,* 73–107.

Cameron-Faulkner, T. (2014). The development of speech acts. In D. Matthews (Ed.), *Pragmatic development in first language acquisition* (pp. 37–52). Philadelphia:John Benjamins.

Campbell, J. K., O'Rourke, M., & Slater, M. H. (2011). *Carving nature at its joints: Natural kinds in metaphysics and science.* Cambridge, MA: MIT Press.

Canivez, G. L., & Youngstrom, E. A. (2019). Challenges to the Cattell–Horn–Carroll theory: Empirical, clinical, and policy implications. *Applied Measurement in Education, 32,* 232–248.

Cantrell, L., & Smith, L. B. (2013). Open questions and a proposal: A critical review of the evidence on infant numerical abilities. *Cognition, 128,* 331–352.

Caplan, D., & Waters, G. S. (1999). Verbal working memory and sentence comprehension. *Behavioral and Brain Sciences, 22,* 77–126.

Caplan, J. B., Legge, E. L. G., Cheng, B., & Madan, C. R. (2019). Effectiveness of the method of loci is only minimally related to factors that should influence imagined navigation. *Quarterly Journal of Experimental Psychology, 72,* 2541–2553.

Carey, S. (1985). *Conceptual change in childhood.* Cambridge, MA: MIT Press.

Carey, S., & Barner, D. (2019). Ontogenetic origins of human integer representations. *Trends in Cognitive Sciences, 23,* 823–835.

Carlson, S. M., Shoda, Y., Ayduk, O., Aber, L., Schaefer, C., Sethi, A., . . . Mischel, W. (2018). Cohort effects in children's delay of gratification. *Developmental Psychology, 54*(8), 1395–1407.

Carpenter, P. A., & Just, M. A. (1987). *The psychology of reading and language comprehension.* Boston: Allyn & Bacon.

Carpenter, P. A., Miyake, A., & Just, M. A. (1995). Language comprehension: Sentence and discourse processing. *Annual Review of Psychology, 46,* 91–120.

Carretti, B., Cornoldi, C., De Beni, R., & Romano, M. (2005). Updating in working memory: A comparison of good and poor comprehenders. *Journal of Experimental Child Psychology, 91,* 45–66.

Carroll, J. B. (1963). A model of school learning. *Teachers College Record, 64,* 723–733.

Carroll, J. B. (1993). *Human cognitive abilities: A survey of factor analytic studies.* New York: Cambridge University Press.

Carver, C. S., Johnson, S. L., Joormann, J., & Scheier, M. F. (2015). An evolving view of the structure of self-regulation. In G. H. E. Gendolla, M. Tops, & S. L. Koole (Eds.), *Handbook of biobehavioral approaches to self-regulation* (pp. 9–23). New York: Springer.

Castles, E. E. (2012). *Inventing intelligence: How America came to worship IQ.* Santa Barbara, CA: Praeger.

Catania, A. C. (1998). *Learning* (4th ed.). Englewood Cliffs, NJ: Prentice-Hall.

Catania, A. C. (2013). *Learning.* New York: Sloan.

Cauffman, E., Shulman, E. P., Steinberg, L., Claus, E., Banich, M. T., Graham, S., & Woolard, J. (2010). Age differences in affective decision making as indexed by performance on the Iowa Gambling Task. *Developmental Psychology, 46,* 193–207.

Caviola, S., Mammarella I. C., Pastore, M., & LeFevre, J.-A. (2018). Children's strategy choices on complex subtraction problems: Individual differences and developmental changes. *Frontiers in Psychology, 9*(1209), 1–9.

Chall, J. S. (1983). *Stages of reading development.* New York: McGraw-Hill.

Chan, W. W. L., Au, T. K., Lau, N. T. T., & Tang, J. (2017). Counting errors as a window onto children's place-value concept. *Contemporary Educational Psychology, 51,* 123–130.

Cheng, Z.-J. (2012). Teaching young children decomposition strategies to solve addition problems: An experimental study. *Journal of Mathematical Behavior, 31,* 29–47.

Cheung, P., Rubenson, M., & Barner, D. (2017). To infinity and beyond: Children generalize the successor function to all possible numbers years after learning to count. *Cognitive Psychology, 92,* 22–36.

Chi, M. T. H. (2008). Three types of conceptual change: Belief revision, mental model transformation, and categorical shift. In S. Vosniadou (Ed.), *Handbook of research on conceptual change* (pp. 61–82). Hillsdale, NJ: Erlbaum.

Chi, M. T. H., Glaser, R., & Farr, M. J. (Eds.). (1988). *The nature of expertise.* Mahwah, NJ: Erlbaum.

Chomsky, N. (1957). *Syntactic structures.* The Hague, the Netherlands: Mouton.

Chomsky, N. (1959). Review of Skinner's Verbal Behavior. *Language, 35,* 26–58.

Chomsky, N. (1965). *Aspects of the theory of syntax.* Cambridge, MA: MIT Press.

Chomsky, N. (1980). *Rules and representations.* New York: Columbia University Press.

Chomsky, N. (1981). On cognitive structures and their development: A reply to Piaget. In M. Piatelli-Palmerini (Ed.), *Language and learning: The debate between Jean Piaget and Noam Chomsky* (pp. 23–55). Cambridge, MA: MIT Press.

Chow, B. W. Y., McBride-Chang, C., & Burgess, S. (2005). Phonological processing skills and early reading abilities in Hong Kong in Chinese kindergarteners learning to read English as a second language. *Journal of Educational Psychology, 97,* 81–87.

Christenson, S. L., Reschly, A. L., & Wylie, C. (Eds.). (2012). *Handbook of research on student engagement.* New York: Springer Science + Business Media.

Christodoulou, J., Lac, A., & Moore, D. S. (2017). Babies and math: A meta-analysis of infants' simple arithmetic competence. *Developmental Psychology, 53,* 1405–1417.

Chu, J., Rittle, J. B., & Fyfe, E. R. (2017). Diagrams benefit symbolic problem-solving. *British Journal of Educational Psychology, 87,* 273–287.

Cipielewski, J., & Stanovich, K. E. (1992). Predicting growth in reading ability from children's exposure to print. *Journal of Experimental Child Psychology, 54*, 74–89.

Clay, M. (1985). *The early detection of reading difficulties*. Auckland, New Zealand: Heinemann.

Clements, D. H., Sarama, J., Wolfe, C. B., & Spitler, M. E. (2013). Longitudinal evaluation of a scale-up model for teaching mathematics with trajectories and technologies: Persistence of effects in the third year. *American Educational Research Journal, 50*, 812–850.

Clerc, J., Miller, P. H., & Cosnefroy, L. (2014). Young children's transfer of strategies: Utilization deficiencies, executive function, and metacognition. *Developmental Review, 34*, 378–393.

Clifton, C., Jr. (2015). The role of phonology in reading: A selective review. In L. Frazier & E. Gibson (Eds.), *Explicit and implicit prosody in sentence processing: Studies in honor of Janet Fodor* (pp. 161–176). New York: Springer.

Clinton, V., Alibali, M. W., Nathan, M. J. (2016). Learning about posterior probability: Do diagrams and elaborative interrogation help? *Journal of Experimental Education, 84*, 579–599.

Coley, J. D., Arenson, M., Xu, Y., & Tanner, K. D. (2017). Intuitive biological thought: Developmental changes and effects of biology education in late adolescence. *Cognitive Psychology, 92*, 1–21.

Colomé, A., & Noël, M.-P. (2012). One first?: Acquisition of the cardinal and ordinal uses of numbers in preschoolers. *Journal of Experimental Child Psychology, 113*, 233–247.

Common Core State Standards Initiative. (2020). The number system. Retrieved from *www.corestandards.org/Math/Content/NS*.

Connor, C. M., Dombek, J., Crowe, E. C., Spencer, M., Tighe, E. L., Coffinger, S., . . . Petscher, Y. (2017). Acquiring science and social studies knowledge in kindergarten through fourth grade: Conceptualization, design, implementation, and efficacy testing of content-area literacy instruction (CALI). *Journal of Educational Psychology, 109*, 301–320.

Connor, C. M., Morrison, F. J., Fishman, B., Crowe, E. C., Al Otaiba, S., & Schatschneider, C. (2013). A longitudinal cluster-randomized controlled study on the accumulating effects of individualized literacy instruction on students' reading from first through third grade. *Psychological Science, 24*, 1408–1419.

Conway, A. R. A., & Kovacs, K. (2018). The nature of the general factor of intelligence. In R. J. Sternberg (Ed.), *The nature of human intelligence* (pp. 49–63). New York: Cambridge University Press.

Corno, L., Cronbach, L. J., Kupermintz, H., Lohman, D. F., Mandinach, E. B., Porteus, A. W., & Talbert, J. E. (2002). *Remaking the concept of aptitude: Extending the legacy of Richard E. Snow*. New York: Routledge.

Corriveau, K. H., & Kurkul, K. E. (2014). "Why does rain fall?": Children prefer to learn from an informant who uses noncircular explanations. *Child Development, 85*, 1827–1835.

Cowan, N. (2014). Short term and working memory in childhood. In P. J. Bauer & R. Fivush (Eds.), *The Wiley handbook on the development of children's memory* (pp. 202–229). New York: Wiley.

Craik, F. I. M., & Lockhart, R. S. (1972). Levels of processing: A framework for memory research. *Journal of Verbal Learning and Verbal Behavior, 11,* 671–684.

Crain, S., & Thornton, R. (2012). Syntax acquisition. *WIREs Cognitive Science, 3,* 185–203.

Credé, M., Tynan, M. C., & Harms, P. D. (2017). Much ado about grit: A meta-analytic synthesis of the grit literature. *Journal of Personality and Social Psychology, 113,* 492–511.

Creusere, M. A. (1999). Theories of adults' understanding and use of irony and sarcasm: Applications to and evidence from research with children. *Developmental Review, 19,* 213–262.

Cromley, J. G., & Azevedo, R. (2007). Testing and refining the direct and inferential mediation model of reading comprehension. *Journal of Educational Psychology, 99,* 311–325.

Cronbach, L. J., & Snow, R. E. (1977). *Aptitudes and instructional methods: A handbook for research on interactions.* New York: Irvington.

Crowley, R., Bendor, D., & Javadia, A.-H. (2019). A review of neurobiological factors underlying the selective enhancement of memory at encoding, consolidation, and retrieval. *Progress in Neurobiology, 179,* 101615.

Csikszentmihalyi, M., Montijo, M. N., & Mouton, A. R. (2018). Flow theory: Optimizing elite performance in the creative realm. In S. I. Pfeiffer, E. Shaunessy-Dedrick, & M. Foley-Nicpon (Eds.), *APA handbook of giftedness and talent* (pp. 215–229). Washington, DC: American Psychological Association.

Cunningham, S. J., Brebner, J. L., Quinn, F., & Turk, D. J. (2014). The self-reference effect in early childhood. *Child Development, 85,* 808–823.

Cutler, L., & Graham, S. (2008). Primary grade writing instruction: A national survey. *Journal of Educational Psychology, 100*(4), 907–919.

Cutting, L. E., & Scarborough, H. S. (2006). Prediction of reading comprehension: Relative contributions of word recognition, language proficiency, and other cognitive skills can depend on how comprehension is measured. *Scientific Studies of Reading, 10,* 277–299.

D'Argembeau, A., Jeunehomme, O., Majerus, S., Bastin, C., & Salmon, E. (2015). The neural basis of temporal order processing in past and future thought. *Journal of Cognitive Neuroscience, 27,* 185–197.

Daiute, C. (2002). Social relational knowing in writing development. In E. Amsel & J. P. Byrnes (Eds.), *Language, literacy, and cognitive development* (pp. 193–229). Mahwah, NJ: Erlbaum.

Danner, F. (1976). Children's understanding of intersentence organization in the recall of short descriptive passages. *Journal of Educational Psychology, 68,* 174–183.

Davis, C., Fox, J., Patte, K., Curtis, C., Strimas, R., Reid, C., & McCool, C. (2008). Education level moderates learning on two versions of the Iowa Gambling Task. *Journal of the International Neuropsychological Society, 14*(6), 1063–1068.

de Groot-Reuvekamp, M., Ros, A., & van Boxtel, C. (2018). Improving elementary school students' understanding of historical time: Effects of teaching with "Timewise." *Theory and Research in Social Education, 46,* 35–67.

De La Paz, D., & McCutchen, D. (2011). Learning to write. In R. Mayer, & P. Alexander (Eds.), *Handbook of research on learning and instruction* (pp. 32–54). New York: Routledge.

de Silva, P. N. (2018). Do patterns of synaptic pruning underlie psychoses, autism and ADHD? *British Journal of Psychology Advances, 24,* 212–217.

De Visscher, A., & Noël, M.-P. (2014). Arithmetic facts storage deficit: The hypersensitivity-to-interference in memory hypothesis. *Developmental Science, 17,* 434–442.

De Visscher, A., Noël, M.-P., & De Smedt, B. (2016). The role of physical digit representation and numerical magnitude representation in children's multiplication fact retrieval. *Journal of Experimental Child Psychology, 152,* 41–53.

Dehaene, S. (1992). Varieties of numerical abilities. *Cognition, 44,* 1–42.

Dehili, V. M., Prevatt, F., & Coffman, T. P. (2017). An analysis of the Barkley Deficits in Executive Functioning Scale in a college population: Does it predict symptoms of ADHD better than a visual-search task? *Journal of Attention Disorders, 21,* 567–574.

Dempster, F. N. (1992). The rise and fall of the inhibitory mechanism: Toward a unified theory of cognitive development and aging. *Developmental Review, 12,* 45–75.

Dent, A. L., & Koenka, A. C. (2016). The relation between self-regulated learning and academic achievement across childhood and adolescence: A meta-analysis. *Educational Psychology Review, 28,* 425–474.

Deoni, S., Dean. D., Joelson, S., O'Regan, J., & Schneider, N. (2018). Early nutrition influences developmental myelination and cognition in infants and young children. *NeuroImage, 178,* 649–659.

Detterman, D. K. (2014). Introduction to the intelligence special issue on the development of expertise: Is ability necessary? *Intelligence, 45,* 1–5.

Dewitz, P., Carr, E., & Patberg, J. P. (1987). Effects of inference training on comprehension and comprehension monitoring. *Reading Research Quarterly, 22,* 99–121.

DeWolf, M., Bassok M., & Holyoak, K. J. (2015). From rational numbers to algebra: Separable contributions of decimal magnitude and relational understanding of fractions. *Journal of Experimental Child Psychology, 133,* 72–84.

Dimino, J., Taylor, R. M., & Gersten, R. M. (1995). Synthesis of the research on story grammar as a means to increase comprehension. *Reading and Writing Quarterly: Overcoming Learning Difficulties, 11,* 53–72.

Ding, M. (2016). Opportunities to learn: Inverse relations in U.S. and Chinese textbooks. *Mathematical Thinking and Learning, 18,* 45–68.

Ding, M., & Auxter, A. (2017). Children's strategies to solving additive inverse problems: A preliminary analysis. *Mathematics Education Research Journal, 29,* 73–92.

Ding, M., Byrnes, J. P., & Ke, X. (in preparation). *Does instruction grounded in cognitive science promote children's understanding of inverses?: A cross-cultural opportunity-propensity study.*

diSessa, A. A. (2013). A bird's eye view of the "pieces" vs. "coherence" controversy (from the "pieces side of the fence). In S. Vosniadou (Ed.), *International handbook of research on conceptual change* (pp. 31–48). London: Routledge.

Donovan, C. A., & Smolkin, L. B. (2006). Children's understanding of genre and writing development. In C. A. MacArthur, S. Graham, & J. Fitzgerald (Eds.), *Handbook of writing research* (pp. 131–143). New York: Guilford Press.

Dore, J. (1975). Holophrases, speech acts, and language universals. *Journal of Child Language, 2,* 20–40.

Duckworth, A. L., Peterson, C., Matthews, M. D., & Kelly, D. R. (2007). Grit: Perseverance and passion for long-term goals. *Journal of Personality and Social Psychology, 92,* 1087–1101.

Duffy, G., & Roehler, L. (1987). Improving classroom reading instruction through the use of responsive elaboration. *The Reading Teacher, 40,* 514–521.

Duncan, G. J., Dowsett, C. J., Claessens, A., Magnuson, K., Huston, A. C., Klebanov, P., & Japel, C. (2007). School readiness and later achievement. *Developmental Psychology, 43,* 1428–1446.

Durkin, K., & Rittle-Johnson, B. (2015). Diagnosing misconceptions: Revealing changing decimal fraction knowledge. *Learning and Instruction, 37,* 21–29.

Dweck, C. S., & Yeager, D. S. (2019). Mindsets: A view from two eras. Perspectives on *Psychological Science, 14,* 481–496.

Eccles, J., & Wang, M.-T. (2012). Part I commentary: So what is student engagement anyway? In S. L. Christenson, A. L. Reschly, & C. Wylie (Eds.), *Handbook of research on student engagement* (pp. 133–145). New York: Springer Science + Business Media.

Eccles, J. S., & Wigfield, A. (1995). In the mind of the actor: The structure of adolescents' achievement task values and expectancy-related beliefs. *Personality and Social Psychology Bulletin, 21,* 215–225.

Eccles, J. S., Wigfield, A., & Byrnes, J. P. (2003). Cognitive development during adolescence. In R. M. Lerner, A. M. Easterbrooks, & J. Mistry (Eds.), *Handbook of psychology: Vol. 6. Developmental psychology* (pp. 325–350). New York: Wiley.

Eckler, J. A., & Weininger, O. (1989). Structural parallels between pretend play and narratives. *Developmental Psychology, 25,* 736–743.

Edgin, J. O., Spanò, G., Kawa, K., & Nadel, L. (2014). Remembering things without context: Development matters. *Child Development, 85,* 1491–1502.

Edossa, A. K., Neuenhaus, N., Artelt, C., Lingel, K., & Schneider, W. (2018). Developmental relationship between declarative metacognitive knowledge and reading comprehension during secondary school. *European Journal of Psychology of Education, 34,* 397–416.

Ehri, L. C. (1995). Phases of development in learning to read words by sight. *Journal of Research in Reading, 18,* 116–125.

Eisenberg, N., & Zhou, Q. (2016). Conceptions of executive function and regulation: When and to what degree do they overlap? In J. A. Griffin, P. McCardle, & L. S. Freund (Eds.), *Executive function in preschool-age children: Integrating measurement, neurodevelopment, and translational research* (pp. 115–136). Washington, DC: American Psychological Association.

Elman, J. L., & McRae, K. (2019). A model of event knowledge. *Psychological Review, 126,* 252–291.

Engelhardt, L. E., Mann, F. D., Briley, D. A., Church, J. A., Harden, K. P., & Tucker-Drob, E. M. (2016). Strong genetic overlap between executive functions and intelligence. *Journal of Experimental Psychology: General, 145*(9), 1141–1159.

Engle, M., Claessens, A., & Finch, M. A. (2013). Teaching students what they already know?: The (Mis)alignment between mathematics instructional content and student knowledge in kindergarten. *Educational Evaluation and Policy Analysis, 35,* 157–178.

Englert, C. S., Stewart, S. R., & Hiebert, E. H. (1988). Young writer's use of text structure in expository text generation. *Journal of Educational Psychology, 80,* 143–151.

Ericsson, K. A. (1996). *The road to excellence: The acquisition of expert performance in the arts, science, sports, and games.* Mahwah, NJ: Erlbaum.

Ericsson, K. A. (2014). Why expert performance is special and cannot be extrapolated from studies of performance in the general population: A response to criticisms. *Intelligence, 45,* 81–103.

Escorcia, D., Passerault, J.-M., Ros, C., & Pylouster, J. (2017). Profiling writers: Analysis of writing dynamics among college students. *Metacognition and Learning, 12,* 233–273.

Espy, K. A. (Ed.). (2016). The changing nature of executive control in preschool. *Monographs of the Society for Research in Child Development, 81,* 1–179.

Etchell, A., Adhikari, A., Weinberg, L. S., Choo, A. L., Garnett, E. O., Chow, H. M., & Chang, S.-E. (2018). A systematic literature review of sex differences in childhood language and brain development. *Neuropsychologia, 114,* 19–31.

Eysenck, M. W., & Brysbaert, M. (2018). *Fundamentals of cognition.* New York: Routledge.

Fagginger Auer, M. F., Hickendorff, M., van Putten, C. M., Béguin, A. A., & Heiser, W. J. (2016). Multilevel latent class analysis for large-scale educational assessment data: Exploring the relation between the curriculum and students' mathematical strategies. *Applied Measurement in Education, 29,* 144–159.

Fandakova, Y., & Ghetti, S. (2017). Memory. In B. Hopkins, E. Geangu, & S. Linkenauger (Eds.), *The Cambridge encyclopedia of child development* (2nd ed., pp. 322–329). New York: Cambridge University Press.

Feitelson, D., Tehori, B. Z., & Levinberg-Green, D. (1982). How effective is early instruction in reading?: Experimental evidence. *Merrill-Palmer Quarterly, 28,* 485–494.

Feltovich, P. J., Prietula, M. J., & Ericsson, K. A. (2018). Studies of expertise from psychological perspectives: Historical foundations and recurrent themes. In K. A. Ericsson, R. R. Hoffman, A. Kozbelt, & A. M. Williams (Eds.), *The Cambridge handbook of expertise and expert performance* (2nd ed., pp. 59–83). New York: Cambridge University Press.

Ferreira, A. C., Sousa, N., Bessa, J. M., Sousa, J. C., & Marques, F. (2018). Metabolism and adult neurogenesis: Towards an understanding of the role of lipocalin-2 and iron-related oxidative stress. *Neuroscience and Biobehavioral Reviews, 95,* 73–84.

Ferretti, R. P., & Graham, S. (2019). Argumentative writing: Theory, assessment, and instruction. *Reading and Writing, 32,* 1345–1357.

Ferretti, R. P., Lewis, W. E., & Andrews-Weckerly, S. (2009). Do goals affect the structure of students' argumentative writing strategies? *Journal of Educational Psychology, 101,* 577–589.

Fielding, L. G., Anderson, R. C., & Pearson, P. D. (1990). *How discussion questions influence children's story understanding* (Tech. Rep. No 490). Urbana: University of Illinois, Center for the Study of Reading.

Fine, A. B., & Jaeger, T. F. (2016). The role of verb repetition in cumulative structural priming in comprehension. *Journal of Experimental Psychology: Learning, Memory, and Cognition, 42*(9), 1362–1376.

Fischer, M. H. (2003). Cognitive representation of negative numbers. *Psychological Science, 14,* 278–282.

Fisher, J. S., & Radvansky, G. A. (2018). Patterns of forgetting. *Journal of Memory and Language, 102,* 130–141.

Fisher, J. S., & Radvansky, G. A. (2019). Linear forgetting. *Journal of Memory and Language, 108,* 104035.

Fitzgerald, J. (1987). Research on revision in writing. *Review of Educational Research, 57,* 481–506.

Flynn, J. R. (2018). Intelligence, society, and human autonomy. In R. J. Sternberg (Ed.), *The nature of human intelligence* (pp. 101–115). New York: Cambridge University Press.

Fodor, J. A. (1975). *The language of thought.* Cambridge, MA: Harvard University Press.

Fodor, J. A. (1983). *The modularity of mind.* Cambridge, MA: MIT Press.

Follmer, D. J. (2018). Executive function and reading comprehension: A meta-analytic review. *Educational Psychologist, 53,* 42–60.

Folmer, A. S., Cole, D. A., Sigal, A. B., Benbow, L. D., Satterwhite, L. F., Swygert, K. E., & Ciesla, J. A. (2008). Age-related changes in children's understanding of effort and ability: Implications for attribution theory and motivation. *Journal of Experimental Child Psychology, 99*(2), 114–134.

Fowler, W. (1971). A developmental learning strategy for early reading in a laboratory nursery school. *Interchange, 2,* 106–124.

Foy, J. G., & Mann, V. (2003). Home literacy environment and phonological awareness in preschool children: Differential effects for rhyme and phoneme awareness. *Applied Psycholinguistics, 24,* 59–88.

Franke, K., Luders, E., May, A., Wilke, M., & Gaser, C. (2012). Brain maturation: Predicting individual BrainAGE in children and adolescents using structural MRI. *NeuroImage, 63,* 1305–1312.

Freedman, A. (1987). Development in story writing. *Applied Psycholinguistics, 8,* 153–170.

Friedman, N. P., & Miyake, A. (2017). Unity and diversity of executive functions: Individual differences as a window on cognitive structure. *Cortex: Journal Devoted to the Study of the Nervous System and Behavior, 86,* 186–204.

Fritz, C. O., Morris, P. E., Acton, M., Voelkel, A. R., & Etkind, R. (2007). Comparing and combining retrieval practice and the keyword mnemonic for foreign vocabulary learning. *Applied Cognitive Psychology, 21,* 499–526.

Fuchs, L. S., Compton, D. L., Fuchs, D., Hollenbeck, K. N., Craddock, C. F., & Hamlett, C. L. (2008). Dynamic assessment of algebraic learning in predicting third graders' development of mathematical problem solving. *Journal of Educational Psychology, 100,* 829–850.

Fuchs, L. S., Gilbert, J. K., Fuchs, D., Seethaler, P. M., & Martin, B. N. (2018). Text comprehension and oral language as predictors of word-problem solving:

Insights into word-problem solving as a form of text comprehension. *Scientific Studies of Reading, 22,* 152–166.

Fuhs, M. W., Hornburg, C. B., & McNeil, N. M. (2016). Specific early number skills mediate the association between executive functioning skills and mathematics achievement. *Developmental Psychology, 52,* 1217–1235.

Furtak, E. M., Seidel, T., Iverson, H., & Briggs, D. C. (2012). Experimental and quasi-experimental studies of inquiry-based science teaching: A meta-analysis. *Review of Educational Research, 82,* 300–329.

Fuster, J. M. (1993). Frontal lobes. *Current Opinion in Neurobiology, 3,* 160–165.

Fyfe, E. R., & Rittle-Johnson, B. (2017). Mathematics practice without feedback: A desirable difficulty in a classroom setting. *Instructional Science, 45,* 177–194.

Gaffigan, J. (2013). *Dad is fat.* New York: Crown Archetype.

Gage, N. L. (2009). *A conception of teaching.* New York: Springer.

Gardner, H. (1993). *Multiple intelligences: The theory in practice.* New York: Basic Books.

Garner, R. (1981). Monitoring of passage inconsistency among poor comprehenders: A preliminary test of the "piecemeal processing" explanation. *Journal of Educational Research, 74,* 159–162.

Garner, R. (1987). Strategies for reading and studying expository texts. *Educational Psychologist, 22,* 299–312.

Garner, R., Alexander, P., Slater, W., Hare, V. C., Smith, T., & Reis, R. (1986). Children's knowledge of structural properties of expository text. *Journal of Educational Psychology, 78,* 411–416.

Garrett, M. F. (1990). Sentence processing. In D. N. Osherson & H. Lasnik (Eds.), *An invitation to cognitive science: Vol. 1. Language* (pp. 133–175). Cambridge, MA: MIT Press.

Gathercole, S. E., Pickering, S. J., Ambridge, B., & Wearing, H. (2004). The structure of working memory from 4 to 15 years of age. *Developmental Psychology, 40*(2), 177–190.

Geary, D. C. (2011). Cognitive predictors of individual differences in achievement growth in mathematics: A five-year longitudinal study. *Developmental Psychology, 47,* 1539–1552.

Geary, D. C., & vanMarle, K. (2018). Growth of symbolic number knowledge accelerates after children understand cardinality. *Cognition, 177,* 69–78.

Geary, D. C., vanMarle, K., Chu, F. W., Hoard, M. K., & Nugent, L. (2019). Predicting age of becoming a cardinal principle knower. *Journal of Educational Psychology, 111,* 256–267.

Gedena, M. J., Romero, S. E., & Deshmukh, M. (2019). Apoptosis versus axon pruning: Molecular intersection of two distinct pathways for axon degeneration. *Neuroscience Research, 139,* 3–8.

Gelman, R., & Gallistel, C. R. (1978). *The child's understanding of number.* Cambridge, MA: Harvard University Press.

Gerde, H. K., Bingham, G. E., & Pendergast, M. L. (2015). Reliability and validity of the Writing Resources and Interactions in Teaching Environments (WRITE) for preschool classrooms. *Early Childhood Research Quarterly, 31,* 34–46.

Gernsbacher, M. A. (1996). The Structure-Building Framework: What it is, what it might also be, and why. In B. K. Britton & A. C. Graesser (Eds.), *Models of understanding text* (pp. 289–311). Mahwah, NJ: Erlbaum.

Gernsbacher, M. A., & Kaschak, M. (2013). Text comprehension. In D. Reisberg (Ed.), *The Oxford handbook of cognitive psychology* (pp. 462–474). London: Oxford University Press.

Geshwind, D. H., & Rakic, P. (2013). Cortical evolution: Judge the brain by its cover. *Neuron, 80,* 633–647.

Gettinger, M. (1984). Individual differences in time needed for learning: A review of literature. *Educational Psychologist, 19,* 15–29.

Gibson, D. J., Gunderson, E. A., Spaepen, E., Levine, S. C., & Goldin-Meadow, S. (2019). Number gestures predict learning of number words. *Developmental Science, 22,* 1–9.

Gierhan, S. M. E. (2013). Connections for auditory language in the human brain. *Brain and Language, 127,* 205–221.

Gillespie Rouse, A., Graham, S., & Compton, D. (2017). Writing to learn in science: Effects on grade 4 students' understanding of balance. *Journal of Educational Research, 110*(4), 366–379.

Gilmore, C. K., & Bryant, P. (2008). Can children construct inverse relations in arithmetic?: Evidence for individual differences in the development of conceptual understanding and computational skill. *British Journal of Developmental Psychology, 26,* 301–316.

Giuliani, N. R., & Pfeifer, J. H. (2015). Age-related changes in reappraisal of appetitive cravings during adolescence. *NeuroImage, 108,* 173–181.

Gleitman, L. R. (1990). The structural sources of verb meanings. *Language Acquisition, 1,* 3–55.

Glenberg, A. M., Gutierrez, T., Levin, J. R., Japuntich, S., & Kaschak, M. (2004). Activity and imagined activity can enhance young children's reading comprehension. *Journal of Educational Psychology, 96,* 424–436.

Glover, J. A., Ronning, R. R., & Bruning, R. H. (1990). *Cognitive psychology for teachers.* New York: Macmillan.

Godden, D. R., & Baddeley, A. D. (1975). Context-dependent memory in two natural environments: On land and underwater. *British Journal of Psychology, 66,* 325–331.

Goldman-Rakic, P. S. (1987). Development of cortical circuitry and cognitive function. *Child Development, 58,* 601–622.

Goldstein, D. M. (1976). Cognitive–linguistic functioning and learning to read in preschoolers. *Journal of Educational Psychology, 68,* 680–688.

Gombert, J. E., & Fayol, M. (1992). Writing in preliterate children. *Learning and Instruction, 2,* 23–41.

Gómez, R. L., & Edgin, J. O. (2016). The extended trajectory of hippocampal development: Implications for early memory development and disorder. *Developmental Cognitive Neuroscience, 18,* 57–69.

Gopnik, A., & Wellman, H. M. (2012). Reconstructing constructivism: Causal models, Bayesian learning mechanisms, and the theory theory. *Psychological Bulletin, 138,* 1085–1108.

Gottfredson, L. S. (1997). Mainstream science on intelligence: An editorial with 52 signatories, history and bibliography. *Intelligence, 24,* 13–23.

Gottfredson, M. R., & Hirschi, T. (1990). *A general theory of crime.* Stanford, CA: Stanford University Press.

Gough, P. B., Hoover, W. A., & Peterson, C. L. (1996). Some observations on a simple view of reading. In C. Cornoldi & J. Oakhill (Eds.), *Reading comprehension difficulties: Processes and intervention* (pp. 1–13). Mahwah, NJ: Erlbaum.

Gould, J. M., Smith, P. J., Airey, C. J., Mort, E. J., Airey, L. E., Warricker, F. D. M., . . . Willaime-Morawek, S. (2018). Mouse maternal protein restriction during preimplantation alone permanently alters brain neuron proportion and adult short-term memory. *PNAS Proceedings of the National Academy of Sciences of the USA, 115,* E7398–E7407.

Graesser, A., Golding, J. M., & Long, D. L. (1991). Narrative representation and comprehension. In R. Barr, M. L. Kamil, P. Mosenthal, & P. D. Pearson (Eds.), *Handbook of reading research* (Vol. 2, pp. 171–205). New York: Longman.

Graesser, A. C., Millis, K. K., & Zwaan, R. A. (1997). Discourse comprehension. *Annual Review of Psychology, 48,* 163–189.

Graf, P., & Schacter, D. L. (1985). Implicit and explicit memory for new associations in normal and amnesic subjects. *Journal of Experimental Psychology: Learning, Memory, and Cognition, 11,* 501–518.

Graham, S. (1997). Executive control in the revising of students with learning and writing difficulties. *Journal of Educational Psychology, 89,* 223–234.

Graham, S. (2006). Writing. In P. A. Alexander & P. H. Winne (Eds.), *Handbook of educational psychology* (pp. 457–478). Mahwah, NJ: Erlbaum.

Graham, S., Berninger, V. W., Abbott, R. D., Abbott, S. P., & Whitaker, D. (1997). Role of mechanics in composing of elementary school students: A new methodological approach. *Journal of Educational Psychology, 89,* 170–182.

Graham, S., Capizzi, A., Harris, K. R., Hebert, M., & Morphy, P. (2014). Teaching writing to middle school students: A national survey. *Reading and Writing, 27,* 1015–1042.

Graham, S., Fishman, E. J., Reid, R., & Hebert, M. (2016). Writing characteristics of students with attention deficit hyperactive disorder: A meta-analysis. *Learning Disabilities Research and Practice, 31,* 75–89.

Graham, S., & Harris, K. R. (1996). Self-regulation and strategy instruction for students who find writing and learning challenging. In C. M. Levy & S. Ransdell (Eds.), *The science of writing: Theories, methods, individual differences, and applications* (pp. 347–360). Mahwah, NJ: Erlbaum.

Graham, S., Harris, K. R., Fink-Chorzempa, B., & MacArthur, C. (2003). Primary grade teachers' instructional adaptations for struggling writers: A national survey. *Journal of Educational Psychology, 95,* 279–292.

Graham, S., Liu, X., Aitken, A., Ng, C., Bartlett, B., Harris, K. R., & Holzapfel, J. (2018). Effectiveness of literacy programs balancing reading and writing instruction: A meta-analysis. *Reading Research Quarterly, 53,* 279–304.

Graham, S., Morphy, P., Harris, K. R., Fink-Chorzempa, B., Saddler, B., Moran, S., & Mason, L. (2008). Teaching spelling in the primary grades: A national survey of instructional practices and adaptations. *American Educational Research Journal, 45,* 796–825.

Graham, S., & Perin, D. (2007). *Writing next: Effective strategies to improve writing of adolescents in middle and high schools—A report to Carnegie Corporation of New York.* Washington, DC: Alliance for Excellent Education. Retrieved from *www.carnegie.org/media/filer_public/3c/f5/3cf58727-34f4-4140-a014-723a00ac56f7/ccny_report_2007_writing.pdf.*

Gray, S. A., & Reeve, R. A. (2016). Number-specific and general cognitive markers of preschoolers' math ability profiles. *Journal of Experimental Child Psychology, 147,* 1–21.

Greany, V. (1980). Factors related to amount and time of leisure reading. *Reading Research Quarterly, 15,* 337–357.

Greany, V., & Hegarty, M. (1987). Correlates of leisure-time reading. *Journal of Research in Reading, 10,* 3–20.

Green, L., Fry, A. F., & Myerson, J. (1994). Discounting of delayed rewards: A lifespan comparison. *Psychological Science, 5,* 33–36.

Greene, J. A., Cartiff, B. M., & Duke, R. F. (2018). A meta-analytic review of the relationship between epistemic cognition and academic achievement. *Journal of Educational Psychology, 110,* 1084–1111.

Greenwald, E. A., Persky, H. R., Campbell, J. R., & Mazzeo, J. (1999). *The NAEP 1998 Writing Report Card for the Nation and the States.* Washington, DC: U.S. Department of Education, Office of Educational Research and Improvement, National Center for Education Statistics.

Grice, H. (1975). Logic and conversation. In P. Cole & J. Morgan (Eds.), *Syntax and semantics: Vol. 3. Speech acts* (pp. 41–58). New York: Academic Press.

Guiton, G., & Oakes, J. (1995). Opportunity to learn and conceptions of educational equality. *Educational Evaluation and Policy Analysis, 17,* 323–336.

Gullick, M. M., & Wolford, G. (2013). Understanding less than nothing: Children's neural responses to negative numbers shifts across age and accuracy. *Frontiers in Psychology, 4*(584), 1–17.

Guthrie, J. T., Cox, K. E., Knowles, K. T., Buehl, M., Mazzoni, S. A., & Fasulo, L. (2000). Building toward coherent instruction. In L. Baker, M. J. Dreher, & J. T. Guthrie (Eds.), *Engaging young readers: Promoting achievement and motivation* (pp. 209–236). New York: Guilford Press.

Halliday, S. E., Calkins, S. D., & Leerkes, E. M. (2018). Measuring preschool learning engagement in the laboratory. *Journal of Experimental Child Psychology, 167,* 93–116.

Hamilton, E. W., Nolen, S. B., & Abbott, R. D. (2013). Developing measures of motivational orientation to read and write: A longitudinal study. *Learning and Individual Differences, 28,* 151–166.

Hanselman, P. (2018). Do school learning opportunities compound or compensate for background inequalities: Evidence from the case of assignment to effective teachers. *Sociology of Education, 91,* 132–158.

Hansen, J., & Pearson, P. D. (1983). An instructional study: Improving the inferential comprehension of good and poor fourth-grade readers. *Journal of Educational Psychology, 75,* 821–829.

Harm, M. W., & Seidenberg, M. S. (2004). Computing the meanings of words in reading: Cooperative division of labor between visual and phonological processes. *Psychological Review, 111,* 662–720.

Hart, B., & Risley, T. R. (1995). *Meaningful differences in the everyday experience of young children.* New York: Brookes.

Harter, S. (1981). A new self-report scale of intrinsic versus extrinsic orientation in the classroom: Motivational and informational components. *Developmental Psychology, 17*(3), 300–312.

Hasselhorn, M., & Grube, D. (2003). The phonological similarity effect on memory span in children: Does it depend on age, speech rate, and articulatory suppression? *International Journal of Behavioral Development, 27*, 145–152.

Hast, M. (2018). It's all relative: The role of object weight in toddlers' gravity bias. *Journal of Experimental Child Psychology, 166*, 696–704.

Hattikudur, S., & Alibali, M. W. (2010). Learning about the equal sign: Does comparing with inequality symbols help? *Journal of Experimental Child Psychology, 107*, 15–30.

Hayes, J. R. (1996). A new framework for understanding cognition and affect in writing. In C. M. Levy & S. Ransdell (Eds.), *The science of writing: Theories, methods, individual differences, and applications* (pp. 1–27). Mahwah, NJ: Erlbaum.

Hayes, J. R. (2012). Modeling and remodeling writing. *Written Communication, 29*, 369–388.

Hayes, J. R., & Bajzek, D. (2008). Understanding and reducing the knowledge effect: Implications for writers. *Written Communication, 25*, 104–118.

Hayes, J. R., & Flower, L. S. (1980). Identifying the organization of writing processes. In L. Gregg & E. Steinberg (Eds.), *Cognitive processes in writing: An interdisciplinary approach* (pp. 3–30). Mahwah, NJ: Erlbaum.

Hayes, J. R., & Flower, L. S. (1986). Writing research and the writer. *American Psychologist, 41*, 1106–1113.

Hayes, J. R., Flower, L. S., Schriver, K. S., Stratman, J., & Carey, L. (1987). Cognitive processes in revision. In S. Rosenberg (Ed.), *Advances in psycholinguistics: Vol. 2. Reading, writing, and language processing* (pp. 176–240). New York: Cambridge University Press.

Hedlund, J., & Sternberg, R. J. (2000). Too many intelligences? Integrating social, emotional, and practical intelligence. In R. Bar-On & J. D. A. Parker (Eds.), *The handbook of emotional intelligence: Theory, development, assessment, and application at home, school, and in the workplace* (pp. 136–167). Hoboken, NJ: Jossey-Bass.

Heidekum, A. E., Grabner, R. H., De Smedt, B., De Visscher, A., & Vogel, S. E. (2019). Interference during the retrieval of arithmetic and lexico-semantic knowledge modulates similar brain regions: Evidence from functional magnetic resonance imaging (fMRI). *Cortex, 120*, 375–393.

Heiss, C. N., & Olofsson, L. E. (2019). The role of the gut microbiota in development, function and disorders of the central nervous system and the enteric nervous system. *Journal of Neuroendocrinology, 31*(e12684), 1–11.

Helge, K. (2002). *Quantum generations: A history of physics in the twentieth century* (reprint ed.). Princeton, NJ: Princeton University Press.

Henderson, L., Snowling, M., & Clarke, P. (2013). Accessing, integrating, and inhibiting word meaning in poor comprehenders. *Scientific Studies of Reading, 17*, 177–198.

Henderson, L., Weighall, A., & Gaskell, G. (2013). Learning new vocabulary during childhood: Effects of semantic training on lexical consolidation and integration. *Journal of Experimental Child Psychology, 116*(3), 572–592.

Herculano-Houzel, S. (2017). Numbers of neurons as biological correlates of cognitive capability. *Current Opinion in Behavioral Sciences, 16*, 1–7.

Heyns, B. (1978). *Summer learning and the effects of schooling*. New York: Academic Press.

Hidi, S., & Boscolo, P. (2006). Motivation and writing. In C. A. MacArthur, S. Graham, & J. Fitzgerald (Eds.), *Handbook of writing research* (pp. 144–157). New York: Guilford Press.

Hintzman, D. L. (1986). "Schema abstraction" in a multiple-trace memory model. *Psychological Review, 93,* 411–428.

Hoff, E. (2006). How social contexts support and shape language development. *Developmental Review, 26,* 55–88.

Hoff, E. (2013). *Language development* (5th ed.). Belmont, CA: Wadsworth/Thomson Learning.

Hopper, P. J. (2015). An emergentist approach to grammar. In B. MacWhinney & W. O' Grady (Eds.), *The handbook of language emergence* (pp. 314–327). New York: Wiley.

Horn, J. L., & Noll, J. (1997). Human cognitive capabilities: Gf-Gc theory. In D. P. Flanagan, J. L. Genshaft, & P. L. Harrison (Eds.), *Contemporary intellectual assessment: Theories, tests, and issues* (pp. 53–91). New York: Guilford Press.

Howe, M. L. (2014). The co-emergence of the self and autobiographical memory: An adaptive view of early memory. In P. J. Bauer & R. Fivush (Eds.), *The Wiley handbook on the development of children's memory* (pp. 545–567). New York: Wiley.

Howe, M. L. (2015). Memory development. In L. S. Liben, U. Müller, & R. M. Lerner (Eds.), *Handbook of child psychology and developmental science: Cognitive processes, Volume 2* (7th ed., pp. 203–249). New York: Wiley.

Howe, M. L., Candel, I., Otgaar, H., Malone, C., & Wimmer, M. C. (2010). Valence and the development of immediate and long-term false memory illusions. *Memory, 18,* 58–75.

Howe, L. J., Sharp, G. C., Hemani, G., Zuccolo, L., Richmond, S., & Lewis, S. J. (2019). Prenatal alcohol exposure and facial morphology in a UK cohort. *Drug and Alcohol Dependence, 197,* 42–47.

Hoyer, K. M., & Sparks, D. (2017). Instructional time for third- and eighth-graders in public and private schools: School year 2011–2012. Available at *https://nces.ed.gov/pubsearch/pubsinfo.asp?pubid=2017076.*

Hudson, J. A., & Grysman, A. (2014). Extending the Life of a Memory Effects of Reminders on Children's Long-term Event Memory. In P. J. Bauer & R. Fivush (Eds.), *The Wiley handbook on the development of children's memory* (pp. 255–284). New York: Wiley.

Hunt, K. W. (1970). Syntactic maturity in school children and adults. *Monographs of the Society for Research in Child Development, 35*(134), 1–67.

Huttenlocher, J., Vasilyeva, M., Cymerman, E., & Levine, S. (2002). Language input and child syntax. *Cognitive Psychology, 45,* 337–374.

Huttenlocher, J., Waterfall, H., Vasilyeva, M., Vevea, J., & Hedges, L. V. (2010). Sources of variability in children's language growth. *Cognitive Psychology, 61,* 343–365.

Hyönä, J., Lorch, R. F., & Kaakinen, J. K. (2002). Individual differences in reading to summarize expository text: Evidence from eye fixation patterns. *Journal of Educational Psychology, 94,* 44–55.

Ifrah, G. (1998). *The universal history of numbers.* London: Harvill Press.

Ingels, S. J., & Dalton, B. (2013). *High School Longitudinal Study of 2009 (HSLS:09) First follow-up: A first look at fall 2009 ninth-graders in 2012*

(NCES 2014-360). U.S. Department of Education. Washington, DC: National Center for Education Statistics. Retrieved April 27, 2020, from *http://nces.ed.gov/pubsearch*.

Inhelder, B., & Piaget, J. (1958). *The growth of logical thinking from childhood to adolescence*. New York: Basic Books.

Jackson, N. E. (1992). Precocious reading of English: Origins, structure, and predictive significance. In P. S. Klein & A. J. Tannebaum (Eds.), *To be young and gifted* (pp. 171–203). Norwood, NJ: Ablex.

Jacob, R., & Parkinson, J. (2015). The potential for school-based interventions that target executive function to improve academic achievement: A review. *Review of Educational Research, 85,* 512–552.

Jara-Ettinger, J., Floyd, S., Tenenbaum, J. B., & Schulz, L. E. (2017). Children understand that agents maximize expected utilities. *Journal of Experimental Psychology: General, 146,* 1574–1585.

Jara-Ettinger, J., Piantadosi, S., Spelke, E. S., Levy, R., & Gibson, E. (2017). Mastery of the logic of natural numbers is not the result of mastery of counting: Evidence from late counters. *Developmental Science, 20,* 1–11.

Jarrold, C., Cocksey, J., & Dockerill, E. (2008). Phonological similarity and lexicality effects in children's verbal short-term memory: Concerns about the interpretation of probed recall data. *Quarterly Journal of Experimental Psychology, 61,* 324–340.

Jetha, M. K., & Segalowitz, S. J. (2012). Structural brain development in late childhood, adolescence and early adulthood. In M. K. Jetha & S. J. Segalowitz (Eds.), *Adolescent brain development* (pp. 1–18). New York: Academic Press.

Johnson, M. H. (1997). *Developmental cognitive neuroscience: An introduction*. Cambridge, MA: Blackwell.

Johnson, M. H., & de Haan, M. (2015). *Developmental cognitive neuroscience* (4th ed.). New York: Wiley/Blackwell.

Johnston, P., & Afflerbach, P. (1985). The process of constructing main ideas from text. *Cognition and Instruction, 2,* 207–232.

Jones, K. K., & Byrnes, J. P. (2006). Characteristics of students who benefit from high quality math instruction. *Contemporary Educational Psychology, 31,* 328–343.

Joyce, J. (1914/2014). *Dubliners*. London: Wordsworth.

Jusczyk, P. W. (1997). *The discovery of spoken language*. Cambridge, MA: MIT Press.

Just, M. A., & Carpenter, P. A. (1987). *The psychology of reading and language comprehension*. Boston: Allyn & Bacon.

Kail, R. V., & Ferrer, E. (2007). Processing speed in childhood and adolescence: Longitudinal models for examining developmental change. *Child Development, 78,* 1760–1770.

Kail, R. V., Lervåg, A., & Hulme, C. (2016). Longitudinal evidence linking processing speed to the development of reasoning. *Developmental Science, 19,* 1067–1074.

Kamps, F. S., Julian, J. B., Battaglia, P., Landau, B., Kanwisher, N., & Dilks, D. D. (2017). Dissociating intuitive physics from intuitive psychology: Evidence from Williams syndrome. *Cognition, 168,* 146–153.

Karp, A., & Furinghetti, F. (2016). *History of mathematics teaching and learning achievements, problems, prospects*. New York: Springer.

Karr, J. E., Areshenkoff, C. N., Rast, P., Hofer, S. M., Iverson, G. L., & Garcia-Barrera, M. A. (2018). The unity and diversity of executive functions: A systematic review and re-analysis of latent variable studies. *Psychological Bulletin, 144*(11), 1147–1185.

Kellogg, R. T. (1996). A model of working memory in writing. In C. M. Levy & S. Ransdell (Eds.), *The science of writing: Theories, methods, individual differences, and applications* (pp. 57–72). Mahwah, NJ: Erlbaum.

Kent, S. C., & Wanzek, J. (2016). The relationship between component skills and writing quality and production across developmental levels: A meta-analysis of the last 25 years. *Review of Educational Research, 86,* 570–601.

Kessler, B., & Treiman, R. (1997). Syllable structure and the distribution of phonemes in English syllables. *Journal of Memory and Language, 37,* 295–311.

Kievit, R. A., Lindenberger, U., Goodyer, I. M., Jones, P. B., Fonagy, P., Bullmore, E. T., . . . Dolan, R. J. (2017). Mutualistic coupling between vocabulary and reasoning supports cognitive development during late adolescence and early adulthood. *Psychological Science, 28,* 1419–1431.

Kim, S., Fernandez, S., & Terrier, L. (2017). Procrastination, personality traits, and academic performance: When active and passive procrastination tell a different story. *Personality and Individual Differences, 108,* 154–157.

King, S. (2000). *On writing.* New York: Simon & Schuster.

Kintsch, W. (1982). Text representations. In W. Otto & S. White (Eds.), *Reading expository material* (pp. 87–102). New York: Academic Press.

Kipp, K., Pope, S., & Digby, S. E. (1998). The development of cognitive inhibition in a reading comprehension task. *European Review of Applied Psychology, 48,* 19–25.

Klahr, D., & MacWhinney, B. (1998). Information processing. In W. Damon (Ed.), *Handbook of child psychology: Vol. 2. Cognition, perception, and language* (pp. 631–678). New York: Wiley.

Klauda, S. L., & Guthrie, J. T. (2008). Relationships of three components of reading fluency to reading comprehension. *Journal of Educational Psychology, 100,* 310–321.

Knudson, R. E. (1992). The development of written argumentation: An analysis and comparison of argumentative writing at four grade levels. *Child Study Journal, 22,* 167–181.

Koedinger, K. R., Alibali, M. W., & Nathan, M. J. (2008). Trade-offs between grounded and abstract representations: Evidence from algebra problem solving. *Cognitive Science, 32,* 366–397.

Koponen, T., Aunola, K., & Nurmi, J.-K. (2019). Verbal counting skill predicts later math performance and difficulties in middle school. *Contemporary Educational Psychology, 59.*

Kosovich, J. J., Hulleman, C. S., Barron, K. E., & Getty, S. (2015). A practical measure of student motivation: Establishing validity evidence for the Expectancy–Value–Cost Scale in middle school. *Journal of Early Adolescence, 35,* 790–816.

Kuhn, D. (2011). What is scientific thinking and how does it develop? In U. Goswami (Ed.), *The Wiley–Blackwell handbook of childhood cognitive development* (2nd ed., pp. 497–523). New York: Wiley-Blackwell.

Kuhn, D. (2020). Why is reconciling divergent views a challenge? *Current Directions in Psychological Science, 29,* 27–32.

Kuhn, D., Ramsey, S., & Arvidsson, T. S. (2015). Developing multivariable thinkers. *Cognitive Development, 35,* 92–110.

Kuhn, M. R., & Rasinski, T. V. (2015). Best practices in fluency instruction. In L. M. Morrow & L. B. Gambrell, (Eds.), *Best practices in literacy instruction* (5th ed., pp. 268–287). New York: Guilford Press.

Kyllonen, P. C. (2015). Human cognitive abilities: Their organization, development and use. In L. Corno & E. M. Anderman (Eds.), *Handbook of educational psychology* (pp. 119–134). New York: Routledge.

Langer, J. A. (1986). *Children's reading and writing: Structures and strategies.* Norwood, NJ: Ablex.

Langner, R., Leiberg, S., Hoffstaedter, F., & Eickhoff, S. B. (2018). Towards a human self-regulation system: Common and distinct neural signatures of emotional and behavioural control. *Neuroscience and Biobehavioral Reviews, 90,* 400–410.

Lauren, L., & Allen, L. (1999). Factors that predict success in an early literacy intervention project. *Reading Research Quarterly, 34,* 404–424.

Lawson, G. M., Hook, C. J., & Farah, M. J. (2018). A meta-analysis of the relationship between socioeconomic status and executive function performance among children. *Developmental Science, 21*(2), 1–22.

Lee, J., & Schallert, D. L. (2016). Exploring the reading–writing connection: A year-long classroom-based experimental study of middle school students developing literacy in a new language. *Reading Research Quarterly, 51*(2), 143–164.

Lee, S. J., Brown, R. E., & Orrill, C. H. (2011). Mathematics teachers' reasoning about fractions and decimals using drawn representations. *Mathematical Thinking and Learning, 13,* 198–220.

Lehmann, M. (2015). Rehearsal development as development of iterative recall processes. *Frontiers in Psychology, 6,* 1–14.

Lehrer, R., & Schauble, L. (2015). The development of scientific thinking. In L. S. Liben, U. Müller, & R. M. Lerner (Eds.), *Handbook of child psychology and developmental science: Vol. 2. Cognitive processes* (7th ed., pp. 671–714). New York: Wiley.

Leno, V. C., Chandler, S., White, P., Pickles, A., Baird, G., Hobson, C., . . . Simonoff, E. (2018). Testing the specificity of executive functioning impairments in adolescents with ADHD, ODD/CD and ASD. *European Child and Adolescent Psychiatry, 27*(7), 899–908.

Lensing, N., & Elsner, B. (2018). Development of hot and cool executive functions in middle childhood: Three-year growth curves of decision making and working memory updating. *Journal of Experimental Child Psychology, 173,* 187–204.

Lenz, K., Dreher, A., Holzäpfel, L., & Wittmann, G. (2020). Are conceptual knowledge and procedural knowledge empirically separable?: The case of fractions. *British Journal of Educational Psychology, 90,* 809–829.

Lepper, M. R., Corpus, J. H., & Iyengar, S. S. (2005). Intrinsic and extrinsic motivational orientations in the classroom: Age differences and academic correlates. *Journal of Educational Psychology, 97*(2), 184–196.

Levin, I., & Bus, A. (2003). How is emergent writing based on drawing? Analyses of children's products and their sorting by children and mothers. *Developmental Psychology, 39,* 891–905.

Levine, S. C., Jordan, N. C., & Huttenlocher, J. (1992). Development of calculation abilities in young children. *Journal of Experimental Child Psychology, 53*(1), 72–103.

Levstik, L. S., & Thornton, S. J. (2020). Reconceptualizing history for early childhood through early adolescence. In S. A. Metzger & L. M. Harris (Eds.), *The Wiley international handbook of history teaching and learning* (pp. 473–501). New York. Wiley.

Lewis, S. J., Zuccolo, L., Smith, G. D., Macleod, J., Rodriguez, S., Draper, E. S., . . . Gray, R. (2012). Fetal alcohol exposure and IQ at age 8: Evidence from a population-based birth-cohort study. *PLOS ONE, 7*(e49407), 1–8.

Leyland, A., Rowse, G., & Emerson, L.-M. (2019). Experimental effects of mindfulness inductions on self-regulation: Systematic review and meta-analysis. *Emotion, 19*(1), 108–122.

Lidz, J. (2007). The abstract nature of syntactic representations: Consequences for theories of learning. In E. Hoff & M. Shatz (Eds.), *Blackwell handbook of language development* (pp. 277–303). New York: Blackwell.

Lin, L., Lee, T., & Snyder, L. A. (2018). Math self-efficacy and STEM intentions: A person-centered approach. *Frontiers in Psychology, 9.*

Linderholm, T., & van den Broek, P. (2002). The effects of reading purpose and working memory capacity on the processing of expository text. *Journal of Educational Psychology, 94,* 778–784.

Lindgren, J. (2019). Comprehension and production of narrative macrostructure in Swedish: A longitudinal study from age 4 to 7. *First Language, 39*(4), 412–432.

Lin-Siegler, X., Ahn, J. N., Chen, J., Fang, F.-F. A., & Luna-Lucero, M. (2016). Even Einstein struggled: Effects of learning about great scientists' struggles on high school students' motivation to learn science. *Journal of Educational Psychology, 108,* 314–328.

Lipowski, S. L., Pyc, M. A., Dunlosky, J., & Rawson, K. A. (2014). Establishing and explaining the testing effect in free recall for young children. *Developmental Psychology, 50,* 994–1000.

Liu, D., Wellman, H. M., Tardif, T., & Sabbagh, M. A. (2008). Theory of mind development in Chinese children: A meta-analysis of false-belief understanding across cultures and languages. *Developmental Psychology, 44,* 523–531.

Loban, D. W. (1976). *Language development: Kindergarten through grade twelve* (Research Report No. 18). Urbana, IL: National Council of Teachers of English.

Locke, E. A. (2005). Why emotional intelligence is an invalid concept. *Journal of Organizational Behavior, 26,* 425–431.

Locke, E. A., & Latham, G. P. (2013). Goal setting theory: The current state. In E. A. Locke & G. P. Latham (Eds.), *New developments in goal setting and task performance* (pp. 623–630). New York: Routledge.

Locke, J. L. (1993). *The child's path to spoken language.* Cambridge, MA: Harvard University Press.

Loftus, E. F., & Palmer, J. C. (1974). Reconstruction of auto-mobile destruction: An example of the interaction between language and memory. *Journal of Verbal Learning and Verbal Behavior, 13,* 585–589.

Lombardi, D., Bickel, E. S., Bailey, J. M., & Burrell, S. (2018). High school students' evaluations, plausibility (re)appraisals, and knowledge about topics in Earth science. *Science Education, 102,* 153–177.

Lombardi, D., Nussbaum, E. M., & Sinatra, G. M. (2016). Plausibility judgments in conceptual change and epistemic cognition. *Educational Psychologist, 51,* 35–56.

Lonigan, C. J. (2015). Literacy development. In L. S. Liben, U. Muller (Vol. Eds.) & R. M. Lerner (Ed.-in-Chief), *Handbook of child psychology and developmental science: Vol. 2. Cognitive processes* (pp. 763–805). Hoboken, NJ: Wiley.

Loveless, T. (2013). *How well are American students learning? The 2013 Brown Center Report on American Education.* Washington, DC: Brookings Institution. Available at *www.brookings.edu/wp-content/uploads/2016/06/2013-brown-center-report-web-3.pdf.*

Lupien, S. J., McEwen, B. S., Gunnar, M. R., & Heim, C. (2009). Effects of stress throughout the lifespan on the brain, behaviour and cognition. *Nature Reviews Neuroscience, 10,* 434–445.

Luria, A. R. (1973). *The working brain.* New York: Basic Books.

MacCann, C., Jiang, Y., Brown, L. E. R., Double, K. S., Bucich, M., & Minbashian, A. (2020). Emotional intelligence predicts academic performance: A meta-analysis. *Psychological Bulletin, 146,* 150–186.

Maddox, G. B., Pyc, M. A., Kauffman, Z. S., Gatewood, J. D., & Schonhoff, A. M. (2018). Examining the contributions of desirable difficulty and reminding to the spacing effect. *Memory and Cognition, 46,* 1376–1388.

Magliano, J. P., Trabasso, T., & Graesser, A. C. (1999). Strategic processing during comprehension. *Journal of Educational Psychology, 91,* 615–629.

Magnuson, J. S., Mirman, D., & Myers, E. (2013). Spoken word recognition. In D. Reisberg (Ed.), *Oxford handbook of cognitive psychology* (pp. 412–441). New York: Oxford University Press.

Malachowski, A. (2004). *Pragmatism.* London: SAGE.

Mandler, J. M., & Johnson, N. S. (1977). Remembrance of things parsed: Story structure and recall. *Cognitive Psychology, 9,* 111–151.

Mani, N., & Ackermann, L. (2018). Why do children learn the words they do? *Child Development Perspectives, 12*(4), 253–257.

Maratsos, M. (1983). Some current issues in the study of the acquisition of grammar. In P. Mussen (Series Ed.), J. H. Flavell & E. M. Markman (Vol. Eds.), *Handbook of child psychology: Vol. 3. Cognition, perception, and language* (4th ed., pp. 707–786). New York: Wiley.

Markman, E. M. (1979). Realizing that you don't understand: Elementary school children's awareness of inconsistencies. *Child Development, 50,* 643–655.

Markman, E. M. (1981). Comprehension monitoring. In W. P. Dickson (Ed.), *Children's oral communication skills.* New York: Academic Press.

Martella, A. M., Klahr, D., & Li, W. (2020). The relative effectiveness of different active learning implementations in teaching elementary school students how to design simple experiments. *Journal of Educational Psychology, 112,* 1582–1596.

Martens, B. K., & Witt, J. C. (2004). Competence, persistence, and success: The positive psychology of behavioral skill instruction. *Psychology in the Schools, 41*(1), 19–30.

Martinek, D., Hofmann, F., & Kipman, U. (2016). Academic self-regulation as a function of age: The mediating role of autonomy support and differentiation in school. *Social Psychology of Education: An International Journal, 19*(4), 729–748.

Matthews, D. (2014). *Pragmatic development in first language acquisition*. Philadelphia: John Benjamins.

Matuchniak, T., Olson, C. B., & Scarcella, R. (2014). Examining the text-based, on-demand, analytical writing of mainstreamed Latino English learners in a randomized field trial of the Pathway Project intervention. *Reading and Writing, 27,* 973–994.

Mayer, D. P. (1999). Measuring instructional practice: Can policymakers trust survey data? *Educational Evaluation and Policy Analysis, 21,* 29–45.

Mayer, J. D. (2018). Intelligences about things and intelligences about people. In R. J. Sternberg (Ed.), *The nature of human intelligence* (pp. 270–286). New York: Cambridge University Press.

McCann, T. M. (1989). Student argumentative writing knowledge and ability at three grade levels. *Research in the Teaching of English, 23,* 62–72.

McCarthy, R. A., & Warrington, E. K. (1990). *Cognitive neuropsychology: A clinical introduction*. San Diego, CA: Academic Press.

McClelland, J. L., & Rumelhart, D. E. (1981). An interactive model of context effects in letter perception: I. An account of the basic findings. *Psychological Review, 88,* 375–407.

McClelland, M. M., Geldhof, G. J., Cameron, C. E., & Wanless, S. B. (2015). Development and self-regulation. In R. M. Lerner (Ed.-in-Chief), W. F. Overton & P. Molenaar (Vol. Eds.), *Handbook of child development and developmental science: Vol. 1. Theory and method* (pp. 523–565). New York: Wiley.

McCloskey, M. (1983). Naïve theories of motion. In D. Gentner & A. Stevens (Eds.), *Mental models* (pp. 299–324). Hillsdale, NJ: Erlbaum.

McCormack, T. (2015). The development of temporal cognition. In L. S. Liben, U. Müller, & R. M. Lerner (Eds.), *Handbook of child psychology and developmental science: Vol. 2. Cognitive processes* (7th ed., pp. 624–670). New York: Wiley.

McCrae, R. R. (2009). The five-factor model of personality traits: Consensus and controversy. In P. J. Corr & G. Matthews (Eds.), *The Cambridge handbook of personality psychology* (pp. 148–161). Cambridge, UK: Cambridge University Press.

McCurdy, M. P., Leach, R. C., & Leshikar, E. D. (2017). The generation effect revisited: Fewer generation constraints enhances item and context memory. *Journal of Memory and Language, 92,* 202–216.

McCutchen, D. (1986). Domain knowledge and linguistic knowledge in the development of writing ability. *Journal of Memory and Language, 25,* 431–444.

McCutchen, D. (2006). Cognitive factors in the development of children's writing. In C. A. MacArthur, S. Graham, & J. Fitzgerald (Eds.), *Handbook of writing research* (pp. 115–130). New York: Guilford Press.

McCutchen, D., Covill, A., Hoyne, S. H., & Mildes, K. (1994). Individual differences in writing: Implications of translating fluency. *Journal of Educational Psychology, 86,* 256–266.

McCutchen, D., Francis, M., & Kerr, S. (1997). Revising for meaning: Effects of knowledge and strategy. *Journal of Educational Psychology, 89,* 667–676.

McCutchen, D., & Perfetti, C. A. (1982). Coherence and connectedness in the development of discourse production. *Text, 2,* 113–139.

McCutchen, K. L., Jones, M. H., Carbonneau, K. J., & Mueller, C. E. (2016). Mindset and standardized testing over time. *Learning and Individual Differences, 45,* 208–213.

McGill, R. J., & Dombrowski, S. C. (2019). Critically reflecting on the origins, evolution, and impact of the Cattell–Horn–Carroll (CHC) Mode. *Applied Measurement in Education, 32,* 216–231.

McGrew, K. S., & Wendling, B. J. (2010). Cattell–Horn–Carroll cognitive-achievement relations: What we have learned from the past 20 years of research. *Psychology in the Schools, 47*(7), 651–675.

McKoon, G., & Ratcliff, R. (1992). Inference during reading. *Psychological Review, 99,* 440–466.

McNamara, D. S. (2017). Self-explanation and reading strategy training (SERT) improves low-knowledge students' science course performance. *Discourse Processes, 54,* 479–492.

McNamara, D. S., & Magliano, J. (2009). Toward a comprehensive model of comprehension. *Psychology of Learning and Motivation, 51,* 298–384.

McNeil, N. M., Hornburg, C. B., Brletic-Shipley, H., & Matthews, J. M. (2019). Improving children's understanding of mathematical equivalence via an intervention that goes beyond nontraditional arithmetic practice. *Journal of Educational Psychology, 111*(6), 1023–1044.

McNeil, N. M., Rittle-Johnson, B., Hattikudur, S., & Petersen, L. A. (2010). Continuity in representation between children and adults: Arithmetic knowledge hinders undergraduates' algebraic problem solving. *Journal of Cognition and Development, 11*(4), 437–457.

McRae, K., & Gross, J. J. (2020). Introduction. *Emotion, 20,* 1–9.

Menn, L., & Stoel-Gammon, C. (2005). Phonological development: Learning sounds and sound patterns. In J. Berko Gleason (Ed.), *The development of language* (6th ed., pp. 62–111). Needham Heights, MA: Allyn & Bacon.

Mercier, H., Boudry, M., Paglieri, F., & Trouche, E. (2017). Natural-born arguers: Teaching how to make the best of our reasoning abilities. *Educational Psychologist, 52*(1), 1–16.

Mercier, H., & Sperber, D. (2011). Why do humans reason?: Arguments for an argumentative theory. *Behavioral and Brain Sciences, 34,* 57–111.

Mervis, C. B., & Crisafi, M. A. (1982). Order of acquisition of subordinate-, basic-, and superordinate-level categories. *Child Development, 53,* 258–266.

Metcalfe, J, & Finn, B, (2008). Evidence that judgments of learning are causally related to study choice. *Psychonomic Bulletin and Review, 15,* 174–179.

Metsala, J. L. (1999). Young children's phonological awareness and nonword repetition as a function of vocabulary development. *Journal of Educational Psychology, 91,* 3–19.

Metsala, J. L., & Walley, A. C. (1998). Spoken vocabulary growth and the segmental restructuring of lexical representations: Precursors to phonemic awareness and early reading ability. In J. L. Metsala & L. C. Ehri (Eds.), *Word recognition in beginning literacy* (pp. 89–120). Mahwah, NJ: Erlbaum.

Metzger, R. L., Warren, A. R., Shelton, J. T., Price, J., Reed, A. W., & Williams, D. (2008). Do children "DRM" like adults?: False memory production in children. *Developmental Psychology, 44*(1), 169–181.

Meyer, B. J. F. (1985). Prose analysis: Purposes, procedures, and problems. In B. K. Britton & J. Black (Eds.), *Understanding expository text* (pp. 11–66). Hillsdale, NJ: Erlbaum.

Meyer, B. J. F., Brandt, D. M., & Bluth, G. J. (1980). Use of top-level structure in text: Key for reading comprehension of ninth-grade students. *Reading Research Quarterly, 16,* 73–103.

Meyer, B. J. F., Wijekumar, K. K., & Lin, Y.-C. (2011). Individualizing a web-based structure strategy intervention for fifth graders' comprehension of nonfiction. *Journal of Educational Psychology, 103,* 140–168.

Miller, L. M. S., Stine-Morrow, E. A. L., Kirkorian, H. L., & Conroy, M. L. (2004). Adult age differences in knowledge-driven reading. *Journal of Educational Psychology, 96,* 811–821.

Miller-Cotto, D., & Byrnes, J. P. (2020). What's the best way to characterize the relationship between working memory and achievement?: An initial examination of competing theories. *Journal of Educational Psychology, 112,* 1074–1084.

Minor, E. C. (2015). Classroom composition and racial differences in opportunities to learn. *Journal of Education for Students Placed at Risk, 20,* 238–262.

Mix, K. S., Huttenlocher, J., & Levine, S. C. (2002). Multiple cues for quantification in infancy: Is number one of them? *Psychological Bulletin, 128,* 278–294.

Mix, K. S., Levene, S. C., & Huttenlocher, J. (1999). Early fraction calculation ability. *Developmental Psychology, 35,* 164–174.

Miyake, A., Friedman, N. P., Emerson, M. J., Witzki, A. H., Howerter, A., & Wager, T. D. (2000). The unity and diversity of executive functions and their contributions to complex "frontal lobe" tasks: A latent variable analysis. *Cognitive Psychology, 41,* 49–100.

Morgan, P. L., Farkas, G., Hillemeier, M. M., & Maczuga, S. (2016). Science achievement gaps begin very early, persist, and are largely explained by modifiable factors. *Educational Researcher, 45,* 18–35.

Morphett, M., & Washburn, C. (1931). When should children begin to read? *Elementary School Journal, 31,* 496–503.

Morris, P. E., & Fritz, C. O. (2015). Conscientiousness and procrastination predict academic coursework marks rather than examination performance. *Learning and Individual Differences, 39,* 193–198.

Mou, Y., Berteletti, I., & Hyde, D. C. (2018). What counts in preschool number knowledge?: A Bayes factor analytic approach toward theoretical model development. *Journal of Experimental Child Psychology, 166,* 116–133.

Muenks, K., & Miele, D. B. (2017). Students' thinking about effort and ability: The role of developmental, contextual, and individual difference factors. *Review of Educational Research, 87*(4), 707–735.

Muenks, K., Wigfield, A., & Eccles, J. S. (2018). I can do this!: The development and calibration of children's expectations for success and competence beliefs. *Developmental Review, 48,* 24–39.

Muenks, K., Wigfield, A., Yang, J. S., & O'Neal, C. R. (2017). How true is grit?: Assessing its relations to high school and college students' personality characteristics, self-regulation, engagement, and achievement. *Journal of Educational Psychology, 109*(5), 599–620.

Müller, U., & Kerns, K. (2015). The development of executive function. In L. S.

Liben, U. Müller, & R. M. Lerner (Eds.), *Handbook of child psychology and developmental science: Vol. 2. Cognitive processes* (7th ed., pp. 571–623). New York: Wiley.

Murayama, K., Miyatsu, T., Buchli, D., & Storm, B. C. (2014). Forgetting as a consequence of retrieval: A meta-analytic review of retrieval-induced forgetting. *Psychological Bulletin, 140*(5), 1383–1409.

Murphy, G. L. (2002). *The big book of concepts.* Cambridge, MA: MIT Press.

Naigles, L. R., & Swensen, L. D. (2007). Syntactic supports for word learning. In E. Hoff & M. Shatz (Eds.), *Blackwell handbook of language development* (pp. 211–231). New York: Blackwell.

Nairne, J. S., Coverdale, M. E., & Pandeirada, J. N. S. (2019). Adaptive memory: The mnemonic power of survival-based generation. *Journal of Experimental Psychology: Learning, Memory, and Cognition, 45*(11), 1970–1982.

Nakano-Kobayashi, A., Awaya, T., Kii, I., Sumida, Y., Okuno, Y., Yoshida, S., . . . Hagiwara, M. (2017). Prenatal neurogenesis induction therapy normalizes brain structure and function in Down syndrome mice. *Proceedings of the National Academy of Sciences of the USA, 114*, 10268–10273.

Nash, G. B. (2004). Lynne Cheney's attack on the history standards, 10 years. Retrieved from *https://historynewsnetwork.org/article/8418.*

Nathan, M. J. (2012). Rethinking formalisms in formal education. *Educational Psychologist, 47*(2), 125–148.

National Assessment of Educational Progress. (2011). Questions tool. Retrieved from *http://nces.ed.gov/pubsearch/pubsinfo.asp?pubid=2012465.*

National Association of Colleges and Employers. (2019). STEM majors projected to be class of 2019's top paid. Retrieved May 2020, from *www.naceweb.org/job-market/compensation/stem-majors-projected-to-be-class-of-2019s-top-paid.*

National Center for Education Statistics. (2011a). *The 2011 reading report card.* Washington, DC: U.S. Department of Education.

National Center for Education Statistics. (2011b). *Writing 2011: National assessment of educational progress at Grades 8 and 12.* Washington, DC: U.S. Department of Education.

National Center for Education Statistics. (2015). Percentages at or above each achievement level for grade 12 science, by all students [TOTAL] and jurisdiction: 2015 and 2009. Retrieved May 2020, from *www.nationsreportcard.gov/ndecore/xplore/NDE.*

National Center for Education Statistics. (2018). Digest of Educational Statistics. Retrieved from *https://nces.ed.gov/programs/digest/d18/tables/dt18_322.10.asp.*

National Center for Education Statistics. (2020a). How did U.S. students perform on the most recent assessments? Retrieved from *www.nationsreportcard.gov.*

National Center for Education Statistics. (2020b). The NAEP science achievement levels. Retrieved from *https://nces.ed.gov/nationsreportcard/science/achieve.aspx#2009_grade12.*

National Council for the Social Studies (2020). National curriculum standards for social studies: A framework for teaching, learning, and assessment. Retrieved from *www.socialstudies.org/standards/national-curriculum-standards-social-studies.*

National Council of Teachers of Mathematics. (1989). *Curriculum and evaluation standards for school mathematics*. Reston, VA: Author.

National Mathematics Advisory Panel. (2008). *Foundations for success: The final report of the National Mathematics Advisory Panel*. Washington, DC: U.S. Department of Education.

National Research Council. (1996). *National Science Education Standards*. Washington, DC: National Academies Press.

National Research Council. (2001). Adding it up: Helping children learn mathematics. In J. Kilpatrick, J. Swafford, & B. Findell (Eds.), *Mathematics learning study committee, center for education, division of behavioral and social sciences, and education*. Washington, DC: National Academies Press.

National Research Council. (2012). *A framework for K–12 science education: Practices, crosscutting concepts, and core ideas*. Washington, DC: National Academies Press.

Neisser, U. (Ed.). (1998). *The rising curve: Long-term gains in IQ and related measures*. Washington, DC: American Psychological Association.

Nell, V. (1988). The psychology of reading for pleasure: Needs and gratification. *Reading Research Quarterly, 23*, 6–50.

Nelson, K. (1996). *Language in cognitive development: Emergence of the mediated mind*. New York: Cambridge University Press.

Newell, G. E., Beach, R., Smith, J., & VanDerHeide, J. (2011). Teaching and learning argumentative reading and writing: A review of research. *Reading Research Quarterly, 46*, 273–304.

Niedo, J., Abbott, R. D., & Berninger, V. W. (2014). Predicting levels of reading and writing achievement in typically developing, English-speaking 2nd and 5th graders. *Learning and Individual Differences, 32*, 54–68.

Niessen, A. S. M., & Meijer, R. R. (2017). On the use of broadened admission criteria in higher education. *Perspectives on Psychological Science, 12*(3), 436–448.

Nigg, J. T. (2017). Annual research review: On the relations among self-regulation, self-control, executive functioning, effortful control, cognitive control, impulsivity, risk-taking, and inhibition for developmental psychopathology. *Journal of Child Psychology and Psychiatry, 58*, 361–383.

Ninio, A., & Snow, C. E. (1999). The development of pragmatics: Learning to use language appropriately. In N. C. Ritchie & T. K. Bhatia (Eds.), *Handbook of child language acquisition* (pp. 347–383). Orlando, FL: Academic Press.

Nokes, J. D. (2017). Exploring patterns of historical thinking through 8th-grade students' argumentative writing. *Journal of Writing Research, 8*, 437–467.

Norris, J. A., & Bruning, R. H. (1988). Cohesion in the narratives of good and poor readers. *Journal of Speech and Hearing Disorders, 53*, 416–424.

Nunes, T., & Bryant, P. (2015). The development of mathematical reasoning. In L. S. Liben, U. Müller, & R. M. Lerner (Eds.), *Handbook of child psychology and developmental science: Vol. 2. Cognitive processes* (7th ed., pp. 715–762). New York: Wiley.

Nussbaum, E. M. (2011). Argumentation, dialogue theory, and probability modeling: Alternative frameworks for argumentation research in education. *Educational Psychologist, 46*(2), 84–106.

Nussbaum, E. M., & Kardash, C. M. (2005). The effects of goal instructions and text on the generation of counterarguments during writing. *Journal of Educational Psychology, 97,* 157–169.

Nye, C. D., Butt, S. M., Bradburn, J., & Prasad, J. (2018). Interests as predictors of performance: An omitted and underappreciated variable. *Journal of Vocational Behavior, 108,* 178–189.

Nygaard, L. C., & Pisoni, D. B. (1995). Speech perception: New directions in research and theory. In J. L. Miller & P. D. Eimas (Eds.), *Speech, language, and communication* (pp. 63–96). Orlando, FL: Academic Press.

Oakes, J. (1985). *Keeping track. How schools structure inequality.* New Haven, CT: Yale University Press.

Obersteiner, A., Reiss, K., Van Dooren, W., & Van Hoof, J. (2019). Understanding rational numbers: Obstacles for learners with and without mathematical learning difficulties. In A. Fritz, V. Geraldi, & P. Rasanen (Eds.), *International handbook of mathematical learning difficulties: From the laboratory to the classroom* (pp. 581–594). New York: Springer International.

Obersteiner, A., Van Dooren, W., Van Hoof, J., & Verschaffel, L. (2013). The natural number bias and magnitude representation in fraction comparison by expert mathematicians. *Learning and Instruction, 28,* 64–72.

Okkinga, M., van Steensel, R., van Gelderen, A. J. S., van Schooten, E., Sleegers, P. J. C., Arends, L. R. (2018). Effectiveness of reading-strategy interventions in whole classrooms: A meta-analysis. *Educational Psychology Review, 30,* 1215–1239.

Olinghouse, N. G., Graham, S., & Gillespie, A. (2014). The relationship of discourse and topic knowledge to fifth graders' writing performance. *Journal of Educational Psychology, 107,* 391–406.

O'Leary, D. D. M., Stocker, A. M., & Zembrzycki, A. (2013). Area patterning of the mammalian cortex. In D. D. M. O'Leary, A. M. Stocker, A. Zembrzycki, J. Rubenstein, & P. Rakic (Eds.), *Patterning and cell type specification in the developing Cns and Pns* (pp. 61–85). Oxford, UK: Elsevier.

Ollers, D. K., Eilers, R. E., Basinger, D., Steffens, M. L., & Urbano, R. (1995). Extreme poverty and the development of precursors to the speech capacity. *First Language, 15,* 167–189.

Olson, L. A., Evans, J. R., & Keckler, W. T. (2006). Precocious readers: Past, present, and future. *Journal for the Education of the Gifted, 30,* 205–235.

Olson, I. R., & Newcombe, N. S. (2014). Binding together the elements of episodes: Relational memory and the developmental trajectory of the hippocampus. In P. J. Bauer & R. Fivush (Eds.), *The Wiley handbook on the development of children's memory* (vols. I–III, pp. 285–308). New York: Wiley Blackwell.

Organisation for Economic Co-operation and Development. (2016). *PISA 2015 results: Vol. I. Excellence and equity in education.* Paris: OECD.

Organisation for Economic Co-operation and Development. (2020). Science performance (PISA). Retrieved May 28, 2020, from *www.oecd-ilibrary.org/education/science-performance-pisa/indicator/english_91952204-en.*

Ostarek, M., & Vigliocco, G. (2017). Reading sky and seeing a cloud: On the relevance of events for perceptual simulation. *Journal of Experimental Psychology: Learning, Memory, and Cognition, 43,* 579–590.

Palardy, G., Rumberger, R., & Butler, T. (2015). The effect of high school socioeconomic, racial, and linguistic segregation on academic performance and school behaviors. *Teachers College Record, 117,* 1–52.

Palincsar, A. M., & Brown, A. L. (1984). Reciprocal teaching of comprehension-fostering and comprehension-monitoring activities. *Cognition and Instruction, 1,* 117–175.

Pan, B. A. (2005). Semantic development: Learning the meaning of words. In J. Berko Gleason (Ed.), *The development of language* (6th ed., pp. 112–147). Needham Heights, MA: Allyn & Bacon.

Pantsar, M. (2019). The enculturated move from proto-arithmetic to arithmetic. *Frontiers in Psychology, 10,* 1454.

Paris, S. G. (1975). Integration and inference in children's comprehension and memory. In F. Restle, R. Shiffrin, J. Castellan, H. Lindman, & D. Pisoni (Eds.), *Cognitive theory* (pp. 223–246). Hillsdale, NJ: Erlbaum.

Paris, S. G. (1978). Coordination of means and goals in the development of mnemonic skills. In P. A. Ornstein (Ed.), *Memory development in children* (pp. 259–274). Hillsdale, NJ: Erlbaum.

Paris, S. G., Byrnes, J. P., & Paris, A. H. (2001). Constructing theories, identities, and actions of self-regulated learners. In B. Zimmerman & D. Schunk (Eds.), *Self-regulated learning: Theories, research, practice* (2nd ed., pp. 253–287). New York: Guilford Press.

Paris, S. G., Wasik, B. A., & Turner, J. C. (1991). The development of strategic readers. In R. Barr, M. L. Kamil, P. B. Mosenthal, & P. D. Pearson (Eds.), *Handbook of reading research* (Vol. 2, pp. 609–640). New York: Longman.

Parkerson, J. A., Lomax, R. G., Schiller, D. P., & Walberg, H. J. (1984). Exploring causal models of education achievement. *Journal of Educational Psychology, 76,* 638–646.

Pashler, H., Bain, P., Bottge, B., Graesser, A., Koedinger, K., McDaniel, M., & Metcalfe, J. (2007). *Organizing instruction and study to improve student learning* (NCER 2007-2004). Washington, DC: National Center for Education Research, Institute of Education Sciences, U.S. Department of Education. Retrieved from *http://ncer.ed.gov.*

Patros, C. H. G., Tarle, S. J., Alderson, R. M., Lea, S. E., & Arrington, E. F. (2019). Planning deficits in children with attention-deficit/hyperactivity disorder (ADHD): A meta-analytic review of tower task performance. *Neuropsychology, 33*(3), 425–444.

Pearson, P. D., & Fielding, L. (1991). Comprehension instruction. In M. Barr, M. L. Kamil, P. B. Mosenthal, & P. D. Pearson (Eds.), *Handbook of reading research* (Vol. 2, pp. 815–861). New York: Longman.

Pekrun, R., & Linnenbrink-Garcia, L. (2012). Academic emotions and student engagement. In S. L. Christenson, A. L. Reschly, & C. Wylie (Eds.), *Handbook of research on student engagement* (pp. 259–282). New York: Springer.

Peng, P., Barnes, M., Wang, C., Wang, W., Li, S., Swanson, H. L., . . . Tao, S. (2018). A meta-analysis on the relation between reading and working memory. *Psychological Bulletin, 144*(1), 48–76.

Peng, P., & Fuchs, D. (2016). A meta-analysis of working memory deficits in children with learning difficulties: Is there a difference between verbal domain and numerical domain? *Journal of Learning Disabilities, 49*(1), 3–20.

Peng, P., Namkung, J., Barnes, M., & Sun, C. (2016). A meta-analysis of mathematics and working memory: Moderating effects of working memory domain, type of mathematics skill, and sample characteristics. *Journal of Educational Psychology, 108*(4), 455–473.

Peng, P., Wang, T., Wang, C. C., & Lin, X. (2019). A meta-analysis on the relation between fluid intelligence and reading/mathematics: Effects of tasks, age, and social economics status. *Psychological Bulletin, 145,* 189–236.

Perez, A. C. (2012). Valuing STEM majors: The role of occupational-academic ego-identity status and task values in STEM persistence [ProQuest Information & Learning]. *Dissertation Abstracts International Section A: Humanities and Social Sciences 73*(5-A), 1651.

Perfetti, C. A. (1985). *Reading ability.* New York: Oxford University Press.

Perfetti, C. A. (2007). Reading ability: Lexical quality to comprehension. *Scientific Studies of Reading, 11,* 357–383.

Perfetti, C. A., & McCutchen, D. (1987). Schooled language competence: Linguistic abilities in reading and writing. In S. Rosenberg (Ed.), *Advances in applied psycholinguistics* (pp. 105–141). Cambridge, UK: Cambridge University Press.

Perfetti, C., & Stafura, J. (2014). Word knowledge in a theory of reading comprehension. *Scientific Studies of Reading, 18,* 22–37.

Perszyk, D. R., & Waxman, S. R. (2018). Linking language and cognition in infancy. *Annual Review of Psychology, 69,* 231–250.

Pfost, M., Hattie, J., Dörfler, T., & Artelt, C. (2014). Individual differences in reading development: A review of 25 years of empirical research on Matthew effects in reading. *Review of Educational Research, 84,* 203–244.

Phillips, M., & Pozzo-Miller, L. (2015). Dendritic spine dysgenesis in autism related disorders. *Neuroscience Letters, 601,* 30–40.

Piaget, J. (1952). *The origins of intelligence in children* (M. Cook, Trans.). New York: International Universities Press.

Piaget, J. (1964). Cognitive development in children development and learning. *Journal of Research in Science Teaching, 2,* 176–186.

Piaget, J. (1965). *The child's conception of number.* New York: Norton.

Pinker, S. (1989). Language acquisition. In M. I. Posner (Ed.), *Foundations of cognitive science* (pp. 359–400). Cambridge, MA: MIT Press.

Pinker, S. (1994). *The language instinct.* New York: Morrow.

Pinker, S. (2011). *The better angels of our better nature: Why violence has declined.* New York: Penguin Books.

Polspoel, B., Peters, L., Vandermosten, M., & De Smedt, B. (2017). Strategy over operation: Neural activation in subtraction and multiplication during fact retrieval and procedural strategy use in children. *Human Brain Mapping, 38*(9), 4657–4670.

Poon, K. (2018). Hot and cool executive functions in adolescence: Development and contributions to important developmental outcomes. *Frontiers in Psychology, 8,* 1–18.

Poppa, T., & Bechara, A. (2018). The somatic marker hypothesis: Revisiting the role of the 'body-loop' in decision-making. *Current Opinion in Behavioral Sciences, 19,* 61–66.

Prado, E. L., & Dewey, K. G. (2014). Nutrition and brain development in early life. *Nutrition Reviews, 72,* 267–284.

Preiss, D. D., Castillo, J. C., Grigorenko, E. L., & Manzi, J. (2013). Argumentative writing and academic achievement: A longitudinal study. *Learning and Individual Differences, 28,* 204–211.

Pressley, M. (1997). The cognitive science of reading: Comments. *Contemporary Educational Psychology, 22,* 247–259.

Pressley, M., Almasi, J., Schuder, T., Bergman, J., Hite, S., El-Dinary, P. B., & Brown, R. (1994). Transactional instruction of comprehension strategies: The Montgomery County Maryland SAIL program. *Reading and Writing Quarterly, 10,* 5–19.

Pressley, M., & Hilden, K. (2006). Cognitive strategies. In W. Damon & R. M. Lerner (Series Eds.), D. Kuhn & R. S. Siegler (Vol. Eds.), *Handbook of child psychology: Vol. 2. Cognition, perception, and language* (6th ed., pp. 511–556). New York: Wiley.

Pressley, M., Johnson, C. J., Symons, S., McGoldrick, J. A., & Kurita, J. A. (1989). Strategies that improve children's memory and comprehension of text. *Elementary School Journal, 90,* 3–32.

Price, C. J. (2012). A review and synthesis of the first 20 years of PET and fMRI studies of heard speech, spoken language and reading. *NeuroImage, 62,* 816–847.

Price, I. K., Witzel, N., & Witzel, J. (2015). Orthographic and phonological form interference during silent reading. *Journal of Experimental Psychology: Learning, Memory, and Cognition, 41*(6), 1628–1647.

Pritchard, S. C., Coltheart, M., Marinus, E., & Castles, A. (2018). A computational model of the self-teaching hypothesis based on the dual-route cascaded model of reading. *Cognitive Science, 42,* 722–770.

Proctor, C. P., Carlo, M., August, D., & Snow, C. (2005). Native Spanish-speaking children reading in English: Toward a model of comprehension. *Journal of Educational Psychology, 97,* 246–256.

Purpura, D. J., Logan, J. A. R., Hassinger-Das, B., & Napoli, A. R. (2017). Why do early mathematics skills predict later reading?: The role of mathematical language. *Developmental Psychology, 53,* 1633–1642.

Putnam, H. (1975). The nature of mental states. In *Mind, language and reality: Philosophical papers* (Vol. 2, pp. 51–58). Cambridge, UK: Cambridge University Press.

Pylyshyn, Z. (1984). *Computation and cognition: Toward a foundation for cognitive science.* Cambridge, MA: The MIT Press.

Quilici, J. L., & Mayer, R. E. (2002). Teaching students to recognize structural similarities between statistics word problems. *Applied Cognitive Psychology, 16,* 325–342.

Ramani, G. B., & Siegler, R. S. (2008). Promoting broad and stable improvements in low-income children's numerical knowledge through playing number board games. *Child Development, 79,* 375–394.

Ransdell, S., & Levy, C. M. (1996). Working memory constraints on writing quality and fluency. In C. M. Levy & S. Ransdell (Eds.), *The science of writing: Theories, methods, individual differences, and applications* (pp. 93–106). Mahwah, NJ: Erlbaum.

Rantala, J., & van den Berg, M. (2015). Finnish high school and university students' ability to handle multiple source documents in history. *Historical Encounters: A Journal of Historical Consciousness, Historical Cultures, and History Education, 2,* 70–88.

Rapp, D. N., van den Broek, P., McMaster, K. L., Kendeou, P., & Espin, C. A. (2007). Higher-order comprehension processes in struggling readers: A perspective for research and intervention. *Scientific Studies of Reading, 11,* 289–312.

Ravitch, D. (2010). *The death and life of the great American school system: How testing and choice are undermining education.* New York: Basic Books

Rawson, K. A., & Dunlosky, J. (2011). Optimizing schedules of retrieval practice for durable and efficient learning: How much is enough? *Journal of Experimental Psychology: General, 140*(3), 283–302.

Rayner, K., & Reichle, E. D. (2010). Models of the reading process. *WIREs Cognitive Science, 1,* 787–799.

Recht, D. R., & Leslie, L. (1988). Effect of prior knowledge on good and poor readers' memory of text. *Journal of Educational Psychology, 80,* 16–20.

Regier, T., Kemp, C., & Kay, P. (2015). Word meanings across languages support efficient communication. In B. MacWhinney & W. O'Grady (Eds.), *The handbook of language emergence* (pp. 237–263). New York: Wiley.

Reisman, A. (2012). Reading like a historian: A document-based history curriculum intervention in urban high schools. *Cognition and Instruction, 30,* 86–112.

Reisman, A. (2015). Entering the historical problem space: Whole-class text-based discussion in history class. *Teachers College Record, 117,* 1–44.

Reisman, A., Brimsek, E., & Hollywood, C. (2019). Assessment of historical analysis and argumentation (ahaa): A new measure of document-based historical thinking. *Cognition and Instruction, 37*(3), 1–28.

Resnick, I., Jordan, N. C., Hansen, N., Rajan, V., Rodrigues, J., Siegler, R. S., & Fuchs, L. S. (2016). Developmental growth trajectories in understanding of fraction magnitude from fourth through sixth grade. *Developmental Psychology, 52*(5), 746–757.

Reyna, V. F., Corbin, J. C., Weldon, R. B., & Brainerd, C. J. (2016). How fuzzy-trace theory predicts true and false memories for words, sentences, and narratives. *Journal of Applied Research in Memory and Cognition, 5,* 1–9.

Rheingold, H. L., Gewirtz, J. L., & Ross, H. W. (1959). Social conditioning of vocalizations in the infant. *Journal of Comparative and Physiological Psychology, 52,* 68–73.

Ribner, A., Harvey, E., Gervais, R., & Fitzpatrick, C. (2019). Explaining school entry math and reading achievement in Canadian children using the opportunity–propensity framework. *Learning and Instruction, 59,* 65–75.

Riccomagno, M. M., & Kolodkin, A. L. (2015). Sculpting neural circuits by axon and dendrite pruning. *Annual Review of Cell and Developmental Biology, 31,* 779–805.

Rinehart, S. D., Stahl, S. A., & Erickson, L. G. (1986). Some effects of summarization training on reading and studying. *Reading Research Quarterly, 21,* 422–438.

Rittle-Johnson, B. (2019). Iterative development of conceptual and procedural knowledge in mathematics learning and instruction. In J. Dunlosky & K. A. Rawson (Eds.), *The Cambridge handbook of cognition and education* (pp. 124–147). New York: Cambridge University Press.

Rittle-Johnson, B., & Star, J. R. (2007). Does comparing solution methods facilitate conceptual and procedural knowledge?: An experimental study on learning to solve equations. *Journal of Educational Psychology, 99*(3), 561–574.

Robson, D. A., Allen, M. S., & Howard, S. J. (2020). Self-regulation in childhood as a predictor of future outcomes: A meta-analytic review, *Psychological Bulletin, 146,* 1–31.

Roebers, C. M. (2014). Children's deliberate memory development: The contribution of strategies and metacognitive processes. In P. J. Bauer & R. Fivush (Eds.), *The Wiley handbook on the development of children's memory* (Vols. 1–3, pp. 865–894). New York: Wiley.

Roediger, H. L. (1980). The effectiveness of four mnemonics in ordering recall. *Journal of Experimental Psychology: Human Learning and Memory, 6*(5), 558–567.

Roller, C. M. (1990). The interaction between knowledge and structure variables in the processing of expository prose. *Reading Research Quarterly, 25,* 80–89.

Rosch, E. (1975). Cognitive representations of semantic categories. *Journal of Experimental Psychology: General, 104,* 192–233.

Rosenshine, B., & Meister, C. (1994). Reciprocal teaching: A review of the research. *Review of Educational Research, 64,* 479–530.

Rosenzweig, E. Q., & Wigfield, A. (2016). STEM motivation interventions for adolescents: A promising start, but further to go. *Educational Psychologist, 51,* 146–163.

Ross, J., Anderson, J. R., & Campbell, R. N. (2011). I remember me: Mnemonic self-reference effects in preschool children: II. The impact of physical self-reference on preschoolers' memory for depicted actions. *Monographs of the Society for Research in Child Development, 76,* 17–24.

Roth, B., Becker, N., Romeyke, S., Schäfer, S., Domnick, F., & Spinath, F. M. (2015). Intelligence and school grades: A meta-analysis. *Intelligence, 53,* 118–137.

Rowe, M. (2015). Input versus intake—A commentary on Ambridge, Kidd, Rowland, and Theakson's "The ubiquity of frequency effects in first language acquisition." *Journal of Child Language, 42,* 301–305.

Rowland, C. A. (2014). The effect of testing versus restudy on retention: A meta-analytic review of the testing effect. *Psychological Bulletin, 140,* 1432–1463.

Ryan, R. M., & Deci, E. L. (2006). Self-regulation and the problem of human autonomy: Does psychology need choice, self-determination, and will? *Journal of Personality, 74,* 1557–1585.

Ryan, R. M., & Deci, E. L. (2017). *Self-determination theory: Basic psychological needs in motivation, development, and wellness.* New York: Guilford Press.

Sackes, M., Trundle, K. C., Bell, R. L., & O'Connell, A. A. (2011). The influence of early science experience in kindergarten on children's immediate and later science achievement: Evidence from the Early Childhood Longitudinal Study. *Journal of Research in Science Teaching, 48,* 217–235.

Saffran, E. M. (2003). Evidence from language breakdown: Implications for the neural and functional organization of language. In M. T. Banich & M. Mack (Eds.), *Mind, brain, and language: Multidisciplinary perspectives* (pp. 251–281). Mahwah, NJ: Erlbaum.

Salovey, P., & Mayer, J. D. (1989). Emotional intelligence. *Imagination, Cognition and Personality, 9*(3), 185–211.

Sameroff, A. J., & Haith, M. M. (Eds.). (1996). *The five to seven year shift: The age of reason and responsibility.* Chicago: University of Chicago Press.

Santayana, G. (1905). *Reason in common sense.* London: Archibald Constable.

Sarnecka, B. W., & Wright, C. E. (2013). The idea of an exact number: Children's understanding of cardinality and equinumerosity. *Cognitive Science, 37*(8), 1493–1506.

Savage, R., Cornish, K., Manley, T., & Hollis, C. (2006). Cognitive processes in children's reading and attention: The role of working memory, divided attention, and response inhibition. *British Journal of Psychology, 97,* 365–385.

Scarborough, H. S., & Dobrich, W. (1994). On the efficacy of reading to preschoolers. *Developmental Review, 14,* 245–302.

Scardamalia, M., & Bereiter, C. (1986). Research on written composition. In M. C. Wittrock (Ed.), *Handbook of research on teaching* (3rd ed., pp. 778–803). New York: Macmillan.

Scardamalia, M., Bereiter, C., & Goelman, H. (1982). The role of production factors in writing ability. In M. Nystrand (Ed.), *What writers know: The language, process, and structure of written discourse.* New York: Academic Press.

Schacter, D. L. (1999). The seven sins of memory: Insights from psychology and cognitive neuroscience. *American Psychologist, 54,* 182–203.

Schacter, D. L. (2012). Adaptive constructive processes and the future of memory. *American Psychologist, 67,* 603–613.

Schacter, D. L. (2019). Implicit memory, constructive memory, and imagining the future: A career perspective. *Perspectives on Psychological Science, 14,* 256–272.

Schneider, M., Beeres, K., Coban, L., Merz, S., Schmidt, S. S., Stricker, J., & De Smedt, B. (2017). Associations of non-symbolic and symbolic numerical magnitude processing with mathematical competence: A meta-analysis. *Developmental Science, 20,* 1–16.

Schneider, W., & Bjorklund, D. F. (1992). Expertise, aptitude, and strategic remembering. *Child Development, 63,* 461–473.

Schneider, M., & Hardy, I. (2013). Profiles of inconsistent knowledge in children's pathways of conceptual change. *Developmental Psychology, 49*(9), 1639–1649.

Schneider, W. J., & McGrew, K. S. (2012). The Cattell–Horn–Carroll model of intelligence. In D. P. Flanagan & P. L. Harrison (Eds.), *Contemporary intellectual assessment: Theories, tests, and issues* (3rd ed., pp. 99–144). New York: Guilford Press.

Schneider, W., Niklas, F., & Schmiedeler, S. (2014). Intellectual development from early childhood to early adulthood: The impact of early IQ differences on stability and change over time. *Learning and Individual Differences, 32,* 156–162.

Schneider, W., & Ornstein, P. A. (2018). Determinants of memory development in childhood and adolescence. *International Journal of Psychology, 54,* 307–315.

Schneider, M., & Preckel, F. (2017). Variables associated with achievement in higher education: A systematic review of meta-analyses. *Psychological Bulletin, 143*(6), 565–600.

Schneider, W., & Pressley, M. (1997). *Memory development between two and twenty* (2nd ed). Mahwah, NJ: Erlbaum.

Schulz, A. (2018). Relational reasoning about numbers and operations—Foundation for calculation strategy use in multi-digit multiplication and division. *Mathematical Thinking and Learning, 20,* 108–141.

Schulz, A., & Leuders, T. (2018). Learning trajectories towards strategy proficiency in multi-digit division—A latent transition analysis of strategy and error profiles. *Learning and Individual Differences, 66,* 54–69.

Schünemann, N., Spörer, N., Völlinger, V. A., & Brunstein, J. C. (2017). Peer feedback mediates the impact of self-regulation procedures on strategy use and reading comprehension in reciprocal teaching groups. *Instructional Science, 45*, 395–415.

Schunk, D. H., & Mullen, C. A. (2012). Self-efficacy as an engaged learner. In S. L. Christenson, A. L. Reschly, & C. Wylie (Eds.), *Handbook of research on student engagement* (pp. 219–235). New York: Springer Science + Business Media.

Schunk, D. H., & Zimmerman, B. J. (2013). Self-regulation and learning. In W. M. Reynolds, G. E. Miller, & I. B. Weiner (Eds.), *Handbook of psychology: Vol. 7. Educational psychology* (2nd ed., pp. 45–68). New York: Wiley.

Schwanenflugel, P. J., & Kuhn, M. R. (2015). Reading fluency. In P. Afflerbach (Ed.), *Handbook of individual differences in reading: Reader, text and context* (pp. 107–119). New York: Routledge.

Schwenck, C., Bjorklund, D. F., & Schneider, W. (2009). Developmental and individual differences in young children's use and maintenance of a selective memory strategy. *Developmental Psychology, 45*(4), 1034–1050.

Schwichow, M., Croker, S., Zimmerman, C., Höffler, T., & Härtig, H. (2016). Teaching the control-of-variables strategy: A meta-analysis. *Developmental Review, 39*, 37–63.

Schwinger, M., Wirthwein, L., Lemmer, G., & Steinmayr, R. (2014). Academic self-handicapping and achievement: A meta-analysis. *Journal of Educational Psychology, 106*(3), 744–761.

Searle, J. R. (1969). *Speech acts: An essay in the philosophy of language.* Cambridge, UK: Cambridge University Press.

Searle, J. R. (1983). *Intentionality: An essay in the philosophy of mind.* New York: Cambridge University Press.

Seidenberg, M. S., & McClelland, J. L. (1989). A distributed, developmental model of word recognition and naming. *Psychological Review, 96*, 523–568.

Seixas, P. (1994). Students' understanding of historical significance. *Theory and Research in Social Education, 22*, 281–304.

Shahzadi, K., & Walker, B. R. (2019). Reinforcement sensitivity theory and relationship satisfaction via mastery. *Personality and Individual Differences, 139*, 46–52.

Shapiro, L. R., & Hudson, J. A. (1991). Tell me a make-believe story: Coherence and cohesion in young children's picture-elicited narratives. *Developmental Psychology, 27*, 960–974.

Share, D., & Levin, I. (1999). Learning to read and write in Hebrew. In M. Harris & G. Hatano (Eds.), *Learning to read and write: A cross-linguistic perspective* (pp. 89–111). New York: Cambridge University Press.

Shaywitz, S. E., Shaywitz, B., Pugh, K. R., Fulbright, R. K., Constable, R. T., Mencl, W. E., . . . Gore, J. C. (1998). Functional disruption in the organization of the brain for reading in dyslexia. *Proceedings of the National Academy of Sciences of the USA, 95*, 2636–2641.

Shin, D. D., Lee, M., Ha, J. E., Park, J. H., Ahn, H. S., Son, E., . . . Bong, M. (2019). Science for all: Boosting the science motivation of elementary school students with utility value intervention. *Learning and Instruction, 60*, 104–116.

Shipstead, Z., & Engle, R. W. (2018). Mechanisms of working memory capacity and fluid intelligence and their common dependence on executive attention. In R. J. Sternberg (Ed.), *The nature of human intelligence* (pp. 287–307). New York: Cambridge University Press.

Shoda, Y., Mischel, W., & Peake, P. K. (1990). Predicting adolescent cognitive and self-regulatory competencies from preschool delay of gratification: Identifying diagnostic conditions. *Developmental Psychology, 26,* 978–986.

Siegler, R. S. (1988). Strategy choice procedures and the development of multiplication skill. *Journal of Experimental Psychology: General, 117*(3), 258–275.

Siegler, R. S. (2016). Continuity and change in the field of cognitive development and in the perspectives of one cognitive developmentalist. *Child Development Perspectives, 10,* 128–133.

Siegler, R. S., & Araya, R. (2005). A computational model of conscious and unconscious strategy discovery. *Advances in Child Development and Behavior, 33,* 1–42.

Siegler, R. S., Duncan, G. J., Davis-Kean, P. E., Duckworth, K., Claessens, A., Engel, M., . . . Chen, M. (2012). Early predictors of high school mathematics achievement. *Psychological Science, 23*(7), 691–697.

Siegler, R. S., & Lortie-Forgues, H. (2015). Conceptual knowledge of fraction arithmetic. *Journal of Educational Psychology, 107*(3), 909–918.

Siegler, R. S., & Pyke, A. A. (2013). Developmental and individual differences in understanding of fractions. *Developmental Psychology, 49,* 1994–2004.

Silverman, R. D., Speece, D. L., Harring, J. R., & Ritchey, K. D. (2013). Fluency was a role in the simple view of reading. *Scientific Studies of Reading, 17,* 108–133.

Singley, M., & Anderson, J. R. (1989). *The transfer of cognitive skill.* Cambridge, MA: Harvard University Press.

Sinopoli, K. J., Schachar, R., & Dennis, M. (2011). Traumatic brain injury and secondary attention-deficit/hyperactivity disorder in children and adolescents: The effect of reward on inhibitory control. *Journal of Clinical and Experimental Neuropsychology, 33*(7), 805–819.

Skinner, B. F. (1957). *Verbal behavior.* New York: Appleton-Century-Crofts.

Skinner, B. F. (1974). *About behaviorism.* New York: Knopf.

Skinner, E. A., & Saxton, E. A. (2019). The development of academic coping in children and youth: A comprehensive review and critique. *Developmental Review, 53,* 100870.

Sloutsky, V. (2015). Conceptual development. In L. S. Liben, U. Müller, & R. M. Lerner (Eds.), *Handbook of child psychology and developmental science: Vol. 2. Cognitive processes* (7th ed., pp. 469–518). New York: Wiley.

Sloutsky, V. M., Yim, H., Yao, X., & Dennis, S. (2017). An associative account of word learning. *Cognitive Psychology, 97,* 1–30.

Smith, C. L., Maclin, D., Houghton, C., & Hennessey, M. G. (2000). Sixth-grade students' epistemologies of science: The impact of school science experiences on epistemological development. *Cognition and Instruction, 18*(3), 349–422.

Smith, E. E. (1989). Concepts and induction. In M. I. Posner (Ed.), *Foundations of cognitive science* (pp. 501–526). Cambridge, MA: MIT Press.

Smith, E. E., & Medin, D. L. (1981). *Categories and concepts.* Cambridge, MA: Harvard University Press.

Snow, C. E., Burns, M. S., & Griffin, P. (1998). *Preventing reading difficulties in young children*. Washington, DC: National Academies Press.

Sobczak, J. M., & Gaskell, M. G. (2019). Implicit versus explicit mechanisms of vocabulary learning and consolidation. *Journal of Memory and Language, 106*, 1–17.

Solomon, G. E. A., & Cassimatis, N. L. (1999). On facts and conceptual systems: Young children's integration of their understandings of germs and contagion. *Developmental Psychology, 35*, 113–126.

Spaepen, E., Gunderson, E. A., Gibson, D., Goldin-Meadow, S., & Levine, S. C. (2018). Meaning before order: Cardinal principle knowledge predicts improvement in understanding the successor principle and exact ordering. *Cognition, 180*, 59–81.

Spencer, M., Quinn, J. M., & Wagner, R. K. (2017). Vocabulary, morphology, and reading comprehension. In K. Cain, D. L. Compton, & R. K. Parrila (Eds.), *Theories of reading development* (pp. 239–256). Amsterdam, the Netherlands: John Benjamins.

Spencer, M., & Wagner, R. K. (2018). The comprehension problems of children with poor reading comprehension despite adequate decoding: A meta-analysis. *Review of Educational Research, 88*, 366–400.

Spires, H. A., Gallini, J., & Riggsbee, J. (1992). Effects of schema-based and text structure-based cues on expository prose comprehension in fourth graders. *Journal of Experimental Education, 60*, 307–320.

Stanovich, K. E. (1986). Matthew effects in reading: Some consequences of individual differences in the acquisition of literacy. *Reading Research Quarterly, 21*, 360–407.

Stanovich, K. E., & Cunningham, A. E. (1992). Studying the consequences of literacy within a literate society: The cognitive correlates of print exposure. *Memory and Cognition, 20*, 51–68.

Stanovich, K. E., & Siegel, L. S. (1994). Phenotypic performance profile of children with reading disabilities: A regression-based test of the phonological-core variable-difference model. *Journal of Educational Psychology, 86*, 24–53.

Stanovich, K. E., West, R. F., & Harrison, M. R. (1995). Knowledge growth and maintenance across the lifespan: The role of print exposure. *Developmental Psychology, 31*, 811–826.

Star, J. R., Newton, K., Pollack, C., Kokka, K., Rittle-Johnson, B., & Durkin, K. (2015). Student, teacher, and instructional characteristics related to students' gains in flexibility. *Contemporary Educational Psychology, 41*, 198–208.

Stark, R. E. (1986). Prespeech segmental feature development. In P. Fletcher & M. Garman (Eds.), *Language acquisition* (2nd ed., pp. 149–173). Cambridge, UK: Cambridge University Press.

Starkey, P., & Cooper, R. G. (1980). Perception of numbers by human infants. *Science, 210*, 1033–1035.

Stathopoulou, C., & Vosniadou, S. (2007). Exploring the relationship between physics-related epistemological beliefs and physics understanding. *Contemporary Educational Psychology, 32*(3), 255–281.

Staub, A. (2015). Reading sentences: Syntactic parsing and semantic interpretation. In A. Pollatsek & R. Treiman (Eds.), *The Oxford handbook of reading* (pp. 1–27). New York: Oxford University Press.

Stein, I. S., & Zito, K. (2019). Dendritic spine elimination: Molecular mechanisms and implications. *The Neuroscientist, 25,* 27–47.

Stein, N. L. (1982). What's in a story: Interpreting the interpretations of story grammars. *Discourse Processes, 5,* 319–335.

Stein, N. L., & Glenn, C. G. (1979). An analysis of story comprehension in elementary school children. In R. O. Freedle (Ed.), *New directions in discourse processing.* Norwood, NJ: Ablex.

Stein, N. L., & Policastro, T. (1984). The story: A comparison between children's and teacher's viewpoints. In H. Mandel, N. L. Stein, & T. Trabasso (Eds.), *Learning and comprehension of text.* Hillsdale, NJ: Erlbaum.

Steinberg, L. (2008). A social neuroscience perspective on adolescent risk-taking. *Developmental Review, 28,* 78–106.

Steinberg, L., Graham, S., O'Brien, L., Woolard, J., Cauffman, E., & Banich, M. (2009). Age differences in future orientation and delay discounting. *Child Development, 80,* 28–44.

Steinberg, L., Icenogle, G., Shulman, E. P., Breiner, K., Chein, J., Bacchini, D., . . . Takash, H. M. S. (2018). Around the world, adolescence is a time of heightened sensation seeking and immature self-regulation. *Developmental Science, 21*(2), 1–13.

Sternberg, R. J. (1985). *Beyond IQ: A triarchic theory of human intelligence.* New York: Cambridge University Press.

Sternberg, R. J. (2005). Intelligence. In K. J. Holyoak & R. G. Morrison (Eds.), *The Cambridge handbook of thinking and reasoning* (pp. 751–773). New York: Cambridge University Press.

Sternberg, R. J. (2013a). Intelligence. In D. K. Freedheim & I. B. Weiner (eds.), *Handbook of psychology: Vol. 1. History of psychology* (2nd ed., pp. 155–176). New York: Wiley.

Sternberg, R. J. (2013b). If you read one recent book on intelligence, make it this one. *PsycCRITIQUES, 58.*

Sternberg, R. J. (2018). Successful intelligence in theory, research, and practice. In R. J. Sternberg (Ed.), *The nature of human intelligence* (pp. 308–322). New York: Cambridge University Press.

Sternberg, R. J., Grigorenko, E. L., & Bundy, D. A. (2001). The predictive value of IQ. *Merrill–Palmer Quarterly, 47,* 1–41.

Stigler, J. W., Gallimore, R., & Hiebert, J. (2000). Using video surveys to compare classrooms and teaching across cultures: Examples and lessons from the TIMSS video studies. *Educational Psychologist, 35,* 87–100.

Stiles, J., & Jernigan, T. L. (2010). The basics of brain development. *Neuropsychology Review, 20,* 327–348.

Stoel, G., Logtenberg, A., Wansink, H., Huijgen, T., van Boxtel, C., & van Drie, J. (2017). Measuring epistemological beliefs in history education: An exploration of naïve and nuanced beliefs. *International Journal of Educational Research, 83,* 120–134.

Stoel-Gammon, C. (2011). Relationships between lexical and phonological development in young children. *Journal of Child Language, 38,* 1–34.

Strauss, M. S., & Curtis, L. E. (1981). Infant perception of numerosity. *Child Development, 52,* 1146–1152.

Sulzby, E. (1991). Assessment of emergent literacy: Storybook reading. *The Reading Teacher, 44*, 498–500.

Swanson, H. L. (1999). What develops in working memory?: A life span perspective. *Developmental Psychology, 35*, 986–1000.

Symons, C. S., & Johnson, B. T. (1997). The self-reference effect in memory: A meta-analysis. *Psychological Bulletin, 121*, 371–394.

Tafa, E., & Manolitsis, G. (2012). The literacy profile of Greek precocious readers: A follow-up study. *Journal of Research in Reading, 35*, 337–352.

Taft, M. (2015). The nature of lexical representation in visual word recognition. In A. Pollatsek & R. Treiman (Eds.), *The Oxford handbook of reading* (pp. 1–16). New York: Oxford University Press.

Takacs, Z. K., & Kassai, R. (2019). The efficacy of different interventions to foster children's executive function skills: A series of meta-analyses. *Psychological Bulletin, 145*(7), 653–697.

Talwar, A., Tighe, E., & Greenberg, D. (2018). Augmenting the simple view of reading for struggling adult readers: A unique role for background knowledge. *Scientific Studies of Reading, 22*, 351–366.

Tamnes, C. K., Herting, M. M., Goddings, A.-L., Meuwese, R., Blakemore, S.-J., Dahl, R. E., . . . Mills, K. L. (2017). Development of the cerebral cortex across adolescence: A multisample study of inter-related longitudinal changes in cortical volume, surface area, and thickness. *Journal of Neuroscience, 37*(12), 3402–3412.

Taquet, M., Quoidbach, J., de Montjoye, Y.-A., Desseilles, M., & Gross, J. J. (2016). Hedonism and the choice of everyday activities. *Proceedings of the National Academy of Sciences of the USA, 113*(35), 9769–9773.

Tarchi, C., & Pinto, G. (2016). Reciprocal teaching: Analyzing interactive dynamics in the co-construction of a text's meaning. *Journal of Educational Research, 109*, 518–530.

Tate, W. F. (1995). Returning to the root: A culturally relevant approach to mathematics pedagogy. *Theory into Practice, 34*, 166–173.

Tauber, S. K., Dunlosky, J., & Rawson, K. A. (2015). The influence of retrieval practice versus delayed judgments of learning on memory: Resolving a memory-metamemory paradox. *Experimental Psychology, 62*(4), 254–263.

Tăut, D., Băban, A., Giese, H., de Matos, M. G., Schupp, H., & Renner, B. (2015). Developmental trends in eating self-regulation and dietary intake in adolescents. *Applied Psychology: Health and Well-Being, 7*(1), 4–21.

Taylor, B. M. (1986). Summary writing by young children. *Reading Research Quarterly, 21*, 193–208.

Taylor, B. M., Frye, B. J., & Maruyama, G. M. (1990). Time spent reading and reading growth. *American Educational Research Journal, 27*, 351–362.

Teale, W. H., & Sulzby, E. (1986). *Emergent literacy.* Norwood, NJ: Ablex.

Thiede, K. W., Anderson, M. C. M., & Therriault, D. (2003). Accuracy of metacognitive monitoring affects learning of texts. *Journal of Educational Psychology, 95*, 66–73.

Thorndike, E. L. (1913). *Educational psychology* (Vols. 1 and 2). New York: Teachers College Press.

Thornton, S. J. (2017). A concise historiography of the social studies. In M. M.

Manfra & C. M. Bolick (Eds.), *The Wiley handbook of social studies research* (pp. 9–41). New York: Wiley.

Tian, J., & Siegler, R. S. (2017). Fractions learning in children with mathematics difficulties. *Journal of Learning Disabilities, 50*(6), 614–620.

Tomasello, M. (1992). *First verbs: A case study of early grammatical development.* New York: Cambridge University Press.

Tomasello, M. (2011). Language development. In U. Goswami (Ed.), *The Wiley–Blackwell handbook of childhood cognitive development* (pp. 239–257). New York: Wiley.

Tomasello, M., & Brooks, P. J. (1999). Early syntactic development: A construction grammar approach. In M. Barrett (Ed.), *The development of language* (pp. 161–190). New York: Psychology Press.

Tomasello, M., & Merriman, W. E. (1995). *Beyond names for things: Young children's acquisition of verbs.* Hillsdale, NJ: Erlbaum.

Tong, Y., Wang, F., & Danovitch, J. (2019). The role of epistemic and social characteristics in children's selective trust: Three meta-analyses. *Developmental Science, 23*(2), 1–19.

Trakhman, L. M. S., Alexander, P. A., & Berkowitz, L. E. (2019). Effects of processing time on comprehension and calibration in print and digital mediums. *Journal of Experimental Education, 87*(1), 101–115.

Traxler, M. J., Tooley, K. M., & Pickering, M. J. (2014). Syntactic priming during sentence comprehension: Evidence for the lexical boost. *Journal of Experimental Psychology: Learning, Memory, and Cognition, 40,* 905–918.

Treiman, R., Mullennix, J., Bijeljac-Babic, R., & Richmond-Welty, E. D. (1995). The special role of rimes in the description, use, and acquisition of English orthography. *Journal of Experimental Psychology: General, 124,* 107–136.

Treiman, R., & Tincoff, R. (1997). The fragility of the alphabetic principle: Children's knowledge of letter names can cause them to spell syllabically rather than alphabetically. *Journal of Experimental Child Psychology, 64,* 425–451.

Treiman, R., & Zukowski, A. (1996). Children's sensitivity to syllables, onsets, rimes, and phonemes. *Journal of Experimental Child Psychology, 61,* 193–215.

Troia, G. A. (2006). Writing instruction for students with learning disabilities. In C. A. MacArthur, S. Graham, & J. Fitzgerald (Eds.), *Handbook of writing research* (pp. 324–336). New York: Guilford Press.

Tsalas, N., Sodian, B., & Paulus, M. (2017). Correlates of metacognitive control in 10-year old children and adults. *Metacognition and Learning, 12*(3), 297–314.

Tullis, J. G., Fiechter, J. L., & Benjamin, A. S. (2018). The efficacy of learners' testing choices. *Journal of Experimental Psychology: Learning, Memory, and Cognition, 44*(4), 540–552.

Turner, S. L., Joeng, J. R., Sims, M. D., Dade, S. N., & Reid, M. F. (2019). SES, gender, and STEM career interests, goals, and actions: A test of SCCT. *Journal of Career Assessment, 27*(1), 134–150.

Tyack, D. B., & Cuban, L. (1995). *Tinkering toward utopia: A century of public school reform.* Cambridge, MA: Harvard University Press.

Ullrich, V. (2016). *Hitler: Assent: 1889–1939.* New York: Knopf.

van den Broek, P. (1989). Causal reasoning and inference making in judging the importance of story statements. *Child Development, 60,* 286–297.

van den Broek, P., Lorch, E. P., & Thurlow, R. (1996). Children's and adults' memory for television stories: The role of causal factors, story-grammar categories, and hierarchical level. *Child Development, 67,* 3010–3028.

Van der Ven, S. H., Boom, J., Kroesbergen, E. H., & Leseman, P. P. (2012). Microgenetic patterns of children's multiplication learning: Confirming the overlapping waves model by latent growth modeling. *Journal of Experimental Child Psychology, 113,* 1–19.

van Dijk, T. A., & Kintsch, W. (1983). *Strategies of discourse comprehension.* New York: Academic Press.

van Drie, J., & van Boxtel, C. (2008). Historical reasoning: Towards a framework for analyzing students' reasoning about the past. *Educational Psychology Review, 20*(2), 87–110.

van Gelderen, A., Schoonen, R., de Gloppen, K., Hulstijn, J., Simis, A., Snellings, P., & Stevenson, M. (2004). Linguistic knowledge, processing speed, and metacognitive knowledge in first and second language reading comprehension: A componential analysis. *Journal of Educational Psychology, 96,* 19–30.

van Putten, C. M., van den Brom-Snijders, P. A., & Beishuizen, M. (2005). Progressive mathematization of long division strategies in Dutch primary schools. *Journal for Research in Mathematics Education, 36*(1), 44–73.

Van Straaten, D., Wilschut, A., Oostdam, R., & Fukkink, R. (2019). Fostering students' appraisals of the relevance of history by comparing analogous cases of an enduring human issue: A quasi-experimental study. *Cognition and Instruction, 37,* 512–533.

VanSledright, B. A. (2014). *Assessing historical thinking and understanding: Innovative designs for new standards.* New York: Routledge.

VanSledright, B., & Maggioni, L. (2016). Epistemic cognition in history. In J. A. Green, W. A. Sandoval, & I. Braten (Eds.), *Handbook of epistemic cognition* (pp. 128–146). New York: Routledge.

Varma, S., & Schwartz, D. L. (2011). The mental representation of integers: An abstract-to-concrete shift in the understanding of mathematical concepts. *Cognition, 121,* 363–385.

Vasilyeva, M., Dearing, E., Ivanova, A., Shen, C., & Kardanova, E. (2018). Testing the family investment model in Russia: Estimating indirect effects of SES and parental beliefs on the literacy skills of first-graders. *Early Childhood Research Quarterly, 42,* 11–20.

Velikonja, T., Fett, A.-K., & Velthorst, E. (2019). Patterns of nonsocial and social cognitive functioning in adults with autism spectrum disorder: A systematic review and meta-analysis. *JAMA Psychiatry, 76*(2), 135–151.

Verhoeven, L., Voeten, M., & Vermeer, A. (2019). Beyond the simple view of early first and second language reading: The impact of lexical quality. *Journal of Neurolinguistics, 50,* 28–36.

Vihman, M. M. (1993). Variable paths to early word production. *Journal of Phonetics, 21,* 61–82.

Vihman, M. M. (2017). Learning words and learning sounds: Advances in language development. *British Journal of Psychology, 108,* 1–27.

Vohs, K., & Baumeister, R. F. (Eds.). (2016). *Handbook of self-regulation: Theory, research, and applications* (3rd ed.). New York: Guilford Press.

von Bartheld, C. S. (2018). Myths and truths about the cellular composition of the human brain: A review of influential concepts *Journal of Chemical Neuroanatomy, 93,* 2–15.

Vosniadou, S., & Skopeliti, I. (2017). Is it the Earth that turns or the sun that goes behind the mountains? Students' misconceptions about the day/night cycle after reading a science text. *International Journal of Science Education, 39,* 2027–2051.

Vygotsky, L. S. (1978). *Mind in society.* Cambridge, MA: Harvard University Press.

Waggoner, J. E., Messe, R., & Palermo, D. (1985). Grasping the meaning of metaphor: Story recall and comprehension. *Child Development, 56,* 1156–1166.

Walberg, H. J., & Tsai, S. (1984). Reading achievement and diminishing returns to time. *Journal of Educational Psychology, 76,* 442–451.

Walker, C. H. (1987). Relative importance of domain knowledge and overall aptitude on acquisition of domain-related information. *Cognition and Instruction, 4,* 25–42.

Wang, A. H., Firmender, J. H., Power, J. R., & Byrnes, J. P. (2016). Understanding program effectiveness of early mathematics interventions for pre-kindergarten and kindergarten environments: A meta-analytic review. *Early Education and Development, 27,* 692–713.

Wang, A. H., & Fitzpatrick, C. (2019). Which early childhood experiences and skills predict kindergarteners' working memory? *Journal of Developmental and Behavioral Pediatrics, 40*(1), 40–48.

Wang, A. H., Shen, F., & Byrnes, J. (2013). Does the opportunity-propensity framework predict early mathematics skills for low-income pre-kindergarten children? *Contemporary Educational Psychology, 38,* 259–270.

Wang, M.-T., Eccles, J. S., & Kenny, S. (2013). Not lack of ability but more choice: Individual and gender differences in choice of careers in science, technology, engineering, and mathematics. *Psychological Science, 24,* 770–775.

Wang, S., Harvey, L., Martin, R., van der Beek, E. M., Knol, J., Cryan, J. F., & Renes, I. B. (2018). Targeting the gut microbiota to influence brain development and function in early life. *Neuroscience and Biobehavioral Reviews, 95,* 191–201.

Wasik, B. A. (1986). *Familiarity of content and inference making in young children.* Unpublished doctoral dissertation, Temple University, Philadelphia, PA.

Wasik, B. A., & Hindman, A. H. (2020). Increasing preschoolers' vocabulary development through a streamlined teacher professional development intervention. *Early Childhood Research Quarterly, 50*(Pt. 1), 101–113.

Wasserman, J. D. (2018). A history of intelligence assessment: The unfinished tapestry. In D. P. Flanagan & E. M. McDonough (Eds.), *Contemporary intellectual assessment: Theories, tests, and issues* (4th ed., pp. 3–55). New York: Guilford Press.

Water, E., Cillessen, A. H. N., & Scheres, A. (2014). Distinct age-related differences in temporal discounting and risk taking in adolescents and young adults. *Child Development, 85*(5), 1881–1897.

Watson, J. B. (1913). Psychology as the behaviorist views it. *Psychological Review, 20,* 158–177.

Weaver, C. A., & Kintsch, W. (1991). Expository text. In R. Barr, M. L. Kamil, P. Mosenthal, & P. D. Pearson (Eds.), *Handbook of reading research* (Vol. 2, pp. 230–245). New York: Longman.

Wechsler, D. (1939). *The measurement of adult intelligence.* Baltimore: Williams & Wilkins.

Weiner, B. (2010). The development of an attribution-based theory of motivation: A history of ideas. *Educational Psychologist, 45*(1), 28–36.

Weiner, B. (2012). An attribution theory of motivation. In P. A. M. Van Lange, A. W. Kruglanski, & E. T. Higgins (Eds.), *Handbook of theories of social psychology* (Vol. 1, pp. 135–155). Thousand Oaks, CA: SAGE.

Weiner, B. (2014). The attribution approach to emotion and motivation: History, hypotheses, home runs, headaches/heartaches. *Emotion Review, 6*(4), 353–361.

Welie, C., Schoonen, R., & Kuiken, F. (2018). The role text structure inference skill plays for eighth graders' expository text comprehension. *Reading and Writing: An Interdisciplinary Journal, 31*(9), 2065–2094.

Wentzel, K. R., Muenks, K., McNeish, D., & Russell, S. (2018). Emotional support, social goals, and classroom behavior: A multilevel, multisite study. *Journal of Educational Psychology, 110*(5), 611–627.

Wentzel, K. R., & Wigfield, A. (2009). *Handbook of motivation at school.* New York: Routledge/Taylor & Francis.

Whitacre, I., Azuz, B., Lamb, L. L. C., Bishop, J. P., Schappelle, B. P., & Philipp, R. A. (2017). Integer comparisons across the grades: Students' justifications and ways of reasoning. *Journal of Mathematical Behavior, 45,* 47–62.

Whitehurst, G. J., & Lonigan, C. J. (1998). Child development and emergent literacy. *Child Development, 69,* 848–872.

Whitney, P., & Kunen, S. (1983). Development of hierarchical conceptual relationships in children's semantic memories. *Journal of Experimental Child Psychology, 35,* 278–293.

Whittlesea, B. W. A., & Cantwell, A. L. (1987). Enduring influence of the purpose of experiences: Encoding-retrieval interactions in word and pseudoword perception. *Memory and Cognition, 15,* 465–472.

Wigfield, A., Eccles, J. S., Fredricks, J. A., Simpkins, S., Roeser, R. W., & Schiefele, U. (2015). Development of achievement motivation and engagement. In M. E. Lamb & R. M. Lerner (Eds.), *Handbook of child psychology and developmental science: Socioemotional processes* (Vol. 3, 7th ed., pp. 657–700). New York: Wiley.

Wigfield, A., Rosenzweig, E. Q., & Eccles, J. S. (2017). Achievement values: Interactions, interventions, and future directions. In A. J. Elliot & D. S. Yeager (Eds.), *Handbook of competence and motivation: Theory and application* (2nd ed., pp. 116–134). New York: Guilford Press.

Wijekumar, K., Graham, S., Harris, K. R., Lei, P.-W., Barkel, A., Aitken, A., . . . Houston, J. (2018). The roles of writing knowledge, motivation, strategic behaviors, and skills in predicting elementary students' persuasive writing from source material. *Reading and Writing, 32,* 1431–1457.

Wiley, J., Griffin, T. D., Steffens, B., & Britt, M. A. (2020). Epistemic beliefs about the value of integrating information across multiple documents in history. *Learning and Instruction, 65.*

Wilkening, F., & Cacchione, T. (2011). Children's intuitive physics. In U. Goswami (Ed.), *The Wiley–Blackwell handbook of childhood cognitive development* (2nd ed., pp. 473–496). New York: Wiley-Blackwell.

Williams, G. J., & Larkin, R. F. (2013). Narrative writing, reading and cognitive processes in middle childhood: What are the links? *Learning and Individual Differences, 28,* 142–150.

Willoughby, M. T. (2016). Commentary. In K. Espy (Ed.), The changing nature of executive control in preschool. *Monographs of the Society for Research in Child Development, 81,* 151–165.

Willoughby, M. T., Wylie, A. C., & Little, M. H. (2019). Testing longitudinal associations between executive function and academic achievement. *Developmental Psychology, 55,* 767–779.

Windschitl, M., & Barton, A. C. (2016). Rigor and equity by design: Locating a set of core teaching practices for the science education community. In D. Gitomer & C. Bell (Eds.), *Handbook of research on teaching* (pp. 1099–1158). Washington, DC: AERA.

Wittgenstein, L. (1953). *Philosophical investigations.* New York: Macmillan.

Wolff, F., Wigfield, A., Möller, J., Dicke, A.-L., & Eccles, J. S. (2020). Social, dimensional, and temporal comparisons by students and parents: An investigation of the 2I/E model at the transition from elementary to junior high school. *Journal of Educational Psychology, 112,* 1644–1660.

Won, S., Hensley, L. C., & Wolters, C. A. (2019). Brief research report: Sense of belonging and academic help-seeking as self-regulated learning. *Journal of Experimental Education, 89*(1), 1–13.

Wong, A. P.-Y., French, L., Leonard, G., Perron, M., Pike, G. B., Richer, L., . . . Paus, T. (2018). Inter-regional variations in gene expression and age-related cortical thinning in the adolescent brain. *Cerebral Cortex, 28,* 1272–1281.

Wood, E., Willoughby, T., McDermott, C., Motz, M., Kaspar, V., & Ducharme, M. J. (1999). Developmental differences in study behavior. *Journal of Educational Psychology, 91*(3), 527–536.

Wright, R. E., & Rosenberg, S. (1993). Knowledge of text coherence and expository writing: A developmental study. *Journal of Educational Psychology, 85,* 152–158.

Wylie, C., & Hodgen, E. (2012). Trajectories and patterns of student engagement: Evidence from a longitudinal study. In S. L. Christenson, A. L. Reschly, & C. Wylie (Eds.), *Handbook of research on student engagement* (pp. 585–589). New York: Springer.

Wynn, K. (1992). Addition and subtraction by human infants. *Nature, 360*(6406), 749–750.

Yeh, S. S. (2017). Contradictions resolved: An analysis of two theories of the achievement gap. *Teachers College Record, 119,* 1–42.

Yeniad, N., Malda, M., Mesman, J., van IJzendoorn, M. H., & Pieper, S. (2013). Shifting ability predicts math and reading performance in children: A meta-analytical study. *Learning and Individual Differences, 23,* 1–9.

Young, D. J., Reynolds, A. J., & Walberg, H. J. (1996). Science achievement and educational productivity: A hierarchical linear model. *Journal of Educational Research, 89,* 272–278.

Young, L. K., & Booth, J. L. (2015). Student magnitude knowledge of negative numbers. *Journal of Numerical Cognition, 1,* 38–55.

Young, L. K., & Booth, J. L. (2020). Don't eliminate the negative: Influences of negative number magnitude knowledge on algebra performance and learning. *Journal of Educational Psychology, 112*(2), 384–396.

Yu, H., McCoach, D. B., Gottfried, A. W., & Gottfried, A. E. (2018). Stability of intelligence from infancy through adolescence: An autoregressive latent variable model. *Intelligence, 69,* 8–15.

Zatorre, R. J., Douglas Fields, R., & Johansen-Berg, H. (2012). Plasticity in gray and white: Neuroimaging changes in brain structure during learning. *Nature Neuroscience, 15*(4), 528–536.

Zelazo, P. D. (2015). Executive function: Reflection, iterative reprocessing, complexity, and the developing brain. *Developmental Review, 38,* 55–68.

Zepeda, C. D., Richey, J. E., Ronevich, P., & Nokes-Malach, T. J. (2015). Direct instruction of metacognition benefits adolescent science learning, transfer, and motivation: An *in vivo* study. *Journal of Educational Psychology, 107,* 954–970.

Zerr, C. L., Berg, J. J., Nelson, S. M., Fishell, A. K., Savalia, N. K., & McDermott, K. B. (2018). Learning efficiency: Identifying individual differences in learning rate and retention in healthy adults. *Psychological Science, 29,* 1436–1450.

Zhang, D., Ding, Y., Lee, S., & Chen, J. (2017). Strategic development of multiplication problem solving: Patterns of students' strategy choices. *Journal of Educational Research, 110,* 159–170.

Zimmerman, B. J. (2008). Investigating self-regulation and motivation: Historical background, methodological developments, and future prospects. *American Educational Research Journal, 45,* 166–183.

Zimmerman, B. J., & Moylan, A. R. (2009). Self-regulation: Where metacognition and motivation intersect. In D. J. Hacker, J. Dunlosky, & A. C. Graesser (Eds.), *Handbook of metacognition in education* (pp. 299–315). New York: Routledge.

Zinar, S. (1990). Fifth graders' recall of propositional content and causal relationships from expository prose. *Journal of Reading Behavior, 22,* 181–199.

Index

Note. f or *t* following a page number indicates figure or a table.

435

emotions and, 100–101
engagement and, 101–102
and goals and mind-sets, 95–97
and interests and values, 98–99
intrinsic *versus* extrinsic, 97–98
nature of, 94–105
outcome expectancies and, 98
phonological competence and, 171–172
progress monitoring and, 102
scientific competence and, 346
vocabulary development and, 178
of writers, 271–272
Motivation development, 105–110
ability beliefs and, 106–107
attributions, postactivity emotions and,
110
effort, persistence, grit and, 109–110
emotions and, 108
engagement and, 108
goals, mind-sets and, 105–106
interest, values, cost and, 108
intrinsic, extrinsic, 107
outcome expectancies and, 107
progress monitoring and, 108
Motivation theory, assumptions of, 95
Multiplication/division skills, 307–310
Mutualism theory of intelligence, 149
Myelination, 15–16, 20

N

National Assessment of Educational
Progress (NAEP)
historical knowledge report, 357, 359
history instruction standards of, 359–361
implications for instructional practices,
382
math proficiency report, 294
motivation for science report, 346
of reading proficiency report, 209
science framework of, 329
scientific competence report, 327–328,
338–339
National Council of Teachers of
Mathematics (NCTM), reform
efforts of, 319
National Mathematics Advisory Panel,
recommendations from, 320–323
National Research Council (NRC)
argument skills report, 344
panel on reading, 210, 227
scientific reasoning report, 327, 328–329

Nativist orientation, 47
Nativist theories
alternatives to, 195–199
grammatical development and, 192–195
Nazism, contributing factors, 350–351
Neurons
excretions of, 13
structures of, 14*f*
synaptogenesis and, 13, 15
Neuroscientific findings
Educators' approach to, 10 (*see also*
Areal structure of cortex; Brain
maturation; Learning disabilities)
frontal lobe function and, 113
psychological theories and, 26–27
Neurotransmitters, excretion of, 13
Nondeclarative memory, *versus* declarative
memory, 65–66
Number sense, in preschool children, 303
Numeracy, attainment of, 294
Nutrition, brain development and, 20–22

O

Object permanence, Piaget's concept of, 40
Operant conditioning
appropriate applications of, 189
implicit memory and, 84
problematic applications of, 190, 192,
194
Skinner's theory of, 35–39
Opportunity–propensity achievement
model, 365–382
antecedent factors in, 368*f*, 370–373
and interdependence among factors, 381
opportunity factors in, 368*f*, 369–370,
373–376
original and current versions of, 368*f*
propensity factors in, 368*f*, 369–370,
376–380, 377*f*, 380*f*
sources for, 366–367
Oppositional defiant disorder (ODD), EF/
SR and, 129
Organization for Economic Cooperation
and Development (OECD)
and student math competence ratings,
294
and student scientific competence
ratings, 327–328, 330, 337, 346
Orthographic processor, 220–222, 220*f*
Outcome expectancies, 98
age changes in, 107